Ophthalmic Care

Full the full range of M&K Publishing books please visit our website:
www.mkupdate.co.uk

Ophthalmic Care

Second edition

Edited by Janet Marsden

Ophthalmic Care

Janet Marsden

ISBN: 978-1-910451-04-5

First published by Wiley, Chichester, 2006.
This revised 2nd edition published by M&K Publishing, 2017

British Library Cataloguing in Publication Data

A catalogue record for this book is available from the British Library

Notice

Clinical practice and medical knowledge constantly evolve. Standard safety precautions must be followed, but, as knowledge is broadened by research, changes in practice, treatment and drug therapy may become necessary or appropriate. Readers must check the most current product information provided by the manufacturer of each drug to be administered and verify the dosages and correct administration, as well as contraindications. It is the responsibility of the practitioner, utilising the experience and knowledge of the patient, to determine dosages and the best treatment for each individual patient. Any brands mentioned in this book are as examples only and are not endorsed by the publisher. Neither the publisher nor the authors assume any liability for any injury and/or damage to persons or property arising from this publication.

To contact M&K Publishing write to:

M&K Update Ltd · The Old Bakery · St. John's Street

Keswick · Cumbria CA12 5AS

Tel: 01768 773030 · Fax: 01768 781099

publishing@mkupdate.co.uk

www.mkupdate.co.uk

Designed and typeset by Mary Blood

Printed in England by McKanes Printers, Keswick

Contents

List of contributors

Sharon Andrew MRPharmS Regional Scientific Services Manager – Ophthalmology, Allergan, UK

Rosie Auld CBE DBO(T) Head of Orthoptic Services, Birmingham and Midland Eye Centre, UK

Jilly Bradshaw, RGN, RSCN Lecturer in Child Nursing. Canterbury Christchurch University, UK

Olga HL Brochner RGON PgDip Senior Nurse, Ophthalmology, Auckland DHB, NZ

John Cooper MSc MRes BSc(Hons) Advanced Nurse Practitioner and Oculoplastic Specialist Nurse, Manchester Royal Eye Hospital, UK

Stephen Craig MSc, BA(Hons), RN1, RN3, OND, LPE Senior Lecturer (Nursing) School of Health and Life Sciences, Northumbria University, UK

Dorothy E. Field Ed D, MA, BscHons, RGN, OND formerly Senior Lecturer Practitioner at Royal Bournemouth Hospital and Bournemouth University, UK

Helen Gibbons MSc RT BA(Hons) RGN Head of Clinical Nursing Education and Research, Moorfields Eye Hospital, London, UK

Margaret Gurney RN, OND, BSc(Hons), MSc formerly Consultant Nurse, Maidstone and Tunbridge Wells NHS Trust, UK

Helen Juckes-Hughes MSc RN Matron of Ophthalmology BCUHB, North Wales UK

Bradley Kirkwood BApplSc(Optom)(Hons), GradCert(OculTher), MA, BN, ONC, FFACNP Optometrist Private Practice, Mackay, Queensland, Australia; Adjunct Lecturer Optometry and Vision Science, Flinders University, Adelaide, South Australia.

Agnes Lee MPhil, BSc(Hons), DipN, RGN, SCM, OND Formally Senior Nurse, Ophthalmology, Northamptonshire Healthcare NHS FT, UK

Robert Lindfield MBChB, MRCOphth, FFPH Clinical Lecturer, London School of Hygiene and Tropical Medicine

Heather Machin, RN, MBA Project Officer, Lions Eye Donation Service, Centre for Eye Research Australia; Royal Victorian Eye and Ear Hospital, Ophthalmology, University of Melbourne, Department of Surgery, Australia; and Nurse Consultant to the Fred Hollows Foundation, NZ.

Janet Marsden, PhD, RGN, OND Professor of Ophthalmology and Emergency Care, Manchester Metropolitan University, UK

Yvonne Needham MSC, BSc, RN, RNT Formerly Senior Lecturer, Hull University, UK

Dr Graeme Pollock MPH PhD, Director, Lions Eye Donation Service, Centre for Eye Research, Australia; Royal Victorian Eye and Ear Hospital, Ophthalmology, University of Melbourne, Department of Surgery, Australia

Susanne Raynel MA RGON AND BHSc OND, Reseach Manager, Department of Ophthalmology, University of Auckland, NZ

Ramesh Seewoodhary BSc(Hons), RGN, OND(Hons), RCNT, RNT, CertEd. Senior Lecturer in Ophthalmic Nursing and Adult Nursing, University of West London, UK

Mary E. Shaw MSc, BA, Cert Ed, FETC 730, RGN, RNT, OND Senior Lecturer, University of Manchester, UK

Carol Slight MN, RN Nurse Practitioner Ophthalmology, Auckland DHB, NZ

David M. Spence BSc(Hons) Dip Optom, Optometrist, UK

Julie Tillotson RGN, OND, BSc(Hons) Formerly Advanced Nurse Practitioner, Bournemouth Eye Unit and Adams Practice Community Eye Clinic, UK

Linda Whitaker RGN, OND (Hons), RCNT, BA in Nursing Education & MA in Applied Research and Quality Evaluation in Healthcare Retired Nurse Researcher, UK

Additional material by **Allyson Ryder, Les McQueen, Gayle Catt, Bronwyn Ward,** contributors to the first edition of this book

Anatomical illustrations by **Stuart E. Lee DipAd, ATD**

Diagrams on pages 8 & 424 by **Mary Blood DipAd**

Preface

The original concept of this book arose out of a recognition by ophthalmic nurses that, in general, existing textbooks for nurses working in the specialty did not have the depth of content required to inform and evidence their practice. This book was therefore designed to meet the needs of ophthalmic professionals and, most especially, ophthalmic nurses, whose practice has expanded exponentially over the past few years, into areas we would never previously have dreamed possible. This expansion, though, has often been accompanied by a lack of accessible evidence to underpin it and this book aims to bridge that gap.

It was written by an international team of ophthalmic practitioners, all experts in their fields, who gave up a large amount of time, immensely willingly, to make this dream a reality because of their passion for, and dedication to, their area of practice.

In the ten years since the first edition, practice has moved on, as has the evidence for practice.

This second edition draws on the passion and goodwill of the original team, complemented by other colleagues, to fully revise and update the text in line with new findings, new practice and new and exciting treatments.

It is hoped that the book combines depth and breadth of content, but does this in an accessible manner which enables it to be used as a comprehensive resource not just by ophthalmic professionals, but by any healthcare professional who ever cares for a patient with an eye problem, thus enabling them to develop the knowledge and skills to incorporate consideration of their patients' eye problems into their practice.

The book is divided into three parts. The first section considers some general aspects relating to the understanding of the function and structure of the eye. The first two chapters cover the physiology of vision including embryology (in order to give an overview of how we see), and basic optics as applied to the eye. This section goes on to consider how drugs affect the eye and the main categories of ophthalmic drugs and delivery systems as well as some of the adverse effects of systemic and ophthalmic drugs. The eye examination chapter considers the requirements for effective assessment of the patient, including physical surroundings, taking a history and obtaining accurate visual acuity. It stresses the need for systematic eye examination and considers both the structures that may be examined and what the examiner should be looking for.

The second section of the book considers issues surrounding patient care. It begins by considering visual impairment, its effects on the patient and strategies that may be used both by the patient, and by carers and health professionals in order to maximise autonomy and independence. Patient education is considered, both in general terms and for this particular client group and the chapter entitled 'Work and the eye' considers some work-related issues and some of the legislation pertaining to eye care and visual standards. The next five chapters deal with care of the patient in ophthalmic settings, considering, in turn, care of the adult in inpatient settings, care of the child with ophthalmic problems, care of the patient undergoing day surgery, care of the ophthalmic patient in the ophthalmic theatre and, finally, care of the patient in the acute setting. This section concludes with two entirely new chapters on eye banking and global eye health.

The third section takes a systematic approach to the care of patients with ophthalmic problems. The work of all ophthalmic health professionals is very closely intertwined and this is reflected in the structure of these chapters. Following the theme developed in the discussion of systematic eye examination and working from the front to the back of the eye, each chapter considers the anatomy and physiology of a structure (such as the lens or cornea) or group of structures (such as the eyelids and lacrimal drainage system). Each chapter discusses some of the common disorders affecting these structures, including their causes, presentation, special tests, diagnosis and treatment, as well as care of the patient. The final chapter considers the ocular manifestations of some of the more common systemic diseases that may be encountered by healthcare professionals.

Ophthalmology has a language of its own, which can be confusing for people new to the specialty, those outside it and even, occasionally, some very experienced practitioners. The book therefore concludes with a glossary of terms.

Some aspects of practice discussed in the text are, of necessity, UK based, but these are clearly indicated and, wherever possible, principles (rather than specifics) are addressed and readers are directed to local policies and interpretations.

The first edition became a core text for ophthalmic nursing, in particular, and for the education of ophthalmic nurses across the world. I hope this second, revised and updated edition will add to the body of evidence-based, informed and thinking practice for all those with eye problems, via those who care for them.

Janet Marsden
March 2016

Foreword to the second edition

It is a little over a decade since the first version of this textbook was launched, and since that time it has become an essential text for those wanting to learn about, or update their knowledge of, best ophthalmic practice. In this second edition, an exemplary, multidisciplinary team of experts has been assembled under the direction of Professor Janet Marsden. The authors have updated, expanded and improved the text, while maintaining its readability, which was core to the wide success of the original version.

This book brings together all those directly involved in eye disease – nurses, ophthalmologists, optometrists, orthoptists, technicians and vision scientists – to reveal the many inter-related facets of the discipline. Soundly based on good practice and the evidence base, this book will be equally useful in the developed and developing world.

In 25 highly illustrated chapters, the authors comprehensively build the reader's knowledge, from consideration of the essential aspects of the applied basic sciences of anatomy, pharmacology and optics, through a step-by-step guide to clinical examination of the eye in health and disease.

Specific sections deal with patient education, ocular issues in the workplace and the causes and burdens of visual impairment. The discussion of care of the ophthalmic patient includes aspects of management in the inpatient setting and specific consideration of eye theatre nursing. Acute eye emergencies are covered in detail, as are aspects of the eyelids, lachrymal drainage system and conjunctiva. A new section deals with corneal transplantation and eye banking. The chapters are extremely well-illustrated in colour to make the text easily understandable – even to those who are new to the subject.

Marsden *et al.* seem to have achieved the impossible with this second edition by making an excellent textbook even better! Although aimed primarily at nurses dealing with eye disease, the use of a multidisciplinary team of authors, and the strong emphasis on a solid evidence base, give the text sufficient breadth and depth to appeal to all those involved in the ophthalmic field. I am sure, like its forerunner, this latest version of *Ophthalmic Care* will become a standard feature on the bookshelves of those wishing to provide the best care for patients with eye diseases.

Professor Charles N.J. McGhee, MB ChB PhD DSc FRCS
Maurice Paykel Professor and Chair of Ophthalmology,
Director, New Zealand National Eye Centre, University of Auckland

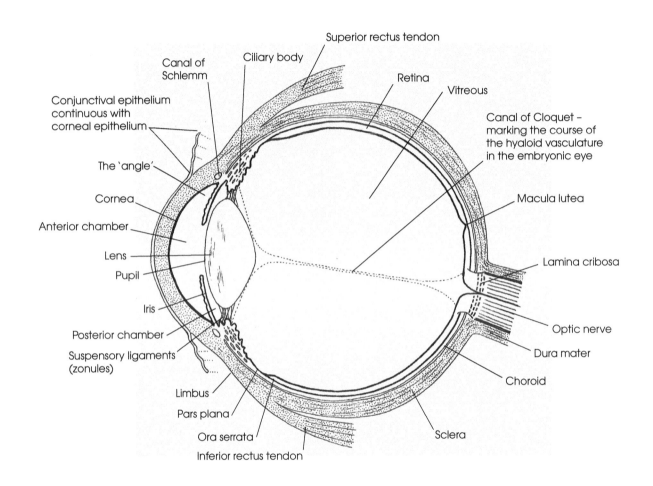

Section through the globe.

Foreword to the first edition

To paraphrase Bill Clinton's celebrated campaign slogan, the adage 'it's the patient, stupid' would seem to sum up perfectly the essential message of this new treatise on eye care written for and by ophthalmic professionals. As the book's editor Janet Marsden herself points out whilst discussing emergency service provision: 'It is irrelevant who cares for the patient, as long as the clinician who does so is competent to undertake the role, understands the parameters of the role, is able and willing to refer when necessary to more appropriate care and that the care of the patient as well as his presenting problem is paramount.'

This role statement differs in no material respect from the essence of the Royal College of Ophthalmologists' description of what an ophthalmologist can and should be doing. Yet this book is being published at a time when the Royal Colleges in the UK (and especially the surgical Colleges) are in disarray over the extent to which, and the circumstances under which, care that they perceive to be the primary prerogative of medical school-trained practitioners should be undertaken by others, and not least by nurses. It is fully acknowledged that the depth of understanding, the mastery of surgical techniques and the experience required of medical specialists (who are ultimately responsible for the patients' care) will exceed that of other members of the multidisciplinary team in certain areas of practice. However, it is also arguably the case that the need for a book of this nature signals a current failure to put the patient's needs squarely at the centre of the training agenda for the variety of health professionals with whom the patient may have contact. That is not to say that 'one-size-fits-all' educational material would be appropriate, but rather that 'fit-for-purpose' is the basic aspiration for training of a range of practitioners whose contributions should overlap wherever possible if eye care is to be other than an exercise in passing the parcel.

The management needs of the majority of ophthalmic patients, including drug prescribing and technical procedures, can be met by appropriately trained individuals who have not had recourse to a dozen or more years of progressively specialised medical and surgical training. Admittedly, high standards of practical expertise can only be acquired through on-the-job experience and guidance, but this manual by an international panel of contributors will underpin in-service development, and its concise readability will surely help to encourage enthusiasm for our subject. Happily, generic caring skills and attitudes are entirely transferable to the small world of ophthalmology and, once its vocabulary has been addressed if not mastered, learning to provide expert care for those with eye afflictions can be intensely rewarding, a sentiment that this book subliminally conveys throughout.

The pre-qualification training of health professionals in 'ophthalmics' is universally disproportionate (i.e. inversely proportionate) to the frequency with which patients present themselves with their wide array of eye- and vision-related problems. Fortunately, obtaining a good history remains the key to successful diagnosis and management – notwithstanding the extraordinary brevity accorded to history-taking and recording by the majority of ophthalmologists. Eliciting an accurate history contributes enormously to the safety of telephone triage and advice, a key role often undertaken by nurses in our modern-day eye service. Indeed, one of the great attractions of our specialty is the considerable extent to which the professional-of-first-encounter with the patient can come to an accurate conclusion about the clinical problem without recourse to extensive laboratory tests and distressing, expensive or time-consuming investigations (making it all the more surprising that general medical practitioners have largely abdicated from this particular area of patient care). This presumes, of course, that the individual involved has the necessary examination skills and is secure in their knowledge of eye anatomy, physiology and pathology. Fostering the acquisition of such comprehensive and fundamental knowledge in nurses, while maintaining an emphasis on the holistic approach and on clarity regarding professional roles and responsibilities, is both the challenge and success of this book.

David McLeod
Professor of Ophthalmology and Honorary Consultant
Ophthalmic Surgeon, Manchester Royal Eye Hospital
May 2005

CHAPTER ONE

Physiology of vision

Ramesh Seewoodhary

The aim of this chapter is to explore the physiology of vision. It is divided into six parts to give the reader an understanding of the concept of sight:

- Embryological development of the eye
- Development of visual perception and mechanisms involved in vision
- Mechanism of vision in dim light and bright light
- Light detection and dark adaptation
- Colour vision
- Control of eye movements and binocular vision.

Embryological development of the eye

The development of the eye takes place between week 3 and week 10 and involves ectoderm, neural crest cells and mesenchyme. The neural tube ectoderm gives rise to the retina, the iris and ciliary body epithelia, the optic nerve, the smooth muscles of the iris, and some of the vitreous humour. Surface ectoderm gives rise to the lens, the conjunctival and corneal epithelia, the eyelids, and the lacrimal apparatus. The remaining ocular structures form from mesenchyme.

Early eye development starts around day 22 of the embryo's life, and the eye measures 2–3mm in length. The neural folds fuse to form the neural tube, but, before they complete their closure, the optic sulci appear as shallow grooves or pits in the inner part of the neural folds (Figure 1.1a).

The folds fuse shortly afterwards to form the forebrain, and the optic sulci evaginate to form the optic vesicles (Figure 1.1b). Invagination of the lower surface of the optic stalk and the optic vesicle occur simultaneously, creating a groove known as the choroidal fissure. At the same time, the lens plate also invaginates to form the lens vesicle. By about 4 weeks, the lens vesicle separates completely from the surface ectoderm to lie free in the rim of the optic cup.

1

The choroidal fissure allows entrance into the optic stalk of the vascular mesoderm, which eventually forms the hyaloid system. As invagination is completed, the choroidal fissure narrows until it is closed by 6 weeks, leaving one small permanent opening at the anterior end of the optic stalk. Through this opening pass the hyaloid artery by the fourth month and the central retinal artery and vein thereafter (Figure 1.1c).

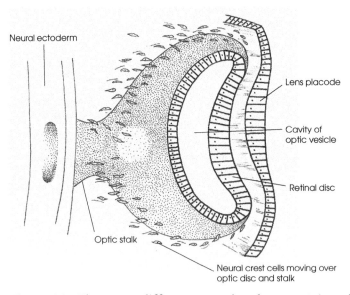

Figure 1.1a The eye at different gestational ages: at 4 weeks

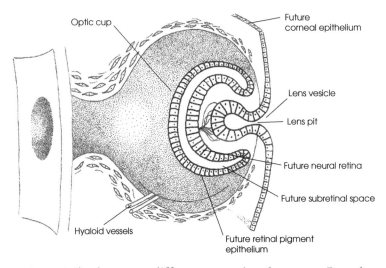

Figure 1.1b The eye at different gestational ages: at 5 weeks

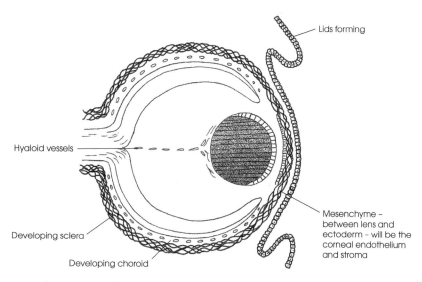

Figure 1.1c The eye at different gestational ages: at 7 weeks

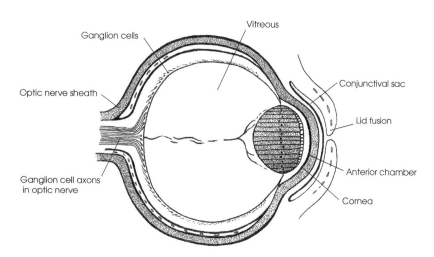

Figure 1.1d The eye at different gestational ages: at 8 weeks

After the fourth month, the general structure of the eye has been determined. Development after this consists of differentiation into individual structures, which occurs more rapidly in the posterior than in the anterior segment early in gestation, and more rapidly in the anterior segment later in gestation (Riordan-Eva & Cunningham 2011).

Generally, the eye is derived from three embryonic layers, namely, surface ectoderm, neural ectoderm and mesoderm

- The surface ectoderm gives rise to the lens, the lacrimal gland, corneal epithelium, conjunctiva, adnexal glands and epidermis of the lid.
- The neural ectoderm gives rise to the optic vesicle and optic cup, and is responsible for the formation of the retina, ciliary body, pupillary muscle sphincter and dilator, optic nerve and glia.
- The mesoderm contributes to the extraocular muscles, sclera, and orbital and ocular vascular endothelium.

The timeline of ocular embryogenesis is summarised in Table 1.1.

Table 1.1 Timeline of ocular embryogenesis

Period after conception	Event	Period after conception	Event
Day 22	Optic groove appears	Week 5	Lens pit forms and depends into lens vesicle Hyaloid vessels develop
Day 25	Optic vesicle forms from optic pit		Primary vitreous develops Osseous structures of the orbit begin to develop
Day 26	Primordia of superior rectus, inferior rectus, medial rectus, and inferior oblique appear	Week 6	Closure of embryonic fissure Corneal epithelial cells develop interconnections
Day 27	Formation of lens plate from surface ectoderm Primordium of lateral rectus appears		Differentiation of retinal pigment epithelium Proliferation of neural retinal cells
Day 28	Embryonic fissure forms Cells destined to become retinal pigment Epithelium acquires pigmentation		Formation of secondary vitreous Formation of primary lens fibres Development of periocular vasculature
Day 29	Primordium of superior oblique appears		Appearance of eyelids folds and nasolacrimal duct Ciliary ganglion appears

Healthy eyes and good vision play a critical role in how infants and children learn to see. Poor vision in infants can cause developmental delays. It is important to detect any sight problems early to ensure that babies have the opportunity to develop the visual abilities they need to grow and learn. The next section discusses development of visual perception.

Development of visual perception

Vision, and how the brain uses visual information, are learned skills. Perception of the environment is the end product of the reinterpretation or processing by the visual cortex of the retina's responses to visual stimuli. There is no strict separation of cortical and retinal function because some processing takes place in the retina and the cortex may not be solely responsible for other processes.

There must be discrimination by means of brightness gradients in the cortex, as well as in the retina. The cortex must be precisely aware of the form and shape of objects and, finally, of the identity of these objects. In the adult, all these processes occur rapidly; we perceive only the objects' identities and react to them automatically and appropriately, often without being fully conscious of them. In the infant, these processes occur slowly and the final stages of form perception and object identification may not occur at all. Although form perception develops automatically with maturation, identification depends on the capacity to acquire and store information and also on the accumulation of experiences on which identification is based.

Retinal response to light, and to moving objects by reflex responses of blinking, pupillary contraction and eye movements, occurs even in the short-gestation infant and is well established in the normal neonate. According to Gesell *et al.* (1949), during the first few weeks the infant begins to gaze around and sometimes to fixate objects. Sporadic body activity then ceases and respiration rate alters; there seems to be some awareness of and attention to the environment. This visual exploration of the environment increases with age, especially when infants are handled or situated in complex and unrestricted environments (White & Castle 1964). In young infants the information is fragmentary. Infants aged 2 months cannot store and retain information for more than a very brief period of about 1 second. Each successive appearance of a stimulus is perceived as a new event, so that the environment is experienced in a disconnected manner. At 6 months, the span of attention is so narrow that a single stimulus may capture it entirely. The infant will concentrate on a stimulus in an indiscriminate manner, in order to obtain all possible information from it, and cannot attend selectively. Babies need to learn how to use the visual information the eyes send to the brain in order to understand the world around them and interact with it appropriately (Bowling 2015).

Awareness of an object involves discrimination between it and its surroundings; brightness and colour discrimination also contribute to this. Infants are known to gaze longer at blue and green stimuli and least at yellow. Experiments by Fantz (1958) suggest that, from a very early age, there is some discrimination between patterns. He claimed that within the first week or so of life infants gazed longer at a picture of a face than at a half-black, half-pink shape. It has been found that infants under 1 month tend to look longer at very simple patterns (such as a half-white, half-black field or one with four quadrants) than at more complex patterns. This is a result of the retinal images being too blurred for finer perception.

Accommodation develops during the second month and it is comparable to that of a normal adult by 4 months. Infants look relatively longer at chequered patterns with four squares by week 3. This increases to 64 squares at week 8, and 576 squares at week 14. Attention to pictures and photographs of faces emerges at 3–4 months. Kagan *et al.* (1966) found that this is followed by the infant smiling more and more, suggesting that some degree of familiarity is involved.

Development in the accuracy of shape perception takes place in close conjunction with tactile exploration. Before the age of 3 months, infants are unaware of any association between the visual and the tactile sensory patterns and do not attempt to handle objects that they perceive visually, or to examine visually the objects that they handle. At 3 months, White and Castle (1964) found that infants stretch out a hand towards an object that they see, and glance repeatedly to and fro between the hand and the object. At about 4 months they grasp the object and cease to look at the hand. They explore the object with their fingers, comparing the shape that they feel with the shape that they see (Piaget 1952). Infants thus discover the nature of three-dimensional solid form and also that, as an object is turned round in space, the visual pattern changes regularly, although the object as felt remains the same. It is not until 8–9 months that the infant realises this fully.

By means of visual and tactile exploration of objects, infants learn not only to discriminate between similar objects but to remember and identify them. In the latter part of their first year, they begin to realise that objects have a permanent identity and that when they are hidden from sight they do not cease to exist but may reappear. Complex shapes are not perceived with complete accuracy until 5–6 years.

Understanding of the relationships of objects to their surroundings also develops gradually. Discrimination of distance, by means of parallactic movement, between fairly near solid objects develops before 2 months (Bower 1965). Infants then learn that they can stretch for and obtain objects within their reach, whereas they can get more distant ones only by crying for someone to give them to them. During the first year of life, infants hardly notice the existence of far-distant objects or else they may suppose that these can also be obtained by crying for them. However, once they begin to move about, infants gain a better awareness of the relative distances of further objects. The exact nature of environmental spatial relationships is not understood until the age of 6–7 years or even more. By 2 years of age, a child's eye–hand coordination and depth perception should be well developed. Children aged 1 and 2 are very interested in exploring their environment and in looking and listening. They recognise familiar objects and pictures in books and can scribble with pencil.

Thus, it is evident that perception of the environment and the objects that it contains, which occurs in older children and adults, is acquired only gradually. The processes of attention, discrimination, form perception, identification and spatial location, requiring both maturation and learning through experience, develop to some extent independently of each other and are not accurately coordinated and integrated, especially with complex precepts, until much later.

Mechanisms involved in the physiology of vision

The physiology of vision is a complex phenomenon. The main mechanisms involved are:

- Initiation of vision (phototransduction), a function of photoreceptors.
- Processing and transmission of visual sensation, a function of image processing cells of retina and visual pathway.
- Visual perception, a function of visual cortex and related areas of cerebral cortex.

Initiation

Initiation of vision (known as phototransduction) is when the rods and cones serve as sensory nerve endings for visual sensation. Light falling upon the retina causes photochemical changes, which in turn trigger a cascade of biochemical reactions that result in electrical impulses. Photochemical changes occur in both rods and cones which are essentially similar processes. The whole phenomenon of conversion of light energy into nerve impulse is known as phototransduction.

Processing and transmission of visual impulse

When there is an electrical activity in the photoreceptors of the retina, the direct flow of electric current passes to other cells such as horizontal cells, amacrine cells and ganglion cells. The ganglion cells then transmit the visual signals by means of action potential to the neurons of lateral geniculate body and later to the primary visual cortex. The processing of visual impulse is complicated. Visual image is deciphered and analysed in both serial and parallel manners.

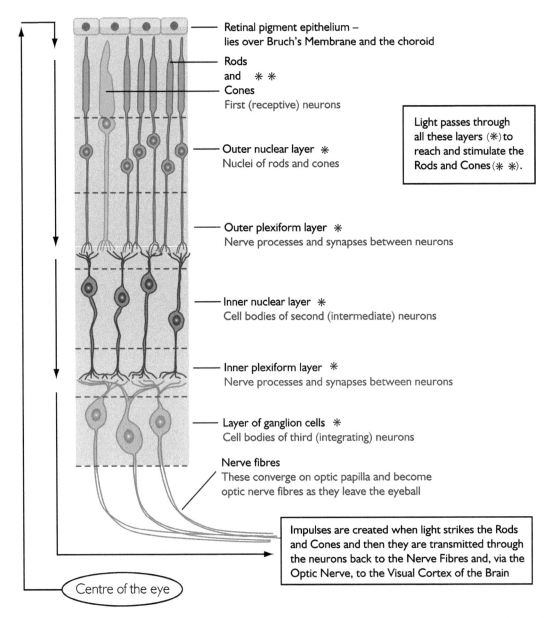

Figure 1.2 Schematic of the retina, showing the passage of light through the retina to the rods and cones, and the nerve impulse through the neural tissue and out of the eye to the brain.

Serial processing

The successive cells in the visual pathway (starting from the photoreceptors and moving to the cells of lateral geniculate body) are involved in increasingly complex analysis of image. This is also referred to as sequential or serial processing of visual information.

Parallel processing

There are several functionally distinct populations of retinal ganglion cells and the two of most interest in humans are the M and P groups, which are related to the magnocellular and parvocellular pathways. M cells have larger cell bodies and axons than P cells. M ganglion cells have larger receptive fields and their axons have faster conduction velocity. These cell axons terminate in different areas of the lateral geniculate nucleus.

The parvocellular pathway consists of around 80% of the nerve fibres and transfers all colour information and high-contrast black and white information. Its nerve fibres are thin and transfer information relatively slowly. The magnocellular pathway is particularly concerned with information about the movement of objects in space and transfers low-resolution black and white information at high speed.

Visual perception

This is a complex integration of light sense and form sense, sense of contrast and colour sense. The receptive fields of organisation of the retina and cortex are used to encode this information about a visual image. The light sense is an awareness of the light. The minimum brightness needed to evoke a sensation of light is called the light minimum. It should be measured when the eye is dark adapted for at least 20 to 30 minutes. In its ordinary use throughout the day, the eye is capable of functioning normally over an exceedingly wide range of illumination by a complex phenomenon known as visual adaptation. This process of visual adaptation primarily involves adaptation to dim light and bright light. This is discussed next.

Mechanism of vision in dim light and bright light

The mechanism of vision in both dim light and bright light involves the retinal photoreceptors known as rods (for dim light) and cones (for bright light and colour vision). The rod and cone photoreceptors are illustrated in Figure 1.3.

Mechanism of vision in dim light (scotopic vision)

Visual photoreceptors contain pigments that break down chemically in the presence of low illumination. This forms a chemical stimulus, which triggers nerve impulses that travel from the retina to the cerebral cortex.

Scotopic vision is vision in dim light. It depends on rod photoreceptors. Rods are one type of photoreceptor and give monochromatic vision. They contain rhodopsin, which is also known as visual purple. When light of low intensity enters the eye, rhodopsin is immediately changed into lumirhodopsin. However, lumirhodopsin is a very unstable compound that can last in the retina only about a tenth of a second. It decays almost immediately into another substance, known as metarhodopsin. This compound, which is also unstable, decays very rapidly into retinene and scotopsin. In the process of splitting rhodopsin, the rods become excited by ionic charges that last only a split second. This results in nerve signals being generated in the rod and transmitted to the brain via the optic nerve.

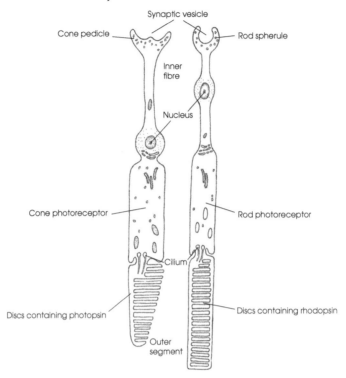

Figure 1.3 Photoreceptors

Figure 1.4 shows how, after rhodopsin has been decomposed by light energy, its decomposition products (retinene and scotopsin) are recombined again during the next few minutes by the cell's metabolic processes to form new rhodopsin. The new rhodopsin can be used again to provide more rod excitation, resulting in a continuous cycle. Rhodopsin is being formed continuously and is broken down by light energy to excite the rods. After decomposition, recombination takes place and vitamin A is needed to achieve this.

When people pass from a brightly lit scene to darkness they are temporarily blinded as a result of the low light levels. In the dark, the eye becomes progressively more sensitive to stimulation by light until a maximum threshold is reached after 30 minutes. The eye then sees much smaller light stimuli than it would in light conditions. This adjustment or increase in sensitivity is called dark adaptation. As light brightness or intensity increases, rods lose their sensitivity and cease to respond.

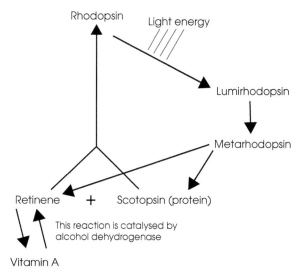

Figure 1.4 The retinene–rhodopsin chemical cycle
responsible for light sensitivity of the rods
(adapted from Guyton 1979)

Rhodopsin bleaching is said to occur when light rays falling on the rods convert 11-cis-retinal into all-trans-retinal through the various stages. The all-trans-retinal is soon separated from the opsin (a process known as photodecomposition) and the opsin is said to be bleached by the action of light.

Rhodopsin regeneration occurs when all the 11-cis-retinal is formed from all the trans-retinal, separated from the opsin and vitamin A supplied from the blood. The 11-cis-retinal reunites with opsin in the rod cells to form the rhodopsin (a process known as rhodopsin regeneration). Thus, the bleaching of the rhodopsin occurs under the influence of light, whereas the regeneration process is independent of light and proceeds equally well in light and darkness.

Mechanism of vision in bright light (photopic vision)

Photopic vision occurs in bright light and is dependent on cone photoreceptors. There are three types of cones, thus giving trichromatic vision. Each type has a different photosensitive visual pigment, with its own wavelength to which it is sensitive. It absorbs this wavelength and is broken down by it to form the chemical stimulus.

The visual pigments in the cone photoreceptors respond to red, green and blue light (the long, medium and short wavelengths of the visible spectrum). All three types of photopsins are stimulated in roughly equal proportions when white light falls on the retina. The various types of colour blindness could be explained in terms of the absence or deficiency of one or more of these special receptors.

Almost exactly the same chemical processes occur in the cones as in the rods, except that the protein scotopsin of the rods is replaced by one of three similar proteins called photopsins. The chemical differences among the photopsins make the three different types of cones selectively sensitive to different colours. A colour sensation has three qualities:

- Hue: depends largely on the wavelength
- Saturation: a saturated colour has no white light mixed with it; an unsaturated colour has some white light mixed with it
- Intensity: brightness depends largely on the strength of the light.

As the intensity of light is reduced, the cones cease to respond and the rods take over. This explains why, in dark conditions, colour is perceived only very dimly, often just as various shades of grey rather than individual colours.

When one passes suddenly from a dim light to a brightly lit environment, the light seems intensely and even uncomfortably bright until the eyes adapt to the increased illumination and the visual threshold rises. Exposure of the dark adapted eye to bright light results in a marked decrease in sensitivity to light which takes place over a period of about 1 minute, during which the rhodopsin is bleached and the pupil constricts to let less light into the eye. This adjustment on exposure to bright light is called light adaptation.

Light detection and dark adaptation

The effect of a visual stimulus is not uniform because it depends on the state of adaptation of the retina at the time of stimulus. In a state of light adaptation, vision is mediated largely by the cones, which deal with the appreciation of form and colour. This is known as photopic vision.

In a state of dark adaptation, the vision is mediated by the rod photoreceptors, which are concerned essentially with the appreciation of light and movement. This is known as scotopic vision.

It is a common experience to be almost totally blinded when first entering a very bright area from a darkened room, and when entering a darkened room from a brightly lit area. The reason for this is that the sensitivity of the retina is temporarily not attuned to the intensity of the light. To discern the shape, texture and other qualities of an object, it is necessary to see both the bright and dark areas of the object at the same time. Fortunately, the retina automatically adjusts its sensitivity in proportion to the degree of light energy available. This phenomenon is called light and dark adaptation.

When large quantities of light energy strike the rods, large amounts of rhodopsin are broken into retinene and scotopsin., Because rhodopsin formation is a slow process, requiring several minutes, the concentration of rhodopsin in the rods falls to a very low value as the person remains in the bright light. Essentially, the same effects occur in the cones. Therefore, the sensitivity of the retina soon becomes greatly depressed in bright light.

The mechanism of dark adaptation is the opposite to that of light adaptation. When the person enters a darkened room from a lighted area, the quantity of rhodopsin in the rods (and colour-sensitive chemicals in the cones) is at first very slight. As a result, the person cannot see anything. Yet the amount of light energy in the darkened room is also very slight, which means that very little of the rhodopsin being formed in the rods is broken down. Therefore, the concentration of rhodopsin builds up during the ensuing minutes until it finally becomes high enough for even a very minute amount of light to stimulate the rods.

During dark adaptation, the sensitivity of the retina can increase as much as 1000-fold in only a few minutes and as much as 100,000 times in an hour or more. This effect is illustrated in Figure 1.6, which shows the retinal sensitivity increasing from an arbitrary light-adapted value of 1 up to a dark-adapted value of 100,000 in 1 hour after the person has left a very bright area and moved into a completely darkened room. Then, on re-entering the bright area, light adaptation occurs and retinal sensitivity decreases from 100,000 back down to 1 in another 10 minutes, which is a more rapid process than dark adaptation.

The transition from scotopic to photopic conditions causes a shift in the wavelength of peak sensitivity of the retina, a relative increase in sensitivity to low wavelengths and a relative decrease in sensitivity to shorter wavelengths (known as the Purkinje shift) During the transition, colours, for example, appear differently from the way we would expect.

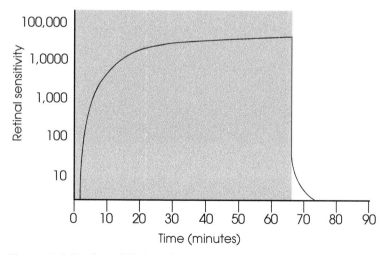

Figure 1.5 Dark and light adaptation. (Adapted from Guyton 1979.)

Mesopic vision

Mesopic vision is a combination of photopic and scotopic vision in low but not quite dark situations. The operating ranges of rods and cones overlap and so, for a significant range of lighting, both are working to an extent. This mesopic area will include most night-time situations where there is street lighting or even a bright moon or a clear sky with many stars.

Colour vision

The process of colour analysis starts in the retina and is not entirely a function of the brain. Colour is detected by cone photoreceptors and it is advisable for colour vision testing to be done in early life, between the ages of 8 and 12. Colour vision is important in many occupations, such as electronic engineering, air pilot traffic control and ophthalmology (see Chapter 7, 'Work and the eye').

Colour vision is not complete until 6 months after birth when, at the same time, the macula is fully developed. Colour appreciation in the retina is ill understood and the only acceptable theory that supports colour appreciation is the Young–Helmholtz theory.

This theory assumes that the cone photoreceptors are the perceiving colour elements and are concerned with three essential colours (Figure 1.6):

- Red (700nm light wavelength)
- Green (600nm light wavelength)
- Blue (420nm light wavelength).

In 1802, Thomas Young proposed that the human eye could detect different colours, because it contained three types of receptor, each sensitive to a particular hue. His theory was referred to as the trichromatic theory:

- Blue pigment absorbing maximally at 420nm
- Green absorbing at 530nm (mid-wavelength pigment)
- Red absorbing at 565nm (long-wavelength pigment).

(The dotted line in Figure 1.6b represents red pigment = 499 nm.)

There are three types of cone photoreceptors and all colours are produced by varying degrees of stimulation of all three types. The eye can recognise a few hundreds of variations of colour, although it can probably distinguish millions.

A white light is produced when all three are equally stimulated. Therefore, if light of a short wavelength is predominant, blue cone photoreceptors will be stimulated and the person sees a blue colour.

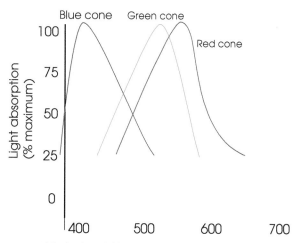

Figure 1.6 (a) Visible light: different cones respond to different wavelengths, e.g. blue cones respond to light of wavelength 400 nm.

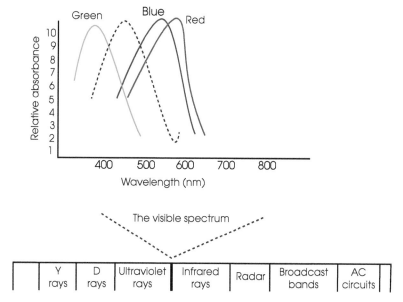

Figure 1.6 (b) Retinal colour vision: spectral absorbance curves in the human.
(Adapted from Tovee 1996)

Specific colour is seen if a light wavelength is of a specific length, e.g. 700nm → red colour perception. A person with normal colour appreciation has all three factors present, i.e.

- blue
- green
- red

and is said to have 'trichromatism'.

Colours depend on:

- Hue: this is related to various shades/reflection.
- Saturation: this is an index of purity of a hue, e.g. scarlet is more saturated than pink.
- Brightness: this is related to light intensity.

Colour blindness

- Total colour blindness is very rare.
- Most colour-blind people have colour deficiency, e.g. the blue factor is weak.
- Most of them have normal visual acuity.

Occasionally, one of the three primary types of cones is lacking because of failure to inherit the appropriate gene for formation of the cone. The colour genes are sex linked and are found in the female sex chromosome. As females have two of these chromosomes, they almost never have a deficiency of a colour gene. However, because males have only one female chromosome, one or more of the colour genes is absent in about 4% of all males. For this reason, almost all colour-blind people are males.

If a person has a complete lack of red cones, they are able to see green, yellow, orange and orange–red colours by using their green cones. However, they are not able to distinguish satisfactorily between these colours because they have no red cones to contrast with the green ones. Likewise, if a person has a deficit of green cones, they are able to see all the colours, but not able to distinguish between green, yellow, orange and red colours because the green cones are not available to contrast with the red. Thus, loss of either the red or the green cones makes it difficult or impossible to distinguish between the colours of the longer wavelengths. This is called red–green colour blindness.

In very rare instances a person lacks blue cones, in which case they have difficulty distinguishing violet, blue and green. This type of colour blindness is frequently called blue weakness.

Abnormal colour appreciation

There are three classifications of abnormal colour vision:

Normal colour vision is trichromatic

1. Anomalous trichromatism shows an *anomaly* of one factor.

    a) Protanomalous – red factor is weak (1:100 males)

    Any redness seen in a colour by a normal observer is seen more weakly by the protanomalous viewer, both in terms of its 'colouring power' (saturation, or depth of colour) and its brightness.

    Red, orange, yellow, and yellow–green appear shifted in hue towards green, and all appear paler than they do to the normal observer.

The redness component that a normal observer sees in a violet or lavender is so weakened that it may not be detected, and therefore only the blue component is seen. Hence, 'violet' may look only like another shade of blue.

b) Deuteranomalous – green factor is weak (5:100 males)

Similar to the protanomalous person, poor at discriminating small differences in hues in the red, orange, yellow, green region of the spectrum.

Errors in the naming of hues in this region because they appear shifted towards red. One very important difference between deuteranomalous individuals and protanomalous individuals is that deuteranomalous individuals do not have the loss of 'brightness' problem

c) Tritanomalous – blue factor is weak

2. Dichromatism shows an *absence* of one factor.

a) Protanopia red factor is missing 1:100 males

b) Deuteranopia green factor is missing 1:100 males

3. Monochromatism shows an absence of colour appreciation and the person is therefore totally colour blind. Cone monochromatism is associated with progressive loss of colour vision. Rod monochromatism is a more severe form, associated with lower visual acuity, nystagmus and photophobia.

- Sex-linked colour 'blindness 'occurs in 8% of males and 0.4% of females (the father must be affected and the mother carry a deficiency of a colour gene).

A colour-blind female (0.4%) must have a colour-blind father and a colour-blind mother in order for the disease to be expressed. Such a combination is very unusual. A colour-blind male (8% of males) need have only a mother who has an abnormal gene (heterozygous) for colour blindness. His father can be normal.

- Disturbance of green factor is more common than red.
- Blue disturbance is very rare.

Psychology of colour

Colour perception is a subjective psychological phenomenon and is not only associated with physiological absolutes. Perception of colour depends on the context in which an object is presented and colour may be interpreted very differently depending on experience. Many protanomalous and deuteranomalous people have very little difficulty in doing tasks that require normal colour vision, as their perception of the world is unique to them and they recognise as a particular colour what people with 'normal' colour vision call that colour. Many do not recognise that their colour vision is in any way distorted.

Control of eye movements and binocular vision

Continuous fine eye movements occur as part of normal viewing. This is an important concept in ensuring that constant stimulation of the photoreceptors maintains image perception – a perception that remains popular. It has been shown that images received by peripheral receptors fade rapidly if fixation is deliberately maintained in one position. Eyes in the alert state are never at rest (Forrester *et al.* 2016). Eye movements are paired when they move in different directions.

Each eye is moved by four rectus muscles (superior, inferior, medial and lateral) and two oblique muscles (superior and inferior). The insertions on the eye of these muscles are such that they have a main and a secondary action. Only the medial and lateral recti move the eye in a simple horizontal direction. The superior rectus muscle elevates the eye and has a secondary action of adducting and intorting the eye.

Torsion of the eye occurs about an anteroposterior axis. While the superior rectus is contracting, the opposite inferior oblique (contralateral synergist) will move the other eye in the same direction. Conjugate movements require reciprocal innervation of the muscles, which can therefore be described as conjugate pairs of muscles for each direction of gaze.

The eye muscles in the primary position of gaze are in a state of tonic activity. Each muscle is, however, activated when the eye moves in its field of action and is inhibited in the opposite direction. The final pathway for neuronal control of eye movement occurs via the cranial nerves, namely the third (oculomotor), fourth (trochlear) and sixth (abducens) cranial nerves.

The extraocular muscles are under both reflex control and higher centre control, with the frontal cortex regulating voluntary activity and the occipital cortex and superior colliculus acting as coordinating centres. The superior colliculus is situated in the midbrain and is the coordinating centre for reflex eye movement. Both eyes normally move together so that images continue to fall on corresponding points of both retinas.

The ability to fixate a bright light is a basic reflex within a few days of birth, but the binocular reflex (involving conjugate eye movements and a sustained response) takes several months to be fully developed. Foveal fixation is the end point of the searching movement of the muscles and may be considered the point of peak activity in the nerve and muscle response. The nerve response is tuned to foveal fixation. The very small fine eye movements for sustained foveal fixation are the result of reflex attempts by the oculomotor centre to achieve the best perceived image.

Voluntary eye movements are initiated in the frontal cortex. Eye position and fixation are maintained via neural integrators situated in the midbrain. The vertical gaze centre is situated in the reticular medial longitudinal fasciculus, which is above the nucleus of the third cranial nerve. Therefore, loss of supranuclear control by lesions affecting the midbrain and brain stem can give rise to a variety of clinical features. For instance, multiple sclerosis can involve the medial longitudinal fasciculus, resulting in abnormal horizontal gaze.

Binocular vision is achieved by using both eyes together so that the separate images arising in each eye are appreciated as a single image by a process of fusion. Binocular single vision is an acquired ability, not simply an inborn one, and is built up gradually during the early weeks and months of life, provided that there is clear coordination of various abilities:

- The ability of each retina to function properly from a visual point of view, especially the fovea centralis. This requires an intact healthy retina and a clear transparent medium, i.e. cornea, lens and vitreous humour.

- The ability of the visual areas of the brain to promote fusion of the two separate images transmitted to them from each eye, so that a single mental impression of the object is achieved. This is made possible by the forward direction of the eyes in humans, so that the visual field of one eye almost completely overlaps the visual field of the other eye (the binocular field of vision).

- The ability of each eye to lie correctly in its bony orbit, so that the visual axis of each eye is directed to the same object at rest and during movement.

- The ability of the mechanism that turns the eyes inwards to a near object (convergence) or outwards from a convergent position to a distant object (divergence), and the focusing mechanisms of the eye (accommodation) to achieve an adequate degree of harmony.

The advantages of binocular single vision include an enlarged visual field and three-dimensional vision with, in addition, improved visual acuity and compensation for the blind spot of each eye by the other.

Normal binocular vision is acquired by the age of 3 years but alterations in vision can occur up to the age of 7 or 8 years. Babies learn to see over a period of time, as they are not born with all the visual abilities they need in life. They must gradually learn to focus their eyes, move them accurately, and use them together. For this reason, it is essential to manage and correct squints early – to prevent amblyopia.

References

Bowling, B. (2015) *Kanski's Clinical Ophthalmology, a systematic approach.* 8th edn. London: Elsevier.

Bower, T.G.R. (1965) Stimulus variables determining space perception in infants. *Science.* **149**, 88.

Fantz, R.L. (1958) Pattern vision in young patients. *The Psychological Record.* **8**, 43.

Forrester, J. V., Dick, A. D., McMenamin, P. G., Roberts, F. & Pearlman, E. (2016) *The Eye: Basic sciences in practice.* 4th edn. Edinburgh: Elsevier.

Gessell, A., Ilg F.L.. & Bullis, G.E. (1949) *Vision: Its development in infant and child.* New York: Hoeber.

Guyton, A.C. (1979) *Physiology of the Human Body.* Philadelphia: Saunders College Publishing.

Kagan, J., Henker, B.A., Hen-Tov, A., Levine, J. & Lewis, M. (1966) Infants' differential reactions to familiar and distorted faces. *Child Development.* **37**, 519.

Piaget, J. (1952) *The Origins of Intelligence in Children.* New York: International Universities Press.

Riordan-Eva, P. & Cunningham, E.T. Jr. (2011) *Vaughan and Astbury's General Ophthalmology.* 18th edn. McGraw-Hill

Snell, R.S. & Lemp, M.A. (1998) *Clinical Anatomy of the Eye.* 2nd edn. USA: Blackwell Science.

Tovee, M.J. (1996) *An Introduction to the Visual System.* Cambridge: Cambridge University Press.

White, B.L. & Castle, P.W. (1964) Visual exploratory behaviour following postnatal handling of human infants. *Perceptual and Motor Skills* 18, 497.

Yanoff, M. & Duker, J.S. (2014) *Ophthalmology.* 4th edn. USA: Elsevier Saunders.

CHAPTER TWO

Optics

Janet Marsden and David M Spence

Light

Light is a type of energy to which the eye is sensitive. It is an electromagnetic radiation, travelling at 300,000km per second, and is part of a spectrum based on wavelength. The path of light is always straight unless an obstacle is encountered. It is usually represented by a straight line or ray with an arrow to demonstrate the direction of travel.

Although the nature of light is not, as yet, fully understood by scientists, it is recognised that, rather than behaving only as a ray, light also behaves as though it is made up of particles (photons) and, finally, as a wave. The focus of this chapter is the transmission of light through media – air, eye tissue, etc.; the ray and wave characteristics are most important and the particle characteristics of light are not considered. In general, wave motion is the disturbance of the medium caused by the energy passing through it (Figure 2.1).

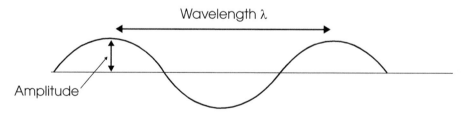

Figure 2.1 Wavelength.

The wavelength is the distance between two symmetrical points on the wave and is often represented by the Greek letter lambda (λ). It is usually expressed in nanometres (nm), a distance that is one-millionth part of a millimetre ($10{-}6$mm) or one thousand-millionth part of a metre ($10{-}9$m). The electromagnetic spectrum consists of a range of wavelengths of radiation (Figure 2.2).

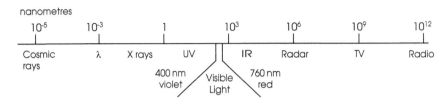

Figure 2.2 The electromagnetic spectrum consists of a range of wavelengths of radiation.

The eye is normally able to discriminate between the wavelengths in the visible spectrum in order to discriminate between different colours. The longest wavelength is red and the shortest violet, with the rainbow spectrum in between. White light is an amalgam of all the different colours. The lens absorbs ultraviolet (UV) light and therefore the eye does not normally see UV light. The patient with aphakia often perceives some very violet or blue colours because the UV end of the spectrum is able to impact on the retina. Waves of light travel randomly. They travel 'out of phase' and in all planes. A single beam of light coming out of the page at the reader would contain waves travelling in all planes. If the beam were cut across, it would appear as in Figure 2.3.

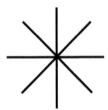

Figure 2.3 A section through an unpolarised 'beam' of light.

If light travels through a medium that lets through only those waves travelling in a single plane, the light is said to be polarised – the cross-section of the beam coming towards the reader would therefore be represented as shown in Figure 2.4. Polarising lenses therefore work by cutting out all light except that going in a single direction; consequently, when used in spectacles, they cut out a degree of the light passing through the lens and remove any scattered light and therefore glare from, for example, water.

Figure 2.4 A section through a polarised 'beam' of light.

LASERs

The word laser is derived from the way they work: **L**ight **A**mplification by **S**timulated **E**mission of **R**adiation. A laser consists of a light source that is usually gaseous. Energy, usually electrical, is 'pumped' into the source. The gas is in a tube with a mirror at each end and the tube has a length equal to a multiple of the wavelength of the light emitted by the gas. The electrons in the gas become 'excited' and are stimulated to emit light, which is in phase.

The light emitted is reflected and re-reflected in the tube by the mirrors and, because of the precise length of the tube, the light remains in phase with itself on reflection and therefore reinforces itself. It becomes stronger and stronger while remaining in phase (coherent). If one of the mirrors allows light to leave the tube, the light will be in phase (coherent), monochromatic (of one wavelength), with all rays parallel (collimated) and usually of high energy.

The eye focuses parallel light on to the retina. If the laser light is of sufficient intensity, it will cause retinal burns, which is obviously the intention of some ophthalmic lasers. The immensely high-intensity light can also be focused on other structures, where it can be used to burn or vaporise tissue in the case of other ophthalmic applications.

The protective goggles used by workers when operating lasers are designed to absorb the wavelength emitted by the laser, while transmitting other wavelengths so that the worker can see.

The behaviour of light

Reflection of light

When light waves hit an object, their behaviour depends on the nature of the medium in which they are travelling and the medium that they 'hit'. Light may be transmitted on through the medium, absorbed by it or reflected back into the first medium. Reflection allows us to see objects around us. There are a number of physical laws associated with reflection:

The incident ray, reflected ray and normal (a line at 90° perpendicular to the surface at the point of reflection) all lie in the same plane

The angle of incidence (i) is equal to the angle of reflection (r) (Figure 2.5).

Irregular surfaces scatter light in many directions – and this is called diffuse reflection. It is by this means that we see objects around us.

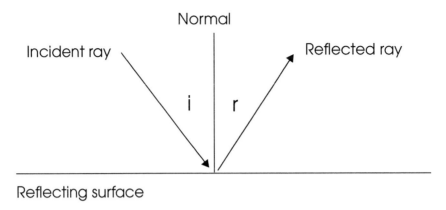

Figure 2.5 *Reflections at a surface –*
the angle of incidence (i) is equal to the angle of reflection (r).

Reflection at a flat surface (such as a mirror)

It is easy to demonstrate this reflection if we look at text in a mirror. The text in the mirror is upright, as in the object we are holding up; it is inverted laterally and it appears as far behind the mirror as the book we are holding is in front of it (Figure 2.6b).

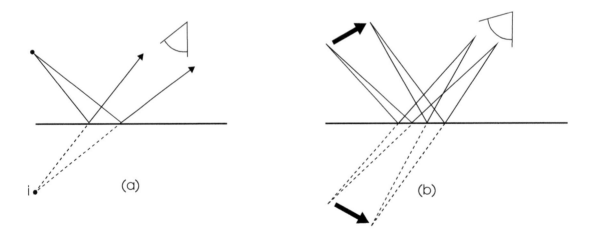

Figure 2.6 (a) The rays are reflected according to the laws of reflection. The brain assumes that the point is situated in the direction from which light enters the eye. The eye therefore 'sees' the point behind the surface. There is no real image at point i and it is therefore known as a virtual image. (b) In this case, the reflected object is a solid shape rather than a point. The image is upright, virtual and inverted laterally, and it appears as far behind the surface as the object is in front of it.

Refraction of light

Refraction is the change in direction of light when it passes from one transparent medium to another (it is easier to show this by representing light as a wave). The speed of light depends on the density of the medium in which it travels – the denser the medium, the slower the speed (Figure 2.7).

As the edge of the wavefront is slowed down, as it hits the denser medium, and the opposite side of the beam carries on at the original speed, the beam is deviated towards a line perpendicular to the surface (normal).

The optical density or refractive index of a particular medium is measured by comparing the speed of light through it with the speed of light in a vacuum (air is used under normal circumstances because its optical density is negligible):

$$\text{Refractive index of material} = \frac{\text{Speed (velocity) of light in air}}{\text{Speed (velocity) of light in medium}}$$

It can therefore be seen that light changes direction at every surface within the eye so that the light may be focused on the retina.

Some common refractive indexes:

Air   1
Aqueous and water   1.33
Cornea   1.37
Physiological lens   1.38–1.42
Glass   1.52

(From Elkington *et al.* 1999)

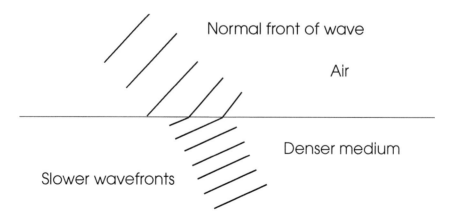

Figure 2.7 Refraction of light: the wavefront changes direction.

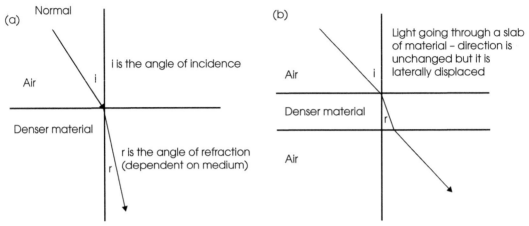

(a) Normal

i is the angle of incidence

Air

Denser material

r is the angle of refraction
(dependent on medium)

(b)

Light going through a slab
of material – direction is
unchanged but it is
laterally displaced

Air

Denser material

Air

Figure 2.8 (a) Refraction of light showing the change of direction; in (b) the light is going through a slab of material – direction is unchanged but it is laterally displaced. In the figure i is the angle of incidence and r the angle of refraction (depending on the medium).

Refraction at a curved surface

A convex surface causes parallel light to converge to a focus if the refractive index of the first medium (N_1) is less than that of the second (N_2), or to diverge as if from a focus (Figure 2.9).

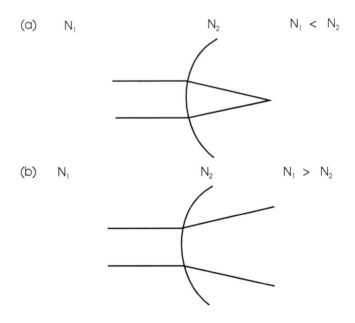

(a) N_1 N_2 $N_1 < N_2$

(b) N_1 N_2 $N_1 > N_2$

Figure 2.9 A convex surface causes parallel light to converge to a focus if the refractive index of the medium (N_1) is less than that of the second medium (N_2), or to diverge as if from a focus. (a) Air: cornea and (b) glass: air.

Surface power is measured in dioptres (D) – positive for converging surfaces and negative for diverging surfaces. The anterior surface of the cornea is a positive refracting surface and its power accounts for most of the refracting power of the eye. The power of a convex or concave surface or lens is determined by its focal length, which is a measure of the distance from the lens to the point where it focuses parallel rays of light (F) (Figure 2.10).

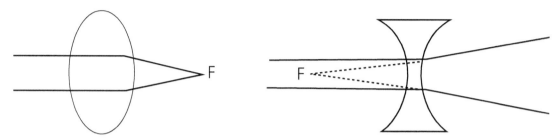

Figure 2.10 The action of a convex and concave lens.

A lens with a focal length of 1 metre is termed a 1-dioptre lens (1 D) and one with a focal length of 0.5 metres, a 2-dioptre lens (2 D):

Dioptric power = 1/Focal length in metres

So a lens with a focal length of 2 metres will have a power of 0.5 D.

Convex and concave lenses are distinguished from each other by a + for convex lenses and a – for concave lenses.

Optics and the eye

The power of the refractive structures within the eye, the cornea and the lens are important factors in the effective focusing of light on to the retinal receptors.

The axial length of the eye

The dioptric power of the eye is around 58 D. The cornea contributes about 43 D and the lens 15 D (although its actual power is around 20 D, it is separated from the cornea and therefore the power is not a simple sum) (Snell & Lemp 1998, Remington 2012).

The lens can change its dioptric power, allowing both distant and near objects to focus on the retina. The lens is normally held in place by the suspensory ligament, which attaches it to the ciliary muscle. Contraction of the ciliary muscle reduces tension on the ligaments and the lens, allowing it to assume a more rounded shape. The curvature of the lens and its thickness increase and therefore its dioptric power increases (accommodation). The range of dioptric power of the lens changes with age – about 8 D at age 40 and only 1 or 2 D by age 60. When accommodation becomes weaker, the eye becomes presbyopic and reading spectacles are needed.

Emmetropia

The eye is considered to be emmetropic if parallel light rays (from infinity or, in effect, greater than 6m away) are focused on the retina when the eye is in a relaxed state. The eye will have a clear image of a distant object without any adjustment to its optics. Most emmetropic eyes are around 23–24mm in length (axial length) but smaller or larger eyes may be emmetropic if their optical components are correspondingly stronger or weaker.

Ammetropia

If the rays of light do not fall on the retina, the eye is ammetropic and a refractive error is present.

Refractive errors of the eye

Myopia

When the focused image is in front of the retina, the eye is 'too long' and is considered myopic. This is also known as short- or near-sightedness because there is a point less than 6m away from the eye from which light will focus on the retina when the eye is at rest.

Patient experience

Individuals with myopia will complain of blurred distance vision. Their near vision is often much better. They may attempt to see better by narrowing the palpebral fissure or 'screwing their eyes up'. (Myopia is a Greek word meaning 'to screw up or close the eyes'.) This attempts to replicate a pinhole effect in which only a very narrow beam of light enters the eye and does not need focusing, thus negating refractive error.

Causes of myopia

Myopia may be caused by a larger axial length than normal, by a greater curvature of the cornea or lens, or by a higher refractive index of the lens. If the eye is longer than normal, the anterior segment will be deeper than normal. There is therefore a smaller possibility of angle-closure glaucoma in myopic individuals. The posterior segment is also affected; choroidal atrophy may occur, usually around the temporal border of the disc, but sometimes around the nasal border or even around the whole disc (peripapillary atrophy). Degenerative changes may occur in the submacular area after choroidal degeneration in this area, and individuals with extreme myopia are more likely to develop retinal detachments.

Simple myopia

Simple myopia usually develops in childhood or adolescence and needs correcting to ensure that a normal accommodation–convergence reflex develops and to ensure satisfactory progress at school. This type of myopia progresses, necessitating regular testing and changes of spectacles, but usually stabilises after adolescence.

Other causes of myopia

Myopia may be associated with an abnormality in which the axial length of the eye is excessive and continues to enlarge. It is rare and associated with vitreous floaters and chorioretinal changes (pathological, progressive or degenerative myopia). Myopia carries on increasing and may reach 40–50 D.

Congenital high myopia is usually a refractive error of around 10 D and can be detected in infants. It is not usually progressive (Pavan-Langston 2007).

Changes in the curvature of the cornea in keratoconus will lead to myopia.

Lens curvature changes caused by hyperglycaemia, causing lens tumescence, will give the diabetic patient myopia. This usually stabilises as their blood glucose levels are controlled.

Nuclear sclerosis, causing an increased refractive index of the lens, will also cause a myopic shift.

Hypermetropia

In the hypermetropic eye, the focus point for the parallel light rays is behind the retina so no clear image is formed on the retina. This may be caused by a shorter axial length than normal, by an insufficient degree of corneal or lens curvature or by a low refractive index of the lens.

Patient experience

The accommodative power of the eye is used to add to the dioptric power of the eye to focus light on the retina and correct the hypermetropia. Distance vision may therefore be as good as near vision. The eye has to work even harder to accommodate for near vision, so it is often near vision that is blurred if the degree of hypermetropia is more than minimal. The eye is never at rest and the individual may experience headaches associated with reading and 'other near-vision tasks. Light sensitivity is common in individuals with hypermetropia and is relieved by correcting the hypermetropia. Individuals with hypermetropia may get a spasm of accommodation, leading to sudden blurred vision (pseudomyopia). This is also relieved by correction of the refractive error.

Causes of hypermetropia

As hypermetropia may be caused by a shorter axial length than normal or by a lesser curvature of the refracting structures of the eye, the hypermetropic eye is usually smaller than normal. This affects the anterior segment, and the anterior chamber tends to be shallower than normal with a crowded drainage angle that may contribute to the development of angle-closure glaucoma. The posterior segment is also affected and the optic disc may look small or blurred (pseudopapilloedema).

Classification of hypermetropia

- Absolute or total hypermetropia is the amount of hypermetropia with all accommodation suspended, as in cycloplegia.
- Manifest hypermetropia is the maximum degree of hypermetropia that can be corrected with a lens when accommodation is active.
- Latent hypermetropia is the difference between absolute and manifest hypermetropia – that part of the refractive error corrected by accommodation (Newell 1996).

As the person ages, the degree of possible accommodation reduces and the degree of manifest hypermetropia will therefore increase.

Most hypermetropia is 'simple'. Pathological hypermetropia may be caused by microphthalmos, aphakia and forward movement of the retina as a result of a tumour or oedema.

Astigmatism

Astigmatism occurs when the curvature of a refracting surface of the eye varies in different meridians (a toric surface). Light rays passing through a shallow meridian are deflected less than those passing through a steeper meridian, resulting in the formation of a complex image. The directions of greatest and least curvature are usually at right angles to each other. Astigmatism may be associated with emmetropia, myopia or hypermetropia.

Patient experience

The patient often experiences blurred vision and may tilt or turn the head in order to achieve the best image. 'Screwing up the eyes' may occur in order to get a pinhole image, and reading material may be held close to the face in order to see the largest (albeit blurred) image possible. The patient may suffer from 'tired eyes', headaches or transient blurred vision associated with visual concentration. (Astigmat means 'not to a point' – so an individual with astigmatism looking at, for example, a star will observe an elongated streak of light.)

Causes and classification of astigmatism

Differences in the curvature of the cornea in different meridians account for most of the astigmatism of the eye.

Regular astigmatism

On a regular curved surface, the meridians of greatest and least curvature lie 90° apart.

If the meridians of ocular astigmatism are constant across the cornea, and the amount of astigmatism is the same at each point on the meridian, the refractive condition is known as regular astigmatism (American Academy of Ophthalmology 1996). If the vertical meridian is steeper, it is referred to as 'with the rule' and if the horizontal meridian is steeper it is known as 'against the rule'. In the cornea, these meridians are often horizontal and vertical or close to those planes. If the meridians are more than 20° away from the horizontal and vertical meridians, the refractive condition is known as oblique astigmatism.

Irregular astigmatism

This occurs when the principal meridians are not at 90° all the way across the cornea, or the amount of astigmatism changes from one point to another, i.e. the corneal surface is irregular. The American Academy of Ophthalmology (1996) suggests that all eyes have at least a small amount of irregular astigmatism, but the term is usually reserved for those eyes that have gross irregularities. This may be caused by keratoconus or corneal scarring.

Presbyopia

Presbyopia is a gradual loss of the accommodative response as a result of loss of elasticity of the lens capsule and hardening of the lens. When the eye tries to accommodate, there is less change in the shape of the lens for the same amount of effort. Accommodation decreases with age, and symptoms of presbyopia, when these affect the ability of the patient to carry out normal tasks, begin at around the age of 40.

Correction of refractive error

Figure 2.11 shows the apparent position of the image, the focus point, in the emmetropic eye (on the retina), the myopic eye (in front of the retina because the eye is too long or its refractive power too weak) and the hypermetropic eye (behind the retina because the eye is too short or its refractive power is too weak). The images in both the myopic eye and the hypermetropic eye are blurred.

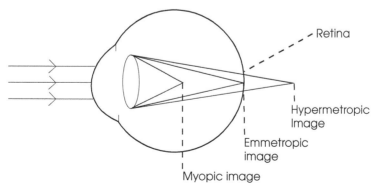

Figure 2.11 Refractive errors.

If the correct lens is placed in front of the ammetropic eye, it will change the direction of the light rays entering the eye, thus enabling the cornea and the lens to focus them at the retina and allowing the person to see a clear image.

In the hypermetropic eye, a convex or plus lens will add to the power of the cornea and lens and enable it to bring the image forward, on to the retina (Figure 2.12).

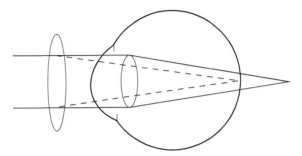

Figure 2.12 Correction of hypermetropia by a convex (+) lens.

In the myopic eye, a concave or minus lens will diverge the light rays before they hit the cornea and the focus point will therefore move backwards to the retina allowing a clear image to be seen (Figure 2.13).

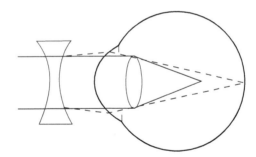

Figure 2.13 Correction of myopia by a concave (–) lens.

Assessment of refractive error
Retinoscopy

Retinoscopy is the objective test that measures ammetropia of the eye. The retinoscope is an instrument that uses a mirror to reflect light along a line connecting the examiner's and the patient's pupils, and has an aperture in the mirror to allow the examiner to observe the patient's illuminated pupil. The examiner observes the reflex created by light reflected from the retina and refracted by the media of the eye. The area of illumination on the retina moves in the same direction as the retinoscope is moved. The observer, however, sees only a tiny beam of light, which appears to come from the eye's far point: infinity in an emmetropic eye, behind the eye in a hypermetropic eye and in front of the eye in a myopic eye. The observer sees the small reflection from the retina move in the same direction as the retinoscope in the emmetropic or hypermetropic eye and in the opposite direction in the myopic eye. Lenses are placed in front of the eye and the retinoscope beam is moved until the pupil is filled with light that does not move. The lenses have corrected the degree of ammetropia at that point. Positive or convex lenses will neutralise hypermetropia, whereas a combination of negative or concave lenses will neutralise myopia.

In practice, the observer is at a distance of 0.5–0.67m from the eye (arm's length), which induces an error of +2 D to +1.5 D; this will be deducted from the final reading to ascertain the amount of ammetropia. This is called the 'working distance lens'. Thus, an emmetropic eye is one in which the working distance lens causes the neutralisation of the movement of the illuminated retinal area.

A similar procedure will be performed at 90° away from the initial meridian to evaluate any correction for astigmatism. A clear medium, good fixation and reasonably sized pupils are prerequisites for accurate retinoscopy. Therefore, although the technique can be very accurate, a subjective refraction is usually carried out to ensure that the patient can tolerate the prescription that is eventually prescribed.

Cycloplegic refraction

Cycloplegic refraction is often performed in order to negate the effects of accommodation, so that an accurate refraction (without the eye doing any work) can be obtained. This is used particularly in children who have high levels of accommodation, so that the correct amount of hypermetropic error may be measured. However, it may also be carried out in adults with hypermetropia, to measure the absolute amount of refractive error.

Subjective refraction

Subjective refraction relies on the patient's response to obtain the refractive correction that obtains the best visual results (visual acuity). Retinoscopy findings may be the starting point for subjective refraction. Alternatively, a small dioptre lens (either plus or minus) may be placed in front of the patient's eye while they are asked if the distance visual acuity chart becomes more, or less, clear. If there is no astigmatism, the refraction consists of adding more plus or minus lenses until the patient has the best possible correction that is comfortable. The eye may be 'fogged' first by using too strong a convex (+) or too weak a concave (–) lens to blur the vision to relax accommodation if the eye is hypermetropic.

Astigmatic correction

Astigmatism requires that a cylindrical lens be added to the basic correction at an appropriate meridian in order to achieve the best correction. One method of ascertaining both the correct meridian of astigmatism and the power of lens needed is to use the 'fogging technique'.

Placing a large plus lens in front of the eye makes the eye artificially myopic and inhibits accommodation. An astigmatic fan (Figure 2.14) is placed in front of the eye and the patient is asked to identify which line on it is darkest and most distinct. This is marked with the angle of the astigmatic meridian.

A minus power cylindrical lens is placed with its axis along this meridian and increases in power until all the lines on the fan become equal. The patient is kept artificially myopic by continually adding positive spherical lenses. The patient is then asked to look at a distance vision chart and spherical lenses are removed until maximum clarity of vision is achieved. If the patient has never worn spectacles before, a reduced form of the prescription may be prescribed initially to avoid intolerance and discomfort. For instance:

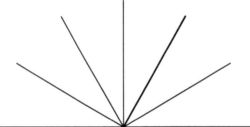

Figure 2.14 The astigmatic meridian (darker line).

- + 2.00 fogs vision to 6/18
- 120° is the axis on the fan which is clearest
- −1.00 at 120° evens out darkness of the fan lines
- reducing plus lenses to + 0.25 gives sharpest vision on distance reading chart.

Reading 'add'

The patient with presbyopia will need a correction to replace that part of the accommodative reflex that is no longer available. This is done with plus lenses that supplement the remaining accommodative power of the eye. The person with emmetropia will need a correction for reading only. If a person has myopia or hypermetropia, they will need a near vision prescription to add to the prescription for distance. This is known as the reading 'add'.

Autorefraction

Sophisticated instruments are available that can refract patients and are felt to be reasonably accurate. Alignment of the eye with the machine is critical as is fixation, which makes these instruments less useful for some patients. Some refractors measure only through very small portions of the optics of the eye, achieving a result that may not be representative of the eye as a whole. The tendency to accommodate when looking into instruments has also proved problematic, but fogging techniques may be used to overcome this. The autorefraction readings must be checked by retinoscopy and refined by subjective testing before prescribing. Failure to ensure that this is carried out by an appropriate professional (such as a registered optometrist, ophthalmic medical practitioner or an ophthalmologist qualified to refract) is a breach of the law.

Prescriptions

As in the astigmatism example ($+0.25 -1.00 \times 120$), shown again in Figure 2.15, it can be seen that the final written prescription is interpreted as follows: the first figure is a spherical lens to correct myopia or hypermetropia depending on whether the symbol in front of it is minus (myopia) or plus (hypermetropia). The second figure is the correction, in the form of a spherical lens, for astigmatism (again, either positive or negative), which is added to the initial correction. The third figure is the axis at which the lens is placed in order to correct the astigmatism. The reading add is documented separately. The prism is the lens needed (if any) to align the eyes (a prism is a lens that bends the path of light without altering its focus and can be used where the eyes are not aligned – for example, in cranial nerve palsies). The 'VA' box contains the visual acuity for each eye when corrected and usually uses Snellen notation. The 'Add' box contains any additional positive power needed to enable the eye to focus for close work such as reading. It is the correction for presbyopia. The final box notes the level of near vision achieved with this correction. The example (Figure 2.15) shows the astigmatism prescription previously described with a reading addition, the person achieving 6/6 and N5.

	Sph	Cyl	Axis	Prism	VA	Add	Near
Right (OD)	+0.25	-1.00	120		6/6	+1.00	N5
Left (OS)							

Figure 2.15 An optometric prescription.

Transposition of prescriptions

There is more than one way to write the same optical prescription! Some ophthalmologists like to work in 'positive cylinder' (or plus cyl) notation and some prefer to use a negative cylinder (minus cyl) prescription. There are a number of reasons for this; optical laboratories tend to work in minus cylinder notations, as this is the way lenses are ground for the final product (*Optician World* 2015). Within the NHS, the category of voucher to offset the cost of lenses is determined by the highest spherical power in the prescription, so it may need to be transposed to achieve this (NHS England 2015). Prescriptions may appear to have changed significantly from eye test to eye test when the prescription is written in two different notations. It is therefore a useful skill to be able to transpose the prescription to ascertain if actual change has taken place.

Transposition is very straightforward as can be seen by the worked examples (Figure 2.16):

- First, add the power of the sphere and the cylinder together, this gives the new power of the sphere
- Change the cylinder sign but keep the numerical power
- Rotate the axis of the sphere through 90° (add 90 if the original is less than 90°; subtract 90 if the original is more than 90°).

	Sph	Cyl	Axis
Prescription in Plus (or positive) Cylinder	+5.00	+2.00	80
Transposed to Minus (or negative) Cylinder	+7.00	-2.00	170

Here, +5.00 added to +2.00 gives a spherical power of +7.00

The cylinder power changes to minus

The axis adds 90 to 80 to make 170 degrees

	Sph	Cyl	Axis
Prescription in Minus Cylinder	-3.50	-0.75	45
Transposed to Plus Cylinder	-4.25	+0.75	135

	Sph	Cyl	Axis
Prescription in Plus Cylinder	-3.00	+8.00	150
Transposed to Minus Cylinder	+5.00	-8.00	60

Figure 2.16 Transposition of cyls.

Correction of refractive error in practice
Spectacles

Most ammetropia may be corrected with spectacle lenses. As stated previously, convex (plus) lenses are used to correct hypermetropia and presbyopia and concave (minus) lenses are used to correct myopia. Although lenses ore often drawn as biconvex or biconcave, other forms of the lenses exist – planoconvex and planoconcave – and those that are most often used for spectacle lenses to reduce distortion and, for best cosmetic effect, meniscus lenses (Figure 2.17).

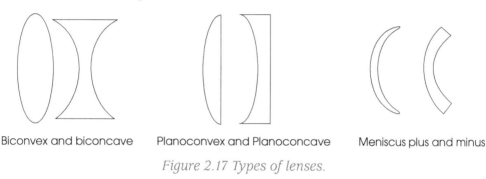

Biconvex and biconcave   Planoconvex and Planoconcave   Meniscus plus and minus

Figure 2.17 Types of lenses.

Lenses prescribed for one distance (reading or distance vision) are termed 'single vision lenses'. Bifocal lenses have a reading add in addition to the distance vision part of the lens and this is placed inferiorly in the lens so that the person can look down to read. Progressive addition lenses (PALs) have a distance correction in the superior portion of the lens and then a zone of gradual reduction in distance power, leading to a reading zone inferiorly.

Spectacle lenses may be made from glass or various forms of plastic material. Glass does not usually scratch as easily as plastic but is less impact resistant (unless toughened) and therefore less safe in case of accident. Plastics are much lighter and therefore less tiring to wear.

Lenses need to be centred both horizontally and vertically in their frame and on the patient's face to ensure that the patient is looking through the correct portion of the lens. The intrapupillary distance must also be taken into account.

Contact lenses

Contact lenses are most commonly used to correct refractive errors. They may be used therapeutically (as in the case of bandage lenses that protect the cornea from external factors and allow healing of corneal disorders), or cosmetically to cover an unsightly damaged eye or to enhance eye colour.

The prime motivating factor for contact lens correction of refractive errors in most patients is cosmetic, in that they are less obvious and cumbersome than spectacles. Contact lenses will improve the quality of vision for individuals with high myopia in particular and the field of view is enhanced for all users. A contact lens aids in the 'smoothing out' of an irregular corneal surface and thus in the enhancement of the retinal image formed, and rigid or hard contact lenses may also help to eliminate astigmatism. Contact lenses are also very useful in the initial correction of keratoconus.

All contact lenses can cause a reversible change in the curvature of the cornea, which may resolve within minutes of removing the lenses or may take a number of days. Patients may find that their vision is slightly blurred for a while when they swap from contact lenses to their normal spectacle prescription.

Types of contact lens

Contact lenses are categorised by size and material. The smallest of the lens types are corneal lenses, which are confined to covering the cornea. These are generally hard lenses, made of polymethylmethacrylate (PMMA), or gas-permeable lenses, which are also hard and made out of cellulose acetate butyrate (CAB), silicone and other similar materials.

Slightly larger than these are semiscleral lenses, which bridge the limbus and lie partially on the conjunctiva that overlies the sclera at the limbus. These are soft lenses that are made from a variety of polymers and are all hydrophilic to various degrees (hydrophilic means 'having an affinity with or taking in water'). The water content of these lenses may be anything from 30% to around 85%.

The final classification of lens based on size is the scleral lens, which covers the cornea and most of the conjunctiva overlying sclera. These are usually made of PMMA but newer developments include gas-permeable scleral lenses. Extended-wear lenses are often used when the patient's ability to use daily-wear soft lenses is impaired.

Each type of lens works in a slightly different way. Hard lenses float on a film of tears, which also forms a type of lens. In this way, corneal irregularities are evened out and astigmatism may be corrected up to a certain level. After about 2 D of astigmatism, a cylindrical or toric lens must be incorporated into the back surface of the lens. Soft lenses adapt to the shape of the cornea without a tear film layer and so will not correct any degree of astigmatism unless a toric lens is incorporated into them. Soft lenses are often categorised by their replacement frequency. Replacement may be daily (daily disposable), and in variable timescales from two weekly to six monthly. The most commonly used contact lenses in the UK are daily disposable. All other lenses will need to be cleaned in between wear.

Bifocal and multifocal lenses are all available in soft materials, along with 'toric' lenses to correct astigmatism. Coloured and special-effect soft lenses, to change the colour or appearance of the eyes rather than correct vision, are known as 'plano cosmetic' lenses and can also be used to mask eye injury or disfigurement. Many soft contact lenses incorporate an ultraviolet filter to help protect the eye.

Lenses and corneal oxygenation

The PMMA lens (the traditional hard lens) floats on a film of tears, which provides the cornea with an oxygen supply. They are in themselves impermeable to oxygen. The lenses need to fit correctly, with an adequate space between the edge and the cornea to allow for an exchange of tears between the lens and the cornea, and to give a comfortable fit. Corneal epithelium has a very high metabolic rate and therefore needs high levels of oxygen. Oxygen solubility in the tear film is limited and, therefore, unless a very good flow of tears is maintained, oxygenation of the corneal tissue is limited by PMMA lenses. Lactic acid and carbon dioxide can accumulate under the lens. Moderate oxygen deprivation of the cornea can lead to degrees of corneal oedema, associated with blurring of vision and haloes around lights. Damage to epithelial cells may lead to punctate corneal erosions on the cornea and, consequently, a degree of pain.

Gas-permeable lenses have varying degrees of permeability to oxygen and therefore interfere less with corneal epithelial metabolism. Little or no corneal oedema results, although a decrease in corneal sensitivity occurs, which is common to all types of contact lens.

Soft lenses retain a large amount of water and therefore cause minimal problems associated with lack of oxygen. They are much easier to adapt to than hard lenses, where tolerance has to be built up over a number of days. They are also much more comfortable to wear than hard lenses and there is less chance that they will be accidentally dislodged. They are, however, much more easily damaged by handling. Over-wear is more likely to cause physical or pathological changes than with other lens types.

Care of contact lenses

All lenses accumulate deposits of lipid, proteins, minerals and other matter. These deposits may lead to reduced vision, poor contact lens fit, infection caused by the presence of organisms adhering to the lens and decreased oxygen transmission, and therefore any potential problems associated with this. A variety of solutions and systems for use in the care of contact lenses are available and are broadly split into four categories.

Cleaning agents

These remove deposits from the lens. Surfactants dissolve and clean off adhered protein, lipid and minerals from the surface of the lens, and enable more effective disinfection. Enzyme cleaners digest the deposits. Even if using a 'no rub' product, it is recommended that the lens is rubbed in the palm of the hand with a few drops of solution, as mechanical rubbing removes most debris. The lens should then be rinsed for as long as the cleaning regime suggests.

Disinfecting agents

Various systems are available but are divided into three common methods:

- Thermal disinfection involves boiling the lenses but has the disadvantage that, if inadequately cleaned before boiling, any deposits of protein on the lens will become permanent. Thermal disinfection is not recommended for high water content soft lenses because it changes their molecular structure.

- The effectiveness of hydrogen peroxide disinfection depends on how long the lens is left soaking in the solution. More than 20 minutes is necessary for adequate disinfection (American Academy of Ophthalmology 1996). The hydrogen peroxide must then be neutralised. Some systems have a built-in neutraliser, to convert the hydrogen peroxide to water, so that the eyes are not damaged by strong solution. Others need a neutralising tablet to be added.

- Chemical disinfection systems take much longer to remove all contamination from the lens and require good cleaning of the lens beforehand.

Rinsing agents

A rinsing solution is necessary after cleaning or disinfecting the lens. Unpreserved sterile saline is commonly the solution of choice and is widely available in a variety of presentations such as single-dose containers and aerosols. Other systems use the same solution to clean, disinfect and rinse.

Whatever regime is used, the instructions should be adhered to in order to prevent eye or lens damage.

Wetting agents

Wetting agents are used to lubricate PMMA and gas-permeable lenses before insertion into the eye.

Note that contact lens cases are a common source of corneal infection. There is little point in cleaning a lens adequately if it is immediately put back into a contaminated container. Lens cases must be disinfected, along with the lens, and changed regularly.

Potential problems associated with contact lens wear

Epithelial problems

Contact lenses may cause thinning of the corneal epithelium (and areas of variable density that are seen as microcysts). They may also cause a reduction in the density of structures anchoring the epithelium to its basement membrane (hemidesmosomes and anchoring fibrils), and therefore cause reduced adhesion to the basement membrane (Forrester et al. 2016). Corneal abrasions may be caused by mechanical damage and punctate epithelial erosions by over-wear or chemical damage caused by poor neutralisation of cleaning or disinfecting solutions.

Corneal infection

Infected corneal ulcers are a very serious complication that may be associated with contact lens wear. They occur with all types of lenses but are much more frequently associated with soft lens wear. Many factors are linked to the development of corneal infection, including poor hand-washing technique, inadequate lens disinfection, over-wear leading to corneal epithelial problems, and contaminated solutions and contact lens cases.

Although many corneal ulcers are bacterial in origin, a growing cause of corneal ulcers associated with contact lens wear is Acanthamoeba sp. The main source of contamination is the fluid in the contact lens case. Showering or swimming with lenses in place is also a source of this organism. Acanthamoeba keratitis causes pain out of all proportion to the clinical findings and responds very slowly to therapy (Forrester *et al.* 2016).

Corneal neovascularisation

This is caused by chronic hypoxia associated with contact lens wear, especially if the lenses are thick, or badly fitting, or lens cleaning is inadequate over a period of time. New vessels may extend onto the visual axis if ignored, causing an impairment in vision. Discontinuation of lens wear often leads to regression of the new vessels although ghost vessels may still be seen on the cornea.

Other methods of ammetropia correction

A number of other methods of ammetropia correction are possible and these are listed below.

Orthokeratology

This is a technique whereby the patient is fitted with a contact lens that is flatter than the corneal curvature – in order to induce corneal flattening and so reduce myopia. The patient may have to wear lenses for only part of the time in order to induce the changes in the cornea all the time. However, the effect is only transient and will disappear if the lens is not worn for the necessary time.

Corneal surgery

For information on corneal surgery, see Chapter 17.

Correction of aphakia

It is most unusual for the crystalline lens not to be replaced with an intraocular lens during cataract surgery. However, occasionally, due to complications of the eye or the surgery, this may be the case.

Correction of aphakia may be achieved by replacing the crystalline lens with a strong convex (+) lens in front of the eye in the form of a spectacle lens. Moving the refracting surface to the front of the eye results in a change in the size of the image of 25–30% (Pavan-Langston 2007). Coming to terms with this new image needs considerable adaptation on the part of the patient and, if only one eye is aphakic, this adaptation is impossible because the brain is incapable of coping with the two different-sized images. Strong plus lenses also cause a lot of visual distortion.

Contact lenses are a better solution to aphakia correction. Magnification is reduced to 5–10%, which causes the brain fewer problems. Elderly people who have undergone cataract extraction may be unable to handle contact lenses easily, leading to the need for extended-wear lenses with their inherent problems.

Intraocular lenses

The cataractous lens is replaced by one made usually of polymethylmethacrylate (PMMA) which is rigid, or one made of silicon, acrylic or hydrogel compounds which are foldable. The lens power needed to correct aphakia is calculated using measurements of the curvature of the cornea (ascertained by keratometry), the axial length of the eye (by A-scan biometry), the expected position of the intraocular lens (using a constant for a particular type of lens) and the refraction required after surgery. This is described more fully in Chapter 19.

Intraocular lenses may be situated in the anterior chamber, with the optical part of the lens (optic) in front of the pupil and the supporting structures (haptic) in the anterior chamber angle. The more common position is in the posterior chamber, which is more anatomically correct. The lens is supported by its haptic, which is placed in the capsular bag or ciliary sulcus. Iris clip lenses are used less often. Multifocal intraocular lenses are available, often designed with concentric zones of different powers. Foldable lenses are becoming more common for use in small incision surgery that results in less astigmatism.

Clear lens extraction/clear lens exchange/refractive lens exchange/refractive lensectomy are interchangeable terms for a procedure where the clear, non-cataractous lens is replaced with an intraocular lens in a procedure similar to cataract surgery. This surgery is designed to deliver ammetropia without the need for external lenses or corneal surgery. This is becoming a more popular elective procedure but carries with it the risks of intraocular surgery

References

American Academy of Ophthalmology (2015) *Clinical Optics*. San Francisco, CA: American Academy of Ophthalmology.

Elkington, A.R., Frank, H.J. & Greaney, M.J. (1999) *Clinical Optics*. 3rd edn. London: Wiley.

Forrester, J.V., Dick, A. D., McMenamin, P.G, Roberts, F. & Pearlman, E. (2016) *The Eye: Basic sciences in practice*. 4th edn. Edinburgh: Elsevier.

Newell, F.W. (1996) *Ophthalmology: Principles and concepts*. St Louis, MO: Mosby.

NHS Choices (2016) *NHS voucher values*. http://www.nhs.uk/NHSEngland/Healthcosts/Pages/nhs-voucher-values.aspx (Accessed 10 July 2016).

Optician World (2009) *How To Transpose an Eyewear Prescription Easily*. http://opticianworld.com/opticianry/how-to-transpose-a-prescription-easily (Accessed 10 July 2016).

Pavan-Langston, D. (2007) *Manual of Ocular Diagnosis and Therapy*. 6th edn. Boston, MA: Lippincott Williams and Wilkins.

Remington, L.A. (2012) *Clinical Anatomy and Physiology of the Visual System*. 3rd edn. Butterworth-Heinemann.

Snell, R.S. & Lemp, M.A. (1998) *Clinical Anatomy of the Eye*. 2nd edn. USA: Blackwell Science.

CHAPTER THREE

Pharmacology

Julie Tillotson and Sharon Andrew

Pharmacology is the study of how drugs act in the body. This chapter is concerned with the action and interaction of drugs on the eye. The main categories of ophthalmic drugs and their uses, and the delivery methods of ophthalmic drugs (along with the major adverse side effects) are covered. The chapter concludes with a discussion of the nurse's role in relation to the effective use of eye treatment and an overview of the current UK legislation on prescribing.

In general terms pharmacology can be divided into two parts: pharmacodynamics and pharmacokinetics.

Pharmacodynamics

This deals with the effects of drugs, and where and how these effects are produced. Attention must also be given to adverse drug actions and interactions.

To achieve their effects, drugs act on receptors; these can be inside the cell or on the cell membranes. The receptors can be either stimulated or inhibited by a drug. The drug's effect is determined by its concentration, its affinity for the receptors (strength of attraction) and the presence of other drugs that may be in competition for the same receptors.

Unwanted side effects elsewhere in the body may also occur (such as dyspnoea with timolol and paraesthesia with acetazolamide), resulting from the high affinity of these drugs for their receptors.

Pharmacokinetics

This deals with the role of various factors in controlling rates of absorption of drugs from the sites of administration, distribution within the body or eye, metabolism and elimination.

The response to a drug and any adverse effects will vary from person to person, and factors such as age, general health, genetic background and the presence of other drugs must be taken into account.

Delivery methods

Systemically administered drugs such as antibiotics, anti-inflammatories and analgesics

Absorption

The route of administration will play a major role in the absorption of a drug. Most drugs are given orally and are absorbed mainly in the stomach and small intestine. Factors such as the solubility of the drug, the dissolution rate of the tablet or capsule, the gastrointestinal enzymes and pH, and the presence of food will determine the degree and rate of absorption.

Some drugs are given by injection (intravenously, intramuscularly or subcutaneously). If given intravenously, the total amount of drug reaches the bloodstream, and to a slightly lesser extent if given by the other two routes. However, higher, consistent and more predictable plasma levels can be maintained by using these routes rather than the oral route.

Distribution

Many drugs bind to plasma proteins such as albumin and establish a balance between the bound and unbound fractions of the drugs. Only the free (unbound) fraction of the drug is able to move out of the bloodstream. The amount of the drug in the free form can be influenced by the amount of drug given. It can also be affected by other drugs present in the plasma, which are competing for the binding sites on the plasma proteins.

Most drugs can penetrate from the bloodstream into extracellular tissues, except for the brain, aqueous humour and retina, where they must have some fat solubility (blood–brain and blood–eye barrier).

Metabolism

Most drugs given systemically are broken down in the liver, either by conjugation or by various chemical reactions such as oxidation and reduction. However, some drugs, such as acetazolamide, are not metabolised at all and are excreted unchanged in the urine.

Excretion

The kidneys excrete most water-soluble drugs and the biliary system the large-molecular-weight compounds. Some drugs, such as aspirin, appear in the tears (which is important for contact lens wearers to be aware of). Other drugs are excreted in saliva and breast milk; and, even though the quantity may be small, this may affect the breast-fed baby, a factor that must be taken into account when a drug is prescribed to a nursing mother.

After absorption, the time for one-half of the plasma concentration of the drug to be eliminated is called the biological half-life ($t_{1/2}$). This has important implications when considering frequency of doses in order to achieve steady-state plasma concentrations, rather than peak (high) and trough (low) plasma levels.

Locally administered drugs
Topical application
Topical drugs for extraocular conditions such as conjunctivitis are effective if their concentration is maintained. The concentration will be affected by dilution with tears, drainage through the nasolacrimal duct, and loss through the blood vessels of the conjunctiva and eyelids into the systemic circulation.

For the treatment of intraocular conditions, the topically applied drugs have to penetrate into the eye and must therefore be capable of crossing the cornea. The areas that they have to cross include the precorneal film, corneal epithelium, stroma and endothelium. To do this, the drug has to be available in both the un-ionised (lipid-soluble) and the ionised (water-soluble) forms. Initially, to pass through the corneal epithelium, it needs to be in the un-ionised form and then in the ionised form to pass through the stroma, before changing again to the un-ionised form to pass through the endothelium into the aqueous.

The penetration of any topically administered drug will alter if there is damage or inflammation of the cornea. For instance, fluorescein exists only in the water-soluble form and will not normally penetrate the cornea, so it is used to assess whether there is any corneal damage.

Topically administered drugs may have improved penetration if applied as an ointment, due to the extended ocular contact time.

The uptake of a drug by ocular tissues is also regulated by the amount of time that it sits in contact with the epithelium. Aqueous solutions will stay within the lower fornix and tear film for less time than suspensions (particles suspended in fluid, rather than dissolved in it). Drugs in more viscous carriers (such as polyvinyl alcohol, hyaluronic acid or gels) have a prolonged contact time, and the highest contact time may be achieved by the use of an ointment. Although ointments may not release lipophilic drugs well, gels allow five times more drug to enter the cornea and act as a reservoir, gradually releasing the drug and prolonging its effect (Fechner & Teichmann 1998).

Practical issues of topical administration
To maximise benefits and minimise adverse effects from topical administration, it is recommended that systemic absorption through the nasal mucosa be minimised

by occlusion of the punctum or simply closing the eye for a count of 60. Leaving a sufficient interval between drops to minimise dilution and overflow, and adhering to recommendations about order of application (a synergistic action effect occurs in some cases, e.g. by using pilocarpine after latanoprost), will help to maximise benefits.

Drop size

German *et al.* (1999) recognised that the drop volume varied significantly between manufacturers, and that concentration and viscosity was related to drop size – with higher concentrations of drug giving rise to larger drops. Repeatability and consistency of drop size from the same bottle varied as well. The handling angle of the drop bottle also affected drop size. There is still no standard drop size in the UK or US. As different drop bottles give different drop volumes, and the same drop bottle will give different drop volumes, the dose of drug in one drop is therefore variable. It is important not to flood the eye with drops. However, if it is felt that the drop has not gone into the conjunctival sac, it would seem better to repeat the drop rather than run the risk of the patient missing a dose

Subconjunctival injection

Drug penetration is by local diffusion through the tissues. There are advantages and disadvantages to this route of administration:

- Advantages include high local concentrations, high tissue concentrations and possibly avoiding the need for topical or systemic medication.
- Disadvantages include very low tissue concentrations between injections, local side effects and (perhaps most importantly) patient apprehension.

Intravitreal injection

The drug gets immediately to the site of action but most intravitreal drugs require repeated injections and each one carries the special risks of infection associated with intraocular penetration.

Metabolism

Local agents applied to the eye are metabolised by enzymes within the globe, although the exact mechanisms are unknown.

Properties of topical preparations

Preservatives

Preservatives (such as benzalkonium chloride and thiomersal) are germicidal at very weak concentrations and so preserve the sterility of eye drops. In a single-drop dispenser unit, such as Minims, a preservative is unnecessary because the unit is disposable. Some drop bottles now have systems that prevent bacteria from entering and allow preservative-free solutions to be administered from a multi-dose dispenser. However, these are only currently available for lubricating eye drops. Eye preparations containing preservatives should not be used by contact lens wearers because some preservatives can accumulate in hydrogel lenses and may induce toxic reactions.

Isotonicity

Isotonicity with tear fluid is desirable because it facilitates the acceptance of the eye drop by the patient.

Oxidation

Some substances, such as phenylephrine, are oxidised and so a reducing agent, such as sodium metabisulphite, is added.

Hydrogen ion concentration (pH)

The H^+ concentration is expressed as the pH, with the neutral value being 7.4. The eye can withstand a pH range of 4.5–10, but extremes are to be avoided, so solutions known as buffers (e.g. sodium citrate) are used to remove excess H^+. It is not only for ocular comfort that a desirable pH is needed; some drugs are physiologically active only at a particular pH, so a balance has to be struck between comfort and activity.

Viscosity

As a result of tear drainage, overflow and blinking, a topical agent remains in the lower fornix for only a short time. To prolong the presence of a drug and enhance corneal uptake, substances with a higher viscosity than tear fluid (e.g. polyvinyl alcohol and methylcellulose) are added to drops.

Light

Light may cause oxidation or hydrolysis. Some products therefore need to be packaged in dark, light-resistant containers.

Sterility

Drops/Ointments

Those products intended to be sterile should be terminally sterilised in their final container. Where it is not possible to carry out terminal sterilisation by heating due to formulation instability, a decision needs to be taken to use an alternative method of terminal sterilisation such as filtration and/or aseptic processing. It has been accepted that other factors (such as the type of container, route of administration and patient benefit) have contributed to the choice of a particular container type that will not withstand terminal heat sterilisation. Certain ophthalmic products are therefore manufactured by validated aseptic processing. The European Agency for Evaluation of Medicinal Products (EMEA) has set out decision trees for selection of sterilisation methods, involving sterilisation by moist heat at 121°C for 15 minutes, by dry heat at 160°C for 120 minutes or by filtration through a microbial retentive filter.

Drugs for injection

These come in ampoules, either in powder form for reconstitution with appropriate diluent, such as water, for injection, or in liquid form. All of these have to be prepared aseptically, according to local clinical policies.

Recommended expiry dates

It is generally recommended that eye drops and ointments for domiciliary use by patients are used for no longer than 1 month after opening (28 days), although an increasing number of, particularly drops for dry eye conditions, have novel non-chemical preservation systems. These mean that they can be used for, in some cases, 6 months or more without compromising their sterility. This is useful, as it cuts down costs of re-prescription and allows larger volumes of eye drop to be supplied.

For hospital ward use by patients, they are used for no longer than 1 week (7 days) after opening, with individual containers for each patient.

For hospital outpatient clinic and theatre use, they are used once and then the remainder is discarded.

Classification of ophthalmic drugs

Drugs acting on the eye may be classified under a variety of headings and in this chapter have been classified as:

- Antimicrobial agents, including antibiotics, antiviral and antifungal agents
- Anti-inflammatory agents, including steroids and antihistamines
- Drugs affecting the autonomic nervous system
- Drugs used in the treatment of glaucoma
- Ocular lubricants
- Local anaesthetic agents
- Diagnostic agents
- Anti-VEGF treatments.

Antimicrobial agents

Antibiotics

These can be classified as either bactericidal or bacteriostatic:

- Bactericidal is when the drug destroys the bacteria during active multiplication.
- Bacteriostatic is when the drug diminishes the rate of multiplication.

Antibiotics may act by one or more bacteriostatic means:

- Interference with the synthesis of the cell wall of the bacterium, e.g. penicillin.

- Prevention of protein synthesis inside the micro-organism, e.g. erythromycin.
- Disturbance of cell wall permeability so that the bacteria lyse, e.g. polymyxin B.
- Inhibiting the enzyme responsible for supercoiling of the DNA helix (DNA gyrase), e.g. ofloxacin.

Most acute superficial eye infections can be treated topically, although systemic treatment may occasionally be required.

Antibiotics can have a narrow or broad spectrum of activity; those with a narrow spectrum are effective against a specific type of bacterium (such as Gram positive); those that have a broad spectrum are effective against a wider range of bacteria. It should be noted that resistance to antibiotics can develop quite quickly and antibiotics should therefore be used only when an accurate diagnosis has been made and ideally after antibiotic sensitivity has been determined. In practice a broad-spectrum antibiotic, such as chloramphenicol, is usually prescribed in the first instance for a presumed bacterial infection and is generally well tolerated by the patient. There have been recommendations that topical chloramphenicol should be avoided because of an increased risk of aplastic anaemia but this does not appear to be an evidence- based suggestion (Field *et al.* 1999). It may, however, be worth avoiding if the patient has a family history of blood dyscrasias.

When prescribing systemic antibiotics, various factors should be taken into consideration, including the age of the patient, any liver or kidney problems the patient may have, and whether they are pregnant or breast-feeding.

As with all classes of drugs, adverse effects can occur with antibiotics and these should also be taken into account when prescribing treatment. For instance, gentamicin is ototoxic and penicillin may cause serious allergic reactions in susceptible patients. Local toxic reactions may also occur in response to the presence of preservative in eye drops, especially after prolonged use. Many antibacterial preparations also incorporate a corticosteroid (e.g. Maxitrol), but these should *not* be used unless a patient is under close specialist supervision because they may mask a more serious condition. In particular, they should never be used for an undiagnosed 'red eye', which is sometimes caused by the herpes simplex virus and may be difficult to diagnose.

Eye drops can be used up to every 2 hours, with the frequency reducing as the infection is controlled, although it should be continued for 48 hours after resolution. Eye ointments should be administered either at night (when used in conjunction with eye drops) or three to four times daily if used alone.

Antivirals

Viruses proliferate inside cells so antiviral agents must be able to penetrate the cells to prevent viral multiplication. There are several viruses that may affect the eye but effective treatment is only available for the herpes viruses.

The drugs work by inhibiting the viral deoxyribonucleic acid (DNA) synthesis, including aciclovir and trifluorothymidine (F_3T). Aciclovir acts by blocking viral replication within the infected cells only because it needs an enzyme produced by the virus to convert the drug into its active form and is the treatment of choice in ointment form for herpes simplex keratitis. Trifluorothymidine acts by bringing about the substitution of a base in the chain for DNA synthesis. However, it acts on uninfected cells too and is therefore more toxic, but is a useful alternative in those patients who are intolerant of (for whatever reason) or unresponsive to aciclovir.

Ganciclovir, valganciclovir (a prodrug of ganciclovir), foscarnet and cidofovir are used in the treatment of cytomegalovirus (CMV) retinitis. Valganciclovir has high oral bioavailability and, because of its once or twice a day dosing, has replaced other treatment as the first line. Foscarnet and cidofovir have become second-line treatments because of their lack of an oral form and the need for long-term intravenous access. Ganciclovir is available as a slow-release intravitreal implant but, although these are used less since oral forms of treatment have become available, they are still needed in patients who have a reactivation of retinitis or who cannot tolerate oral treatment. It must be remembered that local treatments do not protect against systemic infection or infection in the other eye.

Antifungals

These are rarely required in ocular disease. However, fungal infections can occur after agricultural injuries, especially in hot and humid climates. Many different fungi are capable of producing ocular infection and they should be identified by appropriate laboratory procedures. Antifungal preparations for the eye are not generally commercially available, so treatment will need to be carried out at specialist centres, although requests for information about supplies of preparations should be addressed to the local health authority or the nearest hospital ophthalmology unit.

Antifungal drugs that have been used in ocular infections include amphotericin B and natamicin. Amphotericin B is effective against candida and filamentous fungi and needs to be administered every 30 minutes in the first 24 hours, every hour for the second 24 hours, and then slowly tapered in response to clinical change. Natamicin is the only commercially available antifungal and is effective against filamentous fungi but has poor ocular penetration so tends to be used only for superficial corneal infection. Oral fluconazole and ketoconazole are absorbed systemically, with good levels of drug found in the anterior chamber and cornea, and can be used for deeper infection (Singh & Verma 2015).

Anti-inflammatory drugs

Corticosteroids

Steroids are substances that are normally produced in the cortex of the adrenal gland. Cortisol or hydrocortisone is the important steroid in this context and is released in response to a pituitary hormone, adrenocorticotrophic hormone (ACTH), with negative feedback between the level of hydrocortisone and ACTH in the circulation, which is monitored by the hypothalamus. Hydrocortisone has many physiological effects but the one with which we are concerned here is its anti-inflammatory effect. This effect is used in the treatment of many different inflammatory disorders, but generally large doses need to be used; however, newer agents are now available that have greater potency but with accompanying adverse effects.

Local and systemic steroids are used in the treatment of eye disease. Corticosteroids administered locally (as eye drops, eye ointments or subconjunctival injection) have an important place in the treatment of anterior segment inflammation, including that which results from surgery.

Local steroids; eye drops

There are many different preparations available, such as prednisolone, prednisolone acetate, betamethasone, dexamethasone, fluorometholone and rimexolone. Rimexolone appears least likely to cause a rise in intraocular pressure.

Steroids can also be combined with an antibiotic (e.g. betamethasone and neomycin).

Local steroids; ointments

Ointments stay longer on the corneal surface, thus increasing the retention time and effect of the drug, though some temporary visual disturbance will be experienced. Again, many different preparations are available, with or without antibiotic components.

Local steroids; subconjunctival injection

There are two commonly used preparations: betamethasone (useful for short-term effect – 24 hours) and methylprednisolone (for longer effect – 10 days or more).

Local steroids; intravitreal injection

Steroids are now being implanted by intravitreal injection to treat macular oedema. Both dexamethasone 0.7mg (Ozurdex) and fluocinalone acetonide 190 micrograms (Iluvien) are used for slightly different indications. Both drugs are recommended only for those who are pseudophakic, as the steroid implant will induce cataract.

Systemic steroids; oral

Prednisolone is the usual oral anti-inflammatory of choice in the treatment of ocular inflammation. The starting dose in certain conditions is high – up to 80mg daily.

Enteric coated tablets are available and are preferable to minimise the risk of intestinal ulceration. Reduction in dosage has to be gradual, but the degree of dose reduction, and for how long each reduced dose is taken, will vary according to the individual patient's condition and response. All patients on oral steroids should be issued with a steroid card detailing their current dose and regimen duration.

Adverse effects of steroids

Topical corticosteroids should normally only be used under expert supervision. There are three main dangers associated with their use:

1. A 'red eye' where the diagnosis is unconfirmed may result from herpes simplex virus and a corticosteroid may aggravate the condition, leading to corneal ulceration, possible damage to vision and even loss of an eye. Bacterial and fungal infections pose a similar hazard, because the corticosteroid may not only mask symptoms but may also predispose a patient to these infections if used long term.

2. 'Steroid glaucoma' may follow the prolonged use of a corticosteroid and it is therefore important to monitor the intraocular pressure (IOP) of patients on long-term steroids.

3. 'Steroid cataract' may follow prolonged use.

About 30% of the general population will respond to steroids with a rise in IOP of 6–15mm. Around 4–5% will have a marked IOP rise >15mmHg. This steroid response may occur immediately, or after 2–3 weeks of topical application. There may even be a delay of 4–6 months. Discontinuing steroids generally results in a reduction of pressure elevation (Fechner & Teichmann 1998). Other side effects include thinning of the cornea and sclera.

In certain conditions, topical steroids should be withdrawn gradually, in order to avoid relapse or rebound effects (e.g. in anterior uveitis). Some patients may even have to remain on a very weak-strength preparation indefinitely.

Prolonged systemic treatment will be accompanied by exaggerated physiological effects of steroids (cushingoid appearance, raised blood sugar); this may also be accompanied by dramatic mood changes. The high level of steroids in the circulation also leads to disruption of the negative feedback mechanism between the adrenal cortex and the anterior pituitary. If the treatment is prolonged, it may lead to atrophy of the adrenal cortex; this, in turn, could result in the patient taking lifelong replacement therapy. Other adverse effects that can be expected are osteoporosis, peptic ulcers and retarded growth in children. In the eye, systemic corticosteroids have a high risk (75%) of producing a 'steroid cataract' if the equivalent of more than 15mg prednisolone is given daily for several years.

Non-steroidal anti-inflammatory drugs

These are drugs that block the effects of prostaglandins, which are found in almost all tissues including the eye. Prostaglandins are released in inflammatory reactions and are said to be mediators in the process. Several drugs (such as such as indometacin and flurbiprofen) have been shown to block the synthesis of prostaglandins. These drugs are generally given systemically, although indometacin, diclofenac, flurbiprofen and ketorolac are available as topical eye drops. It is becoming common practice for these to replace the use of topical steroids in the treatment of episcleritis, and they have also been shown to be very useful in the treatment of corneal pain after trauma.

Drugs used to treat allergy

Allergy is a common cause of conjunctivitis, and the principal cause of allergy signs and symptoms is the release of histamine. Treatment can be offered by:

- Using drops that block histamine receptors, e.g. emedastine (antihistamine)
- Using drops that prevent the release of histamine, e.g. lodoxamide, sodium cromoglicate (mast cell stabiliser).

Once an allergic reaction has taken place, an antihistamine will block histamine receptors, thus preventing or relieving the symptoms of the allergic reaction. This action is relatively rapid. It will take some time for the mast cell membrane to stabilise and therefore a mast cell stabiliser will have no immediate effect and it is likely to be 7–10 days before its effect is noticed. For patients who have seasonal allergic disorders such as hay fever, a mast cell stabiliser should therefore be used from the beginning of the season to its end. This will prevent the cell membrane from breaking down, releasing histamine and causing the symptoms of allergy. When an allergic reaction has occurred and histamine has been released, an antihistamine is useful to prevent symptoms.

Preparations that both block histamine receptors and prevent the release of histamine (such as olopatidine) are useful when there has been an allergic reaction which is part of an ongoing issue. This type of preparation will treat the antihistamine reaction and can continue to be used, to keep the mast cell membrane stable, to prevent further reaction. As it is used twice daily, it fits in well with school and work attendance.

Drugs affecting the autonomic nervous system

Anatomy

The autonomic nervous system is divided into the sympathetic and parasympathetic pathways. The sympathetic pathway originates in the hypothalamus, passes down the spinal cord and emerges in the thorax. The fibres then pass upwards, towards the superior cervical ganglion lying at the carotid bifurcation where they synapse. The neurotransmitter here is acetylcholine. The postganglionic fibres run towards the eye, wrapped round the internal carotid artery, and finally reach the eye via the ophthalmic artery. They supply the dilator pupillae, the trabecular meshwork and the blood vessels in the eye. The chemical transmitter is noradrenaline (norepinephrine), which acts on both α (alpha) and β (beta) receptors.

The parasympathetic pathway originates in the midbrain; fibres run in the third nerve towards the eye and synapse in the ciliary ganglion, which lies within the muscle cone between the lateral rectus muscle and the optic nerve. The transmitter is acetylcholine. The postganglionic fibres then innervate the constrictor pupillae and ciliary muscle as well as sending branches to the lacrimal gland and trabecular meshwork.

Drugs that affect the autonomic nervous system can be one of the following types:

- A drug that mimics the action of the chemical transmitter of the sympathetic nervous system, called a sympathomimetic, e.g. brimonidine
- One that mimics the action of the chemical transmitter of the parasympathetic nervous system, called a parasympathomimetic, e.g. pilocarpine
- One that blocks the action of the sympathetic nervous system, called a sympatholytic, e.g. guanethidine
- One that blocks the action of the parasympathetic nervous system, called a parasympatholytic, e.g. atropine.

Drugs affecting the sympathetic nervous system

Sympathomimetic agents mimic the actions of the transmitter and so will produce some or all of the following effects:

- Dilatation of the pupil
- Reduction in the rate of production of aqueous humour
- Increase in outflow through the trabecular meshwork by lowering outflow resistance
- Constriction of the conjunctival vessels.

Phenylephrine reduces IOP but is more often used as a mydriatic. It should be used with care in patients with hypertension because it may interact with systemic monoamine oxidase (MAO) inhibitors. It is usually recommended that the 2.5% strength be used, with care in hypertension.

The only sympatholytic agent of note is guanethidine, which is present in Ganda eye drops alongside adrenaline (epinephrine) and is used to enhance and prolong the effect of adrenaline (a sympathomimetic).

Drugs affecting the parasympathetic nervous system

The parasympathomimetics (miotics) may work:

- Directly, e.g. pilocarpine, which causes miosis – increased outflow of aqueous by opening up the inefficient drainage channels in the trabecular meshwork resulting from contraction or spasm of the ciliary muscle
- Indirectly, e.g. by acting on enzymes that normally metabolise acetylcholine and therefore potentiate its action.

The parasympatholytic (antimuscarinic) agents work by blocking acetylcholine. Hence, they cause pupil dilatation and varying degrees of cycloplegia. They vary in potency and duration of action. Atropine is the most powerful, long-acting agent; tropicamide is a short-acting drug that dilates the pupil but has limited effect on accommodation and is therefore an ideal agent for examining the fundus.

It should be remembered that a darkly pigmented iris is more resistant to pupillary dilatation and caution should be exercised to avoid over-dosage. Patients should also be warned not to drive for 1–2 hours after mydriasis due to the possibilities of glare.

Drugs used to treat glaucoma

Glaucoma is usually (but not always) associated with an abnormally high IOP. The rise in pressure is almost always the result of reduced outflow of aqueous humour, the inflow remaining constant. Treatment is aimed at reducing IOP.

Sympathomimetics and miotics, as detailed previously, are used in the treatment of glaucoma for their effect on increasing outflow of aqueous humour through the trabecular meshwork. Other drugs used in the treatment of glaucoma include the following.

Beta (β) blockers

Topical application of a β blocker reduces IOP effectively, probably by reducing the rate of production of aqueous humour. Topical β blockers include betaxolol, timolol, levobunalol and carteolol.

Systemic absorption and subsequent side effects may follow topical application and therefore eye drops containing β blockers are contraindicated in patients with bradycardia, heart block or uncontrolled heart failure. The Committee on Safety of Medicines has also advised that β blockers (even those with apparent cardioselectivity, such as betaxolol), should not be used in patients with asthma or a history of obstructive airway disease unless no alternative treatment is available.

β blockers have a number of important properties in addition to β-adrenoceptor blockade. These include intrinsic sympathomimetic activity (ISA), cardioselectivity and

57

membrane-stabilising activity, which are all of importance when considering the side effects seen with these agents.

The property of membrane stabilisation is relevant to the incidence of ocular side effects. The absence of anaesthetic properties reduces the frequency and severity of foreign body and dryness sensations, anaesthesia of the cornea and dry eye syndrome. It has been suggested that those β blockers that show ISA are less likely to produce bronchospasm and peripheral side effects. The selectivity of cardioselective β blockers diminishes with increasing dosage, even within the therapeutic range. A degree of bradycardia and hypotension is commonly seen with all β blockers but is more marked with non-selective agents.

The precipitation of bronchospasm in susceptible patients can occur with the administration of as little as 1 drop of timolol. Those β blockers that show cardioselectivity or ISA are less likely to cause bronchoconstriction.

Ocular β blockers are generally not contraindicated in diabetes, although a cardioselective agent may be preferable. However, they are best avoided in patients who have frequent hypoglycaemic attacks because they do produce a slight impairment of glucose tolerance.

The long-term beneficial effects of β blockers on visual field preservation have been shown to be less than would be expected. This may be a result of adverse effects on the ocular microcirculation, whereby the β blockers interfere with endogenous vasodilatation and cause optic nerve head arteriolar vasoconstriction. The various βblockers demonstrate marked differences in their vasoconstrictive effect, with betaxolol possibly showing the least vasoconstriction.

Adrenergic agonists

The adrenergic system consists of both α_1 and α_2 receptor cells as well as β_1 and β_2 receptor cells. Adrenergic agonists work by decreasing aqueous production mediated by the β-adrenergic system and an increase in outflow is mediated by the α-adrenergic system. The two most common adrenergic agonist drugs are apraclonidine and brimonidine. Both these drugs are selective α_2 agonists. Apraclonidine carries a high allergy rate and has been restricted to short-term therapy such as postoperative laser trabeculoplasty and YAG (yttrium–aluminium–garnet) laser iridotomy. Brimonidine, on the other hand, has a good safety profile as well as a good efficacy level. It may also provide an intrinsic neuroprotective property. Some of the side effects include headache, insomnia, nervousness, depression and anxiety attacks. Ocular side effects include follicular conjunctivitis, ocular dryness and conjunctival oedema.

Carbonic anhydrase inhibitors

These reduce aqueous humour production by blocking the carbonic anhydrase enzyme involved in aqueous humour production in the ciliary body. Two carbonic anhydrase inhibitors are available for topical use: brinzolamide and dorzolamide. Of the two, brinzolamide appears to cause less burning and stinging on instillation. Acetazolamide is available for systemic use in the form of injection, tablets or slow-release capsules. Although this agent is among the most potent ocular hypotensive agents available, it has limited use in the long-term management of glaucoma as a result of poor patient adherence after the occurrence of side effects such as paraesthesia and gastrointestinal complaints.

It must be remembered that drugs of this class are sulphonamides and that blood disorders (such as thrombocytopenia), rashes and other sulphonamide-related side effects occur occasionally. If severe, these may require discontinuation of the drug.

Prostaglandin analogues

Prostaglandins are hormones found in most tissues, and prostaglandin analogues are biologically active products of arachidonic acid. These drugs act by increasing the uveoscleral outflow and four drugs are commercially available: travoprost, latanoprost, tafluprost and bimatoprost (a synthetic prostamide). They are all administered once daily, at night, and are generally well tolerated. They are relatively free of systemic side effects but have some interesting local side effects such as pigmentation of the iris, which occurs in patients with mixed colour irides and is a result of increased deposition of melanin in the melanocytes. An increase in the length and thickness of the eyelashes and pigmentation of the palpebral skin are also noted side effects.

Hyperosmotic agents

These substances are used effectively to reduce IOP in the short term in emergency situations because of their speed of action; they include intravenous mannitol and oral glycerol (50% solution, 1g/kg), which is usually given with orange juice or ice to disguise its unpalatable taste. Isosorbide is also used, because it has no caloric value, in patients with diabetes. Hyperosmotic agents increase the osmotic pressure of plasma in relation to aqueous and vitreous, which has the effect of drawing fluid out of the eye and so decreasing IOP. The maximal effect of glycerol is seen within 1 hour and lasts for about 3 hours, whereas mannitol acts within 30 minutes with effects lasting 4–6 hours.

Ocular lubricants

The precorneal tear film is made up of lipid, aqueous and mucin components. The lipid layer is on the outside (and helps to decrease evaporative loss); the aqueous layer is in the middle; and the mucin layer is on the epithelium, to provide a hydrophilic surface, allowing the aqueous layer to maintain contact with the cornea. Disturbance in any one of these layers affects the function of the others, leading to a dry eye condition.

There is an abundance of preparations designed to treat dry eye states and the severity of the condition should guide the choice of preparation. Drops including one or combinations of the substances below are available:

- Hypromellose: traditional choice, may need to be instilled frequently, useful when aqueous deficient; can be combined with acetylcysteine, a mucolytic
- Polyvinyl alcohol: hydrophilic, increasing the persistence of the tear film, mucomimetic
- Sodium hyaluronate drops: often need to be used less frequently
- Carbomers: cling to corneal surface, improve tear film stability and prolong tear break-up time
- Paraffin eye ointments: decrease evaporative loss; useful in corneal erosion
- Systane: HP guar with demulcents; a gelling and lubricating polymer system.
- Acetylcysteine: acts as a mucolytic and is useful in tear film conditions with abnormal mucous production such as filamentary keratitis
- Carmellose sodium drops: relatively viscous and useful in moderate to severe dry eyes.

The ideal solution would be one that normalises tear film to prevent evaporative loss; increases hormonal support for the lacrimal glands, meibomian glands and other ocular structures; restores the health of the ocular surface; decreases or eliminates ocular surface and lacrimal gland inflammation; and increases tear production.

Local anaesthetic agents

These topical agents are all useful for examination and treatment in simple procedures such as removal of foreign bodies from the cornea, but they should never be used for the management of ocular symptoms.

Oxybuprocaine and tetracaine are probably the most widely used topical local anaesthetics. Oxybuprocaine or a combined preparation of lidocaine (lignocaine) and fluorescein is useful in tonometry. Tetracaine produces a more profound anaesthesia and is suitable for use before minor surgical procedures; however, it does have a temporary disruptive effect on the corneal epithelium. Proxymetacaine causes less initial stinging and is useful for children.

Side effects of topical anaesthetics include dose-related toxicity to corneal epithelium, causing superficial punctate epithelial defects to occur; although oxybuprocaine appears to be less toxic to epithelium than tetracaine or lidocaine. Topical anaesthetics also inhibit epithelial healing because they interfere with cell mitosis. Use of topical anaesthetic for anything other than examination purposes is generally contraindicated.

Lidocaine, with or without adrenaline, is injected into the eyelids for minor surgery, whereas retrobulbar or peribulbar injections are used for surgery of the globe itself.

Diagnostic agents (dyes)

Fluorescein sodium

This is the most commonly used diagnostic agent and is available in a number of different forms:

- A 1% or 2% solution for topical use
- Dry paper impregnated with 1mg fluorescein
- In combination with lidocaine for tonometry
- An intravenous form that can be obtained in various strengths.

It is termed a 'vital' dye because it stains living tissue without damaging it. Fluorescein sodium absorbs light of a certain wavelength and emits light of a longer wavelength. In other words, it fluoresces in certain conditions, particularly when illuminated by cobalt blue light. The water-soluble dye molecules diffuse into the intercellular spaces between living cells. The intensity of the stain is increased in areas of cellular degeneration or death, where the damage to cells allows higher penetration by the dye. It is very useful for observing permeability in corneal epithelial and endothelial cells. The principal clinical uses of this dye are:

- Demonstrating surface defects on the cornea and conjunctiva
- Performing Seidel's test (for penetrating injury)
- Applanation tonometry (with topical anaesthetic)
- Demonstrating patency of nasolacrimal ducts
- Performing fluorescein angiography.

Rose Bengal

Rose Bengal is a dye that is a derivative of fluorescein. It stains all tissue (live as well as dead and dying cells) but the presence of molecules such as mucin, albumin and artificial tear film compounds stop it from staining the corneal surface. Where there are breaks in the tear film or defects in the ocular surface, it penetrates and stains. It is therefore useful for considering issues of dry eye and staining conjunctiva. It stings excessively and has been discontinued in the UK

Lissamine green

Lissamine green is a synthetically produced organic dye which stains dead and devitalised cells and mucus. It does not stain healthy ocular cells and does not damage cell viability. It is not very visible within the tear film, and therefore excess dye in the tear film does not obscure any staining pattern that is present. It has become the premier dye for staining conjunctiva and is not as effective as fluorescein for investigation of corneal staining. It is available in paper impregnated strips.

Anti-VEGF treatments

These include a group of drugs used to counteract the effects of the vascular endothelial growth factor that leads to haemorrhage in wet age-related macular degeneration (ARMD) and can result in severe loss of vision. Intravitreal injection of the anti-VEGF drug has been shown to reduce new blood vessel growth and oedema, thereby improving the vision of patients who have treatable wet ARMD. Anti-VEGFs are also becoming useful in the treatment, particualrly pre-vitrectomy of proliferative retinopathy and, in some areas as a treatment for retinopathy of prematurity.

Adverse effects of systemic drugs

As a result of its rich blood supply and relatively small mass, the eye is unusually sensitive to adverse drug reactions (ADRs). ADRs can occur in response to systemic medications, as they may enter the bloodstream, from where they can reach ocular structures across the limbal, uveal and retinal vasculature. An important mechanism for ocular ADRs is the selective deposition of drug molecules in the specialised ocular tissues, including the cornea, lens and retina, which may therefore show individual susceptibilities to toxicity.

There are various determining factors when looking at the possibility of ADRs occurring. These include the physicochemical properties of the drug itself, including protein binding, lipid solubility, molecular size and active transport. Also, the integrity of the blood–ocular barriers is important because, when the eye is inflamed, the blood–aqueous barrier becomes more permeable, thus allowing increased amounts of the drug to enter the eye from the bloodstream.

Drugs that may cause ocular ADRs

Numerous drugs used in general medicine may cause ocular ADRs and here are some examples according to the part of the eye that is affected.

Cornea

- Amiodarone: whorl-like corneal epithelial opacities
- Ciprofloxacin: epithelial deposition
- Chlorpromazine: pigmentation of corneal endothelium
- Indometacin: corneal stromal opacities.

Lens

- Corticosteroids: cataract and lenticular deposits
- Phenothiazines: anterior cortical opacities.

Conjunctiva

- Isotretinoin: blepharoconjunctivitis
- Chlorpromazine: deposition.

Lacrimal apparatus

- Antihistamines: tear production
- Rifampicin: coloration of tears.

Retina

- Tamoxifen: maculopathy
- Vigabatrin: field defects
- Digoxin: colour vision defects.

Drugs that may cause significant ocular ADRs

There are certain drugs that are known to cause significant ocular ADRs and these are listed below.

Vigabatrin (antiepileptic)

ADRs reported with vigabatrin include:

- Colour vision deficiencies: selective short wavelength impairment consistent with GABAergic (GABA is γ-aminobutyric acid) inhibition at retinal level.

- Contrast sensitivity impairment.

- Visual field abnormalities: up to a third of patients receiving vigabatrin at a normal therapeutic level will have these. This visual field loss appears to be dose dependent and permanent. It usually presents as concentric, binasal, peripheral constriction with temporal and central sparing.

- Retinal disorders: narrowing of retinal arterioles, atrophy of the peripheral retina, surface wrinkling retinopathy of the macula, abnormalities of retinal pigment epithelium, irregularities of macula reflex and optic disc pallor.

The Committee on Safety of Medicines (1998) has advised that onset of symptoms varies from 1 month to several years after starting treatment. In most cases, visual field defects have persisted despite discontinuation. Visual field testing is therefore recommended before treatment commences and at 6-monthly intervals. Patients should be warned to report any new visual symptoms that develop and those with symptoms should be referred for an urgent ophthalmological opinion.

Levodopa (anti-parkinsonian)

Adverse drug reactions reported with levodopa include:

- Mydriasis, visual hallucinations, ptosis and/or blepharospasm

- Hallucination sufferers had abnormal rapid eye movement (REM) sleep patterns
- May lead to melanomas in any part of the epithelial or ocular pigmented tissues
- Secondary Meigs' syndrome with long-term usage (ocular dystonia).

Hydroxychloroquine/chloroquine (antimalarials)

ADRs reported with hydroxychloroquine/chloroquine include:

- Irreversible retinal damage
- Corneal opacity.

Patients on these drugs should have their eyes checked annually and the Royal College of Ophthalmologists (2009) has advised that a screening protocol for chloroquine should be negotiated with local ophthalmologists. Recommendations also exist for patients on hydroxychloroquine, with examination suggested both before treatment is started and once it has started.

Drugs that may cause oculogyric crisis

A number of drugs may precipitate oculogyric crisis, a condition characterised by maximal upward deviation of the eyes, associated with backward, lateral flexion of the neck, an open mouth with tongue protrusion and ocular pain. Other features may include an increased blood pressure and heart rate with flushing, and psychiatric symptoms such as depression, paranoia and anxiety.

Precipitating drugs include neuroleptics, benzodiazepines, carbamazepine, chloroquine, metoclopramide, nifedipine, tricyclic antidepressants and cetirizine. Treatment in the acute phase involves reassurance, diphenhydramine and/or diazepam or lorazepam. Recovery is rapid after treatment.

Adverse effects of ophthalmic drugs

It must also be remembered that drugs applied topically to the eye may also cause systemic ADRs. The occurrence of systemic ADRs may be decreased but not eradicated by occlusion of the punctum or by closing the eye for a count of 60 following administration, to minimise systemic absorption.

Topical β blockers

Systemic ADRs reported following use of topical β blockers include:

- Bronchoconstriction
- Hypotension
- Bradycardia
- Nausea/diarrhoea

- Anxiety/depression
- Hallucinations
- Fatigue.

Topical sympathomimetic agents

Systemic ADRs reported after use of topical sympathomimetic agents include:

- Dry mouth/nose
- Headache
- Asthenia
- Bradycardia
- Depression.

Topical carbonic anhydrase inhibitors

Systemic ADRs reported after use of topical carbonic anhydrase inhibitors include:

- Fatigue
- Headache
- Dry mouth
- Nausea
- Dyspnoea
- Taste perversion.

Drugs and the nurse

The Nursing and Midwifery Council's (NMC) Standards for Medicine Management (NMC 2007, p. 18) are clear that:

> As a registrant, you are accountable for your actions and omissions. In administering any medication, or assisting or overseeing any self-administration of medication, you must exercise your professional judgment and apply your knowledge and skill in the given situation.

They go on to state that (NMC 2007, p. 24):

> In exercising your professional accountability in the best interests of your patients, you must know the therapeutic uses of the medicine to be administered, its normal dosage, side effects, precautions and contra-indications.

Although this applies only to nurses registered in the UK, it forms a general statement of good practice for the use of good professional judgement in relation to the administration of prescribed drugs.

Prescription, supply and administration of drugs by nurses in the UK

Policy and legislation has changed over the past 20 years to allow nurses in the UK to prescribe drugs. Previously, this facility was limited to medical practitioners and dentists, but it has now been extended to other professionals allied to medicine.

Two types of prescribing are possible. After completion of a recognised educational programme and assessment, nursing staff can become either independent or supplementary nurse and midwife prescribers. Community nurse prescribers are a distinct group (under independent prescribers) but differ slightly in that they consist of district nurses, health visitors and school nurses, who are allowed to independently prescribe from a limited formulary, which includes over-the-counter drugs, wound dressings and applications (RCN 2012).

Independent prescribing

In 2006 legislation was passed (DoH 2004) that enabled nurses to independently prescribe any licensed medicines for any condition within their area of competence, as well as a number of controlled drugs. Further changes in legislation in 2009 allowed independent prescribers to prescribe unlicensed drugs, controlled drugs and also to mix medicines themselves or direct others to do so (Courtenay & Griffiths 2010). Independent prescribing for optometrists was introduced in 2007 (DoH 2007) and this allows optometrists, like independent nurse prescribers, to prescribe any ophthalmic medication for any eye condition within their area of competence. Independent prescribing means that the prescriber takes responsibility for the clinical assessment of the patient, establishing a diagnosis and the clinical management required, as well as responsibility for prescribing where necessary and the appropriateness of any prescription.

Supplementary prescribing

Supplementary prescribing is defined by the Department of Health (2004, p.1) as:

> ...a voluntary partnership between an independent prescriber (a doctor or dentist) and a supplementary prescriber, to implement an agreed patient specific Clinical Management Plan with the patient's agreement.

There are no legal restrictions on the clinical conditions that may be treated under supplementary prescribing, although the Department of Health intends that supplementary prescribing will be used mainly for the management of chronic medical conditions and health needs.

Provided that medicines are prescribable by a doctor, and that they are referred to in the patient's clinical management plan, supplementary prescribers are able to prescribe any general sales list (CSL) and P medicines and all prescription-only medicines (POMs), including those used 'off label' and unlicensed drugs used as part of a clinical trial.

Training for supplementary prescribing for nurses is the same as for independent nurse prescribing, with the addition of a short module covering the context and concept of supplementary prescribing.

In 2006 the Nursing and Midwifery Council released *Standards of proficiency for nurse and midwife prescribers*. Nurses should be familiar with these standards and adhere strictly to these and *The Code* (NMC 2015), which contains the professional standards that registered nurses and midwives must uphold.

There are some situations where patients may have a POM supplied and/or medicine administered directly to them by a range of healthcare professionals without the legal necessity of a signed prescription. This can be achieved in one of two ways.

Patient group direction

Patient group directions (PGDs) were introduced in August 2000 to replace standing orders. They constitute a legal framework that allows certain healthcare professionals to supply and/or administer specified medicines to groups of patients who fit the criteria laid out in the PGD. A healthcare professional can supply (e.g. provide tablets) and/or administer a medicine (e.g. give an injection or eye drops) directly to a patient without the need for a prescription or an instruction from a prescriber. Where medicines are supplied in this way, patients must be counselled and provided with a patient information leaflet. The PGD applies to groups of patients who may not be individually identified before presenting for treatment.

PGDs fit best within services where medicine use follows a predictable pattern and they are generally most appropriate to manage a specific treatment episode where supply or administration of a medicine is necessary. In ophthalmic practice, PGDs might be used for administration of eye drops for ocular examination and for defined situations such as provision of topical antibiotics after corneal abrasion or removal of a corneal foreign body.

The list of practitioners who may use PGDs is defined at present as: nurse, midwife, pharmacist, optometrist, orthoptist, chiropodist and podiatrist, radiographer, physiotherapist, ambulance paramedic, dietician, prosthetist, occupational therapist, speech and language therapist, dental hygienist and dental therapist.

It must be noted that unregistered practitioners, such as healthcare assistants and assistant practitioners, are not included. Individual practitioners using the PGD must be named on a list kept by the employing authority (NICE 2013).

Patient-specific direction

A patient-specific direction (PSD) is used once a patient has been assessed by a prescriber and that prescriber instructs another healthcare professional, in writing, to supply or administer a medicine directly to that named patient or to several named patients. This might be an instruction in the patient's notes or an instruction on a clinic list containing names of patients attending that clinic. PSDs do not require an assessment of the patient by the healthcare worker instructed to supply and/or administer the medication. Where a PSD exists, there is no need for a PGD. This might be used for a clinic list of patients whose pupils need to be dilated before eye examination.

The role of the clinician

The ophthalmic clinician has a major role in ensuring that patients receive optimum drug therapy for their condition. The role includes the obvious instillation or provision of prescribed medication, but also as a patient educator to ensure that the patient is not only able to use the medication, but also understands the consequences of using it or of choosing not to. Patients cannot be expected to agree with our conclusions about their therapy if they do not understand them.

'Compliance' is a term that is often used by clinicians, but compliance has connotations of power – we, the ophthalmic clinicians, tell the patient what they should do and they do what we say. Compliance and non-compliance are both patient-related phenomena, and non-compliant behaviour may represent a conscious decision or choice by the patient (Kyngas *et al.* 2000).

Concordance is an approach to the prescribing and taking of medicines that suggests an agreement reached after negotiation between a patient and a healthcare professional who respects the beliefs and wishes of the patient in determining whether and how medicines are to be taken (Wilson & O'Mahony 1999). Often, the biggest factor in concordance is nurses – we too must ensure our understanding, the understanding of the patient and the patient's ability to undertake the tasks that we ask of them. The message should be consistent regardless of whether the patient is being cared for by specialist ophthalmic clinicians, or those in other settings. The message about all therapy (ophthalmic and general) needs to be consistent so that trust in the information is maintained and the patient is able to make the best personal choices (Marsden & Shaw 2003).

General rules for optimal topical drug therapy

- The patient must be given adequate knowledge of each drug, the intended therapeutic effect, possible side effects and how to deal with them, as well as the optimal timing between doses and any particular order in which drugs should be used.
- One drop into the lower fornix is enough – excess will overflow from the fornix, down the cheek and will also exit the fornix via the puncta and canaliculi into the naso-lacrimal duct. Excessive systemic absorption may take place through the nasal mucosa.

- Ideally 5 (but at least 3) minutes should be left between drops to the same eye – otherwise, the previous drop will be washed away and will not be absorbed in any therapeutic amount.
- All drops should be instilled before any ointment – ointment 'waterproofs' the eye and any drops instilled will not be absorbed but will overflow and the drug will be lost to the eye.
- Although drop size is variable, the dose of a liquid eye medication is 1 drop. However, there is no similar dosage for an eye ointment. As ointments are often prescribed because of their lubricant properties as well as therapeutic properties, it is important that enough is given for the purpose.
- Adverse systemic effects can be minimised by asking the patient to close the eye gently and count slowly to 60 after drop instillation or by occluding the punctum.
- In elderly people or a disabled population, physical disability may be responsible for lack of concordance – instillation aids are available and the clinician should be aware of different types, which might work best for the patient and where to obtain them.

Table 3.1 The order in which topical drug therapy should be instilled

Order	Drug
A	Local anaesthetics Miotics Mydriatics
B	Sympathomimetics Tear deficiency products
C	Non-steroidal preparations Steroids
D	Antibiotics, antifungals, anti-inflammatories Beta blockers Carbonic anhydrase inhibitors Prostaglandin analogues
E	Ointments

(Adapted from Andrew (2004) and Shaw (2014).

References

Andrew, S. (2004) *Order of Eye Drop/Ointment (2014) Administration.* Manchester: Central Manchester FT.

Committee on Safety of Medicines; Medicines Control Agency (1998) Vigabatrin (Sabril) and visual field defects. *Current problems in pharmacovigilance.* **24**.1

Courtenay, M. & Griffiths, M. (2010) *Independent and Supplementary Prescribing: An essential guide.* Cambridge: Cambridge University Press.

Department of Health (2004) *Mechanisms for Nurse and Pharmacist Prescribing and Supply of Medicines.* London: DoH.

Department of Health (2007) *Optometrists to get Independent Prescribing Rights (Press Release).* London: DoH.

Fechner, P.U. & Teichmann, K.D. (1998) *Ocular Therapeutics.* Thorofare, NJ: Slack.

Field, D., Martin, D., & Witchell, L. (1999) Ophthalmic chloramphenicol: friend or foe? *Ophthalmic Nursing.* **2**(4), 4–7

German, E.J., Hurst, M.A. & Wood, D. (1999) Reliability of drop size from multi-dose bottles: is it cause for concern? *Eye.* **13**, 93–100.

Kyngas, H., Duffy, M.E. & Kroll, T. (2000) Conceptual analysis of compliance. *Journal of Clinical Nursing.* **9**, 5–12.

Marsden, J. & Shaw, M. (2003) Correct administration of topical eye treatment. *Nursing Standard.* **17**(30), 42–4.

National Institute for Health and Care Excellence (2013) *Patient Group Directions.* http://www.nice.org.uk/guidance/mpg2 (accessed 12 July 2016).

Nursing and Midwifery Council (2006) *Standards of proficiency for nurse and midwife prescribers.* London: NMC.

Nursing and Midwifery Council (2007) *Standards for medicine management.* London: NMC.

Nursing and Midwifery Council (2015) *The Code.* London: NMC.

Royal College of Nursing (2012) *RCN Fact Sheet – Nurse Prescribing in the UK.* London: RCN.

Royal College of Ophthalmologists (2009) *Hydroxychloroquine and Ocular Toxicity: Recommendations on Screening.* London: RCOphth

Shaw, M. (2014) How to administer eye drops and ointment. *Nursing Times.* **110**(40), 16–18.

Singh, D. & Verma, A. (2015) *Fungal Keratitis Treatment & Management.* http://emedicine.medscape.com/article/1194167-treatment (accessed 12 July 2016).

Wilson, C.G. & O'Mahony, B. (1999) Non-compliance in glaucoma management. *Eye News.* **5**, 6.

CHAPTER FOUR

Examination of the eye

Mary E. Shaw

Although examination of the eye is at the forefront of the ophthalmic health professional's mind, it is important when making a diagnosis to consider the patient as a whole. The general impression of the patient gained by the examiner can provide clues to diagnosis or cues for subsequent action(s) that need to be taken.

Identifying the patient

Scrutiny of the patient's demographic details is not only essential to ensure that you have the correct patient but it also helps to break the ice and establish the first line of communication. When doing this, take care not to breach confidentiality or embarrass the patient – for example if there are others in the clinical area at the same time. Identification of the patient should include:

- Full name
- Date of birth
- Age
- Address.

You should also ask about other sources of information such as:

- Source of referral
- Reasons for referral.

Initial assessment

When you greet a patient, make a general assessment, taking into consideration the following:

- The patient's general appearance.
- Mobility: is the patient in a wheelchair or using walking aids or fully mobile? This may give clues to systemic conditions that affect the eye, and will also alert you to whether or not the patient requires assistance to get into position at the slit-lamp or

examination chair. Assess whether moving and handling equipment or techniques are needed to maintain safety for yourself and the patient.

- Race/ethnicity: some races and ethnicities are more susceptible to certain ocular diseases than others, e.g. people of African–Caribbean origin are more susceptible to developing primary open angle glaucoma (POAG).

- Gender is significant in relation to some hereditary conditions and susceptibility to some diseases.

- Assess any visible physical impairment that might interfere with compliance, especially with topical medications.

- Check for large or small stature relative to age.

- Is the patient overweight or underweight? This could affect mobility and could also give clues to ocular pathology in some cases.

- General state: is the patient calm/nervous/agitated? Agitation or nervousness may affect the patient's ability to communicate effectively. If you put the patient at ease, you will get more out of your encounter.

- Is the patient is accompanied by a relative or care-giver? Does the patient want the relative or care-giver/relative with them in the consultation? They do not have an automatic right to be there, and the patient should be asked if they want to be accompanied.

- Mental capability of the patient: this is a difficult judgement to make – learning disability may be obvious in the case of the patient who has, for example, Down's syndrome, but such a diagnosis does not mean that the patient is not capable of complete engagement in the consultation.

- Sensory deficit: look out for evidence of poor hearing; a hearing aid is an obvious clue but do not assume that it is working properly! If you suspect poor hearing, speak clearly and directly to the patient. If it is known ahead of the appointment that the patient is profoundly deaf, arrange for an interpreter or facilitator to sign for the patient. Respect patient confidentiality; do not use relatives, especially children. They may not give the patient accurate information or they may not understand medical terms.

- Speech impairment or impediment may not be an obvious thing to consider, but it could affect how well you communicate with the patient. If the patient stammers, avoid closing their sentences or filling in words.

- Communication issues including language barriers: if you are aware of any such barriers ahead of time, an official interpreter should be arranged. It is important that communication is with the patient via a disinterested third party, rather than a relative or carer.

The examination room

The room should afford privacy for the patient. Attempting to examine the patient in an open environment is not recommended unless it is an emergency/first-aid measure, because the patient needs to feel secure, and not be embarrassed. It is not just medical information that should remain confidential. For example, the patient whose first language is not English or who is illiterate will not enjoy others knowing of these difficulties during vision testing or at any point during the consultation.

Ideally the examination room should have good lighting and a comfortable chair for the patient to sit in that offers head and neck support.

Equipment needed

For a simple examination, a good-quality pen-torch will normally suffice to examine the eye and adnexa. An ophthalmoscope provides added magnification, light filters and cobalt blue illumination. A slit-lamp biomicroscope is a most adaptable piece of equipment. An indirect ophthalmoscope is another useful tool.

Charts to test visual acuity of the Snellen (Figure 4.1) or logMAR (logarithm of the minimum angle of resolution) (Figure 4.2) type should be available, along with near vision and colour testing equipment. An occluder, or occluder combined with pinholes (more usual), should also be available. Pinholes compensate for refractive error or corneal irregularity when testing visual acuity.

The Snellen test chart should be 6 metres distant from where the patient will sit or stand; alternatively, a mirror at a distance of 3m (reflecting the chart) should be used. The Snellen chart should be well illuminated. Some testing charts may also be available to you on computers. LogMAR charts come in illuminated boxes and different charts are available for testing distance vision at distances of 2, 3 or 4 metres. It is therefore essential to establish that the correct charts for distance of patient from the chart are being used.

Diagnostic fluorescein strips and other stains (depending on local policy), sterile saline, dilating drops as well as cotton buds (used to facilitate eversion of the eyelids when examining the subtarsal conjunctiva) are required.

It should be possible to dim the lighting in the room.

Preparing the patient

The patient should be comfortable and ideally pain free to facilitate a good examination. If the patient is in pain following trauma, instillation of topical local anaesthetic may improve compliance. This will of course have to be prescribed, unless there are local arrangements in place such as a patient group directive, or the examiner is qualified to prescribe. With some conditions such as iritis, it is not appropriate to instil topical anaesthetic drops because they will not affect the pain. However, as the examiner is not making a diagnosis at this stage, it may not be obvious that the patient has iritis and a drop of topical anaesthetic will do no harm to a painful eye.

Oral analgesia (such as paracetamol 500g) may be an option for pain, providing this is not contraindicated.

The patient needs to be informed at the outset about what to expect in the examination to ensure informed consent and cooperation.

Taking a history

The process of history taking and clinical examination performs several vital functions:

- Helps to establish a rapport between the examiner and the patient
- Establishes physical contact between the examiner and patient
- Enables the establishment of an accurate diagnosis (about 70–90% of all diagnoses are established by the end of the history and examination and before tests are performed)
- Identifies the severity of signs and symptoms
- Determines diagnosis
- Commences treatment if appropriate
- Monitors treatment.

Patient assessment should always begin with a careful history. The order of history taking is usually as follows:

- Presenting symptoms: find out from the patient if they are experiencing any problems with vision. Check what the visual acuity or refraction is for both distance and near. Is the patient myopic or hypermetropic?
- History of presenting illness, if any (as, for example, patients with POAG are likely to be asymptomatic). If the referral is from an optometric practice, find out if the patient's visit was a routine appointment or if they went to the optometrist for a specific reason. If the patient is experiencing visual problems, establish the onset/duration/severity and location of symptoms.
- Past medical/surgical history, paying particular attention to any history of hypertension/hypotension, diabetes, history of vascular disease such as hypertension or myocardial infarction, cerebrovascular accident and elevated

cholesterol levels. Attention must be paid to any respiratory disorders such as asthma or chronic obstructive airway disease. History of any renal problems or blood transfusion should also be noted, because they could influence diagnosis and decisions about relevant treatment.

- Ask whether the patient suffers from migraine, cold hands or feet (sign of vasospasm).
- Past ophthalmic history: any history of trauma, ocular disease such as iritis, previous ophthalmic surgery? Is the patient registered blind or partially sighted?
- Any family history of eye problems, including POAG?
- Current medication: systemic, intramuscular, intravenous, subcutaneous or topical, whether prescribed or over the counter.
- Any allergies?
- Social history as appropriate: smoking habit (cigarettes, pipe, cigars), illegal substances, consumption of alcohol, occupation, interests, family circumstances, and perhaps job role as it might have a bearing on diagnosis, care and treatment.

Testing visual acuity

The science of visual acuity testing

Testing charts are designed with black notation on a white background to achieve the best contrast possible. Any testing regime is intended to test the macular area, differentiating the white from the black areas of chart

The Snellen chart dates back to the late 1880s. Herman Snellen defined 'standard vision' as the ability to discriminate a shape which subtended 5 minutes of arc at the macula, where the different parts of the letter subtend 1 minute of arc and were separated from other shapes by a gap subtending 1 minute of arc. Each of the Snellen letters subtends 5 minutes of arc at the distance specified; on the line marked '36' each letter subtends 5 minutes of arc at the macula, at 36 metres from the patient. There are differing numbers of symbols on each line, which presents the patient with different levels of difficulty at each distance. Because of the different number of symbols on each line, it is difficult to get an absolute score when part of a line is read.

Ian Bailey and Jan E. Lovie-Kitchin designed the logMAR at the National Vision Research Institute of Australia in order to standardise the test chart. It has the same number of letters on each line, and the letter size varies logarithmically on each line (as does the distance between the lines) so it is easier to use at non- standard viewing distances. The logMAR score takes every letter or symbol seen into account. A Snellen symbol subtends an angle of 5 minutes of arc at the distance specified, with each part subtending 1 minute of arc (the minimum angle of resolution MAR). The logarithm of the MAR for a 6/6 size letter at 6m is 0. This method of visual acuity recording was designed for use, initially, in research settings but its enhanced accuracy has led to it being widely used in clinical settings as well.

Snellen was conservative in his definition of 'normal' vision and it is recognised that 'normal' vision for a healthy eye is one or 2 lines below Snellen's 6/6.

A record of visual acuity (VA) (distance vision) should be taken for each patient presenting with an ocular condition and documented in the patient's record. This provides a baseline for later comparisons to be made and may also assist diagnosis. VA is normally done after taking an ocular history and is a test of macular function.

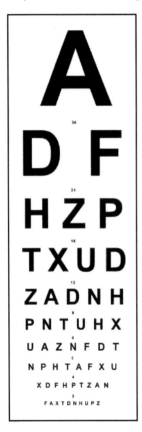

Figure 4.2 LogMAR
(logarithm of the minimum angle of resolution)
visual acuity chart.

Figure 4.1 Snellen visual acuity chart

Privacy is essential to prevent embarrassment and also to prevent patients from learning the chart.

If the patient normally wears distance correction, they should continue to wear them, with a note being made when recording VA that glasses (or contact lenses) were worn. As the examination is carried out to ascertain the best possible visual acuity of the patient, there seems little point in recording visual acuity without correction except, perhaps, on the very first visit to a clinic, in order to demonstrate the patient's uncorrected VA (the patient's glasses prescription would be a good proxy for this). Undertaking VA twice at each clinic visit as a matter of routine is pointless, unless the treatment is expected to have an effect on uncorrected visual acuity (as in the treatment of keratoconus).

Be systematic with your testing, either always testing the right eye (oculodexter or OD) first, then the left (oculosinister or OS) or, more usefully, always test the 'worse' eye first and the 'better' eye second, to prevent the patient remembering some of the letters seen with the 'better' eye.

The examiner should observe the patient (and not the chart) during the test; the examiner will therefore need to know the test chart by heart, or have a reminder copy of it next to them. This is to ensure that the patient does not try to 'cheat' – for example, by peeking over the occluder – and thus provide an erroneous result. If the patient is using eccentric viewing (looking at the chart with a head position that is 'off centre'), this should be recorded in the patient's notes, as it could be an indicator of some disorder such as macular degeneration.

If the patient cannot read letters, they may be able to read a number chart. If they can do neither because of language or literacy problems, the tumbling 'E' test can be used, where each letter on every line is an E but in a different position. The patient is asked to point to a sheet of Es and indicate the corresponding position of the E. Alternatively, they could be given an E to hold and position appropriately. VA is recorded as usual. It is not appropriate to use an interpreter because they could bias the test.

This test is difficult for both patient and tester and is rarely used now. It is much easier and quicker to use other strategies, such as letter matching where the letters on the chart are printed in a random order (and in as large a font as possible) onto a piece of paper, which may be laminated (to facilitate cleaning), and the patient is asked to match letters that the tester is pointing to. This is considerably easier than trying to decide whether the patient is matching an E incorrectly or whether the operator has lost their place on the chart! Charts are available with pictures of familiar objects (such as the Kay picture test) for both Snellen and logMAR. These can be used when ascertaining children's visual acuity but an adult may see them as demeaning.

The patient should be 6m distant from the Snellen chart. They should be instructed to cover one eye (the best eye) with the occluder, and to read every letter on each line, starting from the top, out loud. Encourage the patient to try to read as far down the chart as possible, noting the smallest line that the patient can read. Also note if the patient misses or gets a letter or letters wrong. Follow the same steps, occluding the other eye, to note and record the VA of the weaker eye. The VA should be recorded, e.g. VA; R(OD) 6/6 L(OS) 6/6. The numerator is the line on the test chart and the denominator the distance from the chart, 6m in this case.

If the patient cannot read the largest letter on the chart from 6m, move the patient nearer to the chart, usually in 1-m increments. The distance from the chart is duly noted (e.g. VA; R 3/36 L 3/60), indicating that the chart was read at a distance of 3m.

If the patient cannot see the top letter even when moved nearer to the chart (e.g. 1m), ask the patient to count the number of fingers (CF) that you are holding up. The test distance is usually 1 foot or 30cm. If the patient can count fingers, record as CF in the notes. (This should be undertaken more than once because guessing can sometimes be accurate when there are only 5 numbers to guess.) Contrast against a different-coloured background should be taken into account. Both Snellen and logMAR charts are black-on-white for complete contrast. Light skin against a light background, or dark skin against a dark background, does not provide optimum contrast for the patient

Should the patient not be able to count fingers, they should be asked if they can see any hand movement (HM). Again this is done at 1 foot (30cm). It needs to be a movement of the hand only and, again, contrast should be taken into account. Record as HM for that eye. If HM cannot be noticed by the patient, ask them to locate a light source such as a pen-torch. Hold the light at about 2 feet (60cm) from the patient, and shine it from different areas of the patient's field of vision, asking where the light is coming from, If the patient can see the light, record as PL (perception of light) and state where the patient can see the light. In the event that light cannot be seen, record as NPL (no perception of light).

Where VA is less than 6/9 in either eye, pinhole (PH) VA should be recorded. The pinhole lets only a very fine beam of light through, removing any need for refraction. This gives an indication as to whether vision can be corrected with spectacles or contact lenses, which is indicated by improvements in VA with the pinhole.

Use of pinholes

If usually worn, the patient should wear distance spectacles. The patient should be asked to hold the pinhole to the right eye and the occluder over the left, and to adjust the position of the pinhole until they can view the chart through it and read the smallest line of letters that is visible. It may be necessary to encourage the patient to try a smaller line of letters even if they make some errors.

Record VA as before but adding PH to the measurement.

Some clinical areas do not have the 6m space (or 3-m with a mirror) needed for the test. A 3-metre Snellen chart is available for use in confined places. It gives the result as if at 6m.

LogMAR charts and testing

Charts are designed so that there are five letters on each row. The spacing between each letter is equal and the spacing between rows is equal to the height of the letters on the smaller row. The letter size follows a geometric progression, with a ratio equal to 0.1 log units (1.26). The chart is designed for a standard testing distance of 4m, which is much more manageable in most settings than 6m. The chart is marked on the left with the equivalent Snellen notation; on the right, the notation is the logMAR of the letters concerned. The value of 0.0 logMAR is equivalent to 4/4 or 6/6.

The patient should be asked to read from left to right, from the 0.5 logMAR, or the 4/2 line if the VA is sufficient. The patient should be encouraged to continue to read down the chart until they fail to identify any letters on one line.

Scoring allows the inclusion of each individual letter missed or read incorrectly. Each line is 0.1 logMAR and so each letter is 0.02 logMAR. In practice, the total number of letters read incorrectly is noted and 0.02 logMAR unit assigned to each. This sum is added to the logMAR value for the last line on which any letters were read correctly and recorded as the final logMAR score.

To use the chart at 3m, 0.1 logMAR unit should be added to the final score; at 2m, 0.3 should be added; and at 1m, 0.6. The equivalent of 0.0 logMAR is 6/6 Snellen; 0.3 is equivalent to 6/12, 0.6 to 6/24 and 1 to 6/60.

A much easier way of recording logMAR visual acuity is by a simple letter count. As each chart has the same number of letters, the letter count is accurate for all charts. When looking for progression of visual loss or gain for a particular patient, this method works very well.

Visual acuity scales			
Foot	Metre	Decimal	LogMAR
20/200	6/60	0.10	1.00
20/160	6/48	0.125	0.90
20/125	6/38	0.16	0.80
20/100	6/30	0.20	0.70
20/80	6/24	0.25	0.60
20/63	6/19	0.32	0.50
20/50	6/15	0.40	0.40
20/40	6/12	0.50	0.30
20/32	6/9.5	0.63	0.20
20/25	6/7.5	0.80	0.10
20/20	6/6	1.00	0.00
20/16	6/4.8	1.25	-0.10
20/12.5	6/3.8	1.60	-0.20
20/10	6/3	2.00	-0.30

Figure 4.3 LogMAR/Snellen conversion chart.

A criticism of logMAR in a busy outpatient department is that there are more letters to read per line than the Snellen, but this also makes it more accurate.

Colour vision testing

Colour vision is tested to determine whether there is any acquired and/or hereditary defect of colour vision. Testing colour vision will also enable the examiner to determine whether there are problems with the macular or optic nerve, one of the first indicators of which is colour desaturation.

Some jobs depend on the person having normal colour vision, e.g. British train drivers. According to Birch (2003) there is a duty to ensure that colour vision testing equipment meets quality standards and must therefore be 'fit for purpose'.

The patient should wear their near-vision spectacles for the test. The most common colour vision test is the Ishihara plates. More detailed examination tools are available to determine hue discrimination, but the operator must have specialist skill.

Eye examination

Examination of the eye is essential for the diagnosis and management of ocular disease and trauma. Within a specialist ophthalmic unit, the health professional will have access to a slit-lamp (Figure 4.3). However, this is unlikely to be the case in other settings, such as the primary care physician's surgery or the treatment room. Anyone caring for an ophthalmic patient should be able to perform a basic systematic examination of the eye (including pupil reaction), adnexae and anterior chamber.

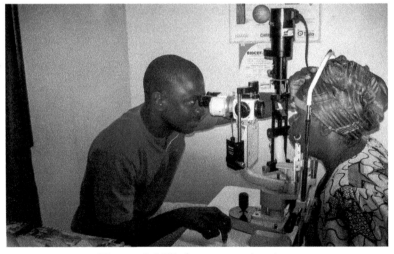

Figure 4.4 Slit-lamp examination.
(Photo reprinted by permission of the International Centre for Eye Health – ICEH.)

Examination of the eye without a slit-lamp

A pen-torch examination of the eye can reveal findings that are significant to making a diagnosis. It may demonstrate that the eye is in fact healthy or diseased, or detect the presence of trauma or a foreign body (FB).

Equipment needed

A good pen-torch (or similar light source) is essential, with batteries that are well charged. Dull light will not highlight anomalies and will prevent adequate examination of the pupil response and determination of the depth of the anterior chamber.

A source of magnification will enable the examiner to view and, if appropriate, remove foreign bodies. It will also enable the examiner to view structures better.

Eye examination technique

Much of the patient's confidence in the practitioner is based on the practitioner having a good examination technique. In addition, the practitioner needs to develop the ability to explain clinically what is seen during the examination process, so that they can give the patient a step-by-step account of what is seen. This will help to explain the symptoms experienced by the patient as well as the rationale behind subsequent treatment choices. It is helpful to use simple diagrams or leaflets to aid explanations, or to develop drawing skills so that you can quickly produce simple sketches of what is seen to share with patients and help understanding. The diagrams can then be given to patients to take away with them.

Examination of the eye should be systematic. It is usual to look first at the eye that is thought to be diseased or injured; if it is a general check, follow the systematic process and examine the right eye first. Beforehand, the patient's face should be considered:

- Does it look normal?
- Is there facial symmetry?
- Are there any signs of disease or trauma, such as a port wine stain, the presence of which could indicate a risk of glaucoma?
- Are the eyes proptosed?
- Is the patient using the brow to open the eyelids?
- Does the patient adopt a particular inclination of the head that could indicate visual problems such as macular degeneration?
- It is also important to establish and note whether or not the patient has an artificial eye. Modern prosthetics provide excellent cosmesis and are not always apparent to the novice examiner.

Before you shine the torch directly into the patient's eye, warn them – to prevent screwing up of the eyes.

Eyelids

Observe the lids; do they look anatomically normal and symmetrical? Then look for anomalies, such as: ptosis, inflammation, redness, oedema, trauma (old and new) such as lacerations, cysts, lesions, and swelling (particularly over the lacrimal sac). Examine lid margins for: redness, scales and dandruff. Then examine the eyelashes:

- Are they turning in (trichiasis)?
- Is the lid turned out (ectropion) or inwards (entropion)?
- Are lashes missing?
- Are the lid margins swollen?
- Are foreign bodies (FBs), or even parasites present?

Ask the patient to close their eyes gently, and observe whether the margins are in apposition or if closure is incomplete. Is the blink rate normal (every 3–6 seconds) or is there some blepharospasm? Check that the lids and puncta are in good apposition to the globe.

Conjunctiva

Each of the following areas of the conjunctiva should be examined carefully: bulbar area, palpebral area and area of the fornices (Figure 4.5).

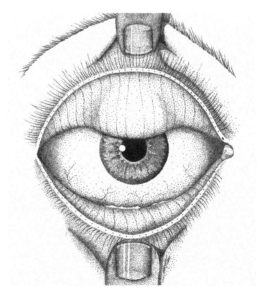

Figure 4.5 Eversion of the upper and lower lids.

Gently pull down the lower lids to expose the lower bulbar conjunctiva. After viewing this area, gently push up the upper lid, asking the patient to look down in order to expose the superior bulbar areas. By asking the patient to look in all directions of gaze, you can view almost all of the conjunctiva. The conjunctiva is normally transparent, with visible conjunctival blood vessels. The sclera should be visible below and is normally white in appearance.

To view the palpebral conjunctiva, you will need to evert the lids. The lower lid can be gently pulled down to expose the conjunctiva, although it is necessary to evert the upper lid manually. Look for foreign bodies, papillae, follicles and cysts.

Everting the upper lid

Having asked the patient to look down, grasp the lashes of the upper lid with the thumb underneath the lashes. Hold the lid, down and slightly away from the globe, taking care not to pull it tight. Using the tip of a cotton-tipped applicator, held in the other hand like a pen, press down on the centre of the lid. The lid will evert along the edge of the tarsal plate. The cotton bud may be removed as the thumb presses the everted part of the lid backwards and anchors it against the upper orbital rim.

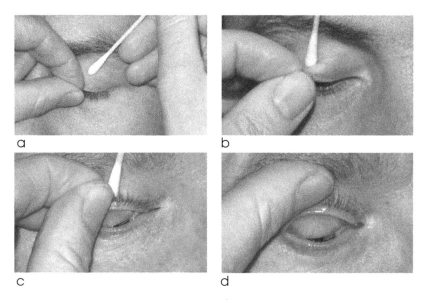

a   b

c   d

Figure 4.6 Lid eversion.

In a healthy conjunctiva you should be able to view the vasculature clear of signs of injection. Note the presence, degree, depth and location of hyperaemia. Note also the presence or absence of subconjunctival haemorrhage. The superficial vessels that you see move with the tissue and are therefore conjunctival. The deeper vessels do not move and are episcleral. Recognising this distinction will help you differentiate between conjunctival and episcleral inflammation. Differential diagnosis may require further slit-lamp examination. Look for cysts, lacerations, papillae, pinguecula, pterygium and FBs.

Episcleral vessels are visible below the conjunctiva and should normally show no signs of injection.

Sclera

The sclera should be white. It is hyperaemic in cases of episcleritis, scleritis or uveitis. In the case of scleritis, the sclera appears to have a bluish/purple tinge.

Cornea

A healthy cornea should appear clear, with no opacities or vasculature and no encroachment of conjunctival tissue. Note the curvature: is it abnormally conical as in keratoconus?

Anterior chamber

Anterior chamber (AC) examination is possible using a pen-torch. Each eye is assessed individually. Shine the torch on the cornea centrally and observe the AC from the temporal aspect; this gives a rough estimate of AC depth but not how shallow the angle may be. The angle is better estimated using the slit-lamp, although a rough estimate can be made by shining the pen-torch on to the nasal side of the cornea and noting the angle depth.

Looking through the cornea to the AC, you should normally have an uninterrupted view of the iris and pupil. After blunt or penetrating trauma, including surgery and laser, hyphaema may be present. You should note how much of the AC is filled. In extreme cases, the whole of the AC may be filled.

In infected or inflammatory conditions, including corneal ulcer endophthalmitis or uveitis, hypopyon (a level of white matter in the AC which may be sterile or infective) may be detected.

The iris

Note the colour – usually both irides are a very similar colour. If there is normally a difference in iris colour, the patient will know. Look for presence of iris atrophy or evidence of trauma such as iris prolapse. Iridodonesis (iris tremor) may be noted if the patient has had a cataract extraction. Note sphincter tears.

Assess the pupils by checking:

- Shape and size (compare with the other eye)
- Reaction to light (direct and consensual)
- Reaction to near objects
- Relative afferent pupillary defect.

Pupillary assessment

It is important to evaluate the pupillary reactions of both eyes. A relative afferent pupillary defect indicates that there is a problem with the afferent pathway to the brain. Careful evaluation and documentation will provide a baseline for future evaluations.

Lens

Some lens opacities can be viewed with the naked eye through the pupil. Note whether the patient is aphakic or pseudophakic (you may be able to see a reflection from a posterior chamber intraocular lens).

Tear film

It is difficult to estimate tear film break-up time with a pen-torch unless you have a blue filter cover. Instil fluorescein into the lower fornix. Ask the patient to blink and then stare without blinking. Shine the pen-torch on to the cornea, observing how long it takes before the tear film starts to break up and disperse. The break-up time is normally 15–20 seconds, after which streaks are noted in the fluorescein.

A more in-depth examination of the ocular structures requires a source of magnification, ideally with a stereoscopic view using a slit-lamp or an indirect ophthalmoscope for the posterior segment.

Slit-lamp examination technique

Slit-lamp examination follows a similar pattern of examination. Do not expect to achieve competence with the use of a slit-lamp after a single practice session. It may take weeks or months of practice under supervision before you gain enough confidence to begin to use it independently as a diagnostic tool.

It is not possible to provide a short description of how to set up and use a slit-lamp. Any reader wishing to learn more about setting up the slit-lamp should review the manufacturer's handbook.

It is important to practise and become familiar with the slit-lamp. It needs to be used regularly to achieve competence, and it can be helpful to get feedback on your performance from an expert. It is rather like driving a car and getting used to the controls, highway code, road conditions and other road users. Confidence will be gained gradually. If you are a novice, it may be helpful to find a willing volunteer to sit on the other side of the slit-lamp and go through the practical aspects of setting the slit-lamp to your requirements and getting the individual sitting correctly at the slit-lamp. Patients who are waiting for appointments are often willing to be guinea pigs to while away the time!

The principle of the slit-lamp is the narrow 'slit' beam of very bright light produced by the lamp. This beam is focused on to the eye, which is then viewed under magnification with a microscope. These are the key points to remember when carrying out slit-lamp examination:

- The patient's comfort and your comfort at the slit-lamp are of the utmost importance so make sure you have at least one chair that is adjustable so you can change its height.
- Provide a good explanation of the procedure to ensure the patient's cooperation.
- Game playing can facilitate the examination of children, as can demonstrating on a parent.
- Carry out your slit-lamp examination systematically and methodically, to reduce the likelihood of missing something.
- Ensure that the eyepieces are correctly adjusted to your prescription before commencing the examination, e.g. your refractive errors (if any) are accounted for and that you have adjusted your pupillary apertures accordingly.
- Document findings accurately and legibly.

The slit-lamp has many uses, including examination and monitoring of:

- Ocular adnexae including lids, lid margins, punctum, lashes
- Ocular structures: cornea, anterior chamber, iris, lens, lens capsule and anterior vitreous face
- Signs, symptoms and progress of anterior segment disease or injury
- Posterior segment of the eye by the use of auxiliary lenses.

Further 'special' investigations include: Goldmann applanation tonometry (applanation tonometry is explained in Chapter 20); Van Herick's estimation of anterior chamber depth; and gonioscopic examination of the angle.

Components of the slit-lamp include:

- The microscope, which houses the viewing system, composed of the oculars and the magnification changers
- The illumination arm, which houses the illumination system
- The remainder of the instrument, e.g. chin rest, fixation light.

The microscope and adjustment of ocular eyepieces

The slit-lamp is a binocular microscope, which means that it gives the examiner a three-dimensional view of the eye and surrounding structures. The prime advantage of a three-dimensional view is that ocular abnormalities can be detected with greater precision. All slit-lamps are slightly different – the explanations here should be modified to suit individual slit-lamps.

The viewing system of the microscope can be adjusted to account for any refractive error; alternatively, you may choose to wear glasses during the examination. If you are unsure what your refractive correction is, a focusing rod, which is supplied with the slit-lamp, can be used to measure your refractive error. Slide off the footplate and insert the focusing rod with the flat side facing you. Turn on the slit-lamp and, using a slit beam of light (about 1–2mm in width), focus the light on to the rod. Close one eye and with the other eye look through the slit-lamp and start turning the wheel of the ocular eyepiece from the plus side of the scale, stopping immediately once the image of the light through the eyepiece is clear and in focus. Where possible (if you know your own refraction readings), check whether the scale readings in dioptres actually correspond to your own spectacle correction.

You will have to adjust the interpupillary distance of the eyepieces to your own eyes, as some people's eyes are more widely or narrowly spaced than others. To adjust the eyepieces to suit your interpupillary distance, first take a look down the binocular eyepieces of the slit-lamp. You should not be aware of seeing any black shading in your field of vision; this indicates poor adjustment. If black shading is noted, you will need to adjust the interpupillary aperture by either squeezing the eyepieces together or pulling them further apart. When the pupillary apertures are correctly set, you will have an unobstructed view when looking through the eyepieces.

Magnification adjustment of the binoculars of the microscope depends on the model or manufacturer; some have a flip switch, whereas others have a dial. If your magnification changer is a lever switch, you will have two different settings on $10\times$ and $16\times$. If your magnification changer is a knob, you will normally have five different magnification settings: $6\times$, $10\times$, $16\times$, $25\times$ and $40\times$. Magnifications of $10\times$ and $16\times$ are adequate for most examination purposes.

The illumination arm houses the light source. The illumination arm is capable of being moved from 0° to 90° on either side of the microscope. The illumination arm houses the following components:

1. Two slit controls that can be used to vary the height and width of the slit beam. In addition, the orientation of the beam can be altered from a vertical to a horizontal plane. The slit control is also used for interposing the blue filter.

2. Filters that control the heat and light intensity of the beam. In addition, colour filters (cobalt blue and cyan) are available and these are used are in conjunction with different eye drops.

The position of the illumination system in relation to the observation system can be measured by a graded index, which is located at the bottom of the illumination column. Knowledge of the angle of the illumination to the illumination column is important for examining/grading certain structures of the eye.

The movement of the slit-lamp is controlled by the joystick, which is situated on the base of the slit-lamp; by moving the joystick left to right and back to front, the slit-lamp column can be moved. The slit-lamp column is raised by turning the joystick clockwise (to elevate) and lowered by turning the joystick counter-clockwise.

Further adjustment to the slit-lamp can be achieved by using a lever located at the base of the slit-lamp table. By releasing the lever, the height of the whole table (including the slit-lamp) can be adjusted to accommodate the height of the individual patient. Take care to control this movement because you could cause the patient some injury.

Patient comfort at the slit-lamp can be further achieved by moving the chin rest up and down by means of the adjustment knob located on the side frame of the slit-lamp. When the patient is in the correct position, the patient's outer canthus will be aligned with a black mark or notch on the headrest bar. The patient's forehead should be snug against the forehead rest.

An explanation of the examination to the patient is vital in order to ensure cooperation and to obtain informed consent. It can also be explained that, although the machine may look formidable, it is only a glorified microscope or pair of binoculars used to magnify the different structures of the eye.

Advise patients that to facilitate accurate examination they need to ensure that their forehead rests against the bar and that their chin should be in the chin rest; they should keep their mouth closed and both eyes open. Note also that they should be warned that the light from the slit- lamp can be bright; this is especially important if the patient is photophobic.

The position of the slit-lamp is equally important to ensure cooperation. Be patient with elderly and very young people. If the patient is in a wheelchair, where possible transfer them to an examination chair. If this is not possible, manoeuvre the slit-lamp as close as you can to the patient by removing the arms and footrests of the wheelchair. For shorter patients or children, it may be possible to examine them standing right in front of the slit-lamp. Patients with head tremors should have their head supported from behind by an assistant. Above all, be patient. Align the slit-lamp to the patient and make yourself comfortable. Set your slit-lamp on the lower magnification and turn it on at the control box to the lowest voltage setting. Use one hand to operate the joystick and the other to operate the illumination arm. If examining the patient's left eye, have the illumination unit on the left-hand side, and vice versa for the right eye.

To focus the light onto the slit-lamp, you can look at the patient's eyes by looking from the side of the slit-lamp machine and grossly aligning the eye. Then look through the oculars and fine-tune the focus by using the joystick and movement of the illumination arm. The second method of alignment is to look through the oculars from the start and, by using the joystick, move the slit-lamp and illumination arm until the eye is in focus. For beginners, this may require some practice before confidence is developed. Do not despair if you do not get the hang of this skill at the first few attempts. Use of the slit-lamp gets easier with practice. It's important to be methodical in your examination. In this way, you are less likely to miss anything. You can then start your examination.

Use of 78 and 90 dioptre lenses, as well as superfield lenses, allows direct viewing of the retina through a dilated pupil. This is a skill in itself and takes a lot of practice, but has replaced indirect ophthalmoscopy in many examinations.

Here are some final tips on using the slit-lamp:

- Ask patients to look at your right ear when you examine their right eye and at your left ear when you examine their left eye.

- Some machines have a fixation light, which is useful when removing FBs.

- There is a latch that tilts the slit-lamp, which is useful for posterior examination work or to see the depth of FB penetration.

Using an ophthalmoscope

Fundal examination can be by direct ophthalmoscopy, using an ophthalmoscope (providing a binocular view); or by indirect methods that often provide a stereoscopic view, as with a slit-lamp. An ophthalmoscope is a useful piece of equipment because it provides sources of magnification, illumination and light filters (usually cobalt blue and cyan – blue–green). It is also portable.

- Ensure that the ophthalmoscope is working properly: check the light source is working (battery charge and light bulb) and ensure that the light source is the largest circle at the beginning of your examination. Adjust the lens setting to 0.

- Hold the ophthalmoscope in your right hand when examining the right eye and the left hand when examining the left eye. In either hand, adjustments to the lens rotator of the ophthalmoscope are made using the index finger.

- Fundal examination is made easier if the pupil is dilated with short-acting drops such as tropicamide 0.5% or 1%, although some would suggest that this is not essential.

- The patient should be sitting comfortably in a chair that allows you easy access to both eyes; they should be asked to remove their spectacles or contact lenses.

- The examination room should be dimly lit, and the patient should be asked to focus on a set distant target. Patients need to be encouraged to maintain their gaze throughout the examination.

- When examining the patient's left eye use your left eye, and your right eye to examine the right eye. Hold the ophthalmoscope comfortably against the arch of your eyebrow.
- If you can whisper in the patient's ear, you are approaching correctly. If you could kiss them, you are not.
- You should look towards the patient's eye through the aperture of the ophthalmoscope, directing the light onto it. Aim to move closer towards the patient's eye in a mid-vertical plane, and at about 20–30° laterally, so that you look first at the optic disc rather than the macula.
- At between 50 and 30cm distance from the patient (and as you move closer), you should be able to observe the 'red light reflex'. If there are any lens or corneal opacities, these will appear black against the red reflex. As you draw closer to the patient, you may find placing your hand on the patient's shoulder stabilises you both.
- As you keep moving closer with the ophthalmoscope, you will find that the retina will come into focus. If you cannot then find the clearest image, use the lenses to assist you. Try to locate the optic nerve head.
- Observe the margins of the disc and note whether they are well defined or notched.
- Look at the colour of the rim, noting its colour, which is normally pink.
- Estimate the size of the optic disc and the cup:disc ratio, noting whether or not the cup takes up a large part of the disc.
- Note the presence of optic disc haemorrhages, peripapillary atrophy and bared circumlinear blood vessels.
- Identify the retinal arteries and veins and whether these are following their normal path.
- If you find a patch of retina and don't know where you are, find a vessel and when it reaches a junction, follow the arrow made by the joining vessel. This will always take you back to the optic disc.
- Finish by asking the patient to look into the light and examine the macula. This is the area of the retina with the highest visual resolution, corresponding to central vision. Any abnormalities, such as haemorrhages, exudates or cotton wool spots, should be noted.

Record your findings (separately for each eye) accurately in the patient's case notes, usually with a diagram.

Indirect ophthalmoscopy

This piece of equipment is a binocular, stereoscopic, head-set device that allows the examiner to gain a wide-field view of both the vitreous and the retina. Some indirect ophthalmoscopes have a teaching mirror attachment. This allows learners to 'see' the same view as the examiner, who can describe what they are viewing. The indirect ophthalmoscope also leaves the examiner with both hands free.

It is usual to dilate the patient's pupils before the examination, and to have the patient lying recumbent on an examination couch with the examiner at the head of the couch. If the patient cannot lie flat, the head of the couch can be raised slightly.

A light source from the indirect ophthalmoscope, positioned on the examiner's head, is directed into the patient's eye by an adjustable mirror; the reflected light is then gathered by a condensing lens to provide an image of the retina. Note that this image will be inverted. The oculars should be close to the examiner's eyes.

As a general principle, the low-powered condensing lenses must be held further from the eye; while stronger condensing lenses need to be held closer, because of the focal length of the condensing lens. Aim to focus the light from the condensing lens perfectly in the centre of the patient's pupil. The condensing lens will thus form an image of the retina, in front of the condensing lens, which fills the whole lens.

There are several factors that could affect the field of view, including: the size of the patient's pupil; the power of the condensing lens used; the size of the condensing lens; any refractive error; and the distance the condensing lens is held from the patient's eye.

To help ensure that the condensing lens is properly directed, it should be noted that most lenses are coded with either a white or a silver ring, indicating that that side should be on the side of the patient's eye. Another tip is that, if the light reflection images from the front and back surfaces are of equal size, the lens is being held correctly.

Both eyes should be examined at the same time to enable comparison of both peripheral fundi, including pigmentation and appearance. It may be necessary to elevate the patient's head in order to examine the superior fundus, thus allowing for a maximum superior view by the examiner. The nasal region, temporal region and retina directly above and below the posterior poles are examined, followed by the inferior fundus. The posterior pole of the optic nerve and macula are usually examined last.

Beginners should practise on non-dilated eyes. Initially, practise with ophthalmoscopes that have converging systems. As a steady hand is essential, try resting part of the hand on the patient's forehead. This is particularly helpful with non-dilated pupils.

A better peripheral view will be obtained using a +28-D or +30-D lens and scleral indentation. Note that a higher-power lens will reduce magnification. Conversely, a better view of the optic disc will be gained using lenses of a power in the +15 D range.

Scleral indentation

Indentation is a technique that moves areas of retina into the field illuminated by the indirect ophthalmoscope by pressing (indenting) the sclera. It is not nearly as difficult or as uncomfortable for the patient as might be imagined. It should be noted that indentation will not cause or worsen retinal detachment.

Conclusion

Clinical examination can be as simple or as complex as time or equipment allows. However, even the simplest of tools, in the right hands, can be used to aid diagnosis and to facilitate treatment interventions.

References

Birch, J. (2003) 'Colour vision examination' in S. Doshi & W. Harvey (eds) *Investigative Techniques and Ocular Examination*. Edinburgh: Butterworth-Heinemann, pp. 13–26.

CHAPTER FIVE

Visual impairment

Helen Gibbons and Linda Whitaker

Visual impairment can have a profound effect on individuals, both in their own lives and in having to come to terms with the stigma attached to 'disabled' people by society. Visual impairment has been shown to reduce a person's functional status and wellbeing, with a magnitude comparable to that of a major medical condition, and to have a major impact on quality of life (Chia *et al.* 2004).

Many visually impaired people have been so since childhood and have learned to adapt to living in a world where we take sight for granted and cannot envisage being without visual stimulus, on which we place great importance. Those people losing their sight later in life can often find it difficult to cope with, and visual impairment is associated with lower subjective wellbeing, reduced competence in everyday activities and greater depression in older people.

In contrast, those who have been visually impaired from childhood have grown up in a non-sighted environment and are often able to cope with their daily lives independently with little or no assistance from sighted individuals. Wahl *et al.* (1998) found that they were generally better adapted than adults who had impairment in later years. However, Rees *et al.* (2010) found that those dealing with visual impairment at a relatively young age (as an adult) may experience greater distress due to experiencing greater disruption in life roles than older adults. Other studies, such as Evans *et al.* (2007), found high levels of depression in visually impaired older adults. Whatever the age of the person who experiences visual impairment, it is clearly life changing. It is also clear that, whenever visual impairment occurs, being aware of issues and suitable coping strategies can aid a person in coming to terms with their impairment, and assist in their rehabilitation.

Myths surrounding blindness

The term 'blind' leads many people to conclude that the person is in total darkness. However, according to the RNIB (2015), only 4% of those who are blind live in complete darkness. Most will have some residual vision, and will use that in learning to cope with their environment and its hazards.

It is also a myth that visually impaired people have better hearing than sighted individuals, and they are no more musically gifted than the sighted population. Visually impaired people therefore have similar characteristics to the sighted population. As such, they are pleasant, grumpy, musical, non-musical, academic, non-academic, sports enthusiasts, non-sports enthusiasts, home owners and non-home owners, just as one would expect to find in the population as a whole. Observations of healthcare staff over several years have shown them, when talking to visually impaired people, inadvertently raising their voices (thinking that this will help with more effective communication) or assuming that just because the patient is visually impaired and elderly they are hearing impaired as well. As healthcare professionals, we need to ascertain from our patient how much residual sight, if any, they have, and whether they have any hearing problems, which may in fact be the result of aging rather than of any association with their visual impairment. People need to be treated as individuals, rather than being expected to behave as we might believe or expect them to.

Stigma and blindness

In society as a whole, people who are blind are often treated as being different from 'normal' members of society. A stigma is usually attached to a person with some sort of a distinguishing mark, leading to disapproval and exclusion from society. This view of disabled people can lead to their non-integration into society as a whole, which has an effect on their personal self-esteem. Stigma is therefore a labelling by society, whereby generalisations are made about individuals in a particular group, usually based on minimal experience of either the group or the individuals who make it up.

Fourie (2007, p. 224) supports this theory by suggesting that individuals who lose their sight may feel threatened by the perceived sudden loss of 'normality' in a society that values the 'normal'. Southwell (2012) reports how many of her clients have lost friends because of their sight loss. It is linked to the stereotyping and labelling mentioned earlier, which can have a negative effect on the individual coming to terms with a visual loss. Common strategies used by visually impaired people to minimise the impact of visual impairment include folding the cane out of sight in the presence of others, wearing dark glasses to disguise an abnormal appearance of the eyes and maintaining eye contact during conversations with others (Allen 1989).

Healthcare workers are also members of society and must therefore face up to their own values and attitudes in relation to people with a visual impairment. Society needs to recognise the process by which it stigmatises individuals. The focus must change from an emphasis on the blindness to an emphasis on the person who happens to be blind. Sadly, in some countries it is assumed that people are visually impaired because they are evil or have been cursed. The charity Sightsavers (2015) highlights this as an area that is a cause for concern and they are working hard to change these negative attitudes.

Altered body image

Linked to the notion of stigma and visual impairment is the concept of body image. When a person is visually impaired, there can often be an obvious defect of the eyes, which is noticeable to the sighted person. This can pose problems to the visually impaired individual, because they are often aware of their altered body image and can become uncomfortable with it. Sometimes this discomfort stems from other people's reactions and not just those of the person with the altered body image, which is why it is linked to the notion of stigma.

It is well documented that society views attractiveness in a positive light and people perceived as ugly tend to be treated with derision. Whitehead (1995) suggests that attractive people are more likely to receive greater consideration. Less attractive people are more likely to experience lower self-esteem and this must surely be associated with the way that they are treated by others. As members of society, it is up to us to attempt to educate people who may 'make fun' of those with altered body image. We can use the media (such as newspapers, magazines, television and radio) and ourselves as role models to get a more positive, inclusive message across.

Many visually impaired people will attempt to conceal their appearance by wearing dark glasses and, if they are comfortable with this option, they should be encouraged. We should, however, be under no illusion that this option is for the benefit of sighted individuals, because the wearing of dark glasses has no therapeutic effect on the visually impaired person, other than to alert others to the possibility of an eye issue and prevent others discussing their appearance.

One of the most obvious situations that can lead to problems with altered body image is when a person has an orbital exenteration for an ocular tumour. This can present great challenges to the individual, because it is not as easy to hide defects involving the face as it can be with other parts of the body. People needing to have an eye removed, for whatever reason, will need a great deal of psychological support from nurses involved in their care. With today's advances in technology, a good cosmetic effect can usually be expected from prostheses, and this can be conveyed to the patient. It may be helpful to have an ocular prosthetist visit the patient preoperatively (if there is one available) to discuss any concerns. Likewise, patients who have had similar surgery and have a good cosmetic appearance are often willing to visit patients who are faced with these operations, and this could be encouraged. Many larger ophthalmic units will have access to counsellors or be able to offer a referral to a counsellor to help these patients address their changing body image.

Registration in the UK

When considering registration for blind and visually impaired people, it is necessary to be aware of the relevant legislation. Registration means that the person will be on the Social Services register of people who are either severely sight impaired (blind) or sight impaired (partially sighted)

Registration in the UK has changed significantly. The old form, the BD8, was developed out of the National Assistance Act of 1948 and was seen as a starting point for access to services and a register of visual impairment and to gather epidemiological data. The BD8 form was updated in 1990, but was superseded by the Certificate of Visual Impairment (CVI) form in 2005 in England and Wales. The CVI form was the result of collaboration between service users and experts and it offered opportunities for patients to get access to a Social Services assessment and therefore get assistance prior to the CVI being completed.

The registration process involves:

- Referral to an ophthalmologist.

- Ophthalmologist assessment of eligibility for certification with the completion of the certificate (Certificate of Visual Impairment (CVI) in England and Wales, BP1 in Scotland and A655 in Northern Ireland). The ophthalmologist will indicate on the certificate whether the person qualifies as 'severely sight impaired or blind' or 'sight impaired or partially sighted'. There is a diagnostic section with tick boxes for the most common causes of sight loss and an expanded section about the patient's needs (emotional, physical and social) and circumstances, which can be filled in by eye clinic staff. A section where clinical staff can express an opinion about the urgency of social needs assessment should also be filled in. Copies of the certificate go to the patient, their GP and local Social Services.

- Social Services contact the patient and ask if they wish to be placed on the register. If the person says yes, they become registered.

Registration leads to a community care assessment. However, if the patient chooses not to be registered, they can still access Social Services assistance.

Documents needed include:

1. Letter LV1 'Optometrist Identification of a Person with Significant Sight Problems': this is a letter concerning visual impairment needs and is given by optometrists

to relevant patients so that they can self-refer for social care. It enables patients to be aware of what types of help are available so that they or their carers can make informed choices. There is no diagnostic information included and these patients are referred to an ophthalmologist in the usual way.

2. Referral form RV1 'Hospital Eye Service Referral of Vision Impaired Patient for Social Needs Assessment': this is completed by staff in the hospital eye service to refer patients (with their consent) for assessment of their social needs. All eye clinic staff can use the form and it can be used where registration is not currently appropriate (e.g. where medical intervention may alter the situation but there are problems in the meantime). If the patient has declined registration, this can be used to obtain advice

3. Certificate of Vision Impairment CVI: this document establishes formal eligibility for registration and any benefits that are directly linked to registration.

All forms are available to download from the Department of Health Website so they are always accessible and the information is current and up to date. The registration form itself has explanatory notes to support its completion and this can only be done if the patient gives their consent. The guidance suggests that patients should be involved in completing the forms.

The National Assistance Act of 1948 gave a definition (which is still used today) that a person can be certified as 'severely sight impaired' if they are 'so blind as to be unable to perform any work for which eye sight is essential'.

The Department of Health classifies people being registered as 'severely sight impaired or blind' if, when wearing appropriate glasses or contact lenses, they have;

- Vision below 3/60 recorded on a Snellen visual acuity chart
- Vision of 3/60 but below 6/60 on a Snellen visual acuity chart with severe reduction of visual field
- Vision of 6/60 or above with a very reduced visual field.

For certification of sight impairment, there are no legal definitions to abide by. However, the CVI guidelines suggest that 'a person can be certified as sight impaired if they are "substantially and permanently handicapped by defective vision caused by a congenital defect, illness or injury"'. As a general rule, these patients can be certified if, while wearing appropriate glasses or contact lenses:

- They have visual acuity of 3/60 to 6/60 on a Snellen visual acuity chart with a full field
- Visual acuity up to 6/24 with moderate visual field defects, or with central blurring
- Have a Snellen visual acuity of 6/17 or better if they have a gross visual field defect or a marked visual field defect (in the case of glaucoma, for example).

This improved form not only offers greater clarity for those registering the patients but also allows for the transfer of information between council services if a patient moves, thus ensuring a smooth transition of support services. There is a much larger and more important role for clinic staff who can initiate the process and help the patient to access help while the process of formal registration is in process. The clinic staff can also influence the speed of response from Social Services.

It is essential that anyone who is new to working in the field of ophthalmology (whether clinical or non-clinical) is made aware of the certification process. Inevitably, at some point they will either see a form or be asked by a patient or relative about one.

It is widely recognised that there is massive under-registration of blind and partially sighted people. This is partly because of the continuing unwieldiness of the system, but also because many people prefer not to register. This can be for a number of reasons, including the fact that registration is still seen as the end of the road for hopes of better sight. The new process allows data on visual impairment to be collected even if the patient eventually chooses not to register.

Rehabilitation

For a patient who is diagnosed as being visually impaired, adjustments will need to be made so that they can try to resume their everyday activities. Many ophthalmic units will employ an eye clinic liaison officer (ECLO) who can advise the patient regarding:

- Their eye condition
- How to register their sight loss and the benefits of registration
- How to apply for welfare benefits
- Employment issues (such as job retention or retraining)
- How to gain access to emotional support and counselling
- How to get advice on local organisations and support groups.

Considerable consideration needs to be given to the patient's anxieties and it is important to consider issues such as rehabilitation, work and leisure for the visually impaired person. To be rehabilitated, as a visually impaired person, it is necessary for the individual to come to terms with the impairment. The five stages described are not unlike those found in the grieving process generally:

- Denial
- Anger
- Bargaining
- Depression
- Acceptance.

It is essential that these patients are offered the high level of support that patients who are receiving bad news from other specialties do. It is not uncommon for people losing their sight to experience anxiety about what the future might hold for them, their family and friends. The personal experience of visual impairment varies but adjustment is progressive, with stages sometimes identified as pre-impact, realisation of loss and the decision to live with the impairment, concluding with adjustment and readjustment (Allen 1989).

Ultimately, the visually impaired person will learn to adapt previously learned skills, or find coping strategies in order to carry out daily living activities. This will, however, be an ongoing process, because individuals will continue to be faced with new situations to which they have not previously been exposed. Visually impaired people therefore continually have to learn to adjust.

It is also necessary to consider the family in relation to individuals with visual impairment, because this situation can affect all family members. The family will need to be involved at all stages in the care and rehabilitation of visually impaired members. The family's questions will need to be identified and discussed, and solutions sought and offered so that the family (and other significant people in the patient's life) do not feel isolated and subsequently become stressed by the situation, as this will hamper the visually impaired family member's rehabilitation and adjustment to their loss. This must all be done with sensitivity to the needs of the visually impaired person first and, at all times, with their explicit consent.

Patients of working ages need to be given information on access to work, including a government and employers' joint funded scheme to provide equipment to enable them to continue with their employment (for example, voice-activated equipment and larger screens and keyboards). The Royal National Institute of Blind People (2015) has an extensive catalogue of resources available to support the visually impaired person to stay in employment.

Mobility

When considering mobility for visually impaired people, it should be remembered, as mentioned earlier, that most individuals will have some residual vision, and this should be used in order to promote orientation and mobility. The most significant factor in orientation and mobility performance has been identified as the visual field, with the central 37° radius zone and the right, left and inferior mid-peripheral zones being the most important (Haymes *et al.* 1996).

Orientation and mobility are, however, complicated areas and can be affected by the amount of light available. The indoor environment can be more easily manipulated to create the best possible conditions for the visually impaired person for orientation and mobility, but it is not possible to manipulate the external environment to any significant extent. Individuals may therefore have good indoor orientation and mobility, but poor outdoor orientation and mobility. In addition, the individual's personality and intelligence can have a bearing on how they cope with orientation and mobility, and so physical factors (such as the degree of visual acuity, visual field and lighting issues) may only be part of the puzzle.

The practical issues that should concern us are those that can make the environment less hazardous for those with a visual impairment who are travelling. Obstacles that most of us take for granted and avoid, because we can see them, can be dangerous for the visually impaired traveller. Unfortunately, the sighted general public do not consider the visually impaired when they are parking their car, half on the road and half on the pavement, and would not consider it a danger to the visually impaired person attempting to negotiate the environment (if they have no personal knowledge or experience of a visually impaired person). In addition, pedestrian areas in a lot of city centres have rubbish bins placed in the middle of the pavement, which again can prove hazardous for visually impaired individuals. Roadworks and drain maintenance, with barriers around them, provide an additional hazard, as do overhanging tree branches at the side of roads or in parks. The present move towards 'shared spaces', without obvious barriers between cars and pedestrians, causes major problems for those who cannot see well.

In public indoor areas, wet floors obviously present a hazard, as do the signs that are usually left behind to indicate that the floor is wet. By taking care to consider safe environments and involve visually impaired people in community issues (such as provision of access to buildings, designing of pedestrian precincts, and informing about road and pavement works with essential service maintenance) a lot of these problems could be addressed. Improvements have been made (including the introduction of 'talking lifts' in newer buildings, providing railings and bevelled surfaces at pedestrian crossings, and audible warnings at crossings), but there is still a long way to go.

Railway station staff and airport staff are now trained to help those with visual impairments with boarding. However, this requires careful planning, as assistance needs to be booked in advance.

Individuals nevertheless need instruction in independent travel before they can endeavour to negotiate the external environment independently. For this reason, mobility officers are usually employed by local authorities to assist with mobility training, especially the use of the long cane, so that individuals can learn to negotiate the environment.

The visually impaired person with a white stick is a familiar sight but there is an important distinction between a white stick and a long white cane. A stick may be painted white to show that the person is visually impaired but its function is still support. A white cane is used only as a mobility aid. A visually impaired person mobilising with a long cane needs to use it to detect any obstacles in their path. To do this, the cane is swept in an arc in front of the person's body, with the cane touching the ground in front of the 'trailing foot, rather than the forward foot'. This has been identified as the single most important point in the best use of the cane. By doing this, the individual is able to determine any obstacles in the path of where their next foot will fall.

An additional problem experienced by visually impaired people in relation to orientation and mobility is that of veering or moving away from their intended path. Kallie *et al.* (2007) support this and define veering as 'any deviation from an intended path'. For the visually impaired, veering can be particularly hazardous, as they can easily walk into pedestrians or stationary objects, potentially posing a risk to safety, particularly when crossing a busy street.

Guide dogs can be a useful aid to mobility, but they are not suitable for everybody, because the visually impaired person will need to have good balance. Also, the individual and family must be prepared to accept the dog into the family, and there must be an area in which the dog can play and exercise (just like any other dog) because they cannot be expected to be working at all times. Guide dogs cannot see and interpret the world as a human can; they are trained to respond to instruction, and the visually impaired person is normally expected to attend a training programme (often residential) before they can acquire a guide dog.

Sighted guiding

There are times when visually impaired people may need help from sighted people to enable them to move around. This is known as 'sighted guiding'. Visually impaired people should always be asked if they actually want help. Some may neither need nor want it. It is not appropriate to assume that they do, or to 'grab' the person and take charge.

To guide someone, the visually impaired person should take the arm of the sighted guide (rather than, as is often seen, the guider holding the visually impaired person and attempting to 'steer' them). Using the correct method will place the visually impaired person slightly behind the sighted guide and so they will be more confident that they will not be guided into any obstacle. It also allows the person to feel the guide's body movement, and this enables them to turn to the left or right with minimal verbal instruction.

When guiding someone on a level surface, it is usually necessary to verbally describe any change in floor surface or obstacles in the path so that no collisions or falls occur. It is important to remember, as a sighted guide, that the minute the visually impaired person is allowed to bump into an object, they will lose all faith in you as a guide, and it will be difficult to retrieve their trust.

When guiding someone to a chair, it is necessary to describe to them the type of chair it is, whether or not it has arms, and how it is positioned. If the chair is against a wall, the person should be guided to it from a front-facing position, allowed to feel the chair and, unless there are any mobility or balance problems, be allowed to sit down independently. If the chair is not against a wall, it may be better to approach the chair from the rear, and again allow the individual to feel the chair before sitting down.

When guiding through a doorway, it is usual to allow the visually impaired individual to be on the hinge side of the door, so that they can have control of it and shut it behind them, without you having to stop, turn around and shut the door yourself. Before passing through the door, you need to say whether the door opens towards or away from you, and whether or not it is a spring-loaded door, in order to avoid accidents.

When negotiating stairs, it is necessary to verbalise whether the stairs are ascending or descending. If a rail is present, allow the visually impaired person to hold the rail so that they feel more secure. At the first stair, it is prudent to pause, and for the sighted guide to explain that they will go onto the stairway first. After stepping onto the first step, again pause, so the visually impaired person can feel for the edge of the step with a foot, before proceeding. Keep one full step ahead of the visually impaired person, and verbally indicate when the end of the stairs is imminent. If there are only a small number of stairs, it may be possible to count them and verbalise this to the individual. If there are a lot, it is more useful to explain that you will say when you are nearing the end, rather than waste time and effort counting.

The main point to remember, when acting as a sighted guide, is that anything you see should be verbally described to the visually impaired person. You may often see obstacles and hazards and avoid them without too much thought but, to a visually impaired person, the hazards and obstacles are not always apparent, and so must be verbalised.

Further advice can be obtained from the Guide Dogs for the Blind (2015), a charity that offers leaflets and a training DVD to assist sighted people in guiding the visually impaired.

Communication

The presence of a visual impairment does not, in itself, prevent that individual from communicating. Although deafness can be apparent in a visually impaired person, not all blind people are deaf; nor have they suddenly lost their mental faculties because of their visual loss. It is therefore wrong to assume that a person with visual impairment is mentally affected or that you need to shout to make yourself heard.

It is true, however, that people with a visual impairment may not be as aware of certain aspects of non-verbal communication that we take for granted. They may not be able to see clearly the face of the person to whom they are talking and consequently may not be able to rely on the visual cues presented during normal conversation. For instance, it is normal when talking to increase the amount of eye contact as a clue for that individual that it is their turn to speak, and this may not be apparent. Also, we normally tend to watch the face and mouth of the person who is speaking, especially in noisy situations. These facial cues are sometimes not applicable for those with a visual impairment, and this can exacerbate the myth of deafness and mental insufficiency if the individual does not understand what we are saying initially. It is therefore important to be aware of the environment, because undue noise can affect the transmission and reception of information.

We have probably all been in the position of answering a question, or responding to a statement, when it was not directed at us, and have experienced the embarrassment that can ensue. For this reason, when you are walking into a room or area where a visually impaired patient is, it is essential to address the individual by their name so that they are aware that you are talking to them. Always introduce yourself and explain clearly what you are going to be doing. Similarly, when talking to a visually impaired person, it is important to indicate if you have to leave the vicinity, because again it can be embarrassing if that person suddenly finds that they are talking to themselves.

Visual impairment in children

When a visual impairment is present or occurs in childhood, it is essential to consider the parents' requirements as well as those of the child. Babies can be born with visual problems, which can have a devastating effect on the family. Most parents just wish for their children to be healthy and, if a child is born with a visual impairment, they suffer the same grieving process that accompanies adult sight loss. They will go through different stages of grief for their 'normal child', including denial, anger and blame. They may blame themselves for producing an 'unhealthy baby', or they may blame chance or possibly at the medical profession. Support is essential in helping them come to terms with the situation, and to provide them with information to help them raise their visually impaired child.

Most parents prefer to receive information about their child's problems as soon as possible (Speedwell *et al.* 2003). They need to know about the degree of visual disability and the possibilities and probabilities for the future. Clinicians should be extremely sensitive to the needs of the family in order to equip them with the knowledge they need to help them plan for the future. This may be by referring them to specialist social workers, education teams, or local and national support groups. Although this information may not be appropriate immediately on diagnosis, parents will need to know very soon afterwards where to go for help.

It is generally accepted that children who are blind will lag behind their sighted peers in attaining motor skills. They will take longer to reach developmental milestones such as reaching for objects, sitting up independently, crawling and walking. Further milestones attainable throughout the child's development will subsequently be delayed.

Children with a visual impairment cannot always mimic the behaviour of others, which is a normal process of learning while growing up. Most sighted children will mimic adult behaviour in their play by, for example, dressing up, making cups of tea and meals, pretending to serve in a shop, using biscuit tins as drums, and dancing. A study by Troster and Brambring (1994) suggested that sighted children engaged in more complex levels of play at an earlier age than blind children did. They found that blind children interacted less frequently with other children than the sighted children did and that blind children preferred games and toys involving touch and sound, rather than those involving imagination. It is therefore a necessity to structure a blind child's play and provide playthings that are meaningful in order to develop the child's cognitive, social and emotional skills. Examples of suitable materials include auditory toys (such as musical chimes, building blocks and electronic musical keyboards) and non-toxic play materials that can be manipulated. They should also be encouraged to mix and play with other children, to develop their social skills. This may prove to be a trying period for them, due to the different play styles adopted by sighted and blind children.

Visually impaired or blind children usually have to be shown things by touch, before they can be learnt, which will involve a lot of handling of objects. They will also need to handle materials to give them a perception of the world. They will need to handle, for example, sand, sugar, flour and water to learn what is meant by the different words given to these different substances.

Nielsen (1996) sounds a note of caution in reference to guiding the hands of a visually impaired child on to specific objects or different parts of the environment. She suggests that this can disrupt children's opportunities to build up strategies for themselves. She also suggests that it is better to allow children to reach and feel the objects so that they can take the time needed to make sense of the object themselves. She concludes that, if visually impaired children have the opportunity to explore objects without interference, a strategy for mapping will be developed, which can later be corrected and developed according to enhanced motor capability, enhanced capacity for memorising and enhanced cognitive development.

Visual impairment in childhood affects development and education in terms of the way the child is cared for, and shapes the adult that the child becomes. It is imperative that each child receives the best possible care, information and education, and is encouraged to achieve their aspirations, rather than having those aspirations limited by their disability.

The visually impaired person in hospitals and care settings

All the topics dealt with in this chapter are relevant to nurses when caring for visually impaired patients in any healthcare setting. It is not only specialist ophthalmic units that deal with patients with a visual problem. As has been explained, the population is generally living to a greater age, and therefore other health-related problems may necessitate admission to care settings for those with sight problems. People often manage very well in their own environment but become disorientated and even confused in new settings.

Orientation to the hospital ward or care setting is of paramount importance and normal sighted guide techniques should be used. However, it is often the case that the individual's normal mobility techniques may not be of use to them during an inpatient stay. For instance, the use of long canes may prove to be hazardous for other patients, and guide dogs may not be welcome in surgical units because of infection control risks. This can result in a loss of independence for the individual and therefore needs to be considered by the nursing staff.

If leaving food or water nearby, ensure that the visually impaired person is aware of its position to prevent spillages and potentially dangerous accidents. Food should be placed on non-slip mats and the plate's contents can be explained in relation to a clock face. Using this strategy, independence in eating can be maintained.

The communication strategies outlined earlier should also be used while the patient is in a hospital or other care setting. The problem of undue noise interfering with the communication process is one that is readily apparent in the hospital setting, because noise levels tend to be rather high at times. Strategies should therefore be implemented to assist the process of communication between healthcare staff and visually impaired patients.

For further discussion of the visually impaired person in hospital, see Chapter 8.

References

Allen, M.N. (1989) The meaning of visual impairment to visually impaired adults. *Journal of Advanced Nursing.* **14**, 640–46.

Chia, E.M., Wong, J.J., Rochtchina, E., Smith, W., Cumming, R. & Mitchel, P. (2004) Impact of bilateral visual impairment on health related quality of life: the Blue Mountains Eye Study. *Investigative Ophthalmology & Visual Science.* **41**, 171–76.

Department of Health (DoH) (2015) *Certificate of Visual Impairment Explanatory Notes for Consultant Ophthalmologists and Hospital Eye Clinic Staff.* https://www.gov.uk/government/uploads/system/uploads/attachment_data/file/213286/CVI-Explanatory-notes-in-DH-template.pdf (accessed 15 July 2016).

Evans, J.R., Fletcher, A.E. & Wormald, R.P.L. (2007) Depression and Anxiety in Visually Impaired Older People. *Ophthalmology.* **114**(2), 283–88

Fourie, R. (2007) A qualitative self study of Retinitis Pigmentosa. *British Journal of Visual Impairment.* **25**(3), 217–32.

Guide Dogs for the Blind (2015) *Guidance on leading and guiding.* https://www.guidedogs.org.uk/aboutus/how-to-help-a-blind-or-partially-sighted-person/request-the-sighted-guide-dvd/#.Vdc5gBRViko (accessed 15 July 2016).

Haymes, S.A., Guest, D.J., Heyes, A.D. & Johnston, A.W. (1996) The relationship of vision and psychological variables to the orientation and mobility of visually impaired persons. *Journal of Visual Impairment & Blindness.* **90**, 314–24.

Kallie, C.S., Schrater, P.R. & Legge, G.E. (2007) Variability in Stepping Direction Explains the Veering Behavior of Blind Walkers. *Journal of Experimental Psychology: Human Perception and Performance.* **33**(1), 183–200.

National Assistance Act of 1948 (2015) *Welfare arrangements for the blind.* http://www.legislation.gov.uk/ukpga/Geo6/11-12/29/section/29 (accessed 15 July 2016).

Nielsen, L. (1996) How the approach of guiding hands of the visually impaired child can disturb his opportunity to build up strategies for tactile orientation. *British Journal of Visual Impairment.* **14**, 29–31.

Rees, G., Tee, H.W., Marella, M., Fenwick, E., Dirani, M. & Lamoureux, E.L. (2010) Vision-Specific Distress and Depressive Symptoms in People with Vision Impairment. *Investigative Ophthalmology and Visual Science.* **51**(6), 2891–96.

Royal National Institute for the Blind (RNIB) (2015) *Myths and visual impairment.* https://www.rnib.org.uk/sites/default/files/ks1_lb_blind_teachersfaq.doc (accessed 15 July 2016).

Royal National Institute for the Blind (RNIB) Online Shop. http://shop.rnib.org.uk/?utm_source=mainsite&utm_medium=crosslink&utm_campaign=topnavshop (accessed 15 July 2016).

Sightsavers (2015) *Stigma.* http://www.sightsavers.org/what-we-do/equality/ (accessed 15 July 2016).

Southwell, P. (2012) The psycho-social challenge of adapting to visual impairment. *British Journal of Visual Impairment.* **30**(2), 108–14.

Speedwell, L., Stanton, F. & Nischal, K.K. (2003) Informing parents of visually impaired children: who should do it and when? *Child Care Health Development.* **29**, 219–24.

Troster, H. & Brambring, M. (1994) cited in Silverstone, B., Rosenthal, B. & Lang, M. (2000) *The Lighthouse handbook on Visual impairment and Rehabilitation.* Oxford: Oxford University Press. p. 1143.p

Wahl, H.W., Heyl, V., Oswald, F. & Winkler, U. (1998) Visual impairment in old age. *Ophthalmology.* **95**, 389–99.

Whitehead, E. (1995) Prejudice in practice. *Nursing Times.* **91**(21), 40–41.

CHAPTER SIX

Patient education

Helen Juckes-Hughes

We face vast challenges as we advance through the twenty-first century and there has never been a greater need for effective patient health education. Unfortunately, as Scriven (2010) indicates, contemporary life is not always as conducive to health and wellbeing as we would wish. Ophthalmic practice, in particular, has seen a dramatic shift in its approach to the needs of patients. Surgical techniques and technical developments, such as foldable intraocular lenses, have increased efficiency and helped to streamline the patient pathway (RCO 2010), allowing the ophthalmic clinician to embrace day surgery as the preferred option, while still ensuring improved visual outcomes and safe practice (NHS Executive 2000).

Patient education within the patient care pathway

Day surgery can result in a high throughput of patients if approached in an organised fashion. However, an increase in patient volume may also increase possible risk to patient outcomes. To compensate for any increased surgical risks, clear performance specifications are required. The development of professional and organisational performance specification structures can in turn clarify work roles and education programmes, and ultimately help healthcare staff to meet patient needs.

Such performance specifications are frequently drawn up as part of an 'integrated patient care pathway'. The purpose of such a pathway is to standardise care and record a patient's progress in a manner that can be used to audit the effectiveness of the care. Evans (2002) argues that the fundamental principle of integrated care pathways is to make explicit the most appropriate care for an identified patient group, based on available evidence and consensus of best practice. Agreed standardised care will, through consistent management, result in a reduction in unnecessary variations in treatment and outcome. Patient pathways should also incorporate all aspects of care aimed at patient education, to enable patients to take a more active role in their treatment and recovery.

The importance of patient education in ophthalmic care

Throughout the history of ophthalmic nursing, in particular, the importance of patient education has been recognised. However, patient education now takes precedence over many aspects of traditional ophthalmic nursing care. This is largely a consequence of reduced patient–nurse contact time. Three decades ago, ophthalmic units would admit patients for cataract surgery for a 3–5-day admission period. The average length of patient stay in most units today may be 3–5 hours! Such a reduction in contact time highlights the need for good-quality patient information at all points in the patient journey to ensure that a positive outcome is achieved from a surgical intervention.

The document *Action on Cataracts* (NHS Executive 2000) provides a guide to the way forward in service delivery in England and is incorporated within the Royal College of Ophthalmologists guidelines (RCO 2010) to create a clear, comprehensive plan for the clinical management of patients with cataract. This offers a model for streamlined care that aims to reduce the number of visits a patient makes to the hospital setting. This model highlights the importance of spending time effectively with the patient and other family members when they visit the ophthalmic department. The key point of contact for patients tends to be a nurse and nurses are therefore responsible for a significant amount of patient education. Opportunities for patient education can be limited and they need to be sensitively included in all areas of practice to support and enhance information gathered at each stage of the patient's care pathway.

Defining health

At this stage, patient education terminology should be discussed in more depth. To achieve any degree of patient education, the general aims and purpose of the action should be addressed. In most cases, any nursing intervention aimed at patient education relates to maintaining or improving the patient's health status, which first needs to be defined.

However, defining health is not a simple exercise because it involves personally held values, beliefs and experiences. The concept of health is multi-dimensional and may alter over time. Health has both an objective and a subjective dimension. The objective dimension of health provides a solid fundamental approach to healthcare and health education. Although it is important to acknowledge the objective dimension of health, the nurse must also consider the patient's subjective interpretation of health.

Health holds a fundamental position in the discipline of nursing, although lay beliefs about health vary and may differ from those of health professionals. It is therefore important to reflect on the complexity of health in order to develop nursing interventions that encompass all aspects of health (Larson 1999). Thus, the definition of health can direct the education of nurses and other clinicians as well as the application of patient education within clinical practice.

The difficulties in identifying a standardised definition of health mean that approaches to patient health education and health promotion are also non-standardised, and this can lead to difficulties in clinical practice. Patient education is seen as integral to the ophthalmic nursing role. However, Norton (1998) suggests that it is sometimes difficult to distinguish clearly between enthusiastic education and persuasion (or even manipulation) when health professionals attempt to promote their patients' health. Nevertheless, development of the nurse's role ensures that nurses are best placed to recognise patients' potential health deficits or needs and can inform patients sufficiently for them to make their own personal choices about their own health management. Health promotion and education by nurses can lead to many positive outcomes, including adherence to treatment, greater patient knowledge of their medical condition, and enhanced quality of life (Bosch-Capblanc *et al.* 2009; Keleher *et al.* 2009).

Patient education strategies

Patient education is a dynamic process that is conducted in a variety of settings, both formally and informally, with numerous interactions between patient and nurse that appear to occur in an ad hoc manner – as is sometimes the case! Although this informal approach can complement the nursing and medical approach to patient education, it remains important for ophthalmic nurses to follow a strategic framework in order to achieve optimum patient interaction and the best decision-making on health. Nursing practice is made up of a combination of beliefs, values, knowledge, practice and skills. Nursing models utilised by ophthalmic nurses therefore provide an important foundation for patient health education and health promotion approaches. As in nursing, there is no single approach to patient education that can act as a 'one size fits all' solution. In comparison to other established fields (such as psychology, medicine or nursing), the specialism of health promotion and patient education has only recently been established.

Health promotion has its roots in a variety of specialist fields and incorporates elements from medicine, psychology, nursing, sociology, epidemiology and political awareness. Approaches to positive patient education can involve information giving, teaching or preventive measures or they can be driven legislatively. The health promotion model developed by Tannahill (1985) demonstrates the wider application of health promotion by incorporating three overlapping spheres – health education, disease prevention and health protection (Figure 6.1). Stuckey (1999) promotes the application of Tannahill's model to health promotion in its attempt to enhance health and prevent ill-health through the overlapped parameters of education, prevention and protection (Downie *et al.* 1992). However, Stuckey goes on to point out that even this model presents some difficulties, despite its relevance to a wider audience through its involvement in public health, community and political issues.

There are numerous models of health promotion that nurses can apply when planning a strategic approach to patient education. Some are descriptive and others are prescriptive in style, with the trend in patient education now changing from a top-down approach to a more democratic involvement of the individual.

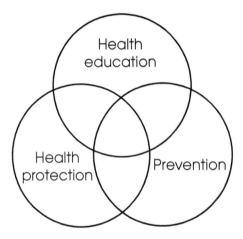

Figure 6.1 A model of health promotion
(adapted from Downie et al. 1992).

The traditionalist medical prevention model

One of the earliest models used in patient education was the traditionalist medical model of prevention. This model largely focuses on activity aimed at reducing morbidity and premature mortality rates. It encourages dependence on medical knowledge, requiring compliance from the patient, as advised/prescribed by the professional medic. This in turn reinforces the medical hierarchical system, creating a climate in which victim blaming can occur.

The holistic patient-centred healthcare model

Although many aspects of ophthalmic healthcare rely on medical intervention and diagnostic techniques, it is part of the nurse's role to ensure that patients receive a holistic approach to their care. This means providing wider educational opportunities to ensure that patient empowerment and choice can occur, despite the tendency of medical colleagues to rely entirely on the medical model. Understanding the patient as a whole person gives healthcare professionals an insight into their personal history and how they have dealt with challenges in their life. Understanding the patient as a whole person enables nurses to provide a more patient-centred approach to their care, seeing them as unique human beings, and acknowledging their experience, rather than seeing them merely as a number or diagnosis (Stuart *et al.* 2014). One of the strengths of a patient-centred approach is that it seeks to go beyond some of the distinctions and limitations that are intrinsic in the conventional medical model; specifically the dichotomy between art and science, feeling and thinking, subjective and objective, and tacit and explicit knowledge. Patient-centred care and evidence-based care and treatment are synergistic in creating improved clinical care for patients.

The health belief model

Human behaviour is complex and an individual's health behaviour is determined in many ways. In the field of health promotion and patient education, interest has been concentrated on the individual's motivation and attitude to their own health and health behaviours. The health belief model (Rosenstock 1966, Maiman & Becker 1974) was formulated to explain preventive health behaviour and examine the interaction of values, beliefs and the perception of cost versus benefit. The model highlights the role of beliefs that stimulate preventive health actions by providing a cue to change an individual behaviour. The health belief model hypothesises that the decision to take health-related action depends on the simultaneous occurrence of sufficient motivation, levels of vulnerability and belief in perceived benefit. It is very clinically oriented because fear of disease or potential illness is again the motivating factor, relying on perceived threat and susceptibility. This was the approach used in the early 1980s when informing the public about HIV and AIDS.

The patient empowerment model

More recently, there has been a greater emphasis on the concept of voluntarism in the field of patient education. This approach aims to facilitate patient choice and encourage individualism more widely. Tones' empowerment model (Tones & Tilford 2001) combines educational and radical aspects, encouraging the nurse to provide information to increase patients' knowledge and raise consciousness of any potential problem areas. Tones' approach to patient education adopts a bottom-up strategy to assist patients in developing their decision-making skills. For effective patient education, self-empowerment skills are essential and more ethically justifiable.

Nurses' perceptions of health promotion

Sadly, in Ward's 1997 study of nurses' perceptions of health promotion and professional nursing practice, most respondents used only the preventive medical model. Casey (2007) found that health promotion occurs as an add-on, when time allows, and is not individualised. As nursing works so closely alongside medicine, its environment and infrastructure offer little opportunity to adapt views from the traditional, medically oriented, preventive approach to those of the alternative holistic models, which encompass radical and empowerment issues. Realistically, true freedom of patient choice remains a rare commodity – even in ophthalmic nursing practice. By applying a sound theoretical basis to patient education, nurses can more fully understand the needs and desires of the individual patient, adopting a flexible approach that is suited to each individual situation.

Written healthcare information

Patient education is a valuable part of professional nurses' practice. Written information is a cost-effective intervention that complements the verbal advice offered by nurses and other health professionals. With increased access to the internet, the public have many opportunities to seek information about their condition. Some sites are highly professional and informative, whereas others can be misleading. The need for patients and the public to have accurate and clear written information relevant to their condition is therefore obvious and should reflect the local services that are available (Nicklin 2002).

Appropriate information that is understood by the patient can encourage participation in the decision-making process. Semple and McGowan (2002) found that many patient information leaflets are produced using language that is difficult for the public to understand. Readability indices are often included as part of word-processing programs and should be used to ensure that the majority of the public can comprehend the information provided. The visually impaired will have differing information needs, as will those with cognitive difficulties; and in a multicultural society it is important that information is in a language and format that is accessible to all patients and their carers. As part of the nurses' assessment, it is important also to recognise the level of individual patient participation and desire for knowledge expressed by the patient about their condition. All patients' coping mechanisms vary and information overload can become destructive.

In practice, patient–nurse contact time is limited; and it is therefore vital to provide written information as an accurate reference and back-up to any verbal information that has been given during the ophthalmic consultation. National organisations in the UK, such as the Royal National Institute for the Blind (RNIB) and the International Glaucoma Association (IGA), provide written information on ophthalmic conditions. This material can provide a wealth of generic information written according to best practice. When presenting patients with reduced vision with written information it is important to consider best practice guidance (see Table 6.1). Such information is, however, produced with a national audience in mind, and patients and their relatives also require specific information relevant to their condition to avoid conflicting information. Arditi (2010) advises on best practice regarding the use of colour and colour contrast to assist with written information. Printed information is of little use if the patient is unable to read it; an appropriate size of type must therefore be used in booklets, with photocopies avoided because distortion can occur. Any visual impairment can reduce the effectiveness of written information if the information is produced in the wrong format.

Table 6.1 Recommendations for written information

Type size	A minimum of 14 point type (approx. 4mm in height), and consider using 16–22 point for some readers
Contrast	Black text on white background
Typeface	Select a clear sans-serif or serif typeface, e.g. **Arial/Univers** or New Century Schoolbook
Type style	Avoid CONTINUOUS CAPITAL LETTERS Avoid *italics* Choose **bold** or **semi-bold** type to emphasise point
Print material	Use matt (non-glossy) paper to print information

Patients need to understand their health information quickly, as they get less face-to-face time with their healthcare providers than they used to. Patients are increasingly seen as active participants in their care, rather than passive recipients. Health information is communicated in many ways. This includes individual conversations and printed materials as well as websites, text messages, pictures, telephone calls and group meetings. However, regardless of the method of communication, the aim is always to promote health understanding.

Some people may have difficulty understanding health information for a number of reasons, including age, culture, disability, language, literacy and emotion. Health literacy is about communicating health information clearly and understanding it correctly. It is relevant at all points of the care continuum, from disease prevention, detection and diagnosis, to decision making, treatment and self-care. Osborne's (2013) working definition of health literacy recognises the shared responsibility between patients and healthcare providers; she defines health literacy as communicating in ways that both parties can understand.

Teaching healthcare skills and techniques

The provision of information is merely a foundation for good patient education. For some patients, additional skills have to be learnt in order to maintain a healthy continuum. These skills may include hand washing, the safe insertion of contact lenses and prosthetics or the ability to instil eye drop medication. Once a patient has accepted that they need to replicate such a skill independently, the nurse has to ensure that retention and motivation to learn and assimilate are achieved (Bandura 1977).

Adults aged 65 years and over are an important and growing part of our population and therefore make up the majority of attendees at our eye clinics and surgical areas. However, older adults are a diverse group, as people in their sixties are likely to have very different needs and abilities from those who are one or two decades older. Individually, older adults can of course differ even more. Despite this diversity, it is true that everyone is increasingly likely to be diagnosed with acute illness and chronic conditions as they get older (Osborne 2013). Older adults therefore need to learn a great deal about health and wellness, treatment and care, but learning these details is not easy. Health information is intrinsically complex: filled with new words and phrases, instructions and devices. In addition, older adults may have to take medications that affect their sight, hearing, alertness and attention span. Emotional issues can also hinder learning; it is understandably difficult for anyone to focus on detailed information when dealing with the anxiety of moving home or losing a loved one or close friend.

The importance of treatment with eye drops is widely known (Tsai *et al.* 2007) but many factors can influence patients' adherence to eye drop medications. An important factor (which is often disregarded) is the method of eye drop administration. This includes the handling, storing and actual administration of eye drops. Safe eye drop instillation is a fundamental aspect of many ophthalmic patients' treatment regimens. For this to be successfully adopted by patients, a combination of clear information about why medication is prescribed and the technique for administering it needs to be imparted.

Demonstration of a skill is useful; however, the ophthalmic nurse needs to develop lateral thinking in their educational approach. The patient's home environment should be considered, as should physical abilities, lifestyle and time. These factors should all be taken into account, with the aim of introducing as few changes as possible into a person's daily routine.

It is also important to create an environment that is suitable for learning and communicating well. If possible, provide well-lit rooms and quiet open spaces that make it easy to talk and hear one another. Speak slowly, clearly and concisely, covering one thing at a time and using everyday language. Show (don't just tell) patients about health information. For example, supplement spoken and written information with illustrations, CDs and DVDs, or demonstrate, using real objects or simulated models. Nurses should consider sharing stories of their own to help their patients connect with health information at a more personal level.

Precious time can be wasted teaching people something that they already know, so a good starting point is to find out what the patient already knows, with the nurse aiming to convey new health information or skills, building on what is already known.

When nurses assist their patients in developing a practical skill, such as drop instillation, not only does communication become relevant but the empathetic qualities of the nurse are also drawn upon. Stuart *et al.* (2014) recommend that, when giving feedback, it is helpful to focus on suggestions about improvement, rather than provide a list of weaknesses. This is because positive feedback tends to produce feelings of wellbeing and energy, whereas negative feedback arouses feelings of anxiety. If the nurse comments favourably on what has been done well or correctly, this reinforces the behaviour and makes it more likely to be repeated.

The three-stage approach to teaching a skill

Teaching a skill is not just about giving patients information and demonstrating new practical skills; it is also important for the nurse to consider how the patient feels about learning new skills. If a person is afraid to do something because they are concerned that they may look foolish or do something incorrectly, they are unlikely to succeed. Encouragement and staged development are needed in order to progress. If a patient or relative is anxious about the process, the nurse will need to alter their approach in teaching the skill. Building confidence is as important a part of patient education as developing a patient's practical skills. Scriven (2010) believes that a three-stage approach is most effective when developing a patient's ability to perform a particular healthcare technique:

1. Demonstrate
2. Rehearse
3. Practise.

Adapting techniques to individual patients

Confidence building thus becomes an integral part of health education. Developing a patient's skills requires the nurse to demonstrate the task, to rehearse it with the patient and then to enable the patient to practise it. This involves patient interaction, it is important that the environment is conducive to allow the patient to see the demonstration, hear the instructions and understand the process. Ideally, the environment chosen can replicate a similar area that the patient may select at home or in the work area. It is therefore important for the nurse to build up a picture with of where the patient will be when instilling their eye drops – for instance, at home, on the train, in the office, in a mechanic's garage or on a building site. Each location will require adaptation from the process carried out in a clinical environment.

Other considerations include:

- Hand-washing facilities
- Lighting
- Availability of shelving or a mirror
- Seating/standing
- Whether head and neck support is required
- Storage of drops in between administration
- Finger and thumb movement
- Grip
- Special awareness when instilling drops
- Technique
- Memory and suitable triggers to remind the patient when medication is due.

It should also be noted that all learners need to progress their skills acquisition at their own pace and it is worth investing time and effort to help patients get the techniques and skills right from the outset.

In a clinical setting, the nurse follows clear guidelines to maintain safe practice and reduce risk. For the patient, it is important that the nurse provides advice and guidance while also accepting that patient compliance may occur only if the patient chooses to take this advice. As mentioned earlier, the approach selected when educating patients may not necessarily result in the patient selecting the nurse's favoured option; and this is sometimes a difficult adjustment for some nurses to make. In view of potential litigation relating to practice, there should always be clear legible documentation of verbal advice given and/or written documentation (including version or edition number), with a dated signature to identify your practice.

Furthermore, by taking an empathetic approach, the nurse can target advice more realistically. For example, timing of drop administration may be adjusted for the construction site worker if cross-infection may occur as a result of the dirty environment and lack of hand-washing facilities. By making adjustments to recommended treatment regimens, the likelihood of the patient completing the course of treatment can be increased (McKie 1994).

Long-term treatment compliance

Some conditions, such as glaucoma, require long-term eye drop instillation, and the nurse is limited in the options available to offer patients, to control their condition. Glaucoma is the second leading cause of blindness worldwide so people's understanding of their eye condition is important, as is their ability to self-care. Chronic open angle glaucoma (COAG) is asymptomatic in the early stages, and the number of diagnosed glaucoma patients is likely to rise in the coming decades as the population ages and longevity increases.

There can be little doubt that non-compliance with prescribed medication is a major factor in glaucoma treatment failure. For this group of patients, compliance plays a significant part in their lifestyle adjustment, as they require lifelong therapy (often involving daily instillation of eye drops). These patients have to take greater responsibility for their own care and become skilled in managing their symptoms and communicating their needs and concerns to health professionals.

Seewoodhary and Watkinson (2011) have found that the ophthalmic nurse contributes to concordance by using effective communication, information giving and interpersonal skills to promote health through individualised exploration of health beliefs and attitudes.

In 2005 the Department of Health established the Expert Patient Programme, designed to support people living with long-term health conditions. The aim of such programmes is to support people by increasing their confidence, helping them to better manage their condition and improve their quality of life. However, unfortunately, none of the courses were designed for patients with chronic eye conditions. With this in mind, Amro *et al.* (2011) set about developing and implementing the Glaucoma Expert Programme (GEPP) with the specific aim of improving glaucoma patients' expectations and adherence to treatment. The expert patients were trained to act as facilitators of learning and may go on to inspire and motivate fellow patients. Supporting positive attitudes with a set of skills, including self-administration, fitting medication-taking into daily life routines, acquiring family and social support, is likely to result in positive adherence behaviours.

Progressing from singular patient education approaches, Richardson *et al.* (2013) advocate group-based education for patients with glaucoma as an effective complementary strategy to increase understanding of their condition and to promote continued adherence to medication. Waterman *et al.* (2014) support this by concluding that group-based education is acceptable to both patients and nurses and is viewed as a positive and appropriate means of giving patients the information they need to make informed choices. In her study, Waterman showed that incorporating group-based education sessions into routine clinical practice for newly diagnosed glaucoma patients considerably increased patient understanding of their condition, assisted ophthalmology departments in achieving the NICE (2011) quality standard for glaucoma information provision and subsequently improving patient outcomes.

The number of adjustments made to a patient's medication can create confusion for patients. Taking medicines home requires multiple skills, from obtaining the prescription to taking it to a pharmacy to bringing the medication home (Osborne 2013). The instructions on the label need to be read and understood; if the patients are taking more than one medication they need to be able to differentiate between each medication and note the appropriate time to take each one. Patients need to be familiar with using the clock and calendar to coordinate the frequency and duration of their medication and to ensure that they do not run out. It is therefore useful for the nurse to discuss these multiple options and treatment approaches with the patient at the outset. Taking time to get to know the patient's day-to-day lifestyle can help the nurse advise on how to arrange drop instillation times to coincide with a radio or television programme or a regular activity such as shaving.

Finally, it is important to acknowledge that eye drops and ointments are governed by the same controls as other medications and the nurse must therefore be able to inform the patient of the proposed effect of the medication. Information on the duration of treatment, frequency and possible side effects should all be imparted to the patient so that they can share the responsibility of care (Nursing and Midwifery Council 2010).

Opportunities for patient education

The Royal College of Nursing (RCN) recognises that the ophthalmic nurse has the knowledge and skills to provide educational guidance and opportunities to the ophthalmic patient and the wider population, with the aim of maintaining ocular health (RCN 2009). Nurses therefore have a professional duty to ensure that patients have sufficient understanding of their treatment to be able to decide whether or not to comply with recommended therapy.

Preoperative patient education

One area in which ophthalmic nursing has led the way for a long time is preoperative nursing assessment. For most ophthalmic departments or even larger specialist units, the fundamentals of ophthalmic nursing relate to surgical intervention. In the UK, there has recently been a focus patient-centred healthcare and education. Casey and Ormrod (2003) recognise the development and value of nurse-led surgical preassessment clinics for a variety of surgical procedures. For ophthalmic nurses, involvement in the preoperative assessment process through a planned systematic approach is a major and long-established part of their role (Fathers 1998).

For much of the population, the prospect of undergoing surgery is daunting; raised anxiety levels can cause stress, which may in turn result in a longer stay in hospital (Beddows 1997). The much-publicised disadvantages of inpatient surgery include: communal sleeping arrangements leading to lack of sleep, poor-quality hospital food and the risk of hospital-borne infection. All these factors make daycare surgery appear far more attractive (Solly 2004). However, with a decrease in length of stay comes a decrease in actual nurse–patient contact. The challenge then is for good preoperative nursing assessment to ensure that patients and their families are suitably prepared physically, psychologically and socially to cope with their postoperative needs.

Patient education and counselling are the focus of preoperative nursing assessment. Preoperative assessment opportunities vary widely; the most effective will be structured and built into the routine working day to become an integral part of the nursing process and patient surgical care pathway (Garretson 2004). Preoperative assessment should therefore include nurse–patient interviews, discussion about choices, provision of written information to support verbal interaction, diagnostic testing and documentation, skills training or viewing of postoperative equipment if required, and a departmental tour that may include the relatives' waiting room, patient seating/bedded areas, locker/storage facilities and treatment area. The benefits of a well-structured preoperative assessment can include a streamlined service for the patient on the day of surgery, an increase in surgical throughput (and hence a reduction in the surgical waiting list) and increased patient satisfaction.

In some instances, patients do not have the luxury of planned surgery. For instance, in the case of some retinal conditions patients are admitted to hospital for emergency treatment. The surgeon aims to identify the cause of the detachment and respond by closing or sealing the tears or holes or relieving any vitreoretinal traction. Although the procedures carried out to rectify the condition are relatively routine in some ophthalmic units, the experience is usually unique for the patient. The anticipation of surgery and fear of permanent loss of vision create added stress. The nurse has to ensure that all relevant information is presented to the patient in an orderly and succinct manner. In an urgent surgical situation, patients need to be made aware of potential outcomes, risks and benefits in order to make informed decisions with as balanced a view as possible. Psychological support and allowing sufficient time to discuss issues are important factors in the patient education process.

Postoperative patient education
Patient education and involvement increase patient awareness and understanding of postoperative expectations, such as positioning and medication regimens (Shelswell 2002), thus increasing the likelihood of patient compliance. For subspecialties, such as

vitreoretinal nursing, the level of nursing knowledge on the topic can vary and result in conflicting communication. In McLauchlan *et al.*'s study (2002), patients said that lack of preoperative information exacerbated some of their problems involving postoperative posturing. The study identified that standardisation of information is imperative and, in this instance, acknowledged the appointment of a nurse specialist as a positive move towards addressing patient and staff education deficits.

Patient education at eye clinics

When surgical intervention is not an option (or at least a later consideration), many ophthalmic patients find themselves attending the eye outpatient department. This area in ophthalmic services is synonymous with lengthy periods spent sitting in clinic corridors or cramped waiting areas – and few ophthalmic units have managed to overcome this problem for patients. For the glaucoma patient, the visit will include a number of interventions such as recording distance vision and a peripheral field test. At some point during the visit, such patients may also need pupillary dilatation for an examination of the optic disc; all this adds to the time patients spend in the clinic.

For Oermann *et al.* (2001), this problem provided an opportunity to explore the potential benefits of structured patient education about glaucoma. The identified group were played video-taped information during the clinic visit and provided with audiotapes and information booklets. Using the time spent waiting to see the practitioner or medical officer in this structured manner, to enhance patient understanding of their eye condition, appeared to be effective and increased the patients' knowledge of glaucoma.

There are several ways in which patient education can be structured to give patients information during their wait in clinics. Videotape instruction is cost-effective, reaches a wide audience and provides consistent advice. Teaching videos are available, such as those from the London School of Hygiene and Tropical Medicine, which offer practical advice on the administration of eye drops and ointment, rehabilitation and mobility. However, when selecting patient videos or DVDs, it is important to ensure that they are aimed at the public and not health professionals because this can lead to confusion and misunderstanding for some listeners. Video instruction does have some limitations, including a lack of opportunities for interaction, and difficulty in hearing the advice given. As with all patient education, it is important to provide a diverse range of approaches in order to enhance care and avoid restricting patient choice.

Group patient education

As acknowledged by Taylor (2015), costly approaches that reach one individual at a time are giving way to group methods that are more cost-effective, including self-help groups. Support groups represent a resource for patients and families of those with chronic conditions. Some of these groups are set up by a nurse or therapist or in some cases they are patient-led. Support groups discuss issues of shared concern that arise as a consequence of developments in people's health. They can provide feedback and guidance about how others in the group have dealt with problems and give people an opportunity to share their emotional responses with others who are experiencing similar issues. Support groups can satisfy unmet needs for social support for family members and caregivers or may act as an additional source of support.

Online and mobile patient education

The Internet is increasingly a source of information and social support for patients, with websites providing instant access to other people in similar circumstances. Websites can bring people together who were once remote, so that they can address issues through shared knowledge and experience. However, Taylor (2015) cautions that websites are only as good as the information they contain and there is always a risk of misinformation, although some of the better-known websites are scrupulously careful about the information they post.

The development of mobile technology is transforming the accessibility, affordability and availability of healthcare and patient health education, with advances in mobile phone and wireless technology opening up new possibilities for both healthcare professionals and patients. Machin *et al.* (2014) recognise that in the near future smartphones may provide a platform for refraction, anterior and posterior segment assessment, which should assist in early referral of patients in low-resource locations. Technology needs to be embraced, and emails and text messages are now everyday methods of communicating for many people of all ages. Every year thousands of patients miss their hospital appointments because they forget when they are. Each missed appointment costs the NHS money (in terms of wasted staff time) but, more importantly, it means that an appointment slot cannot be offered to another patient and this increases waiting times for everyone. Many hospitals have started sending patients an appointment reminder either by text message to their mobile or an interactive voice message on their landline (Hospital Appointment reminders service 2015).

Wanger (2011) proposes that hospital appointment reminders do not only have to be hospital generated, as technical advances have created an array of computer programs colloquially known as 'apps' (short for 'applications') that can be run on smartphones, enabling the patient to have control and independence in planning their attendance at their hospital appointment. A number of apps may be suitable for eye care. For example, the appointment reminder app sends customised text messages and/or email reminders to patients (Appointmentreminder 2015). Likewise, 'My Eye Drops' and 'Pocket Nurse' (avilable from various 'app' stores) can provide the patient with up-to-date information on their medication, offer interactive information regarding related conditions for the medication prescribed and reminders about instillation of eye drops during the day, and can also remind patients about future clinic appointments.

Conclusion

Clearly, there are many and varied approaches to patient education in ophthalmic care, with each approach being seen to support and complement nursing practice and patient interaction. A skilled and competent nursing workforce is required to improve patient eye health outcomes; nurses have a duty of care to contribute towards patient education and to motivate family members too. Through patient empowerment, the patient can learn about their own condition and take responsibility for concordance and self-caring. At the same time, the role of the ophthalmic nurse remains pivotal in ophthalmic nursing care.

References

Amro, R., Cox, C.L., Waddington, K. & Siriwardena, D. (2011) Glaucoma expert patient programme. *International Journal of Ophthalmic Practice*. **2**(1), 32–8.

Appointment reminder. http://www.appointmentreminder.org (accessed 21 July 2016).

Arditi, A. *Making Text Legible: Designing for People with Partial Sight*. Lighthouse International. Li129-107.members.linode.com (accessed 3 August 2016).

Bandura, B. (1977) *Social Learning Theory*. Englewood Cliffs, NJ: Prentice-Hall.

Beddows, J. (1997) Alleviating pre-operative anxiety in patients: a study. *Nursing Standard*. **11**(37), 35–38.

Bosch-Capblanc, X., Abba, K., Prictor, M. & Garner, P. (2009) *Contracts between patients and healthcare practitioners for improving patients' adherence to treatment, prevention and health promotion activities*. The Cochrane Collaboration, Oxford: John Wiley & Sons, Ltd.

Casey, D. (2007) Nurses' perceptions, understanding and experiences of health promotion. *Journal of Clinical Nursing*. **16**(6), 1039–49.

Casey, D. & Ormrod, G. (2003) The effectiveness of nurse-led surgical preassessment clinics. *Professional Nurse*. **18**, 685–87.

Downie, R.S., Tannahill, C. & Tannahill, A. (1996) *Health Promotion Models and Values*. 2nd edn. Oxford: Oxford University Press.

Evans, T. (2002) *An Introduction to Surgical Care Pathways. Conference lecture notes*. London: Royal College of Surgeons.

Fathers, C.P. (1998) Health promoting by nurses in the ophthalmic care setting. *Ophthalmic Nursing*. **1**(4), 13–17.

Garretson, S. (2004) Benefits of pre-operative information programmes. *Nursing Standard*. **18**(47), 33–37.

Hospital Appointment Reminder Service http://www.wales.nhs.uk/sitesplus/861/page/71663 (accessed 21 July 2016).

Keleher, H., Parker, R., Abdulwadud, O. & Francis, K. (2009) Systematic review of the effectiveness of primary care nursing. *International Journal of Nursing Practice*. **15**, 16–24.

Larson, J.S. (1999) The conceptualisation of health. *Medical Care Research Review*. **56**, 123–36.

McKie, L. (1994) *Risky Behaviours – Healthy Lifestyles*. Lancaster: Quay Publishing Ltd.

McLauchlan, R., Harker, R., MacDonald, H., Waterman, C. & Waterman, H. (2002) Using research to improve ophthalmic nursing care. *Nursing Times*. **98**(2), 39–40.

Machin, H., Chakrabarti, R. & Perera, C.M. (2014) From iPHones to eye care: novel uses of Smartphones in ophthalmology. *International Journal of Ophthalmic Practice*. **5**(1), 28–29.

Maiman, L.A. & Becker, M.H. (1974) The health belief model: origins and correlates in psychological theory. *Health Education Monographs*. **2**, 336–53.

Marcum, J., Ridenour, M., Shaff, G., Hammons, M. & Taylor, M. (2002) A study of professional nurses' perceptions of patient education. *Journal of Continuing Education in Nursing*. **33**, 112–18.

National Institute of Health and Clinical Effectiveness (NICE) (2009) *Glaucoma: diagnosis and management of chronic open angle glaucoma and ocular hypotension*. London: NICE.

National Institute of Health and Clinical Effectiveness (NICE) (2011) *Glaucoma in Adults; Nice Quality Standard*. London NICE

NHS Executive (2000) *Action on Cataracts: Good practice guidance*. London: Department of Health. p. 7.

Nicklin, J. (2002) Improving the quality of written information for patients. *Nursing Standard*. **16**(49), 39–44.

Norton, L. (1998) Health promotion and health education: what role should the nurse adopt in practice? *Journal of Advanced Nursing*. **28**, 1269–75.

Nursing and Midwifery Council (NMC) (2010) *Standards for Medicine Management*. London: NMC.

Oermann, M.H., Needham, C.A., Dobai, M.T., Sinashtaj, L. & Lange, M.P. (2001) Filling the waiting time in the clinic with education about glaucoma. *Insight.* **26**(3), 77–80.

Osborne, H. (2013) *Health Literacy from A to Z.* 2nd edn. Burlington: Jones & Bartlett Learning.

Richardson, C., Brunton, L., Olleveant, N., Henson, D.B., Pilling, M., Mottershead, J., Fenerty, C.H., Spencer, A.F. & Waterman, H. (2013) A study to assess the feasibility of undertaking a randomized controlled trial of adherence with eye drops in glaucoma patients. *Patient Preference and Adherence.* **7**, 1025–39.

Rosenstock, I.M. (1966) *Why People Use Health Services.* Millbank Memorial Fund Quarterly Centennial Edition. **44**, 94–127.

Royal College of Nursing (RCN) (2009) *The Nature, Scope and Value of Ophthalmic Nursing.* London: RCN.

Royal College of Ophthalmologists (RCO) (2010) *Cataract Surgery Guidelines.* 4th edn. London: RCO.

Scriven, A. (2010) *Promoting Health: A Practical Guide: Ewles & Simnett.* 6th edn. Kent: Bailliere Tindall.

Seewoodhary, R. & Watkinson, S. (2011) Public health knowledge of glaucoma: implications for the ophthalmic nurse. *International Journal of Ophthalmic Practice.* **2**(4), 170–77.

Semple, C.J. & McGowan, B. (2002) Need for appropriate written information for patients, with particular reference to head and neck cancer. *Journal of Clinical Nursing.* 11, 585–93.

Shelswell, N.L. (2002) *Perioperative patient education for retinal surgery.* AORN. 75, 801–807.

Solly, J. (2004) A nursing leader in surgery. *Nursing Standard.* **100**(32): 26–29.

Stuart, M., Brown, J.B., Weston, W.W., McWhinney, I.R., McWilliam, C.L. & Freeman, T.R. (2014) *Patient-Centred Medicine: Transforming the Clinical Method.* 3rd edn. London: Radcliffe Publishing Ltd.

Stuckey, B. (1999) Health promotion for cataract day-case patients. *Professional Nurse.* 14, 638–41.

Tannahill, A. (1985) What is health promotion? *Health Education Journal.* **44**, 167–68.

Taylor, S.E. (2015) *Health Psychology.* 9th edn. New York: McGraw-Hill Education.

Tones, K. & Tilford, S. (2001) *Health Education: Effectiveness, efficiency and equity.* 3rd edn. Cheltenham: Nelson Thornes.

Tsai, T., Robin, A.L. & Smith, J.P. (2007) An evaluation of how glaucoma patients use topical medications: a pilot study. *Transactions of the American Ophthalmology Society.* **105**, 29–35.

Wanger, P. (2011) Cellphones in ophthalmic care: review of current developments. *International Journal of Ophthalmic Practice.* **2**(3),144–147.

Ward, M. (1997) Student nurses' perceptions of health promotion: a study. *Nursing Standard.* 11(4), 37.

Waterman, H., Richards, C. & Bull, S. (2014) *Training nurses to deliver group based education to people with glaucoma to meet NICE information 11 guidelines: the G-TRAIN study: A report for the IGA.* Unpublished.

CHAPTER SEVEN

Work and the eye

Janet Marsden

Work is what many people do for a significant proportion of their day, for many days of the year and for many years. Work is therefore a very important part of people's lives and the need to see to be able to work effectively is implicit in many roles. This chapter describes some aspects of the eye and vision that are relevant to the working environment. The first section describes the functions of the visual system related to work; and the second considers aspects of health and safety related to the protection of the eye and vision in the working environment. Driving is also covered here, as it is an integral part of working life. As regulations tend to differ from one country to another, some aspects of this chapter relate specifically to the UK or Europe. The reader should apply local conditions, laws and regulations to the principles considered here.

Visual performance

An individual must be able to see adequately in relation to the demands of a particular task, and each task will require different standards of performance. The functions of the visual system can be divided into four main groups:

1. Detection
2. Recognition
3. Colour discrimination
4. Depth perception.

Detection

Detection includes many factors, such as the visual field. The normal stationary eye can detect visual stimulus within a defined area – a total horizontal field of around 190°. This consists of a 145° monocular field and a 120° binocular overlap. The eye can see an area of about 60° superiorly, 70° inferiorly, 95° laterally and 60° medially (quoted figures vary). The retina is most sensitive at the macula and least sensitive at the periphery; and the blind spot is situated in the temporal visual fields, 15° temporal to fixation and just below the horizontal meridian.

Some occupations require a full field of vision whereas others, perhaps involving close work, make little use of the peripheral field. Age influences the visual field; senile enophthalmia results in contraction of the lateral field. The visual field may also be reduced mechanically, by spectacles or lens types, or by types of protective eyewear. Monocular vision results in a loss of visual field and many people need a considerable adaptation period before resuming previous tasks.

Detection ability is enhanced by head and eye movements. Different types of eye movement include saccadic (fast eye movements that locate an object on the macula) and smooth pursuit movements (that maintain fixation on the object). The vestibular system enables stabilisation of the eyes with respect to the environment when the head moves; and the vergence system allows accurate fixation at any distance in the visual field, acting as a range-finding system. Different amounts of accommodation and convergence are needed for viewing objects at different distances; and tasks that require a frequent change of direction of gaze can be fatiguing and cause discomfort. Conversely, tasks such as visual display unit (VDU) operation, which require a fixed direction of gaze and fixed accommodation for long periods, can also cause some problems.

Other aspects of detection include the light levels at which the person perceives light (light perception) and their adaptability to different levels of light (visual adaptation including dark adaptation – see Chapter 1). Contrast sensitivity allows the person to detect border contrast (the object against its background), and flicker frequency, to resolve a rapidly flickering object into a fused one.

Recognition

The main component of recognition is the static visual acuity, which is discussed more fully in Chapters 2 and 4. Static visual acuity is influenced by luminance. This means that visual acuity is increased in brighter situations until a threshold is reached, at which point glare may actually reduce acuity. Contrast also affects the eye's ability to discriminate between two objects, and has its maximum effects at low levels of illumination and its least effect at high levels of illumination. Visual acuity is also influenced by the time available to recognise the object. The longer an object is visible for, the more likely the person is to be able to recognise it. Rapidly moving or changing objects may therefore be seen less easily than static ones, and this dynamic visual acuity is not directly related to static visual acuity (North 2001). Pathology may reduce visual acuity and thus the recognition component of visual performance.

Colour discrimination

The physiology of colour vision is discussed more fully in Chapter 1. The identification of colour is subjective but can be analysed in terms of hue, saturation and luminous intensity (North 2001). The human visual system can detect and discriminate between millions of colours and this discrimination depends on:

- The state of adaptation of the retina: in photopic or light conditions the retina is best able to detect colour.

- The region of the retina that is stimulated: colour vision extends only 20–30° from the fovea where the cones are situated. Other areas of the retina are not able to distinguish colour.

- Contrast: the ability to detect a colour depends to a great extent on the colour of the background. The greater the contrast between the colour and its background, the greater the ability to distinguish it. The colour perceived may change depending on the background (simultaneous contrast). This means that the colour of the object tends to appear as a colour nearer to the complementary colour of the background (a grey spot viewed against a red background may appear slightly green) (North 2001). After-images may also appear after exposure to colour, the after-image taking the appearance of a complementary colour to the initial image (successive contrast).

Depth perception

Both monocular and binocular clues are used by the visual system in order to judge depth. Binocular clues are the most sensitive and it may therefore take some time for a person to adapt to perceiving depth correctly after losing vision in one eye. Monocular depth perception relies on perspective, parallax (the movement of an object in relation to another object), and the appearance of light, shade and size. As the two eyes see slightly different images that are resolved by the brain, binocular clues are based on this stereopsis and also on convergence. Depth perception can be affected by a large variety of factors, including uncorrected refractive errors and squint. In low light levels, depth perception is also reduced.

As well as the capability to see an object, its visibility has an effect on the ability of the person to see it. Many factors influence visibility, including size, colour, contrast, the illumination of the object or the area, the distance of the object from the eye, the movement and speed of the object and the conditions in which it is seen. This applies to any object, but also to any task that must be undertaken. A person's visual ability to perform a task (their visual performance) therefore relies on both the visual capability of the person and the visibility of the task.

The visibility of a task is often fixed (depending on the task) so the factor that impacts most on a person's ability to undertake a task or occupation is their visual capability. Some tasks (and therefore occupations) need a very high level of visual performance and some less.

Occupational visual standards

Many occupations have a standard for visual performance. Most of these concentrate on visual acuity but others include colour vision and visual field. The first occupational visual standard was reportedly set for Dutch railway workers in 1877 (Vingrys & Cole 1986) and the British Army specified a standard in 1917. Clearly, it is important that the employee should be able to do the job that they are employed for; and visual standards tend to exist where reduced vision would not only cause problems with the task, but could also cause danger to the person or to others.

Refractive surgery can remove the need for visual correction. While institutions such as the United States military have embraced this to the extent of providing it for their personnel, the UK military are rather more conservative, allowing minimally invasive (LASIK, LASEK, etc.) surgery in some cases, but no refractive surgery in aviation, diving, airborne forces or marines. Personnel who have laser correction while serving are medically downgraded for a year to allow their vision to stabilise, the eye to become as strong as possible and any complications to resolve.

Some other examples of occupational vision standards are shown below.

Flying

In the UK, flying is controlled by the Civil Aviation Authority and their standards generally apply. Class 1 medical assessments apply to commercial pilots and transport pilots and class 2 to private pilots. The class 1 test is 'that there shall be no abnormality of the function of the eyes or their adnexae, or any active pathological condition, congenital or acquired, acute or chronic, or any sequelae of eye surgery or trauma which is likely to interfere with the safe exercise of the privileges of the applicable licence' (CAA 2015).

Class 2 requirements are slightly less stringent and both these regulations may be varied slightly if the pilot is examined for re-certification. Other flight officers may have slightly lower levels of corrected acuity (6/9) and normal binocular vision. Refractive surgery is not a bar to flying, once vision is stable and glare and contrast sensitivity are not a problem. Vision is regularly tested, and the tests include unaided acuity and acuity with spectacles as well as contact lenses. Cataract, glaucoma and retinal surgery render a pilot unfit to fly and an assessment of fitness will be done after 3–6 months. All applicants who wear contact lenses must carry a spare pair of spectacles. Glider pilots flying solo must meet driving standards and class 2 flying standards if carrying passengers.

Seafarers and coastguards

Most seafarers undergo visual acuity and colour vision testing as part of their medical examinations. Standards vary but 6/6 and 6/12 apply for some duties, and 6/18 and 6/18 for others, with a reading acuity of N8. The final standard is 'sufficient to undertake duties efficiently'. Binocular vision is normally necessary and full colour vision is required. The test is valid for 2 years.

The standard for coastguards is, again, sufficient for them to do their duties. Lifeboat crew members must have good visual acuity. Although spectacles may be provided by the Royal National Lifeboat Institution, they may not be worn on the lifeboat. Contact lenses are not permitted in lifeboats at sea.

Police force

Different standards apply in different branches of the service – for instance, for the mounted branch or driving, and in different areas of the UK. Generally, however, good vision is required, including reasonable colour vision.

Railways

Drivers must have a minimum of 6/9 corrected in one eye and 6/12 in the other. Unaided vision must be more than 3/60 and near vision N8. All types of spectacle lens are allowed, as are contact lenses, although spectacles should be carried in case lenses are lost. Guards, and other railway workers, have the same requirements, except for the near vision requirement.

Electrical engineering

Electrical engineering as a speciality contains a lot of colour coding of components and wires. Lack of colour vision could therefore have serious consequences; no other vision tests for the industry are specified, although trainee engineers undertaking apprenticeships must have colour vision testing.

Teaching

There are no standards for vision in teaching. Although teachers with visual impairment are not barred from teaching, qualified teacher status (QTS) requires individuals with sensory impairment to teach mainstream classes. An individual assessment of teachers with impairment would therefore be necessary, bearing in mind that reasonable adjustments to the environment (including the provision of support staff) can be made to facilitate the teacher's practice.

Vision screening

It is important to know, at the beginning of employment, what the visual standard of the employee is, especially if there are visual standards for the particular role they are employed in. Periodic visual screening may also take place. For example, pilots must prove their visual capacity at each medical examination, but it is also important in occupations where the job itself can have an effect on vision.

Colour vision disturbance, for example, can be acquired throughout life, as a result of ocular or general disease, as a consequence of exposure to a chemical, as a side effect of a wide range of medications and post head injury. It is estimated that 5% of the population have an acquired defect as severe as the 8% with an inherited defect (HSE 2005). The general aging process can also cause subtle change in vision. For example, with aging changes of the lens, observable colours change, as less light (particularly, less blue light) is allowed through to the retina. Colour vision testing would therefore take place before a person takes up an occupation where colour vision is important and periodically thereafter, or before taking up a role in an area where, for example, chemicals may affect vision, and periodically thereafter.

Occupational colour vision testing with an Ishihara plate book

The subject must wear the vision correction that they normally wear; and the examiner must be screened to ensure that they have normal colour vision before they test others.

As the illumination of the test area can affect the appearance of colours, it must have adequate lighting: a natural north sky illumination in the northern hemisphere or artificial natural daylight fluorescent illumination. Daylight lamps may only hold the stated level of illumination for 6 months and should then be tested.

- The light source should be bright enough (different tests specify required brightness) and should be testable and brighter for people aged over 50
- Any materials (books, etc.) used should be kept closed when not in use, in a box and away from sunlight
- Plates should not be touched
- Detailed lists of test results should be kept
- Each eye should be tested separately.

The examiner instructs the subject to 'Tell me the numbers that you can see as I turn the pages. Sometimes you will not see a number and then I will turn to the next page'. The pages are turned and the viewing time controlled. A period of about 4 seconds is allowed for each plate. Undue hesitation can be a sign of colour deficiency.

The City University Test (3rd edition)

This is a two-part test recorded on a sheet provided with the test. Part 1 is a screening aid for detecting defects in colour vision and part 2 characterises the defect. Part 1 takes around 30 seconds. The charts consist of four columns of spots and the subject must identify the presence and position of any different-coloured spot. Part 2 displays a central colour and four surrounding colours, and the subject selects one of the outer colours which looks most like the central colour.

Lantern tests

Where the recognition of coloured signals (as in the Civil Aviation Authority standard) is required, the colour vision test uses a lantern which imitates actual signal systems. The test requires the naming of standardised coloured lights of controlled colour, size and luminance, usually in a darkened room. The usual lantern test is the Fletcher-Evans CAM (Clinical, Aviation, Maritime) test. Other lanterns may be in use but are no longer produced (HSE 2005).

Trade tests

Colour discrimination is needed for various trades – as in electrical work. Colour naming is not used and subjects must distinguish a coloured shape in a pattern, arrange colours in a sequence or match colours. Asking the person to name a few coloured components does not constitute an accurate test but can be used in borderline decisions to assess their capacity to do the task.

Vision testing for other occupations

Screeners (such as the Keystone VS-5) test eye coordination, depth perception, colour blindness, vision at different distances and vision in low light. The person should wear appropriate vision correction and should be referred if they have problems with any of the tests.

Protecting the eye(s) at work

The Health and Safety at Work Act was implemented in 1974 and replaced a number of acts including the Factories Act (1961), which had become rather dated and confusing. The Health and Safety at Work Act is supported by a number of different regulations.

The Protection of Eyes Regulations were drawn up in 1974 to complement the new Act. They were replaced in 1992 by the Personal Protective Equipment at Work Regulations, which drew together all aspects of protective equipment in the workplace. These have been amended by the Personal Protective Equipment Regulations (2002) but remain substantially as they were written in 1992.

The Safety, Health and Welfare at Work (General Application) Regulations 2007 require all employers to identity and assess the risks to health and safety in the workplace, so that the most appropriate means may be taken to reduce those risks to acceptable levels. This suggests that there is a hierarchy of control measures, and personal protective equipment (PPE) should always be regarded as a last resort when all other systems, engineering controls and safe systems of work have failed to protect against a risk. This is because PPE protects only the person wearing it, whereas other methods of risk control may protect everyone in the workplace.

PPE is effective only if suitable, correctly fitted, maintained and, above all, worn. Maximum protection levels are seldom achieved. PPE may also restrict the wearer by limiting visibility and therefore introduce new risks. In many cases, however, PPE is still required and employers must provide employees with adequate equipment and train them in its use wherever there is a risk to health and safety that cannot be controlled by other means. Employees must have access to the equipment and, although most must be provided on a personal basis, some might be shared if it is used for only limited periods. No charge can be made to the worker for the provision of PPE that is used only at work. PPE should offer the best protection in the circumstances and it must not be worn if the danger of using it is greater than the risk against which it is worn to protect. PPE should comply with all applicable legislation.

In the context of eye protection, the employer should first identify the types of hazard present, such as dust, projectiles or chemical splashes, and then assess the degree of risk (in terms of size and velocity of projectile). They can select the suitable PPE from a range of approved equipment, which should be comfortable for the person for whom it is chosen. PPE should always be in good order and well maintained, and should be replaced as soon as it becomes unfit for its purpose.

Eye protection serves to guard against the hazards of impact, splashes (from chemicals or molten substances, liquid droplets, mists and sprays), dust, gas, welding arc, radiation (non-ionising) and laser light.

Safety spectacles are similar in appearance to prescription spectacles but may have lateral shields incorporated to prevent impact from the side. To prevent against impact, lenses are made from tough, optical-quality plastics such as polymethylmethacrylate (PMMA) and polycarbonate. Polycarbonate has the highest impact resistance of all lens materials and is very light. Plastics tend to be quite soft so they are easily scratched. They age well and do not warp or discolour. They are easily made with an integral prescription.

Eye shields are like safety spectacles but heavier, in one piece and frameless. Vision correction is not usually possible, although many types of eye shield can be used over prescription lenses.

Safety goggles are heavier and less convenient to use than either safety spectacles or eye shields. They give the eyes total protection from all angles because the whole periphery of the goggle is in contact with the face. They may have toughened glass or plastic one-piece lenses. Because of the seal around the face, goggles are more prone to misting than spectacles and some may have built-in vents, which must be specially designed if they are to protect against liquids, dust, gas or vapour. Double-glazed goggles with anti-mist coatings are also used.

Face shields are heavier and bulkier than other types of protector but can be comfortable if fitted with an adjustable head harness. They protect the face but do not fully protect the eyes and will not therefore protect against dust and gases. Thy can be worn over prescription spectacles and do not generally mist.

Helmets may be worn when welding and can protect the head and face from radiation and spatter. The light filter for welding may be adjustable so that the wearer can move it in order to see for grinding or chipping purposes.

Accident and incident reporting

The Reporting of Injuries, Diseases and Dangerous Occurrences Regulations 2013 (RIDDOR) dictate that certain classes of accident at work must be reported to the Health and Safety Executive. RIDDOR (1997) applies in Northern Ireland. All employers have a legal duty to report or record the following work-related health and safety incidents:

- Deaths
- Specified injuries
- Over seven-day incapacitation; where a worker is away from work or unable to perform their normal duties for more than seven consecutive days following their injury. This does not include the day of the accident but does include weekends
- Injuries to members of the public that result in the need to go to hospital
- Occupational diseases
- Specified 'near miss' events.

All other accidents should be recorded by an employer, and the employee should make sure that they are recorded in case there are any long-term sequelae. If the employee is injured as a result of dangerous or faulty equipment or premises, unsafe working practices or lack of supervision, training or instruction on lifting, or as a result of inadequate safety equipment or protective clothing, they may be able to claim compensation. In actions for damages for personal injury, the limitation period is 3 years, starting either from the date on which the injury occurred or from the date the person first had knowledge of the injury; the courts have wide powers to extend the normal time limits.

Ophthalmic clinicians see the results of many work-related accidents, most of them relatively minor. However, it is important that correct information be given to ophthalmic patients about their right to adequate protection against work-related injury, and clinicians should take every opportunity to reinforce information about safety eyewear and the possible consequences to the eye, vision and person of accidents at work.

Life outside work also presents many hazards for the eye. Do-it-yourself (DIY) and sport, in particular, present emergency departments with large numbers of eye injuries each year, with potential long-term visual problems for some of these patients. Ophthalmic clinicians are often unable to give advice about eye protection before the injury takes place, but must take every opportunity to assist the person to make decisions about eye protection to prevent injury in the future. One of the most important ways in which clinicians can help is perhaps by setting an example by wearing appropriate eye protection in situations where it is necessary.

Display screen regulations

The Health and Safety (Display Screen Equipment) Regulations (1992) are for the protection of people, both employees and the self-employed, who habitually use display screen equipment as a significant part of their normal work. The regulations apply to protect them, whether they are at an employer's workstation or a workstation at home. A display screen user is someone who uses equipment where the job depends on the use of the equipment, they use it for continuous spells of an hour or more and there is no alternative to its use.

Workstation analysis must take place and the employee must be provided with suitable equipment to enable them to use the display screen for long periods without risk of harm (footrests, appropriate chairs, wrist supports, etc). The aspects of the regulations relating to vision include the employer ensuring that the employee is provided with an eye test at their request and then that they would have further tests of an appropriate nature at regular intervals. Display screen users are not obliged to have eye tests but, when they wish to, the examination should be by an optometrist or a doctor with suitable qualifications. If the employee is found to need correction for display screen use, it must be provided by the employer. (Regulations also apply to self-employed people, who have a duty of care towards themselves.)

People who use display screens often complain of fatigue that is generally unrelated to the need for correction. A fixed focus for long periods can lead to fatigue and it should be suggested that users take advantage of breaks and changes of work, and regularly change the focus of the eyes, looking beyond the screen in front of them, to avoid fatigue. Concentration on a single object tends to reduce blinking. This can lead to dry eyes and, again, feelings of eye fatigue. This can be alleviated by ocular lubricants in severe cases or in patients with existing dry eye. Often, just being informed that reduced blinking can lead to these symptoms can help the user to remember to change focus and blink.

Vision and driving

The single most important sense for driving is vision. It is estimated that a driver receives up to 90% of the information needed to carry out this task safely through the visual system. It is clear, then, that people without vision should not drive. There is a continuum, however, between perfect vision, poor vision and no vision; and there need to be standards so that, at some point along this continuum, a person is deemed fit to drive with respect to vision.

In the UK, the law states that the driver must be able to read (with correction if required) a registration plate, attached to a vehicle, with letters 79mm high and 57mm wide at a distance of 20.5m (if the vehicle was registered before September 2001) or letters 50mm wide at 20m (if registered during or after September 2001) – equating to around 6/10 acuity. The driver must also meet the minimum eyesight standard for driving, of 6/12 Snellen, with correction if necessary, using both eyes together or monocularly if the driver only has one eye. This is the only eye test that drivers in the UK are likely to take to assess vision for driving, unless they come to the attention of the Driver Vehicle Licensing Authority (DVLA) for some reason. Although the standard for the UK appears clear, Currie *et al.* (2000) found that 26% of patients with 6/9 vision failed the number plate test, and 34% with 6/12 vision passed it. They also found that optometric, ophthalmological and GP advice on whether or not particular individuals could drive was inconsistent.

Other countries use more rigorous tests, including visual field, stereopsis, glare recovery and dark adaptation, and measure vision periodically throughout the person's driving 'career'. One of the problems with visual acuity and driving is that there are no agreed international standards and the research on what constitutes adequate vision for driving is incomplete. In an extensive literature review, Charman (1997) found that, although visual performance by most tests declines at middle age and beyond, older drivers have fewer accidents than their younger counterparts, whose visual performance is better. Older drivers are more likely to hurt themselves than put others at risk and the fatality rate for drivers over the age of 75 is five times higher than the average (European Commission on Road Safety 2011). Kulikov (2011) found that the older driver's decision to reduce or cease driving was affected by licence renewal policies. Renewal in person, mental and peripheral vision testing, and the possibility of restricted licensing all tended to accelerate decisions about driving ability.

In a later study, Owsley and McGuin (1999) found that visual acuity was only weakly related to a driver being involved in crashes and felt that peripheral vision played a more critical role. They also felt that colour vision problems were not in themselves a threat to safe driving and the same stance is taken by the DVLA in the UK. More recently, Desapriya *et al.* (2014) updated and reflected on these earlier studies, finding that there was insufficient evidence to assess the effects of vision screening tests on vehicle crash reduction.

Although older people perform less well in visual performance testing, West *et al.* (2003) found that many elderly drivers appear to recognise their limitations and restrict their driving, even though they may not attribute this to visual impairment.

Even though the acuity test for driving in the UK is simple, drivers are obliged to report any change in their circumstances (such as eye disease or injury) to the DVLA so that a decision can be made about fitness to drive. The regulations are divided into two groups, corresponding to licence type. A group 1 licence includes cars, motor cycles and light goods vehicles, whereas a group 2 licence includes large (previously heavy) goods vehicles, passenger-carrying vehicles, medium goods vehicles and minibuses (see Table 7.1 below).

Table 7.1 Visual standards for driving (DVLA 2015)

	Group 1 entitlement	Group 2 entitlement
Visual acuity	Able to meet the number plate test and achieve 6/12 binocularly.	New applicants are barred if the acuity using corrective lenses is worse than 6/7.5 in the better eye and 6/60 in the other eye. Corrective lenses must be less than 8 dioptres in any meridian.
Monocular vision	Complete loss of vision in one eye. The person must inform the DVLA but will be able to drive when advised that he or she has adapted to the disability and acuity in the remaining eye fulfils the requirement, and there is a normal monocular field in the remaining eye.	Complete loss of an eye or vision of less than 3/60 uncorrected in one eye. Applicants are barred from holding a group 2 licence.
Visual field defects, glaucoma, retinopathy, retinitis pigmentosa, hemianopia, etc.	Driving must cease unless the person is confirmed to have a field of at least 120° on the horizon, measured using a target equivalent to the white Goldman III4e setting. There should be no significant defect in the binocular field which encroaches within 20° of fixation above or below the horizontal meridian. Extenskjo should be at least 50° left and right.	The horizontal fields should be 160° with 70° left and right and 30° up and down. No defect within 30° of the centre.

	Group 1 entitlement	Group 2 entitlement
Diplopia	Cease driving on diagnosis – resumption on confirmation to the DVLA that diplopia is controlled by spectacles or a patch that the driver undertakes to wear while driving. In exceptional cases, a stable diplopia may be compatible with driving, with consultant support.	Permanent refusal or revocation of licence. Patching is not acceptable.
Night blindness	Cases considered on an individual basis.	Cases considered on an individual basis.
Colour blindness	Need not notify the DVLA.	Need not notify the DVLA.
Blepharospasm	Consultant opinion is required. Control with botulinum toxin may be acceptable.	Consultant opinion is required. Control with botulinum toxin may be acceptable.

It is clear from the field requirements that many patients should be screened for field defects, particularly those with neurological problems (such as stroke), who may not normally be screened, because homonymous or bitemporal field defects that come close to fixation are a bar to driving. Certain static defects that have been present for a long time may be considered as exceptional cases. For some holders of group 2 licences, grandfather rights apply. If they have had a type 2 licence before the more stringent regulations came into force (particularly those about complete loss of vision in one eye), licences were not revoked.

People who should not be driving

In practice, it is likely that clinicians will encounter people who should not be driving. Certain groups are easier to deal with than others, including those with temporary visual impairment.

Padding

If a patient has an eye padded for any reason, they should not drive. Such individuals have effectively been rendered monocular and the regulations state that they should not drive if monocular until they have adapted to the disability. Driving while padded is likely to render them open to prosecution because their licence to drive is compromised by this change in circumstances. If they are involved in an accident, it may invalidate any insurance because the company is likely to state that the person's visual status has changed and they were not informed.

Dilatation

The only standard for driving in the UK is the number plate test (and field of vision).

A dilated pupil does not affect the patient's distance visual acuity and therefore they are likely to be able to fulfil the requirements for driving. A recent study (Potamitis *et al.* 2000) suggested that pupillary dilatation may lead to a small decrease in vision and daylight driving performance in young people, but it considered only a sample of 12 people and concludes that the changes were not significant. Chew *et al.* (2007) supports this conclusion. At present, therefore, there is no regulation that stops people with dilated pupils from driving, although they should be warned about glare and lack of accommodation and that, if they do not feel able to drive, they should not do so. Whether or not a patient drives after dilation remains entirely their decision. It would be supportive of the patient's decision to check their visual acuity as they leave the clinic and record it to reassure them, and the clinician, that they meet the visual standard.

Reduced acuity resulting from lack of correction

Patients should be informed that, without correction, they do not have visual acuity of a legal standard for driving. Unfortunately, unless they have an accident and someone actually checks their acuity at the scene, this is not likely to be picked up by any authority. However, the legal aspects of driving should be highlighted, along with the consequences for their insurance cover and the safety of other road users.

Inability to meet the visual standard

It is the responsibility of patients to inform the DVLA of any changes in their visual function. If they do not, clinicians have a problem about what to do. Information given to the patient should be repeated, a second opinion may be suggested and advice given should be recorded in the patient's notes.

Patient confidentiality undoubtedly applies in this case but if a patient continues to ignore advice, it can be argued that the duty to the public overrides the duty of confidentiality and this is supported by the General Medical Council (GMC 2009).

Multidisciplinary discussion should take place and be recorded, including any decisions made. Patients should be told of any decision made, to give them an opportunity to decide to inform the DVLA themselves.

Bioptics

Technological solutions to vision problems can give a much enhanced quality of life. Bioptics are telescopes mounted on spectacles or used independently, which magnify, but also restrict, visual field. In the UK these are not acceptable for driving. The DVLA stress that, if these are used in order to meet the vision requirement for driving, it is without the DVLA's knowledge and the resulting licence will be invalid (DVLA 2011) Some US states allow bioptic use after specialist rehabilitation training.

References

Charman, W.N. (1997) Vision and driving – a literature review and commentary. *Ophthalmic and Physiological Optics.* **17**, 371–91.

Chew, H.F., Markowitz, S.N., Flanagan J. & Buys, Y.M. (2007) The effect of pupil dilation on driving vision in Canada. *Canadian Journal of Ophthalmology.* **42**, 585–91.

Civil Aviation Authority (2016) *Visual system guidance material.* https://www.caa.co.uk/Aeromedical-Examiners/Medical-standards/Pilots-(EASA)/Conditions/Visual/Visual-system-guidance-material-GM/ (accessed 24 July 2016).

Currie, Z., Bhan, A. & Pepper, I. (2000) Reliability of Snellen charts for testing visual acuity for driving: prospective study and postal questionnaire. *British Medical Journal.* **321**, 990–92.

Desapriya, E., Wijeratne, H., Subzwari, S., Babul-Wellar S., Turcotte K., Rajabali F., Kinney J. & Pike, I. (2014) *Vision screening of older drivers for preventing road traffic injuries and fatalities.* The Cochrane Library.

Driver and Vehicle Licensing Authority (2011) *Bioptics – Current GB driving standards.* https://www.gov.uk/government/uploads/system/uploads/attachment_data/file/193663/Bioptics.pdf (accessed 24 July 2016).

Driver and Vehicle Licensing Authority (2015) *For medical practitioners. At a glance guide to the current medical standards of fitness to drive.* Swansea: DVLA.

European Commission on Road Safety (2011) *Assessing the fitness to drive.* http://ec.europa.eu/transport/road_safety/specialist/knowledge/old/what_can_be_done_about_it/assessing_the_fitness_to_drive_en.htm (accessed 24 July 2016).

General Medical Council (2015) *Confidentiality: reporting concerns about patients to the DVLA or DVA.* http://www.gmc-uk.org/Confidentiality___reporting_concerns_to_the_DVLA_or_DVA.pdf_58821800.pdf (accessed 24 July 2016).

Health and Safety Executive (2005) *Colour Vision Examination.* London: HSE.

Jude, E.B., Ryan, B., O'Leary, B.M., Gibson, J.M. & Dodson, P.M. (1998) Pupillary dilatation and driving in diabetic patients. *Diabetic Medicine.* 15, 143–47.

Kulikov, E. (2011) The social and policy predictors of driving mobility among older adults. *Journal of Aging and Social Policy.* **23**(1), 1–18.

North, R.V. (2001) *Work and the Eye.* 2nd edn. Oxford: Butterworth Heinemann.

Owsley, C. & McGuin, G. (1999) Vision impairment and driving survey. *Ophthalmology.* **43**, 535–50.

Potamitis, T., Slade, S.V., Fitt, A.W. McLaughlin, J., Mallen, E., Auld, R.J., Dunne, M.C. & Murray, P.I. (2000) The effect of pupil dilation with tropicamide on vision and driving simulator performance. *Eye.* **14**, 302–6.

Vingrys, A.J. & Cole, B.L. (1986) Origins of colour vision standards within the transport industry. *Ophthalmic and Physiological Optics.* **6**, 369–75.

West, C.G., Gildengorin, G., Haegerstrom-Portnoy, G., Lott, L.A., Schneck, M.E. & Brabyn, J.A. (2003) Vision and driving self-restriction in older adults. *Journal of the American Geriatric Society.* **51**, 1348–55.

CHAPTER EIGHT

Care of the adult ophthalmic patient in an inpatient setting

Mary E. Shaw

The aims of this chapter are to help the reader to understand the general needs of ophthalmic patients admitted for medical and surgical interventions and to address their specific needs relative to their condition and treatment. The health education needs of the patient, the family/significant others and the carers are also considered.

General introduction

Despite the growing trend to treat most patients in outpatient or day-case settings, some people will still need to be admitted for their treatment. This may be because of the complexity of the treatment or surgical intervention – for example, a patient admitted for intensive treatment of a corneal ulcer or someone with type 1 diabetes attending for vitreoretinal surgery. On the other hand, patients may have been selected purely, and perhaps unnecessarily, on the grounds that they have a 'social' problem – perhaps living alone or with mobility problems. In parts of the UK and in some countries, patients are admitted to inpatient beds because of the distance they would have to travel for treatment or follow-up. Throughout this chapter, the reasonableness or otherwise of such decisions is explored.

It is recognised that activities and approaches to patient management will be strongly influenced by the nature and location of the ophthalmic unit and the unit setting. Smaller units may have no inpatient facilities at all, referring those who require a hospital stay to other centres. Other hospitals may have beds for ophthalmic patients attached to other specialties, meaning that the nurse caring for the ophthalmic patient may not have any ophthalmic training but only experience gained 'on the job'. In addition, some smaller units are likely to refer complex cases to specialist tertiary referral hospitals. Government policy, including matters relating to patient choice, affects the way treatment centres are organised (Royal College of Ophthalmologists 2012).

Regardless of where they are nursed, ophthalmic patients should be cared for by nursing staff with appropriate competence and experience, which ideally should include an ophthalmic qualification. Many inpatients are people requiring surgical interventions. These can range from cataract extraction to more complex oculoplastic surgery, as well as surgery for ocular trauma. Other people are admitted for medical management of ocular disease, such as acute glaucoma, corneal ulcer and orbital cellulitis. This is sometimes difficult to achieve, as (in the UK, for instance) paediatric patients are normally cared for by paediatric nurses in non-ophthalmic settings. Very few paediatric nurses have an ophthalmic qualification and some may have only limited experience of children with eye problems.

Any nurse working in an inpatient ophthalmic unit should have a broad range of highly specialist knowledge and skills relating not just to ophthalmology but also to medicine, social work, care of elderly people and those with learning disabilities, and counselling. On a daily basis, they will be challenged with what is likely to be an unpredictable workload. Although most patients may be admitted for routine surgery and procedures, they frequently bring with them complex medical and social histories which will impact on their nursing and medical management, including discharge planning. Frequently, out of normal hours, the ophthalmic ward-based nurse will be triaging ophthalmic emergencies or fielding calls from patients or relatives who are worried about postoperative problems or difficulties. The age range of people admitted to the adult ward for treatment can be from 16 to over 100. Dealing with this wide range of clients clearly calls on all the ophthalmic nurse's skills and judgement. As mentioned earlier, children and infants who are admitted to hospital in the UK must be cared for in paediatric centres and by specialist paediatric nurses.

Selection for inpatient stay

In many ophthalmic units, the decision to admit to a hospital bed is determined by agreed protocols. These relate to decisions to admit as a medical emergency or for routine surgery. It is not unusual for a decision to admit to be taken as a last resort, all other options having been considered. The following are examples of criteria for ward admission:

- Patient is not happy to have day surgery
- Adverse health problems, e.g. heart disease or unstable diabetes mellitus
- Surgical intervention requires careful monitoring postoperatively
- Poor health
- No adult support at home if patient undergoes general anaesthetic
- No access to a telephone for use in an emergency
- Patient has no transport or there is an issue with the distance to travel.

The ward environment

Many wards are designed to accommodate both men and women, albeit in separate bays or rooms. It is imperative that all patients are afforded the opportunity to maintain their privacy and dignity at all times. Separate toilet and bathroom facilities must be available for each sex and must be signed appropriately so that people with visual problems can access them. Ideally, rooms should have en-suite facilities; this can help prevent the spread of infection and makes the isolation of infected cases easier to manage.

It should be emphasised that the need to care for a patient in a single room should not result in any patient feeling isolated or neglected, albeit unintentionally, by nursing, medical or other staff.

Inevitably many patients attending the ward for medical and surgical interventions will have some degree of problem with their visual acuity and/or field of vision. Ophthalmic outpatient facilities have been criticised for failing to meet the needs of those with visual impairment in terms of both the service they offer and the environment in which care is given (McBride 2000, 2001). Ward settings are equally open to criticism if the facilities and staff fail to meet the needs of ophthalmic patients. Staff should be encouraged to review the care setting and ensure that it meets the special needs of people with visual problems. It should be borne in mind that the patient may be admitted to the ward with good vision but that treatment and interventions may temporarily affect their vision. For instance, a patient who has had lid surgery may return to the ward with a pad and pressure bandage. Such patients will have had no time to adapt to their new situation. Another example is the patient undergoing vitrectomy and repair of detachment who has silicone oil inserted intraoperatively. How well will they be able to navigate around the ward (with the resulting distorted vision) if support is not provided?

Consider practice routines for which a reasonable amount of vision may be needed, such as patient education or obtaining written informed consent from the patient. If patients are having dilating drops instilled for examination of the posterior segment just before they are expected to read some important information about their condition or treatment, they may not be able to read any documents shown to them easily.

Letters inviting the patient to attend should be clear, and written using 14-point font. The detail within the letter should be sufficient for the patient to be able to respond to any specific instructions, such as date and time of admission, and fasting requirements. The patient will also need clear directions to the ward and there should be adequate signage at the hospital to direct them. If preferred, the patient should also be able to access the information in Braille (though few people read Braille now), on tape or CD. It may be of much more use to the patient to have letters and other information emailed so that text can be enhanced on a large screen, or to have details are texted to a mobile phone so that text can be spoken by the technology, to the patient.

Hospital admission

Simple things can help to smooth admission to hospital. For example, cross-checking the findings of the case note review the day before admission against admission lists and theatre lists will enable judgements to be made and will help staff identify priorities to address in the morning.

Reviewing case notes before admission

Before admission (perhaps the night before admission), a review of the patient's case notes could highlight important matters that will enable staff to ensure that admission and transfer to surgery goes smoothly on the day. Issues for consideration include: diagnosis; type of surgery; whether the patient is arriving by hospital transport (and may therefore be late in arriving); mobility problems; special needs, including link worker or interpreter and/or carer requirements; comorbidity issues; whether or not relevant investigations have been performed; fasting instructions; whether the patient has given written consent to the procedure.

The reception staff should greet the patient and anyone with them in an efficient and welcoming manner. If the bed is not immediately available, the patient should be shown to the waiting room/admission lounge and advised as to how long a wait they will have. Any specific instructions must be given before leaving the patient, such as not to eat or drink until advised otherwise. All patients must be shown how to call for assistance if needed and where the nearest toilet facilities are.

The waiting area should be uncluttered, well lit and with sufficient materials to prevent boredom while waiting. Diversion activities can include television or radio but this should not cause a nuisance to others.

Care should be taken to keep those waiting up to date on the length of any ongoing delays. This is because their level of anxiety is likely to increase if they are kept in the dark about when their bed will be ready.

General care on admission

The recommended steps nurses should take when admitting a patient are listed below.

- Greet the patient and relatives or friends, making them feel welcome and at ease.
- Introduce yourself.
- Identify their named nurse if that is not you.
- Ensure that the patient or escort is aware of your presence and also when you are leaving.

- Confirm the patient's identity.
- Escort the patient to their bed.
- Orient them to the ward environment, including mealtimes and drink arrangements.
- Ensure patient confidentiality.
- Maintain patient dignity at all times.
- Ensure that the patient is shown how to locate the toilets and bathroom/shower nearest to the room where they are staying.
- Show them the call bell system and how to work this to contact staff when needed, including in an emergency. Ensure the call bell is within easy reach.
- Give advice on visiting times and telephone contact details.
- Infection control matters should be discussed, including staff and visitor hand washing, and visitor numbers and minimum age for visitors (as appropriate to your setting).
- Allow time to place clothing and other items in the locker.
- Advise about local policy relating to storage of valuable items.
- Advise the patient on self-medication policy, if appropriate, or remove medication for safe storage and dispensing.
- Apply an identity bracelet, having confirmed the patient's identity.
- Apply a wrist bracelet to alert staff to known allergies.
- Undertake a moving and handling risk assessment.
- Measure and record the patient's vital signs: temperature, pulse, respirations, blood pressure.
- Record the patient's visual acuity.

Post-admission discharge planning

If not already started at the preassessment or outpatient clinic appointment, discharge arrangements must be reviewed at the earliest opportunity after admission, with the following being assessed:

- Transport arrangements: how will the patient get home? Relatives or friends may be able to help; remind the patient to make such arrangements. In some cases, with criteria determined locally, patients may be provided with hospital transport.
- Availability of a responsible adult in the event of an emergency after a general anaesthetic (some patients attend the ward as a day case).

- Availability of a telephone at home to ring for advice.
- Drop instillation and/or ointment application: can the patient manage or is help available or is a district nurse required?
- Eye care/first dressing.
- Eyelid hygiene (if necessary).
- Wound care (in the case of lid surgery or other oculoplastic surgery).
- Ability to recognise and respond appropriately to complications.
- Ability to manage everyday activities of living.

Admission of patients undergoing surgical intervention

- Verbal fasting instructions are given to the patient that are appropriate to the day and time of anaesthetic. Or, if the patient is admitted already fasting, note when they last ate or drank.
- Nil-by-mouth signage, as appropriate.
- If the patient is on medication, establish whether it has been omitted or taken as normal that day. Some medications need to be taken as usual (e.g. anti-hypertensives), whereas others need to be omitted.
- Take and record the weight of patient (if necessary).
- Change into theatre gown, if local policy to do so.
- Ensure that needs of people with disabilities are met.
- Ensure that needs of ethnic minority groups are met, e.g. provide an official interpreter if necessary.
- Confirm the patient's written consent to the procedure.

Organising patient care priorities on admission

The nursing goal will be to admit patients quickly and efficiently, while making them feel welcome and reassured that those involved in their care understand their specific needs. The speed with which admission activities are carried out will be dictated by patient need and when the patient is having surgery. The patient who is admitted at 08:00, for surgery at 08:30, will therefore be dealt with before the patient arriving at the same time but whose surgery is not until later that same morning. In either case, it is important to let the patients know what is happening, and why, to ensure cooperation and reduce anxiety.

The nurse, doctor or anaesthetist may need to spend extra time with a patient to examine and prepare them for their operation. This could affect the theatre list schedule and so it is imperative that staff in the theatre are kept informed about patient progress.

The patient's preoperative assessment should be reviewed and any changes or additional matters duly recorded in the care pathway document. Preassessment ensures that vital investigations are carried out ahead of time so that appropriate action, based on findings, can be taken in a timely manner. Where there is no preassessment, the necessary information gathering and investigations must take place as quickly and efficiently as possible.

Assessment on the day of surgery, although it sometimes happens, is not recommended because there is a risk that important and relevant matters may be missed or that findings could result in delays in transfer to theatre. Vital signs are usually taken and recorded on the day of admission as a baseline for comparison in the immediate postoperative period. Any abnormal findings are re-checked before appropriate action is taken.

Patients with diabetes should have their blood glucose monitored hourly while fasting preoperatively. Postoperatively, patients should be monitored at least hourly until they are eating and drinking normally. If patients have type 1 diabetes, the usual insulin is resumed when they are eating and drinking normally. Locally, specific regimens will be available for the management of unstable diabetes pre- and postoperatively and these should be followed.

Where hearing aids are worn, the patients should be reassured that they can wear them to theatre so that they can hear and join in conversations and follow instructions in the anaesthetic room. Patients may wish to keep spectacles on until they are in the anaesthetic room, to retain independence and to facilitate good communication with others. If they are having a general anaesthetic, the nurse/care worker should ensure that the hearing aid and/or spectacles are safely returned to a patient's locker and are available for the recovery period.

Link workers are vital where English is not the patient's first language. Asking relatives or friends to translate is not to be recommended, for reasons of confidentiality and accuracy of information. Local clinical governance guidelines must be followed.

Contact lenses, if worn, should be removed and placed in the appropriate receptacle in cleaning/storage fluid.

The nurse must ensure that the necessary tests and investigations have been performed and that the results are available in the case notes.

Care and management of patients undergoing cataract extraction

Cataract (opacity of the crystalline lens) is a common cause of treatable blindness. Cataract extraction is one of the most commonly performed ophthalmic operations; and most people with this condition are treated as day cases. The most common operation is phacoemulsification of the lens with implant of an artificial intraocular lens (IOL). This surgery may be done under general, local or topical anaesthetic. (Further details of this procedure can be found in Chapter 19.)

Preoperative care of cataract patients

To be admitted for this type of surgery, there is generally some relevant history such as a health and/or social problem(s). Despite these problems, admission to the ward may be on the actual day of surgery, with discharge later that evening or the next morning. In such circumstances it could be argued that the ward is in effect acting as an extension of the day-surgery unit. Occasionally, admission will be organised for the day before surgery for reasons such as the need to stabilise brittle diabetes mellitus. One could question the reasonableness of treating the person with diabetes as an inpatient, on the grounds that admission itself could contribute to the destabilisation of their diabetic state. Other reasons for pre-admission may include ensuring that transport difficulties do not interfere with surgery, or because the patient requires some other test or intervention preoperatively.

Preoperative assessment is likely to have been completed at the outpatient stage in a preassessment unit. Nursing, medical and ocular history will have already been obtained and specific investigations already undertaken.

Local protocols or guidelines will dictate which other tests and investigations are carried out: for instance, electrocardiogram (ECG); blood tests such as urea, electrolytes and full blood count; chest radiograph and screening for methicillin-resistant *Staphylococcus aureus* (MRSA); and whether the results are available or need to be obtained. The nurse must ensure that the necessary tests and investigations have been performed and that the results are available in the case notes.

To view and access the cataract during surgery, it is essential to achieve pupillary dilatation (mydriasis) in the eye to be operated on. This is the case even if the patient is undergoing a combined procedure, such as phacoemulsification and IOL with trabeculectomy (drainage surgery).

The type of drops used to achieve pupil dilatation will vary depending on local patient group direction (PGD) or consultant requirement in the form of a prescription (see example below). On no account should verbal instructions be taken (Nursing and Midwifery Council 2015). Obtaining standard dilatation instructions is by far the safest system because multiple systems will add to the risk of error. PGDs have their limits, in that they can be used only in the circumstances for which they have been prepared, and only by staff groups able to use them. Any variation in requirement will necessitate an individual prescription. So, for example, if a PGD was for dilatation before phacoemulsification and an IOL, it could not be used for a combined procedure.

A typical preoperative prescription for dilating the pupil prior to surgery

Cyclopentolate 1% x 3 to right eye and

Phenylephrine 2.5% to right eye x 3

or

Tropicamide 0.5% or 1% to right eye x 3

Estimating the depth of the anterior chamber will indicate whether it is safe to go ahead and dilate the pupil. A simple test is the shadow test, for which you will need to use a good pen-torch. The van Herick test, using the slit-lamp and a narrow beam, or the Shaffer grading system using a gonioscope, will indicate the likelihood (or otherwise) of a rise in IOP if the pupil is dilated.

Whichever drops are prescribed, the nurse or other member of staff instilling them must follow relevant checking procedures to ensure that the right patient gets the correct drops at the correct time, and that they are instilled into the correct eye. The consent-to-operation form should be examined for patient and doctor/nurse signature and details of the eye to be operated on. A verbal check, asking the patient which eye is being operated on, may also be undertaken to confirm that the patient is aware which eye it is. The drops should be in date and the patient should not be allergic to them or have a medical condition contrary to their use. It is usual to use Minims rather than bottled drops, because they are free of preservative and they are single use.

It is becoming increasingly common to give the patient dilating drops at the preassessment clinic and to ask them to begin instillation before coming into the hospital on the day of surgery.

The patient should be allowed to void urine before being taken to theatre. If the patient has a urinary catheter, this should be emptied or, where incontinence briefs are worn, the patient should be given an opportunity or assistance to change. If the patient has a stoma bag, they should also be given the chance to ensure that it is empty and secure. Assistance should be provided as appropriate, taking care to maintain privacy and dignity.

Where used, the preoperative theatre communication sheet/checklist should be completed. This can assist handover of important information to the anaesthetic/theatre team. This, in turn, can be a source of reassurance to the patient.

Patients undergoing general anaesthetic may require a premedication and this should be given at the time prescribed. For those having a local anaesthetic, a premedication is rarely prescribed because the patient's cooperation is needed; it is also potentially catastrophic if the patient falls asleep and suddenly awakens during surgery.

However, if the patient is particularly anxious, local anaesthetic with sedation may be arranged.

During transfer to theatre, the patient may walk there if able or be transferred in a chair or on a theatre trolley. The staff escorting the patient should maintain direct communication with the patient. This will help to calm and reassure the patient.

Postoperative care of cataract patients

Postoperatively, the patient will require the standard routine care relative to the type of anaesthetic used. The operated eye may be protected with only a cartella shield, secured with non-allergenic tape. This allows for some useful vision, which can be important if the fellow eye has poor vision or no useful vision at all, as in a previous enucleation. Excess blood-stained tearing on to the cheek is often seen; this is normal and should be dabbed away, using tissues. (Ensure that the patient does not rub the skin because this leads to excoriation.) As this is body fluid, standard precautions (gloves and correct disposal) should be used to prevent cross-infection. Hand washing is essential before and after patient contact.

Pain assessment is a vital aspect of postoperative care; and most patients with mild pain can have their pain or discomfort relieved with paracetamol given orally.

The cartella shield is removed the next morning before the eye is cleaned for the first time. The shield should be washed in warm soapy water and stored dry. It is reapplied each night for 1 or 2 weeks, secured with tape. This is to prevent rubbing of the eye, thus reducing the theoretical risk of dislocating the IOL.

Pain is normally minimal after cataract extraction but it must still be addressed. A pain score should be taken, asking the patient about the location, nature and type of the pain. This can also assist the diagnosis of postoperative complications, especially raised IOP. Appropriate analgesia should be given. For minor discomfort, paracetamol 1g can be given, as per local PGD or formulary for nurse prescribing.

Vision in the operated eye is likely to show improvement soon after the operation. After some types of local anaesthetic, this improvement may be delayed, but only by a matter of hours. In the interim period the patient should be assisted with activities of daily living as necessary, based on assessment of need. This includes mobility, personal hygiene, elimination, and eating and drinking.

The patient should have access to a call bell at all times.

Postoperative complications, although rare, do nonetheless occur and may include:

- Iris prolapse
- Striate keratopathy
- Hyphaema

- Hypopyon
- Allergy to topical medication
- Subluxation of the IOL
- Endophthalmitis.

In the immediate postoperative period, those caring for the patient should be alert to any of these complications. The patient and/or carer should be made aware of how to recognise complications and of the action to be taken should they arise. Signs and symptoms to look for include:

- Eye ache/pain not relieved with paracetamol
- Reduction in vision
- Other visual disturbance, including flashing lights and floaters
- Conjunctival injection (redness)
- Conjunctival oedema
- Corneal oedema
- Sticky eye.

The patient or carer should be advised to contact the ward should any symptoms appear after discharge. The ward staff should maintain a telephone triage record (Figure 8.1) of the presenting complaint and current treatment and patient details. It is imperative that details of any advice given are recorded and retained.

```
Date . . . . . . . . . . . . . . . . . . . . Name of patient . . . . . . . . . . . . . . . . . . . . . . . . . . . . . . . . . . . . . . . . . . . . . . . . . . .

Name of caller. . . . . . . . . . . . .Time of call . . . . . . . . . . . . . . . . . . . . . . . . . . . . . . . . . . . . . . . . . . . . . . . . . .

Patient problem. . . . . . . . . . . . . . . . . . . . . . . . . . . . . . . . . . . . . . . . . . . . . . . . . . . . . . . . . . . . . . . . . . . . . .

Information/advice given . . . . . . . . . . . . . . . . . . . . . . . . . . . . . . . . . . . . . . . . . . . . . . . . . . . . . . . . . . .

. . . . . . . . . . . . . . . . . . . . . . . . . . . . . . . . . . . . . . . . . . . . . . . . . . . . . . . . . . . . . . . . . . . . . . . . . . . . . . . . .

. . . . . . . . . . . . . . . . . . . . . . . . . . . . . . . . . . . . . . . . . . . . . . . . . . . . . . . . . . . . . . . . . . . . . . . . . . . . . . . . .

Signed . . . . . . . . . . . . . . . . . . . . . . . . . . . . . . . . . . . . . . . . . . . . . . . . . . . . . . . . . . . . . . . . . . . . . . . . . . . . .
```

Figure 8.1 Example of telephone triage record.

On the first day postoperatively, the eye should be cleaned. As the wound is on the globe, not on the lids, the nurse is essentially performing lid hygiene. Cotton-wool balls can safely be used for cleaning the eyelids in such cases. It is usual to use an aseptic technique in hospital to prevent cross-infection. Patients should be encouraged to clean their own eyelids under supervision and to instil their own drops. This will enable the nurse to determine whether patients need additional help or support to instil their drops. Hospitalisation is not a rationale for automatic referral to the district nursing service. Such referrals should be a last resort and must be carefully considered. Drop aids may make it easier for the patient to maintain independence. As there is no single style of drop bottle, there is as yet no single universal drop aid, so a patient on multi-drop therapy may need more than one type of drop aid.

If, having been assessed, the patient is found to have difficulty with memory, memory aids can be tried such as written or pictorial images.

Once cleaned, the eye can be examined using a bright pen-torch or a slit-lamp. Examination of the eye is necessary before any postoperative drops are instilled because some findings may contraindicate drops. For instance, if a prolapsed iris is seen, cyclopentolate should not be instilled. Eye drops are instilled as per prescription. It is usual to use anti-inflammatory drops combined with a broad-spectrum antibiotic.

Discharge to the usual place of residence is normally the day after surgery. Patient education beforehand is essential. Information should be given verbally (and also in writing) on managing the drops, cleaning the eye, specific instructions relating to identifying complications and what action to take should they occur, getting back into normal routine and follow-up appointment.

Generally speaking, the patient should be able to resume normal activities within 24–48 hours. Swimming and contact sports should be avoided for 3 weeks. Some centres no longer routinely see patients postoperatively but rather advise them to visit their optometrist for refraction and, where appropriate, corrective lenses. Others see the patient at 3 or 4 weeks. Telephone preassessment for listing for the second eye is becoming quite routine practice.

Trabeculectomy

This aim of this type of operation is to create an artificial drainage outlet for aqueous humour to reduce IOP. A scleral flap is made and a sclerectomy performed to improve aqueous outflow into the suprachoroidal space. In addition, a peripheral iridectomy is performed to ensure that the internal opening is not obstructed by peripheral iris. The scleral flap is sutured but, as it is hoped that it does not heal, the result is a filtration bleb that can be seen under the conjunctiva. Filtration surgery is usually performed when conservative treatment or laser trabeculoplasty has failed to stabilise the IOP or where the patient's health, age or circumstances dictate. This may or may not be used in conjunction with antimetabolites such as 5-fluorouracil (5-FU) to prevent healing of the scleral tissue (Bowling 2015). (See Chapter 21 for further details.)

Specific preoperative care

Trabeculectomy may be performed under local or general anaesthetic. The patient will require little specific preparation for this type of surgery. Topical or oral medication to reduce the production of aqueous humour should not be taken on the day of the operation. This helps to increase the amount of aqueous filtering through the bleb. The patient requires a full explanation of the procedure and postoperative care. A care pathway or theatre communication sheet should be completed by the nurse. The surgeon will determine whether any drops (such as pilocarpine) are required preoperatively, but these are by no means given routinely.

Specific postoperative management

On their return to the ward, the patient will have a cartella shield in place over the operated eye. This will be removed the next morning and is normally discarded because it is no longer required. Assistance with activities of daily living should be provided as required. Pain, which is normally minimal, should be addressed, making an accurate assessment of the nature and type of pain. Where present, it should be treated with appropriate analgesic agents and/or referred to the medical staff in cases of suspected elevated IOP.

Complications after surgery can include:

- Leaking bleb
- Flat anterior chamber
- Elevated IOP
- Infected bleb.

The patient should be monitored for any signs of complications, especially elevated IOP. Accurate pain assessment will help to determine the cause of pain and should result in timely and appropriate treatment. Elevated IOP is usually characterised by brow ache or headache, nausea and vomiting. If IOP is thought to be elevated, urgent medical intervention should be sought.

Repair of perforating injury

A patient with a perforating injury will normally be admitted as an emergency. They may be in shock as well as being overwhelmed by the speed of events as they have occurred. The patient will be anxious about what is happening with the eye as well as, perhaps, home or work matters. The trauma could have occurred at home, at work or in an accident while travelling. Whatever the cause of the trauma, the patient will require expert nursing attention.

The patient needs to be admitted to the ward and made comfortable, including provision of pain relief where appropriate. The nurse needs to introduce themselves and (if not done already) ask the patient if they want anyone to be notified about their admission. If the patient has been scheduled for surgery, they need to be physically and psychologically prepared for this, and a nursing assessment should be completed before transfer to theatre. Additional tests and investigations ordered should be completed; these may include photographs, scans and blood tests. If transfer to surgery is imminent, sufficient nursing assessment to ensure patient safety should be undertaken and completed in a timely fashion upon return from theatre.

Postoperatively, the patient must be safely transferred into bed, their vital signs being monitored and a pain assessment undertaken. Analgesia, which may be intramuscular, must be given in a timely fashion. If intravenous antibiotics are in progress, these should be given as prescribed and the infusion site monitored for signs of extravasation or inflammation. If the antibiotic is being given via a volumetric pump, this should be set at the correct rate and it too should be monitored for accuracy. Postoperative care will depend on the nature and type of injury.

Vitrectomy

Vitrectomy (see Chapter 22) is the surgical removal of vitreous. It is performed for a variety of reasons, including repair of retinal detachment and macular hole. This type of surgery is performed on a planned, routine basis unless there is an ocular emergency. This gives the opportunity to preassess and plan the admission and postoperative management. As with other ocular surgery, the trend is towards day case surgery, so inpatient admission is usually associated with other medical, social or logistical issues.

The operation can be performed under local or general anaesthetic. The patient needs to be carefully assessed to find out whether they can manage to lie flat and remain still for a prolonged period (sometimes for as much as 3 hours).

Routine preoperative care should be instigated by the nurse. As the surgeon needs to have a good view of the retina, preoperative dilating drops will be prescribed. It is not unusual for dilating drops to be prescribed for the fellow eye to give the surgeon the opportunity to examine for the presence or otherwise of ocular pathology, but this will need to have been part of the patient consent process.

If there is a need to posture the patient postoperatively to maintain tamponade on a particular area of the retina, the patient can be given the opportunity to practise and experience the effect on their body and activities of living. Occasionally, the nature of the condition may actually indicate the need to posture preoperatively. In either case, the patient needs to be prepared psychologically and physically to posture, because the regimen could last for up to 6 weeks. If available, specific equipment for support should be utilised or, where not available, existing equipment should be safely adapted (e.g. pillows on a lowered bed table) and use of aids such as pillows could be deployed to support face-down posturing.

Patients should be consulted and involved in planning to prevent the complications of immobility, as well as how they will manage their activities of living in the postoperative period. Boredom, difficulty eating and drinking, rest and sleep are aspects of life that can potentially be affected.

Postoperative management will involve routine nursing management plus supporting the patient with any posturing requirement. Positioning the patient who is posturing in the immediate postoperative period can prove challenging for the nursing team. The posture to be adopted should be ordered by the surgeon, e.g. strictly face down or upright cheek to pillow. If patients have had general anaesthetic and/or postoperative analgesia, they may forget they have to posture and will need to be reminded to adopt their posturing position. Should it be necessary to assist the patient to adopt a posturing position, safe moving and handling principles must be followed, including the use of mechanical lifting aids as appropriate.

Pain management is essential to ensure patient comfort and to detect early complications, including elevated IOP. Appropriate action should be taken and care documented.

Routine postoperative care should be carried out, including monitoring and recording vital signs. Fluids and diet should be introduced as appropriate. Note whether there is any nausea and vomiting and assess whether this is likely to be a response to anaesthetic or elevated IOP. Take appropriate action in either case to make the patient comfortable. It is challenging for the nurse to support the patient experiencing such complications while assisting them to maintain posture to ensure positive outcome of surgery. If patients do vomit, they will need to have a vomit bowl and tissues close at hand, plus a call bell to get prompt assistance. A mouthwash should be offered afterwards.

For the first 24 hours or overnight, a double pad is worn on the operated eye. (Occasionally a cartella shield is used instead.) This is removed the following day, and the first dressing and pen-torch or slit-lamp examination of the eye performed and drops instilled. This is an opportunity for the nurse to educate the patient about aftercare, especially drop instillation.

The patient will, in all probability, be discharged on the first day postoperatively; having been examined by the doctor and declared fit for discharge, plans made preoperatively need to be implemented. The patient or carer needs to be instructed on eye care and also given verbal and written information on the drop and posturing regimens. Patients need to be aware of the complications of surgery and posturing, and how to prevent and detect them. They also need a 24-hour contact number so that they can discuss progress. An appointment should be made for them to return for routine postoperative review.

Oculoplastic surgery

Although oculoplastic surgery may be performed on a day-case basis, there are times when, for clinical reasons, the patient will need to be admitted for pre- and postoperative management. Some surgery requires careful postoperative monitoring of the patient to prevent and detect complications of surgery.

Entropion

This is involution of the lids, leading to the patient experiencing tearing and pain (because of corneal irritation). The cornea may also become ulcerated and ultimately opacity may result. Causes include age-related, spasticity and cicatricial factors. The lower lid is affected but, in the case of cicatricial entropion, the upper lid may also be involved.

Ectropion

This is drooping of the lower lid, resulting in tearing that can lead to excoriation of the skin on the cheek, corneal exposure and corneal ulceration.

The following are specific needs with both types of surgery:

- A careful preoperative assessment to prepare the patient and/or the carer for the surgery and postoperative period of care.

- If both eyes require surgery, patients may have pads on both eyes postoperatively to prevent haemorrhage. This will render patients temporarily blind. In such circumstances they need to be certain that they can get assistance when required. A call bell must be at hand and the patient needs to know how to use this. Preoperatively, the patient needs to be oriented to the ward, the nursing and support staff and the routine of the ward.

- Standard preoperative preparation is needed.

Postoperative management will include the routine needs, including monitoring vital signs and observing for signs of haemorrhage. However, it will be affected by the dressing or lid oedema and how this impacts on the patient's visual acuity and/or depth perception.

If patients are not used to having little or no vision, they will be very nervous and anxious about such a catastrophic lack of independence, even though it is temporary.

They need assurance that they will be assisted to manage their routines in the immediate postoperative phase. Expert care is essential. Patients need to know why the dressings are needed and that assistance with eating and drinking, toileting, etc. will be provided.

Mohs reconstruction

This type of surgery is undertaken in order to treat basal and squamous cell carcinomas affecting the eyelids. The surgery is in two parts: first, removal of the carcinoma; and, second, reconstructive surgery.

The patient usually attends the ophthalmic ward after the excision of the ulcer and will have a pad in place on the operated eye to prevent haemorrhage. Patients need routine preoperative care and management, supplemented with support and explanation about what must be a frightening experience for them. Despite reassurance that this type of cancer does not usually metastasise, patients are frequently worried about the long-term implications as well as what they will look like after the surgery.

Nursing staff need to provide honest explanations to patients about their condition and care, reinforcing detail given by medical staff. As part of preoperative care, patients need to have visual acuity taken and recorded – note especially that of the opposite side to the surgery because, if vision is poor in this eye and it cannot be corrected, this will influence nursing management.

If not already undertaken, the patient's face and surgical wound will need to be photographed, which means that the dressing has to be removed by a nurse (following standard precautions) who also knows how to manage if a haemorrhage occurs. Unless they have been specially trained, it is not appropriate to expect ophthalmic imaging staff to manage the dressing.

Many specialist centres have nurses who specialise in oculoplastic nursing. The expertise of these individuals should be routinely called upon to support the patient's care. They can advise patients and carers about the surgery and aftercare.

The reconstruction may require tissue to be taken from a graft site. This means that, in the postoperative period, the nurse will have at least two operation sites to monitor. It is also not unusual for the graft site to cause the patient more pain and discomfort than the site of the reconstruction.

Both sites need to be monitored for signs of haemorrhage. If bleeding is noted, a pressure pad and bandage must be applied over the existing dressing and the medical staff contacted as a matter of urgency. The patient's general health and vital signs should be recorded and documented during this period. Often, the pressure bandage is sufficient to halt the bleeding, but occasionally it is necessary to return to theatre to stop the bleeding.

Pain management is essential postoperatively. Patients need to be aware that the dressings will normally be left in place (undisturbed) for a week. They will be given

routine analgesia to take home as well as oral antibiotics. They need to be pain free for their journey home. Verbal and written instructions should be given about aftercare and complications. A contact number to use for emergencies and other enquiries should be given.

As they will temporarily have monocular vision, patients need to be advised that they may not be able to judge depth that well.

Dacryocystorhinostomy

Blockage within the nasolacrimal apparatus causes tearing that is constant and results in patient discomfort and irritation of the cheek. Surgery is carried out either via the external route or as an endoscopic procedure.

Other than routine preparation for surgery plus physical and psychological preparation, no specific preparation is needed. The patient should be visited by the oculoplastic nurse specialist to discuss postoperative management.

In the postoperative period, the external approach to surgery will require pad and bandage with or without a nasal pack; the patient having endoscopic surgery will normally have a nasal pack *in situ*. As haemorrhage is a possible complication, a tray should be set up for dealing with epistaxis in an emergency, with a nasal pack (which may be kept in refrigerator), nasal forceps and nasal speculum.

Also in the postoperative period, but for routine management, the patient needs to be monitored for signs of haemorrhage. This could be from the external wound or from the operative site as epistaxis. Epistaxis can be severe, and in any case it must be treated as a medical emergency with appropriate first-aid action taken. Epistaxis may not be overt through the nose; it could be trickling down the back of the throat. The patient must be kept calm, sitting upright (not flat), leaning slightly forward and pinching the bridge of the nose. Tissues and a receptacle should be used to collect any blood (not to be discarded until seen by the medical team) to estimate total blood loss. The emergency epistaxis tray should be brought to the bedside. The medical staff will pack the wound in an attempt to halt the bleeding. If this is not successful, the patient may have to return to theatre. Routinely, the dressing and nasal pack are removed before discharge home.

Written and verbal instructions should be given to the patient on how to manage care at home. Antibiotics and analgesia are given as prescribed to take home. With an external dacryocystorhinostomy, chloramphenicol ointment may be given with which to massage the wound. An appointment for follow-up will also be given.

Enucleation

This involves complete removal of the globe but with conservation of the remaining orbital content, including the extraocular muscles.

Evisceration

This involves removal of the contents of the globe, retaining the sclera. This type of surgery provides a better chance of long-term success for any implant or prosthesis because the body is less likely to reject the implant.

Exenteration

This involves surgical removal of the globe and the orbital content. In some cases, it may include the loss of bone. If the lids can be conserved, they may be used to line the cavity.

Throughout the admission, the nursing staff should implement the care prescribed by the specialist nurse. Waterman *et al.* (1999) found that patients undergoing these types of surgery experienced marked postoperative nausea and vomiting and were often in pain. For this reason, these patients will normally remain in hospital for up to 48 hours postoperatively. During this time, they can be supported to begin to overcome some of the physical and psychological trauma associated with the loss of an eye. Postoperative pain and nausea should be assessed and treated appropriately.

The patient should be monitored for haemorrhage. This will manifest overtly through the pressure pad and dressing, which should not be disturbed. If bleeding is noted, an additional pad and bandage should be applied and the patient should rest, semi-recumbent, in bed. Urgent medical assistance is required.

Analgesia, anti-inflammatories and antibiotics should be given as prescribed. Pain assessment should be made and recorded. The patient should be subsequently approached to ensure that the analgesics are working.

It has been identified that there is a paucity of research in relation to the type of postoperative dressing to use with such wound cavities because there are often fissures and cavities connecting to other structures. Although the dressings are normally left in place for 1 week, the nurse needs to understand the dressings used, both to inform practice and so that correct information and advice can be given to the patient.

On the day of discharge, the patient needs written and verbal postoperative advice, including what to do if the dressing comes loose (contact the ward and return for it to be re-applied). The patient or a family member should be able to help re-apply the bandage only. They need to know that the dressing will ooze and may have a slight odour. However, if there is any cause for concern, such as fever or uncontrollable pain or bleeding, the patient should be instructed to contact the ward as a matter of urgency.

Admission for medical treatment

Such admissions tend to be unplanned and such patients come via accident and emergency or outpatient departments. Preassessment is unlikely to have been undertaken so the nurse needs to complete one in order to determine the patient's care needs.

MRSA status may be significant in determining where to nurse the patient. It may be necessary to isolate the patient until their status is known; this will be determined by local and/or national policies.

Hyphaema

Hyphaema (blood in the anterior chamber) may be the result of an accidental injury such as a blow to the eye with a squash ball, or surgical trauma. It is also seen occasionally following YAG (yttrium–aluminium–garnet) laser iridotomy.

Admission is not usual unless there are exceptional circumstances such as elevated IOP or total hyphaema, and depending on the cause, e.g. if it is associated with penetrating injury. The patient could be cared for at home, provided that they are prepared to rest in an upright position and they are able to return for a follow-up appointment. Total hyphaema will affect the patient's vision.

If admitted, the patient will be anxious and will require explanation as to why they have to rest in bed, nursed upright. Keeping a young fit person at rest is not the easiest task but if complications (such as raised IOP) are to be avoided or detected early, the patient needs to be supported to rest. Remember, this could be the person's first experience of hospital admission.

Unless on strict bed rest, the patient should be allowed to mobilise to the toilet to void urine or open their bowels and to the bathroom to wash. While on bed rest, patients are at risk of the complications of immobility so a suitable assessment should be made, together with the patient, and a care plan developed to prevent their occurrence. Diet and fluids must be considered in such assessment to prevent dehydration and constipation. The latter could be compounded by codeine-based analgesia given for pain relief.

Corneal ulcers

A corneal ulcer (see also Chapter 17) is a regular reason for admission to the ophthalmic ward. Patients may be elderly, confused and disoriented. In addition, they may have other health problems that need to be addressed during the admission. Younger patients with severe corneal ulcers may also be admitted but they are usually supported or self-caring at home. Patients with corneal ulcers need not necessarily be isolated as part of their care. This is only necessary if the ulcer is infected with a virulent organism. In such a situation, patients need to be isolated in a single room with en-suite facilities. Staff and visitors need to know how to follow standard precautions to prevent cross-infection. It is vital that medical isolation does not lead to social isolation. The patient should have access to TV, radio and books/newspapers, but most importantly to people during their stay in hospital.

Pain needs to be managed. The cornea is very sensitive, and acute or chronic pain must be managed with oral medication given in response to pain assessment. Pain may arise from other causes, which must be identified and dealt with appropriately. Discomfort may be an issue rather than overt pain; patients occasionally need education about not putting up with routine ocular discomfort, but trying mild analgesics or anti-inflammatories to relieve it.

Frequent/intensive drop therapy will normally be prescribed, the antibiotic being determined by culture of a swab or a corneal scrape. The nurse may be instilling drops as frequently as every 15 minutes, day and night, for the first 24 hours. This can lead to sleep disturbance, poor appetite, and resentment of the care regimen and the people delivering it. The patient needs to understand the rationale for this care. Intravenous or oral antibiotics should be given as prescribed.

Sleep disturbance may have been a feature of the patient's problem before admission, compounded by the intensive drop regimen. The nurse must not omit drops if the patient is sleeping; such action could unwittingly prolong the need for such treatment.

The patient needs to have an adequate intake of fluids and a nutritious diet. It may be necessary in some cases to refer the patient to the dietician. The patient is likely to feel generally unwell on admission and will need nursing interventions as appropriate, while avoiding unnecessary dependence on others.

Patient education is essential. Take the opportunity to assess the patient's drop technique during their stay, once they are well enough. In chronic ulcer management, acute episodes could be the result of the patient missing drops or not being able to instil drops for physical/mechanical reasons or memory loss. Drop and memory aids could be tried. If these do not work, alternatives need to be considered, including district nurse or care manager (social worker) review.

Loneliness and social isolation could be at the root of the acute episode of corneal ulceration. The care manager and voluntary agencies or support groups may assist in developing a care package if the patient will permit it.

Discharge planning will have started on admission and the plan should be implemented in a timely fashion to support transfer home or into temporary or permanent residential or nursing home care. A follow-up appointment must be given, along with consideration of transport to the appointment.

Acute glaucoma

As suggested by the name, the onset of this condition is acute, the IOP elevated, the glaucoma is usually unilateral, and there is a fixed semi-dilated pupil and reduced vision because of corneal oedema, which leads to the patient seeing haloes around lights. As well as feeling generally unwell, the patient is likely to be frightened or anxious about the admission.

Patients will probably still be in some pain or discomfort despite emergency treatment. They should be assessed for pain and, if necessary, analgesia given as prescribed. This could be intramuscular pethidine, often accompanied by an antiemetic.

Nausea and vomiting are features of acute glaucoma and so a vomit bowl and tissues should be available in easy reach if the patient needs them. Should the patient vomit, it may relieve some of the discomfort. They should be offered a mouthwash or the opportunity to brush their teeth. Patients should be nursed in a side room with dim lighting because of the photophobia experienced.

Reduction of IOP with drop therapy should be continued as prescribed. Drinking fluids and eating should be encouraged. Fluid intake is particularly important, to prevent dehydration.

Preparation for laser iridotomy the following day is done by explaining the procedure to patients and answering any queries that they may have. If assessed as needed, oral analgesia should be given before the procedure to ensure cooperation. The pupils should already be constricted by the pilocarpine drops. The patient should be reassured that the procedure is relatively pain free but that topical analgesia will be administered in the laser department.

Discharge advice and information should be given verbally and in writing. (See Chapter 21 for more details of glaucoma.)

Orbital cellulitis

This is a rare but distressing condition that may be bilateral. If severe enough, admission to hospital is warranted. The patient will be generally debilitated and also pyrexial. Assessment on admission, and planning of care, are essential to improving wellbeing.

Patients need to be nursed in a quiet, dimly lit room; however, if hourly visual acuity and test for relative afferent pupillary defect (RAPD) have been requested, illumination will be necessary. Warn patients about the change in light intensity so that they can prepare for it.

Pain management is essential, as is the introduction of topical and intravenous antibiotics as prescribed. Cold compresses are normally found to be soothing and can relieve some ocular discomfort. Moistened eye pads can be utilised, using clean pads each time, and safely discarding the used pads.

If the lids are crusty or purulent, they need to be cleansed using an aseptic technique. Swabs should ideally be taken before any antibiotics are started. As the patient will be in pain, ensure that adequate analgesia has been given before performing eye care. The decision as to whether or not to isolate the patient will be determined by the cause of the cellulitis, but this is not usual.

Physical care should include care related to rest and sleep, adequate oral fluid and nutrition intake, personal and oral hygiene, temperature regulation and elimination needs. Bed rest is indicated in the first 24 hours until the patient is well enough to sit out for increasing periods of time, and then until well enough to return home.

As the cause of orbital cellulitis is not always known, the patient should be reassured that recurrence is rare. Prompt and timely intervention can prevent permanent damage to visual function. Discharge home is normally being planned from admission so that systems are in place to support the patient as required. Unless advised by the doctors, patients should refrain from work until they have been discharged by the hospital.

Conclusion

Although care of the ophthalmic patient as an inpatient is less and less common, due to a reduction in the number of inpatient beds and a recognition of the benefits of day surgery, there are some occasions, as demonstrated in this chapter, when inpatient care is essential. Good care for the ophthalmic patient in hospital requires a battery of skills and knowledge that are less and less available to the ophthalmic unit, and this area should be recognised as a highly specialised area of ophthalmic nursing.

References

Bowling, B. (2015) *Kanski's Clinical Ophthalmology, a systematic approach.* 8th edn. London: Elsevier.

McBride, S. (2000) *Patients Talking: Hospital outpatient eye services – the sight impaired user's view.* London: RNIB.

McBride, S. (2001) *Patients Talking 2: The eye clinic journey experienced by blind and partially sighted adults.* London: RNIB.

Nursing and Midwifery Council (2015) *Standards for Medicines Management.* London: NMC.

Royal College of Ophthalmologists (2012) *Ophthalmic Services Guidance. Ophthalmic daycare and inpatient facilities.* London: RCOphth.

Waterman, H., Leatherbarrow, B., Slater, R. & Waterman, C. (1999) Post-operative pain, nausea and vomiting: qualitative perspectives from telephone interviews. *Journal of Advanced Nursing.* 29, 690–96.

CHAPTER NINE

The care of the child undergoing ophthalmic treatment

Janet Marsden and Jilly Bradshaw

Defining childhood

The United Nations Convention on the Rights of the Child defines children as persons under the age of 18 and, although this is aspirational rather than enforceable, it reflects practice in many areas of the world. In the UK, the age of majority is 18, except in Scotland, where it is 16. The UK is a signatory to the Council of Europe Declaration on Child Friendly Healthcare (2011) which is based on a model of service delivery identified in the UN convention. The UK ratified the convention in 1991 with reservations and finally agreed to the convention in 2008. One of the key outcomes of the Children and Young People's Health Outcomes Forum, which reported in 2012, is that children and young people and their families should be at the heart of what happens and where this happens, health outcomes are better.

While the sections on parental responsibility and consent in this chapter are informed by legislation used in England and Wales, this is not an international, or even whole UK, standard. It is important to be aware of the legislation that applies in individual settings. However, the principles of partnership working and respect for the child should apply across all settings where children and their families are cared for.

The child and the hospital

The National Service Framework for Children in Hospital (DH 2003) set standards that apply to every department and service in a hospital that delivers care to children and young people. In terms of quality and safety of care, it states that 'children and young people should receive appropriate high quality, evidence-based hospital care developed through clinical governance and delivered by staff who have the right set of skills' (p. 9). It goes on to state that staff treating and caring for children should have the education, training, knowledge and skills to provide this care. While it is clearly hugely important that registered children's nurses are involved in the perioperative care of children with eye problems, the ophthalmic nursing skills required should not be underestimated. As nurses qualified in both areas are somewhat rare, effective collaboration between paediatric and ophthalmic clinicians is required to ensure that the child's ophthalmic care is not compromised while they are being cared for in an appropriate paediatric area.

Children are most often cared for in general and specialist ophthalmic outpatient areas where the skills of a paediatric nurse would often be under-utilised. In these areas, it is arguably more important that the ophthalmic specialist nurse is available to work with the child and their family to achieve the best ophthalmic outcomes. However, paediatric nursing input in these areas can also be hugely beneficial to the child's experience and can help to prevent them developing long-lasting anxiety about going to hospital. Clearly, the ophthalmic nurse needs some specialist skills in working with children and their families, but it should also be remembered that most children are accompanied at all times by their parents or main carers, who know them best and upon whom they depend for their emotional and physical wellbeing. Ophthalmic nurses must therefore work as part of a team, which includes the family and the child, listening and responding to cues from parents and using their ophthalmic nursing skills and knowledge to best advantage. A set of paediatric ophthalmic nursing competencies is available, developed by the RCN Ophthalmic Nursing Forum (RCN 2012). These competencies are widely used to develop and demonstrate competence in this area.

Developmental stages of the child

Birth to 12 months

This is a period of enormous growth and development, beginning with a completely helpless infant, who weighs an average of 3.5kg, and ending with a child who is beginning to take a few steps, say a couple of words and eat solid food. It is a period of attachment and trust and the child/carer bond is hugely important and very strong. Recognising developmental milestones is key to adapting care to children of this age range. Recognising that many children develop 'stranger anxiety' at around 11 months of age will help the health professional adapt their approach to examination, care and treatment.

12 months to 2 years

Growing independence is a key feature of this age range, with negativity as a feature of growing autonomy. 'NO' is a very common word! Toddlers are egocentric and feel that they are the centre of their world. They are not able to understand any other point of view but their own and may feel that they are responsible for things that are actually outside their control. Verbal skills are limited and they will not be able to express themselves so they may show fear, upset and anxiety.

Pre-school children

Interaction with the pre-school child is much easier than with a toddler and many pre-school children are outgoing and unafraid, as long as they know what is going to happen and they do not lose contact with their parent or carer. Their communication skills are getting better and the child often understands explanations, especially when accompanied by pictures or models and dolls with which the child can interact. Encouraging the child to help teddy to do things first, for example, can instil confidence. Praise and encouragement are useful tools. As memory and imagination are developing rapidly in this phase of childhood, fact and fantasy can become mixed up and it is vital that communication is direct, clear and unambiguous, using words that cannot be misunderstood. For instance, it's best to refer to 'checking temperature' rather than 'taking temperature' (Barnes & Smart 2003) and use words that the child normally uses.

Age 5–adolescence

There is a huge continuum here but the child is often curious and a willing participant in examination and care. They begin to understand cause and effect but their thinking initially remains concrete and clinicians must check that they have understood what has been discussed, perhaps by asking the child to paraphrase the information given. The story from the parent and the child may well be different, with both attributing cause and effect in different ways, and the child may seek to avoid telling a complete story if they perceive that it will get them into 'trouble'. Younger children may see illness or unpleasant procedures as a punishment and may not understand that some of the unpleasantness is part of the treatment needed to make them feel better.

Adolescents

Physical, emotional and cognitive growth characterise this period of development. Increasing independence from carers and family, and increasing dependence on friends and peer group, are normal. The adolescent will be trying to establish their own identity by testing boundaries and experimenting. They are capable of abstract thought and will have their own opinions on health and illness. Any management will have to be negotiated, rather than stated, and the older adolescent is likely to prefer consultation and treatment in private, often without parental presence, although separation from parents and peers is still likely to promote anxiety.

It is recognised that adolescents in inpatient settings should be cared for in discrete areas and with their peer group, rather than with younger children. Their needs are entirely different, and visiting friends and an awareness of their stage of development will help to keep things as 'normal' as possible for them. Remember that it is very important to adolescents not to look different from their peer group and this may need to be taken into account when planning treatment.

The child and their family

Children and young people need to be in control of their own health and well- being and must therefore be involved in the process of their care, as appropriate for the individual child. Many children are capable of giving informed consent, provided they are given information and made aware of the particular issues, in an appropriate way for their age, stage, knowledge, life experience and culture (DH 2003, DH 2012).

If the child is too young, or they have extra needs that limit their ability to participate in decision making, their parents or carers must have an opportunity to express views and opinions. It is essential that the voices of parents and carers are heard – as well as, but not instead of, the voices of their children (DH 2012).

Clear information (given in a form that is appropriate to the individual child, to aid understanding and minimise anxiety) promotes confidence and trust in the staff, and lessens children's feelings of powerlessness and loss of control.

The pre-school child will often feel vulnerable and traumatised when separated from their parents; and the parents play a key part in enabling examination and effective care and treatment, particularly as they know the child better than anyone else. Clinical staff should appreciate the natural anxiety and fear of all parents coming into hospital with their child, however minor the reason may seem, and importantly, the crucial importance of parental presence to the child. This alliance between nursing staff and parents is vital but problems can arise if there are misunderstandings between the parents and nurses. For instance, they may have differing expectations about the care to be given to the child. For this reason, good verbal and written communication is essential.

Parents and guardians

It is important to recognise who has parental responsibility for a child. It is also extremely important to identify the adult who is accompanying the child when they attend clinical services, and whether that adult has parental responsibility, so that when decisions need to be made for or with the child, they are being made by a person who is able to do so. Only someone with parental responsibility – or authorisation from a parent – can consent to treatment in children who lack capacity, except in an emergency.

The concept of parental responsibility was first defined in the Children Act 1989. There is no difference in law between mothers and fathers and either may give consent. But if parents are separated, it is prudent to ensure that both parents agree. Where there is disagreement, mediation may be needed to ensure common understanding and decision making.

Who has parental responsibility?

- All mothers, married or unmarried, automatically have parental responsibility for any child they give birth to.
- Fathers who were married to the mother of the child when it was born also automatically have parental responsibility and may acquire it by marrying the mother later.
- Unmarried fathers can acquire parental responsibility by jointly registering the birth of the child with the child's mother (for births after 1 December 2003) or, for pre-December 2003 registrations, by re-registering the birth and adding the father's details.
- If the birth is registered in Northern Ireland, the father has parental responsibility if he is married to the mother at the time of the birth or, if he marries the mother after the birth, as long as the marriage takes place in Northern Ireland.
- He also has parental responsibility if he is named, or becomes named on the child's birth certificate (from 15 April 2002).
- If a father has a residence order from a court, he acquires parental responsibility.
- In Scotland, a father has parental responsibility if he is married to the mother when the child is conceived or at any time afterwards. An unmarried father has parental responsibility if he is named on the birth certificate (from 4 May 2006).
- A birth parent can sign a parental responsibility agreement to give parental responsibility to the child's father.
- A step-parent can have parental responsibility by consent with all those having parental responsibility for the child.
- A court may award parental responsibility.
- An adoption order awards parental responsibility.
- Same sex partners who were civil partners at the time of fertility treatment will both have parental responsibility.
- For same sex partners who are not civil partners, the second parent may apply for parental responsibility with a parental agreement, or by becoming a civil partner and making a parental responsibility agreement, or by jointly registering the birth.

- A mother's partner who is not the father of the child cannot have parental responsibility; this is only achieved by marriage or civil partnership.

Guardians and carers

A 'special guardian' has parental responsibility and this can be exercised without seeking the consent of the birth parent. A guardian of the child, any person with a residence order, and a local authority foster parent with whom the child has lived for more than a year may apply for Special Guardianship. A guardian may also have been appointed by the parents (to take care of the child after their death) and this guardian has parental responsibility.

People without parental responsibility, but who have care of a child, may do what is reasonable in all the circumstances of the case to safeguard or promote the child's welfare. This may include step-parents, grandparents and child-minders (GMC 2007).

Their consent can be relied on if they are authorised by the parents. But clinicians should make sure that their decisions are in line with those of the parents, particularly in relation to contentious or important matters affecting the child's welfare. Such consent does not need to be in writing and the healthcare professional does not need to consult the parents unless there is cause to believe the parents' view would differ significantly.

Consent to treatment

Clinicians should always act in the best interests of children and young people, but sometimes it may be difficult to identify what is actually in their best interests. The law relating to consent to treatment for children and young people is different across the UK and will be differentiated here.

If a young person is able to understand the nature, purpose and possible consequences of investigations and treatment, as well as the consequences of not having treatment, is able to retain and use this information in order to make a decision and communicate this decision to others (in whatever way is appropriate for them) then they can consent to investigation or treatment. Capacity to consent depends more on ability than on age (GMC 2007). However, at 16, a young person can be presumed to have the capacity to consent. A young person under 16 may also have capacity to consent and this is often known as 'Gillick competence', after a House of Lords' decision in Gillick (1985).

If a child lacks capacity to consent, the parent may consent on behalf of the child. It is usually sufficient to have consent from one person and if there is a dispute between the parents, it is often worth seeking legal advice from institutional legal teams about applying to the courts for a ruling.

The legal framework for 16- and 17-year-olds who lack the capacity to consent differs across the UK:

- In England, Wales and Northern Ireland, parents can consent to investigations and treatment that are in the young person's best interests.
- In England and Wales, treatment can also be provided in the young person's best interests without parental consent.
- In Northern Ireland, treatment can be provided in the young person's best interests if a parent cannot be contacted, although legal advice should be sought for other than emergency interventions.
- In Scotland, 16- and 17-year-olds who do not have the capacity to consent must be treated as adults who lack capacity and treatment may be given in their best interests.

Parents cannot override the competent consent of a young person to treatment that the doctor agrees is in their best interests.

Young people who withhold consent

In Scotland, parents cannot authorise treatment a young person has refused. However, in England, Wales and Northern Ireland, their decision can be overruled. This should be done with legal advice and, usually, by a court as it could be suggested that overruling the competent child's decision conflicts with their human rights and this would be subject to legal challenge. The graver the potential outcome of withholding consent, the higher the standard of proof required that the young person withholding it is competent.

Specific issues affecting children in ophthalmic settings

There are key issues for children who have eye and vision problems and their families. Firstly, when asked, most people say that they 'live' in their eyes and that vision is their most important sense. Children can be very distressed if there is disruption to their vision during eye examination, following the instillation of eye drops or postoperatively. Children of all ages are frequently teased about their appearance – for example, if they have a squint or cyst, which can make them unhappy and sometimes withdrawn. Parents are usually extremely concerned and emotional about treatment and surgery on such a small yet vital organ and frequently assume, with horror, that the eye will have to be removed during surgery. Both parents and children worry about the cosmetic results of surgery, the healing process and the visual outcome. Finally, what may seem just routine eye treatment to staff, is always a major event to the child and their family. The parent is often almost as much a focus of care as the child.

Therapeutic holding

There may be occasions when the child needs to be immobilised so that a procedure can be carried out. It may be a method of helping the child, with their permission if at all possible, to manage a painful procedure quickly and effectively. Alternative terms for therapeutic holding include 'supportive holding' or 'clinical holding' (Jeffery 2008, Lambrenos & McArthur 2003).

This technique should only be undertaken without the child's consent as a last resort. It must be undertaken only in the child's best interest and any decision should be made with the involvement of the parent or guardian. The method to be used, when and for how long, must be agreed and documented at all stages. Holding without the child's consent can result in feelings of distress and anxiety and lack of control. The nurse must make skilled use of age-appropriate techniques, such as wrapping the child up and explaining to the child what is going to happen, comforting them and explaining clearly why therapeutic holding is necessary. Comprehensive guidelines and best practice are published by the Royal College of Nursing (RCN 2010).

Partnership working

Partnership with children and families, and encouraging the participation of both in all aspects of care, are key to effective service provision. Both healthcare professionals and parents have a responsibility within this partnership. Healthcare professionals need to recognise when the culture of the family is a barrier to optimal involvement of the child – for example, where the parent inhibits choice or overrides the child's decision making by acting *for* them rather than *with* them, or dominates the consultation. In this situation, the healthcare professional should work with the parent to move to a more participatory way of working.

High levels of partnership and participation can be facilitated by:

- Recognising the age and capacity of the individual child to understand and engage in a consultation or clinical encounter.
- Ensuring that all healthcare professionals communicate directly with any child irrespective of age or disability, throughout the consultation or clinical encounter, and have the skills to address the child in a way that is appropriate to their level of comprehension.
- Using age-appropriate language to facilitate understanding.
- Involving the child as much as possible in decision making, and encouraging the child to take part in discussions, allowing time to consider and discuss options, inviting questions, and anticipating concerns if they are unexpressed.

- Providing a child-friendly environment, including colourful decor, posters (using large print and simple language), and a range of age-appropriate toys and interactive condition-appropriate props. Play is vital to enable children to normalise stressful situations and is used by the child as a coping strategy
- Privacy and dignity are as important for the child in the ophthalmic setting as they are for the adult. This, along with any confidentiality of information issues, should be borne in mind when dealing with children of any age.
- Providing age-appropriate seating, furniture, etc.
- Drawing diagrams or using objects (real or models) to illustrate treatment or care processes.
- Providing information in a number of age-appropriate formats, in a timely fashion as the condition changes.
- Appreciating, acknowledging and addressing the emotional and psychological needs of the child and parent. This includes having the capacity to anticipate what these needs may be, in the light of the clinician's experience of the condition.

The importance of information and communication

One of the key outcomes of the Children and Young People's Health Outcomes Forum, which reported in 2012, is that children and young people and their families should be at the heart of what happens and that communication and information should be age appropriate. Williams *et al.* (2011) make the following points:

- Parents and children require individually targeted interventions and support to enable them to participate fully in consultations and decision-making.
- Verbal information needs to be backed up with written and other forms of appropriate additional information in child-centred and age-appropriate ways, and also for parents.
- Children and young people require continued access to high-quality information at strategic points in their lifespan. Resources provided over time should include information on: accessing and choice of services; the condition, signs and symptoms, treatment options and choices; managing the condition and self-care; managing the condition at home and at school; growing up with the condition and lifestyle issues; transition to adulthood; and individual information needs that have been identified or raised.
- Children's information provision and follow-up should be included in the clinical record to ensure continuity of care.

- Clinicians should only keep information from children and young people if it would cause them serious harm (and not just upset them or make them more likely to refuse treatment), or they are asked to by the child or young person (GMC 2007).

The child in the hospital

Many children are admitted to the ophthalmic unit as day cases for elective surgery, usually under a general anaesthetic. Day surgery is beneficial to children in several ways. Firstly, it minimises the overall emotional stress and disruption to the child and their family. Secondly, it facilitates the continual presence of the parent, which is so vital to every child's wellbeing, and the cost to the hospital is considerably reduced. However, if the psychological advantages are to be maximised, it is very important that children who are admitted, whether as day cases or with an overnight stay for elective surgery, are properly prepared preoperatively and looked after efficiently throughout their stay in hospital (Kelly & Adkins 2003).

Pre-admission assessment

The first crucial step in planning the care of a child to be admitted for elective surgery is a pre-admission visit to the ward, and an assessment of each child and his parents by a paediatric nurse (Kelly & Adkins 2003). Research over many years has confirmed that good preoperative preparation reduces perioperative problems, such as pain and anxiety, and hastens discharge (Kain *et al.* 2009). The nurse is therefore uniquely placed to agree an individualised plan of management with the parents as partners in the care (Kenyon & Barnett 2001).

Ideally, the visit should take place 1–2 weeks before admission and will offer the child a safe time to play, meet their nurses and have fun! This can effectively help the child feel secure and realise that time in hospital can be enjoyable. The nurse should be relaxed, friendly and unhurried. The nurse should record information about the child's individual routine and personality, past medical history, their weight, allergies, immunisation status and medication. The parents must be given clear, accurate verbal and written instructions about the preparations at home before admission – most importantly, how to manage the preoperative starvation period successfully (parents of babies will be most concerned about this particular aspect). They need to know the course of events on the operation day, especially the anaesthetic procedure. A thorough plan for discharge and care at home to ensure seamless care must be established at this stage. This will include sorting out domestic arrangements, parental jobs, arranging time off playschool/school for the child, care of siblings and all aspects of caring for the child at home afterwards.

An explanation must be given to the child about their role when they come back into hospital for surgery, appropriate to their age, stage of development and life experience. This is best explained to children by allowing them to play with teddies and dolls, displaying equipment that they are likely to see, such as a theatre gown, anaesthetic mask and tubing, syringe and stethoscope. This type of therapeutic play can really help the child to understand what is going to happen, assimilate the information and cope better with hospitalisation (Dix 2004, Li *et al.* 2007, Li & Lopez 2008). Adolescents need more detail and choices about what is to happen to them, in order to feel more confident and in control. All children should be treated with respect, and their opinions and wishes should be taken into consideration when planning care with them.

Much reassurance must be given to families because a prospective hospital admission can be distressing for them and may also bring back memories of a bad experience for another member of the family. Even a single negative encounter can significantly alter an individual's subsequent ability to cope. Every encounter (even for a 'minor' procedure) therefore requires attention to the psychosocial needs of the child and their family (Harris *et al.* 2013).

The family must be shown around the ward and the available facilities explained. If appropriate, they may be shown into the anaesthetic room, which is usually less threatening than people imagine and can effectively allay fears before the 'big day'.

Admission and the day of surgery

The child should be greeted by name, shown their bed and introduced to other families. The children's ward should be safe, homely and cheerful, and offer a wide range of toys and games for all age groups. Parents should be encouraged to be with their child for all procedures.

Any changes in the child's circumstances since the pre-admission visit are noted and the child's fitness for surgery ascertained. Parents should support their child for all procedures, however seemingly minor, and implement care with help from the nurse. Identity bands must be checked and put round the child's ankles, leaving the hands free.

On the day of surgery, long waiting times (which can cause anxiety and boredom) should be avoided. This will also reduce the length of time needed for preoperative fasting.

The child may need to put on a theatre gown, and a baseline set of vital signs is recorded. A local anaesthetic cream is applied over veins on the back of the hands at the correct time before surgery; parents are asked to help ensure that the young child does not tamper with this 'magic' cream so that it stays *in situ*. The child should be sensitively reminded about what the operation will involve, and how they are likely to feel afterwards, in a way appropriate to their age and developmental stage. This will help the child feel less alarmed later on. Appropriate explanations should be given to the child and their parents as necessary throughout the day, whilst always maintaining confidentiality.

A pen mark on the forehead will denote the correct eye for surgery; it is essential to check this carefully against the consent form, medical notes and operating list.

Any prescribed preoperative premedication (e.g. midazolam 0.5mg/kg), and any preoperative eye drops, must be administered at the correct time. Children and parents must understand the reason for and effects of all medication given. The nurse may need to use play and distraction techniques in order to succeed with this! Verbal informed consent from the child and parents will be needed if holding techniques need to be employed. Often, however, if the child is given adequate explanation and encouragement, they will cooperate.

Throughout these preparations, the paediatric nurse should treat the child with tact and sensitivity. Their natural need for privacy and dignity must also be taken into consideration in all circumstances. In this way the nurse will increase the child's trust and confidence in what is happening, and help them feel happy and in control, and therefore more likely to be cooperative.

One or both parents and the child's teddy, blanket or other comforter may accompany the child and nurse to go directly into the anaesthetic room. There should be no waiting around at any point during this journey, because this heightens the inevitable stress felt by both child and parent. The nurse must support the parent after the child is anaesthetised. This is usually a very upsetting stage for parents, however smoothly the anaesthetic procedure has gone. It is good practice to accompany parents discreetly back to the ward and, after being told approximately how long the operation will take, they should be advised to take a break for a drink or fresh air.

Postoperative care

Before the child's return to the ward, parents should be forewarned about what changes to expect in the child's appearance and behaviour. Many anaesthetists welcome parents into the recovery room to comfort the child and accompany them back to the ward with the nurse. If possible, the bed area or room should be kept quiet to promote sleep, and darkened to minimise sensitivity to light. Parental presence and their caring for the child are vital components of relieving the child's discomfort and distress postoperatively. Parents are usually anxious to see their child after surgery, but are also nervous about how they will be. Support of parents involves advising them how to care for their children by reassuring them, lying on the bed and cuddling them, stroking their forehead and wiping their face with a cool flannel, and gently distracting them with a story or a nursery rhyme. These interventions work well and the child will usually sleep with the parent close by.

Postoperative observations are essential to monitor the child's recovery and promptly identify problems in the early stages. Assessment is made of the following: child's consciousness level and skin colour; pulse, respiratory rate/effort and temperature. These are recorded until the child is conscious. Further observations of O_2 saturations, peripheral pulses and capillary refill time should be taken, and medical staff should be alerted if the child's condition deteriorates in any way. The condition of the eye should be monitored – for instance, the presence of any swelling or haematoma, blood in the tears noted or remarks indicating that the child has diplopia (double vision). Eye movements should be discreetly observed and concern about any aspect of the eye discussed with the surgeon. The child should be gently discouraged from rubbing the eye.

Rectal analgesia, e.g. diclofenac (Voltarol) 1–3mg/kg or paracetamol 10–15mg/kg, can be given intraoperatively, with good effect, to minimise postoperative pain. An intravenous antiemetic, e.g. ondansetron 100μg/kg for over-2-year-olds, may be given at the same stage. Any further discomfort later on can be treated with a simple analgesic, such as paracetamol elixir. Parents must be informed about the medication given and its effects.

As the child recovers, tepid drinks and light snacks should be offered. When the child wakes and is feeling better, gentle play is allowed and activity re-established while maintaining safety. The intravenous cannula is removed only when the child's overall condition is good, mobility has been regained and fluids/diet are tolerated.

Planned discharge

The parent and child, as appropriate, must understand the process of how the eye will recover after surgery and be shown how to clean the eye and administer eye drops. Little children loathe eye drops and the gentle restraint often needed, and other strategies, must be passed on to parents for this to be successful, getting a relative or friend to help if possible. Instructing the child to look at a toy held above them, counting to 20 after the eye drops to focus their attention, and giving a small reward (chocolate or stickers) for compliance, will all help.

Parents also need advice about administering appropriate regular analgesia for 2–4 days postoperatively. This is an important aspect of care to minimise discomfort and stop the child rubbing the eye, making it sore. Being free of pain also helps the child re-establish their normal level of play and activity, and helps them look back more favourably on their recent experience in hospital.

Advice must be given about recreation, activities and schooling. Swimming and contact sports should be curtailed until the eye has settled. This will usually take 2–6 weeks, depending on the surgery performed. All aspects of care of the eyes, and general childcare, must be discussed with the parent and child before discharge. Teenagers should be advised not to wear eye make-up for 2–3 weeks after surgery.

Research shows that children can be disrupted by even a short stay in hospital, especially the under-5s, and parents should be made aware of this (While & Wilcox 1994). This may be shown by clingy and tearful behaviour, which will pass if plenty of extra love, praise and encouragement are offered to the child. Attention should be given to siblings too and small tasks devised for them to 'help', so that they do not feel left out. Parents should therefore be advised to plan a quiet few days based at home after surgery, allowing each member of the family to settle down, and limiting visitors and long trips.

A useful strategy is to ensure that the family receive a postoperative telephone call from the ward the day after surgery, to ensure that all is well and provide further advice where necessary; this is always greatly appreciated by the family (Feasey 2000). They should have a hospital contact telephone number and be assured that they may ring at any time for advice about the eye.

The child will usually have a follow-up appointment after surgery. Further help and support for families may be sought from the community paediatric nurses, the health visitor and family doctor, and this must be organised before discharge.

The care of the child as an inpatient: reasons for admission

On some occasions a child who has undergone eye surgery as a day case does not meet the discharge criteria and needs to stay overnight. This delay may be the result of postoperative problems, e.g. failure to tolerate fluids, the need for further observation or a domestic situation that warrants a longer stay in hospital. Other indications for inpatient care may include:

- Severe infections
- Eye drop therapy
- Occlusion therapy
- Trauma.

Severe infections

Orbital cellulitis (see also Chapter 23) is a potentially life-threatening and vision-threatening condition, arising from bacterial infection in the nasal sinuses, after a penetrating injury or eye surgery (Bowling et al. 2015). It is more common in children than adults and causes an acute, purulent infection of the tissue of the eye and orbit, resulting in a tender, swollen and painful eye. It is generally treated by a multidisciplinary team, due to the sinus involvement and potential neurological infection

The child will be febrile and unwell, with a painful eye and may have altered vision. Treatment will involve regular and effective analgesia (a child will often refuse medication if they do not think it works) and antipyretic medication, systemic antibiotics intravenously or orally, and antibiotic eye drops. Nursing care of this sick child includes allowing adequate rest, gentle play, careful cleansing of the eye and face, instillation of eye drops and IV or oral antibiotic therapy as well as monitoring the child's general condition

Ophthalmia neonatorum is any eye infection that occurs within 21 days of birth. It may be caused by bacteria, such as gonococci or pneumococci, but most commonly by *Chlamydia sp.* (see also Chapter 16). Gonococci cause a severe bacterial eye infection and may require admission to hospital. The infection is transmitted to the baby during vaginal delivery. Sexually transmitted disease in the parents must be excluded.

Gonococcal infection causes the eyelids to swell with a profuse, purulent discharge from the baby's eyes, and there is a real risk that the cornea may become ulcerated or even perforate. The baby's eyes require regular lid toilet, intensive treatment with antibiotic eye drops and often a systemic antibiotic as well. Scrupulous attention to the hygienic care of the infant, including care of the umbilicus, is essential, to prevent cross-infection. At the same time, attention must be paid to all the other needs of a newborn baby, including nutrition, adequate warmth and the comforting of a baby who may feel unwell.

If a young baby is admitted, the mother also needs careful nursing. She may well be feeling the physical and emotional effects of the birth, and may require a midwife's attention. If the mother has chosen to breast-feed she will need guidance and support, because establishing breast-feeding is demanding and tiring. The mother needs regular updates about her baby's condition and support to allow her to contribute to her baby's general care, to promote bonding and affection between mother and baby.

The family will need very sensitive emotional support through this upsetting and difficult time, and appropriate support and follow-up should be planned before discharge.

Eye drop therapy

A child may be admitted as an inpatient for the instillation of essential eye drops if they are refusing to cooperate with treatment at home, the parent is unable to cope, or the social situation is such that the treatment is difficult or impossible. Sometimes a child who has just undergone a cataract extraction will require frequent eye drop administration and this can be demanding and difficult for some parents to achieve at home. The nurse will require great patience and ingenuity to teach parents and the child the best way to cope with the eye drop routine at home and thus ensure a good outcome from this admission. Further support at home may be offered by health visitors, school nurses and community paediatric nurses.

Occlusion therapy (see also Chapter 23)

Amblyopia, or 'lazy eye', is reduced visual acuity in an affected eye that lacks visual experience and use in early life, when the visual pathways are developing. A squint or refractive error may also be present but otherwise the eye is structurally normal.

Occlusion treatment has been successfully used for over 200 years and involves use of an occlusive patch to cover the unaffected eye, thus encouraging the amblyopic eye's use and function. This is possible up to the age of 8 years, but it is generally accepted that, after that age, the visual system has matured and visual acuity cannot be improved upon. Compliance with treatment is pivotal to treatment success, and failure to develop binocular vision has psychosocial effects and limits certain career options in adult life.

Most children will tolerate 'patching' at home, but some resist strongly, exhibiting very 'challenging' behaviour if parents even attempt to apply the patch! Some hospitals admit non-compliant children for a few days, with the aims of teaching them to wear an eye patch and establish a routine for them to wear it for a designated time each day. Parents must fully understand the aim of occlusion therapy and how this will be achieved. Success depends very much on good information being given to parents and teaching them effective practical strategies to use at home with their child.

Parents often feel a sense of failure and exasperation if they do not succeed in carrying out such seemingly simple treatment at home. They therefore need much support and encouragement themselves during admission and afterwards at home.

It is also crucial for a parent to stay with their child in hospital, first to support them but crucially to learn how to manage the occlusion at home after discharge. The child's normal routine and discipline – mealtimes, bathing, bedtimes, etc. – should be maintained as far as possible, while they are in hospital, to help them feel secure.

It is essential to work directly with the child throughout the period of treatment. A simple, clear explanation must be given and they must understand why they have to wear an eye patch and that they may not be able to see very well at first. But with lots of fun, different toys, puzzles and games, the exposed eye will work hard and vision can, on occasions, improve enough on the first day, making the wearing of the 'patch' more tolerable. The first few hours are usually the most demanding for the nurse and parent or carer, who is persuading and enticing the child to leave the patch alone. Constant distraction is essential!

The use of a simple reward scheme (such as a colourful chart and an attractive book to stick used patches in and record the patching time achieved) will often appeal to the natural competitiveness of the young child. While the child is on the ward, they should be kept fully occupied with good play facilities as it is often boredom or frustration that can make a child remove their patch, in order to gain the adult's attention. There may well be certain times when the child finds it particularly difficult to cope with wearing the 'patch', such as at playschool, and strategies should be sought to improve matters. Siblings can be encouraged to visit, to prevent them worrying about the parent and child in hospital. Parents should be offered frequent breaks, because this is a demanding and emotional time for them.

Following their admission, children are closely monitored in the orthoptic clinic, to assess improvement, avoid amblyopia in the occluded eye, and offer parents, and indeed the child, further support.

The health visitor should be made aware of the admission, because they will be well placed to continue advising parents about problems at home. If the child is of school age, the school nurse and teacher can be instrumental in helping the child succeed with 'patching' at school.

Trauma (see also Chapter 12)

Trauma is one of the most common reasons for a child's admission to the eye ward. Children are at special risk from eye injuries because they are less aware of potential dangers and are often fearless in their outlook. They love to experiment and can easily stray into dangerous situations. The injuries sustained by children are usually unilateral and often severe. They are more often suffered by boys than girls. The human eye is protected from trauma by the eyelids and the blink reflex, the lids closing spontaneously if a hazard threatens, and by movement of the head to avoid injury. The eye is also protected by the orbital bones and a surrounding layer of fat. However, the orbit of a child's eyes is also smaller than an adult's, and therefore offers relatively less protection.

Emergency admission

On admission, it is essential that an accurate history of the incident be obtained so that no injury is missed. This may prove difficult because young children in particular may not be able to articulate or to recall the circumstances of the injury, and older children may give a vague account of events, wanting to protect themselves or friends from blame.

Management may involve an examination under anaesthetic (EUA), immediate surgery to repair the injury or a period of observation. The nursing staff can help facilitate this examination by taking a few minutes to talk to the child in a straightforward way and familiarise them with the consulting room: the slit-lamp and lights; how and why they will have to sit, perhaps on Mummy's knee; why they must sit still. Again, turning this into a game, examining 'teddy' first and using distraction toys, can effectively promote a quick and successful examination, whereas 'muddying the water' by missing out this valuable stage can cause real problems later on. It is important to give the child and parents a clear explanation of the chain of events at an early stage; they will all require much support and reassurance to lessen stress at this worrying time.

When a child is admitted to the eye ward with a serious eye injury, they will be frightened, quiet and pale, and may vomit. The child should be nursed in a quiet, darkened room and encouraged not to rub the affected eye. As their sight has been adversely affected, maintaining a safe environment is crucial, particularly because the child will be relying more on their non-visual senses than usual.

The nurse must observe the eye carefully and immediately report any change in its appearance, including swelling, the level of vision, diplopia, an increase in pain or discomfort and any other symptoms. In particular, the nurse must observe and report any change in the child's level of consciousness and pupil reaction, or general condition that may indicate the presence of another injury, particularly a head injury. The importance of rest may be difficult for young children to comprehend and it will require a resourceful nurse and family to keep them happy and occupied.

A child in discomfort or pain will be distressed and uncooperative; this must be avoided. Effective analgesia is therefore important and needs close monitoring, using pain assessment tools and analgesia/anti-emetic ladders. If the child is comfortable, they will be more relaxed and tolerate treatment better. They may also feel frightened and confused, especially if vision is much reduced or absent, and will need regular, straightforward, appropriate explanations about what is happening, helped by diagrams and models. The child will also need much support and emotional care. It is important that the child is encouraged to be as independent in washing, dressing and eating as their condition allows. Play, which is so vital to children's wellbeing, can be gently introduced when the child is well enough. This will help normalise a strange and stressful situation for the child and distract them from the more unpleasant aspects of their care.

The child will usually require eye drops. It often takes much ingenuity on the nurse's part to administer them accurately and without undue distress to the child. Supervising a willing parent may be the best way; distraction techniques and play may help, together with much praise and encouragement. The eye will also require regular gentle cleansing, using an aseptic technique; this may be more easily done with a young child if their teddy has his eye cleaned first.

If surgery is planned, preoperative preparation (including psychological preparation) of the child is needed. It is essential to obtain informed consent to surgery from the child, who is often very frightened, and the adult with parental responsibility. It must be accurately established at what time the child last ate and drank, and the required period of starvation observed. The child is then prepared for theatre in the usual way. Even if time is limited, play therapy using equipment that the child will see (syringe, anaesthetic tubing and mask, plaster, etc.) will help familiarise them with anaesthetic procedure. Time spent in this way is really valuable in helping the child to cope with a stressful situation.

Postoperative nursing care should be followed, as suggested previously, with special attention to the emotional wellbeing of the child and parent, and regular updates about progress to both child and parent. As the child recovers further, their general hygiene, elimination, nutrition, activity, play and possibly school work also need the attention of the nurse. Boredom should be avoided but sufficient rest taken too.

It is hard for parents to see their child in pain, and they often feel guilty or angry about how the injury occurred, so they too need much sensitive help and support. Such support will include clear and accurate information, reassurance and strategies for how to give the best emotional and physical help to their injured child. They may also need guidance about their domestic situation and the care of any other children at home, who will be worried about their sibling.

As discussed, the care of the child must be talked over with both the child and the parents so that they can all participate in the care at a level with which they are comfortable, bearing in mind the type and nature of the injury, and that they are all upset and worried.

Parents should be encouraged to stay with their child, as far as is practicable, particularly when the child undergoes *any* nursing procedure or treatment, however small. Parents need to be shown ward facilities, offered accommodation and meals, and enough time to rest and look after other members of their family.

Before the discharge, the parents must be fully advised about the care of the child at home. Written information can be taken home and referred to, which is helpful for busy parents. Parents should be proficient at cleansing the eye and administering eye drops and analgesia. They need advice about what kinds of activity, recreation and schooling are appropriate for the child. The child themselves may feel dispirited and sad, especially if visual loss is permanent, and they will need much sensitive support.

The child who experiences a significant loss of vision, their parents and siblings will need much ongoing practical help and psychological support from the various health agencies. Ongoing support from the hospital (and a telephone number with which to access this) will also be welcomed and support groups may be helpful. The child will also be closely followed up as an outpatient.

Minor trauma

Many children with eye complaints visit the eye A&E or indeed the main A&E department of a hospital without a dedicated eye unit. As discussed above, children are prone to experiment with all sorts of household and garden objects that they perceive as intriguing and fun to play with. This spirit of adventure means that little children, in particular, can be injured quickly and easily and a wide range of accidents may occur.

It is important to begin by examining the child's eyes carefully, to establish the nature and extent of the injury. However, this is often easier said than done, because superficial injuries to the eye can be exquisitely painful and often cause the eye to 'water' profusely. The young child arriving in the department is therefore often fractious, tired and uncomfortable, and unwilling to let anyone near their eyes!

Under these circumstances, it is wisest to attend to the child's basic needs before attempting to examine the eye – if the condition allows. This involves ensuring that they are not overheated in a thick jumper, that they have a drink and a snack if they are hungry (and surgery is not imminent), that they use the lavatory if needed, and that they are distracted with toys and books while parents are reassured and given an explanation of the management of the child and how they can help. But, perhaps *most importantly*, especially if the child is in pain or discomfort (usually obviously shown by body language and challenging behaviour, i.e. crying, grumpy, head down, eyes screwed up and arm shielding face) is to give a topical anaesthetic (after explanations and maybe a 'trial' on a toy or mum) and/or a simple analgesic, such as paracetamol syrup, *first*. It is far more likely that the child will cooperate with the staff once they are comfortable.

Lastly, *before* examination and treatment, you need to sit with the child and explain what is going to happen and thereby, if possible, gain informed consent. They must understand exactly what is to happen, particularly if eye drops are involved (either analgesic drops and/or fluorescein drops to distinguish an abrasion), and what they will feel. Encourage them to look at and touch equipment, and see teddy go through it all first! The child should be talked through each step of the examination, to maintain cooperation, by a member of staff who has got to know the child a little and hopefully established some rapport with them. The second person can then more easily carry out the examination.

This whole respectful, planned approach, enlisting the help of the child and parent, with the assurance of stickers or a bravery award afterwards, can very often win the child's favour, with the examination being carried out successfully on the *first* attempt and with minimal fuss.

The care of the child in the outpatient department

It is important to remember that a child's referral to the outpatient department may well be their first personal experience of entering a hospital. How they interpret this experience may affect them considerably, so it is vital to make the time as positive and enjoyable as possible. Depending on their age and life experience, they may feel frightened and anxious or, conversely, quite excited about the visit. They and their family will need a sensitive and confident approach from the clinical staff to gain their cooperation and help them feel at ease. Age-appropriate facilities should be available (such as toys and puzzles).

The waiting time, for young children in particular, should be kept to a minimum to prevent them becoming bored and miserable. Parents will often have other children with them, and children to collect from school, or be travelling on public transport, so a lengthy wait may make them feel more anxious.

Before the test or examination begins, the child (whatever their age) must be given an explanation about what is about to happen. This should be delivered in a language-appropriate way, in short sentences, with clear and straightforward instructions. The child needs a little time to think about what has been put to them and should not be rushed. Involvement of the child may be enough to expedite the examination.

If eye drops need to be given, verbal informed consent must be obtained and 'holding still' techniques discussed with parent and child, should the child not be in a cooperative mood. The resourceful nurse can often distract the child sufficiently to facilitate the examination by turning it into a game, perhaps with the child's teddy and the use of 'distraction toys', which can immediately capture a child's attention; such toys may be kept in each consulting room. The nurse can also appeal to the child's competitive side by offering him 'fun' stickers and a bravery certificate after the examination! Positive praise and encouragement will also help. A large model of the eye or large diagrams can be helpful when explaining the condition to families.

The nurse should ensure that the family fully understands what has been said before they leave. They can be given information leaflets on the various eye conditions that are helpful to refer to at home. If their child is to be listed for surgery, the family should be told that they will receive a date for a pre-admission visit, where all the procedures and details will be explained to them, which will reassure them.

Contact with, and referrals to, other healthcare professionals may be needed, and this link should be well established in the outpatient department, as in any other dealing with children. Information should be passed both to and from the hospital service by all professionals concerned with the care of the child, so that a seamless service can be ensured.

References

9th Council of Europe Conference of Health Ministers (2011) *Child-friendly Healthcare: Building a Health Future for and with Children.* Lisbon.

Barnes K. & Sart F. (2003) 'A developmental approach to the history and physical examination in paediatrics' in K. Barnes (ed.) *Paediatrics: a clinical guide for nurse practitioners.* Edinburgh, Butterworth Heinemann.

Bowling, B. (2015) *Kanski's Clinical Ophthalmology, a systematic approach.* 8th edn. London: Elsevier.

Dix, A. (2004) Let us play. *Health Service Journal.* **22**, 26–7.

Department of Health (DH) (2003) *Getting the Right Start: National Service Framework for Children in Hospital. Standard for Hospital Services.* London: DH.

Department of Health (DH) (2012) *Report of the Children and Young People's Health Outcomes Forum.* London: DH.

Feasey, S. (2000) Quality counts: auditing day-surgery services. *Journal of Child Health Care.* **4**(2), 73–77.

General Medical Council (GMC) (2007) *0–18 years: guidance for all doctors.* London: GMC.

Harris, T.B., Sibley, A., Rodriguez, C. & Brandt, M.L. (2013) Teaching the psychosocial aspects of pediatric surgery. *Seminars in Pediatric Surgery.* **22**, 161–66.

Healy, K. (2012) A Descriptive Survey of the Information Needs of Parents of Children Admitted for Same Day Surgery. *Journal of Pediatric Nursing.* **28**(2), 179–85.

Jeffery, K. (2008) 'Supportive holding of children during therapeutic interventions' in J. Kelsey & G. McEwing (eds) *Clinical skills in child health practice.* London: Churchill Livingstone Elsevier.

Lambrenos, K. & McArthur, K. (2003) Introducing a clinical holding policy. *Paediatric Nursing.* **15**(4), 30–33.

Kain, Z.N. & Caldwell-Andrews, A.A. (2005) Preoperative psychological preparation of the child for surgery: an update. *Anesthesiology Clinics of North America.* **23**, 597–614.

Kain, Z., Caldwell-Andrews, A. & Mayes, L. (2009) 'Perioperative behavior stress in children' in C. Cote, J., Lerman & I. Todres (eds) *A Practice of Anesthesia for Infants and Children.* 4th edn. Philadelphia: Saunders Elsevier. pp. 25–35.

Kelly, M. & Adkins, L. (2003) Ingredients for a successful paediatric pre-operative care process. *AORN Journal.* **77**, 1006–11.

Kenyon, E. & Barnett, N. (2001) Partnership in nursing care: the Blackburn model. *Journal of Child Healthcare.* **5**, 35–38.

Li, H.C.W. & Lopez, V. (2008) Effectiveness and Appropriateness of Therapeutic Play Intervention in Preparing Children for Surgery: A Randomized Controlled Trial Study. *Journal for Specialists in Pediatric Nursing.* **13**(2), 63–73.

Li, H.C.W., Lopez, V. & Lee, T.L. (2007) Effects of preoperative therapeutic play on outcomes of school-age children undergoing surgery. *Research in Nursing and Health.* **30**, 320–32.

Royal College of Nursing (RCN) Ophthalmic Nursing Forum (2012) *Ophthalmic Nursing; a career and competence framework.* London: RCN.

Royal College of Nursing (RCN) (2010) *Restrictive physical intervention and therapeutic holding for children and young people, Guidance for nursing staff.* London: RCN.

While, A. & Wilcox, V. (1994) Paediatric day surgery: day-case unit admission compared with general ward admission. *Journal of Advanced Nursing.* **19**.1, 52–7.

Williams, A., Noyes, J., Chandler-Oatts, J., Allen, D., Brocklehurst, P., Carter, C., Gregory, J.W., Leonton, S., Lewis, M., Lowes, L. & Threadgold, T. (2011) *Children's Health Information Matters: Researching the practice of and requirements for age appropriate health information for children and young people.* London: HMSO.

CHAPTER TEN

Developments in care in day surgery for ophthalmic patients

Margaret Gurney

The trend towards day surgery for ophthalmic patients in the UK has grown rapidly following the development of:

- New technology
- Changes in the way the NHS delivers care
- The influence of politics on healthcare
- Evidence-based practice
- New approaches to local anaesthesia
- Changes in patient expectations.

Numerous changes in the delivery of healthcare have opened up the opportunity for private providers to contract for care provision in a number of specialties, including ophthalmology. With fewer inpatient beds available for ophthalmology in many hospitals, day case surgery is now the norm for most ophthalmic procedures, and settings can include both NHS treatment centres and private hospitals.

The history of ophthalmic day surgery in the UK

Day case surgery has a much longer history in the UK than many people realise. An early proponent was James Nicholl, a paediatric surgeon who reported regularly to the British Medical Association between 1899 and 1908 on his success with operations on 9000 children as day cases at his Glasgow hospital. Despite this pioneering work, day case surgery was extremely slow to develop in the UK.

An enquiry into the 'Management of the NHS' (the Griffiths Report – Department of Health and Social Security 1983) identified an urgent need to reform the NHS so that it could become a more effective service, able to meet the challenges of the twenty-first century. One area identified as needing urgent review was the length of time people stayed in hospital before and after surgery for routine procedures.

This was followed by a number of studies in the early days from the Audit Commission (1990, 1991) and the NHS Management Executive (1991). An investigation into the provision of day case surgery (Audit Commission 1990) identified that at least 40% of ophthalmic operations could be undertaken as day cases. When the Audit Commission reviewed costs, it estimated in 1990 that a shift in emphasis towards day surgery would save between £10 million and £19 million annually. Day surgery was regarded by health service economists as an opportunity to reduce expenditure and as a method of reducing waiting lists. These studies determined that increased use of day surgery would lead to improved organisation in the delivery of care and would be tailored to suit the needs of the individual.

The benefits of day surgery have been well documented. They include:

- Shorter waiting time for treatment
- Reduced costs
- Shorter procedure time
- Better postoperative recovery
- Minimum waits and cancellations
- Higher levels of technical expertise by surgeons and anaesthetists
- Less psychological trauma for elderly people and children
- Minimum disruption to normal lifestyle
- More holistic nursing care.

A political change in 1997 introduced sweeping changes to the NHS in a 10-year plan of modernisation – *A First Class Service* (DH 1998). This was followed by *Making a Difference* (DH 1999), which set out to strengthen the contribution of nursing, midwifery and health visiting in a restructured NHS. Ophthalmology services have been greatly influenced by these policy documents and, even more so, by the publication of *Action on Cataracts* (NHS Executive 2000) and *The NHS Plan* (DH 2000), which identified wide areas in ophthalmology that could be better provided by nurses.

Qualitative studies conducted since the move to day surgery have demonstrated very high levels of satisfaction with it. In a survey by the Audit Commission (1991), over 80% of respondents reported that they preferred day surgery and would recommend it. One of the early ophthalmic day surgery studies (Law 1997) reported similar findings but found that there was still a lot of work to be done in the area of giving information in the right manner and in alleviating patient anxiety. This is a continuing issue for patients undergoing day surgery (Mitchell 2012).

Throughout the country, day-surgery units were being set up to cope with the increasing demand. Although there were many positive reports at first, it soon became evident that this change in culture had raised a number of issues in relation to the quality of care and nurse–patient contact time.

Markandy and Platzer (1994) expressed concern that reports such as those by the Audit Commission (1990, 1991) ignored the role of nurses in patient selection and preassessment. These reports focused on cost-effectiveness and efficiency, whereas Markandy and Platzer (1994) identified areas of concern such as patient anxiety, information giving and education. The reduced contact time between nurse and patient meant that clearly defined roles for nurses were needed in order to maintain quality in nursing care.

Day case ophthalmic surgery

Cataracts and strabismus operations were the first surgical procedures to be identified as suitable for day case admission. Reports discussing the merits of day case ophthalmic surgery by Gregory and Lowe (1991) and Smith (1993) indicate that patients displayed high satisfaction levels. In addition, research by Strong et al. (1991) on the clinical effectiveness of an ophthalmic day surgery unit (ODSU) demonstrated that a carefully planned service could deliver an increased throughput of patients with improved quality of care and outcomes cost-effectively. This model formed an example of good practice that was drawn on by other ophthalmic departments wishing to change. Day case surgery has now become the norm for most ophthalmic procedures, with cataracts forming the greatest proportion of the procedures undertaken. The important issues that arise with this diversity of surgery in relation to information giving and streamlined care will be discussed further.

Action on Cataracts and Focus on Cataracts

The implications for ophthalmic practice in the UK changed dramatically in February 2000 with the publication of *Action on Cataracts* (NHS Executive 2000). This guidance to good practice set out to reduce the very long waits that were occurring for patients needing cataract surgery; in the worst case scenarios, patients were waiting as long as 2 years.

A new model of care was proposed that aimed to:

- Reduce the wait for outpatient appointments
- Make surgery more accessible
- Reduce the number of visits to hospital
- Introduce an integrated care pathway

- Provide a booked admissions project

- Streamline the role of the nurse in preassessment and pre- and postoperative care. (DH 2008).

Focus on Cataracts, published by the NHS Centre for Innovation and Improvement (2008), built on *Action on Cataracts*, recommending an even more streamlined pathway and identifying that day case cataract rates had increased from 88% in 2001 to 96% in 2007.

This theme of streamlined care is echoed in ophthalmic settings everywhere, with the realisation of the possibilities of day surgery. Whichever model is chosen, however, it must be ensured that, while the patient's journey is streamlined, patient care is not compromised. It is important to remember, for instance, that most day case ophthalmic patients are elderly, and many are frail with concurrent medical conditions. They may need to take things rather more slowly than other patients so these models, should always be adapted to the individual.

Bearing all this in mind, for many patients with ophthalmic conditions, day surgery is preferable to inpatient surgery for all the reasons identified and it also gives satisfaction to all the staff involved in its delivery. There appear to be huge benefits to service providers and patients alike and these are well demonstrated by both qualitative and qualitative research findings.

Changing the model of care

Early models of ophthalmic day care were seen to be protracted. For example, the pathway shown in Figure 10.1 (below) was the traditional model adopted when day case ophthalmic surgery was first introduced. This was a long drawn-out process and was a service-focused model, rather than a patient-focused one, with multiple journeys to the hospital, including multiple postoperative visits.

Old pathway

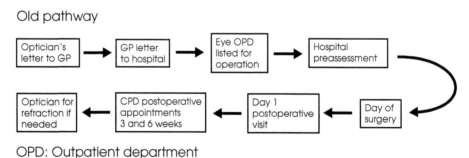

OPD: Outpatient department

Figure 10.1 Old pathway for model of care for ophthalmic day-care cataract surgery.

Patient visits optometrist and is referred directly to hospital

Optometrist discusses risks and benefits of surgery.

Provides patient with information leaflet.

Discusses patient lifestyle and ensures patient wishes to proceed with surgery.

Offers choice of provider. Completes cataract referral form, including current refraction.

Sends referral to hospital with a copy to patient's GP and CCG.

CCG: Clinical commissioning group

Patient booked directly to a cataract clinic

Preassessment to include biometry, health assessment, medicines, allergies and examination by ophthalmologist.

Consent form, booking of operation date and postoperative appointment.

Arranging INR where applicable and in line with local policy.

INR: International normalised ratio (blood coagulation test)

Figure 10.2 Revised cataract pathway (adapted from Focus on Cataracts 2008)

With the introduction of a more streamlined pathway such as this, for cataract, clinicians tend to have less time than ever to spend on patient assessment and care (Lala *et al.* 2010). Criteria for day surgery vary wildly and, in order to enhance throughput and fulfil targets for day-surgery rates, they have often changed to allow more vulnerable patients access to day surgery. Although this is not necessarily a bad thing, packages of care must be in place to ensure that day surgery works for the patient rather than just for the ophthalmic unit.

The role of the nurse in preassessment

Nursing practice is greatly influenced by the need to concentrate on the clinical suitability of patients, to the extent that emphasis can be placed in this area rather than on therapeutic nursing interventions. Ophthalmic nurses are now the pivotal point in the preassessment of patients for day case surgery. Many patients have their entire assessment carried out by ophthalmic trained nurses and the appointment usually occurs 2–3 weeks before surgery. Each ophthalmic unit will develop its own criteria and protocols, which reflect the organisation's philosophy and the needs of the population that it serves. In particular, there will be different criteria for patients having general or local anaesthesia (Table 10.1).

Table 10.1 Common criteria for ophthalmic day surgery

Inclusion criteria:

- Patient must want day surgery, although (with the rise in multiple providers) this may be the only choice
- Patient must be able to understand the self-care that is expected
- Patient must have access to a telephone
- Patient must be able to lie still for the required operative period
- Patient must have transport arranged if necessary
- Patient must have someone at home if surgery is under general anaesthesia.

Exclusion criteria:

- Patients with complex health problems
- Patients with body mass index (BMI) > 36 if having general anaesthetic
- Patients with uncontrolled diabetes.

The consequence for patients of not being able to access day surgery procedures may be a longer wait for surgery. Patients may therefore give false or misleading information to the nurse at preassessment to ensure that they fit the criteria. Accurate assessment is therefore the key to safe day surgery.

Assessment of the patient

An ophthalmic nurse with recognised competencies in ophthalmic assessment and examination should carry out the ophthalmic preassessment. The timing of preassessment varies from hospital to hospital. It may be conducted as a purely nurse-led service or may be incorporated into a one-stop clinic, involving the ophthalmologist, for patients going through a cataract pathway. For other ophthalmic conditions, the preassessment will generally be 1–3 weeks before surgery.

Traditionally, a nursing model of care has formed an intrinsic part of a framework of care, but formalised care pathways and personal constructs are replacing these models. However, this does not remove the nurse's responsibility for assessing and planning the appropriate care for the individual. The use of pathways can make managers and clinicians complacent because they try to fit the patient into the pathway, rather than adjusting the pathway to suit the needs of the patient.

It is easy to assume, when pre-assessing, that patients already know why they have come to the clinic, but it is surprising how many people do not understand what their ocular problem is. Patients with complex conditions, such as those with oculoplastic or vitreoretinal problems, have often not had their eye problem explained to them comprehensively or have not understood or remembered the information, so time will need to be set aside for explanation before full assessment begins. Many patients may still be unaware of their actual problem.

Although assessing, planning and implementing care is a core nursing activity, it is useful to have guidelines to follow when assessing suitability for ophthalmic day surgery.

General preassessment considerations

The patient's general mobility and safety are a consideration at all times. Co-existing medical conditions, such as poorly controlled diabetes and frequent hypoglycaemic attacks, might suggest that the patient would be at less risk if an overnight stay were considered (although admission to hospital may also destabilise previously stable situations). Patients who are frail, with no support at home, whose vision in their unoperated eye is poor, so that they might be unsafe at home after their surgery, should also be considered for an overnight stay; or robust packages of care must be in place preoperatively to facilitate day surgery.

Many areas now use care pathways in which nursing assessment is reduced to the minimum. In these settings, the focus is on general health, medications, allergies, communication, breathing and mobility. Preassessment acts as a data collection point, from which interventions will be planned. However, unless nurses are prepared to individualise care pathways where appropriate, this minimalist approach fails to recognise that patients are individuals with a variety of needs and it may lead to less than optimum care in the very fast pace of the day surgery setting.

Suitability for local anaesthesia (see also Chapter 11)

To achieve successful surgery under local anaesthetic, the patient must be able to lie flat for 30 minutes for cataract surgery but even longer for other ophthalmic procedures. A 'trial lie' at preassessment may help to identify their suitability for this. For example, patients with Parkinson's disease or uncontrolled head tremor may not be suitable for local anaesthetic and, because of this, a general anaesthetic may be considered.

Learning disability or confusion/dementia may also preclude the use of local anaesthesia. Similarly, inability to communicate with patients (due to language barriers or deafness) may be alleviated by arranging for an interpreter to be present during surgery.

Anticoagulant therapy

Patients on warfarin need an international normalised ratio (INR) < 3.5 for cataract surgery but the level required for vitreoretinal surgery is even lower. This aspect therefore needs to be given particular attention. The last result should be reviewed at preassessment and checked on the day of surgery. If the last result is within the required level, check on the day of surgery or in line with local policy. Patients with levels consistently >3.5 should be discussed with the ophthalmologist, anaesthetist and haematologist if necessary.

Patients needing surgery for oculoplastic problems also need to stop aspirin before surgery, and advice needs to be sought for those on other anticoagulants.

Blood pressure

When diastolic pressure is 100 or above, the patient should be referred to their primary care physician or nurse for a check before admission. Studies suggest that raised blood pressure is not a valid reason for cancelling ophthalmic surgery. However, local policies should be followed if the diastolic pressure remains > 100.

Pulse

An ECG may be indicated if the patient's pulse is irregular or if they are bradycardic or tachycardic. If the ECG is abnormal, an anaesthetic opinion should be sought.

Urinalysis

Although it would be most helpful if this were assessed in the primary care setting, before preassessment, urinalysis is a good indicator of diabetes, renal function and infection. Findings at preassessment, such as blood, nitrates or glucose in urine, should precipitate a referral back to primary care so that these can be investigated further.

Open wounds

Open wounds should be swabbed and cultured, and abnormal results should be managed accordingly.

Haematological investigations

There is little evidence of the need for preoperative blood tests before local anaesthesia, unless there is a clinical need. However, anaesthetists undertaking the management of local anaesthesia often require haematological tests. Local policy should therefore be followed but clinicians should endeavour to modify non-evidence-based practices!

Blood tests are indicated in the following circumstances.

Full blood count (FBC):

- Patients with anaemia
- History of alcoholism, liver disease, or on warfarin or chemotherapy
- Haematuria.

Urea and electrolytes (U&Es):

- Patients with diabetes having general anaesthetic
- Multiple drug therapy
- Significant diuretic therapy.

Technical assessment

Many nurses acquired the technical skills of keratometry and biometry when preassessment for ophthalmic patients became a fundamental part of care. With a multidisciplinary approach and the growth of one-stop clinics, this is increasingly being undertaken by hospital opticians, orthoptists and technicians.

Clinical governance has also had an impact on who performs keratometry and biometry, as continuous audit reports have highlighted variances in the refractive outcome of patients after cataract surgery. Accuracy is of paramount importance and the outcome of cataract surgery can be heavily influenced by the accuracy of biometry. It is therefore vital that the biometrist is skilled in all the techniques associated with measurement and is able to adapt to the individual needs of the patient.

Slit-lamp examination at preassessment

Slit-lamp examination of the patient is essential and this will normally be done by an ophthalmologist if it is a one-stop clinic. If preassessment is purely nurse-led, slit-lamp examination will highlight problems such as blepharitis, dry eyes and any variations in intraocular pressure from previous examinations. Findings should be documented and any necessary health education or treatment requirements can be instigated. The fundus should be assessed at some point before surgery because this may have implications for visual outcome. The patient needs to know of any changes in the retina (such as age-related macular degeneration) before surgery if at all possible, so that truly informed consent can be given for the surgery and expectations for the visual outcome after surgery are realistic.

Informed consent

The term 'informed consent' is an ethical one that underpins the legal requirement for healthcare professionals to obtain consent for any procedure performed on a patient. Their consent is valid only if you have explained properly. Clinicians are required to inform patients about the procedure to which they are being asked to agree, and to explain the risks, benefits and alternatives available to them. Failure to do this negates the validity of consent and leaves both the patient and healthcare professional in a vulnerable position.

Although it is best for the person carrying out the procedure to obtain consent, this is often delegated to others who have been trained to seek consent for that procedure, such as preassessment nurses. It is useful to confirm the 12 key principles of consent, as formulated by the Department of Health (2002) and listed in Table 10.2 below.

Table 10.2 Twelve key principles for informed consent: the law in England and Wales

When do health professionals need consent from patients?

1. Before you examine, treat or care for competent adult patients you must obtain their consent.

2. Adults are always assumed to be competent unless demonstrated otherwise. If you have doubts about their competence, the question to ask is: 'Can this patient understand and weigh up the information needed to make this decision?' Unexpected decisions do not prove the patient is incompetent, but may indicate a need for further information or explanation.

3. Patients may be competent to make some health-care decisions, even if they are not competent to make others.

4. Giving and obtaining consent is usually a process, not a one-off event. Patients can change their minds and withdraw consent at any time. If there is any doubt, you should always check that the patient still consents to your caring for or treating him or her.

Can children give consent for themselves?

5. Before examining, treating or caring for a child, you must also seek consent. Young people aged 16 and 17 are presumed to have the competence to give consent for themselves. Younger children who understand fully what is involved in the proposed procedure can also give consent (although their parents will ideally be involved). In other cases, someone with parental responsibility must give consent on the child's behalf, unless they cannot be reached in an emergency. If a competent child consents to treatment, a parent cannot over-ride that consent. Legally, a parent can consent if a competent child refuses, but it is likely that taking such a serious step will be rare.

Who is the right person to seek consent?

6. It is always best for the person actually treating the patient to seek the patient's consent. However, you may seek consent on behalf of colleagues if you are capable of performing the procedure in question, or if you have been specially trained to seek consent for that procedure.

What information should be provided?

7. Patients need sufficient information before they can decide whether to give their consent, e.g. information about the benefits and risks of the proposed treatment and alternative treatments. If the patients are not offered as much information as they reasonably need to make their decision, and in a form that they can understand, their consent may not be valid.

8. Consent must be given voluntarily, not under any form of duress or undue influence from health professionals, family or friends.

Does it matter how the patient gives consent?

9. No! Consent can be written, oral or non-verbal. A signature on a consent form does not itself prove that the consent is valid – the point of the form is to record the patient's decision, and also increasingly the discussions that have taken place. Your trust or organisation may have a policy setting out when you need to obtain written consent.

Refusal of treatment

10. Competent adult patients are entitled to refuse treatment, even when it would clearly benefit their health. The only exception to this rule is where the treatment is for a mental disorder and the patient is detained under the Mental Health Act 1983. A competent pregnant woman may refuse any treatment, even if this would be detrimental to the fetus.

Adults who are not competent to give consent

11. No one can give consent on behalf of an incompetent adult. However, you may still treat such a patient if the treatment would be in their best interests. 'Best interests' go wider than best medical interests, to include factors such as the wishes and beliefs of the patient when competent, their current wishes, their general wellbeing, and their spiritual and religious welfare. People close to the patient may be able to give you information on some of these factors. Where the patient has never been competent, relatives, carers and friends may be best placed to advise on the patient's needs and preferences.

12. If an incompetent patient has clearly indicated in the past, while competent, that he or she would refuse treatment in certain circumstances (an 'advance refusal'), and those circumstances arise, you must abide by that refusal.

It is important for all nurses to be aware of the principles of consent for the healthcare system in which they are working. The principle, on the whole, remains the same although the age of majority may be different and hospital requirements for written consent may be normal practice.

It is important to remember that consent is an ongoing process and it may be withdrawn at any time. It is advisable to check that consent is still current on the day of admission. It is incumbent on the person obtaining consent to ensure that the individual is competent to consent to treatment.

The educational and psychosocial needs of patients having day surgery

With the decreased contact time between patient and nurse, it is important that the psychological needs of patients are not overlooked (see also Chapter 6). There is a need to manage preoperative information, anxiety and postoperative recovery to a high standard, as the patient's journey through the system is so fast. Written and verbal information about the ophthalmic problem and treatment should be given to the patient and any concerns explored fully. Many patients require detailed information (Blandford *et al.* 2011), but information overload can also cause anxiety (Oldman *et al.* 2004). Visual presentations, such as the use of an eye model or video, increase interest and often aid retention of information. It is of paramount importance that nurses are well versed in the numerous types of surgery and are able to give the correct verbal and written information.

It is useful in practice to have a framework for health education and health promotion, such as that of Downie *et al.* (1996), to enhance patient knowledge and awareness of preventive measures. This model asserts that health education empowers individuals by providing information that helps them develop skills and self-esteem.

Pain, even if minimal, is a normal consequence of surgery and this may be a cause of worry for the patient. Pain and its management should be discussed at the preassessment visit so that the patient knows what level of pain to expect and that clinicians will help them to manage it.

One of the most important components of patient education in ophthalmology is the teaching of eye drop instillation. It is essential to assess the patient's ability to do this because postoperative drops are generally required for several weeks after surgery. If a patient cannot safely perform this or is confused, arrangements need to be made with a relative, carer or district nurse before admission. If practice with drops is required, ocular lubricants could be given, under an agreed patient group direction or other appropriate strategy.

Agree the date and time of admission and provide a contact number for patients and relatives, should they have any questions. Discharge planning should commence at preassessment and any transport or social care needs should be agreed at this time, along with arrangements for district nurse care if required. Follow your local policies in relation to this.

On the day of admission

Ideally patients should be given a time of admission that is staggered and convenient to them. This enables efficient use of the care team and a calm environment without overcrowding. However, for the convenience of the service and to reduce delay and optimise theatre time, patients for surgery in the morning may all be told to arrive at 07:30 and afternoon patients at 12:30 or 13:00. This causes a number of problems for patients and can increase anxiety levels, as some people will be waiting 3–4 hours before their surgery. It is recommended that patients should ideally spend no more than 90 minutes in the day stay unit but this is often not the case. Even in the most efficient service, it is important to respond to individual patients' needs, and this may be just too fast a throughput for some elderly patients.

Providing a welcoming environment with good facilities will help to reduce the stress on patients. On admission, patients should receive a warm welcome and have their details checked and baseline observations taken and documented, ideally by the nurse who pre-assessed them. Familiarisation with the environment is necessary to enhance safety, particularly if there is a significant degree of visual impairment.

Preparation for theatre should follow local policies. Patients having cataract extraction or retinal/vitreoretinal procedures will need dilating drops and the safety of patients following this procedure needs careful attention. For cataract patients it is vital that the correct keratometry and biometry readings are in the notes and are legible. If they are not, then they should be repeated prior to surgery.

Although cataract pathways are often robust, patients undergoing other types of surgery may not have attended a preassessment clinic and this must be taken into account so that they are given adequate information and support at this time.

Patients having a general anaesthetic for ophthalmic surgery must have the results of any tests or investigations available with their notes and a check on the last time food or drink was taken. Preoperative fasting remains a contentious issue, despite research and best practice evidence, and local policy should be followed.

The intraoperative period

Patients having local anaesthesia often feel vulnerable. To alleviate this, many settings adopt the use of therapeutic touch, which can be carried out by the nurse who is caring for the patient or a member of the theatre team. It also provides a communication link for the patient (see Chapter 11).

The postoperative period

The postoperative period after ophthalmic surgery is often very short before discharge; it is therefore important to observe patients carefully. On return to the ward or day case area after local anaesthesia, patients should be able to recover in a chair and be offered refreshments. Their blood pressure and pulse should be taken and documented. Patients who have had general anaesthesia need to recover safely in a bed. Analgesia and anti-emetics should be available if required.

Discharge

Good discharge of ophthalmic patients is imperative and should encompass the following:

- Provision of eye drops and any oral medications
- Full verbal and written instructions on the actions and any expected side effects of the medications
- What to expect during recovery (which symptoms are 'normal' and which are not, and what to do about abnormal symptoms)
- Pain and discomfort and how to manage it
- Written advice that is relevant and can be easily read and understood
- Advice about return to normal daily activities
- Contact number for any problems or advice
- Outpatient appointment.

Many departments operate a follow-up service by telephone to check on the patient's well-being. This might be felt to be an example of good practice, although the patients should give consent for the call and a convenient time should be arranged.

Arranging an outpatient appointment

Previously, patients were reviewed the morning following surgery by both the nurses for a 'first dressing' and then by the doctor for clinical review. In most departments this no longer happens and the negative aspect of this is that a valuable teaching point has been lost to nurses. The potential for reassurance on the first postoperative day is also lost at a time when many patients may feel anxious about their ability to look after themselves.

For patients who have had uncomplicated cataract surgery, many hospitals have a nurse-led discharge service that sees the patient once and then discharges them from hospital care. This may also be developed to locally trained optometrists. Patients who have undergone other surgical procedures are generally seen the following day, in either the day-stay unit or the clinic. It is important to ensure that patients/relatives know this and can attend. Follow-up appointments for other procedures should follow local policy.

Conclusion

Day case surgery in ophthalmology has been very successful in reducing the time patients wait for treatment. Innovative ophthalmic nurses who have created new roles in practice to enhance patient care and develop professional practice have driven a large part of that success. It is clear that, to be successful, day case surgery should be in the best interests of the patient as well as the service, and the needs of elderly and frail people must be paramount in this fast-paced setting.

References

Audit Commission (1990) *A Short Cut to Better Services: Day surgery in England and Wales.* Abingdon: Audit Commission Publications.

Audit Commission (1991) *Measuring Quality: The patient's view of day surgery. NHS Occasional paper 3.* London: HMSO.

Blandford, C., Gupta, B., Montgomery, J. & Stocker, M. (2011) Ability of patients to retain and recall new information in the post-anaesthetic recovery period: a prospective clinical study in day surgery. *Anaesthesia.* **66**(12), 1088–92.

Department of Health (1998) *A First Class Service – quality in the new NHS.* London: DH.

Department of Health (1999) *Making a Difference – strengthening the nursing, midwifery and health visiting contribution to health and healthcare.* London: DH.

Department of Health (2000) *The NHS Plan.* London: DH.

Department of Health (2002) *12 Key Principles of Informed Consent.* London: DH.

Department of Health and Social Security (1983) *NHS Management Inquiry.* (Griffiths report) London: DHSS.

Downie, R.S., Tannahill, C. & Tannahill, A. (1996) *Health Promotion Models and Values.* 2nd edition. Oxford: Oxford University Press.

Gregory, D. & Lowe, K. (1991) An enhanced role for the ophthalmic nurse. *Professional Nurse.* **1**, 43–50

Lala, H.A., French, J.L., Foxall, G.L., Hardmann, J.G. & Bedforth, N.M. (2010) Effect of preoperative multimedia information on perioperative anxiety in patients undergoing procedures under regional anaesthesia. *British Journal of Anaesthesia.* **104**(3), 369–74.

Law, M. (1997) A telephone survey of day-surgery eye patients. *Journal of Advanced Nursing.* **25**, 355–63.

Markanday, L. & Platzer, H. (1994) Brief encounters. *Nursing Times.* **90**(7), 38–42.

Mitchell, M. (2012) Anxiety management in minimal stay surgery. *Nursing Times.* **108**(48), 14–16.

NHS Executive (2000) *Action on Cataracts: Good practice guidance.* London: Department of Health.

NHS Institute for Innovation and Improvement (2008) *Focus on Cataracts.* London: DH.

NHS Management Executive (1991) *Day Surgery: Making it happen. Value for Money Unit.* London: HMSO.

Oldman, M., Moore, D. & Collins, S. (2004) Drug patient information leaflets in anaesthesia: effect on anxiety and patient satisfaction. *British Journal of Anaesthesia.* **92**(6), 854–58.

Smith, H. (1993) Day release cataracts. *Nursing Times.* **89**(39): 29–33.

Strong, J.P., Wigmore, W., Smithson, S., Rhodes, S., Woodruff, G. & Rosenthal, A.R. (1991) Day case cataract surgery. *British Journal of Ophthalmology.* **75**, 731–33.

CHAPTER ELEVEN

Ophthalmic theatre nursing

Heather Machin

Introduction

Patients undergoing ophthalmic surgery enter a highly technical and sophisticated environment where the outcome of their surgery can have a significant impact on the future quality of their vision. Nurses in the operating theatre (OT), also referred to as the operating room in some countries, are responsible for balancing the needs of the patient and surgeon with the organisation's objectives within their facility. They have to ensure that care is safe, ethical, efficient and economically viable, while also making sure that postoperative outcomes are optimised.

The ophthalmic OT is known to be one of the fastest-flowing OT settings within the healthcare environment. Some OT teams turn around the OT in under a few minutes in order to meet the political and economic pressure and the waitlist demands of this 'high-volume, high-quality' surgical sector (NHS Executive 2000).

The nurse's role in the OT extends beyond the evidenced role of scrub and scout nurse, also known as 'a Circulator' in some countries, to include patient care support areas (such as preoperative and postoperative care, anaesthetics and instrument care) and non-direct patient support areas (such as risk assessment, managing resources, surgical-assisting, quality, management and education). These roles are often intertwined with modern systems management technologies such as Electronic Medical Records (EMR) and e-Supply Change Management (SCM) systems, all of which extend beyond the usual, basic, perceived role of the OT nurse.

OT nurses also work as key members within the multidisciplinary team, both at senior management level and within each OT where they are responsible and active patient advocates and role models for safety. This has been encouraged in recent times through such developments as the WHO's Safe Site Surgery (SSS checklist) initiative. Additionally, the implementation of both local/national and hospital level competency programmes has become mainstream and these competencies are now widely accepted as positive markers for the provision of a uniform level of service and safety throughout the world.

OT nurses are also required to be aware of global recommendations and local implementation of disability inclusivity frameworks when planning and working within the OT. This is to ensure that care is allocated and provided without discrimination and takes into account the needs of patients with a variety of presenting issues, such as people who have hearing impairments, intellectual disability or use wheelchairs.

Objectives

This chapter will provide key, globally translatable recommendations. It supports practice for OT nurses working in multidisciplinary teams within a variety of settings, including a general hospital OT, stand-alone ambulatory facility (day surgery), minor procedural clinic and mobile health facility. Professional and technical aspects have also been integrated to reflect clinical practice. Additional consideration has been given to the contextual resource differences facing ophthalmic OT nurses around the world and emphasis has been placed on global commonality.

It has not been possible to address everything in detail, but references for further reading are given where possible to other websites and other chapters in this book. The focus is on day-to-day operations, which directly affect patients, colleagues and individual nurses as members of the multidisciplinary team. Further information on the organisation and management of the department, and the legal aspects of OT practice and OT design, can generally be found within each country's local nursing college guidelines or, where available, a perioperative OT nursing association, ophthalmic nurses' association or day surgery nursing association. Many of these professional bodies can provide peer and regulatory level standards, statements and practice guidelines.

An emphasis on team work will remain central to this chapter, as it is of fundamental importance in the OT. Team work will be intertwined with three core underpinning concepts:

1. Principles of patient care in the ophthalmic OT
2. Risk management issues in ophthalmic surgery
3. Specific nursing considerations of common surgical procedures.

Principles of patient care in the ophthalmic OT

The following points should be highlighted and remembered when caring for ophthalmic surgical patients:

- Patients may be visually impaired as a result of their underlying pathology
- The use of miotics or mydriatics, or surgery on the eye, will further disrupt their vision
- The patient may be anxious about the forthcoming surgical procedure

- Patients may be unable to read any documents (e.g. consent forms) you give them
- The patient's physical environment may need to be checked to prevent falls and injury (e.g. removing tripping hazards)
- Patients with otherwise functioning vision (e.g. patients who are undergoing oculoplastic surgery) may find temporary loss of vision (e.g. from postoperative dressings) difficult to manage.

Planning care in the ophthalmic OT

Planning starts when a patient is scheduled for surgery on an operating list. Sometimes this is a regular list and at other times it is an emergency list. Each facility needs to have in place a routine scheduling system that works for that particular OT facility. This will ensure that the OT can gather as much information about the patient as possible within the available timeframe. Without this information, the surgeon and facility run the risk of being unable to provide the patient with the best care option. Having good-quality patient information will also help prevent delay or cancellation (e.g. due to missing instruments, incorrect consumables or poor preoperative patient education).

The information the OT will need to gather includes:

- Patient's personal details, including key patient identifiers and contact details
- Patient's medical, surgical and social history
- Type of surgery planned
- Type of anaesthetic planned
- Name of anaesthetist if required
- Original or copy of signed informed consent
- List of any prosthetic (implantable devices) needed for the surgery, e.g. intraocular lens, corneal tissue or orbital implant
- List of any other special requirements that the surgeon needs the nurse to know about, e.g. if the surgeon requires a new instrument or if the surgeon will be performing a new pioneering procedure. These points need to be flagged and followed up.

If a procedure is required that the facility has never performed before, the OT nurse has to inform their nurse manager and liaise with the surgeon to ensure this can be prepared for. In some instances (though this may be country-specific), the surgeon and/or the facility may need to check their service licence to ensure they are legally permitted to perform the procedure. This may be the case for research, use of an unauthorised medical device (or even a device that is available but not authorised for use on humans in that country), or even a 'pioneering' new surgical technique. By checking these details early, such issues can be prevented and the facility and surgeon can proceed with their preparations, or work together to find alternative medical devices, apply for a licence change or undergo any other process needed to ensure that surgery is not denied without investigation. It is important that every opportunity is taken to provide the patient with the best and most advanced care option that is legally and practically possible before resorting to cancelling the proposed procedure.

Preparation systems need to be put in place to schedule surgeon start times, patient arrivals and fasting times, checking next of kin details and ensuring postoperative appointments have also been arranged. While arrival and start times need to be planned to reduce gaps in the OT turnaround-times, the planning does need to take into account the patient who may be anxious and often fasting. Care must also be taken to ensure their wait is not prolonged unnecessarily for the convenience of the facility. For this reason, many facilities stagger the arrival time for patients on the same list.

Coordination between the OT and other areas of the ophthalmic setting is vital to achieve a smooth patient journey by ensuring surgical list efficiency, patient preparedness, and best-possible care outcomes by avoiding error, delay and cancellation.

Preoperative assessment and patient interaction

Preoperative assessment aims to identify and minimise risk – as well as providing patient education – to ensure that the patient presents for surgery as fully prepared and fit as possible (Southampton University 2002). Generally, facilities will accept and provide anaesthetic support to patients who fall within a certain category. The category is determined by the licence perimeters of the facility in conjunction with an anaesthetic rating scale called an ASA rating. This rating has been developed by the American Society of Anaesthesiologists (ASA). Depending on licensing, stand-alone day-stay facilities will generally accept ASA I and II patients, while those attached to (or in proximity to) support services such as an intensive care unit (ICU) may accept III and above. The ASA classification, as defined by the American Society of Anaesthesiologists (ASA 2014), is outlined in Table 11.1 (below).

The UK's Royal College of Ophthalmologists and Royal College of Anaesthetists (RCOph/RCA 2001, p. 10) also emphasise that: 'Pre-operative assessment is essential to imbue a sense of confidence in the patient and minimise unexpected problems and late cancellation of the procedure.' It is therefore essential to assess the patient's anxiety level in relation to suitability for local anaesthesia. The assessment process provides the opportunity for information sharing, ensuring that the patient understands not only the surgical procedure and intended outcome, but also what is required from them during the local anaesthesia procedure. This should include a realistic explanation of what this experience is like. It is an essential step in gaining informed consent and managing risk.

Table 11.1 ASA anaesthetic rating scale

ASA PS Classification	Definition	Examples, including but not limited to:
ASA I	A normal healthy patient	Healthy, non-smoking, no or minimal alcohol use
ASA II	A patient with mild systemic disease	Mild diseases only without substantive functional limitations. Examples include (but not limited to): current smoker, social alcohol drinker, pregnancy, obesity (30 < BM < 40), well controlled DM/HTN, mild lung disease.
ASA III	A patient with severe systemic disease	Substantive functional limitations; one or more moderate to severe diseases. Examples include (but not limited to): poorly controlled DM or HTN, COPD, morbid obesity (BMI ≥ 40), active hepatitis, alcohol dependence or abuse, implanted pacemaker, moderate reduction of ejection fraction, ESRD undergoing regularly scheduled dialysis, premature infant PCA < 60 weeks, history (> 3 months) of MI, CVA, TIA, or CAD/stents.
ASA IV	A patient with severe systemic disease that is a constant threat to life	Examples include (but not limited to): recent (< 3 months) MI, CVA, TIA, or CAD/stents, ongoing cardiac ischemia or severe valve dysfunction, severe reduction of ejection fraction, sepsis, DIC, ARD or ESRD not undergoing regularly scheduled dialysis.
ASA V	A moribund patient who is not expected to survive without the operation	Examples include (but not limited to): ruptured abdominal/thoracic aneurysm, massive trauma, intracranial bleed with mass effect, ischemic bowel in the face of significant cardiac pathology or multiple organ/system dysfunction.
ASA VI	A declared brain-dead patient whose organs are being removed for donor purposes	

Note: The addition of 'E' denotes emergency surgery. (An emergency is defined as existing when delay in treatment of the patient would lead to a significant increase in the threat to life or body part.)

Managing patient anxiety

Ophthalmic surgical patients are often highly anxious (Katzen 2002), not only because they are undergoing a surgical procedure but also because the success of the surgery may be directly linked to their visual prognosis. It is essential that the OT nurse makes an individual assessment of each patient's level of anxiety on their arrival at the department and plans care in accordance with the facility's surgical care pathway. Additionally, as ophthalmic patients are often visually impaired, special care needs to be taken with regard to mobility and communication within the department.

Dobson (1991) suggests that care should be taken with communication. Staff should introduce themselves and others, announce when entering or leaving the room, before touching, and to explain noise. They should also try not to leave the patient on their own, and allow extra time to help transfer the patient from one waiting area to another. Staff also need to be familiar with the techniques of guiding a person with vision impairment (i.e. assisted walking/transfer), as their cues and physical prompts are different.

Anxiety during the perioperative phase can, where appropriate and appreciated, be reduced with the use of therapeutic touch, hand-holding and music (Dobson 1991, Allen *et al.* 2001, Moon & Cho 2001, Katzen 2002). As each patient is different, it is important to find out what works best for them.

Additional preoperative information

Depending on the type of procedure, and the medical status of the patient, vision test results (e.g. visual acuity measurements, biometry and perimetry) and medical test results (e.g. International Normalised Ratio (INR) test or people with blood clotting conditions) also need to be accessible and ready for revision prior to commencement of treatment (unless such tests are brought to the facility by the surgeon on the day) and followed up accordingly.

Safety First – Safe Site Surgery

Safe Site Surgery (SSS) influences all phases of care – for all members of the multidisciplinary team.

All over the world, SSS is considered to be routine best practice for the prevention of medical error (injury or death). It is also considered fundamental to reducing the economic burden associated with rectifying or compensating for medical errors. The World Health Organization (WHO) therefore recommends that a SSS check system be utilised whenever a procedure is conducted (WHO – *Guidelines for Safe Site Surgery* 2009).

The OT SSS check system requires a *whole team*-approach, with all members working together, listening to each other and focusing on the patient and the needs at hand. Additionally, a check needs to take place at each phase of the patient's care in order to prevent issues from arising immediately and within the next phase. The phases and SSS action items have been segmented, and colloquially intertwined with the baseball metaphor – *Time Out*. 'Time Out', in the OT context, means *stop what you are doing, examine what is happening and put in place a plan to ensure the best possible care is provided.*

Table 11.2 (below) is an SSS check sheet, amended specifically for cataract, from the WHO checklist.

Table 11.2 Checklist from WHO Safe Site Surgery Checklist, amended for cataract surgery

SIGN IN (to be read out loud)

Before giving anaesthetic
Has the patient confirmed his/her identity, site, procedure and consent? ☐ Yes
Is the surgical site marked? ☐ Yes
Is the designated lens available plus a suitable alternative? ☐ Yes
Is the anaesthesia machine and medication check complete? ☐ Yes ☐ Yes ☐ Yes ☐ Not applicable
Does the patient have a: Known allergy? ☐ No ☐ Yes Difficult airway/aspiration risk? (General Anaesthetic) ☐ No ☐ Yes, and equipment/assistance available Any special requirements for positioning or draping? ☐ No ☐ Yes, surgeon notified Is the patient taking warfarin? ☐ No ☐ Yes, last INR result available Is the patient taking tamsulosin or other alpha blocker? ☐ No ☐ Yes, surgeon notified
Has pre-operative VTE risk assessment been undertaken? ☐ Yes ☐ Not applicable

cont.

The checklist is for Cataract Surgery ONLY

This modified checklist must not be used for other surgical procedures.

TIME OUT (to be read out loud)

Before start of cataract surgery
Have all team members introduced themselves by name and role? ☐ Yes
Surgeon, Scrub Nurse and Registered Practitioner verbally confirm: ☐ What is the patient's name? ☐ What procedure, and which eye? ☐ What refractive outcome is planned? ☐ What lens model and power is to be used? ☐ Is the correct lens implant present?
Anticipated variations and critical events **Surgeon:** ☐ Are there any special equipment requirements or special investigations? ☐ Are any variations to the standard procedure planned or likely? ☐ Is an alternative lens implant available, if needed? **Anaesthetist (GA or sedation):** Are there any patient-specific concerns? ☐ What is the patient's ASA grade? ☐ Any special monitoring requirements? **Scrub Nurse/ODP:** ☐ Has the sterility of the instrumentation been confirmed (including indicator results)? ☐ Are there are equipment issues or concerns?

SIGN OUT (to be read out loud)

Before any member of the team leaves the operating room
Registered Practitioner verbally confirms with the team: ☐ Has the name and side of the procedure been recorded? ☐ Has it been confirmed that instruments, swabs and sharps counts are complete (or not applicable)? ☐ Have any equipment problems been identified that need to be addressed? ☐ Are any variations to standard recovery and discharge protocol planned for this patient?

cont.

PATIENT DETAILS	
Last name:	
First name:	
Date of birth:	
NHS Number*:	
Procedure:	

*If the NHS Number is not immediately available, a temporary number should be used until it is

The phases of SSS are listed below.

Preoperative – Sign In

- Conducted in the preoperative area by the preoperative nurse, and in the peranaesthetic phase by either the anaesthetist or the anaesthetic nurse/assistant.

Pre-Surgery – Time Out

- Conducted inside the OT in the presence of the entire OT team – including any visitors and students. For this to occur, the surgeon, surgical assistant, anaesthetist, anaesthetic nurse, scrub and scout nurse must all be present in the OT.
- The check is completed when the patient is on the bed (surgical trolley/gurney) prior to administration of general anaesthetic agents (if scheduled) and any prepping and draping.
- The OT team members stop what they are doing, introduce themselves, and together (with one person checking the notes, and another person checking the patient), verbally cross-reference and confirm all patient identifiers.
  This includes cross-reference of the consent, proposed surgical site, instruments and equipment, and any other potential risks or issues that are expected.
  On completion, the checklist is signed by one member of the team, on behalf of the whole team. Thereafter, anaesthetic and prepping and draping processes may commence.

Note: Exceptions can be made for paediatric surgeries, whereby the patient can be anaesthetised – but not prepped – prior to the moment of Time-Out. While this is not globally practised, for those who *do* use this method, their premise is that this prevents an escalation of anxiety for the child who would otherwise be waiting for Time-Out to be completed. Nurses are encouraged to be aware of their own facility's policy on this and/or seek direction from local anaesthesia councils in consultation with their anaesthesia medical director.

Post-Surgery – Sign-Out

This is carried out by the OT scrub and scout nurse, who conduct this prior to the surgeon closing the wound. The surgeon must be informed of any discrepancies noted before wound closure. Any issues raised during the surgery (e.g. broken equipment) must be followed up and documented.

The phases of care

In this section we will explore preadmission, preoperative, intraoperative and postoperative aspects of care.

Preadmission

Once a patient has been confirmed for surgery, the OT team is responsible for preparation – unless this has already been carried out by a separate preassessment clinic.

This includes checking, at least 2–3 days beforehand, that the OT has all the items they need (i.e. any special items have been ordered in) and that the surgical list has been set and cross-matched with the Standing Orders (SO) or surgeon's preference sheet. A SO is a medical order (prescription, if you will), signed by the treating surgeon and/or anaesthetist, that provides the nurse with instruction on how to prepare and care for a patient. This SO (or preference sheet) should be in place in the facility so that every patient is prepared for a particular surgeon's surgery requirements.

Depending on the setting, a pre-administrative phone call may take place. In many countries, this is performed by nurses who specialise in care of the preoperative or postoperative surgical patient. In order to make this phone call, they must already know:

- Time and date of surgery
- Name of the surgeon
- Type of operation planned and anaesthetic type (cross-matched against the patient record)
- Name of the anaesthetist (if required) and their fasting and preoperative SO.

During this phone call, the nurse will check the patient's medical, surgical and social history, specifically making sure that the patient is safe for surgery within their facility (see ASA ratings, p. 207). In addition, they are screened again (a second time after their preassessment visit) for surgical and infection risk.

Once the patient has been cleared for surgery, the nurse will inform the patient about:

- Fasting times and any other preoperative requirements
- How to personally prepare – i.e. shower and wash hair
- Arrival time – including location, parking and contact details
- What to expect in general (e.g. how long they will be at the facility)
- What to do after the surgery.

Lastly, if working within an ambulatory or mobile facility, the nurse must ask for the next-of-kin (NOK) details to ensure that there is someone (who is physically healthy and of sound mind) to collect them after surgery and stay with them overnight, depending on the requirements of the particular facility.

On admission

Once the patient has been admitted administratively, the preoperative nurse may invite the patient into the preoperative preparation/waiting area. Within this area, and depending on the facility's policy, the nurse will:

- Check patient identifiers: This can be done by checking the patient's wristband (or similar identification system) against their corresponding consent and personal details form. They can ask the patient (or NOK) to verbally confirm these details. If there is a discrepancy, the nurse must halt proceedings until the issue has been resolved. Often it is just a simple administrative typing error that can be easily rectified. Patient identifiers include (but are not limited to):
  - Name
  - Date of birth (or age, if DOB not known)
  - Name of surgeon
  - Type of surgery planned and which site (i.e. left or right eye)
  - Hospital admission number
  - Patient phone number and home address
  - Confirming surgery via cross-match of the consent to the patient.
- Double-check medical, surgical and social history including allergy status.
- Document routine baseline observations – heart rate, oxygen saturation, blood pressure.
  - Depending on their age, medical status and/or type of surgery – their temperature and blood sugar level may also need to be reviewed.

- Confirm and follow-up on any other medical items, e.g. INR results for individuals with blood clotting conditions.
- Prepare the site/eye as required by the surgeon (i.e. commence the preoperative eye drop regime).
- Dress the patient as required (e.g. surgical gown, hat and feet) as per hospital policy, and ensure valuable items (such as mobile phones and jewellery) have been removed and safely stored. *Note: Practice varies with regard to completely dressing and/or just placing a gown over a patient's day clothes. It depends on local evidence and if the surgery is scheduled for the day-stay facility or the general theatre facility. Nurses are encouraged to check their local policy.*
- Review for issues: This includes assessing for rashes, open wounds, changes in health status since the preoperative phone call (e.g. flu), and concerns (discrepancies) that require the surgeon and/or anaesthetist to review, such as a blood sugar level or blood pressure outside the expected range.
- Administer any other pre-medication ordered by the anaesthetist.
- Complete pre-surgical site wash if required (e.g. some surgeons and facilities require the eye and/or surrounding skin of the surgical site to be pre-washed with povidone iodine).
- The surgical site is marked. Generally, this is done by the treating surgeon. However, in some countries this is done by the preoperative nurse or a surgical assistant, who will be involved in the actual surgery. The mark needs to be made with an indelible pen in a colour that contrasts with the colour of the patient's skin, for visibility.
- Complete the preoperative section of the SSS check, including confirming that the OT is ready with any prosthetic items that may be needed.
- Ensure the patient has had the opportunity to go to the bathroom.

Once the patient has been prepared and any issues have been addressed, the patient can be transferred to the anaesthetic area.

Anaesthetic care

Anaesthesia for ophthalmic surgery has become an increasingly complex topic, due to a wide range of influences, including changes in surgical techniques, new drugs, individual patient needs and expectations, and surgical requirements (i.e. duration).

As most ophthalmic procedures are still carried out under local anaesthesia, general anaesthesia will not be covered in this chapter. This also means that care of the paediatric patient in the OT will be excluded from discussion of anaesthesia in this chapter.

Any facility administering anaesthetics must ensure they have in place a medical emergency preparedness plan, including access to call (help) systems, and an emergency (crash) trolley with frontline drugs, and advanced cardiac emergency items. Additional emergency facility transfer plans, equipment maintenance programmes and a competency programme for staff are all essential to ensure staff preparedness for anaesthetic-related medical emergencies.

Table 11.3 (below) shows the specific medical conditions highlighted by the Royal College of Ophthalmologists and the Royal College of Anaesthetists (2001) for consideration with patients undergoing local anaesthetic ophthalmic surgery and the potential problems and actions required to manage these and other medical contraindications. This is not an exhaustive list but it does provide a starting point for investigation and awareness.

Table 11.3 Potential risks associated with local anaesthetic ophthalmic surgery on patients with specific systemic medical conditions and suggestions for managing these risks

Medical condition	Potential risk and management plan
Hypertension	**Risk of expulsive haemorrhage in intraocular surgery:** Uncontrolled hypertension should be referred to the GP for management before admission. Check BP before sending for the patient. Ensure patient has taken any antihypertensive medication as normal. Ensure supply of necessary equipment is available in the event of an incident and that the scrub nurse is aware of action to take.
Myocardial ischaemia	**Risk of angina attack during procedure:** Induced by stress and anxiety. Patient should not have surgery within 3 months of a myocardial infarction. Patients should bring any glyceryl trinitrate (GTN) spray to theatre with them. Monitor with ECG and pulse oximetry. Intravenous access available. Ensure that all staff have attended regular Basic Life Support (BLS) training. Anaesthetic cover available if required. Nurses should be aware of the controversy surrounding the use of phenylephrine 10% to dilate the pupil in this group of patients and follow local guidelines.
Diabetes mellitus	**Risk of hypoglycaemic attack during the procedure:** Monitor blood sugar level immediately before procedure, whether local or general anaesthetic. For patients undergoing local anaesthetic, their usual regimen is maintained. Hypostop® gel may be administered if required according to local patient group directives (PGDs).
Anticoagulation therapy	**Risk of bleeding:** Ensure recent international normalised ratio (INR) level is within therapeutic range before sending for the patient; this is particularly relevant to orbital lid surgery.
Chronic obstructive pulmonary disease	**Inability to tolerate lying flat and surgical draping covering the face:** Check if the patient has practised lying flat before coming to theatre and evaluate findings. Careful positioning of the patient to support breathing and comfort. Ensure adequate O_2 supply under the drape. Monitor with pulse oximeter. Arrange for patient to bring usual inhaler to theatre.

Anaesthetic types

Options for local anaesthesia include topical, sub-tenon, peribulbar and retrobulbar anaesthetic (all blocks), with sedation as an adjunct.

In many countries, the provision of an intravenous cannula (IVC) – regardless of the use of sedation – is mandatory for all patients entering the OT (other than those receiving topical anaesthetic). The rationale for this mandatory requirement is to ensure venous access in case of potential (life-threatening) emergencies. Every facility should therefore be encouraged to review their policy on the requirement of IVC and should do so in consultation with their country's College of Anaesthetists.

For surgery under local anaesthesia, the patient's involvement in their own care is essential. This is facilitated by explaining to the patient what is about to happen. Ongoing evaluation of how the patient is coping is also important and the care plan may need to be altered in response to changes in patient reactions.

Although a thorough explanation should have been given to the patient before their arrival in the department, it is beneficial to reiterate the essential points at each stage of care to ensure comprehension and compliance.

Initially, an explanation about attachment of any monitoring equipment, and its benefits for safety, is recommended. This should be followed by an explanation about the administration of the anaesthetic. The anaesthetic should be administered in a quiet, private space/room, with good lighting, and with minimal staff present – i.e. an anaesthetist/surgeon and an anaesthetic nurse/operating department practitioner (ODP).

Standards for monitoring have been specified by the Royal College of Ophthalmologists and the Royal College of Anaesthetists (2001) and are as follows:

- A dedicated and trained member of staff to take responsibility for remaining in contact with the patient and reporting any adverse events
- Clinical observation to be carried out, including patient's colour, response to surgical stimuli, respiratory movements and palpation of the pulse
- Pulse oximetry to detect cardiac and respiratory problems promptly
- Intravenous access is essential if peribulbar or retrobulbar techniques are used or if sedation is used.

This monitoring should start before the administration of the anaesthesia and continue until the surgical procedure has ended. Depending on the patient's medical condition, additional monitoring may be required, such as electrocardiogram (ECG or EKG) or blood pressure measurements and monitoring, which should be continued once the anaesthetic has been given. This is especially important when giving blocks and/or sedation to prevent risk of contraindication. This should be indicated in local guidelines.

Table 11.4 Specific nursing considerations with each type of ophthalmic local anaesthesia

Type of local anaesthesia	Nursing implications
Topical – instillation of local anaesthetic drops	Patient's eye will be fully mobile so it is vital that the patient is given a full explanation of the need to keep both eyes open and remain still.
Sub-tenon – anaesthetic placed in potential space between globe and tenon's fascia surrounding the globe using a blunt cannula	Spring scissors are needed to create an opening in conjunctiva and tenon's; local anaesthetic drops are required before start. Provides good anaesthesia and akinesia. This may be a nurse-led procedure. As a sub-tenon's block is considered a 'surgical technique', it is essential that this is completed under sterile conditions.
Retrobulbar – a small amount of anaesthetic is introduced behind the globe in the intraconal space	Topical anaesthesia may be used before administration of retrobulbar. The patient may experience discomfort because of pressure during administration. The risk of haemorrhage, perforation of globe and brain-stem anaesthesia is increased because a long, sharp needle is used. Close monitoring during and after administration is essential (Foss 2001). A Honan's balloon (eye weight) may be used to facilitate diffusion of the anaesthetic agent. This procedure is surgeon or anaesthetist led.
Peribulbar – similar to retrobulbar but uses a shorter needle, placing anaesthetic more anteriorly and using more volume	Topical anaesthesia may be used before administration of peribulbar. A Honan's balloon may be used. A small time gap between administration and start of surgery is recommended by Foss (2001). Same risks as retrobulbar so close monitoring is also recommended. This procedure is surgeon or anaesthetist led

Intravenous sedation may be used during local anaesthetic ophthalmic surgery, and administered via an IVC. The guidelines of the Royal College of Ophthalmologists and the Royal College of Anaesthetists (2001, p. 17) say that sedation 'should only be used to allay anxiety and not to cover for inadequate blocks'. This guideline suggests the use of 'conscious sedation', which minimises the chances of a sleeping patient suddenly waking during surgery and being startled, disoriented and perhaps starting to move (Nordlund *et al.* 2003). Once a patient has been administered a sedative, it is important that a member of the clinical team remain within the area to assist and monitor the patient as needed.

Prior to any administration of anaesthetics, a full patient check needs to take place, including patient identifiers and confirmation of route of administration and allergies. This then needs to be cross-checked on the pre-anaesthetic (Sign-In) section of the SSS Checklist.

OT care

The patient may only be transferred to the OT when the scrub nurse and anaesthetist confirm that the team is ready to accept the patient. This means that the team has cleaned up after the previous patient and has commenced preparation for the next.

Before surgery – getting ready

The anaesthetic and support team transfer the patient to the OT. They explain what is going to happen and position the patient comfortably. They place all monitoring devices on the patient, and ensure that their head is stable. They also position the patient to allow for optimal surgical site access by the surgeon.

To improve airflow under the drape and prevent claustrophobia, a device may be attached to the bed, or placed on the patient's chest, to help elevate the drape away from the patient's face. This makes a small tent-like area – allowing fresh air to circulate under the drape. An adequate oxygen supply can additionally be maintained by administrating 35% oxygen via the Venturi system under the drape and the partial oxygen pressure (pO_2) levels can be monitored by the pulse oximeter. Once the patient is settled, the OT team is required to complete the *Time Out* section of the SSS Checklist. Thereafter, the team may commence surgical site preparation (and/or the general anaesthetic induction).

Any IVC +/− fluid lines also need to be readily accessible to the anaesthetic team prior to draping so that the anaesthetist can administer additional medications as required during the procedure.

Note: For further reading regarding oximetry, please refer to the WHO Pulse Oximetry Patient Safety Project http://www.who.int/patientsafety/safesurgery/pulse_oximetry/en/

The prepping process should not be rushed because it contributes to the successful outcome of the surgery. Most ophthalmic procedures require the patient to be supine with a pillow placed underneath the knees for comfort and to alleviate back strain. Patients should be warned of any sensation that they may experience (Cooper 1999), e.g. fluid trickling down the side of their face during the procedure or the sensation of the surgeon's wrist resting on their forehead or cheek. Research has shown that most patients will experience some visual stimulation, e.g. bright white light or a kaleidoscope of colours (Murdock and Sze 1994), and the patient may continue to have sensation in the eye (Duguid *et al.* 1995, Newsom *et al.* 2001) during the operation.

The patient should be instructed not to speak or move their head during an intraocular procedure, as this will affect the surgeon's ability to perform the surgery. They should be told how to communicate if assistance is required (Reeves 1993). For example, they should be encouraged to speak if they are in pain so that more anaesthetic can be administered. Other alarm mechanisms need to be implemented so the patient knows how to communicate when they need to cough or urinate. It is essential that the 'alarm' mechanism be fully understood by the patient to prevent complications and help the patient feel more in control of the environment (Nordlund *et al.* 2003). Many facilities use a 'hand holder', a volunteer or healthcare practitioner who can hold the patient's hand to reassure them and be a communication conduit during the procedure.

Prepping

Before commencing, the patient positioning needs to be checked. It is also important to check the surgeon's preferences regarding taping closed the non-operative eye with a gentle surgical adhesive tape, securing of the patient's head to prevent movement, placement of equipment and any other surgeon-specific need.

As with any surgical procedure, surgical site prepping requires cleaning from dirty to clean areas in an outward motion with an appropriate antimicrobial agent. Should the surgeon also require the surface of the eye also be prepped (for intraocular procedures), local anaesthetic drops, such as oxybuprocaine hydrochloride 0.4%, may be administered prior to prepping. This is to prevent the antimicrobial agent from causing the surface of the eye to sting.

Additionally, if a patient has an allergy to an antimicrobial agent, e.g. iodine, then the nurse must inform the surgeon and collectively select an alternative solution. Alternatives, such as aqueous chlorhexidine, may be selected; however, if using this, it is imperative that it does not go onto the surface of the eye – and remains only on the lids and surrounding skin. This is because it can dry out the cornea and cause slight opacification. Alternative prepping agents need to be double-checked with the surgeon before use.

The scrub nurse (or surgeon in some facilities) will then prep the surgical area. Prepping over airways (for general anaesthetic) and/or including prepping of non-ocular graft-sites must also be considered. Drapes that provide appropriate cover and access are recommended.

While most countries strive to use single-use disposable drapes, re-usable drapes are still used in several developing and emerging economy nations. In these instances, the scrub nurse must check the integrity of the drape and also ensure that any towel (drape) clips are placed appropriately without harming the patient. The permeability of the drape also needs to be considered for sterility and patient comfort.

Once prepped, the surgical team may move their sterile trolleys and equipment around the patient – in accordance with standard universal aseptic practices.

During the surgery

OT teams routinely play music and converse. Non-scrubbed staff also move around and, both inside and outside the OT. While these are all acceptable, the team needs to be mindful and considerate of the patient and other staff members at all times. Music needs to be appropriate and at an acceptable volume for the workplace. Conversation and language need to be professional and respectful (and exclude confidential matters), and mobile phones need to be turned off (or on silent). Additionally, excessive movement in and out of the OT (or within it) may affect the room's airflow system. Therefore, unless staff need to move around, they are encouraged to stand or sit still.

Volume is important. If noise is too loud, the team cannot communicate or hear alarm tones, or worse still, cannot hear the patient. This can have serious implications for the team and the patient (Phillips 1991, Foss 2001). The patient needs to be able to identify the surgeon's voice in order to follow instructions and notify the surgeon of issues. Noise therefore needs to be kept to a minimum. Whispering should also be avoided, because it may be a distraction for both patient and surgeon. A normal tone of voice is preferable and should be limited to passing on relevant information.

End of the surgery

Prior to closure of the wound, the scrub and scout nurse need to complete the *Sign-Out* section of the SSS Checklist and report any discrepancies. If there are no issues, the surgeon is informed, the wound closed and surgery completed. The patient's drapes are then removed (without contamination or spillage of waste matter), and the surgical site gently washed and dressed (or ointment applied) as per the surgeon's request.

Anaesthetic monitoring devices are then removed (though the IVC must remain in situ) and the patient is transferred to recovery. It is the responsibility of the OT team member who is transferring the patient to provide the recovery team with a full patient–surgical handover including any particular postoperative instructions that may differ from the routine SO or expected care pathway.

All documentation is to be completed (electronically or on paper) prior to the patient exiting the OT.

Positioning and restraint

The operating table needs to be very stable, because slight movements are magnified during microsurgery. Care should be taken not to lean against the table, the surgeon's chair or the microscope. The correct position for most ocular surgery is absolutely horizontal, i.e. the chin and forehead must be at the same level or height because fluid will pool if the head is tilted (Foss 2001). The exception is during some adnexal procedures, when head tilt or reverse Trendelenburg is required to aid haemostasis. Minor adjustments can be made using Gamgee padding or pillows to ensure patient comfort for the duration of the procedure. Heel support or other equipment may be required to prevent venous stasis in the lower limbs. Access underneath the drape also needs to be considered during positioning for general anaesthetic (to prevent dislodgement of an airway device).

A number of different headrests are available, with a variety of different features to aid positioning and surgical access, e.g. Rubens and Halliday. The operating table may have a head clamp (rest) attachment against which the patient can rest their head to help keep them still.

Lastly, while staff must work to ensure the patient is stable and secure, care must be taken to ensure the patient's human rights are not violated by excessive restraint.

Surgeons may often ask for the patient's head to be taped to the bedhead and this is now routine practice in many parts of the world. In this instance, it is important to inform the patient that this will occur so they can prepare for it. Such 'taping' and 'strapping' becomes an issue when hands or limbs are tied down to prevent movement. This may previously have been the practice in some countries, but it is no longer acceptable in most parts of the world. Instead, staff are encouraged to hold the patient's hand in a comforting manner (under the drapes), talk to the patient and ask them to remain still. If this does not help keep the patient still, it indicates that the patient requires more sedation or pain relief to ease their discomfort and distress, and prevent movement.

Postoperative care

Once the patient has been transferred to recovery and the OT team have provided the handover, the recovery team takes on responsibility for the patient. They assess the patient's stability by checking their vital signs within the expected parameters. During this period, the nurse checks the surgical site and dressing, and reports to the surgeon (and/or anaesthetist) on any issues, such as excessive bleeding or pain, that are outside the expected range for the specific type of surgery. The nurse ensures that any postoperative orders prescribed by the surgeon/anaesthetist are followed up.

For general anaesthetic patients, the nurse may be required to stay one-on-one with the patient for an extended period of time or, at least, until their airways are clear and the patient is alert. For local anaesthetic patients, one nurse may be responsible for several patients at a time. Regardless of the type of anaesthetic, the nurse must be prepared to administer emergency support to individual patients in their particular stage of recovery.

Many ambulatory facilities will also provide light refreshments for the patient once their airways are clear and they are sitting up and alert. The nurse needs to be aware of the particular facility's policy on this, and ensure that food is provided at the appropriate phase of recovery.

Discharge from the facility

In large facilities, patient discharge may take place in a separate area, such as a day surgery ward, but often the OT team manage the whole pathway.

Once the patient has met the facility's discharge criteria, the IVC can be removed, the patient can get dressed in their day clothes and all personal belongings should be returned. The patient is then given full discharge education, in the presence of their NOK or carer/supporter, as long as the patient happy with this. The nurse can then sign out the patient and, depending on the country, the NOK may also sign to confirm that they have received all the information.

Discharge education (instructions) can include, but are not necessarily limited to:

- What to do for the first 24 hours
- What to do for the first few weeks
- When the surgeon wants to see them again
- When to take any medications and/or how to use eye drops and ointment
- What to do with any dressings
- When to and how to wash their face and hair without contaminating their surgical site
- What to do if they have any pain, excess bleeding or other emergency issues
- Any other special requirements – e.g. head positioning for post-retinal patients discharged with silicone oil or a gas bubble inside their eye.

The patient should be provided with:

- Instructions in writing – in a typeface and size they can read, and in a language they understand
- Information on what to expect postoperatively, i.e. what level of pain to expect, bleeding, how long they may have bruising for and/or any gritty feeling and sensations they may experience
- Their surgeon's contact details
- Emergency contact details
- Any prescriptions and/or eye drops or ointment provided by the facility; the dispensing of medications by the OT is country and policy specific
- Any dressing materials, or where to obtain them, should the surgeon wish them to be reapplied
- Sunglasses may be provided for patients or they may have been asked to bring their own.

Risk management and environmental issues in ophthalmic surgery

OT design

Ventilation

Airflow in the ophthalmic OT should be designed to the same high specification as in any other OT (Clarke & Jones 1998). Air pressure inside the OT needs to be higher than outside, so that air flows in one direction, away from the OT. This requires air exchanges to occur at least 20–30 times per hour. The system is regulated through a high-efficiency particulate arresting (HEPA) filter system.

At the beginning of each session, the nurse must ensure that this system is working. Adequate checks should be carried out regularly to ensure that the air conditioning system has not been contaminated, e.g. monitoring for contamination and changing filters.

The temperature in the OT and surrounding rooms (such as the sterile store/stock rooms) needs to be constant to prevent the growth of micro-organisms in the air and, especially in hot and humid countries, prevent the build-up of mould. Once mould has set in, it is difficult to remove and can severely damage the structure of the building and equipment (e.g. the inside of the microscope). The OT air-conditioning system therefore needs to be kept on continuously and should be included in routine maintenance checks.

OT patient flow – area design

The OT needs to be designed in such a way that the space is used economically. This means that all the space is utilised and that time is not lost while waiting for patients, staff and equipment to move between rooms. For example, anaesthetic bays need to be adjacent to their corresponding OT so the patient can be prepared and taken directly in within a few seconds. Any OT set-up rooms also need to be readily accessible to the OT and be part of the OT airflow system.

The placement of the sterilisation room needs to be considered to prevent OT staff trailing contaminated (used) instruments and waste a long distance. A dirty corridor may also be incorporated into the design. If this is not possible, alternative closed-in transfer systems are required to prevent cross-contamination. The sterilisation rooms should also be designed to facilitate the ergonomic needs of staff, while simultaneously providing a streamlined system for waste segregation, contaminated instrument washing areas, clean instrument wrapping areas and storage. This is often done through the physical separation of rooms, each with their own unique airflow system.

Lastly, the recovery department needs to have direct access to ambulance waiting areas and emergency evacuation routes. Within the recovery department, the first trolley area should always be allocated to general anaesthetic patients to reduce the transfer time for the patient and prevent any delay in getting the OT team back to the OT.

Infection control

Infections are a potential problem facing all patients who are undergoing surgery. For ophthalmic patients, the risk of infections such as endophthalmitis or toxic anterior segment syndrome, are real and the results can be devastating. Management of both the patient and the facility environment (American Academy of Ophthalmology 2012) is therefore required to prevent cross-contamination. Infection control is the responsibility of all personnel working within the facility.

Patient management – infection prevention

The patient's own eyelids and conjunctival flora are a possible source of wound contamination. The most common causative organism of bacterial endophthalmitis is *Staphylococcus epidermidis*, which is a commensal bacterium of the eyelids. Povidone iodine antiseptic solution in 5% dilution (or less) has been proved effective against common commensals of the skin and certain spores. It is also non-toxic to the eye and is the antiseptic of choice for both skin preparation and instilled into the conjunctival sac (Ciulla *et al.* 2002).

Careful draping, taking the time to tuck the patient's eyelashes under the drape, to prevent contamination by the patient's own microflora, will establish a sterile field and prevent contamination from unprepared areas. It is also good practice to use disposable drapes and equipment where possible because of the higher risk of contamination.

In countries such as the UK, this is of particular concern due to the potential presence of Creutzfeldt–Jakob disease (CJD) – a prion-based disease that is transmissible through surgery (Armitage *et al.* 2009). As science and technology remain unable to remove CJD prions from metal surgical instruments without incineration, instruments must be discarded (at significant cost) to prevent cross-contamination. For the UK, single-use instruments are therefore becoming the norm.

In recent years, the WHO has implemented a global hand hygiene campaign to prevent the spread of micro-organisms through human touch and inanimate objects. In countries such as Australia, general hand hygiene initiatives and routine structured audits are now mandatory in all facilities for all staff and visiting surgeons. The results of these audits are benchmarked against the national average to support the facility in improving their practice.

Surgical hand-washing techniques have also changed over time, due to the advent of alternative waterless scrubbing solutions. These provide quicker and more effective washing technique options for staff.

Cleaning the operating theatre

Special precautions with decontamination of the OT facility and equipment are also necessary and environmental cleaning plans should be routine. This includes cleaning between patients, end-of-day cleaning and routine monthly, quarterly and bi-annual cleaning of certain items. Facilities need to use a hospital-grade germicidal agent that is suitable for eradication of such organisms within the environment.

Decontamination and sterilisation of surgical instruments

Sterilisation is usually defined as the inactivation of all living organisms. However, this does not include prions, which continue to cause problems. At the time of publication, prion-based diseases cannot be terminated (killed) by conventional OT sterilisers, which reach a temperature of 124–135° Celsius. Prions, while not fully understood, are thought to be destroyed only by incineration.

As previously discussed, this is of particular significance in the United Kingdom (UK) which experiences nationwide issues with prion-based CJD hospital-acquired transmission. While prion-based disease remains an issue in the UK and several other developed countries (though to a lesser extent), it is not currently an issue within developing and emerging economy nations. Therefore, as all countries experience different outbreak and transmission levels, and are governed by different regulatory bodies with varied economic positions, the OT nurse must be familiar with their own country's regulations on the use and re-use of surgical instruments, whether they are designed for single use or re-use.

Before sterilisation can start, all the instruments used need to be decontaminated. This means the process of cleaning instruments that have a heavy bio burden (Henning 2011). Decontamination reduces the bacterial load, and removes organic material that could interfere with sterilisation and, if not removed, although killed by the sterilisation process, could still cause intraocular inflammation due to the presence of endotoxins.

Decontamination starts during the surgical procedure, after the surgeon hands the instrument back to the scrub nurse. The scrub nurse should manually remove any gross matter as soon as possible, to prevent drying of blood and other organic debris. Henning (2011) recommends that the scrub nurse should rinse instruments between uses in sterile distilled water. It is vital that no water is left on the instrument if the surgeon wishes to place it back inside the eye. This is because water damages the corneal endothelium (because water is not an isotonic solution). Additionally, 0.9% saline is not recommended for rinsing instruments either because it can damage instruments by staining them and leaving a saline residue.

Prior to transferring the contaminated instruments to the sterilisation department, the scrub nurse must remove all matter (e.g. suture material), remove any sharps (blades), and ensure that all items are accounted for by checking them off against their tray list during the *Sign-Out* process. Any damaged items need to be accounted for and brought to the attention of the sterilisation team for repair or replacement.

Instruments that have been used for injecting surgical oil (e.g. during retinal surgery) also need to be set aside so the sterilisation team can treat them with additional care. This is to prevent the oil from remaining in or on the instrument.

Lastly, instruments used for cytotoxic (anti-metabolite) therapy, also need to be isolated so the sterilisation staff can treat them with appropriate care. It is important to be aware of the facility's policy with regard to the handling and management of cytotoxic waste.

Nursing considerations within the sterilisation room

Decontamination continues in the 'dirty area' of the sterilisation department after the procedure. Staff involved in manual decontamination need to wear personal protective equipment (PPE) at all times.

The first step for the sterilisation team, once they have received a handover from the OT team regarding any damaged, missing or special care items, is to check for sharps (to prevent injury to self). Thereafter, they need to remove any contaminated material from the instruments, dispose of any excess fluid, and then complete an instrument count. Completing the count early is essential to ensure that instruments have not been placed in the waste in error. Once all instruments are accounted for, the sterilisation team may dispose of the OT's waste bags.

Prior to cleaning, instruments are examined one-by-one. Any instrument that has a *screw* or *hinge* needs to be opened, ready for cleaning.

The cleaning (decontamination) process is different in each facility, as some continue to manually hand-wash while others have embraced automated instrument cleaning machines. In either case, the sterilisation team must separate the instruments and equipment, based on the material they are made from (e.g. plastics, glass, silicone, electronic, battery-operated, fibre optics and metals, e.g. titanium), and the machine's capabilities. The team must then follow the manufacturer's recommendations to ensure the item is cleaned and cared for in the appropriate manner without damaging it. Most importantly, any battery-operated items must have the batteries removed prior to decontamination.

Decontamination usually takes place using an enzymatic neutral-based cleaning material, which is gentle on the instruments but also suitable and non-toxic to the eye. The process is completed with a rinse cycle, with all lumen (cannulated) instruments completely cleaned, rinsed and dried through.

Failure to care for a lumen instrument appropriately could potentially lead to toxic anterior segment syndrome (TASS). TASS is a non-infectious type of intraocular inflammation, which occurs after the introduction of a toxic agent intraocularly during anterior segment surgery (Clouser 2004). It should be noted that several incidents of TASS have been attributed to residual detergents left on instruments because of inadequate rinsing after their use in ultrasonic washers or inadequate training of staff in their use (Clouser 2004). Ophthalmic OT personnel should be aware of these risks and take appropriate action to overcome them. TASS can be catastrophic to the patient and, in a worst-case scenario, result in the patient losing their eye.

Once decontaminated, metal instruments are placed in an ultrasonic washer machine to remove any remaining micro-organisms from their surface, and then dried and wrapped, ready for sterilisation. Metal instruments – particularly hinged ones – may also be lubricated in an enzymatic (milk) solution to prevent rusting, surface-pithing and stiffness of the joints. Lubrication regimes vary in different countries, with some facilities lubricating after every use, while the majority do so at scheduled times, depending on how often the item is used.

Once all instruments have been decontaminated (cleaned, rinsed and dried), they are ready for wrapping and sterilisation. It is internationally recommended that internal and external indicators be utilised to show that the item has been sterilised (Henning 2011). Each tray/pouch should also be labelled so the contents can be identified. Tracking systems, including tray identification sheets, are also advised to prevent loss or instruments at all stages and to assist the sterilisation team in tracking and monitoring sterilisation and/or conducting an instrument recall, as required.

Sterilisation

There remain several methods for sterilisation but the most common is heat, via a steam autoclave. In the past, dry and hot ovens were used but these are being globally phased out.

Certain ophthalmic instruments cannot withstand autoclaving or are not suitable for other reasons (e.g. if they are made of glass) and alternative sterilisation methods are required. Ethylene oxide was traditionally used but has been globally phased out because of the health and safety risks (it is explosive and is also toxic to skin and mucous membranes). Due to this, facilities are now encouraged to purchase instruments that can be sterilised via alternative methods or change to single-use instruments only.

Incidents of toxic endothelial cell destruction (TECD) and TASS have also been reported after gas plasma sterilisation, which has been used as an alternative to the above methods (Gimbel & Pereira 2002). TECD is characterised by a profound corneal oedema and opacification within 24 hours of surgery (Duffy *et al.* 2000).

Steam sterilisation

The sterilisation cycle, depending on the machine, includes both pre-vacuum and heat processes. Sterilisation occurs in the machine's chamber when peak steam penetration reaches 135° Celsius. This lasts around 3.5 minutes and is followed by a drying cycle of 40–50 minutes. The process concludes with a de-vacuum of the chamber, which will allow the door to be opened at the end of the cycle. The instruments may then be removed and placed in an area to dry and cool down, prior to being used or placed in the storage area.

Regardless of the method of sterilisation used, or what equipment is being used, a recording and tracking system is recommended. These are essential risk management tools to prove sterility of instruments and to identify problems and trends. Additionally, daily testing of the equipment is required to ensure that it is functioning. Sterilisers, in particular, require daily enzymatic and air penetration (i.e. Bowie Dick) testing.

'Immediate use steam sterilisation' should be used only in emergency situations where another instrument is not available. This should only be done in line with the manufacturer's instructions for the steriliser and the instruments should not be stored.

Machine (equipment) care and use

The ophthalmic OT is home to a variety of machines, each of which serves a particular function. They all require regular maintenance checks and need to be cleaned after use, and covered with a light dust protector when stored. This section provides an overview of some machines found in the OT.

Diathermy machines

While bipolar diathermy can also be provided by some anterior and posterior machines, a separate diathermy machine can provide both bipolar and monopolar capabilities. Staffs need to check that the corresponding monopolar plates, electrical cables and tips correspond with the correct machine to ensure correct and safe electrical circuit.

Cryotherapy machines

Often used in retinal surgery, the 'cryo' machine requires its own mounted trolley. This is because it needs to be connected to liquid nitrogen. An exit flume, to expel gases outside the OT, may also be required.

Microscopes

Microscopes provide illumination as well as the magnification that is essential for microsurgery. In addition, they are useful for video recording and teaching purposes. Nurses need to be competent in setting up their microscope. It is good practice to check that the microscope is clean and in full working order before starting the surgical list. This includes checking that safety locks are tightened, cabling is not a hazard, and foot controls are functioning. Most modern microscopes have a built-in filter to protect against ocular damage to the user during laser treatment. Alternatively, staff members need to be aware if the microscope being used has a built-in filter and/or how to attach a filter if necessary. Staff working within the retinal OT may also be required to attach additional accessory items for magnification of the posterior aspect of the eye (i.e. a biom® set).

Sufficient sets of sterile microscope handles and button-caps should also be available.

While most microscopes are floor- or ceiling-mounted, bed-mounted microscopes are common in some parts of the world. In this instance, care needs to be taken to ensure that the microscope is secure, before placing the patient on the bed.

Lasers

Nursing staff have an important role to play in ensuring good laser practice to prevent hazards to the patient and team. The direct beam can damage the eye so appropriate protective eye wear and filters on microscopes are necessary. As laser wavelength and power varies, safety eye wear needs to be suitable for the wavelength range of the particular device. It is important that safety eyewear is available and used for each specific piece of laser equipment. The standards for laser safety eye wear are based on key international standards. Any kind of reflection of the beam can damage the eye so non-reflective surfaces are required in the surgical field for safety. A laser is a fire hazard so regular maintenance and careful storage are also important.

The OT nurse needs to follow local laser safety rules, in line with international guidelines, and obtain training where available. All staff should be aware of the emergency shutdown procedure. Suitable warning signs at entrance doors and window coverings are needed, as well as regulation of staff movement to avoid accidental exposure (Medical and Healthcare Products Regulatory Agency 2015). A useful source of advice on laser safety is the National Radiological Protection Board within the UK. Additionally, in some countries, staff must be trained in laser safety and physicians must hold a laser licence in order to provide laser treatment.

Radioactive therapy equipment

Radiotherapy provides therapeutic treatment to achieve controlled cell destruction in certain conditions such as malignancies. In ophthalmic practice, radiotherapy is generally organised on a regional or national basis and there are few centres of excellence.

Many of the radioactive sources used in ophthalmic practice emit beta radiation and therefore do not radiate any great distance. However, they do pose a potential health and safety risk, and certain precautions are recommended for storage, handling and monitoring. The use of radioactive sources in medicine requires a licence, naming the person who has permission to use it. Further information is available from the Radiation Protection Services arm of Public Health England (https://www.phe-protectionservices. org.uk). Any centre using radioactive sources should also have 'local rules' in place, regular training (including safe handling techniques), local radiation protection officers and reporting mechanisms to ensure compliance with local regulations. It is the responsibility of the OT nurse to ensure that they are familiar with safe use of radioactive sources.

Ocular medications and surgical therapeutic agents used during ophthalmic surgery

Three main points are stressed when using drugs and fluids during ocular surgery:

- Preparations that contain preservatives should not be used inside the eye because of the risk of damage by toxicity.
- Fluids used inside the eye should be isotonic and preferably buffered.
- At all times, the surgeon must be informed of any solution they are being handed by the scrub nurse, in order to prevent incorrect administration.

Any patient allergies or deviations from the regular brand or strength of drug must always be communicated to the surgeon prior to surgery commencing.

Any drug or therapeutic agent opened onto the OT surgical trolley needs to be carefully managed by the scrub nurse and must be labelled to prevent wrongful administration. Drugs should be isolated on the surgical trolley until they are needed.

Irrigation solutions

Specifically designed intraocular irrigating fluids and viscoelastic agents have been developed to help maintain stable intraocular pressure and the anterior chamber during intraocular surgery, thus preventing haemorrhage and damage to the corneal endothelium. (The corneal endothelium has no regenerating properties and severe damage leads to loss of the essential 'pump mechanism' that maintains corneal fluid balance and therefore transparency.) These irrigation solutions are isotonic, in that they mimic the balance of salts within the aqueous.

If a non-isotonic fluid is used, an imbalance can occur between the ocular cells and the fluid. Fluid and electrolytes may cross the cells' semipermeable membranes in an attempt to achieve a balance, and the cells may be destroyed as a result. Certain salts (such as potassium and calcium) are added to help maintain this balance and keep ocular tissue alive. Buffers are usually also added because the effect of a change in pH can be just as damaging. Common buffers used are lactate (in Hartmann's solution) and acetate or citrate (in Balanced Salt Solution – BSS).

A new intraocular irrigating solution and administration line should be used for each patient. Additives should not be used, with the exception of adrenaline (epinephrine) to BSS for phacoemulsification surgery or Hartmann's solution for vitreoretinal surgery if the surgeon requests it to maintain mydriasis.

Viscoelastics

Viscoelastics have all the properties of fluids, making them easy to manipulate. They are very useful during intraocular surgery to help the anterior chamber retain its shape when the globe is opened by the creation of a surgical wound. It should be remembered that these agents need to be removed at the end of the surgery because they have been implicated in causing raised intraocular pressure postoperatively. In recent times some surgeons have also used viscoelastics on the exterior of the eye, as a corneal lubricant alternative to BSS.

Cell staining agents

Cell staining agents have been developed specifically to aid surgeon visualisation. For example, during cataract surgery, Trypan Blue (a capsular staining agent) is used to stain the lens capsule prior to performing capsulorhexis. Posteriorly, membrane staining agents, such as Indocyanine Green Dye (ICG), have also been developed to enhance the visualisation of the internal limiting membrane tissue on the macular surface. This assists the surgeon to perform a membrane (pucker) peel.

Cytotoxics

Some cytotoxic (anti-metabolite) agents, such as Mitomycin C and 5-Fluorouracil (5FU), may also be used during ophthalmic surgeries such as trabeculectomy, to help with the healing process, and reduce scar formation through cellular death. Handing cytotoxics requires strict adherence to policy regarding the management and handling of cytotoxic agents.

Parasympathomimetic preparations

Agents such as Micohol-E® (acetylcholine chloride) and Miostat® (carbachol), are routinely used in cataract surgery and, to a lesser extent, corneal surgery. When the surgeon administers one of these, it causes miosis of the iris in seconds after delivery – resulting in rapid miosis (drugs.com, 2015).

Retinal oil and gas

Retinal oil and gas (and filtered air) are used therapeutically within the eye during retinal surgery to act as a tamponade to aid the reattachment of the retina.

Appropriate postoperative education should be provided, including advice on head positioning (if requested by the surgeon), prior to discharge. This is especially relevant for patients discharged with gas bubbles – i.e. filtered air, sulphur hexafluoride (SF6) or perfluoropropane (C3F8). Postoperative education needs to include:

- Avoidance of air travel
- Driving to high altitudes – because atmospheric pressure changes can lead to the bubble expanding, thus increasing the IOP and leading to retinal ischaemia
- Deep sea driving, which can (conversely) cause the gas-filled eye to collapse.

SF6 is known to be absorbed within 3 weeks and C3F8 is absorbed over 3 months.

While the gas is in the eye, there is a risk that nitrous oxide (used in general anaesthetic), which tends to move into gas-filled cavities, could enter the eye and cause the intraocular pressure to increase. While there is a gas bubble in the eye, surgery could pose a risk to vision if nitrous oxide is used.

Several key strategies have been recommended (http://beavrs.org/gas-in-your-eye), which are now considered standard practice in developed countries, to ensure the patient's safety after discharge. These include:

- All patients who receive intraocular gas will be advised of its implications by their surgeons
- All patients will wear a nitrous oxide warning band while they have gas in their eye
- All anaesthetists will be educated about this
- All nursing staff working in pre- and perioperative nursing [areas] will acquire this knowledge.

Intravitreal antibiotics

A common practice around the world, particularly for cataract surgery, is the routine administration of antibiotics prior to the close of the surgery to prevent bacterial endophthalmitis (Gan *et al.* 2001). Vancomycin, supplemented with a second antibiotic such as ceftazidime or an aminoglycoside covering for rare Gram negative bacteria, has become the standard treatment. Nurses are required to be mindful of sterile preparation and any patient allergies prior to administration. Additionally, as several antibiotics have similar-sounding names, knowledge of and/or implementation of a Tall Man Lettering system is recommended, to prevent drug identification issues. This is the practice of writing part of a drug's name in upper-case letters, to help distinguish sound-alike drugs from one another in order to reduce medication errors. It is used extensively internationally – for example, in the class of Cephalosporins.

Intravitreal injections

Intravitreal injections are primarily designed to administer therapeutic agents into the eye, while minimising systemic absorption (AAO Hopkins Center for Quality Eye Care 2015). Common agents include Bevacizumab or Avastin®, which is an antivascular endothelial growth factor (anti-VEGF) medication, designed to treat 'wet' age-related macular degeneration.

Vancomycin for endophthalmitis treatment is also administered intravitreally. It may be accompanied by an injection of an antifungal medication (i.e. Amphotericin B) and is preceded by an extraction of fluid from inside the eye's chamber, ready to send to pathology. Depending on the facility, intravitreal injections can take place in an outpatient or OT setting and are generally classified as a minor procedure.

Care and handling of microsurgical instruments during the procedure

Microsurgical ophthalmic instruments have specific care requirements regarding their storage, handling, cleaning, inspection, testing and the protection of delicate tips (Henning 2011). Nursing considerations involve several safety measures. Cannulas should be checked as primed and patent before being handed over to the surgeon. Luer-Lock connections should also be used to prevent accidental trauma.

Avoid drawing up solutions until just before they are needed and use sterile sticky labels attached to each syringe to prevent misidentification of contents (Dobson 1991). During the case, instruments should not be wiped with gauze or towels because this may damage the instruments and leave fibres in the operative site – alternative micro-fibre wipes should be used instead.

Instruments should be passed with the working tips downwards and placed in the surgeon's hand ready for use, alleviating the need to look up from the microscope eye pieces. Extra care needs to be taken with tips and sharps because several ophthalmic procedures are carried out in a darkened room. Effective use of a uniform system (in which instruments are routinely placed in the same spot) enables the scrub nurse to quickly and safely locate the required instrument as and when needed. Local protocols should be followed regarding the counting of instruments and swabs.

Care and handling of specimens and tissue for transplantation

Specimens, once confirmed by the surgeon, need to be carefully transferred from the operative site and into the specimen pot by the scrub and scout nurse – without contamination. Prior to this, the surgeon needs to confirm the specimen transfer method – i.e. fresh or formalin. All corresponding transfer and log documents need to be completed.

Tissue for transplantation (as in corneal surgery) needs to be cared for in accordance with the accompanying instructions from the dispatching eye bank. Chapter 13 provides an in-depth outline of tissue care, including tracking and document checking.

Specific nursing considerations in common ophthalmic surgical procedures

By being familiar with the steps in operative procedures, the scrub nurse can help reduce the length of the surgical procedure. This will enhance the patient's comfort and safety and also help prevent issues such as retinal toxicity, due to prolonged exposure to the microscope lights. This section is not comprehensive but includes common procedures with very specific nursing implications.

Cataract surgery

While extra capsular cataract extraction (ECCE) has largely been phased out in developed and emerging economy nations, phacoemulsification and small incision cataract surgery (SICS) remains the current preferred surgical option around the world. Additional emerging technologies, such as the use of femtosecond laser technologies, have also been introduced. However, at the time of writing, these methods have not yet been widely implemented around the world. Please refer to Chapter 19 (on the lens and cataracts) for further information.

Phacoemulsification surgery uses ultrasonic waves delivered via a small needle vibrating at high speed to emulsify and aspirate the lens matter. This is combined with an irrigation system, which helps maintain the anterior chamber and cool the needle tip. This system allows for the removal of the cataract and replacement with an intraocular lens through a small incision, which means less leakage of irrigation fluid and increased anterior chamber stability. It also greatly reduces the incidence of postoperative astigmatism, because the wound is generally self-sealing.

Specific nursing implications during cataract surgery

Several phacoemulsification machines are available. All machines provide an irrigation, aspiration and emulsification facility, which needs to be regulated in order to maintain the anterior chamber. The nurse should understand the relationships between the following three factors and how they can be varied:

- Infusion pressure
- Vacuum setting
- 'Phaco' tip size.

To achieve aspiration, a vacuum is provided by either a peristaltic pump or a Venturi pump. These two devices use different physical principles and have various pros and cons. Some modern machines combine the two types (for more detailed discussion, see Hope-Ross 2003). The nurse's role is to ensure that the machine is primed and ready for use when required and to be familiar with the various features of the machine being used in order to be able to troubleshoot in the event of a problem. The scrub nurse should also monitor the volume of fluid in the infusion bottle and arrange for this to be replaced when running low.

Small incision cataract surgery (SICS) is a mid-mark technique, between ECCE and phacoemulsification, that is favoured in lower-resource settings, due to its efficacy, self-sealing wound closure and its lower cost to the patient. The Himalayan Cataract Project's (2006) (www.cureblindness.org) *Standard Operating Manual for Modern Small Incision Cataract Surgery*, co-developed by the Tilganga Eye Centre, Nepal, Fred Hollows Foundation, and The Moran Eye Centre, University of Utah is freely available.

The scrub nurse should be familiar with the equipment needed if the procedure is converted to extracapsular cataract extraction or if anterior vitrectomy is required, in the event of a rupture in the posterior capsule (for more detail, see Foss 2001, Wadood & Dhillon 2002) and must be familiar with the lenses available within their facility – including knowing how to prepare the lenses and/or if the lens is pre-loaded.

Glaucoma procedures

The trabeculectomy procedure creates an internal drainage fistula for aqueous fluid. This is combined with the creation of a drainage bleb under the conjunctiva to provide resistance to the new aqueous exit route, allowing for reabsorption back into the circulation.

Several techniques have been described. Wound healing agents are commonly used in conjunction with this procedure to prevent the newly created drainage fistula from healing over. 5-Fluorouracil (5-FU) and Mitomycin C are the two most common agents used in patients who have been identified as being at high risk of failure from scarring. The usual precautions when handling cytotoxic drugs apply: masks, eye protection and gloves are all required.

Particular care needs to be taken when counting swabs that were soaked in an anti-metabolite and inserted over the sclera. These should be counted on insertion and removal, and the application time monitored.

The cytotoxics are always administered before the paracentesis and washed away with lots of fluid to ensure that none gets into the anterior chamber. The 'run-off' needs to be soaked up and disposed of in a cytotoxic bin. A separate trolley is necessary if cytotoxics are being used, in order to prevent accidental introduction of the cytotoxic into the anterior chamber after the paracentesis has occurred. This would be catastrophic, leading to destruction of cells inside the eye. Where possible, only disposable equipment should be used on this trolley. If any reusable items are used, they should be clearly labelled and handled accordingly during the decontamination and sterilisation processes.

Trabeculectomy surgery may be carried out in combination with cataract surgery as either a 'one-site' or 'two-site' procedure. The two conditions frequently coexist and fistulising surgery can speed up the development of a cataract.

Tube and valve surgery may be carried out in a selected group of patients in whom trabeculectomy surgery is inadvisable. This involves the insertion of a silicone tube and/or valve into the anterior chamber, which is connected to a plate anchored to the sclera under the conjunctiva.

Finally, destruction of the ciliary body with a cyclodiode laser may be used for selected cases, such as patients with little useful vision, where previous medical therapy or filtering surgery has failed. Laser safety guidelines and postoperative management of pain are important nursing considerations.

Strabismus (Squint)

The main aim of Strabismus (squint) surgery is to restore alignment of the visual axis, and (if possible) to restore binocular single vision and ensure that both eyes work together. Surgery will involve the repositioning of one or more of the extraocular muscles to straighten the eyes.

Surgery on the extraocular muscles may involve a variety of different techniques to alter the action of the muscles. The action of a muscle can be weakened, strengthened or transposed using different procedures according to the outcome required (see Chapter 23).

Weakening procedures

The most frequently performed procedure to reduce the action of a muscle is that of a recession, whereby the muscle is cut at its point of insertion and reattached with sutures at a measured distance posterior to the original insertion. This will reduce the tension of the muscle and may be documented in the notes as a minus sign in front of the distance in millimetres of the muscle recession.

Other weakening procedures include partial thickness Z incisions on each side of the muscle tendon, without disinserting the muscle. This effectively lengthens the muscle, thereby reducing its action.

Strengthening procedures

The most common method of strengthening a muscle is a resection. The muscle is disinserted and shortened by excising a measured amount, and reattached with sutures back to its original point of insertion. This strengthens its action and is documented as a plus sign in front of the amount to be respected. A muscle action can also be strengthened by advancing its point of insertion anteriorly, nearer to the limbus, thus strengthening it.

One other type of muscle surgery is to transpose the muscle in order to alter its field of action, rather than strengthen or weaken it. This shifts the muscle insertion up or down by half to one insertion width along the original axis. This procedure is used to correct A and V pattern deviations.

Specific nursing implications during squint surgery

Each patient must be assessed individually by the multidisciplinary team beforehand and the theatre nurse must check that results are available from the different tests and investigations carried out by orthoptists, optometrists, paediatricians, neurologists and ophthalmologists. As it is estimated that up to 5% of all children have some degree of squint (Nickerson 2002), it is a relatively common paediatric ophthalmic procedure and requires a family-centred approach to planning care. The parents will need to be carefully prepared, together with the child, for a stress-free visit to the OT. The surgery should be carefully explained and the family made aware that more than one operation may be necessary.

If the scrub nurse is very familiar with the steps in the procedure, they can be ready with the correct equipment to aid the smooth progress of the surgery and assist with holding muscle hooks, etc. The procedure may involve surgery on both eyes because the muscles work together in pairs to allow coordinated movement. Altering the action of one muscle will therefore have an effect on the other. It is not necessary to have separate trolleys set up for a bilateral operation because this is an extraocular procedure. While draping techniques will differ from surgeon to surgeon, bilateral skin preparation remains generally consistent.

The most popular suture currently used is a double-ended, 6/0 Vicryl, on a quarter circle spatulated needle, to control the depth of the suture. The scrub nurse will need to ensure that the suture is cut and mounted on the needle holder (one forehand and one backhand) before holding the squint hook, because this is a difficult single-handed manoeuvre. If an adjustable suture is used for an adult patient, the suture should not be cut but left double ended. This will be tied in a bow for alteration when the patient is awake enough to cooperate.

One final consideration during squint surgery is the oculocardiac reflex, which occurs when there is traction on the orbital structures, the conjunctiva or the extraocular muscles. This reflex produces hypotension, which results in decreased cardiac output (Gavaghan 1998), leading to bradycardia and even asystole. This needs to be reported to the surgeon and the surgery must be halted until cardiac output is restored. Staff also need to be mindful of the placement of the airway when draping and working within the surgical site.

Retinal surgery

There are four main indications for vitrectomy surgery:

- To clear the media, e.g. vitreous haemorrhage and inflammatory debris
- To gain access, e.g. to remove epiretinal membranes, foreign bodies or dropped nucleus
- To create a space, e.g. for gas, air or oil being used as tamponade
- To relieve traction, e.g. proliferative vitreoretinopathy/proliferative diabetic retinopathy (PVR/PDR).

Modern vitrectomy surgery uses the single-function, three-port, 20-, 23- or 25-gauge system. Access to the posterior segment is via three pars plana sclerotomies, created with a fine blade or trocar delivery system. These ports allow access for:

- An infusion of either BSS or Hartmann's solution under the force of gravity and atmospheric pressure in order to maintain the intraocular pressure
- A fibre-optic light source to illuminate the surgical site
- Instrumentation, e.g. vitreous cutter, scissors, forceps, injection of gas or oil.

Specific nursing implications during vitreoretinal surgery

The nurse's role includes ensuring that the vitrectomy machine is primed and ready for use when required, and being familiar with the various features of the machine being used, in order to be able to troubleshoot in the event of a problem. Training of new staff and regular updates will facilitate this. The nurse also needs to check at the start of the list that lasers, diathermies and cryo machines are ready for use.

Careful handling and positioning of the instruments, sharps, plugs, trocars and other equipment is particularly important because the surgery may be carried out in a darkened environment.

Important considerations for nurses are: monitoring the intraocular fluid used and the types used, infection control, maintenance of intraocular pressure (IOP) and addition of drugs. Infusion volume is particularly important, to ensure that IOP is maintained. The nursing team must be mindful of infusion bottle levels. That said, modern vitrectomy machines have much more sophisticated technology, allowing surgeons to monitor, manipulate and maintain the IOP as they require.

Health and safety issues relating to the use of ophthalmic lasers, cryotherapy equipment, and gas and heavy liquid – within a dark room environment – also need careful consideration. The nurse needs to work within local and national policy guidelines, e.g. ensuring appropriate safety filters are in position on the microscope during laser use.

The use of long-acting insoluble gas, e.g. sulphur hexafluoride (SF6), as an internal tamponade, should be discussed with the anaesthetist, because (as previously discussed) there is a risk that nitrous oxide used as part of the anaesthetic will cause the gas bubble to expand and be detrimental to retinal circulation. Postoperatively, patients are required to wear a wristband.

Oculoplastic surgeries

Eyelid surgery

The main function of the eyelids is to protect the globe from injury and excessive light (Snell & Lemp 1998). The lids also spread the tear film over the surface of the globe to lubricate it and they assist in the drainage of the tears through the puncta. Many different surgical techniques have been described to treat pathologies affecting the lids (see Collin 1989 and Leatherbarrow 2010 for more detail). A good understanding of normal anatomy and physiology greatly assists understanding of the procedure being carried out and the intended outcome. Lid surgery also encompasses surgery to the lacrimal system and orbital structures. The topic is therefore too complex for detailed discussion in this chapter and only general nursing considerations are included.

Specific nursing implications during lid surgery

The anatomy of the eyelid is quite complex. Surgical 'identification of the landmarks' is made simpler if the patient is conscious during the surgery. Asking the patient to look up and down during the procedure helps identify structures and assists in predicting the final position of lids after the surgery. Therefore, most lid surgery is carried out on a conscious patient with sedation in certain circumstances and analgesia as required (see Table 11.4, p. 217, for further detail).

Prepping generally involves cleaning the whole face with the selected antiseptic solution, followed by draping the patient's head, or part of the head, in a turban style. A separate drape is used to cover the patient's chin, neck and upper torso. Alternative draping may be required for surgery involving grafting from sites such as behind the ear. In this instance, those areas need to be secured, prepped and draped at the commencement of surgery.

The reverse Trendelenburg (head-up position) is commonly employed. This position has the added advantage of contributing towards haemostasis, although diathermy should also be set up and available at the start of the procedure. The use of monopolar diathermy will require an additional exit fume (via a suction device). Lid surgery does not routinely require the use of a microscope so it is not routinely possible to follow the steps of the procedure on a video monitor. (However, some procedures, such as endoscopic brow lifts or endoscopic dacryocystorhinostomy procedures, can involve cameras and monitors and will therefore require the nurse to be familiar with setting up and using these technologies.)

Several types of suture material and needles may be required (e.g. for traction, muscle and skin closure) and it is recommended that the scrub nurse should discuss in advance what the surgeon's particular preference is. Careful counting of sharps and swabs is a routine component of *Time-Out* and *Sign-Out*.

The eyelids have a rich blood supply from branches of the palpebral arteries (Collin 2006). As a result, surgery can cause excess bleeding, if not managed, as well as swelling and bruising of the lid postoperatively. To minimise or prevent this, a pressure bandage may be applied at the end of surgery, though many surgeons prefer not to bandage and opt for ointment only (depending on the particular case). The scrub nurse will require prescribed ointment and padding (e.g. gauze swabs for the dressing), and elasticated tape is preferable for increased tension.

If bilateral lid surgery has been carried out, some surgeons who do choose to pressure bandage may place the dressing over both eyes, thus leaving the patient sightless. As this is a safety concern for the patient, the surgeon may order an extended recovery period, with the instruction to remove one dressing prior to discharge. Careful preoperative assessment and planning are required to ensure that the patient is fully aware of this and that coping measures are in place for the duration. In addition, if the procedure involves opening the orbital septum, there is an increased risk of haemorrhage into the orbit, with the devastating possibility of blindness as a complication in 1:100,000 cases (Foss 2001).

Trachoma

Trichiasis is an infectious condition caused by the bacteria *Chlamydia trachomatis*, which affects the eyelids and the cornea and can lead to permanent corneal blindness (International Trachoma Initiative 2015). The condition, which is transmitted through poor hygiene, is a significant and leading cause of blindness in lower-resource countries and within indigenous populations of Australia. The condition causes the eyelashes to turn inwards. As a consequence, they rub against the cornea, causing severe discomfort.

While prevention and education regarding transmission and hygiene are essential, a tarsal rotation procedure is required to reinvert the eyelids to their natural position. The OT nurse needs to implement techniques, equipment and consumable items routinely utilised for general eye lid surgeries (see above). If left untreated, the cornea can become permanently damaged and may require a corneal transplant.

Nurses are to prepare and care for patients undergoing trachoma tarsal lid surgery in the same manner as any other oculoplastic procedure.

Enucleation

This procedure may be carried out to remove a painful blind eye, an infection, malignant tumour or after severe trauma. It involves removal of the globe with a small portion of the optic nerve, leaving the conjunctiva and extraocular muscles behind. An orbital implant (hydroxyapatite) is usually inserted to restore lost volume in the socket and provide a good cosmetic appearance. The extraocular muscles are sutured to this and the conjunctiva closed. A retrobulbar injection of Marcain® (bupivacaine) is useful to control postoperative pain in the initial recovery period. A temporary conformer shell (size A–F) is inserted to maintain the shape of the eyelids, and a pressure dressing is applied.

For this group of patients, a preoperative visit by a trained counsellor is recommended in order to ensure the patient is fully informed – and has consented to the procedure at hand. This is to help reduce their stress, allay anxiety, and provide them with relevant information on postoperative outcomes and functions of daily life. One of the greatest fears many patients have, according to Hehir (2000), is that the wrong eye will be removed. For this procedure it is the doctor's responsibility to obtain informed consent and mark the eye carefully. The implementation of the SSS check system is strictly adhered to for this patient.

There are two other different methods that may be used to remove an eye, depending on the underlying pathology and individual circumstances. An evisceration procedure may be indicated after trauma, for a blind painful eye or in severe infection to prevent sympathetic ophthalmia. This technique involves scooping out the entire intraocular contents, leaving a scleral shell and the muscle attachments intact. Particular care is taken to ensure removal of all the uveal tissue. The surgeon may require an irrigation system for this. The postoperative management is the same as for an enucleation procedure.

An exenteration procedure, which is the most radical of all forms of eye removal, is generally indicated in the case of malignancy and therefore requires careful perioperative planning. An exenteration involves removing all the soft tissue of the orbit, including the eyeball, retrobulbar tissue and eyelids. In certain cases, it may be possible to split the lids above the tarsal plate and retain sufficient skin to line the orbit. The patient may require further plastic reconstructive surgery.

The OT nurse needs to ensure that any specimens taken are carefully labelled, recorded and sent to the appropriate department.

Dacryocystorhinostomy (DCR)

DCR surgery involved the unblocking of the nasal-punctal duct to allow tear drainage. This procedure can be performed as a conventional surgical procedure or via endoscopic viewing. This involves using bone-crunchers and punctal dilators to force an opening in the duct. This is concluded by placing tubing to maintain the opening in the long term.

Nurses need to be familiar with the anatomy and physiology of the nasal-punctal region in order to prepare for this surgery. Additionally, the nurse needs to ensure that all steps are taken to reduce bleeding during, and after, this procedure. The patient is also advised to avoid hot food and beverages postoperatively for several days to prevent such bleeding.

Corneal surgery

The replacement of a patient's cornea with donor corneal tissue is known as keratoplasty or corneal graft. This may be full thickness (penetrating keratoplasty) or partial thickness. Please refer to Chapter 17 for an explanation of the partial thickness grafts currently available. There are four main indications for corneal graft surgery (Foss 2001):

● To improve vision which has been lost as a result of trauma or corneal dystrophies such as keratoconus

● To relieve discomfort and prevent issues caused by damaged corneal surface diseases, e.g. bullous oedema

● To eliminate infection (rare, e.g. fungal)

● To seal a perforation.

Specific nursing implications during penetrating graft surgery

The nurse should check that a donor cornea is available and has been cleared for use before the patient arrives for their surgery. Please refer to Chapter 13 on eye banking and the checking process.

Generally, the patient's pupil should be constricted preoperatively to protect the intraocular structures. Structural support for the globe is compromised when the whole cornea is removed, especially in aphakic and myopic patients. Please refer to Chapter 17 (on the cornea), regarding surgical cut types.

The scrub nurse should ensure that the donor material is positioned securely and safely on the scrub trolley until it is required. Handling of the donor material should be restricted to the surgeon only, to reduce the risk of accidental damage to the corneal endothelium.

Prior to the commencement of the surgery, the nurse and surgeon should also check that all trephination devices are set up and functioning correctly, prior to trephination of the patient or donor cornea.

Author's note

Special thanks to Gregory Passanante (Chief Nursing Officer) and Dr Julia Haller, MD, (Ophthalmologist in Chief), Wills Eye Hospital, Philadelphia, USA.

References

AAO Hopkins Center for Quality Eye Care (2015) *Intravitreal Injections – 2015.* American Academy of Ophthalmology.

Allen, K., Golden, L.H., Izzo, J.L., Ching, M.I., Forrest, A., Niles, C.R., Niswander, P.R. & Barlow, J.C. (2001) Normalisation of hypertensive responses during ambulatory surgical stress by perioperative music. *Psychosomatic Medicine.* **63**, 487–92.

American Academy of Ophthalmology (2012) *Infection Prevention in Eye Care Services and Operating Areas and Operating Rooms.* American Academy of Ophthalmology.

American Society of Anaesthesiologists (2014) *ASA Physical Classification System.* https://www.asahq.org/resources/ clinical-information/asa-physical-status-classification-system (accessed 9 August 2016).

Armitage, W.J., Tullo, A.B. & Ironside, J.W. (2009) Risk of Creutzfeldt–Jakob disease transmission by ocular surgery and tissue transplantation. *Eye.* **23**, 1926–30.

Clarke P. & Jones J. (1998) *Brigden's Operating Department Practice.* London: Churchill Livingstone

Clouser, S. (2004) Toxic anterior segment syndrome: How one surgery center recognised and solved its problem. *INSIGHT.* **XXIX** (1), 4–7.

Collin, J.R.O. (2006) *A Manual of Systematic Eyelid Surgery.* 3rd edn. London: Elsevier.

Cooper, J. (1999) Teaching patient in postoperative eye care; the demands of day surgery. *Nursing Standard.* **13**(32), 42–46.

Ciulla, T.A., Starr, M.B. & Masket, S. (2002) Bacterial endophthalmitis prophylaxis for cataract surgery: an evidence-based update. *Ophthalmology.* **109**, 13–24.

Dobson, F. (1991) Perioperative care of the visually impaired. *British Journal of Theatre Nursing.* **July**, 4–9.

Drugs.com (2016) Michol-E. http://www.drugs.com/pro/miochol-e.html (Accessed 9 August 2016).

Duffy, R.E., Brown, S.E., Caldwell, K.L. & Lubniewski, A. (2000) An epidemic of corneal destruction caused by plasma gas sterilization. *Archives of Ophthalmology.* **118**, 1167–77.

Duguid, I.G., Claoue, C.M., Thamby-Rajah, Y., Allan, B.D., Dart, J.K. & Steele, A.D. (1995) Topical anaesthesia for phacoemulsification surgery. *Eye.* **9**(4), 456–59.

Foss, A.J.E. (2001) *Essential Ophthalmic Surgery.* Oxford: Butterworth-Heinemann.

Gan, I.M., van Dissel, J.T., Beekhuis, W.H., Swart, W. & van Meurs, J.C. (2001) Intravitreal vancomycin and gentamicin concentrations in patients with postoperative endophthalmitis. *British Journal of Ophthalmology.* **85**, 1289–93

Gavaghan, M. (1998) Cardiac anatomy and physiology: a review. *AORN Online.* **67**, 802–22.

Gimbel, H.V. & Pereira, C. (2002) Advances in phacoemulsification equipment. *Current Opinion in Ophthalmology.* **13**, 30–32.

Hehir, M. (2000) Removal of an eye: Who cares? A nursing perspective. *Ophthalmology Nursing.* **4**(3), 8–11.

Henning, C. (ed.) (2011). *American Society of Ophthalmic Registered Nurses. Care and Handling of Ophthalmic Microsurgical Instruments.* 3rd edn. Iowa: Kendal/Hunt Publishing Co.

Himalayan Cataract Project, USA (2006). *Standard Operating Manual for Modern Small Incision Cataract Surgery* Tilganga Eye Centre, Nepal.
https://itunes.apple.com/gb/book/standard-operating-procedure/id643318901?mt=13. (accessed 9 August 2016).

Hope-Ross, M. (2003) Phakodynamics. *Refractive Eye News.* August/September, 9–18.

International Trachoma Initiative (2015). *About Trachoma.* http://trachoma.org (accessed 9 August 2016).

Katzen, J. (2002) Management of anxiety in the refractive surgery patient. *INSIGHT.* **XXVII**, 103–7.

Leatherbarrow, B. (2010) *Oculoplastic surgery.* 2nd edn. Informa Healthcare.

Medical and Healthcare Products Regulatory Agency (2015) *Lasers, intense light source systems and LEDs – guidance for safe use in medical, surgical, dental and aesthetic practices.* MHRA.

Moon, J. & Cho, K. (2001) The effects of handholding on anxiety in cataract patients under local anaesthesia. *Journal of Advanced Nursing.* **35**, 407–15.

Murdock, I.E. & Sze, P. (1994) Visual experience during cataract surgery. *Eye.* **8**, 666–7.

Newsom, R.S.B., Wainwright, W.C. & Canning, C.R. (2001) Local anaesthesia for 1221 vitreoretinal procedures. *British Journal of Ophthalmology.* **85**, 225–7.

NHS Executive (2000) *Action on Cataracts: Good practice guidance.* London: Department of Health,

Nickerson, B. (2002) Nursing care of the paediatric patient following strabismus repair surgery. *INSIGHT.* **XXVII**(3), 64–65.

Nordlund, M.L., Marques, D.V., Marques, F.F., Cionni, R.J. & Osher, R.H. (2003) Techniques for managing common complications of cataract surgery. *Current Opinion in Ophthalmology.* **14**(1), 7–19.

Phillips, C. (1991) An eye-opening experience. *British Journal of Theatre Nursing.* **July**, 14–15.

Reeves, W. (1993) Surgical experience of the ophthalmic patient. *INSIGHT.* **XVIII**(l), 16–22.

Royal College of Ophthalmologists (2001) *Cataract Surgery Guidelines.* London: RCOphth.

Royal College of Ophthalmologists (2002) *Creutzfeldt–Jakob Disease (CJD) and Ophthalmology.* London: RCOphth.

Royal College of Ophthalmologists and Royal College of Anaesthetists (2001) *Local Anaesthetic in Ophthalmology Guidelines.* London: RCOphth/RCA.

Snell, R.S. & Lemp, M.A. (1998) *Clinical Anatomy of the Eye.* 2nd edn. USA: Blackwell Science.

Southampton University (2002) *Pre-operative Assessment: Setting a standard through learning.* Southampton: University of Southampton.

Wadood, A.C. & Dhillon, B. (2002). The role of the ophthalmic theatre nurse in phacoemulsification surgery. *Ophthalmology Nursing.* **6**(3), 25–7.

World Health Organization (2009). *WHO Guidelines for Safe Site Surgery 2009.* http://www.who.int/patientsafety/safesurgery/tools_resources/9789241598552/en/ (accessed 9 August 2016).

World Health Organization (2015). *Patient Safety – Pulse Oximetry Page.* http://www.who.int/patientsafety/safesurgery/pulse_oximetry/en/ (accessed 9 August 2016).

CHAPTER TWELVE

The care of patients presenting with acute problems

Janet Marsden

Introduction

This chapter discusses the assessment, investigation, treatment and care of patients presenting with acute eye problems. As acute presentations may include almost all ophthalmic systems, many of the problems described here are also dealt with more fully in other chapters; only the more immediate needs of the patient are included here.

The clinician involved in the care of patients presenting acutely will vary, depending on particular circumstances. In some areas, ophthalmic nurses undertake all the initial assessment and management of this group of patients. In other areas, the clinician is primarily an ophthalmologist, and optometry-led services continue to develop, particularly in primary care. General practitioners are still responsible for much of the eye care for patients presenting acutely, as are emergency clinicians in general emergency units. This chapter aims to describe signs and symptoms displayed by patients who may present in acute settings, and discusses management and care without attributing particular roles to different clinicians. It is irrelevant who cares for the patient, as long as the clinician who does so is competent to undertake the role, understands the parameters of the role and is able and willing to refer (when necessary) to more appropriate care. At all times, care of the patient and their presenting problem is paramount.

Triage

In many acute settings, there is a rapid turnover of patients. They do not attend one by one, with plenty of time to assess and treat each person before the next arrives. It is therefore essential to have some way of discriminating between all those who present, and to have a system in place to ensure that patients are seen in order of clinical need (rather than the order in which they attend).

Triage is a method of prioritising 'casualties', which initially emerged during the Napoleonic wars. The method then was the opposite of medical priorities now, in that the least injured soldiers were treated first to ensure that the fighting force remained strong. Those who were not likely to survive were not treated. Triage emerged in the form that we see now much later and was refined in the Korean and Vietnam conflicts.

Triage involves identifying and giving a high priority to those people who have the most urgent clinical need. There are many ways of achieving this and many systems in place in acute ophthalmic areas, ranging from simple 'urgent', 'soon' and 'delayed' categories, to more complex methods. When undertaken most effectively, triage involves making a decision about clinical priority based on presentation rather than diagnosis. Effective clinical management of the patient and efficient departmental management depend on accurate allocation of the clinical priority in the triage encounter. The triage encounter is not long enough to make a diagnosis; and diagnosis may not be a good indication of clinical priority as a result of, for example, levels of pain.

Whatever system is in place, it must be systematic and rigorous and capable of being audited. It must also be seen to be fair so that patients do not feel that there is discrimination involved in who is seen next.

One such method is that designed by the Manchester Triage Group (Mackway-Jones *et al.* 2014). This method, known as 'emergency triage' or more commonly 'Manchester triage', was designed for use in general emergency departments and has been adopted by most emergency departments in the UK and as a national triage system by a number of countries. It is used to triage the largest number of patients of any triage system internationally. It provides a standard to which ophthalmic acute or emergency settings must aspire and for that reason is discussed in detail here.

Manchester triage uses a series of presentations and a limited number of signs and symptoms at each level of clinical priority. This ensures consistency between triagers and transparency of the decision to allocate a clinical priority. Traditionally, the clinician triaging a patient tends to have a feeling about what might be wrong with the patient and then seeks signs and symptoms from the history to prove or disprove their ideas. The tendency is to consider the common and easy possibilities first and move upwards to consider more severe possibilities only if the patient mentions other symptoms.

Manchester triage is reductive – the method starts with the most severe possibilities and works downwards. A patient must be allocated a higher triage category if a discriminator in that category cannot be ruled out. The system therefore defaults to a safe priority. From a general emergency department perspective, there are 53 presentations and the triage practitioner must decide which to use. From an ophthalmic perspective, there is only one commonly used presentation and that is 'Eye problems' (Mackway-Jones *et al.* 2014). In the UK, the times allocated to areas of the national triage scale are as shown in Table 12.1.

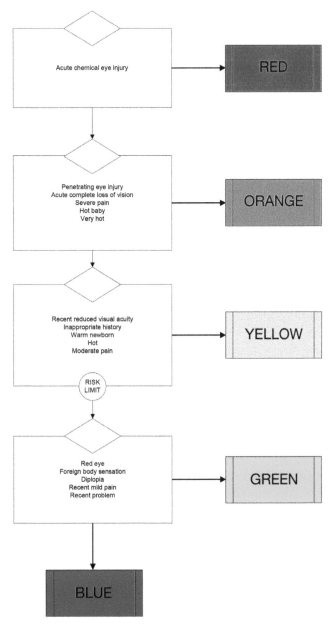

Figure 12.1 Manchester triage system – eye problems.
(From Mackway-Jones et al. 2014, with permission.)

Triage is designed to be a very fast initial assessment of the patient to decide on a clinical priority. Visual acuity is a key component in the decision but, otherwise, all that is required is a brief history, bearing in mind the discriminator and the recording of the chosen discriminator and triage category (see example below).

Table 12.1 Times allocated to areas of the UK national triage scale

Colour	Name	Target time (minutes)
Red	Immediate	0
Orange	Very urgent	10
Yellow	Urgent	60
Green	Standard	120
Blue	Non-urgent	240

This 'blue' target has since been modified, in line with UK government targets that aim for all patients to be discharged from emergency care within 4 hours (Figure 12.1).

Triage example

A patient presents with a red, sore eye for 2 days without trauma and no reduction in vision:

Chemical eye injury can be ruled out, so not red. Moving down...

The level of pain should be discussed: severe pain is 8–10 on a 10-point scale; moderate pain 5–7; and mild pain 1–4. The patient says his level of pain is around 4.

There is no history of trauma so penetrating trauma can be ruled out, as can sudden complete loss of vision. The patient is apyrexial.

The patient does not fall into the orange category. Moving down...

On further questioning, the patient's visual acuity is not reduced, **so not yellow. Moving down...**

The patient falls into the green category, based on the level of pain.

All that need be documented from this triage encounter is, in this case, 'red eye', green.

Management of the workload with an effective triage system will ensure that all patients are cared for in a timely and appropriate fashion, bearing in mind their clinical priority, in a manner that is transparent and reproducible.

Telephone triage

A major expansion of the triage process has been the recognition and development of telephone triage. Giving advice by telephone has always been an integral part of the nurse's role, although not one that has been recognised as having a distinct identity and therefore a hidden part of the workload. Formalised advice giving by telephone has the potential to be a valuable tool in many settings – a fact that was recognised in the development of NHS Direct, the professional telephone advice and helpline which was in place in England until recently.

Telephone triage was first described as a useful tool in the emergency care setting in the UK by Buckles and Carew-McColl in 1991. Since then, several authors have attributed various benefits to the strategy, which include reduced attendance as a result of explanations and self-care advice, redirection of patients to more appropriate agencies, identification of problems before the patient attends the department, cost-effectiveness due to a potentially reduced workload and pre-attendance patient empowerment.

Telephone triage also has its difficulties, however. The patient is not visible so many of the cues that experienced nurses take from the patient's appearance and behaviour are not available. The nurse may not even be able to gain information from the patient but may be talking to an intermediary, such as a relative or neighbour or another health professional, all of whom may know the patient to a greater or lesser degree.

The demarcation line between telephone advice and telephone triage is debatable. However, it is suggested that it occurs when a formalised process of decision-making takes place, allowing identification of clinical priority and allocation to a predetermined category of urgency of need for medical evaluation and care. In the telephone triage encounter, it may be decided that the patient needs to be seen now, that they need to be seen within a number of days or perhaps that advice and self-care are all that is required in this episode. These decisions may be more formalised in terms of the areas to which patients are referred and timescales available, and will depend on local services. However, it is clear that it is even more difficult to make a decision about diagnosis by telephone; advice must be given in the light of the signs and symptoms elicited from the telephone call (which would be easier if a similar framework was employed to that used in face-to-face triage); and, most importantly, that the conversation (including information from the caller and decisions made by the clinician) must be recorded in detail.

Telephone triage, like face-to-face triage, should be undertaken only by experienced practitioners. The availability of protocols and charts does not remove the need for expert clinical knowledge. The decisions made in telephone triage arguably call for a higher level of skill and knowledge than when the patient is present. Certainly, the questioning skills of the practitioner must be very highly developed in order to gain the most useful information from a worried caller, quickly and effectively.

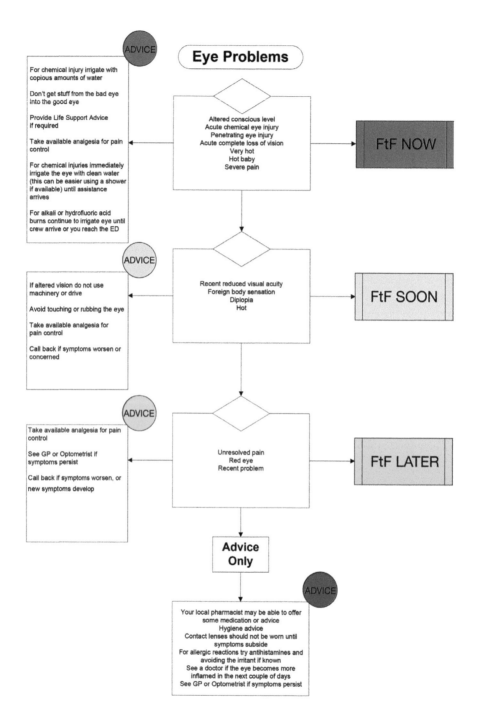

Figure 12.2 Telephone triage and advice, eye chart.
(From Marsden et al. 2016, with permission.)

Like face-to-face triage, telephone triage works well when it is carried out correctly, and less well when corners are cut, or certain aspects (such as pain) are ignored. All triage systems must be auditable and this relies on good training of competent practitioners, using their skills and knowledge, and the tools available to them, to best effect. The telephone iteration of Manchester triage (Marsden *et al.* 2016) is reproduced here in Figure 12.2.

The patient's story

What the clinician needs to know is what has actually happened to the patient and what has prompted them to present today. Has something new happened or have symptoms been going on for some time and the patient has become sufficiently worried to attend? Perhaps the patient has been prompted to attend by another person's intervention. It is important, as in all scenarios, to remain non-judgemental because, if the patient feels that perhaps they should not be attending because the problem is not particularly acute, they may include new symptoms, in order to legitimise attendance and these can confuse any decisions about the condition to a considerable degree. The art of questioning the patient is therefore to make the 'story' rather more specific and tease out signs and symptoms that the patient may not have considered pertinent, without prompting the patient into responses that are not true for them but are those that they think the clinician is looking for.

Minor trauma

'The majority of (eye) injuries are superficial in nature and transient in their effects but place considerable demands on A&E services.' MacEwan (1989, p. 888).

The vast majority of eye injuries are, as MacEwan suggests, 'trivial' in comparison to other presentations to general emergency care settings, but still form a large proportion of those patients presenting acutely to ophthalmic services. It is always important to remember that, however 'trivial' or 'run of the mill' the patient's problem may seem to ophthalmic professionals, to the patient no injury is trivial; it is likely to be a major life event, causing pain, distress and anxiety.

Identifying the extent of surface ocular trauma

A light source and single-use fluorescein Minims or impregnated strips are the crucial elements in identifying the extent of surface trauma. Both white- and cobalt blue-filtered light are necessary and magnification enables much more comprehensive assessment. The tools used may therefore range from a pen-torch or ophthalmoscope, a head loupe or ring light with integral magnification to (in the best case) a slit-lamp and a clinician with the skills to use it!

Fluorescein stains damaged epithelial cells and shows a bright green/yellow stain under cobalt blue light. It is therefore used to show the extent of both conjunctival and corneal epithelial loss. It is relatively non-toxic to ocular tissue so it may be used even where there is suspected perforation.

Traumatic subconjunctival haemorrhage

This is common after a variety of injuries and is, in itself, self-limiting, requiring no treatment. Fluorescein should be instilled and the eye examined using a cobalt blue light on a pen-torch, ophthalmoscope or, ideally, a slit-lamp to rule out a conjunctival laceration. The patient should be reassured that the haemorrhage will resolve, usually over a period of weeks.

A traumatic subconjunctival haemorrhage that extends backwards so that the posterior border is not visible may indicate significant orbital trauma and may need further investigation if the history, and other signs and symptoms are indicative of this.

Corneal trauma

The two main components of the corneal injury are extent and depth, and both must be assessed. The extent may be assessed using simple direct illumination from a pen-torch or ophthalmoscope. Depth is better assessed using a slit-lamp, but may be considered by using a slightly angled view of the cornea, rather than considering the injury just from a 'straight-on' view (Marsden 2001). The degree of epithelial loss is not a good indicator of the severity of injury and, because pain is associated with epithelial loss, a high level of pain may not indicate a severe injury. It is always important to consider the depth of corneal foreign bodies before removal. Occasionally, foreign bodies may perforate the cornea and extend into the anterior chamber, and this must be identified so that appropriate measures may be taken for removal – perhaps in a theatre environment.

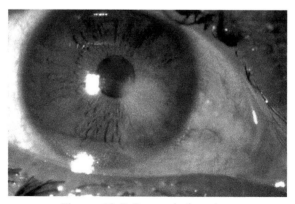

Figure 12.3 Corneal abrasion.
(Photo reprinted by permission of the International Centre for Eye Health – ICEH.)

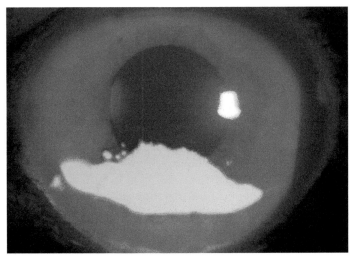

Figure 12.4 Exposure keratitis.
(With permission of Angela Chappell, Ophthalmic Imaging Department,
Flinders Medical Centre, Adelaide, South Australia.)

Findings should be documented, generally by illustrating the location and extent of the injury on a diagram. It is possible, when using a slit-lamp, to measure the extent of injury but, otherwise, as accurate an interpretation as possible should be drawn. This is useful for identifying the progress of healing at any subsequent review visits.

Fluorescein may be used in identifying perforation of the cornea (or sclera) in cases where the eye appears to be intact but there is suspicion of deep penetration. A drop of fluorescein instilled into the lower fornix will spread over the cornea as the patient blinks. If there is corneal or scleral perforation, aqueous fluid will tend to leak out of the perforation and wash away the fluorescein film. If the eye is illuminated by a cobalt blue light, the observer will see black streaks appearing in the fluorescein film under the site of the injury. This will indicate an aqueous leak and is confirmation of perforation.

Treatment of surface ocular trauma

Having identified the extent of trauma, there are a number of decisions to be made about treatment. Treatment decisions will affect patient comfort and the patient's experience of trauma. It is therefore important that care is optimised for each patient.

The three main areas that need consideration are:

- Prevention of infection
- Treatment of pain
- Optimisation of healing.

Prevention of infection

One of the eye's major innate defence mechanisms against pathogens is the integrity of the corneal epithelium. The eye normally has a population of commensal bacteria (diphtheroids, staphylococci, streptococci), which prevent colonisation with pathogenic bacteria (Forrester *et al.* 2016, Newell 1996). Disruption of the corneal epithelium allows penetration of the outer coat of the eye by these and any other opportunistic pathogens, which can result in infection of the cornea itself (infective keratitis) or infection of the interior structures of the eye (endophthalmitis), which can be catastrophic to ocular tissues and any prognosis for useful vision.

Clearly, any breach in the corneal epithelium requires treatment with topical prophylactic antibiotic until the epithelium is healed. Conjunctival epithelial loss is less likely to lead to ocular infection, due to the nature of the specialised conjunctival immune system and the fact that it is close to the globe rather than being part of it. Antibiotic prophylaxis is generally given after conjunctival injury.

Antibiotic as prophylaxis rather than treatment

As antibiotics are for prophylaxis, the choice should be one with a broad spectrum of activity and, in practice, in acute care settings, this is likely to mean either chloramphenicol or fusidic acid preparations (Fucidin). Short courses of topical chloramphenicol do not appear to cause systemic side effects (Besamusca & Bastiensen 1986, Consumers' Association 1997) and it is considered to be a very safe drug, widely used throughout ophthalmology in the UK. Chloramphenicol is available in both drop and ointment form and fusidic acid as a viscous drop, which becomes clear and liquid on hitting the tear film of the eye. Chloramphenicol is usually prescribed four times daily and fusidic acid twice daily; this regimen should be continued until the epithelium is healed. Often, a 5-day course is prescribed but the reasons for this are traditional rather than evidence based. It can be left to the patient's discretion to stop the antibiotic once any pain has resolved, i.e. when the epithelium has healed and the risk of infection has passed.

The choice of antibiotic treatment is often limited by what is available, but consideration must also be given to the vehicle – and whether a drop or ointment form is preferable. Fechner and Teichmann (1998) prefer ointment and Rhee and Pyfer (1999) suggest that both are equally effective. Practitioner experience suggests, however, that ointment provides much more comfort, as it provides a greasy surface between the injured conjunctiva or cornea and the lids. Certainly, if an eye pad is worn, ointment should be used because the antibiotic will be present on the eye for much longer than a drop, underneath the eye pad. Ointment does tend to blur vision for a few minutes but this can be minimised by advising the patient to instil no more than a couple of millimetres of the ointment. Patients should be informed that chloramphenicol has an unpleasant taste and, as the lacrimal drainage system eventually drains down the back of the throat, chloramphenicol drops or ointment will be tasted for some while after instillation.

If perforation of the cornea is suspected or confirmed, a single drop of unpreserved, single-dose chloramphenicol (in Minim form) may be instilled before further assessment. Both preservatives and ointment are toxic to ocular tissues and should not be used.

Dealing with pain

Any breach in the corneal epithelium will cause a degree of discomfort or pain, as the corneal nerves are damaged and exposed and the extent of epithelial loss is likely to be related to the degree of pain experienced by the patient. Corneal pain is difficult to treat, but a number of strategies can be used and accurate assessment of the degree of pain is required. Conjunctival trauma causes much less pain and foreign body sites, whether conjunctival or corneal, are usually described as being irritable rather than painful.

Topical anaesthesia

For examination purposes and to obtain an accurate visual acuity assessment, topical anaesthesia should be used. Literature has suggested that repeated instillation will result in dose-related toxicity to the corneal epithelium and delay in healing caused by inhibition of cell division. However, much of this research has been related to long-term use and abuse of these drops. More recent studies suggest that the short-term use of these drops is not likely to result in problems such as reduced or delayed healing (Verma *et al.* 1995, 1997, Brilakis & Deutsch 2000); and, indeed, these drops are given routinely after corneal laser surgery. If the patient is supplied with drops, the volume of drops should be small so that a 48- or 72-hour supply only is given (for example, a single Minim) and the patient should be told to return if pain persists or gets worse at any point (Waldman *et al.* 2014, Swaminathan *et al.* 2015)

Pupil dilatation

A component of the pain experienced is likely to be a result of ciliary spasm when there is more than a very small area of corneal epithelial loss. This can be seen because the pupil of the affected eye reacts more slowly than that of the uninjured eye. Relief of the spasm, and some of the pain, may be achieved by instilling drops such as tropicamide or cyclopentolate 1% to dilate the pupil. Of these, cyclopentolate 1% lasts longer. The patient should be warned that these drops paralyse the ciliary muscle and so accommodation and the patient's near vision will be blurred because focusing is impossible. Atropine should never be used because it is completely irreversible and lasts from 10 to 14 days.

Topical analgesia

Prostaglandins play a major role in pain sensation, and non-steroidal anti-inflammatory drugs (NSAIDs) are used systemically as analgesics to inhibit the enzyme cyclo-oxygenase and therefore decrease the synthesis of prostaglandins (Fechner & Teichmann 1998). Topical NSAIDs have been evaluated for use in corneal pain (Brahma *et al.* 1996) and found to be extremely useful. Their use does not appear to delay healing and no adverse effects have been found where the cornea is not otherwise compromised and the NSAID is used only for a short time. For patients with corneal pain, topical NSAIDs therefore provide a significant degree of effective pain relief and are usually prescribed four times daily (Brahma *et al.* 1996, Fechner & Teichmann 1998, Rhee &Pyfer 1999).

Three NSAIDs are available in eye drop form: diclofenac sodium and flurbiprofen sodium in single-dose units and ketorolac trometamol and nepafenac as a 5-ml bottle, which may be more cost-effective.

Systemic analgesia

Use of topical analgesia should almost remove the need for systemic analgesia. Pain associated with other branches of the trigeminal nerve is notoriously difficult to treat. Practitioner experience suggests that many common analgesics provide little relief for corneal pain and other strategies, such as those discussed, have a rather better effect. If systemic analgesia is suggested, the analgesic that the patient normally takes is as likely to be effective as anything else, although NSAIDs plus paracetamol (in combination) have been reported to work well.

Padding for corneal abrasion

To pad or not to pad, that is the question. A number of studies have been undertaken that address the question of eye pads and there have been equivocal results, ranging from faster to slower healing and suggesting, over a large sample, little effect on pain. Interpretation of these results suggests that there will be a number of patients below and a number above this mean conclusion. It is clear, therefore, that for some patients padding will make their situation better, whereas for others there is no doubt that their level of pain will increase. If the decision is to pad nobody, a significant number of patients will be denied effective pain relief. A strategy might therefore be devised to pad those patients who have significant pain, while telling them that this is for comfort only and that, if the pad makes the pain worse, they should remove it.

A double eye pad should always be used, one pad folded over the closed lids and the other open on top of it (Figure 12.5). The whole is taped firmly to the face so that the patient cannot open the eye underneath the pad.

Medication (dilating drops, analgesia, antibiotic) should be instilled before padding and antibiotic ointment should be used because it will be present on the cornea for longer than in drop form. If comfortable, the pad should be left intact for 24 hours, then removed and instillation of medication started. If the pad is uncomfortable, it may be removed and medication started.

Do not pad the eyes of patients who are driving home. If they leave the pad on and drive anyway, they are probably breaking the law, and certainly invalidating their insurance and driving extremely dangerously. If they take it off to drive, time, materials and effort have been wasted. Patients are much more likely to comply with advice if they are allowed to drive home and advised on how to apply the eye pad themselves when they arrive. A drop of local anaesthetic will facilitate a safe drive home.

Patients should never have both eyes padded at once because this is extremely disorienting and disabling. If both eyes are affected, the worst should be padded and pads given for use at home for the other eye if necessary.

Figure 12.5 Eye padding: one pad is folded and placed over the closed lid; the other is open over the top and taped down.

Optimisation of healing

Education is needed to persuade the patient of the importance of continuing to use prescribed medication to avoid corneal infection. Decisions as to whether or not to review simple corneal abrasions depend very much on the individual clinician. It is useful to review large abrasions to ensure that healing is taking place and that there is no loose epithelium that needs debriding.

Recurrent erosion syndrome

Recurrent erosion syndrome is a distinct possibility for those patients who have an animal or vegetable cause for their corneal trauma (e.g. plant or fingernail). The filaments that anchor the epithelium to Bowman's membrane may take even longer to heal and, until this happens, the epithelium is unstable and easily damaged. It is helpful to explain this to the patient.

It should also be explained that the patient is most vulnerable to epithelial loss at night because the epithelium sticks to the conjunctiva of the eyelid (rather than to its basement membrane) while the eye is relatively dry, overnight. The epithelium may therefore be peeled off by the mechanical action of the lid opening on waking. This can be prevented, until the epithelium is stable, by using ointment at night before sleeping, to keep the eye lubricated. 'Simple' ointment, or Lubri-Tears or Lacri-Lube (ointment base without drugs), should be used for up to 3 months to prevent this happening. Treatment of recurrent erosion may include bandage contact lenses; and, in refractory cases, photorefractive keratectomy is sometimes used.

Foreign bodies
Subtarsal foreign body

The patient often presents with a foreign body sensation and a history of something falling or blowing into the eye. Management involves everting the upper lid, using a moistened cotton-tipped swab. Any foreign material trapped underneath the lid may be wiped off with the swab. Unless severe pain prevents lid eversion, no local anaesthetic should be instilled. The patient can confirm that all foreign bodies have been removed, as the previously gritty pain disappears (Cheng *et al.* 1997). The eye should then be stained with fluorescein to rule out any corneal abrasion. If corneal abrasions are present, they are often linear and superficial.

If the corneal injury is minimal, a 'stat' instillation of antibiotic ointment is usually sufficient. If larger abrasions are present, they should be treated as corneal abrasions.

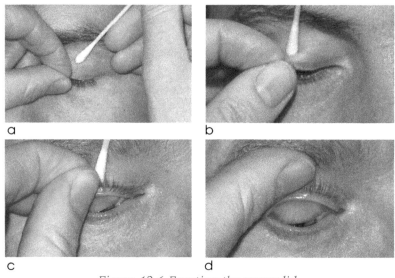

a

b

c

d

Figure 12.6 Everting the upper lid.

Conjunctival foreign body

Foreign bodies do not often penetrate the conjunctiva and are therefore easily wiped off using a moistened cotton bud, after instillation of local anaesthetic. The resultant abrasion and any concurrent abrasion may be treated with antibiotic ointment. A pad is not usually necessary and the degree of pain experienced is much less than with corneal trauma.

Corneal foreign body

Corneal foreign bodies are very common, often resulting from grinding wheels and other industrial machines, DIY and wind-borne foreign bodies. Superficial foreign bodies are often easily removed with a moistened cotton bud after instillation of local anaesthetic, and the resultant small abrasion should be treated with antibiotic ointment.

Impacted corneal foreign bodies need to be removed using the edge of a 21-gauge hypodermic needle held tangentially to the cornea, with the hand resting on the patient's cheek or nose. The needle may be mounted on a cotton-tipped applicator or syringe for easier manipulation. After the initial removal of the foreign body, a rust ring often remains. This must be removed completely, but this is easier after 24–48 hours of treatment with antibiotic ointment.

Removal of a corneal foreign body with a needle is a procedure that must be carried out with extreme care. Although the cornea is tough, it is quite possible to penetrate it with a needle; if the foreign body is 'dug' out too enthusiastically and the deeper layers of the cornea are damaged, a corneal scar will result. This might cause major visual problems if it involves the visual axis. It is therefore important that, if the area possesses a slit-lamp, it is used during the removal of corneal foreign bodies, so that a high degree of magnification and support for the patient's head is possible.

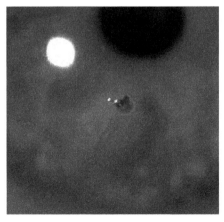

Figure 12.7 Foreign body.

After removal of a foreign body, treatment is as for a corneal abrasion, although, because little corneal epithelium is lost and pain is minimal, a pad is not usually required. Many patients have repeat visits for removal of a corneal foreign body and treat them as an occupational hazard. Opportunities should be taken for health education about eye protection. A battery-operated tool with a tiny rotating burr on the end is sometimes preferred for removal of corneal foreign body. However, tips should be disposable, rather than re-used, so they will not be as cost-effective as a needle. These tools also leave the corneal irregular, with a very clear corneal 'dent', even after healing.

X-ray examination is indicated only if there is a definite history of a high-speed foreign body hitting the eye (e.g. hammer and chisel) and no foreign body can be found. It is most unlikely that one foreign body would penetrate the eye, while another stayed on the cornea.

Superglue injuries

Cyanoacrylate glue is usually instilled into the eye by accident because the container may resemble an eye drop or ointment applicator. The patient usually presents with eyelids stuck together and there is often a degree of pain. The tear film usually prevents adhesion of the glue to the globe; and the pain is often caused by a corneal abrasion, resulting from a plaque of glue that is inside the lids and is rubbing on the cornea.

Treatment consists of separating the lids and removing any pieces of glue from the fornices. The lids are usually separated by cutting the lashes very close to the lid margin because these are often what is holding the lids together. The dried glue must be picked off the lid margins. The procedure may be painful and lengthy. Extreme care must be taken not to injure the lid margin. Instillation of topical anaesthetic drop through any gap in the lids will facilitate cooperation. Children may need a general anaesthetic. Any corneal damage is treated as an abrasion.

Blunt trauma

Blunt trauma occurs when the globe is hit with force. The globe may distort as a result of the pressure placed on it and this distortion may cause damage to any or all of the structures within it. As the force is removed, the globe springs back into shape. The force that this places on tissues within the eye may again cause disruption to them. A history of blunt ocular trauma (squash ball, shuttlecock, elbow to the eye, etc.) should give a high index of suspicion of this type of injury. Children, in particular, are likely to feel ill and drowsy, and parents and carers will need advice regarding symptoms of head injury.

Anterior segment contusion injuries

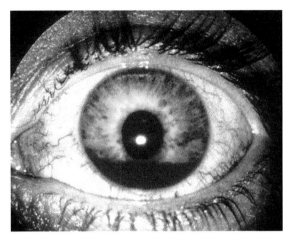

Figure 12.8 Hyphaema.

Traumatic hyphaema may be detected only with a slit-lamp (red blood cells floating in the anterior chamber) or may be visible with the naked eye, to the extent of filling the whole of the anterior chamber. Any hyphaema is likely to result in loss of vision. In cases where the hyphaema is large, red blood cells may block the trabecular meshwork, resulting in raised intraocular pressure (IOP) and severe pain. The pupil may be irregular or sluggish.

Treatment of hyphaema includes rest at home, with regular ophthalmic review to check both the IOP and the process of reabsorption. Sitting and sleeping upright should be encouraged in order to allow the blood cells to settle and absorb, away from the visual axis. Red blood cells that are haemolysed while free in the anterior chamber, or settled on the corneal endothelium, may stain the corneal endothelium with haem pigment, which may affect vision. This stain takes some months to clear and reabsorbs from the periphery inwards. Central staining will cause visual disability and perhaps deprivation amblyopia in a young child (Eagling & Roper-Hall 1986). The patient will need to have a posterior segment examination, generally when the hyphaema has settled and the eye is less tender, in order to assess retinal integrity.

Traumatic uveitis
This is a common effect of blunt trauma and may be the only sign of it. Treatment is as for any uveitis, with pupil dilatation and topical steroids.

Iris and pupil abnormalities
Traumatic mydriasis or miosis may occur as a consequence of blunt trauma and the pupil may be irregular, when compared with the fellow eye, as a result of partial or

complete rupture of the iris sphincter. Disinsertion of the iris base from the ciliary body may cause what appears to be a 'hole' in the iris at its base (iridodialysis) and is often associated with hyphaema. No treatment is immediately necessary and surgery is unlikely to be undertaken unless the visual axis is compromised.

Lens abnormalities

The impact of the iris on the lens as the eye changes shape may leave a circle of iris pigment which can be seen after dilatation (Vossius' ring). Traumatic rupture of the zonules may occur. If 25% or more are ruptured, the lens is no longer held securely behind the iris. Luxation or subluxation of the lens may take place. There may be deepening of the anterior chamber, caused by tilting of the lens posteriorly, or it may appear shallow as a result of anterior displacement. Pupil block and raised IOP may occur if the lens blocks the pupil. Iridodonesis (iris tremble) may be visible.

Treatment may be required urgently if IOP rises or if the lens is dislocated anteriorly because it can compromise the corneal endothelium and cause corneal oedema. Posterior dislocation into the vitreous is likely to be dealt with less urgently and a secondary intraocular lens implanted.

Concussion or contusion cataract may appear as an immediate or long-term consequence of blunt trauma. More rarely, the lens capsule may rupture, releasing soft lens matter into the anterior chamber, and this requires early intervention.

Angle recession

Angle recession is a term used to describe tears into the anterior face of the ciliary body, which alter the appearance of the drainage angle. This type of injury (seen with the aid of a gonioscopy lens) is seen in almost all patients who present with a hyphaema and varies in severity. Angle recession may be associated with permanent damage to the aqueous outflow pathways and this leads, in the long term, to fibrosis of the affected trabecular meshwork and glaucoma of the affected eye. This may develop some years after the initial injury so patients with this type of injury should be encouraged to have regular optometric examinations to have their IOP checked, if they are not to be followed up by an ophthalmologist.

Posterior segment damage
Macular oedema

Macular oedema after blunt trauma may settle quickly or persist for some time. Where it persists for more than a few days, pigment scarring of the retina may develop as the oedema settles and the reduction in vision may be profound. Cystic degeneration of the retina may develop after macular oedema, which may result in a macular hole that needs surgical repair.

Choroidal rupture

Distortion of the globe may stretch the tissues around their attachment at the optic disc. This stretching may cause splits or ruptures in the choroid that are usually arcuate in shape and may occur anywhere in the posterior segment, concentric with the optic disc. They may be associated with haemorrhage. The retina shows a crescent-shaped white area as the underlying sclera is exposed. If peripheral, the impact on the patient's vision may be minor – a peripheral scotoma. If the choroidal rupture occurs within the posterior pole, and particularly in the macular area, central vision may be profoundly affected.

Retinal injury

Commotio retinae results in reduced visual acuity and is the result of damage to the nerve fibre layer. It often resolves over a period of time.

Retinal tears, holes and dialysis

Retinal holes may be a late complication of blunt trauma, caused by atrophy of damaged areas of retina. Retinal dialysis (detachment of the retina at the ora serrata) usually follows impact. Retinal detachment may follow in time, so dialyses are often treated with cryotherapy or laser treatment to prevent this.

Severe blunt trauma to the globe may result in avulsion of the optic nerve. The patient is likely to present with complete loss of vision. Preretinal or vitreous haemorrhage may obscure the optic disc and there is likely to be a complete afferent pupillary defect. There is complete disruption of the retinal circulation, which will not recover. Table 12.2 (see p. 264) lists decision-making criteria when treating minor ocular trauma.

Major trauma

Orbital injury

Both facial and skull trauma can result in orbital injury. The orbits are each composed of seven bones, the thinnest of which are the lamina papyracea over the ethmoid sinuses (along the medial wall) and the maxillary bone on the orbital floor (see also Chapter 23).

Medial orbital fractures

The lacrimal secretory system (especially the nasolacrimal duct) may be damaged and the medial rectus muscle may be trapped within fractures of the lamina papyracea. Dacryocystorhinostomy may be required if the nasolacrimal duct is obstructed. Surgical exploration of the medial orbit may be necessary if mechanical restriction of ocular motility is present.

Orbital floor fractures

These are often referred to as blow-out fractures because they are produced by transmission of forces through the bones and soft tissues of the orbit by a non-penetrating object such as a fist or ball. These fractures may be complicated by the entrapment of muscles and orbital fat, which limit ocular motility. Surgery is not always indicated because oedematous tissues often settle, freeing muscles and allowing correct motility.

Signs and symptoms include diplopia, enophthalmos, emphysema and infraorbital anaesthesia, and a classic presentation involves an injured patient, who would perhaps not have presented to A&E otherwise, blowing their nose and then attending because the eyelids have swollen alarmingly, as air from the sinus has been driven into the tissues of the lid.

The patient should be given advice about avoiding Valsalva's manoeuvre, such as blowing the nose or straining at stool. Investigations should include orthoptic assessment, to accurately assess the effect of the trauma on extraocular movement. Computerised tomography (CT) will be undertaken to identify the extent of trauma and plan repair. Broad-spectrum antibiotics are likely to be prescribed to prevent orbital cellulitis.

Table 12.2 Decision-making: treating surface ocular trauma

	Traumatic subconjunctival haemorrhage (superficial trauma)	Conjunctival abrasion	Conjunctival foreign body	Subtarsal foreign body	Corneal foreign body	Corneal abrasion	Corneal laceration	Conjunctival laceration
Likely degree of pain	Mild	Mild	Mild	Mild to moderate	Mild – irritation	Mild to severe	Mild to severe	Mild to moderate
Dealing with the pain	Ointment for lubrication of irregular ocular surface	Ointment for lubrication between conjunctiva and lid	Ointment as a single dose or depending on the extent of epithelial loss	Ointment as a single dose or depending on the extent of corneal and conjunctival epithelial loss	? dilate Ointment if not a deep cavitiy	? dilate Ointment Non- steroidal systemic ? pad ? topical anaesthetic	? dilate? non-steroidal systemic	ointment
Stopping infection	No need, no break in integrity	Antibiotic ointment until feeling back to normal (conjunctiva healed)	Antibiotic ointment until feeling back to normal (conjunctiva healed)	Antibiotic ointment until feeling back to normal (conjunctiva healed)	Ointment or drops until feeling back to normal (cornea healed) Ensure all rust removed	Ointment or drops until feeling back to normal (cornea healed) Prevent recurrence by ointment at night	Drops until feeling back to normal (cornea healed) May need corneal contact lens	Ointment until feeling back to normal (cornea healed)
Review	Not normally	No need	No need	No need	For rust removal	If large, loose conjunctiva, not healing	Yes	If large
Other							If other than very small and shallow, refer	

Orbital apex trauma

Fractures of the orbital apex may result from direct, non-penetrating, blunt trauma or from penetrating trauma such as with large orbital foreign bodies. Orbital apex fractures present differently, depending on the degree of injury to the vascular and neural structures within the orbital apex, and various syndromes have been defined to describe different presentations (Bater *et al.* 2008).

Optic nerve trauma

Optic nerve injury may occur, commonly as a result of traumatic optic neuropathy from indirect trauma (e.g. fractures of the base of the skull). Haematoma may compress the nerve or the nerve may be damaged by a foreign body or a fracture, which can result in a spectrum of injury from minor trauma to the nerve to complete transection. Injury to the cranial nerves present in the orbit (III, IV and VI) may present as extraocular muscle palsy with diplopia, and injury to the trigeminal nerve (V) as sensory disturbance to areas that it supplies.

It is most likely that patients with this type of injury will present first to general A&E, and clinicians there must be alerted to the possibility of ocular involvement from indirect trauma such as base of skull fractures, as well as from more direct trauma where the eyes themselves do not appear to be involved. Collaboration of ophthalmic units with A&E is necessary to ensure that patients with this type of injury do not lose vision unnecessarily. Patient complaints of loss of or reduction in vision must be taken very seriously; in order to quantify this, visual acuity must be checked regularly in this group of patients and ophthalmological opinion obtained immediately if vision is involved.

Retrobulbar haemorrhage

This may occur from direct or indirect trauma to the orbit and progress rapidly, resulting in pain, proptosis of the globe, lid and conjunctival swelling, and congested conjunctival vessels. Subconjunctival haemorrhage may be dense and extend beyond the visible conjunctiva. If the globe begins to proptose after trauma, an ophthalmologist should be involved immediately. CT or magnetic resonance imaging (MRI) may be required urgently and the patient's visual acuity should be checked very frequently (perhaps every 10 minutes).

If visual acuity reduces, emergency decompression by lateral canthotomy (a horizontal incision at the lateral canthus, through skin and conjunctiva, and then through the lateral canthal tendon, under local anaesthetic) will be required to relieve pressure on the optic nerve. Equipment for this procedure will not be needed very often but should be readily available in any area in which this group of patients is likely to present, so that avoidable loss of vision may be prevented. Wherever the patient presents, regular observation of the appearance of the patient, accompanied by measurement of visual acuity and encouragement of the patient to report new symptoms where they are able, will help to minimise complications of the injury.

Open trauma

An open eye requires immediate assessment. If any retained materials protrude from the globe, no attempt should be made to remove them. The material should be stabilised as far as possible, perhaps by taping it to the cheek if this seems appropriate or by covering the whole area with a plastic shield or small gallipot or receiver.

No pressure should be put on to an eye with a full-thickness injury and, although it might seem appropriate to cover the area with a pad, this should be done only if no other method of covering the eye exists, and should be undertaken only with extreme care. The pad must be loose and taped well away from the globe.

Patients with even very severe eye trauma may not have much pain if there is little corneal epithelial loss. The control of any pain and nausea must be a priority, however, because vomiting with an open eye is likely to lead to loss of the ocular contents. A rise in IOP may be minimised by caring for the patient with them either lying flat or sitting up at around a 30° angle.

Unless both eyes are extensively damaged, there should never be an occasion when both eyes are covered. A patient with one damaged eye is unlikely to be comforted, reassured or relaxed by having both eyes occluded and being unable to see anything going on around them or the person who is talking to them.

Lid trauma

For the eyes to be protected, the lids must be intact, in the correct position and without any disruption to their structure and function. Repair of lid trauma may be delayed as a result of the extremely good vascularisation of the lids and associated structures. The repair may therefore be a planned activity, rather than an emergency one, leading to the best possible functional and cosmetic result for the patient.

Ocular burns

Burns to the eye and surrounding structures present to the acute setting from a variety of domestic and industrial sources. Ocular burns may be divided most commonly into chemical, thermal and radiation; and chemical burns, in particular, can be quite devastating to the eye and to the patient's potential for vision. The degree of injury depends on the type of substance involved, but, most importantly, on the length of contact time. Patients with burns from heat or radiation have been separated from the source of the injury by the time they reach A&E or the ophthalmic unit. However, patients with chemical injury are likely to have residual chemical in and around their eye and therefore need immediate treatment (irrigation) in order to minimise the injury. If the chemical injury is recent (3–4 hours), they will be triaged red – immediate – and all assessment, including visual acuity, should be delayed until irrigation has taken place. A prompt and effective response to a chemical injury is vital in order to minimise tissue damage.

Chemical burns

These are the most urgent category of ocular burns and are usually caused by alkalis, acids or solvents. Alkaline chemicals include:

- Calcium hydroxide (lime), found in plaster and mortar, sodium or potassium hydroxide, which are used as cleaning agents (e.g. drain cleaner)
- Ammonia, which is again used as a cleaning agent
- Ammonium hydroxide, which is found in fertiliser.

Alkalis penetrate rapidly through corneal tissue, combining with cell membrane lipids, and result in cell disruption and tissue softening. A rapid rise in the pH in the anterior chamber may cause damage to the iris, ciliary body and lens. Damage to vascular channels leads to ischaemia.

Acids are less penetrating, and most damage is done during and soon after initial exposure. Acid substances precipitate tissue proteins, forming barriers against deeper penetration and localising damage to the point of contact. Most commonly, domestic acid injuries are the result of contact with car battery (sulphuric) acid. Most acids are used in dilute form; however, given sufficient concentration or volume, they may still cause severe ocular injury. Acid substances include hydrochloric, sulphuric and acetic acids, and also complex organic and inorganic compounds. Hydrofluoric acid (used particularly by stonemasons) is exceptional in that it causes progressive damage similar to an alkaline substance.

Solvents, such as petrol, perfume, alcohol and volatile cleaning fluids, although very painful initially, tend to cause only minor and transient injury. Thermal and/ or contusion injuries caused by the temperature or pressure of the chemical may be superimposed on the chemical injury.

Sequelae of ophthalmic chemical injury

Minor chemical burns of the eye are likely to heal rapidly without residual scarring. More severe burns result in an acute inflammatory response, during which the corneal tissue is at risk of perforation as a result of the release of proteolytic enzymes from the white blood cells. As the eye heals, formation of scar tissue may cause vascularisation and opacification of the cornea. Symblepharon – or adhesions between the conjunctiva that lines the lid and the conjunctiva covering the globe – may form and limit lid closure and eye movement, a problem that will necessitate major reconstructive surgery. The lids may be damaged and this can result in trichiasis, where the lashes grow inwards and rub and irritate the eye. The lid itself may roll inwards (entropion) or outwards (ectropion) as a result of scarring and, again, cause problems with lid closure and exposure of the globe. Dry eyes often follow a chemical injury and are the result of damage to lacrimal ducts and secretory cells, causing reduced tear secretion. It is therefore most important that appropriate treatment starts as rapidly as possible, to minimise long-term problems and maximise visual potential.

Initial management

Irrigation

The initial treatment of any chemical eye injury involves copious irrigation to dilute the chemical and remove particulate matter. Irrigation should start immediately, using whatever source is available. Significant research has taken place on irrigating fluids, mostly in animal models. Rihawi (2008) concluded that a small amount of borate buffer was more effective than sodium chloride (NaCl) for severe alkaline injuries and other studies have suggested that irrigation with NaCl and other high osmolarity solutions causes corneal swelling, damage to intercellular junctions and epithelial sloughing (Kompa *et al.* 2002) and that excessive irrigation has the potential for further, if temporary, corneal damage.

Tap or sterile water has been recommended for irrigation, as a low osmolarity solution; as long as appropriate equipment is available to ensure a controllable, directable flow of fluid, this would provide effective irrigation. Normal (0.9) saline is often used via a giving set as a convenient, directable, controllable jet of sterile fluid.

Whichever source is used, irrigation needs to be timely and effective. Failing the immediate availability of fluid and a giving set, a running tap may be used to irrigate the eye in the interim. Buffer solutions, which neutralise both acid and alkaline chemicals, are available in some areas but are expensive and therefore not widely used.

A drop of local anaesthetic (such as oxybuprocaine 0.4%, amethocaine 1% or proxymetacaine 0.5%) should be instilled before irrigation to assist in patient compliance and to minimise pain. This may need to be repeated during the irrigation. Although repeated instillation of topical anaesthetic is not generally recommended, in order to facilitate effective irrigation and subsequent examination of the patient's eye, repeated instillation may be necessary to relieve pain and is therefore desirable.

During the procedure, the patient needs frequent information, explanations and reassurance. They may be encouraged to hold a container to collect the irrigation fluid and clothes should be protected with waterproof covering such as a cape or plastic sheet. Irrigation should take place with the patient sitting upright in a comfortable chair with their head supported and inclined to the side of the eye to be irrigated. Irrigating patients' eyes while they are lying down only ensures that they get extremely wet and are less likely to be able to cooperate in the procedure, as they strive to protect themselves from what may feel like 'drowning'.

Contact lenses should be removed before irrigation. If left in place, a contact lens will ensure that a reservoir of chemical remains on the surface of the eye. The eyelids should be held open, manually or using a speculum, and all aspects of the cornea and conjunctiva irrigated, including the conjunctiva exposed by everting the upper lid. All particles of chemical matter should be removed, by wiping with a cotton-tipped applicator if necessary. Particles may lodge under the everted upper lid, in the upper fornix. This is usually impossible to visualise but may be reached by sweeping a wet cotton-tipped applicator under the edge of the everted upper lid and up into the upper fornix. Double eversion of the lid may be possible but this is a very uncomfortable procedure; and full explanation, reassurance and perhaps another drop of topical anaesthetic will be required to ensure that the procedure is tolerated.

Any delay caused by attempting to identify the chemical or an appropriate neutralising solution adds to the contact time and increases the risk of more severe injury. It is best to assume that previous irrigation, outside the ophthalmic setting, has been inadequate and therefore effective irrigation must be carried out immediately. It is impossible to specify an exact time for irrigation, or a volume of fluid that should be used, because this depends on the nature of the chemical and its physical state as well as the patient's condition. Clinical decisions about solutions, volume and irrigation times should rely on the strength of the chemical, time between injury and irrigation, the presenting pH and the presence of particles in the chemical. At some point, however, irrigation must be stopped so that assessment, examination and treatment can commence.

The usefulness of pH paper to check for adequate irrigation may be debatable. In alkaline injury, in particular, the chemical will leach out of the eye for a number of hours after injury, thus altering the pH of the tear film. However, delaying therapy for several hours, until the pH is back to normal (neutral = pH 7, the conjunctival sac's normal pH is around 7.4 – Forrester *et al.* 1996), will delay healing and irrigation for this length of time and is therefore not practicable or desirable.

There is little in the literature to suggest when the pH of the tear film should be tested. Several minutes should be left to elapse without irrigation before testing; otherwise, the irrigation fluid may be tested instead and this may lead to inappropriate cessation of irrigation. However, if some time is allowed to elapse before testing the pH of the tear film with indicator paper, and the pH then proves to be abnormal, the eye will have had a long period without irrigation in which further damage may have occurred. Ultimately, indicator paper is no substitute for prompt, adequate and thorough irrigation; the clinical decision-making capabilities of the nurse, coupled with a strong knowledge base, will ensure that the decision to stop irrigation is taken appropriately.

After irrigation, the patient's visual acuity should be checked to provide a baseline. Cheng *et al.* (1997) suggest that patients with epithelial damage, including less than one-third of the corneal epithelium or a similar area of conjunctival epithelium, may be treated in the same way as a patient with a corneal abrasion. However, the eye may look deceptively normal as a result of tissue blanching and ischaemia, which needs urgent assessment and treatment; a totally white eye after chemical injury may in fact be a sign of severe ischaemia with a poor prognosis for vision. Accurate assessment of the condition of the eye is therefore vital.

Initial ophthalmic management

Medication usually includes:

- Topical steroids: to reduce and control inflammation
- Topical antibiotics: prophylactic use to prevent secondary infection
- Ointment: keeping burned surfaces apart with a layer of ointment to stop aberrant healing (symblepharon) and enhance patient comfort
- Mydriatics, such as cyclopentolate 1%, to dilate the pupil, reduce pain caused by ciliary spasm and prevent adhesions between the iris and the lens (posterior synechiae) resulting from intraocular inflammation.

Potassium ascorbate drops or systemic ascorbic acid may be used after alkali injury, as ascorbate levels become depressed. This substance is believed to be necessary for the synthesis of collagen, so it may therefore be prescribed in order to maximise healing, although there is no evidence that it has any effect in humans (Mackway-Jones & Marsden 2003). Instilling a weak acid into a damaged eye is not pleasant for the patient and admission to hospital may therefore be required.

Rodding is a technique involving use of a glass rod and antibiotic ointment. The ointment is instilled into the eye and the rod is used, after instillation of topical anaesthetic, to spread the ointment over all surfaces of the conjunctiva, particularly in the upper and lower fornices, to keep the surfaces of conjunctiva apart and prevent the formation of symblepharon. This may need to be done regularly in a badly burned eye.

Solvent injuries

After injury with a solvent, the patient often experiences acute and severe pain and 'stinging' in the eye, which may have settled somewhat by the time they present to the clinical area. On examination, the eye is likely to be generally 'red' and punctate stains are seen on the cornea after instillation of fluorescein. Treatment of solvent injury is generally with antibiotic ointment to prevent infection and aid comfort. Pupil dilatation may help to minimise pain. The patient should be reassured that this type of injury resolves very quickly and is not likely to have any permanent effects.

Thermal burns

These usually involve damage to the lids, although other external eye structures may be injured. Treatment of burns to lid skin is similar to that of thermal burns elsewhere on the body. Thermal burns range from very mild, such as those caused by tobacco ash, which may be treated as an abrasion (with dilatation of the pupil and chloramphenicol ointment), to the very severe burns caused by molten metal and glass, which may require reconstruction of the globe and surrounding structures. Thermal burns involving the lids can heal aberrantly, with scarring and tethering of lid skin and conjunctiva leading to lid closure and mobility problems. The eye should not be padded if lid burns are present (Onofrey *et al.* 1998).

Children, in particular, may sustain thermal burns to the cornea as a result of accidental exposure to a cigarette end, which – if held by an adult – is often at just the right height for a child to run into. Thermal corneal burns from this source are generally superficial (as a result of the child's immediate reaction and the wetness of the cornea) and may be treated as an abrasion. It would seem unlikely that corneal burns from cigarettes, in children, could be non-accidental, due to the fast reaction to close the eyelids if something is seen coming towards the eye. However, lid burns from cigarettes should evoke suspicion in the clinician and urgent referral to a child protection specialist is advised. The child should be examined for burns elsewhere, but this should take place in an appropriate setting – not necessarily in A&E or the ophthalmic unit.

Radiation burns

Although all radiation can cause eye injury, ultraviolet (UV) radiation is the most common source of injury and, when caused by welding, is often known as 'arc eye'. 'Arc eye' is the result of injury by UV radiation, most commonly after exposure to welding arcs, but also after exposure to UV 'sunlamps'. Sunbeds do not generally cause a problem because the intensity of the UV light is lower (see Figure 12.9).

The UV radiation is absorbed by the corneal epithelial cells, and results in local cell death. There is a latent period 6–12 hours – depending on the amount of exposure – before symptoms are experienced, which explains the traditional midnight to 2am presentation of these patients. The damaged epithelial cells slough off, exposing the nerve fibres underneath. The patient will then present with a gritty, sometimes intensely painful eye(s), with photophobia, watering and blurring of vision. Lid erythema and oedema may also be present.

The patient is likely to need topical anaesthetic drops before assessment of visual acuity and examination of the eye. On staining with fluorescein, punctate staining is seen over the surface of the cornea where some cells have been destroyed.

Treatment is as for a corneal abrasion, with a mydriatic drop and antibiotic ointment as prophylaxis and for comfort. Oral analgesia may be necessary. Padding may help but, as both eyes are often affected, the worst eye only should be padded and the other treated with frequent applications of ointment. Complete recovery is usually within 24–36 hours.

Metal inert gas (MIG) welding equipment uses high-intensity white light, which can burn the retina (in the same way as looking at the sun). Retinal examination may be required for patients whose vision does not return to normal after epithelial healing.

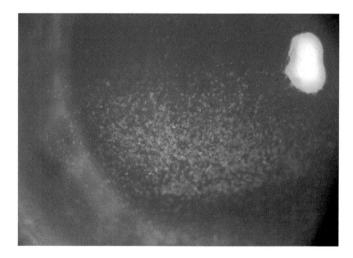

Figure 12.9 Punctate epithelial erosions.

(With permission of Angela Chappell, Ophthalmic Imaging Department, Flinders Medical Centre, Adelaide, South Australia.)

Other presenting problems
Non-traumatic red eye

Patients often present acutely with red eyes that are not associated with any trauma. It is important that all clinicians in contact with these patients are able to recognise signs and symptoms of common 'red eye' presentations so that appropriate and timely treatment can be facilitated. Many of the presentations discussed here are also discussed within other appropriate chapters. The presentation matrix is designed to remind clinicians of the presenting signs and symptoms of red eye so that appropriate decisions may be made about treatment and referral.

Subconjunctival haemorrhage

Patients may present with a spontaneous subconjunctival haemorrhage (see Figure 12.10). Often, the patient has not noticed any irritation but has been prompted to attend by others noticing the haemorrhage. This presents as a deep red patch of blood under the conjunctiva, which may be quite small and circumscribed or may be severe enough for the conjunctiva to resemble 'a bag of blood'.

Provided that there is no history of trauma, no treatment is needed. Subconjunctival haemorrhage may occasionally be associated with hypertension so blood pressure (BP) might be measured and recorded. However, the worry of the condition and 'white coat syndrome' may raise the patient's BP from normal levels. Patients with clotting disorders or those on anticoagulants (including aspirin) may be prone to repeat episodes and they should therefore be warned about this.

As the patient's eye appears much worse than it is, a lot of reassurance may be needed. Subconjunctival haemorrhages take up to 3 weeks to resolve and, because the conjunctiva is an elastic membrane, the blood may spread under it and actually appear worse, before it begins to resolve.

The eye may feel irritable as the conjunctiva is moved from its normal place and may be irregular. Artificial tears may be useful in minimising irritation while the haemorrhage settles. If there is a large amount of blood under the conjunctiva, uneven wetting of the cornea may occur as a result of the lid moving over misplaced conjunctiva rather than corneal epithelium. Corneal exposure may result, including dellen (a local area of corneal dryness). This can be treated if necessary, and further damage prevented, if the patient is encouraged to use frequent applications of lubricating ointment.

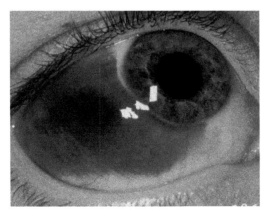

Figure 12.10 Subconjunctival haemorrhage.

Infective conjunctivitis

Inflammation of the conjunctiva is by far the most common cause of red eyes. Organisms involved in infective conjunctivitis include bacteria and viruses. Other causes of infective conjunctivitis are much less common. Bacterial conjunctivitis in adults is, in itself, much less common than often thought (Tullo & Donnelly 1995), and most conjunctivitis in adults is caused by a virus – often a type of adenovirus.

Conjunctivitis in children is more likely to be bacterial. Eye pads should never be suggested for patients with conjunctivitis. The warm, damp atmosphere underneath an eye pad will allow further organism growth and exacerbate the condition.

If a patient presents with a uniocular, chronic conjunctivitis (one that may have been persisting for some weeks, without the other eye becoming involved and with minor irritation and discomfort only) clinicians should have a high degree of suspicion that they may have a chlamydial infection. Appropriate swabs should be taken, followed by referral to an appropriate genitourinary medicine specialist if a positive swab result is received. Generally, there is little point in taking conjunctival swabs in adults (unless this condition is suspected) because a positive result of bacterial or viral conjunctivitis is most unlikely to change the treatment given to the patient.

As conjunctivitis is highly infectious, patients should not generally be offered a review appointment because all viral and bacterial conjunctivitis is self-limiting. If blurring of vision becomes a problem, however, the patient should be encouraged to return because keratitis caused by adenovirus may occasionally, if severe, be treated with steroid drops (see Chapter 16).

Allergic conjunctivitis

This is very common and presents acutely in two distinct ways. The first type of presentation is red eyes with itching and watering and an appearance of large bumps (papillae) on the subtarsal conjunctiva. This presentation is particularly common during the 'hay fever season' and may therefore be associated with a runny nose, sneezing, etc. Systemic antihistamine treatment is effective, as are antihistamine drops such as azelastine (Optilast), emedastine (Emadine) and levocabastine (Livostin Direct).

Mast cell-stabilising drops, such as sodium cromoglicate, help to stabilise the mast cell membranes and therefore prevent an allergic response. They are useful if sufferers of allergic eye symptoms start using them before the symptoms start, and continue them throughout the season, until the allergens are no longer present. Using them for an acute episode is unlikely to be helpful because it takes between a week and 10 days for the mast cell membranes to stabilise so that the drops can begin to work. Olopatadine (Opatanol) has both an antihistamine and a mast cell-stabilising effect and can therefore be used in an acute episode, and then carried on as a preventive measure.

The second presentation is by an acute and frightening atopic reaction (Figure 12.11), which involves massive chemosis or swelling of the conjunctiva, often described by the patient as 'jelly' on the eye. This is usually the result of the patient rubbing the eye with an allergen present on the hand or finger. Common allergens include some plant juices, pollen and animal dander or hairs. This condition is completely self-limiting and requires no treatment, unless the chemosis is severe and protruding from the closed lids. In this case, lubricant drops might be necessary. Reassurance about the condition is likely to be necessary and, if the reaction is severe, the patient may need to be monitored for systemic effects of the allergen.

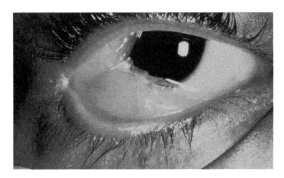

Figure 12.11 Chemosis.

Anterior uveitis

Uveitis is an inflammatory condition that may be associated with systemic disease, such as ankylosing spondylitis, but is often idiopathic. It may also occur secondary to trauma. The most common presenting symptoms are: photophobia; pain caused by iris and ciliary spasm; conjunctival redness (injection), which may be more marked around the corneoscleral junction (limbus); and decreased visual acuity. The reduction in vision is the result of protein and white blood cells that are part of the inflammatory reaction in the anterior chamber. The pupil, because of spasm and inflammation, is likely to be small (miosed) compared with the unaffected eye, and may react sluggishly. There will be a bright reflection of light when the cornea is illuminated, demonstrating the lack of corneal involvement, and there will be no staining with fluorescein (see Chapter 20).

Acute glaucoma (angle-closure glaucoma)

In acute glaucoma, the outflow of aqueous in the eye is obstructed by the peripheral iris covering the trabecular meshwork. As aqueous continues to be produced, the pressure inside the eye increases rapidly. This results in the sudden onset of severe pain (as a result of the increased IOP) and blurred vision (caused by corneal oedema).

Haloes may be seen around lights. The pain is not likely to be localised in the eye, but may involve the whole head and may be accompanied by nausea, vomiting and abdominal pain caused by vagal stimulation. Patients are usually elderly and are likely to be hypermetropic (long-sighted). On examination, the patient's eye will be red and the reflection of light from the cornea will be very diffuse – showing that the cornea is oedematous. The pupil will be semi-dilated, oval and fixed. A great deal of explanation, reassurance and care is needed by these ill and often terrified patients (see Chapter 21).

Table 12.3 Differential diagnosis of the red eye

	Conjunctivitis	Uveitis	Glaucoma	Corneal ulcers
Lids	? swollen Follicles, papillae if allergic	Normal	Normal	May be swollen
Conjunctiva	Injected	Injected	Injected	Injected
Cornea	? punctate staining	Normal, bright reaction	Very hazy	Opacity/stains with fluorescein
Anterior chamber	Deep	Deep	Shallow or flat	Deep
Iris	Normal	May look 'muddy'	May be difficult to see	Normal
Pupil	Normal	Slight miosis (compared with fellow) Sluggish	Fixed, oval, semi-dilated	Usually normal, may be slightly sluggish
Pain	Gritty	Deep pain in eye	Severe pain in and around eye and head	Gritty
Discharge	Pus/watery/sticky in morning	May water	No	May water
Photophobia	If severe	Yes	No	Not usually
Systemically	? flu-like symptoms (urticaria)	Well	Nausea Vomiting Severe abdominal pain Dehydration	Well

Corneal ulcers

There are three main types of corneal ulcer that are likely to be seen as acute presentations. Differentiation between the different types of corneal ulcer is sometimes difficult, and the treatment is completely different:

- Bacterial ulcers occur as 'fluffy' white demarcated areas on the cornea that stain with fluorescein.
- Marginal ulcers appear as ulcerated areas that stain with fluorescein and are usually close to the limbus. They are part of a hypersensitivity response by the eye to staphylococcal exotoxins and are usually treated with steroid eye drops.
- Ulcers caused by herpes simplex virus are known as 'dendritic' ulcers because of their branching, tree-like shape when stained with fluorescein. They are treated with aciclovir eye ointment primarily (see Chapter 17).

Painless loss of vision

There are many causes of painless loss of vision and many patients present with loss of vision acutely. It is often very difficult to differentiate between causes that need immediate care by an ophthalmic service and those that will cope with a delayed referral, and indeed need referral to other specialists.

Classification of loss of vision is also problematic, with a tendency to consider diagnoses rather than presentations. This schematic diagram divides loss of vision into different sections, depending on the patient's presenting problem.

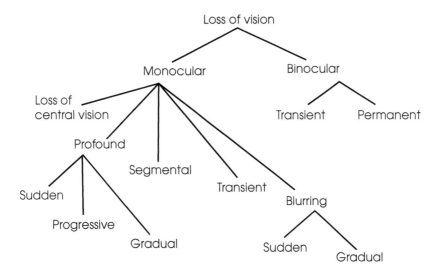

Figure 12.12 Classification of loss of vision (Marsden 1999).

History of vision loss

It is important to ascertain the parameters of the problem by taking a history:

- Was it sudden or gradual loss of vision? If sudden, is it possible that it has been there for a while but the patient has only just noticed. For example, did the patient notice the loss of vision when they covered an eye? If that was the case, it may have been present for some considerable time. If the loss was gradual, over what period of time has it occurred (days, weeks or even months)?

- Are there patches or areas of actual vision loss or is the vision generally blurred?

- Does the loss of vision involve some or all of the vision? Are there sectors of the field of vision that are missing? Is the loss worse centrally or peripherally?

- Was the loss transient? Has it come back now or is it recovering? For how long was vision affected? Or does it seem to be permanent?

- Is the vision now getting better, or worse, or is it staying the same?

- Are there any other symptoms that the patient is experiencing? Often, the patient may not consider other symptoms because the eye problem is the most worrying issue. If the patient is questioned, however, other symptoms may be ascertained that the patient does not readily associate with the eye problem, such as headache, weakness or pain elsewhere.

This information will help to categorise the type of vision loss, in order to rule out some possibilities immediately while leaving other avenues open for further investigation. Depending on the situation, most of these patients will be examined by an ophthalmologist, but the decision about what to do most appropriately for the patient often has to be made by another clinician – for instance, in primary care, in areas remote from ophthalmic medical services or in other areas such as emergency care settings.

Monocular versus binocular loss of vision

Ocular pathology, or optic nerve problems, will cause monocular loss of vision. A problem at or posterior to the optic chiasma, in the brain, will cause binocular loss of vision. It is most unusual for a patient to suffer from bilateral simultaneous eye disease, causing loss of vision. The only exception to this would be in the case of bilateral blurring of vision that has appeared over a number of days. This is characteristic of papilloedema.

A generalisation, but one that almost always works in practice, is that, if a patient complains of binocular loss of vision, the problem is likely to be of neurological rather than ophthalmic origin.

Binocular loss of vision

Migraine

One of the most common causes of transient, bilateral loss of vision is classic migraine. The patient is likely to complain of transient loss of vision and flashing lights; and scintillating images may appear, as may fortification spectra. The patient may experience the loss of large parts or sectors of the visual field. This aura usually lasts for 20–30 minutes and then resolves, followed by a severe headache. In a first episode of migraine, the patient may be very frightened by the visual symptoms and may not associate the headache with the loss of vision.

Another migraine type is known as acephalgic migraine. The patient experiences the aura, but does not go on to develop the headache. It may be quite difficult to explain to the patient that these symptoms do not actually constitute an eye problem.

Homonymous hemianopia

Hemianopia means 'loss of half of the visual field' and homonymous means 'on the same side'. The patient may complain that they are unaware of things approaching from the side of the field defect. The patient may also have trouble with reading because they may not be able to follow a line of print. Visual acuity may be only mildly reduced in each eye because part of the macular function on each side is likely to be intact. Distance visual acuity testing may demonstrate that the patient is unable to see the letters on the Snellen chart on the side of the field defect.

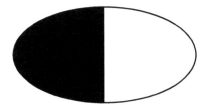 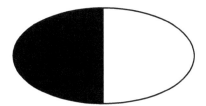

Figure 12.13 Field loss in homonymous hemianopia.

The most common areas of damage are in the optic radiation and the occipital cortex. The hemianopia may be incomplete, and temporal lobe lesions cause predominantly upper field loss.

Causes of homonymous hemianopia include vascular lesions such as embolus or haemorrhage, or tumours and inflammatory lesions in these specific areas of the brain. This type of field defect may accompany obvious systemic symptoms such as hemiparesis or hemiplegia. Referral to settings other than ophthalmology would be most appropriate and the patient needs a neurological assessment.

Bitemporal hemianopia

This means 'loss of the field of vision on the temporal side in each eye'.

Bitemporal field loss usually indicates a lesion in or around the optic chiasma. Most chiasmal lesions result from compression by tumours arising from structures around the chiasma, such as pituitary adenoma, meningioma, craniopharyngiomas or aneurysm (Cheng *et al.* 1997). The patient may complain of blurring of the temporal field. Cranial nerve palsies may also occur as a result of compression by a tumour and the patient should be asked about symptoms of double vision. Evaluation by a neurologist is urgently required for patients presenting in this way.

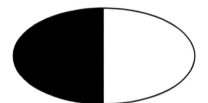 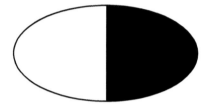

Figure 12.14 Field loss in bitemporal hemianopia.

Monocular loss of vision; profound loss of vision

This is characterised by complete or severely diminished vision affecting the whole of the visual field. This may occur suddenly or gradually over a period of days. Sudden, profound loss of vision suggests a vascular problem and the most likely causes of this are central retinal artery occlusion and vitreous haemorrhage (see Chapter 22).

Vitreous haemorrhage

This is the most likely cause if there is an associated history of diabetes. The patient may not be aware of eye changes related to the diabetes, especially if no regular eye screening takes place. They may be aware of the haemorrhage occurring and may describe a cloud of floaters (the first blood) which becomes denser over a short period, resulting in a profound loss of vision. Any attempt by the clinician to visualise the back of the eye will be unsuccessful, due to the blood in the vitreous cavity. Laser is usually the treatment of choice, once the retina can be visualised. The patient may need a great deal of support and explanation in order to understand the lack of apparent urgency in treating debilitating loss of vision.

Central retinal artery occlusion

In this condition, the patient may describe the vision disappearing 'like someone switching the light off'. The loss may be absolute and is, at best, likely to be 'count fingers' or less. Some patients retain a degree of central vision owing to the presence of a cilioretinal artery, an anatomical anomaly. The retina is likely to be pale, due to swelling within the retina, and the foveal (macular) area is seen as a 'cherry-red spot' because the retina is very thin and the choroid is seen underneath the retina, without swelling to mask the colour. An embolus in the central retinal artery may be seen.

This condition is an ophthalmic emergency. Although investigations into the cause of the condition are necessary (e.g. urgent erythrocyte sedimentation rate or ESR and C-reactive protein or CRP because giant cell arteritis may be a factor; lipid profiles; full blood count – to rule out coagulopathies and ultrasonography of the coronary arteries; and echocardiography – to identify the site of the embolus), immediate treatment can start wherever the patient presents, even before they see an ophthalmologist.

Treatment is aimed at allowing increased perfusion of the retina by reducing the IOP. It includes the administration of intravenous acetazolamide 500mg to reduce IOP and ocular massage to encourage the outflow of aqueous. In addition, the patient is often asked to rebreathe exhaled air by breathing into a paper bag. This increases the carbon dioxide concentration in the body, thus dilating blood vessels and possibly allowing the embolus to move further into the retinal circulation. If this occurs, a sector of visual loss, rather than profound loss, may be a good outcome for the patient. An anoxic retina is irreversibly damaged in 90 minutes (Pavan-Langston 2007). For a patient who wakes up with this condition, or who does not attend immediately (the vast majority), the visual outcome of this condition is usually poor.

In some conditions, vision loss may become progressively more profound over the whole field of vision over a number of days. The most likely cause of this is optic neuritis, which is described under 'Blurring of vision'.

Profound loss of vision that appears gradually, starting with a segment of the visual field and enlarging to cover the whole of it, is likely to be the result of a retinal detachment. This is described under 'Segmental loss of vision' below and in Chapter 22.

Segmental loss of vision

The loss of an area of the visual field in one eye is most likely to be due to vascular causes, such as occlusions of branches of the retinal artery or vein, or retinal detachments. If the onset is sudden and stays the same, the cause is likely to be vascular. If the area of visual loss changes over time, the cause is more likely to be a retinal detachment.

Branch retinal artery and vein occlusions

These may be seen with an ophthalmoscope. The branch artery occlusion will lead to a segment of retina being paler than the rest; all the vessels will appear in the correct location; and an embolus may be seen in one of the vessels. Multiple retinal haemorrhages may be seen if the cause of the loss of vision is a branch retinal vein occlusion. The haemorrhages will be in the area of retina that is served by the blocked vein. Retinal oedema may be seen and an occlusion may be visible. There is no immediate treatment for either of these conditions although follow-up by an ophthalmologist will be necessary. (For more detailed information on these conditions, see Chapter 22.)

Retinal detachment

Spontaneous retinal detachment affects around 1 in 10,000 of the population each year. It is more common in males and in short-sighted (myopic) eyes (Pavan-Langston 2007). It usually occurs in middle age as a result of collapse of the vitreous gel, causing traction on a weak area of retina which produces a hole (rhegmatogenous retinal detachment). Other causes include traction on the retina in conditions where fibrovascular tissue has developed between the retina and vitreous, as in diabetic retinopathy (traction retinal detachment) and subretinal disorders such as tumours or inflammation that allow fluid to pass behind the retina, pushing it off its basement membrane (a condition known as exudative retinal detachment). For more detailed information on retinal detachment, see Chapter 22.

Symptoms characteristic of retinal detachment include:

- Flashing lights – these are the result of traction on the retina or of areas of the retina moving. The only way the brain can interpret movement of the retina is in terms of light so, as the retina moves, the brain interprets and the patient 'sees' flashes of light.

- Floaters – the appearance of a large circular floater is the result of the detachment of the vitreous gel from its attachment at the optic disc. A shower of tiny floaters is likely to be caused by haemorrhage into the vitreous because a small retinal blood vessel is involved in the retinal tear.

A sector of loss of vision may be noticed that tends to enlarge over a period of hours or days. The patient may complain of seeing a 'shadow' that tends to move, or a curtain or cobweb descending over the eye. This is the result of an area of retina that is detached and may be enlarging or moving within the patient's field of vision. Central vision may be lost as a result of macular detachment.

The detached retina will appear grey and may seem slightly wrinkled. If central vision is present, the macula is still attached and it is likely that immediate surgery will be needed to preserve this situation. If central vision is affected, it is likely that the macula is detached. If this has happened within a matter of hours, immediate surgery is again likely to be needed to attempt to reattach it and preserve some of its function. If the macula has been detached for some time, it is likely that a surgical delay of a few days will not adversely affect the outcome for vision because macular function is not likely to be restored (Cheng *et al.* 1997).

Loss of central vision

Common causes of loss of central vision include age-related macular degeneration (AMD), optic neuritis, central serous retinopathy and macular burns.

Age-related macular degeneration

Age-related macular degeneration refers to a gradual degeneration of the macula. It is the most common cause of visual loss in those aged over 75, and affects around 20% of individuals. There is usually a very gradual loss of central vision. The patient may have noticed that they have to use a bright light to read by and that words fade after a few minutes. Although this is not an acute problem, elderly patients may present to acute settings because they have reached a point where they can no longer manage the problems alone. AMD is detailed further in Chapter 22. Any loss of vision that involves distortion of central vision should have an early assessment because the 'wet' form of AMD may respond to treatment.

Optic neuritis

This refers to inflammation of the optic nerve. Episodes are usually monocular, although they may be binocular. It is most common in adults between the ages of 20 and 40 and is more common in women. Around 50% of people who present with optic neuritis go on to develop multiple sclerosis (MS) within 15 years (Optic Neuritis Study Group 2008).

The patient is likely to present with loss of central vision, which may progress to a generalised loss of vision and can become severe. It is maximal after about 2 weeks and tends to recover after 4–6 weeks. Over a period of months, most patients recover 6/12 vision or better. For more detailed information on optic neuritis, see Chapter 24.

Other symptoms include pain around or behind the eye, which is worse on ocular movement (as a result of the inflamed optic nerve moving as the eye moves).

Perception of colour in the affected eye is likely to be reduced. This can be tested using the top of a red pen and comparing the perception of red in each eye. The pupil reactions will be abnormal and the optic nerve head may appear normal or be swollen. Steroids may be prescribed if vision loss becomes profound.

Referral to a neurologist or neuro-ophthalmologist, for further assessment and possible treatment, is the preferred course of action. A possible diagnosis of MS should not be discussed immediately because, even with a confirmed diagnosis of optic neuritis, MS is still only a possibility and the acute setting has neither the time nor the resources for the counselling that may be necessary in this situation.

Central serous retinopathy

Central serous retinopathy (CSR) occurs usually in young adult males and has an unknown cause. Symptoms commonly include a unilateral blurring of central vision and a generalised darkening of the visual field with some distortion. Visual acuity is usually only mildly reduced. It is rare for it to be less than 6/18, but it may reduce to 6/60 (Cheng *et al.* 1997). Although referral to an ophthalmologist is necessary, most episodes of CSR resolve within 3–6 months. Treatment is not usually indicated, although laser treatment has been shown to assist resolution in some cases where the CSR episode persists.

Macular burns

These may be caused by MIG welding equipment, as described earlier. Although very rarely experienced, looking at the sun (for example, during a solar eclipse) can result in macular burns; and indeed the last such eclipse in the UK resulted in a number of patients with irreversible retinal damage. The opportunity for appropriate health education before a solar eclipse is great, as they are extremely predictable. Perhaps ophthalmic professionals should consider disseminating health education information that there are no sunglasses strong enough to prevent eye damage as a result of looking at the sun, to help prevent this avoidable sight loss.

Blurring of vision

Blurring of vision may be the result of problems anywhere from the cornea to the optic nerve and the brain. Many patients will have problems in differentiating between generalised blurring and loss of central vision, and therefore careful questioning is again needed to obtain a full picture of the problem

Sudden onset blurring of vision may be caused by vitreous haemorrhage or vascular occlusions. These have been dealt with elsewhere. Other causes of blurring of vision tend to develop more gradually and may include CSR and optic neuritis. Again, these have been dealt with earlier in this chapter and in other chapters. Patients with papilloedema often present with blurring of vision. This may be worse in one eye and may be exacerbated by, for example, standing up (Cheng *et al.* 1997). Concurrent symptoms may be ignored by the patient in favour of the eye problem. Patients with bilateral swollen optic discs need urgent neurological referral.

Patients occasionally present with refractive errors that they have not noticed previously. It may be that they have covered one eye and noticed that the vision in the remaining eye is not good. This may provoke much anxiety and encourage them to self-refer. Visual acuity should be checked, using pinholes to negate the effect of any refractive error. If vision improves dramatically with pinholes, a large significant proportion of the blurring is likely to be caused by refractive error and, in the absence of any other findings, the patient may be referred to an optometrist.

Opacities in any of the clear structures of the eye will result in blurring of vision because less light is allowed to reach the retina. The most common opacity is the result of cataract (see Chapter 19). Again, the patient may just have noticed the loss of vision, possibly by closing one eye, or worry about the symptoms may have prompted self-referral. A more worrying presentation is if the lens opacity has occurred after trauma, or is in a younger person, and further investigations may be appropriate.

Corneal problems can also result in blurring of vision (see Chapter 17).

Transient loss of vision

Transient loss of vision may be caused by a vast range of conditions. A number of these (such as papilloedema and migraine) have been dealt with earlier. Other, common causes of transient loss include carotid artery disease and giant cell arteritis. Intermittent angle-closure glaucoma is a rare but possible cause of these symptoms.

Carotid artery disease

Retinal emboli from carotid artery disease often produce transient visual loss, known as amaurosis fugax. This may be described as 'a curtain being lowered and then lifted over the vision'. It is likely to last seconds or minutes, rather than hours. It may be a sign of impending cerebrovascular accident and so cardiovascular investigations are appropriate. Turning the head may precipitate an attack and this is characteristic of carotid artery disease.

Giant cell arteritis

Patients with giant cell arteritis often complain of headache and tenderness over the scalp. This may be obvious when they comb their hair. They may also notice jaw claudication and pain on chewing. An urgent ESR is indicated and may be more than 80mm. Treatment is with high doses of steroids; definitive diagnosis is by temporal artery biopsy; and frequent monitoring of the patient's condition will be required.

Intermittent angle-closure glaucoma

Patients may present with symptoms of pain in and around the eye and blurring of vision that begins, usually at night, when the pupil becomes larger as a result of the reduced light levels, and may last a number of hours. It may have resolved by the time the patient presents. If the anterior chamber appears shallow, and the symptoms are as described, intermittent angle-closure glaucoma may be suspected, and urgent prophylactic laser treatment can be undertaken to prevent further attacks.

References

Bater, M.C., Ramchandani, P.L., Ramchandani, M. & Flood, T.R. (2008) An orbital apex fracture resulting in multiple cranial neuropathies. *British Journal of Oral Maxillofacial Surgery.* **46**,163–64.

Besamusca, F. & Bastiensen, L. (1986) Blood dyscrasis and topically applied chloramphenicol in ophthalmology. *Documenta Ophthalmologica.* **64**, 87–95.

Brahma, A.K., Shah, S., Hillier, V.F., McLeod, D., Sabala, T., Brown, A. & Marsden, J. (1996) Topical analgesia for superficial corneal injuries. *Journal of Accident and Emergency Medicine.* **13**, 186–88.

Brilakis, H.S. & Deutsch, T.A. (2000) Topical tetracaine with bandage soft contact lens pain control after photorefractive keratectomy. *Journal of Refractive Surgery.* **16**(4), 444–47.

Buckles, E. & Carew-McColl, M. (1991) Triage by telephone. *Nursing Times.* **87**(6), 26–28.

Cheng, H., Burdon, M.A., Buckley, S.A. & Moorman, C. (1997) *Emergency Ophthalmology.* London: BMJ Publishing Group.

Consumers' Association (1997) *Drugs and Therapeutics Bulletin.* **35**(7), 49–52.

Eagling, E.M. & Roper-Hall, M.J. (1986) *Eye Injuries: An illustrated guide.* London: Gower.

Fechner, P.U. & Teichmann, K.D. (1998) *Ocular Therapeutics.* Thorofare, NJ: Slack.

Forrester, J.V., Dick, A. D., McMenamin, P.G., Roberts, F. & Pearlman, E. (2016) *The Eye: Basic sciences in practice.* 4th edn. Edinburgh: Elsevier.

Kompa, S., Schareck, B., Tympner, J., Wustemeyer, H. & Schrage, M.F. (2002) Comparison of emergency eye-wash products in burned porcine eyes. *Graefe's Archives for Clinical Experimental Ophthalmology.* **240**(4), 308–13.

MacEwan, C.J. (1989) Eye injuries: a prospective survey of 5671 cases. *British Journal of Ophthalmology.* **73**, 888–94.

Mackway-Jones, K. & Marsden, J. (2003) Ascorbate for alkali burns to the eye. *Journal of Emergency Medicine.* **20**, 465–66.

Mackway-Jones, K., Marsden, J. & Windle, J. (2014) *Emergency Triage*, 3rd edition. London: Wiley Blackwell.

Marsden, J. (1999) Painless loss of vision. *Emergency Nurse.* **6**(9), 13–18.

Marsden, J. (2001) Treating corneal trauma. *Emergency Nurse.* **9**(8), 17–20.

Marsden, J., Newton, M., Windle, J. & Mackway-Jones, K. (2016) *Emergency Triage: Telephone triage and advice.* London Wiley Blackwell.

Newell, F.W. (1996) *Ophthalmology: Principles and concepts.* St Louis, MO: Mosby.

Onofrey, B.E., Skorin, L. Jr. & Holdeman, N.R. (1998) *Ocular Therapeutics Handbook.* Philadelphia, PA: Lippincott-Raven.

The Optic Neuritis Study Group (2008) Multiple Sclerosis Risk after Optic Neuritis: Final Optic Neuritis Treatment Trial Follow-Up. *Archives of Neurology.* **65**(6), 727–32.

Pavan-Langston, D. (2007) *Manual of Ocular Diagnosis and Therapy.* 6th edn. Boston, MA: Lippincott Williams and Wilkins.

Rhee, D.J. & Pyfer, M.F. (eds) (1999) *The Wills Eye Manual.* 3rd edn. Philadelphia, PA: Lippincott, Williams & Wilkins.

Rihawi, S., Frentz, M., Reim, M. & Schrage, M.F. (2008) Rinsing with isotonic saline solution for eye burns should be avoided. *Burns.* **34**(7), 1027–32

Swaminathan, A., Otterness, K., Milne, K. & Rezaie, S. (2015) The Safety of Topical Anesthetics in the Treatment of Corneal Abrasions: A Review. *Journal of Emergency Medicine.* **49**(5), 810–15.

Tullo, A.B. & Donnelly, D. (1995) 'Conjunctiva' in J.P. Perry & A.B. Tullo (eds) *Care of the Ophthalmic Patient.* 2nd edn. London: Chapman & Hall.

Verma, S., Corbett, M.C. & Marshall, J. A. (1995) Prospective, randomized, double-masked trial to evaluate the role of topical anesthetics in controlling pain after photorefractive keratectomy. *Ophthalmology.* **102**(12), 1918–24

Verma, S. Corbet, M.C., Patmore, A., Heacock, G. & Marshall, J. (1997) A comparative study of the duration and efficacy of tetracaine 1% and bupivacaine 0.75% in controlling pain following photorefractive keratectomy (PRK). *European Journal of Ophthalmology.* **7**(4), 327–33.

Waldman, N., Densie, I.K. & Herbison, P. (2014) Topical tetracaine used for 24 hours is safe and rated highly effective by patients for the treatment of pain caused by corneal abrasions: a double-blind, randomized clinical trial. *Academic Emergency Medicine.* **21**(4), 374–82.

CHAPTER THIRTEEN

Eye Banking

Heather Machin and Graeme Pollock

Introduction

The Eye Bank (EB) is a department or free-standing unit, which is responsible for the ethical and legal obtaining of human tissue for ocular application (HTO). HTOs, which may also be categorised as medical products of human origin (MPHOs) (Warwick *et al.* 2009), are looked after by the EB who, depending on location, are responsible for the whole process, including: consent, examination of donor and tissue suitability (donor coordination), retrieval (recovery) processing, distribution and associated tissue tracking, and monitoring and service management.

The aim of this chapter is to help educate nurses involved in the preoperative counselling and education of waiting transplant recipients, provide information to surgical teams who receive and prepare tissue for surgery, outline the role and responsibility of the eye bank team (including their regulatory requirements) and finally present this sub-specialty area as a potential career avenue for interested nurses, ophthalmic technicians, orthoptists, optometrists and scientists.

Background

Corneas, which are now the most transplanted MPHO in the world (Doughman & Rogers 2012), became a medical option over 100 years ago, when the first corneal eye transplantation was performed in Moravia (now the Czech Republic) by Dr Eduard Zirm, who performed the first human-to-human transplant (Moffatt *et al.* 2005). This led F.P. Filatov of the Ukraine (1935 – 1937) to lay the foundations for eye banking and corneal preservation (Pels & Pollock 2013).

Having recognised that the donor tissue for corneal transplants could be recovered post-mortem, physicians and scientists discovered that fresh homologus transplants (allograft or allogeneic transplant), rather than animal tissue transplants (xenotransplant), avoided postoperative opacification of the graft and these transplants were less likely to be rejected (Bredehorn-Mayr *et al.* 2009).

In 1944, Townley Paton officially established the world's first eye bank facility in New York, which later led to the foundation of the Eye Bank Association of America in 1961 (Sharma *et al.* 2010). Since that time, EBs have taken responsibility for supplying viable and disease-free cornea (and other HTOs), and have developed into a stand-alone service that ophthalmologists can trust to supply tissue for transplant surgery (Pels & Pollock 2013). Due to these advances, donation has evolved from an immediate procedure (which was prone to recipient risk and surgical scheduling inconvenience) into a formal regulated process that is subject to vigorous testing, regulations and uniform processing by highly trained professionals (Machin 2014).

With the advent of new preservation systems and advanced optic-microscopes, tissues can now be stored longer and can be minutely reviewed for their suitability for transplantation. These measures ensure that recipient needs (and their long-term visual outcomes) are at the forefront of EB decision-making.

Human tissue for ocular application

The term human tissue for ocular application (HTO) refers to any tissue, of human origin, which is prepared for surgical transplantation onto or into the eye of another human. This term is used to differentiate the tissue from man-made or animal materials, which are also commonly associated with medical transplantations and prosthetic devices. The term HTO is also used, in preference to 'eye tissue', because not all human tissue used in eye care is recovered from a donor eye. There are currently four common types of HTO (cornea, sclera, amnion and stem cells) which are prepared for transplantation, each with their own unique testing and processing requirements and each with their own transplant functionality.

Cornea

A human cornea can be utilised for the surgical repair of several types of corneal diseases such as bulbous keratoplasty, kerataconus and chemical burns (see Chapter 17); and it can be either transplanted as a whole cornea – penetrating keratoplasty (PK) – or as a dissected single layer ready for replacement of a specific layer of the recipient's cornea – known as partial thickness transplant surgery. These techniques can be favoured in some cases when the surgeon wants to retain the healthy parts of the cornea and only replace the diseased layer. Such partial techniques also allow for a quick postoperative rehabilitation period for the patient (Armitage 2011). If pre-cut by the EB, they can also obviate the technical and logistical difficulties of cutting the donor cornea in the operating theatre, which can increase surgical time and potentially squander precious donor tissue (Chu *et al.* 2014).

Currently, partial thickness surgical techniques that have been embraced around the world, as alternatives to full thickness penetrating keratoplasty (PK) surgeries, include techniques such as Descemet's stripping endothelial keratoplasty (DSEK) (Dapena *et al.* 2009), Descemet's membrane endothelial keratoplasty (DMEK) and Descemet-stripping automated endothelial keratoplasty (DSAEK), which provide treatment for endothelial disorders such as Fuch's dystrophy and pseudophakic bullous keratopathy (Kitzmann *et al.* 2008). In these procedures the endothelium of the recipient's cornea is replaced with donor endothelium. Additionally, lamellar keratoplasty, such as deep anterior lamellar keratoplasty (DALK), also remains an option for recipients with dysfunctional stroma (stromal dystrophies), such as thinning and scarring, and is often used for keratoconus surgery (Lindquist 2009). With such lamellar techniques, the surgeon need only separate the posterior lamellar graft from the anterior protecting flap and insert it into the recipient's eye (Ruzza *et al.* 2013). In this technique, the recipient's endothelium remains intact.

The preparation of tissue can either be performed by a competency trained EB technician or the surgeon (depending on surgeon preferences and available technology). When the EB prepares the tissue in advance of the surgery, this is often commonly referred to as 'pre-cut' tissue. The process of pre-cutting the tissue requires careful dissection so that the surgeon can access just the layer required for the transplantation. The tissue is then carefully placed inside the anterior of the eye – the posterior part of the cornea – where it is surgically supported to remain in that position. Partial thickness surgery techniques continue to change and develop and there are continuing discussions on their comparative success.

Additionally, some surgeons may request corneal caps for conjunctival patch-grafts of chemical burns, because the thin, clear, appearance of the cornea can mimic that of conjunctival tissue. While this is not commonly available globally (because the EB needs to be set up to provide this tissue cut), there has been increased surgeon demand for cornea for this purpose and this may be an area of HTO requirement that evolves further over time.

Sclera

Scleral tissue is often requested by a surgeon for one of three reasons;

- To provide a cover for a prosthesis – i.e. hydroxyl-apatite after enucleation (Custer & McCaffery 2006) (see Chapter 15)

- To provide a patch-graft for an excised tumour

- To be used as a sutured-in cover over a glaucoma drainage device which extends – externally – from within the eye's trabecular meshwork (i.e. Brarveldt or Ahmed valve) (see Chapter 21).

The EB can prepare the sclera as a whole sclera and/or divide it into smaller pieces, depending on the specific need. The tissue is usually preserved in alcohol or glycerol, or may be provided dehydrated in saline with antibiotics.

Amnion

The Human Amniotic Membrane (AM), which is the innermost layer of the placental membrane (Kheirkhuh *et al.* 2010), is a tough and semi-transparent membrane used in some countries for ocular surface reconstruction – such as a conjunctival patch-graft for burns, Stevens-Johnson Syndrome (dry eye), and corneal stem cell deficiencies, as a permanent or overlaid graft. The AM is obtained from the amnionic layer of the placenta and is divided into smaller pieces, ready for surgical use. While this is not commonly utilised globally, the surgeons who request this tissue do so because they feel AM can suitably mimic the conjunctiva. Alternative options for AM are corneo-scleral discs.

Stem cells

Stem cells are a relatively new component in EB development and, at the time of publication, are not widely available. Currently, the only adult stem cells obtained from tissue stored by EBs are those of the limbal epithelium, which are used to treat limbal stem cell deficiency (LSCD). In some instances, these can be sourced from limbal rims typically discarded after other keratoplasties, though a whole corneo-scleral disc may need to be sacrificed to comply with a particular country's regulatory requirements. The most commonly performed limbal stem cell (LSC) technique is cultured limbal epithelial transplantation (CLET) (Baylis *et al.* 2011). In CLET, explants from the limbal region of a donor cornea are placed on amnion and a sheet of cells is cultured from these explants in the laboratory (Pellegrini *et al.* 1997; Mariappan *et al.* 2010). This cell sheet on an amnion carrier is then delivered to the surgical theatre for transplantation.

Role of the eye bank team

The EB performs a variety of functions, though ultimately their function is to ensure ethical management of quality-tested tissue, from a consenting donor, that is supplied to the recipient and surgeon. The EB ensures that the donor's wishes are adhered to and that the recipient has the best possible postoperative outcome. While the process of recovery and distribution may vary in different parts of the world, the primary functions of the EB include:

- Donation consent process
- Recovering the tissue
- Testing and contraindications
- Tissue preparation

- Preservation and storage
- Distribution
- Labelling
- Monitoring, data reporting (and corneal registry).

Donation consent process

Almost all eye tissue is recovered from cadaveric donation, and the consent and recovery process for this commences when death is determined by the irreversible cessation of circulation. Depending on the geographical location of the death, the EB is either notified by another organ or tissue bank staff member (i.e. skin/bone bank staff) or they are notified by the coroner, hospital or nursing home. Very rarely, a relative contacts the eye bank directly. Generally, those in attendance at the death, such as a religious figure, doctor or nurse, may ask the relative or next-of-kin (NOK), often termed 'a knowledgeable historian', if the deceased had expressed a wish to donate during their lifetime. In some countries, such as Australia, where an opt-in system is in place, the donation process can only commence (Eye Bank Association of Australia and New Zealand 2009) when the consent has been confirmed by the NOK.

Generally, a hospital contact (sometimes called a donor coordinator) will liaise with the family or NOK of the deceased to confirm that they did indeed want to donate. This requires skill, compassion and an understanding of grief and the needs of the family during their time of mourning. This is essential, to ensure that family members are not taken advantage of during such a vulnerable time. Additionally, several countries have developed national professional conduct standards when approaching a family member or NOK for consent. This includes their conduct prior to confirmation of death and their actions thereafter (National Health Service 2013).

There are geographical variations in the donation process, as some countries have implemented an opt-in donation system while others have implemented an opt-out system (Machin 2014). Regardless of the system, the EB will not proceed if the NOK states that the deceased did not wish to donate. In some countries, a donation register may also be available (often online), which can also indicate the intent of the donor and will support the NOK when making the final decision.

The EB will not only confirm consent to donate but will also confirm what will be donated, and how the donation will occur. For example, some EBs (depending on the technology they have available) seek specific confirmation on consent for cornea, sclera or other parts of the eye – though, in general, 'whole eye' consent may be obtained. Additionally, the EB will seek consent for donation for transplantation, donation for research or non-surgical use and/or a combination. It is up to the NOK to confirm how they wish to proceed.

After consent

Once consent is obtained, the EB will continue to discuss with the NOK (and/or medical treating team) the social, medical and ocular history of the deceased. This is to ensure that the tissue is suitable for donation and suitable for transplantation – and to prevent any potential medical/ocular disease transfer and/or infection. Each EB has a national/regional medical standard, government act or regulation that outlines 'contraindications for donation', based on up-to-date evidence. These lists are regularly up dated, based on the latest literature and areas of relevance, and they may vary, depending on the country or region (i.e. the demographic-epidemiological health differences of the donating population group, which may result in legislative differences compared to neighbouring countries).

The ocular history is also carefully examined – specifically to exclude donation from deceased individuals who had corneal pathologies or prior corneal surgery (including corneal transplants and LASIK), as these corneal variations may not provide the best possible surgical outcome for the recipient. The EB also examines for evidence of recent surgery, i.e. if there are sutures in the eye or evidence of possible recent surgery that could alter the corneal shape or pose an infection risk. Otherwise, the EB will generally accept donation from deceased individuals with refractive error, cataracts, intraocular lenses and retinal disease (including evidence of scleral buckles), as these surgical procedures do not alter the function of the cornea (which is an avascular tissue), and do not pose an issue for the obtaining of sclera either. That said, a sclera with a buckle may not be preferred for scleral donation, despite being accepted for corneal donation, due to the permanent change-of-shape made by the buckle over time.

An ocular examination (history and physical assessment) is also required to check for congenital or acquired disorders of the eye, i.e. herpetic keratitis (European Eye Bank Association 2013) and malignancies of the eye. Lastly, solid cancers (non-blood cancers) generally do not prevent a person from being suitable for eye donation.

Overall, the thickness of the cornea is generally independent of other morphometric parameters of the normal human eye, and does not change significantly during life – suggesting that suitability is multifactorial. Therefore, the age of the donor does not necessarily indicate the deterioration of the cornea's cell count, its shape or general tissue suitability. This is why a full social, medical and ocular examination is completed. Depending on the country/location, the EB may accept tissue from all ages because there are generally no upper age limits (European Eye Bank Association 2013). However, there may be a lower age limit – for example, recovery from a child younger than 2 years old (Eye Bank Association of Australia and New Zealand 2009). This is because, despite some variance, infant corneas have a steeper curved shape and tend to be more flaccid. Conversely, in the aging population, thinning or steeper corneas have also been reported by Müller *et al.* (2004) and may also (depending on the case) be excluded for this reason.

Tissue for research or non-surgical use

At the time of consent, the EB will also ask the NOK if the deceased wished to donate for research or non-surgical use. The EB may often recover tissue for research as routine practice or, from time to time, depending on research needs, the EB may accept donation specifically from a deceased person who has a particular medical or ocular history. This is to support approved research into a particular ocular condition (e.g. a researcher studying retinitis pigmentosa (RP) may request a human retina from a deceased person with RP). For this to occur, the researchers are required to demonstrate full ethics approval for the use of human tissue in their research prior to the EB preparing and dispatching the tissue. Depending on the need, the tissue can be supplied fresh to the researchers or it can be cryopreserved for later ethics-approved requests.

Non-surgical use generally refers to the use of tissue in clinical training and education (Eye Bank of Australia and New Zealand 2009). An eye bank trainee or a medical trainee may be assigned to work on some tissues.

Donor and recipient confidentiality

In most countries, common practice and law does not allow HTO donor families to know or contact a recipient or vice-versa; nor may either party select their tissue. This is agreed in order to prevent ethical issues arising. Instead, EB and other government regulations support donation agencies to function as 'go-betweens' by allowing either party to write a de-identified letter to the EB. Having confirmed that the letter has been de-identified, the EB will pass it to the recipient (or donor) on the other party's behalf.

Recovering the tissue

Eye tissue

The tissue is recovered (removed from the donor) as early as possible from the point of death, but generally not exceeding 18 hours for hypothermic preservation and 24 hours for organ-culture preservation (preservation options are discussed later in this chapter). These time limits help to ensure tissue integrity and allow the deceased family to proceed with their funeral arrangements without delay. If it is left much longer, there may be a higher chance of the graft failing during its processing time at the EB or, more importantly, during transplant surgery.

The process takes around 30–45 minutes. If the donor is also donating other organs and tissues, the EB will coordinate to allow those recoveries to be carried out at the same time. The EB staff will recover from the morgue, the coroner's, the funeral director's operating theatre or, at times, the hospital ward. Upon examination, the EB staff member will check all personal identifiers (name, age, hospital/donor number, etc.) – similar to all hospital checking processes.

They may also conduct a physical examination of the body to check for signs of external puncture marks and identifiable features as part of their preventative risk assessment process, such as that of New South Wales Organ and Tissue Donation Service (2014), designed to prevent the transmission of infection and disease. Prior to recovery, the EB technician must therefore carefully inspect the forearms and antecubital fossa for physical signs of recent intravenous drug use (Reinhart 1993), the surface of the skin for evidence of rashes, signs of jaundice (European Eye Bank Association 2013) or open wounds, and other presenting facts that do (or do not) correspond with the social and medical history they have obtained from the NOK and medical team. This includes factors surrounding how the person died.

Additionally, prior to recovery, the EB staff member will examine the eyes to make sure that the eyelids have been closed over the eyes since death (Machin 2014). This is because, once someone dies, their corneas are no longer nourished by the effects of blinking. Therefore, if the eyelids are open, or even half open, the whole eye or sections of the eye will dry out, thus increasing the likelihood that they will be unsuitable for donation. Once the EB staff member has determined that the eyes have been maintained – post-death – in a suitable fashion, they will commence the recovery using all universal precautions and aseptic techniques common within the operating theatre and general hospital areas. This is to ensure their own safety and to maintain the condition of the tissue, to prevent cross-contamination to the recipient.

The recovery can be carried out using one of two methods:

- Whole globe extraction, which is similar to an enucleation, with gauze or other packaging material, placed in the remaining orbital cavity.

- Corneal-scleral rim (disc) extraction, in which an incision is made along the pars-plana, to detach the cornea from the rest of the eye, with a small scleral rim retained. The rim provides the EB and the surgeon with a platform to grasp the tissue without damaging the cornea, and allows for further trephining of the cornea by the surgeon to a diameter to suit the requirements of the transplant.

Whichever method is used, the process is conducted in an aseptic manner, with the eye decontaminated with providine (iodine/betadine), antibiotics, sterile-saline or a combination, prior to draping (European Eye Bank Association 2014).

A prosthetic plastic conformer is placed onto the gauze (for whole eye) or remaining eye/ocular content (for disc excision) and the eyelids are closed back over the prosthetic. This gives the donor a restored normal (closed-eye) appearance for open-casket viewing.

Figure 13.1 Conformers that are placed into the donor's ocular cavity to help maintain the shape of the eyelids post-recovery.

Amnion

The human amniotic membrane (AM) is obtained with consent from the mother, for both placental recovery and to confirm a Caesarean birth will take place. A Caesarean birth is essential, as this means the placenta can be delivered under sterile conditions (Dekaris & Gabric 2009). This is also coordinated with the attending obstetrician, midwife and/or birthing suite nursing team. The placenta is taken to a closed-off air-controlled room, where the EB team carefully wash off any remaining blood clots before removing the AM layer from the placenta until a full sheet layer is separated. This can often require several team members, as the sheet needs to be held out, cut into pieces and placed flat on a membrane support. A full donor (mother) history and blood test is completed and the placenta also undergoes a full blood and sterility test. The mother is also required to undergo another blood test several months later to reconfirm the test results. Once processed and tested, the AM is stored frozen or sometimes freeze-dried (European Eye Bank Association 2014).

Stem cells

At the current time limbal stem cell (LSC) transplants are frequently performed as part of a research project and require appropriate informed consent for donation for research. The limbus is recovered as part of the globe and is therefore subjected to the same testing, contraindications, preparation and preservation as corneo-scleral discs are for other uses. Following recovery, LSC must be cultured in aseptic conditions. Currently, a barrier to the clinical use of LSC is the need to prepare the LSC sheets in accordance with good manufacturing practices and to a standard required by the nation's regulatory agencies (Harkin *et al.* 2013).

Testing and contraindications

Blood tests are performed for all donors, either at the time of tissue recovery or within 24 hours, although there are no significant studies indicating that blood tests carried out after 24 hours will give false negative results (European Eye Bank Association 2013). Alternatively, if a sample was obtained within 7 days prior to death, then that may also be utilised. The bloods are serologically tested for all possible infections that could potentially be transmitted by this type of transplantation (i.e. HIV and hepatitis B and C), and cross-checked with what is known of the donor's medical and social history. Tissue is not released for surgery until the EB has received full confirmed blood test results from the pathologist.

Note: As the full list of medical, surgical and social contraindications is beyond the scope of this chapter, we recommend that you contact your local EB or your national/ regional association and regulatory body to obtain a full list of contraindications.

The eye tissue is processed inside a medical-air cabinet (hood), where the parts of the eye are dissected into cornea, sclera and so on, depending on the requirements of the EB and the donor consent.

The eye tissue itself is also tested for its visual suitability, and the advent of the slit-lamp for biomicroscopy has been invaluable in assessing the tissue while suspended inside its preservation medium (Chu 2000) to detect for the presence or absence of guttata, Descemet folds, infiltrates, and scars. Depending on the degree of presentation, these features could have a negative impact on the visual outcome for the recipient.

Additional specular microscope studies may also be used to assess for morphological changes, issues with the endothelium (Chu 2000) or those who have had anterior segment surgery in the past. Other examination tools include light microscopy (bright field, phase contrast and inverted light microscopy – or a combination) and, more recently, the use of computer-aided analysers (European Eye Bank Association 2014).

Tissue preparation and preservation

Sclera

The sclera is cleaned of ocular content and may be retained as a whole sclera or divided into half, quarter or some other fraction, depending on policy and need. The tissue is then preserved. Depending on the country, this may be done by placing it in 70–100% alcohol (European Eye Bank Association 2014) and storing it at room temperature (which is often validated for use within 12 months from processing). Alternatively, the tissue may be dehydrated in glycerol – though alcohol may be preferred because it has greater bactericidal and antiviral benefits (Romanchuk *et al.* 2003). Alternative, less favoured, preservation methods include cryopreservation and gamma radiation (Eye Bank Association of Australia and New Zealand 2009). Usage (expiration) and validation reports also vary from one location to another.

Once prepared and preserved, the sclera is classified as 'dead' tissue and has no original functionality and can only be used as patch material.

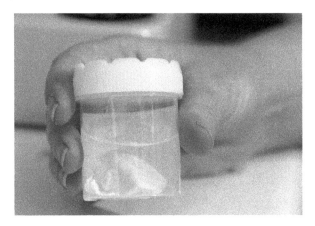

Figure 13.2 Bottle with sclera in alcohol.

Cornea

As the corneal tissue needs to remain as living tissue (Armitage 2011) so that it can function within the recipient's eye, it needs to be prepared in a precise manner to maintain its optimal function. There are several ways to preserve the corneal tissue, depending on the technology available at the particular EB. Either way, this type of tissue is generally prepared as a corneo-scleral disc – a form it retains until the day it is required for surgery, at which point it can be dispatched as a full cornea or prepared for specific layered partial thickness surgery, such as DMEK (discussed below).

Most EBs around the world continue to prepare and cut cornea manually, using the instruments, equipment and technologies commonly found in operating theatres (i.e. microscope, corneal scissors, trephines, etc). However, in recent years, some EBs have started exploring the potential of femtosecond laser technology to provide more precise cutting technique opportunities by preparing the recipient and the donor tissue using incisional patterns that were previously unavailable to the surgeon (Lindquist *et al.* 2009). While commonly associated with cataract-refractive surgery, the femtosecond laser may (or may not) eventually prove to be suitable for EB use in the future.

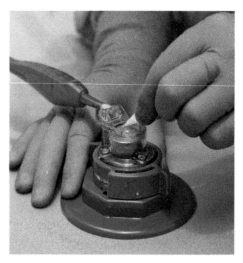

Figure 13.3 Pre-cutting corneo-scleral rim.

The cornea is preserved and stored, normally using one of two methods, depending on the technology available at the EB:

● Hypothermic

● Organ culture preservation (OCP) (also known as normothermic).

Additionally, there are two less common preservation methods, glycerin and cryopreservation, which are used for the purpose of tectonic (structural) keratoplasty (Eye Bank Association of Australia and New Zealand 2009). However, neither of these are currently routinely used around the world. Therefore, in this chapter, we will focus on the two most common types – hypothermic and OCP.

The variation between these two common storage methods is related more to the availability of the technology (and the need for storage space or timelines around tissue availability) than outcomes, as they have comparable tissue preservation and post-transplant success rates.

Table 13.1 Types of storage medium and storage requirements

Appearance	Technical preservation name	Where to store it	How to store it	When to use it by
Warm – pink coloured liquid	Normothermic	Room temperature but not greater than 37° Celsius (though this not required on dispatch)	Secure cupboard in normal air-conditioned space; not too hot and not too cold	As per the expiry date
Cold – pink coloured liquid	Hypothermic	Fridge	Between 0 and 10° Celsius	As per the expiry date

The preservation of the cornea – and which part and how it is stored – is extremely important because the cornea, unlike other HTO and other tissue types in general, is a living tissue. (In contrast, the sclera, submerged in alcohol, is dead and is only used as a patch-graft, rather than to perform a physiological function.) As the cornea is living, it continues to perform its function of taking in and expelling liquid in its environment. Therefore, the medium used to preserve the cornea must be able to retain nourishment and ensure that, by the time the tissue is transplanted, the corneal tissue has been returned to its normal function without too much fluid retention (swelling), as too much swelling will render the cornea non-viable. This is also because the surgeon needs the tissue to be in its normal state in order to ensure correct surgical positioning and suturing – and therefore a successful postoperative outcome.

Some EBs may routinely add antibiotics to the preservation medium at the beginning or mid-stage of the process. This is precautionary, to help prevent contamination. This step is not an indication of the likelihood of infection due to handling or the tissue itself, and is a risk prevention step to eliminate the HTO as the entry point for hospital-acquired infections such as endophthalmitis (Rehany *et al.* 2004).

Organ culture preservation

Organ culture preservation (OCP), which is also referred to as normothermic preservation, retains the tissue close to the normal human body temperature of the cornea (usually 28–37° Celsius). The benefit of this preservation method is that the tissue can be stored in the EB for a period of up to 30 days (Armitage 2011). This means that the surgeon, hospital and patient can plan ahead and schedule the surgery in a more systematic and convenient manner. The cornea remains in a preservation medium until it is required to be dispatched, at which time the EB transfers it to a similar transport medium, sometimes referred to as 'thinning medium' because it reduces the oedema in the cornea that occurs during OCP.

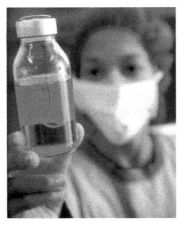

Figure 13.4 Bottle with cornea (in organ culture preservation)

Hypothermic preservation

Hypothermic preserves the cornea in a cold environment of 0–10° Celsius and is supplemented with antibiotics and other agents (dextran and chondroitin sulphate) to prevent corneal swelling and preserve endothelial function (Pels 1997). The benefit of this preservation method is that the medium is cheaper for the EB to set up (although it may be more expensive in the long term) and tissue can be processed quicker. The disadvantage is that the tissue is only suitable to be used within 14 days from the preservation date (Armitage 2011). It takes several days for the EB to receive the pathology results; by the time the tissue is ready for dispatch, the surgeon/hospital therefore often has to schedule in the surgery in less than 5 days. This means that patient/surgical list scheduling can be rushed and surgeons are often under pressure to schedule in patients within already heavily booked operating theatres before the tissue expires and is wasted. If not managed well, this places undue strain on the operating theatre staff.

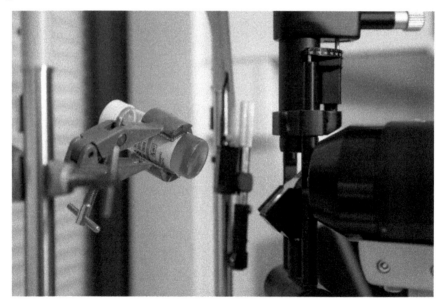

Figure 13.5 Bottle with cornea (in hypothermic preservation) being tested at the slit lamp.

Glycerin (glycerol) preservation

Glycerin corneas are generally used for DALK, where viable endothelium is not required. They may also be used for patches or glaucoma surgery or purely for tectonic surgery where no visual outcome is expected (i.e. as a replacement for sclera). Additionally, in some developing countries or in developed countries who wish to prepare tissue for export to another country, glycerin may be used for its beneficial storage times.

(As it can be stored at room temperature, it is suitable for long-haul transfer and for use by humanitarian agencies.) However, there has been very little uptake of glycerin preservation on the wider global stage and within most domestic EB services because glycerin corneas do not give transplant outcomes that are as clear as those using OCP or hypothermic preservation.

Distribution

Depending on the particular EB, tissue recovery levels can be increased or decreased to support the needs of the waiting recipients. This is because the EB does not wish to waste the generous gift of donation if there are no recipients in their district waiting for a transplant (or no operating theatre slots available). In this situation, they do not want to recover tissue and then destroy it after the expiration date. The EB will therefore generally ask corneal surgeons for estimates of recipient wait lists. This enables the EB to try their best to provide for those recipients as soon as they can. The EB works collaboratively with the surgeon and their rooms, who in turn coordinate with the operating theatre, regarding the surgical need for tissue. This ensures that the EB has also completed all testing and preparing of the tissue. From time to time, an EB that is unable to supply their district may ask a neighbouring EB (with whom they have an agreement) to help provide tissue.

The tissue must be dispatched in a stable environment – for instance, hypothermic tissue requires the transport container to retain its cold temperature for the duration of the journey, regardless of the temperature outside the packaging.

Labelling

The tissue is dispatched with EB labelling, which must correspond with the donor's details (de-identified on dispatch) and the recipient's details as provided by the surgeon's rooms. Additionally, any requests for pre-cut (should that service be available from the EB) must also be completed. EBs are responsible for assigning a unique identification number to the tissue container at all times (Eye Bank Association of Australia and New Zealand 2009) and this number remains with the tissue until transplantation, at which point the corresponding number is allotted to the chart of the recipient.

Labelling is an area of EB service which is currently undergoing worldwide review and, in recent years, EBs have worked with their professional associations, government agencies, the World Health Organization and other bodies involved in tracking HTO to improve the process. Through this collaboration, the EB community has developed a global agreement on labelling nomenclature and labelling styles to ensure that HTO can be tracked (World Health Organization 2011, 2012). This has been developed in response to evident gaps in labelling, which have led to unethical practices (e.g. profiteering, trafficking and transplant tourism) of some organs and tissues in some parts of the world. This labelling, traceability and tracking system should help ensure that any adverse events reported by the surgeon or the EB can be reviewed, and other recipients from the same donor can also be notified for follow-up review. It also means that HTO dispatched into other states/districts or countries can also be tracked.

This global agreement was developed in 2013–2014 by global members of the ISBT128: Eye Tissue Working Group, which included specialists from the World Health Organization, the tracking development company that owns ISBT128 (ICCBBA), and representative corneal surgeons and eye bankers from: the Association of Eye Banks in Asia, Eye Bank Association of America, European Eye Bank Association, Eye Bank Association of India, Pan American Association of Eye Banks (South America) and the Eye Bank Association of Australia and New Zealand. Based on this agreement, several individual EBs have commenced implementation. Some EBs are also exploring integration of this labelling system with electronic donor record systems for national consistency and tracking. As time progresses, the EB sector is expecting a wider global up-take of this labelling system.

The Eye Bank for Sight Restoration in New York, USA, which is the world's first official EB (having opened in 1944), is also one of the first EBs in the world to implement the pioneering new labelling tracking system. Within the labels there are several key pieces of information which the EB, surgeon and the nurses in the operating theatre need to check, to ensure that the paperwork corresponds with the tissue bottle/container and the recipient. These checks should also be incorporated into the routine *Sign-In* and *Time-Out* components of operating theatre safe site surgery checking systems prior to commencement of the surgery (see Chapter 11).

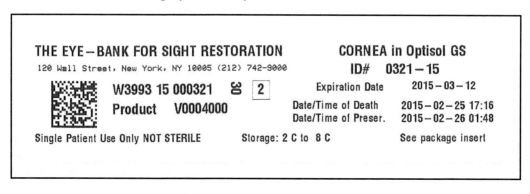

Figure 13.6a Label for donated cornea (reprinted by permission of Pat Dahl).

```
  The Eye-Bank for Sight Restoration, Inc.      212-742-9000
  120 Wall Street, New York  NY  10005    www.eyedonation.org
```

```
                   DONOR INFORMATION REPORT            PAGE 1
  EBAA Accredited                                    03 MAR 2015

  Tissue Type  CORNEA       ID #  0321-15    Exp Date   2015-03-12
```

```
  Age  48.00                       Media/Lot# Optisol GS /W0007703

  Date & Time of Admission       2015-02-13  00:00
  Date & Time of Death           2015-02-25  17:16
  Date & Time of Insitu Excision 2015-02-26  01:20     Tech 0604
  Date & Time of Preservation    2015-02-26  01:48     Tech 0604

  Donor On Vent: N   Length      days  Refrigeration Y at 21:36
  Cause of Death   COMPLICATIONS OF METASTATIC UTERINE CARCINOMA
  Secondary COD
```

```
  Med/Soc Interview   UTERINE CANCER, LARGE NEPHROLITHIASIS, BILATERAL
                      HYDROUTERONEPHROSIS, METS TO LUNG, LIVER,&LAD,DVT,
                      COLONOSCOPY, OOZING RECTAL MASS, TUMOR NECROSIS,
                      TAH, BSO, ANEMIA, CHEMOTHERAPY, S/P IVC PLACEMENT
                      D/T GI BLEED, B/L URETERAL STENT, H/O SEPSIS
                      (CLEARED) D/T TUMOR NECROSIS S/P DEBULKING

  Ocular History      No ocular history noted on chart review

  Blood Sample POST MORTEM         Accession Number  10268282
  Serology Lab VRL
  Serology Tests    NR = Non Reactive   POS = Reactive  QNS = Not tested
  HBsAg           2015-02-28   NR
  HBcore Total    2015-02-28   NR
  HCV Ab          2015-02-28   NR     THE EYE-BANK FOR SIGHT RESTORATION    CORNEA in Optisol GS
  HIVI/II Ab      2015-02-28   NR     120 Wall Street, New York, NY 10005 (212) 742-9000   ID#  0321-15
  RPR             2015-02-28   NR          W3993 15 000321  ☏ 2     Expiration Date   2015-03-12
  HIV-NAT         2015-02-28   NR          Product  V0004000        Date/Time of Death  2015-02-25 17:16
  HCV-NAT         2015-02-28   NR                                   Date/Time of Preser. 2015-02-26 01:48
  HBV-NAT         2015-02-28   NR     Single Patient Use Only NOT STERILE  Storage: 2 C to 8 C   See package insert
```

```
  Cornea Evaluation  Date 2015-02-26        Tech 0112
  Epithelium    SLIGHT EXPOSURE        Lens Status   PHAKIC
  Stroma        8.5MM CLR, S/M EDEMA, S ARCUS
  Descemet's Membrane 2+ FOLDS
  Endothelium          VS IRREG, DIFFUSE SPOT CELL LOSS, PERI STRESS
  Endothelial Cell Density 2877 sq mm  on 2015-02-26
  Pachymetry    530 um  on 2015-02-26
  Comments   EPI: S DIFF XP, PERIPHERAL IRREGULARITIES

  Medical eligibility determined after reviewing information provided by
  MEDICAL CHART REVIEW & PHYSICIAN INTERVIEW
  and approved by Medical Director Designee(s):
  Christopher Ferro, CEBT
```

Figure 13.6b Corresponding donor information report (reprinted by permission of Pat Dahl).

Monitoring, data reporting (and corneal registry)

Once an EB dispatches HTO to the operating theatre, they are generally required to provide de-identified statistical data to their governing agencies to help monitor and track the use and need of HTO. Additionally, the EB is required to report any adverse – and notifiable – events immediately to the authorities and/or the Project Notify Library. This library is a worldwide notification tool, which helps track and alert medical professionals to issues such as infection outbreaks due to transplantation.

In some countries, such as Australia, Sweden and the United Kingdom, a corneal graft registry has also been implemented. The data for these registries is provided by the surgeons postoperatively. These registries can track trends in technique, outcome rates and other possible variables which may affect outcomes (e.g. vascularised recipient beds of glaucoma in the recipient) by collecting de-identified information on recipients, donors, eye bank practices, surgical procedure, subsequent management, complications, graft survival, and visual outcomes after the graft (Keane *et al.* 2013). The outcomes are then reported both to the authorities and to the corneal surgical and EB community so that discussions on outcome and practice change can take place.

Hospital and day surgery duties

Patient education

For any patient scheduled for a transplant, of any kind, a full preoperative informed discussion and consent process must take place between the patient and their physician. Additionally, nursing and allied health staff have a unique opportunity to continue to offer educational support and answer any remaining questions from patients. With regard to the HTO, the patient and/or their relative may or may not know or understand where their HTO comes from (and often they may not wish to know).

Many patients may ask about the history of the donor and ask if they can contact the donor's family to say thank you. While the patient may request this, the law – in almost all countries – does not allow the donor or the recipient to be provided with information and contact details for the other party. This is to respect privacy and observe ethics, to prevent 'selection' or 'payment' issues that could result from this connection. Instead, the EB may offer an opportunity for one party to write a letter to the EB. The EB will then pass those details on to the recipient/donor. Within the letter, there can be no identifiable remarks or details.

Receiving and storing tissue in the operating theatre

When HTO arrives at the operating theatre (OT) facility, the staff must firstly check that the tissue has been transferred in the correct environment (e.g. cold for hypothermic) and the paperwork matches the labelling. Additionally, it is essential to check the surgical list to determine that the correct tissue type has been supplied in preparation for the patients. The HTO must then be stored, in accordance with the requirements outlined on the accompanying paperwork until it is needed for the surgery list start-time. Any noted issues with the paperwork or bottle (including tampering, expiration or a cracked container) need to be reported to the surgeon and/or EB to check for suitability to transplant and/or arrangement for tissue replacement. Such issues need to be reported in an incident report, for quality tracking purposes, by both the operating theatre and the EB.

Generally, HTO should be stored in a restricted area, away from the general public, patients and their relatives, and in close proximity to the OT. Fridges used to store hypothermic tissue need to be regularly checked for their temperature, and room temperatures also need to be checked to ensure that the ambient air is suitable for normothermic tissue storage. The OT should have a tissue-checking system in place, to confirm that the HTO has arrived and to cross-check the expiration date prior to the surgery. All paperwork for the tissue needs to be retained and kept with the tissue at all times.

Commencement of surgery

The HTO needs to be removed from the storage area and presented to the OT, for the surgeon and surgical team to check, prior to commencing the list – and prior to patient preparation. Additionally, the tissue again needs to be checked during *Sign-In* (in preop) and *Time-Out* (intraop) phases of the safe site surgery checking system, prior to commencing site preparation.

During surgery

Once the patient is draped, the surgeon – generally – asks the scout nurse (circulator) to open the HTO and present it to the OT table. This is because the surgeon wants to make sure the tissue is of good quality and prepared, before making a surgical incision into the eye. The scout nurse needs to make sure that the transfer of the HTO is done in a sterile manner, without damage to the tissue and without dropping the tissue. Depending on the type of transport container or packaging, the bottle may be opened by the scout, and the surgeon may remove the tissue, using forceps. Alternatively, the surgeon may instruct the scout to empty the contents of the bottle into a sterile pot on the OT trolley. Either way, it is important that the scout communicates with the surgeon to ascertain their preference and to ensure that asepsis is maintained at all times during the transfer to the operating table.

Once on the sterile field, the surgeon will prepare the tissue to suit the type of corneal surgery being performed. It is important that the scrub/scout nurse prepares the correct instruments for the surgeon's particular technique.

At the end of the surgery, the scrub/scout nurse needs to make sure that any remaining tissue (e.g. scleral rim) is disposed of correctly, with all other human waste. In some instances, remaining HTO may be ethics-approved for further research and the surgeon may ask for the remaining tissue to be re-bottled, ready to be sent to the researcher. In this case, it is important that the scrub/scout nurse handles the tissue carefully, without contamination of the tissue or self, by donning standard personal protective equipment.

Any labelling stickers that have been provided are to be placed in the operating theatre prosthesis logs and also on the patient and surgeon's notes – in the prosthesis section. All other remaining EB paperwork is to be returned to the surgeon, who then uses these documents to complete their outcome reports and submissions, which are required by their governing authorities or registries. If stickers are not provided, the scout nurse needs to manually write the details into each area of their log/patient charts as per their hospital policy.

Checking expiration dates: At all times, HTO must be transplanted prior to its expiration date. This is because the medium it is prepared in is only validated to retain the consistent environment for the period suggested on the label. It is therefore absolutely imperative that tissue – especially corneal tissue which is living – is not transplanted after the expiration date. All expired tissue must be returned to the EB.

Risk prevention/management

EB practices are subject to auditing and visitation by their governing bodies (in a similar way to hospitals going through accreditation cycles) to ensure that best evidence-based practice is followed and the facility is working within a continual quality improvement system (Eye Bank Association of Australia and New Zealand 2009). This also includes staff competency training, tissue and issues (incident) revisions and investment in new technologies.

Additionally, in some countries, the law categorises HTO as a 'medical/surgical implant' that is manufactured just like a metal hip-joint or a packet of Paracetamol (acetaminophen). It therefore requires the tissue to be recovered, prepared and validated in accordance with good manufacturing practice codes as well as the human tissue act for that particular country/state.

Global provision of HTO

In recent years, the World Health Organization (WHO) has worked with professionals in the eye, tissue and organ sectors to help establish ethical principles and practice around transplantation, due to the wide variations in access to tissues and organs, and limited global uniformity and ethical considerations surrounding consent and distribution processes. The global discussions and collaborations now focus on protecting the vulnerable and promoting the altruistic nature of donation (World Health Assembly 2010), resulting from the WHO's development of its *Aide-Memoire: Access to Safe and Effective Cells and Tissues for Transplantation.* (2006), which provides key strategies for education, safety and quality systems to prevent and protect all parties.

This has led to some transplant sectors (e.g. nephrology), which experience the unethical acquisition of organs either illegally or through coercion of vulnerable and displaced persons on a global scale, uniting to develop their own universal bioethical framework of principles and practice. For instance, in 2008 the Society of Nephrologists and the International Transplant Society collaborated to develop and endorse the global Declaration of Istanbul on Organ Trafficking and Transplant Tourism, which encompasses the ethical principles of organ transplantation and strategies to ensure safe and ethical practice.

While there is very little published literature specifically pertaining to ethics around HTO, the EB sector has been proactive in this regard, and in 2014 developed the Global Alliance of Eye Bank Associations to help share recommendations, bridge gaps and connect eye bank and corneal professionals around the world.

EB regional associations have also begun their own discussions and strategies and are striving towards global recommendations and associations. For example, the Eye Bank Association of Australia and New Zealand has taken a pro-active approach by developing its own regional bioethical framework on practice and processes. Inspired and supported by the Declaration of Istanbul on Organ Trafficking and Transplant Tourism (2008) and WHO, this framework was formally ratified on 4 March 2015 (Eye Bank Association of Australia and New Zealand 2015).

The Eye Bank Association of America has also put in place an association-wide agreement for all their eye banks to strive towards ISBT128 labelling by 2017. As this eye bank is the world's greatest exporter of HTO, this agreement will have a profound long-term positive effect on the safety and tracking of tissue around the world. Additionally, the European Eye Bank Association encourages individual eye banks to communicate on surplus tissue, to support regional need, and assists them in doing this through its network.

Authors' note

Special thanks to:

Dr Karl David Brown PhD,
Department of Ophthalmology, University of Melbourne, Australia;

Patricia Dahl,
Executive Director/CEO, the Eye-Bank for Sight Restoration Inc., New York, USA;

Lions Eye Donation Service, Centre for Eye Research Australia, University of Melbourne, Australia.

References

Armitage, W.J. (2011) Preservation of Human Cornea. *Transfusion, Medicine and Hemotherapy.* **38**, 143–147

Baylis, O., Figueiredo, F., Henein, C., Lako M. & Ahmad, S. (2011) 13 years of cultured limbal epithelial cell therapy: a review of the outcomes. *Journal of Cellular Biochemistry.* **112**, 993–1002.

Bredehorn-Mayr, T., Duncker, G.I.W. & Armitage, W.J. (2009) *Eye Banking.* Switzerland: Karger.

Chu, H., Hsieh, M., Chen, Y., Hou, Y., Hu, F. & Chen, W. (2014) Anterior Corneal Buttons From DSAEK Donor Tissue Can Be Stored in Optisol GS for Later Use in Tectonic Lamellar Patch Grafting. *Corneal Journal.* **33**(6), 555–58

Chu, W. (2000) The past twenty-five years in eye banking. *Cornea.* **19**(5), 754–65.

Custer, P.L. & McCaffery, S. (2006) Complications of Sclera-Covered Enucleation Implants. *Ophthalmic Plastic and Reconstructive Surgery.* **22**(4), 269–73.

Dapena, I., Ham, L. & Melles, G.R.J. (2009) Endothelial keratoplasty: DSEK/DSAEK or DMEK – the thinner the better? *Current Opinion in Ophthalmology.* **20**, 299–307.

Dekaris, I. & Gabric, N. (2009) 'Preparation and Preservation of Amniotic Membrane' in T. Bredehorn-Mayr, G.I.W. Duncker & W.J. Armitage (eds) *Eye Banking.* Switzerland: Karger.

Doughman, D.J. & Rogers, C.C. (2012) Eye Banking in the 21st Century: How Far Have We Come? Are We Prepared for what's Ahead? *International Journal of Eye Banking.* 1, 1.

European Eye Bank Association (2013) *Minimum Medical Standards. European Eye Bank Association. Revision 1.* European Eye Bank Association.

European Eye Bank Association (2014) *Directory:* Twenty-Second Edition. European Eye Bank Association.

Eye Bank Association of Australia and New Zealand (April 2009) *Medical and Quality Standards for Eye Donation and Eye Tissue Banking* – 2nd ed. Eye Bank Association of Australia and New Zealand.

Eye Bank Association of Australia and New Zealand (2015) *Bioethical Framework for Policy and Procedure, Version 1.* Eye Bank Association of Australia and New Zealand.

Harkin, D., Apel, A., Di Girolamo, N., Watson, S., Brown, K., Daniell, M., McGhee, J.J. & McGhee, C. (2013) Current status and future prospects for cultured limbal tissue transplants in Australia and New Zealand. *Clinical and Experimental Ophthalmology.* **41**, 272–81.

Keane, M. C., Lowe, M.T., Coster, D.J., Pollock, G.A. & Williams, K.A. (2013). The Influence of Australian Eye Banking Practices on Corneal Graft Survival. *Medical Journal of Australia.* 19th August. 275–79.

Kheirkhuh, A., Sheha, H., Casas, V., Raju, V. K. & Tseng, S.C.G. (2010) 'Amniotic Membrane Transplantation' in R.B. Vajpayee, N. Sharma, G.C. Tabin & H.R. Taylor (eds) *Corneal Transplantation.* 2nd edn. New Delhi: Jaypee-Highlights Medical Publishers.

Kitzmann, A.S., Goins, K.M., Reed, C., Padnick-Silver, L., Macsai, M.S. & Sutphin, S.T. (2008). Eye Bank Survey of Surgeons Using Precut Donor Tissue for Descemet Stripping Automated Endothelial Keratoplasty. *Cornea.* **27**(6), 634–39.

Lindquist, T.D., Miller, T.D., Elsen, J.E. & Lignoski, P.J. (2009) Minimizing the risk of disease transmission during corneal tissue processing. *Cornea.* **28**(5), 481–84.

Machin, H. (2014) Corneal Transplant Tissue – Before it reaches the operating theatre. *International Journal of Ophthalmic Practice.* **5**(6), 205–11.

Mariappan, I., Maddileti, S., Savy, S., Tiwari, S., Gaddipati, S., Fatima, A., Sangwan, V.S., Balasubramanian, D. & Vemuganti, G.K. (2010) In vitro culture and expansion of human limbal epithelial cells. *Nature Protocols.* **5**, 1470–79.

Moffatt, S.L., Cartwright, V.A. & Stumpf, T.H. (2005) Centennial Review of Corneal Transplantation. *Clinical and Experimental Ophthalmology.* **33**, 642–57.

Müller, A., Craig, J.P., Grupcheva, C.N. & McGhee, C.N.J. (2004) The effects of corneal parameters on the assessment of endothelial cell density in the elderly eye. *British Journal of Ophthalmology.* **88**, 325–30.

National Health Service (2013) NHS: *Approaching the families of potential organ donors – best practice guidance*. United Kingdom: National Health Service Blood and Transplant: Consent/Authorization Best Practice Development Group. http://www.odt.nhs.uk/pdf/family_approach_best_practice_guide.pdf (accessed 18 August 2016).

New South Wales Organ and Tissue Donation Service (2014) *Deceased donor physical assessment policy number EATB-C-WI-003*. New South Wales Government, Australia.

Participants in the International Summit on Transplant Tourism and Organ Trafficking Convened by the Transplantation Society and International Society of Nephrology in Istanbul, Turkey, April 30–May 2, 2008. (2008) The Declaration of Istanbul on organ trafficking and transplant tourism. *Transplantation*. **86**(8), 1013–18.

Pellegrini, G., Traverso, C.E., Franzi, A.T, Zingirian, M., Cancedda, R. & de Luca, M. (1997) Long-term restoration of damaged corneal surfaces with autologous cultivated corneal epithelium. *Lancet*. **349**, 990–93.

Pels, L. (1997) Commentary: Organ culture: the method of choice for preservation of human donor corneas. *British Journal of Ophthalmology*. **81**, 523–25.

Pels, E., & Pollock, G. (2013) 'Storage of Donor Cornea for Penetrating and Lamellar Transplantation' in T. Reinhard & F. Larkin, F. (eds) *Corneal Disease: Recent developments in diagnosis and therapy*. London: Springer.

Rehany, U., Balut, G., Lefler, E. & Rumelt, S. (2004). The prevention and risk factors for donor corneal button contamination and its association with ocular infection after transplantation. *Cornea*. **23**(7), 649–54.

Reinhart, W.J. (1993) 'Gross and slit lamp evaluation of the donor eye' in F.S. Brightbill (ed) *Corneal Surgery: Theory, techniques and tissue*. 2nd edn. St Louis: Mosby.

Romanchuk, K.G., Nair, P. & Grahn, B. (2003). How long can donor sclera be safely stored? *Cornea*. **22**(6), 569–72.

Ruzza, A., Salvalaio, G., Bruin, A., Frigo, A.C., Busin, M. & Ponzin, D. (2013) Banking of Donor Tissues for Descemet Stripping Automated Endothelial Keratoplasty. *Cornea*. **32**(1), 70–75.

Sharma, N., Shekhar, C. & Kumar, S. (2010) 'Chapter 1: Evolution of Corneal Grafting Surgery' in R.B. Vajpayee, N. Sharma, G.C. Tabin & H.R. Taylor (eds) *Corneal Transplantation*. 2nd edn. New Delhi: Jaypee-Highlights Medical Publishers.

Warwick, R.M., Fehily, D., Brubaker, S.A. & Eastlund, T. (2009) *Tissue and Cell Donation: An Essential Guide*. Oxford: Wiley-Blackwell.

World Health Assembly (2010) *Organ and Tissue Donation. Sixty-Third World Health Assembly*. 21 March 2010. http://apps.who.int/gb/ebwha/pdf_files/WHA63/A63_R22-en.pdf (accessed 18 August 2016).

World Health Organization (2006) *Aide-Memoire: Access to Safe and Effective Cells and Tissues for Transplantation*. World Health Organization. http://www.who.int/transplantation/AM-HCTTServices.pdf (accessed 18 August 2016).

World Health Organization (2011) *Report: First Advisory Meeting for the SONG Project (Standardization of Organ Nomenclature Globally) in Collaboration with the ICCBBA. World Health Organization. 4-5 May 2011*. http://who.int/patientsafety/SONG-Project-report_Transplantation_Sep-2013.pdf

(Accessed 18 August 2016).

World Health Organization (2012) WHO Standard Organ Transplant Nomenclature-Version 1.0. Collaboratively developed by WHO and ICCBBA through the SONG project. http://www.who.int/patientsafety/WHO-Standard-Organ-Transplant-Nomenclature-1-0.pdf (accessed 18 August 2016).

Resources

Association of Eye Banks of Asia
http://www.eyebankingasia.org/ (accessed 18 August 2016).

The Corneal Society
http://www.corneasociety.org/ (accessed 18 August 2016).

The Declaration of Istanbul on Organ Trafficking and Transplant Tourism
http://www.declarationofistanbul.org (accessed 18 August 2016).

Eye Bank Association of India
http://www.ebai.org/ (accessed 18 August 2016).

Eye Bank Association of Australia & New Zealand (EBAANZ)
http://www.ebaanz.org/ (accessed 18 August 2016).

For EBAANZ information on the handling and care of HTO, see: *National Guidelines – A resource for Australian Hospitals, Operating Theatres and Day Surgery Staff Regarding the Care and Handling of Human Tissue for Ocular Transplantation 2016* © available via http://www.ebaanz.org/medical-standards-and-quality/ under 'Professional documents, guidelines and standards'. (accessed 18 August 2016).
EBAANZ Bioethical Framework
http://www.ebaanz.org/wp-content/uploads/2016/05/EBAANZ-Bioethic-Framework-2015.pdf
(accessed 18 August 2016).

EBAANZ National Guideline http://www.adha.asn.au/uploads/63175/ufiles/Members_pages_Docs/Bulletins/2016_
Bulletins/ADHA_Bulletin_10_-_18_March_2016_-_EBAANZ_NATIONAL_GUIDELINES_2016.pdf
(accessed 18 August 2016).

Eye Bank Association of America
http://www.restoresight.org/ (accessed 18 August 2016).

European Eye Bank Association
http://www.europeaneyebanks.org/ (accessed 18 August 2016).

Global Alliance of Eye Banks
http://www.gaeba.org (accessed 18 August 2016).

ICCBBA, Tissue Tracking ISBT128
https://www.iccbba.org/ (accessed 18 August 2016).

International Journal of Eye Banking
http://www.eyebankingjournal.org (accessed 18 August 2016).

Pan American Association of Eye Banks
http://www.apaboeyebanks.org/ (accessed 18 August 2016).

Universal Declaration of Human Rights
http://www.un.org/en/universal-declaration-human-rights/index.html (accessed 18 August 2016).

World Health Organization, Human Organ Transplantation http://www.who.int/transplantation/organ/en/
(accessed 18 August 2016).

CHAPTER FOURTEEN

Global eye health

Robert Lindfield

Introduction

Approximately 40 million people are blind (visual acuity worse than 3/60 in the better eye with available correction) worldwide. Around 90 % of them live in low- and middle-income countries, with India and China accounting for the majority of blind individuals. Women are more likely to be affected than men, due to their longer life expectancy (many blinding eye conditions are age related) and the difficulty that women have, in some settings, in seeking care.

Figure 14.1 shows the percentage of blindness due to specific conditions. It should be noted that most of the diseases listed occur in every country regardless of development status but rarely cause blindness in high-income countries. This is mainly due to the presence of well-established health services that individuals can readily access.

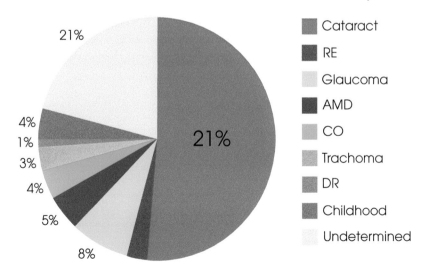

Figure 14.1 Global causes of blindness as percentage of total blindness in 2010
(World Health Organization 2012).

The global initiative 'Vision 2020: the right to sight', aims to eliminate avoidable blindness by the year 2020. This initiative is a collaboration between the World Health Organization (WHO) and the International Agency for the Prevention of Blindness (IAPB). The IAPB is an overarching body representing charities, businesses and academic institutions, which was established in 1999. Its initial focus was on five leading causes of blindness: cataract, refractive error, trachoma, onchocerciasis and childhood blindness.

Vision 2020 has evolved over the last 15 years and has changed its focus to ensure that eye health is embedded in local health systems (see section below on health systems), that all individuals are able to access eye health services, and that services are adequately equipped and staffed, and of high enough quality to deliver the services required. It has amended its list of priority eye diseases to include diabetic retinopathy, age-related macular degeneration (AMD) and genetic eye diseases

The rest of this chapter will describe the leading causes of blindness in more detail and provide an outline of health systems and how they interact with eye health.

Cataract

Cataract is the leading cause of blindness worldwide, with approximately 20 million people affected. Cataract surgery is the only effective treatment and is increasingly being provided throughout the world.

Unfortunately, many people are still unable to access cataract surgery, and the reasons for this can be broadly split into patient and service factors.

Patient factors are those that stop patients from accessing services. These are frequently associated with strongly held beliefs – for example, that blindness is part of growing old (a common perception in many countries) and that there is nothing that can be done to restore vision ('the will of God'). However, studies suggest that issues like cost of services, distance to services and the quality of services are also key drivers of uptake.

Service factors relate to the ability of the health system to provide surgery in a timely manner, when and where it is required, at an affordable price. One of the main limitations on cataract surgical services is the availability of trained surgeons, particularly in rural areas. Surveys routinely show that most ophthalmologists practise in urban centres, leaving the rural areas with limited or no services. Some countries have tried to address this by training non-doctor cataract surgeons and this strategy has met with some success.

The type of cataract surgery routinely used in many developing countries is called small incision cataract surgery (SICS) (see also MSICS in Chapter 19). Unlike phacoemulsification, which is practised widely in developed countries, SICS requires very limited equipment and cheaper consumables (e.g. a rigid instead of foldable intra-ocular lens, no high-tech computerised equipment). Studies have shown that the outcome of SICS is similar to that of phacoemulsification and, in resource-poor settings, is probably a more efficient technique. However, phacoemulsification is being used by a lot of surgeons in developing countries to generate income, as they can charge wealthier patients higher prices for this procedure. Some hospitals are cross-subsidising their services by generating income in this way.

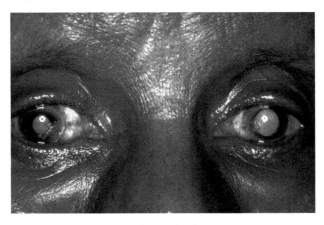

Figure 14.2 Bilateral white cataract.
(Photo reprinted by permission of the International Centre for Eye Health – ICEH.)

Refractive error

Whilst not a leading cause of blindness, refractive error is a major cause of sight loss, with an estimated 150 million people living with visual loss due to uncorrected refractive error worldwide (see also Chapter 2). The two main types of refractive error are near (short) sightedness or myopia, and far (long) sightedness or hypermetropia. Both can be treated with spectacles, contact lenses or laser. A variant of hypermetropia is presbyopia – difficulty with near vision that is associated with increasing age and is almost universal over the age of 50. A commonly held belief is that presbyopia is not a problem in many developing countries because of high rates of illiteracy. However, this ignores the marked rise in literacy globally and the need for good near-vision for activities like sewing.

The ability to secure a cheap, adequate pair of spectacles varies hugely throughout the world. As expected, areas like rural sub-Saharan Africa do not have adequate provision of refractive error services and people often remain visually impaired because they cannot afford a pair of spectacles. Similar issues to cataract surgery affect refractive error, with inequity in distribution of services.

Chronic blinding conditions
Glaucoma

Glaucoma is a chronic, progressive neuropathy of the optic nerve that can lead to sight loss if untreated. It affects approximately 60 million people worldwide and is the cause of blindness in around 8 million people – particularly in low-income countries (see also Chapter 21).

There are two main types of glaucoma, open angle and closed angle, both of which lead to irreversible optic nerve damage, but the method of causing the damage differs slightly. Open angle glaucoma is more common in people of European, South Asian and African origin, whereas closed angle glaucoma is more common in people of East Asian origin.

Chronic open angle glaucoma is known as the 'silent thief of sight', as people are frequently unaware that they are slowly going blind, as the condition is symptom free until the end stage of disease. In many developing countries people present to services with glaucoma when they are already blind, which is too late for any effective treatment, as the damage is irreversible. There are significant difficulties in detecting glaucoma early in these settings, particularly where drops are scarce and expensive and surgery (trabeculectomy) is the only effective treatment.

Patients often struggle with the concept of glaucoma surgery. Although it costs a lot of money, it does not lead to improved vision (and can frequently lead to worse vision). They are often sharing wards with people who have had their vision restored by means of cataract surgery, and it is difficult to explain that the purpose of trabeculectomy is to prevent further visual loss, rather than provide a cure.

Closed angle glaucoma (CAG) is relatively common in East Asia, where it is more prevalent than chronic open angle glaucoma (COAG). Treatment involves lasers; and such services are scarce in many places, meaning that CAG is a relatively common cause of blindness in these settings.

Different modalities of treatment are being trialled in many places, with some promising results from specific laser treatment, but these are a long way from being widely implemented and there is still a need to advertise the importance of glaucoma in communities, particularly amongst first degree relatives of those affected who have an increased risk.

Diabetic retinopathy

Diabetes affects approximately 9% of adults worldwide (see also Chapter 22). Diabetic retinopathy (DR) is a complication of poorly controlled diabetes that, if not managed correctly, can lead to retinal damage and sight loss. Like glaucoma, patients are frequently unaware of the presence of DR until it is too late and an ocular examination is required to detect it, unless or until it affects central vision (called macular oedema). Late presentation is therefore common in many settings.

In countries like the UK, there is an established diabetic retinopathy screening programme, where every diabetic over the age of 10 is assessed for DR every two years. This type of programme is unfeasible in many low- and middle-income countries, as it is very expensive and the infrastructure does not exist to provide it. This has led to a range of different ways of finding those with DR being developed, including opportunistic case finding (anyone found to be diabetic has their eyes examined) and screening programmes using telemedicine. However, in most developing countries, there is still no mechanism for those with diabetes to be assessed for DR systematically.

Treatment for DR involves applying laser burns to the retina to stop the disease progressing. There are many issues in providing effective treatment, such as lasers being expensive to buy and maintain, and staff requiring ongoing training and support to use them. Again, providing this type of service in resource-poor settings is difficult.

Age-related macular degeneration (AMD)

This is the third most common global cause of visual impairment, with a blindness prevalence of 8.7% (see also Chapter 22). It is the primary cause of visual loss in industrialised countries. As its main risk factor is aging, it is much less of a problem in low-income countries, due to their lower life expectancy.

Infectious eye diseases
Trachoma

Trachoma is the leading infectious cause of visual impairment, affecting 1.8 million people globally, and leaving more than 0.5 million irreversibly blind (World Health Organization 2015). It is caused by the chlamydia trachomatis bacterium, which results in a keratoconjunctivitis. Repeated infections with the organism over a period of years, usually starting in early childhood, lead to scarring of the inside of the eyelids and resultant 'rolling' inwards of eye lashes (termed trachomatous trichiasis). The lashes then rub on the cornea, leading to painful irreversible corneal scarring and sight loss. It is believed to be endemic in 51 countries.

The organism spreads from close contact between people but the cycle of infection/reinfection can be broken by good hygiene and sanitation. The disease particularly affects women, as they have regular close contact with infected children. Trachoma tends to occur in places with poor water supplies and limited or no sewerage systems. If you have to walk several kilometres to collect water you will prioritise drinking over washing. As a consequence, blinding trachoma tends to affect the poorest people in the poorest communities in the world.

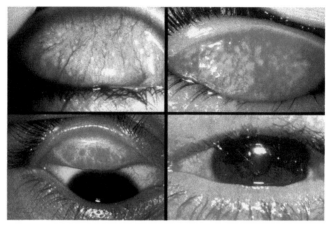

Figure 14.3 Stages in the development of trachoma clockwise from top left; follicles of trachoma (TF); intense inflammation of trachoma (TI); trichiasis of trachoma (TT); conjunctival scarring of trachoma (TS)

(Photos reprinted by permission of the International Centre for Eye Health – ICEH.)

The World Health Organization (WHO) has developed a strategy to deal with trachoma called the SAFE strategy. This focuses on:

- **S** –Surgery on the eyelid to redirect the inward-turning eyelashes away from the corneal surface
- **A** – Antibiotics to treat the infection and break the cycle of infection/reinfection
- **F** – Face washing, emphasising the importance of hygiene factors in breaking the infection/reinfection cycle and preventing transmission
- **E** – Environmental factors, highlighting the need for covered latrines and good sewerage systems that prevent the fly, which transmits the disease, from breeding.

Surgical lid rotation, to redirect the eyelashes away from the cornea, is a relatively simple procedure that can be performed by nursing staff working in local health centres. They receive training in the surgical technique and the equipment required, and they perform surgery in local settings such as clinics or schools. High-quality surgery has been shown to reduce the risk of blindness from trachoma.

The antibiotic to treat the infection (azithromycin) is donated free by Pfizer. The drug is distributed to the whole community at least once a year, with drug administration being led by local community members. Every member of the community receives a dose of antibiotic that reduces the burden of infection in the community and has been shown to reduce the risk of blindness. Data reported to WHO by member states for 2013 showed that nearly 234,000 people with trachomatous trichiasis were provided with corrective surgery that year, and 55 million people were treated with anti-chlamydial antibiotics (World Health Organization 2015).

Both the face washing and environmental factors are addressed through a combination of health education and infrastructure development. Local people are frequently taught about the importance of hand and face hygiene and their association with decreased risk of trachoma (plus other diseases such as diarrhoea and vomiting). They are also encouraged to construct covered latrines and develop safe water sources, although the latter is frequently difficult in arid areas.

Figure 14.4 Availability of water affects the prevalence of trachoma in a community.

There is an international collaboration to eliminate trachoma as a public health problem, termed GET 2020 (Global Elimination of Trachoma). This is a partnership between the WHO and other organisations (NGOs, companies, etc.) to oversee the SAFE strategy and establish best practice. Trachoma is considered a 'neglected tropical disease' (NTD) and is often dealt with alongside other NTDs, including diseases such as leprosy or onchocerciasis.

Onchocerciasis

Onchocerciasis is a blinding eye condition caused by the parasitic worm, Onchocerca Volvulus. This enters the body through the bites of the blackfly, genus Simulium, which breeds in fast-flowing rivers and streams, often adjacent to fertile agricultural land. The worm produces larvae (microfilariae), which migrate to the skin, eyes and other organs, where they cause an intense inflammatory response, particularly when they die, leading to itching, skin lesions (specifically nodules) and eye lesions. The eye lesions can cause blindness. The blackflies ingest blood and microfilariae from an infected human when they bite them and transmit them to another host.

Over 99% of people infected with onchocerciasis live in 31 countries in sub-Saharan Africa. However, onchocerciasis has been controlled in many countries through an approach that includes controlling the vector of the disease (the blackfly) and treating infection with ivermectin (Mectizan), an anti-helminthic drug, donated for free by Merck. There have been very successful community-led distribution programmes of mectizan, where the local population has taken responsibility for ensuring that every member of the community receives the dose of mectizan they require. As a result, the disease has become less of an issue in many places.

Childhood blindness

Blindness in children is rare (1:10000, compared to 1:100 adults) but it is potentially devastating, as it can lead to a life of disability. Consequently, preventing and treating childhood blindness is a priority for many governments and organisations.

Children experience many of the same eye diseases as adults (e.g. cataract, glaucoma and refractive error) but these can be defined as either congenital or acquired causes of blindness. Congenital causes develop in-utero and tend to be genetic, iatrogenic or idiopathic; acquired causes develop after birth and include infective, traumatic or idiopathic. Blindness in children can be further categorised by either aetiology or anatomical site (e.g. rubella blindness or cataract blindness).

An emerging cause of childhood blindness in middle- and low-income countries is retinopathy of prematurity (ROP). This is an iatrogenic cause of blindness in premature infants, associated with excess supplementary oxygen, infection and poor nutrition in the neonatal unit. ROP results from the poor development of retinal vasculature, which can lead to retinal detachment. As poorer countries develop maternal and child health services, the number of children surviving prematurity has increased. However, the quality of neonatal services has not, in many settings, been sufficient to prevent ROP. Early stages of ROP can be identified and treated, predominantly by laser, but this requires a screening programme with retinal examination of premature babies at regular intervals whilst they are in the neonatal unit.

Preventing childhood blindness requires a range of approaches, from vaccination to good nursing care, and is a core component of any childhood blindness programme. Treatment for children is usually more complicated than in adults, as they are smaller and their eyes are more elastic and react more violently to interference. Consequently, there is a need for experience and training in paediatric eye care, which is absent in many low-income settings.

Genetic eye diseases

Because of the low prevalence of blinding eye disease in industrialised/high-income countries, genetic eye pathology represents a significant cause of blindness in these settings (see also Chapter 25). The only current means of prevention of genetic eye disease is genetic counselling.

Although no longer a leading cause of visual impairment due to significant work by health systems in the countries where it is prevalent, leprosy is another 'neglected tropical disease' with significant eye sequelae.

Leprosy (also known as Hansen's disease)

Leprosy is caused by Mycobacterium Leprae and primarily affects the skin, peripheral nerves and the eyes, causing a chronic granulomatous inflammation. Patients present with skin lesions, muscle weakness and peripheral neuropathy. The anterior segment of the eye is often affected with complications, including chronic, low-grade uveitis. Iris 'pearls' are seen, which are collections of dead bacteria. Large areas of iris atrophy occur, as well as interstitial keratitis and complications of corneal hypoaesthesia. The posterior segment of the eye is not affected. Lagophthalmos, with exposure keratitis, in a cornea with reduced sensation, can lead to ulceration and perforation (International Centre for Eye Health 2010).

Figure 14.5. A man showing typical facial symptoms of leprosy. This patient has bilateral facial palsy, lagophthalmos, corneal exposure in the left eye, and corneal ulceration.
(Photo reprinted by permission of J.D.C. Anderson.)

While many countries where leprosy used to be endemic have achieved elimination at a national level and are working at local level, pockets of high prevalence still remain in some areas in Angola, Brazil, the Central African Republic, India, Madagascar, Nepal and the United Republic of Tanzania, as well as in the Democratic Republic of the Congo and Mozambique.

Health systems

From this brief overview of the epidemiology of eye disease in developing countries, it is clear that just focusing on eye health in isolation will not effectively address many of the conditions discussed. This has been widely acknowledged by the WHO and IAPB and, as a result, the most recent World Health Organization global action plan (WHO 2013) focuses on embedding eye care within the health system.

The health system describes the way that health services are provided in each setting. Every health system has the same six 'building blocks': human resources, equipment/consumables, financing, management, IT and delivery. Every building block needs to be present for the health system to function optimally and deliver care to the patient. For example, if finance systems are not in place then staff will not get paid and equipment will not be purchased.

Considering eye health as part of the overall health system is important, as it allows a more efficient and sustainable approach. There are many examples of eye health embedding in the general health system, e.g. centralised procurement, centralised human resource management and centralised IT systems. However, such services must be delivered with a focus on equity and quality.

Universal health coverage

A second area of concern for eye care within the wider health system is the affordability of services. There are alarming figures about the numbers of patients who become dangerously poor through health costs and the WHO has made affordable healthcare a priority.

They suggest that no patient should be adversely affected by out-of-pocket expenses for healthcare and have suggested various ways of making healthcare affordable. In many places, people pay a lot for eye care and it will be challenging to make it affordable but, without doing so, people will continue to lose their sight, and the ambition of eliminating avoidable blindness by the year 2020 will not be achieved.

References

International Centre for Eye Health (2010) *Leprosy and the eye teaching set.* London: ICEH.

World Health Organization (2012) *Global Data on Visual Impairments 2010.* Geneva: WHO.

World Health Organization (2013) *Universal eye health: a global action plan 2014 – 2019.* Geneva: WHO.

World Health Organization (2015) *Trachoma; factsheet No 382.* Geneva: WHO.
http://www.who.int/mediacentre/factsheets/fs382/en/ (accessed 18 August 2016).

CHAPTER FIFTEEN

The eyelids and lacrimal drainage system

John Cooper
with material by Les Mcqueen

Introduction

It would be easy to underestimate the value and function of the eyelids and to consider them merely in terms of two extensions of skin that help to protect the eye. This view is of course grossly simplistic. The eyelids are integral to eye function and protection, and they are relatively intricate and complex structures that are probably rather taken for granted.

Apart from the accepted cosmetic appearance the eyelids afford, functionally they also provide protection and ocular comfort, control light, remove debris and contribute to tear drainage. For these functions to work efficiently, the eyelids have to be structurally intact and approximate against the globe. Even simple defects of the eyelids can significantly prejudice their ability to work efficiently. An example would be the significant reduction in effective tear drainage if the lower eyelid margin is not flush against the eye. Equally, if affected by trauma or surgery, the eyelids can be notoriously difficult to reconstruct, especially if the lacrimal apparatus are involved.

Allied and integral to the eyelids and the eye is the lacrimal system, which produces tears and protects and lubricates the eye. The subsequent drainage of tears via the puncta and the lacrimal sac has to be economical and proficient; any disturbance or blockage of the system can have a profound effect on patients, especially if this leads to some degree of epiphora (watering).

As they play an essential part in eye function, the eyelids and the lacrimal system should be viewed as an important part of the ophthalmic practitioner's knowledge. Understanding the anatomy and physiology of the eyelids will allow for a greater awareness of the aetiology and modality of associated eyelid conditions.

This chapter will outline the normal anatomy and physiology of the eyelids and the lacrimal system in order to facilitate and augment the practitioner's knowledge.

Additionally, further consideration of common eyelid disorders and altered pathology will be described, along with some key nursing considerations.

Functional anatomy and physiology of the eyelids

Basic topography of the eyelids

The function of the eyelids and the blink mechanism are to:

- Provide protection and comfort for the eye
- Contribute to tear drainage (via the lacrimal system)
- Spread lubrication and tears over the eye/cornea
- Assist in the removal of debris
- Cover the eye during sleep
- Control light coming into the eye.

The eyelids have an average horizontal length of 26mm in females and 27mm in males, which shortens slightly over time as we get older (van den Bosch *et al.* 1999). The outer corner of the eyelids, the lateral canthus, is usually slightly higher than the inner corner (medial canthus) by a mean vertical distance of approximately 1.35mm (Rosenstein *et al.* 2000).

The lateral canthus represents the union of the upper and lower eyelids, and the point of fusion is known as the lateral commissure. The distance from the lateral commissure to the lateral bony orbital rim is approximately 7.5mm (Rosenstein *et al.* 2000). The lateral canthus is held in position by the lateral canthal tendon, a fibrous connective tissue band that inserts 1.5mm behind the orbital rim (at Whitnall's tubercle) and is an extension of the orbicularis muscle.

The inner corner of the eye reflects the connection between the medial canthal tendon and the eyelid to the orbital rim at the lacrimal crest and the frontal process of the maxilla. The medial canthal tendon has two limbs, which are also closely associated functionally and surround the lacrimal sac.

Within the eyelid, both the medial and lateral tendons attach to the tarsal plates, which consist of dense connective tissue and provide structure for the eyelids. The upper tarsal plate is semilunar or 'D'-shaped and at its broadest is 10mm in diameter (and directly corresponds with the upper eyelid skin crease); it is 25–29mm in horizontal length and 1mm thick. The smaller lower tarsal plate has a 5mm vertical diameter.

The central vertical distance between the upper and lower eyelid is approximately 10mm (palpebral aperture). The upper eyelid usually rests just below the upper corneal limbus, and the lower eyelid at the lower corneal limbus.

The caruncle is a small pink fleshy eminence in the medial angle of the eye that contains sebaceous and sudoriferous glands.

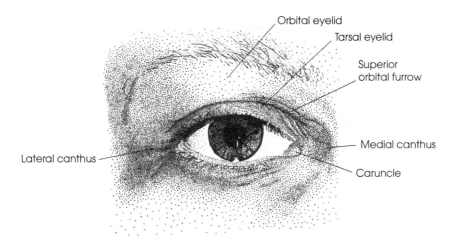

Figure 15.1 External view of the eye and lids

The eyelids essentially comprise four layers of tissues:

- Skin
- Muscle (orbicularis oculi)
- Tarsal plate/orbital septum (connective tissue)
- Conjunctiva (palpebral).

Skin layer

The skin of the eyelids is very thin and consists of epidermis, dermis and appendages of various cell types. It is some of the thinnest skin in the human body measuring 0.04–0.06mm, and varies very slightly between genders, races and age groups (Lee & Hwang 2002). The thickness of the eyelid skin is graduated and gets noticeably thicker, the further distally from the eyelid margin it is – for example, at the brow the skin is 2.8 times thicker than it is at the eyelid (Ha *et al.* 2005).

The outer epidermis of the eyelid skin consists of keratinised, stratified, squamous epithelium and comprises five layers:

- Stratum corneum
- Stratum lucidum
- Stratum granulosum
- Stratum spinosum
- Stratum basale.

327

The surface cells are dead and are largely made up of keratin, which is a fibrous structural protein (also a key component of hair and nails). The epidermis contains no blood vessels and is nourished in its deeper layers by the underlying dermis.

The epidermis contains many keratinocytes, which are continuously produced by the basal layer in a process known as keratinisation. Keratinocytes act as a barrier against several external factors including heat, water loss, ultra violet (UV) radiation and – most importantly – pathogens such as bacteria and viruses. Other specialised cells that can be located in the epidermis include Langerhans (dendritic antigen presenting cells), Merkel (receptor) and melanocytes (skin colour and absorption of UV-B light).

The basal layer contains cuboidal and columnar cells, which in turn contain stem cells that multiply, producing keratinocytes. Merkel cells also reside in the basal layer and are receptors that are sensitive to touch. The basal layer of the epidermis of the eyelids is probably of most significance to the ophthalmic practitioner, as this is the layer associated with basal cell carcinomas (BCCs) or 'rodent ulcers'.

Underlying the epidermis is the dermis, which is largely composed of connective tissue containing elastic fibres and collagen. The irregular finger-like projections of the dermis into the epidermis are known as the dermal papillae, and they contain loops of capillaries and nerve receptors.

Two distinct layers differentiate the dermis. The more superficial papillary region makes up about one-fifth of the dermis and consists of fine elastic fibres. The deeper layer reticular region is composed of connective tissue, with interconnected bundles of collagen and elastic fibres. Within this layer are sweat glands (ducts), nerves, blood vessels, lymphatics, oil glands and hair follicles. The dermis of the lid is also very thin (approximately 0.3mm). The collagen and elastic fibres in the reticular region of the dermis give the skin its strength and elasticity. The dermis reticular region is attached to the underlying muscle at the superficial fascia.

Various glands can found within the deeper dermis layer and these include:

- Sebaceous glands – lobed exocrine (duct) glands that are associated with eyebrow hairs and the caruncle. They secrete sebum, an oily material that serves to waterproof and lubricate the skin. Sebum also contains a small amount of acid that acts as a barrier to bacteria.

- Meibomian glands – a type of modified sebaceous gland that are located within the tarsal plates of both the upper and lower eyelids. There are approximately 50 of these glands in the upper and 25 in the lower eyelid, and the openings (orifices) are in the posterior eyelid margin. The meibomian glands are essential because they constantly produce meibum, a complex secretion that helps to lubricate the eye. Only recently has progress been made in understanding the composition of meibum. Essentially, it is a lipid-rich, oily substance that also contains stabilising factors such as omega-hydroxy fatty acids (Butovich 2009).

- Glands of Zeis – also a modified unilobular sebaceous gland at the eyelid margin, associated with the follicles, that help to maintain and lubricate the eyelash.
- Glands of Moll – sometimes referred to as ciliary glands, are modified sweat or apocrine glands.
- Glands of Krause and Wolfring – accessory lacrimal glands located in the fornices of the eyelids, which further secrete tears onto the eye.

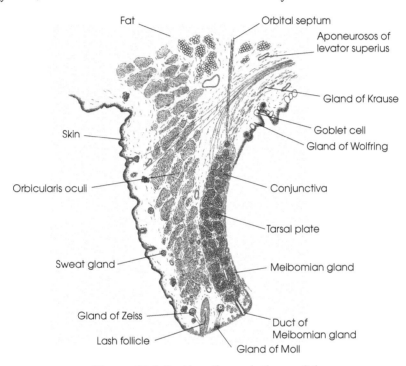

Figure 15.2 Section through the eyelid.

Eyelid muscles

There are three distinct muscles associated with enabling the eyelids to open and close:

- Orbicularis oculi
- Levator muscle
- Müller's muscle.

The orbicularis oculi muscle is associated with closing the eyelids and concentrically encircles the orbit. It arises from the medial canthal area (nasal component of the frontal bone), encompassing the eyelids and the temporal/cheek areas of the face. The upper fibres medially merge into the corrugator muscle and centrally into the frontalis muscle. The orbicularis is largely a voluntary striated muscle and is innovated by the VII cranial nerve (facial). The orbicularis muscle is also anatomically subdivided into pretarsal (over the tarsal plate), preseptal (over the septum), which together are responsible for involuntary blinking, and an orbital segment associated with forced blinking (Nerad 2001).

The levator and Müller's muscles are responsible for opening the eyelid. The levator palpebrae superioris muscle is the more dominant retractor muscle and is associated with involuntary elevation of the upper eyelid. It is made up of skeletal muscle and is innervated by the superior division of cranial nerve III (oculomotor). The levator palpebrae muscle originates from the lesser wing of sphenoid bone and extends forward superiorly in the orbit and is supported by Whitnall's ligament. Eventually it extends as a fibrous aponeurosis into the anterior upper tarsal plate of the eyelid.

Whitnall's ligament is also worth mentioning because it is an important surgical landmark and acts as a 'pulley' for the levator muscle. It extends transversely as a fibrous band from the lacrimal gland supero-laterally to the trochlea medially. It is often visualised during levator advancement surgery when correcting ptosis (drooping eyelid).

Müller's muscle is responsible for involuntary upper eyelid elevation and is also known as the superior tarsal muscle. It is made up of smooth muscle that is innervated by postganglionic sympathetic nerves that originate from the superior cervical ganglion. Some of the nerve fibres communicate with the oculomotor nerve (CN III).

Müller's muscle extends anteriorly from Whitnall's ligament onto the upper tarsal plate. It is sandwiched between the levator aponeurosis and the inner palpebral conjunctiva. Once the levator muscle has raised the eyelid, Müller's muscle helps to maintain elevation of the eyelid, but it generally has a much weaker action than the levator muscle. Damage or restriction in sympathetic innervation of the Müller's muscle can cause a degree of ptosis, as in Horner's syndrome.

It is also important to remember that the frontalis muscle in the forehead has some limited influence in elevating the upper eyelid as well as the brow.

The lower eyelid also has its own stabilising muscles, often collectively known as the inferior retractor muscles. These are made up of various structures, including:

- Capsulopalpebral fascia – a band of fibrous tissue associated with the inferior oblique muscle that is attached to the inferior margin of the lower eyelid tarsal plate.
- Inferior tarsal muscle – the lower eyelid smooth muscle equivalent of the upper eyelid Müller's muscle.
- Inferior suspensory ligaments – a 'hammock' of ligaments surrounding the inferior rectus and oblique muscles that help to support the eye and the fornices.

Both the upper and lower eyelid's structure and shape are maintained by thick connective tissue pads, known as tarsal plates. The dimensions are outlined above, but essentially the upper eyelid tarsal plate is significantly larger than the lower eyelid. The tarsal plates include the meibomian glands.

The orbital septum is a tough fibrous or membranous sheet that forms a layer from the bony orbital rim to the tarsal plates. It provides an anatomical and physiological boundary between the orbit and the eyelids and this is especially significant in relation to infection. Infection anterior to the orbital septum is known as preseptal (cellulitis), whereas posteriorly it is orbital (cellulitis).

The orbital septum also helps to prevent the contents of the orbit from prolapsing forward. This is especially pertinent, given that the septum becomes weaker as we get older and may account for some degree of eyelid bulging or herniation in elderly patients.

Between the overlying orbital septum and the muscle layer, there are several identifiable areas of fat, each of which have names, including: central, lateral, pre-aponeurotic, nasal, medial and lacrimal fat 'pads', obviously depending upon their position.

Eyelid blood supply

The eyelids have a very good blood supply, which relies on branches of the ophthalmic, temporal and facial arteries. These arteries supply several groups of vessels, including the marginal (and inferior), medial (peripheral), superior and inferior arcades. Most of the venous drainage is associated with the superior and inferior ophthalmic veins.

Innervation of the eyelids

The eyelids are innervated by the sensory, maxillary and motor nerves.

The sensory ophthalmic nerve, the first branch of the trigeminal nerve (CN V_1), has three major branches:

- The frontal branch (frontal nerve) subdivides into supraorbital (forehead and scalp) and supratrochlear branches (upper eyelid and superior medial canthus)
- The nasociliary branch, which then subdivides into several sensory branches within the orbit as well as the infratrochlear nerve (inferior medial canthus) and external nasal branches (nose)
- The lacrimal branch (or lacrimal nerve) innervates the lacrimal gland.

The maxillary (V_2) division of the trigeminal nerve includes branches such as the:

- Infraorbital nerve (lower eyelid, cheek, upper gingiva and teeth).

The mandibular (V_3) division ennervates only non-ophthalmic structures

The motor oculomotor (CN III) has two divisions. The upper supplies the levator palpebral muscle, which lifts the eyelid (and innervates the superior and medial rectus muscles).

The lower division supplies the inferior rectus and oblique muscles.

The facial nerve (CN VII) innervates the orbicularis oculi muscle, which is responsible for shutting the eyelids. This has five branches, two of which are associated directly with the eyelids:

- Temporal – orbicularis, procerus, corrugator and frontalis muscles
- Zygomatic – orbicularis of the lower eyelid and the lacrimal gland
- Buccal – mouth
- Mandibular – mouth
- Cervical – neck.

Conjunctiva

The conjunctiva lines the posterior surface of the eyelids and folds back at the fornices to cover the anterior surface of the eye/globe up to the limbus. It has three distinct subdivisions:

- Bulbar – represents the conjunctiva that covers and is tightly adherent to the anterior surface of the eye
- Palpebral – is the posterior eyelid section that completely lines the inner surface of the eyelid, up to the posterior lamellar
- Fornix – corresponds to the loose inner fold of membrane as it translates from palpebral to bulbar conjunctiva.

The conjunctiva is a membrane of non-keratinising stratified and columnar squamous epithelium, which also includes goblet cells that provide lubrication. The epithelial layer of the conjunctiva contains blood vessels and lymphatic channels. The conjunctiva also acts as a defence layer against infection, as it contains lymphocytic cells.

The eyelid margin

The eyelid can physically be divided into two distinct vertical sections, the anterior and posterior lamellae, at the eyelid margin. The anterior lamella consists of the eyelid skin, underlying orbicularis muscle and the eyelashes. The posterior section of the eyelid is the tarsal plate and meibomian glands. The two divisions are separated by a visible demarcation known as the grey-line. The lamellae have particular surgical significance and provide a platform for repair in many conditions.

The eyelashes

The anterior lamellae contain at least one row of eyelashes that provide protection from debris and injury. The morphology of eyelash hair is very similar to that of scalp hair, but eyelashes are significantly stunted in length due to having a shorter hair cycle (approximately 8–12mm in the upper eyelid and 6–8mm in the lower). They usually have a distinct colour between individuals, and a curvature, which varies slightly depending upon ethnic origin. Typically, there are approximately 90–120 lashes in the upper eyelid and 70–80 in the lower (Thiabut *et al.* 2009).

The eyelashes may either fall out naturally or be physically removed (epilation) and regrow over a period of 6–8 weeks.

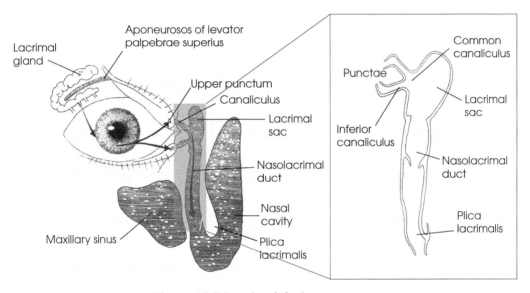

Figure 15.3 Lacrimal drainage system.

Anatomy and physiology of the lacrimal system

The lacrimal gland produces tears, which provide lubrication for the eye, and the subsequent drainage of tears is via the puncta, cannaliculus, lacrimal sac and nasolacrimal duct into the inferior meatus of the nasal cavity.

The lacrimal gland

The lacrimal gland resides superotemporally just posterior and behind the orbital rim in a concavity in the orbital roof (lacrimal gland fossa). The lateral horn of the upper eyelid levator muscle divides the lacrimal gland into two distinct lobes: the palpebral lobe and the orbital lobe. If the upper eyelid is lifted laterally, it may be possible to observe some of the palpebral lobe of the lacrimal gland as a pinkish area under the conjunctiva. In some individuals, the lacrimal gland can sometimes prolapse anteriorly, making it notably obvious when the upper eyelid is lifted.

As a type of tubuloacinar gland, the lacrimal gland is made up of multiple lobules, separated with connective tissue and branched with numerous alveoli.

The lacrimal gland is approximately 17mm in length and 15mm in width. There is no significant difference in size between genders, but the gland does shrink slightly with age (Timboli *et al.* 2011). It is innervated by the lacrimal nerve (parasympathetic) and zygomatic nerve (sensory).

The vascular blood supply to the lacrimal gland is essentially from the lacrimal artery and drained by the superior ophthalmic vein.

Tears

The production of tears by the lacrimal gland is to not only lubricate the eye surface but also to allow for clearer vision, delivery (and excretion) of nutrients, metabolic products and to provide protection against infection (Tiffany 2003).

Within the approximately 1ml of tears that are produced every day, there is a variable amount of water, lipids, immunoglobulins, antibodies, glucose, potassium, sodium, urea, lactoferrin, albumin and mucin.

The tear film consists of three distinct layers:

1. Conjunctival goblet cells produce a thin layer of mucus that adheres to the epithelium of the cornea/conjunctiva (0.2–0.5µm thick).

2. Over this is an aqueous layer, which is produced by both the main and accessory lacrimal gland (7µm).

3. To prevent the tears from evaporating, another thin layer of superficial lipid lies over the aqueous layer, which is provided by the sebaceous glands of the eyelid (meibomian and Zeis) (0.1µm).

Slight variations in the composition of the tear film may result from systemic change – for example, in allergic reactions the immunoglobulin concentration increases. Other variations can lead to specific problems of tear film quality. A general reduction in tear film production can lead to dry eye syndrome or keratoconjunctivitis sicca, which in turn can lead to corneal damage, ulceration and even perforation in the most extreme examples.

The puncta

Normally, during the course of each blink of the eyelids, the tears are evenly distributed across the eye and generally evaporate concordantly with the production of more tears. A small quantity of tears do pass away via the upper and lower eyelid drainage holes, called the puncta. By way of a combination of capillary attraction, eyelid closure and negative pressure within the lacrimal sac, any excessive watering will drain into the lacrimal sac via the puncta.

These tiny openings are approximately 0.3mm in diameter and are usually located some 5–6mm from the medial canthus on both upper and lower eyelids. The inferior punctum is situated 0.5mm laterally to the superior punctum and they are both slightly directed towards the globe. They sit on a pale elevated mound known as the papilla lacrimalis.

The puncta's position in relation to the eye is essential for their correct function and it is important to recognise this when examining the eye in a patient with a history of epiphora. The lower eyelid punctum drains more of the tears away (70%) than the upper (30%); any obstruction of the lower eyelid punctum would therefore have a more devastating effect and consequently create more epiphora.

The canaliculi

Having entered the puncta, tears initially travel vertically along the first segment of the lacrimal drainage system known as the canaliculi for about 2mm. The upper and lower eyelid canaliculi extend horizontally (for approximately 8mm) thereafter until they usually meet to form the common canaliculus. The common canaliculus immediately fuses with the superior end of the lacrimal sac at the common internal punctum.

Special valves, known as Rosemüller valves, are present to prevent retrograde refluxing of tears back along the canaliculi.

The lacrimal sac

The lacrimal sac is essentially a collection bag for the tears before they enter the nasolacrimal duct. It resides in the bony lacrimal fossa and is between 10 and 15mm in length. The lacrimal sac can be divided into the fundus superiorly and the body inferiorly. The body of the lacrimal sac narrows inferiorly to become the nasolacrimal duct.

A double-layered epithelium makes up the lining of the lacrimal sac; and microvilli on the surface of this layer support the notion that some of the components of tear fluid are absorbed while they are in the lacrimal sac (Paulson 2008).

On occasion, if there is congestion or a physical blockage, the 'stagnant' contents of the lacrimal sac can become infected and create a swollen, painful erythematous area inferonasally. This condition is known as dacryocystitis.

The nasolacrimal duct

As the lacrimal sac descends inferiorly, it narrows and becomes the nasolacrimal duct. This continuation of the sac transfers fluid down into the nasal cavity via an opening, the inferior nasal meatus, which lies under the inferior turbinate (conchae). The duct passes through the bony nasolacrimal canal, which is formed between the lacrimal and maxilla bones.

The length of the nasolacrimal duct is approximately 15mm, making the entire length of the lacrimal sac/duct about 30mm (Nerad 2001). At the distal end of the nasolacrimal duct is a valve that partially covers the nasal end of the tube and is known as the valve of Hasner. This valve prevents air from entering the nasolacrimal duct.

Eyelid examination

Before slit-lamp examination of the lids, some time should be taken to look at their general position and appearance. Simple observations of the lids in both the open and closed positions can often give an indication of underlying, or associated, pathologies. This is also an opportunity to look at the mechanics of lid function. Do they open and close smoothly? Is there any evidence of lid lag (delayed movement of the lids on down-gaze associated with thyroid eye disease) or incomplete closure (which can lead to corneal exposure problems due to the eye being exposed during sleep)?

The beginning of the examination should involve facing the patient and looking generally at the position of the lids and the size of the palpebral fissure (the distance between the upper and lower lid margins). In doing so, comparisons can be made between the right and left eyes. The lid margins should be examined, along with the colour and nature of the skin of the lids. The clinician should observe for any 'lumps and bumps' or any excess skin tissue in the upper and lower lids (dermatochalasia) and for the presence of any crusting or signs of discharge along the lid margins. The natural position of the lids should be considered and compared between the right and left eyes, this time in relation to the position of the lashes, lid margins and puncta.

It may be pertinent to assess the (horizontal) eyelid laxity and this can be undertaken by two tests:

- Eyelid distraction test – pulling the eyelid horizontally away from the eyeball, in which eyelid laxity may be associated with the ability to pull the eyelid more than 6mm from the eye (Nerad 2001).

- The Snap test – essentially the lower eyelid is pulled vertically downwards and the test ascertains the time taken for it to return to its normal position (without a blink). If it takes longer than 1 second, it may imply laxity (or it may not even return without blinking).

It was mentioned earlier that the eyelid opening or palpebral aperture (PA) is about 10mm and this can be measured. Further significant measurements associated with the PA include:

- Marginal reflex distance (MRD_1) – the distance from the central pupillary light reflex (centre of the pupil) to the upper eyelid margin, which is usually 4mm.

- Marginal reflex distance (MRD_2) – the distance from the central pupillary light reflex to the lower eyelid margin, which usually measures 6mm.

The initial examination should also include gently touching the lids to feel for discrete 'lumps and bumps' that may not be obvious to the naked eye. Gently pinching the skin folds and tissue of the lids can be useful in order to check skin laxity and elasticity. Lid eversion (turning the lids) to look at the general appearance of the palpebral conjunctiva can also be performed at this point, although it may be more beneficial to do this during slit-lamp examination so that a more detailed look at the conjunctiva can be achieved, and the patient's discomfort can be reduced by having to evert the lids only once.

Eyelid disorders and conditions
Blepharitis

Blepharitis is one of the most common eyelid conditions that the practitioner is likely to come across. It represents an often chronic picture of eyelid margin inflammation, and with that an exhaustive list of signs and symptoms. There are few exact definitions, and the term blepharitis might be a non-specific phrase for a range of complex multifactorial problems that cause the inflammatory eyelid margin irritation. It can be a notoriously difficult condition to diagnose and treat, often involving repeated remissions and flare-ups that are very demoralising for the patient.

Lemp & Nichols (2009) suggest that blepharitis is probably the most common presentation in routine ophthalmic practice and therefore accurate diagnosis and effective treatment are vital. The clinical course of blepharitis can be very mild and self-limiting, but can become chronic, with lid margin scarring, trichiasis, loss of lashes, dry eye due to lack of tear film quality and lid and eye infection.

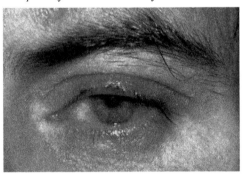

Figure 15.4 Blepharitis.

There are several classifications of blepharitis which relate to the causative factor, they include:

- Staphylococcal – the build-up of colonies of skin commensals, which form pathogenic colonies
- Seborrhoeic – relating to seborrhoeic dermatitis
- Mixed – many patients have both anterior and posterior problems
- Posterior or meibomitis/meibomian gland dysfunction

- Parasitic Demodex mites – eight-legged ectoparasites, which live in hair follicles and sebaceous glands, causing follicular hyperplasia and an increase in keratinisation near the base of the lashes; this, mixed with lipids, produces characteristic cylindrical 'dandruff' on the lid margins

- Allergenic

- Hormonal – menopause and androgen deficiencies are thought to contribute.

However, Powell (2010) suggests that a simpler classification of blepharitis, as either anterior or posterior, would be more clinically effective. Anterior blepharitis (i.e. in front of the grey line) is more commonly associated with bacterial invasion and localised hypersensitivity reactions that typically cause debris build-up and crusting, margin redness and trichiasis. Posterior blepharitis (i.e. behind the grey line) is more associated with the meibomian glands and their dysfunction or blocking, causing chalazia and irritation.

Anterior blepharitis

Anterior blepharitis involves the anterior lid margin and eyelashes and is associated with staphylococcal infection and Demodex mite infestation. Some dermatological conditions, such as acne rosacea, aeborrhoeic dermatitis and eczema, carry an increased risk of anterior blepharitis. The lids may be sticky on waking.

Meibomian gland dysfunction, or meibomitis (chronic posterior blepharitis), is an abnormality of meibomian gland function, characterised by obstruction of the gland openings onto the lid and changes in the glandular secretion.

Bacterial lipases may contribute to raising the 'melting' point of the meibum, making it less viscous and thus affecting its excretion from the glands. Having less phospholipid within the tear film makes the tear film unstable and more likely to evaporate more quickly from the eye surface.

Meibomitis may present as plugged meibomian glands and, when massaged, they may produce a turbid, toothpaste-like material. Alternatively, on slit-lamp examination, goblets of oil may be seen accumulating and covering the meibomian gland orifices. This may result in alteration of the tear film, eye irritation, inflammation and resulting ocular surface problems (Nelson *et al.* 2011)

Blepharitis treatment

There is considerable interaction between these types of blepharitis and addressing the disease; and the subsequent inflammatory reaction requires intense treatment, good patient compliance and an understanding of the causative mechanisms. Often, two or three elements may be at play at any one time. To achieve positive treatment outcomes, it will be necessary to remove causative factors, provide cleaning, treat any underlying infection, and treat dry eyes.

Compliance by the patient will always depend on their understanding of the problem; it is therefore important for the practitioner to spend time explaining the disease. Assessment of the patient's ability to perform cleaning and manual dexterity might be useful to gauge how well they can manage with the various cleaning techniques. This will be particularly important if the patient is visually impaired. Complex cleaning regimes may well be frustrating for someone with limited vision and restricted dexterity. Treatment of blepharitis is based on three important factors: cleaning of eyelids, heat and massage. These elements may also need to be combined with treatment of the underlying inflammation and bacterial colonisation.

1. Eyelid cleansing: Traditionally, a diluted mixture of a small amount of baby shampoo or bicarbonate of soda with water, applied with a cotton bud, is used to clean the eyelids of heavy crusting once or twice a day. This technique is still recommended and is relatively effective and tolerated by many patients, although there is little evidence base and the dilutions used are often according to the preference of the clinician or patient. It may be difficult for some individuals to be able to accurately mix products, using a cotton bud on the lids may be difficult for those with limited dexterity, and it may be just as effective to use clean tepid water and cotton pads to clean the lids. In addition, too much shampoo may strip too much oil from the skin and lids, affecting the oil layer and causing more irritation.

Several commercial over-the-counter products are now available, including Blephasol and Blephaclean wipes (Spectrum Thea) and Lid Care Wipes (Novartis Ophthalmic). However, these come at a relatively high cost, which may make them too expensive for some individuals to afford. They have been proven to be clinically affective (Powell 2010), though simple baby wipes may be just as effective.

2. Heat treatment: Applying heat to the eyelids will enable the glands to secrete oils more fluidly and help to remove crusting. The use of a clean flannel held under a hot water tap, rung out and placed over the eyelids for 5–10 minutes twice a day is well recognised as being effective (Powell 2010). However, it may be difficult to maintain the right or appropriate temperature consistently. Again commercial heat-applying options are available, including reusable 'eye-bags', which can be heated in a microwave and may provide a more constant form of heat application. Bilkhu *et al.* (2014) provided some research evidence of the clinical effectiveness of one particular eye-bag product; although the sample in this study was small, it was found to be safe and effective.

3. Eyelid massage: Using a cotton bud or clean finger, gentle massage of the eyelids might help the expression of oils or blocked glands (in conjunction with heat treatment). However, this is rather a subjective treatment and it is difficult to be precise about how the technique is carried out, how much pressure is applied and how to evaluate its success. Generally, the advice is to massage upwards, against a closed eye, after having applied heat. This may be difficult in patients with reduced dexterity and care has to be taken not to damage the eye in the process.

Treating underlying causes and consequences

4. Artificial tears: As already outlined, dry eyes are commonly associated with blepharitis and the use of artificial tears may provide the necessary comfort for the patient. It may also have the benefit of diluting specific toxins that may be causing irritation. It is recommended that the artificial tears should be used in conjunction with an antimicrobial.

5. Antibiotics: The use of topical antibiotics to reduce the bacterial burden will be important in acute and sub-acute infection, e.g. Fucidic acid or Chloramphenicol. It may be necessary to take a course of oral antibiotics, commonly Doxycycline or Erythromycin, to combat the condition systemically.

6. Topical corticosteroids: Reduction of the associated chronic inflammation by the use of corticosteroids may be reserved for the more persistent and severe cases of blepharitis, given the potential side-effects associated with their prolonged use (such as raised intraocular pressure and cataracts). The lowest effective dose should be used and tapered weaning of the treatment is important to reduce rebound inflammation.
Treating the underlying condition

Associated conditions, such as acne rosacea or dermatitis, may require treatment to reduce their effect upon the eyelids.

7. Remove make-up: It's important for the patient to completely remove eye make-up every day. False eyelashes (and the adhesives used to attach them) should also be completely removed.

8. Dietary considerations: Good systemic hydration is important, as this will affect tear production. Many advocate the use of omega 3 fatty acids in the diet to improve the quality of the tear film.

9. Demodex mites: These small parasitic infestations of the eyelashes can cause blepharitis and can be successfully treated with tea tree oil diluted in a carrier oil (Gao *et al.* 2011).

10. Ongoing review: As a practitioner caring for these patients, it is vitally important to provide a platform for ongoing review and management of their blepharitis. Having a specific clinic can be useful in helping patients with information, guidance, compliance and support.

Assessment, diagnosis and management of patients with blepharitis is challenging and requires significant input from both clinician and patient.

Chalazion (meibomian cyst)

A chalazion is a common benign inflammatory lesion that is associated with retained sebaceous material (usually a plugging of a meibomian gland) leaking into the surrounding tissue. This causes a raised nodule within the tarsal plate that may be tender and, if large enough (especially in the upper eyelid), may press on the cornea, causing a mechanical astigmatism or ptosis.

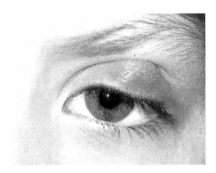

Figure 15.5 Chalazion – external view.

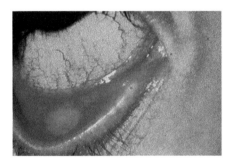

Figure 15.6 Chalazion – inner lower eyelid view.

The clinical presentation of a chalazion can cause some distress for the patient, and it will be important to provide reassurance that it will usually settle on its own. An internal hordeolum is present when the gland becomes infected. Externally, it may present as a small lump with erythema and swelling, which may affect the whole eyelid.

An infection (internal hordeolum) is likely to be painful and treatment is with topical antibiotics (such as chloramphenicol 1% four times daily for up to two weeks), hot compresses, lid massage and lid cleaning. Lid infection in children can spread along and beyond the lid, and systemic antibiotics might be considered to prevent preseptal or orbital cellulitis.

If the cyst does not resolve, surgical intervention may be required. However, surgical intervention should not take place if the cyst is infected because the infection may spread to other structures in the lid.

Once the infection has settled, there may be a small residual lesion (chalazion) that may require further intervention if it does not settle on its own or the patient has discomfort or is unhappy with the cosmetic appearance of the lid. Incision and curettage is generally the surgical intervention of choice. Additionally, a conjunctival palpebral extension of the lesion may cause a fleshy granuloma that might require surgical removal. A chalazion in the upper lid which causes some mechanical astigmatism will be particularly difficult for the patient, and early removal should be considered.

Injections of steroids into chalazia have been shown to be as effective as incision and curettage (I&C) in treating chalazion (Ben Simon *et al.* 2011) but there are several contraindications, including atrophy and discolouration of the area, raised intraocular pressure and corneal perforation.

However, it may be necessary to undertake an incision and curettage of the lesion, and this procedure is outlined in Table 15.1 (below).

Table 15.1 The incision and curettage procedure for a chalazion

1. Identify the location of the chalazion prior to surgery, gain written consent and mark the appropriate site/side for surgery, using the correct Trust-recognised paperwork and protocol.
2. Instil local anaesthetic drops into the affected eye. The practitioner may mark the specific area where the chalazion is, prior to the infiltration of any anaesthetic.
3. The practitioner may clean the skin on the affected side with an antiseptic solution (check allergies).
4. Administer local anaesthetic to the appropriate area requiring surgery.
5. Check and prepare the equipment for use. The practitioner will require an overhead light to provide illumination.
6. Wash hands (six-step handwash) and don sterile gloves.
7. Place the chalazion clamp over the lesion; if taking a posterior approach, evert the eyelid once the clamp is secure.
8. The practitioner will use their non-dominant hand to gently hold the chalazion clamp and will then use the 11 blade, correctly loaded into a Bard-Parker handle (or use a disposable blade) to incise the length of the chalazion. Some references suggest making a cross-incision.
9. The practitioner will then use a curette(s) of the appropriate size to remove the contents of the chalazion. This will be repeated as necessary. Care must be taken to protect the globe from accidental injury throughout the procedure.
10. Once the curettage is complete, apply a stat dose of antibiotic ointment and chalazion clamp and place a double pad and Jelonet in place for 1–2 hours postoperatively.

A 'recurrent chalazion' that repeatedly returns in the same area may, very rarely, represent a sebaceous gland carcinoma. If in any doubt, always consider an incisional biopsy.

External hordeolum (stye)

This presents as a small lesion that is erythematous and inflamed with a yellowish 'head' of pus. The lesion is a staphylococcal infected cyst of Moll or Zeis that opens into the eyelash follicle. It is differentiated from an internal hordeolum in that it will be located much nearer the lid margin and cause localised swelling around the base of the affected lash/es.

The lesion is characterised by being painful, but is usually self-limiting and will resolve within two weeks, with little or no intervention. However, topical antibiotics, hot compresses and removal of the effected eyelashes may expedite recovery.

Other common benign eyelid lesions

Cyst of Moll (apocrine hidrocystoma)

This is a small benign retention cyst of the eyelid margin, which presents as a round translucent lesion, sometimes with a bluish tinge. These lesions are associated with the apocrine sweat glands and often occur singularly, often near the puncta.

Treatment is simple surgical excision, ensuring the entire encapsulated bag is removed or de-roofed (marsupialised). Needle aspiration may not be sufficient, as the lesion may refill.

Cyst of Zeis

These are small round yellowish-white lesions, often occurring on the eyelid margin and arising from sebaceous glands. They contain sebum and are best treated by surgical excision and cautery. Again unless complete excision is guaranteed, they can refill and may require further excision.

Fibroepithelioma (skin tag)

This type of lesion presents as a skin extension, which may be pedunculated (i.e. skin tag) or sessile which is broad-based. They also occur in various other areas of the body and especially within folds of skin, e.g. the armpits and groin.

Skin tags are removed by surgical excision. This ensures that, with pedunculated lesions, a sufficient base is removed.

Epidermal inclusion cyst

Epidermal inclusion cysts are small, round, firm, elevated lesions, containing keratin, that are associated with hair follicles. Very small lesions are often called milia. Surgical removal is usually the preferred treatment. Sometimes these lesions are referred to as 'sebaceous cysts', which is incorrect terminology as they contain keratin rather than sebaceous material.

Seborrheic keratosis

These lesions are relatively common and are described as having a 'stuck-on' appearance.

They vary hugely in colour, shape and size, but are typically tan or brown and round or oval in shape. They don't usually warrant any particular treatment, but can be removed surgically if necessary.

Actinic keratosis

A slow-growing scaly lesion of the eyelids that may also associated with a cutaneous extension. It is associated with UV skin damage and can (extremely rarely) transform into squamous cell carcinoma. Treatment is usually by excisional biopsy.

Xanthelasmata

Usually presents as a bilateral yellowish-white lesion of uniform shape in the upper and/or lower medial canthus areas of the eyelids. Along with corneal arcus, this type of lesion is associated with raised cholesterol levels. It is important to get the patient's cholesterol levels checked. However, more recent research has found more accurate markers attributed to xanthelasmata and raised lipid in the form of apolipoproteins (Pandhi *et al.* 2012).

Treatment of xanthelasmata can involve the application of trichloroacetic acid (90%), destruction with carbon dioxide or argon laser, or surgical excision if these methods are not successful.

Malignant eyelid lesions

Basal cell carcinoma

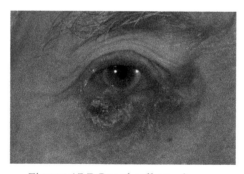

Figure 15.7 Basal cell carcinoma
(reprinted by permission of the Ophthalmic Imaging Department, Manchester Royal Eye Hospital).

The skin is susceptible to ultraviolet (UV) sun damage, and – given that it is almost always exposed – the face is particularly vulnerable. It doesn't therefore come as any surprise that fair-skinned individuals are most commonly associated with basal cell carcinoma (BCC). In some older patients, the appearance of actinic sun-damaged skin changes around the face and head offer good clues to the likelihood of the presence of malignant lesions.

According to Baxter *et al.* (2012), there are two classifications of skin cancer – melanoma and non-melanoma. BCCs make up some 80% of the non- melanoma group and, of these, a further 85% involve the head and neck (Katalinic *et al.* 2003). BCCs of the eyelids most commonly involve the medial canthal region and the lower eyelid.

There are different types of BCCs, depending on their anatomical location. These include:

- Nodular – involving the head and neck and the most common type of BCC in the UK (Nakayama *et al.* 2011)
- Nodular ulcerative BCC – also known as a rodent ulcer
- Superficial – often resembling eczema or psoriasis and slow growing
- Morphoeic (sclerosing) – appearing like a whitish scar, which again is slow growing or an overriding plaque (making it very difficult to delineate).

BCCs are tumours that arise from the regenerative basal layer of the epidermis and are associated with several important characteristics:

- BCCs of the eyelid often present with a painless lesion with pearly edges and telangiectasia (tiny dilated blood vessels)
- Destruction of the eyelid architecture is not uncommon and lashes are often completely lost
- There may be ulceration, which may be associated with bleeding: patients often describe lesions that easily bleed at the most innocuous of touches
- Similarly, the lesions will be firm (indurated) and have an irregular appearance on examination.

Whilst most BCCs are seen as 'low grade' and typically slow growing, they can (if left untreated) invade the orbit and cause considerable damage. These may subsequently only be treated by orbital exenteration.

There are several approaches to managing BCCs in the eyelids:

- Wide surgical excision – in lesions <20mm in diameter a 4mm surgical margin around the lesion may provide up to 95% clearance (Roewert-Huber *et al.* 2007).
- Mohs micrographic surgery – accepted as the gold standard for the excision of BCC. The lesion is excised in horizontal layers and is mapped and prepared histopathologically. It is then inspected via microscope in all dimensions by a specially trained dermatologist. Any spread of the tumour to the edges of the resected specimen leads to further excision of residual tumour from the site of the lesion in that specific area. This makes the success rates for Mohs micrographic surgery very high – as much as 98–99% (Baxter *et al.* 2012) while removing less healthy tissue. All this is undertaken while the patient waits, often over a period

of two or three hours. It may take a couple of excisions to remove the tumour and then, once the wound is stabilised, the eyelids will be reconstructed by an oculoplastic surgeon. However, this service isn't available to all and there is a 'postcode lottery' regarding its accessibility for some patients.

- Topical treatments – Imiquimod has been shown to be effective in treating small BCCs, but its relative success may depend upon the amount of tissue penetration and the size of the lesion (Baxter *et al.* 2012).

- Radiotherapy – this is often reserved for patients for whom surgery may not be an option.

Beyond the physical and anatomical aspects of BCCs, the practitioner has to offer the patient support and information regarding the diagnosis, treatment and management of these lesions. At the mere mention of the words 'tumour' or 'malignant', the patient is likely to be shocked or apprehensive as to the diagnosis and associated treatment modalities. Psychological support will be necessary for some individuals, and the practitioner will need to assess the patient and anticipate potential problems.

Squamous cell carcinoma

This is a more aggressive and potentially destructive malignant tumour affecting the eyelids. It is much less common, representing approximately 5% of eyelid tumours (Nerad 2001). Clinically, it can resemble BCC in many of its characteristics, including: induration, ulceration, scaly skin, diffuse nature and damage to eyelid architecture. The pearly margins and telangiectasia are not normally associated with squamous cell carcinoma (SCC).

SCC can metastasise to surrounding lymph nodes in a significant proportion of cases; checking for lymphadenopathy will therefore be necessary.

SCC is also associated with UV skin damage, fair skin and generally people aged over 60. It more commonly affects the lower eyelid and the medial canthal area. It is important that any suspicious lesions should be biopsied and that the practitioner should be judicious in their history-taking and clinical examination. The patient may present for an entirely different reason and, upon examination, the practitioner may identify a potentially suspicious lesion that requires further investigation.

In most cases, the treatment for SCC is wide surgical excision and combined radiotherapy, and this can obviously be traumatic for the patient. Extensive psychological support may be necessary and the input of a trained clinical psychologist may be required. In the UK there are organisations such as Changing Faces and Let's Face It, which can provide support and advice for patients and professional staff in these cases.

Lid and lash malposition

Trichiasis

The term trichiasis represents a group of conditions that characterise eyelashes that are misdirected and cause discomfort and irritation to the eye. It is an acquired condition and can affect individual lashes or entire rows of eyelashes.

It may be caused by scarring or as a consequence of blepharitis or herpes zoster ophthalmicus, but the actual causative factor isn't known. Consequently, the irritation can cause corneal epithelium trauma, punctate epithelial erosions and infections.

Various treatment modalities are available, including:

- Epilation – pulling the eyelashes out with forceps, which provides temporary relief but inevitably the lashes will grow back (in about 6–8 weeks)
- Electrolysis – fine needle destruction of the hair follicles, using electrocautery diathermy machines; may take several treatments to be successful
- Cryotherapy – using a cryoprobe to freeze-thaw areas of the eyelid where there may be blocks of lashes to treat; however, there are risks of tissue necrosis and skin de-pigmentation
- Argon laser ablation – the use of laser to destroy the lash roots
- Surgery – it may be necessary to remove a section of eyelashes by undertaking a wedge resection.

Entropion

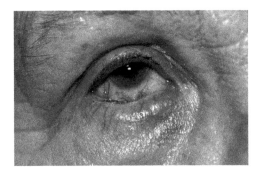

Figure 15.8 Entropion

One of the more common eyelid malformations is where the lid margin turns inward and the eyelashes abrade against the globe (pseudotrichiasis), causing discomfort and irritation of the cornea and conjunctiva. This is known as entropion. In a study undertaken by Damasceno *et al.* (2011), in the population they studied, it had a prevalence of 2.1%, and was marginally more common in females. However, in another similar study, entropion was more common in males and appeared to become more prolific as individuals grew older (Mitchell 2001).

Entropion is generally associated with the lower eyelid, but it can also affect the upper eyelid.

There are five types of entropion:

- Involutional – represents the most common type of entropion as it is age-related. It is caused by the degeneration of the eyelid muscles, which in turn allow both horizontal and vertical eyelid laxity. Most commonly, it is the lower eyelid retractors which are the primary cause.

- Cicatricial – caused by severe scarring of the palpebral conjunctival, which then pulls the eyelid inwards, and the common causes are trachoma, trauma, cicatrising conjunctivitis and chemical injuries.

- Marginal – the more common presentation of cicatricial entropion, which is more representative of this type of entropion seen in practice.

- Spastic – rare type of entropion, which is more transient and caused by continual squeezing of the eyelids possibly postoperatively after surgery.

- Congenital.

As far as the patient is concerned, entropion will often cause discomfort, epiphora, discharge, punctate epithelial erosions, infection, corneal ulcers, swelling, pain and red eye. A quick fix is to educate the patient to tape the lower eyelid and use lubricants. A small piece of surgical paper tape is strategically and firmly placed laterally along the lower eyelid to mimic the action of a lid-tightening procedure. This is fiddly to do, especially with reduced sight or dexterity, but can be repeated to maintain the desired effect until a surgical procedure can be undertaken. A bandage contact lens may be indicated to protect the cornea.

Another option is to perform 'everting' sutures, whereby two or three double-armed stitches (4/0 Vicryl or Chromic) are placed full-thickness into the eyelid to mechanically tighten the levator muscle, which in turn rotates and holds the eyelid outwards. The sutures are passed from the inferior conjunctival fornix, superiorly and anteriorly through the skin 3 or 4mm from the margin below the tarsal plate, and tied off. Ideally, the sutures should be left to dissolve and fall out naturally, as this causes localised scarring which helps to hold the eyelid in place. This procedure is not suitable when the lower eyelid is too lax, as it is likely to create an ectropion. But it is a good stopgap until a more robust method for tightening the eyelid is undertaken.

Generally, however, the main surgical approach to reversing entropion is a levator retractor reinsertion (IRR), often combined with a lateral tarsal strip (LTS). An IRR procedure via a palpebral subciliary approach involves accessing and dissecting the retractor off the conjunctiva and then advancing and reinserting it with sutures. This procedure will correct the entropion but it will also be necessary to tighten the eyelid by undertaking an LTS or similar procedure.

It is important for the practitioner to continue to encourage lubrication of the eye until such time as the patient has had successful correction surgery. Once they have had surgery, it will be necessary to dissuade the patient from rubbing their eye too vigorously. If excessive rubbing can be avoided, the results from a combined IRR/LTS procedure for involutional entropion can be very good.

With cicatricial entropions, it may be important to replace or remove the scarred conjunctiva and replace it with a mucous membrane graft (usually harvested from the mouth) and this may be combined with tarsal rotation surgery.

Congenital entropions are rare and more often associated with Sino-Asian ethnic groups. They may correct themselves over time, but may require surgical involvement at a later stage.

Ectropion

An ectropion is where the eyelid rotates or droops away from the eye, causing irritation, mattering, epiphora, red eye, erythema and chronic thickening of the eyelid.

There are three types of ectropion:

- Cicatricial – caused by extensive scarring or contracture of the skin of the eyelid by trauma or skin disease such as eczema
- Paralytic – associated with ipsilateral facial nerve palsy
- Involutional – age-related relaxation of the eyelid, causing horizontal laxity and medial or lateral canthal laxity.

Short-term treatments might include lubricants and taping the eyelids shut, especially at night. A temporary suture tarsorrhaphy might provide relief and protect the cornea, but will restrict vision to some extent. Botulinum toxin injection into the upper eyelid levator muscle will create a temporary ptosis lasting for approximately three months.

Other surgical approaches might include horizontal lid tightening by resecting a pentagonal wedge of eyelid or an LTS procedure. With cicatricial ectropion, it may be necessary to initially relieve the scarred tissue and (after performing an LTS) then to replace the lost tissue with a full-thickness skin graft (FTSG). There are several potential donor sites for FTSG, including the upper eyelid, pre-auricular area, supra-clavicular area and inner upper arm. These areas all have skin that is thin, provides a reasonable colour match and are relatively hairless.

FTSGs require a lot of postoperative care. Initially, gentle compression will be necessary and it will therefore important to keep a dressing in place for several days after surgery. Once the dressing has been removed, the skin graft needs to be kept meticulously clean with sterile water or cooled boiled water. Topical application of antibiotic ointment may provide protection. Early removal of sutures will reduce irritation, inflammation and granulomas. Don't forget the donor site. It is important to keep the FTSG as dry as possible for the first few weeks after surgery; a macerated skin graft is likely to fail.

Massaging the grafted site postoperatively may reduce the risk of contracture and improve cosmesis. This has to be introduced to the patient carefully at approximately two weeks post-op. Spending time educating the patient in the correct technique will reap long-term benefits. It is important for the patient to appreciate the force/pressure required for this technique. Massaging too hard will damage the graft and hurt the patient; too soft and the patient will be wasting their time. Unfortunately, there is no research evidence that massage is beneficial in this area, but clinically and anecdotally the author has seen significant improvements in FTSGs that are scrupulously massaged by the patient.

Using a clean index finger and lubrication, encourage the patient to firmly massage the grafted site in an upwards direction for 8–10 minutes five or six times a day.

Ptosis

Ptosis relates to the abnormal drooping of the upper eyelid and is a relatively common problem. There are several classifications of ptosis:

- Neurogenic – a rare type of ptosis associated with CN III palsy and Horner's syndrome
- Myogenic – caused by impairment of the transmission of signals to the levator muscle (myopathy) and associated with myasthenia gravis, progressive external ophthalmoplegia
- Aponeurotic – age-related ptosis associated with levator aponeurosis
- Mechanical – physical ptosis associated with gravity and the weight of an element pulling it down, such as a lesion.

It is important to take an initial history and carry out a careful examination, including measurement of the palpebral fissure and marginal reflex distance (see above). Measurement of levator function will also be important. This involves using a thumb pressed firmly against the brow of the patient (to negate the frontalis muscle effect in lifting the lid) and getting them to initially look down and then upwards as far as possible. Then measure the distance between the two, at the upper lid margin (15mm or more is normal, <10mm is fair to poor).

Various surgical techniques are outlined in the literature to correct ptosis, depending on the type, cause and extent of the levator function. The most common surgical procedure is the levator aponeurosis advancement (LAA). Principally, an upper eyelid skin crease incision is made, then isolation and dis-insertion of the levator muscle, followed by advancement of the muscle to provide the correct amount of lift required. This procedure is often carried out under a local anaesthetic (with sedation) to allow the surgeon to assess the height of the eyelid perioperatively.

Postoperatively, the operated eye will require abundant lubricants as the patient may find it difficult to close the eye completely until they learn to compensate.

Brow ptosis

It is important to remember that the brow may also droop, creating the impression of ptosis, especially in the later decades of life. A brow ptosis might require surgical intervention by way of a direct brow lift.

Dermatochalasia

Involutional, age-related changes to the upper eyelid leads to a surplus of skin that may hang over the patient's visual access. This is usually corrected by surgical excision (blepharoplasty).

Floppy eyelid syndrome

This is a condition whereby the eyelids (particularly the upper ones) are excessively lax, essentially floppy and redundant. It is commonly associated with certain general characteristics and especially clinically obese middle-aged men (and incidentally sleep apnoea as well). Consequently, the upper eyelid(s) are so lax they can evert and, especially during the night when asleep, this can cause exposure and rubbing against the pillow. This results in keratoconjunctivitis and irritation of the globe and palpebral conjunctiva.

The treatment option is usually surgical – with removal of the excess eyelid skin with a wedge excision.

Lacrimal system malfunction
Epiphora

The production and composition of tears by the lacrimal gland and the accessory lacrimal glands has been outlined above. However, either as a consequence of hypersecretion or defective drainage, tears can overflow, causing irritation, erythema and infections; this is known as epiphora. It is also a constant frustration for patients, who complain of tears running down their face and having to continually use a tissue to mop them up, especially in dry (air conditioning) or windy conditions.

Hypersecretion is secondary and allied to various ocular surface diseases that cause watering. It is necessary to identify and treat or remove the causative factor, which may reduce the subsequent excess epiphora. Conversely, a common source of hypersecretion is dry eye syndrome.

Defective drainage will exacerbate watering and is usually due to malposition (e.g. puncta due to ectropion), obstruction of the lacrimal drainage system or lacrimal pump failure (secondary to lower eyelid laxity).

Understanding the nature of the blockage or malfunction of the lacrimal system will enable the healthcare professional to choose the appropriate treatment. For example, identifying and correcting an entropion will undoubtedly help to rectify issues with watering, both from the irritation of ocular surface drying and the poor eyelid position. However, an eversion or stenosis of the puncta might be more difficult to observe without the use of a slit-lamp. Moreover, obstruction of the lacrimal system as a whole is not always that obvious and is multifactorial. Ascertaining the exact nature and position of any narrowing (stenosis) and blockage is essential and a common test for this is a sac washout.

Lacrimal system tests
Sac washout test

It has been long established that the function of the lacrimal system can be assessed by carrying out a sac washout (SWO). This test is performed by passing a blunt-tipped, slightly curved cannula (a lacrimal cannula attached to a 2ml syringe) into the canaliculus, via the puncta, and then ejecting normal saline to ascertain the patency of the system. Performing an SWO is much more than a mere patency test; it is also an important diagnostic examination. It is essential to ascertain the amount of fluid, resistance and 'feel' of the canaliculi in order to identify the nature and location of any potential blockage or narrowing (stenosis) in the system.

Initially, it may be difficult to insert the cannula into the puncta, and the puncta may require dilation (using a punctal dilator). It is more conducive to passing the lacrimal cannula if the eyelid is held taut in a horizontal stretch (which essentially overcomes the initial vertical section of the cannaliculus).

Two distinct sensations associated with SWO, 'hard' and 'soft' stop, may be described with the test. A hard stop is in relation to the lacrimal cannula passing through the canaliculus and hitting the medial wall of the lacrimal sac (i.e. the lacrimal bone). Reflux here might suggest an obstruction of the sac or duct. Alternatively, a 'soft' stop would be associated with an obstruction prior to entering the lacrimal sac within the common canaliculus (Weber *et al.* 2007).

On injecting the fluid, there may be resistance and some regurgitation of saline due to stenosis via one or both of the puncta, or total regurgitation if there is a complete obstruction. It is important to note the approximate amount of regurgitation in the clinical notes as a percentage. Sometimes adding a drop of fluorescein into the saline can allow easier observation of the fluid.

Dye disappearance test

Another simple but effective method for assessing whether there is an obstruction is the insertion of a drop of 2% fluorescein into the conjunctival fornix and assessing, after 5 minutes, how much of the dye is retained. Normally, at 5 minutes, all the dye should have disappeared.

Nasal endoscopy

In some specialist clinics, the use of an intranasal endoscope to observe the outward flow of fluid into the nasal cavity via the nasolacrimal duct will provide further useful information. Not only will it illustrate basic anatomical variances such as polyps or septal deviations, but it will allow the practitioner to observe fluorescein-impregnated saline being injected into the nasal cavity. Some individuals may have to be referred to an ENT specialist for this test.

Contrast dacryocystography and scintigraphy

Dacryocystography is a more complex diagnostic test, involving the injection of radio-opaque contrast medium to assess the lacrimal system via x-ray. Alternatively, scintigraphy involves injection of radioisotopes into the lacrimal system and the use of gamma cameras to construct two-dimensional pictures. Both these tests are expensive and time consuming and may have contraindications, but are useful in evaluating particularly challenging cases where the nature and position of potential obstructions are not immediately obvious.

Punctal stenosis

As a consequence of chronic blepharitis, cicatrising conjunctivitis or herpes zoster lid infections, the puncta can become stenosed. Simple dilation may be not be sufficient in the long term; and physical widening of the puncta may therefore be necessary. This is done by cutting and removing part of the punctal wall (two or three snip procedures).

Common canalicular obstruction

There are various causes of common canalicular obstruction, including infection, irradiation or trauma, or it may be congenital. If the obstruction is partial, it may be overcome by intubating it with a silicone stent (inserted with the patient under general anaesthetic), which is left in place for several months. The stent may widen any potential stenosis and allow for better flow of tears on its removal.

Complete obstruction will require surgery to overcome the blockage; the exact type of surgery will depend on whether there is a normal functioning canaliculus between the punctum and the obstruction or not. If not, the main option will be a conjunctivodacryocystorhinostomy and insertion of Lester Jones tubes. Essentially, a new passageway is created between the medial canthal conjunctiva to the nasal cavity (through the lacrimal bone) and a flanged Pyrex glass tube is inserted into the new duct to act as a drainpipe for tears.

Lester Jones tubes (LJTs) come in various lengths and widths to accommodate all sizes. The average size is around 4mm diameter and 14mm in length. Once in place, they require careful maintenance by the patient (for life), including taking special measures to keep it patent by flushing (sniffing up) saline drops inserted into the conjunctival fornices through the tube. Additionally, if the patient feels he need to sneeze they will have to cover the LJT at the distal end with a finger to stop it from being dislodged. Unfortunately, patients do sometimes report the loss of their LJTs for various reasons and they will then need to be replaced.

Nasolacrimal duct obstruction

Idiopathic obstruction of the nasolacrimal duct may be overcome with surgery by undertaking a dacryocystorhinostomy.

Dacryocystitis

Dacryocystitis is an inflammation of the lacrimal sac, often as a result of infection. It may be congenital, acute or chronic. Congenital dacryocystitis is rare and results from lack of patency of the nasolacrimal duct (specifically the valve of Hasner) in infancy. It can be serious, as the orbital septum is not completely formed in children and there is a significant risk of spread – in the form of orbital cellulitis and all its complications.

Acquired dacryocystitis appears to be more common in females, due to narrower lacrimal duct diameter, and in adults aged 40 and above. It may occur due to an idiopathic inflammatory stenosis (primary acquired nasolacrimal duct obstruction) or may be secondary to infection or inflammation of the duct, trauma neoplasm or mechanical obstruction (secondary acquired lacrimal drainage obstruction). Obstruction of the duct leads to stagnation of tears in a closed system, which can result in bacterial growth and infection, leading to dacryocystitis.

Acute dacryocystitis presents as a sudden onset of pain, erythema and oedema overlying the lacrimal sac area, and tenderness may extend to the face. A purulent discharge may come from the puncta. Epiphora is present and a palpable mass is often seen, inferior to the medial canthal tendon. Treatment is with systemic antibiotics, and application of heat may be useful. The sac may rupture and a fistula may form to the skin, which tends to heal after a few days. More deliberate drainage of the abscess may take place.

In chronic dacryocystitis, tearing is the most common presentation and there is likely to be a chronic low-grade bacterial infection inside the lacrimal sac.

In both cases, the definitive treatment is dacryocystorhinostomy which should take place after infection has been dealt with.

Dacryocystorhinostomy (DCR)

This procedure is performed in order to anastomose the lacrimal sac to the nasal mucosa (at the middle meatus). It is usually carried out under a general anaesthetic, but can be undertaken with the patient sedated and with a local anaesthetic (if they are unfit to undergo a general anaesthetic). There are three main approaches:

- External DCR – a 10–15mm incision is made medial to the inner canthus, and the lacrimal bone exposed (the lacrimal sac moved aside). A small bony ostomy is created and the nasal mucosa exposed. Then the lacrimal sac is flayed open with an H-shaped incision. The mucosa are opened with an anterior and posterior fold and they are then attached to the newly created posterior folds of the lacrimal sac. This essentially creates a direct passage from the lacrimal sac into the nasal cavity. The system is often intubated with a silicone stent, which is removed a few weeks later. Success rates for this procedure are 90%.

- Endoscopic DCR – this procedure is undertaken endoscopically via the nose. This approach means there is no external wound and it is therefore cosmetically more satisfying. The nasal mucosa is stripped back and the bone exposed. The bony ostium is created, as required, through the lacrimal bone. The lacrimal sac is then opened and silicone stents passed through and tied up the nose. Surgeons require specialised training to undertake this procedure and the equipment is expensive. This approach also has good success rates of around 90% (Nerad 2001).

- Endolaser DCR – this is principally the same procedure as the endoscopic approach but utilising a laser to create the openings. However, evidence suggests that this approach is generally less successful than external or endoscopic.

Dry eyes

In addition to the production, flow and drainage of tears, the quantity, quality and composition of the tear film are key factors in maintaining ocular comfort, ocular health and visual clarity. Furthermore, tear film quality relies on the additional secretions from the accessory glands of Krause and Wolfring (found in the fornices), on the sebaceous oils from the meibomian glands, and on mucin (the mucus secretions) from the goblet cells in the conjunctiva.

The outer lipid layer of the tear film helps to prevent evaporation of the aqueous layer as the eye is exposed to air. It also lowers the surface tension of the tear film, allowing water to be drawn into it, and acts as a lubricant between the lids and the surface of the globe.

The middle, aqueous layer supplies atmospheric oxygen to the corneal epithelium, washes away debris from the eye and facilitates leukocyte action after injury. It has an important antibacterial action as a result of the presence of lysozyme, immunoglobulin IgA and lactoferrin, and fills any minute irregularities of the corneal surface, allowing more accurate refraction of light.

The inner mucin layer aids in wetting of the corneal surface by the aqueous layer, turning the anterior corneal surface from a hydrophobic to a hydrophilic state (Bowling 2015).

Deficiencies in any of these layers can give rise to types of dry eye and dry eye symptoms. These are described as conditions 'when there is inadequate tear volume or function resulting in an unstable tear film and ocular surface disease' (Kanski & Bowling 2011, p.122).

Causes of dry eye

Dry eye may be caused by immunological conditions such as rheumatoid arthritis, Sjögren's syndrome, systemic lupus erythematosus or inflammatory damage to the lacrimal gland. It is often associated with age and known as keratoconjunctivitis sicca. It has been suggested that dry eye syndrome results from lymphocytes infiltrating the lacrimal gland and causing chronic progressive inflammation (Zoukhri 2006). It is also suggested that levels of androgens that protect the ocular surface from inflammation decrease with age and when the level is reduced (as at the menopause), ocular cells make more cytokines that attract T cells to the conjunctiva, producing surface damage and increasing symptoms of dry eye.

Sjögren's syndrome

This is an autoimmune condition that affects the mucous membranes as a consequence of inflammation and a destruction of the lacrimal and salivary glands. The primary form represents the condition in isolation and the secondary form is associated with other diseases such as connective tissue disorders or rheumatoid arthritis.

Types of dry eye

Dry eye is classified as:

- Abnormalities of the aqueous layer
- Abnormalities of the mucin layer
- Abnormalities of the lipid layer
- Abnormalities of the corneal epithelium
- Abnormalities of the lids.

Abnormalities of the aqueous layer

Insufficient production of the aqueous component of the tear film is the most common cause of dry eye. The resulting condition, known as keratoconjunctivitis sicca (KCS), is usually due to decreased tear production by the accessory lacrimal glands. Inflammation of the lacrimal glands may also be accompanied by inflammation and drying of other mucous membranes, particularly those in the mouth, vagina, and/or respiratory tract.

Abnormalities of the mucin layer

Deficient production of mucin interferes with the even distribution (spreading) of the tear film across the corneal surface, resulting in a very unstable and uneven tear film with a rapid break-up time. Abnormalities in the mucin layer of the precorneal tear film often occur as a result of loss of the goblet cells of the conjunctival epithelium.

Abnormalities of the lipid layer

When abnormalities in the lipid layer of the precorneal tear film occur (due to meibomitis, for example), deficiencies in the lipid layer result in excessive evaporation of the aqueous component of the tear film, which in turn leads to drying of the ocular surface.

Abnormalities of the corneal epithelium

Infections and trauma, resulting in corneal scars and ulcerations, can damage the microvilli of the epithelial cells, causing permanent dry spots. Damage to the corneal surface can also result from exposure to certain drugs, including many types of general anaesthesia.

Abnormalities of the lids

Because the eyelids play such an important role in distributing the tear film, normal blinking is essential to maintain a healthy corneal and conjunctival surface. Thus, anything that interferes with normal blinking, or anatomic abnormalities that interfere with the complete closure of the eyelids during blinking, can result in drying of the ocular surface. (Marsden 2007).

Signs and symptoms of dry eye

The symptoms vary considerably from one individual to another. Most patients complain of a foreign body sensation, burning and general ocular discomfort. The discomfort is typically described as a scratchy, dry, sore, gritty, smarting or burning feeling. Discomfort is the hallmark of dry eye because the cornea is richly supplied with sensory nerve fibres.

A significant percentage of patients also experience photophobia and intermittent blurring or other problems with visual acuity. The tear film makes the refracting surface of the eye smooth and able to fulfil its role. A disrupted tear film will result in disrupted vision.

Individuals with dry eye commonly remark that their eyes tire easily, making it difficult for them to read or watch television. The reason for this difficulty is that the frequency of blinking typically decreases during tasks that require concentration. As blink frequency decreases, there is more time for the tear film to evaporate. If blinking is infrequent enough, the duration of exposure will exceed the tear film break-up time (BUT), resulting in the formation of one or more dry spots on the corneal surface.

Contact lens intolerance can also be a symptom of dry eye. A patient with mild to moderate dry eye may not experience symptoms until contact lenses are fitted. The placement of a contact lens can upset the delicate balance of tear film production and distribution, leading to lens intolerance.

As in blepharitis, the severity of the symptoms and the discomfort experienced by the patient often appear disproportionate to what would be expected from clinical findings. This can be complicated by serious underlying systemic or ocular conditions that need investigation, explanation and treatment, in addition to managing the dry eye symptoms. Those who work with patients with dry eyes often find that the dry eye symptoms can take over the lives of those who have them and these patients require an enormous amount of support, education and empathy to enable them to manage and live with their symptoms.

Management of dry eye

The basic principles of management are:

- To establish the cause of the dry eyes
- To treat any underlying causes
- To assess the quality and quantity of the tear film
- To find the best treatment options that aid compliance and give maximum comfort and resolution of symptoms.

Quantity and quality of tear film are both important and lead to different options for treatment.

Quantity of tear film

Quantity is measured using Schirmer's test (Figure 15.9). The tip of a predesigned small strip of blotting paper is placed in the lateral portion of the lower canthus (to avoid irritation and trauma to the cornea). The patient is asked to keep the eye open and blink normally and, after 5 minutes, the amount of tear secretions that have soaked onto the strip is measured.

Obviously, a piece of paper in the lower fornix may produce some irritation, so this test may be undertaken after topical use of anaesthetic drops to obtain a reading without eye irritation and this is known as Schirmer's test 2. Li *et al.* (2012) feel that this is a better measure of baseline tear production. The normal quantity of tears that would be expected in this 5-minute period without anaesthetic is 15mm or more, and slightly less with anaesthetic. Less than 10mm indicates impaired tear secretion. Quantity can also be observed during slit-lamp examination because there should be a 2–3mm 'pool' of tears sitting on and above the lower lid margin.

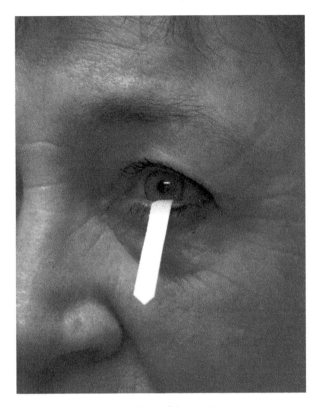

Figure 15.9 Schirmer's test
(reprinted by permission of Angela Chappell, Ophthalmic Imaging Department,
Flinders Medical Centre, Adelaide, South Australia).

Quality of tear film

Tear film break-up time is an indication of tear film stability and therefore of quality of the tear film. Using a slit-lamp, the tear film is observed after instilling a drop of fluorescein 2%. The tear film is examined using a wide beam of light and a cobalt blue filter. The patient is asked to blink, and the time is recorded between this and the moment when black spots or lines begin to appear in the tear film as it starts to dry. A tear break-up time of less than 10 seconds is abnormal.

The tear film should also be studied closely, and clarity, debris and mucus strands should be noted. During examination, the conjunctiva, lid margins and openings of the meibomian ducts should also be considered for any contributing meibomitis, blepharitis or conjunctivitis that could impact on the quality of the tears.

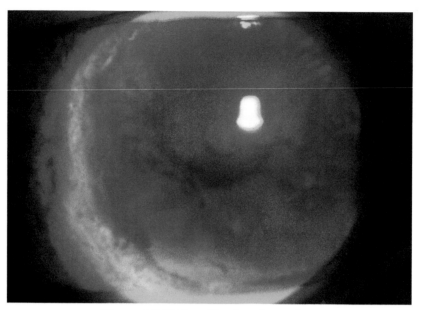

Figure 15.10 Tear film break-up time
(reprinted by permission of Angela Chappell, Ophthalmic Imaging Department,
Flinders Medical Centre, Adelaide, South Australia).

Dysfunction of the lipid layer of the tear film can lead to evaporative dry eye and this may be the result of meibomitis or obstructed meibomian glands causing oil deficiency. Deficiency of the aqueous layer leads to a hyposecretive dry eye (which may result, for example, from age changes in the lacrimal gland or from Sjögren's syndrome) and the two may coexist (Bowling 2015).

Treatment and practical guidance for dry eye

The first line of treatment for most patients with dry eyes will be some form of ocular lubricant, and there are a multitude of drops and ointments designed for this purpose. The plethora of lubricants available all add lubrication to the eyes, although, pharmacologically, they may well have been designed to work on different parts of the tear film layer, depending on any underlying ocular pathology and the nature of the resultant tear film deficiency.

Finding the right ocular lubricant/s for the patient can often be a time-consuming exercise, and may involve a process of trial and error until one lubricant (or a combination of several) is identified that is best tolerated by the patient. This should be the easiest for them to use and, from a compliance point of view, fit in with the patient's lifestyle – being put in as frequently (or, preferably, as infrequently) as necessary to manage the symptoms. The patient needs to know that it is not a 'one size fits all' regime and that they are a key player in managing their dry eye condition and finding the correct regime.

It is worth a patient with dry eye trying drops one at a time until one (or a combination) is found that works well. Each one can be tried at first a minimum of three or four times a day and more frequently if symptoms are present, finding an interval between which the eye is not symptomatic and then reducing the frequency until the longest, asymptomatic interval is found.

It should be explained that there are no drugs in these drops so they may be used extremely frequently if necessary. Drops and gels with different combinations of ingredients can be used and ointments used as adjuncts if required. Many newer dry eye therapies are supplied in larger, preservative-free bottles with novel preservation systems so that they do not have to be discarded after 4 weeks but last significantly longer, up to 6 – 9 months in some cases. Liposomal drops and sprays are available for patients who have deficiencies of the oil layer.

Patients expect the treatment that they are given to work and, if the first bottle of artificial tears does not work, they may lose faith in the clinician and the system. If drops are being used very frequently, provision of preservative-free drops would be appropriate to prevent preservative toxicity.

NB: Ciclosporin eye drops may be used in severe dry eye to suppress the activity of the immune system.

Punctal occlusion

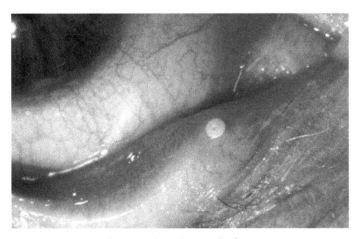

Figure 15.11 Punctal plugs.
(reprinted by permission of Angela Chappell, Ophthalmic Imaging Department,
Flinders Medical Centre, Adelaide, South Australia).

For patients who have severe dry eyes and those who get little symptomatic relief from the use of topical lubricants alone, the insertion of punctal plugs may be considered, to assist in keeping the lubricants/tear film on the surface of the eye for as long as possible (Figure 15.11).

Often, temporary collagen plugs can be inserted through all four puncta into the canaliculi, initially to see if there is any effect on the control of symptoms.

Collagen plugs dissolve over a period of a few weeks; and if symptoms have resolved or at least been reduced to a tolerable level, more permanent occlusion (using silicone plugs) would follow. Some silicone plugs are designed to fit into the puncta (Figure 15.11), while others are designed to fit into the canaliculus. Even with the insertion of silicone plugs, most patients, particularly with severe dry eye symptoms, will have to continue with additional topical lubricant drops. Very occasionally, epiphora can result, following insertion of the more permanent plugs, and the resultant watering can be as distressing for the patient as their dry eye symptoms. If necessary, punctal plugs can simply be removed (canalicular ones using a sac wash out technique), but then treatment options will have to be reconsidered for the management of the dry eye symptoms.

Health education

It is important that the patients get the time, support and education they require to understand and live with the condition. General advice should include:

- In general, the only person who can control their symptoms is the patient and they must be encouraged to find and use a regime that works for them. Ophthalmic healthcare professionals can advise, but are no substitute for a patient who is expert in their own condition

- The possibility of discontinuing contact lens use, reducing wear time – or using frequent, unpreserved drops.

- Avoidance or reduction in activities that reduce blinking, e.g. reading, driving, working on a computer monitor or watching television – or, at least, being aware that these activities will aggravate the condition and using tear substitutes more frequently.

- Reducing exposure to fumes, dust, cigarette smoke and dry air-conditioned or centrally heated environments that can aggravate symptoms; a bowl of water placed in the room may help maintain humidity levels.

References

Baxter, J., Patel, N. & Varma, S. (2012) Facial basal cell carcinoma. *British Medical Journal.* **345**, e5342.

Ben Simon, G.J., Rosen, N., Rosner, M. & Spierer, A. (2011) Intralesional triamcinolone acetonide injection versus incision and curettage for primary chalazia: a prospective, randomized study. *American Journal of Ophthalmology.* **151**(4), 714–16.

Bowling, B. (2015) *Kanski's Clinical Ophthalmology, a systematic approach.* 8th edn. London: Elsevier.

Bilkhu, P., Naroo, S. & Wolffsohn, J. (2014) Randomised masked clinical trial of the MGDRx eyebag for the treatment of meibomian gland dysfunction-related evaporative dry eye. *British Journal of Ophthalmology.* doi:10.1136/bjophthalmol-2014-305220.

Butovich, I. (2009) The Meibomian Puzzle: Combining Pieces Together. *Progress in Retinal and Eye Research.* **28**(6), 483–98.

Damasceno, R., Osaki, M., Dantas, P. & Belfort, R. (2011) Involutional entropion and ectropion of the lower eyelid: prevalence and associated risk factors in the elderly population. *Ophthalmic Plastic Reconstructive Surgery.* **27**(5), 317–20.

Gao, Y.Y., Xu, D.L., Huang, L.J., Wang, R. & Tseng, S.C. (2011) Treatment of ocular itching associated with ocular demodicosis by 5% tea tree oil ointment. *Cornea.* **31**, 14–17.

Ha, R., Nojima, K., Adams, W. & Brown, S. (2005) Analysis of facial skin thickness: defining the relative thickness index. *Plastic and Reconstructive Surgery.* **115**(6), 1769–73.

Kanski, J. & Bowling, B. (eds) (2011) *Clinical Ophthalmology.* 7th edn. London: Elsevier.

Katalinic, A., Kunze, U. & Schäfer, T. (2003) Epidemiology of cutaneous melanoma and non-melanoma skin cancer in Schleswig-Holstein, Germany: incidence, clinical subtypes, tumour stages and localization (epidemiology of skin cancer). *British Journal of Dermatology.* **149**, 1200–206.

Lee, Y. & Hwang, K. (2002) Skin thickness of Korean adults. *Surgical and Radiologic Anatomy.* **24**(3–4), 183–89

Lemp, M. & Nichols, K. (2009) Blepharitis in the United States 2009: a survey-based perspective on prevalence and treatment. *Ocular Surface.* **7**(April), S1–S14.

Li, N., Deng, X.G., & He, M.F. (2012) Comparison of the Schirmer test with and without topical anaesthesia for diagnosing dry eye. *International Journal of Ophthalmology.* **5**(4), 478–81.

Marsden, J. (2007) *An Evidence Base for Ophthalmic Nursing Practice.* London: Wiley.

Mitchell, P., Hinchcliffe, P., Wang, J., Rochtchina, E. & Foran, S. (2001) Prevalence and associations with ectropion in an older population: the Blue Mountains Eye Study. *Clinical and Experimental Ophthalmology.* **29**(3), 108–10.

Nakayama, M., Tabuchi, K., Nakamura, Y. & Hara, A. (2011) Basal cell carcinoma of the head and neck. *Journal of Skin Cancer.* http://dx.doi.org/10.1155/2011/496910 (accessed 29 September 2016).

Nelson, J.D., Shimazaki, J. & Benitez del Castillo, J.M. (2011) The International workshop on Meibomian gland dysfunction: report of the definition and classification subcommittee. *Investigative Ophthalmology & Visual Science.* **52**(4), 1930–37.

Nerad, J. (2001) *The Requisites: Oculoplastic Surgery.* St Louis: Mosby.

Pandhi, D., Gupta, P., Singal, A., Tondon, A., Sharma, S. & Madhu, S.V. (2012) Xanthelasma palpebrarum: a marker of premature atherosclerosis (risk of atherosclerosis in xanthelasma). *Postgraduate Medical Journal.* **88**(1038), 198–204.

Paulson, F. (2008) Anatomy and physiology of efferent tear ducts. *Ophthalmologe.* **105** (4), 339–45.

Powell, D. (2010) *Current findings on blepharitis. Contact Lens Spectrum.* http://www.clspectrum.com/articleviewer.aspx?articleID = 104450 (accessed 23 August 2016).

Rosenstein, T., Talezedah, N. & Progrel A. (2000) Anatomy of the lateral canthal tendon. *Oral Surgery, Oral Medicine, Oral Pathology, Oral Radiation and Endodontology.* **89**(1), 24–28.

Roewert-Huber, J., Lange-Asschenfeldt, B., Stockfleth E. & Kerl, H. (2007) Epidemiology and aetiology of basal cell carcinoma. *British Journal of Dermatology.* **157**, 47–51.

Thiabut, S., De Becker, E., Caisey, L., Bara, D., Karatas, S., Jammayrac, O., Pisella P. & Bernard, B. (2009) Human eyelash characterization. *British Journal of Dermatology.* **162**, 304–10.

Tiffany, J. (2003) Tears in health and disease. *Eye.* **17**, 923–27.

Timboli, D., Harris, M., Hogg, J., Realini, T. & Sivak-Callortt, J. (2011) Computerised Tomography of the lacrimal gland in normal caucasian adults. *Opththalmic Plastic & Reconstructive Surgery.* **6**, 453–56.

van den Bosch, W., Leenders, I. & Mulder, P. (1999) Topographic anatomy of the eyelids, and the effects of sex and age. *British Journal of Ophthalmology.* **83**(3), 347–52.

Weber, R., Keerl, R., Schaefer, S. & Rocca, R (eds) (2007) *Atlas of Lacrimal Surgery.* London: Springer.

Zoukhri, D. (2006) Effect of Inflammation on lacrimal gland function. *Experimental Eye Research.* **82**(5), 885–98.

CHAPTER SIXTEEN

The conjunctiva

Agnes Lee

Anatomy and physiology of the conjunctiva

The conjunctiva is a thin, transparent, mucous membrane that derives its name from the Latin *conjunctus* (meaning 'adjoining, closely connected, continuous') because it is attached to the eyelids and the eyeball. The conjunctiva lines the upper and lower lids (palpebral conjunctiva) and is reflected at the superior and inferior fornices on to the sclera (bulbar conjunctiva) up to the limbus, where its epithelium becomes continuous as the first layer of the corneal epithelium.

It is therefore divided into three parts:

- Palpebral conjunctiva
- Bulbar conjunctiva
- Conjunctiva in the fornices.

The conjunctiva's upper layers consist of stratified columnar epithelium and vary from two layers thick over the tarsal plate to five to seven layers at the corneoscleral limbus. Lymphocytes and melanocytes are scattered throughout the basal layers of the conjunctiva. The conjunctival stroma consists of loosely arranged bundles of collagenous tissues containing fibroblasts. Conjunctiva also contains macrophages, mast cells and leukocytes, all of which play a part in any inflammatory response (Abelson *et al.* 2002).

Palpebral conjunctiva

The palpebral conjunctiva is slightly thicker than the bulbar conjunctiva, is firmly attached to the tarsal plate, and lines the upper and lower lids. The palpebral conjunctiva is extremely thin and transparent and the yellowish tarsal glands can easily be visualised in the posterior surface of the tarsal plate by eversion of the lids. Blood vessels are also clearly visible. The palpebral conjunctiva is divided into three zones.

The marginal zone extends from right across the border of the lid to the back of the eyelid. The tarsal glands and lacrimal punctum can be seen emerging from this point.

It is important to note that, as the conjunctival epithelium is continuous with the lining of the inferior meatus of the nasal cavity, the infection can easily spread between these two structures (O'Rahilly *et al.* 2008).

The tarsal zone is thin, vascular and light red in colour.

The orbital zone contains cylindrical and cuboidal cells. In addition, the accessory lacrimal glands (of Krause and Wolfring) are situated here.

On the posterior edge of the lid margin, along the posterior edge of the openings of the tarsal glands, the conjunctiva joins the skin of the lid. Here, the non-keratinised, squamous epithelium of the conjunctiva is continuous with the keratinised, stratified, squamous epithelium of the skin.

Bulbar conjunctiva

The bulbar conjunctiva is very thin and lines the anterior portion of the eyeball (including the insertions of the extraocular muscles and Tenon's capsule) and is loosely attached to the sclera, except near the limbus where it increases in thickness. It moves over the sclera easily and, as it is transparent, blood vessels are clearly visible.

The plica semilunaris, which is a crescent-shaped fold in the inner canthus, can be seen in the medial fornix of the conjunctiva. It is richly supplied with goblet cells, which secrete mucin, an important component of the precorneal tear film that protects and nourishes the cornea. Lying within the medial side of the plica is the lacrimal caruncle (a small, pinkish, ovoid body of modified skin possessing a few fine colourless hairs), containing sweat and sebaceous glands.

At the corneoscleral limbus, the cells of the conjunctiva change to stratified, squamous, non-keratinised epithelium, which is continuous with the epithelium of the cornea.

Conjunctiva in the fornices

This lines the upper and lower lids and is loosely attached to the underlying fascial expansions of the sheaths of the levator and rectus muscles. Contraction of these muscles can pull on the conjunctiva so that it moves with the eyelid and eyebrow (Snell & Lemp 1998).

Conjunctival glands

The goblet cells are responsible for secreting the mucus part of the tear film and are scattered throughout the conjunctiva. The glands of Krause and Wolfring, also known as the accessory lacrimal glands, secrete some of the watery part of the tear film. These glands have no nervous control.

Conjunctival blood vessels

The arterial supply of the conjunctiva arises from the palpebral and anterior ciliary arteries. The peripheral arterial arch supplies the inferior and superior conjunctival fornices and the bulbar conjunctiva, whereas the marginal arterial arch supplies the palpebral arteries.

Conjunctival lymph drainage

The conjunctival lymph vessels are arranged as a deep and superficial plexus in the submucosa of the conjunctiva. Those vessels on the lateral side of the eye drain into superficial parotid nodes and those from the medial side into the submandibular nodes.

Nerve supply of the conjunctiva

The innervation of the bulbar conjunctiva is from the long ciliary nerves. These are branches of the nasociliary nerve, which in turn is a branch of the ophthalmic division of the trigeminal nerve. The superior bulbar conjunctiva and superior fornix conjunctiva are supplied by the frontal and lacrimal branches of the ophthalmic division. The inferior fornix is from the lacrimal branch of the ophthalmic division, and the infraorbital nerve from the maxillary division of the trigeminal nerve (Snell & Lemp 2013).

Functions of the conjunctiva

The conjunctiva is responsible for production of the mucus component of the tear film (from goblet cells) and its accessory glands help to ensure a continually moist environment. It also has a protective function – evaporation of tears lowers the temperature in the conjunctival sac, effectively inhibiting microbial growth. This is assisted by the junctions of hemidesmosomes to their basement membrane, which may prevent or limit bacterial colonisation. It acts as a physical barrier, preventing foreign bodies from entering the orbit and providing a moist environment so that a clear cornea is maintained.

Mucosa associated lymphoid tissue is a system of lymphoid tissue found in various mucosal sites in the body. It is populated by lymphocytes, such as T and B cells, as well as plasma cells and macrophages and lymphoid follicles. The conjunctival associated tissue is known as CALT and contains all the components necessary for a complete immune response, detecting antigens, expressing immunoglobulins and forming a key part of the immune system of the ocular surface (Knop & Knop 2000).

Abnormal physiology seen in infectious and inflammatory disorders of the conjunctiva

The clinical features that must be considered when diagnosing any conjunctival infection or disorder include the following:

Papillae are caused by a non-specific response of the conjunctival tissue to many acute and chronic inflammatory disorders. The various types of inflammatory cells (such as lymphocytes, plasma cells and eosinophils) are seen to invade the conjunctival stroma, resulting in tiny raised masses which look red, with a central blood vessel. This is seen mainly in bacterial and allergic eye conditions.

Follicles are tiny swellings of the lymph system, appearing milky or pearlescent, translucent and lobular and containing lymphocytes and macrophages. They are seen in viral and chlamydial conditions and in viral conjunctivitis. They form in response to viral particles entering the lymph system, which can also result in the localised preauricular swelling and tenderness associated with viral disease.

Discharges can be of different types, textures and colours, depending on causative organisms and aetiology:

- Mucopurulent discharge is usually a sign of bacterial infection, varying in colour, from cream to yellowish to green
- Serous, watery discharge is usually a sign of viral or allergic-type disorder
- Ropy and stringy serous discharge with mucus thread is associated with vernal conjunctivitis.

Injection/hyperaemia is congestion of conjunctival blood vessels. The distribution of congestion is important in the diagnosis. Diffuse injection in the fornices is normally found in conjunctivitis; sectoral injection indicates episcleritis; and ciliary injection might indicate iritis.

Petechial haemorrhages are pinpoint haemorrhages found in the palpebral or bulbar conjunctiva.

Conjunctival chemosis is swelling of the bulbar conjunctiva in response to infection or inflammation.

Conjunctival staining results from breakdown of the conjunctival epithelial cells, which then allows 'staining' (with fluorescein, rose bengal or lissamine green), the pattern of which represents missing or damaged tissue.

Conjunctival scarring is the end result of a wide variety of types of severe inflammation found in conditions such as severe dry eyes, entropion, trichiasis, chemical injury and trachoma.

Symblepharon is adhesions between the palpebral and bulbar conjunctiva after trauma, burns and infections.

Pseudomembrane is seen in severe infection, resulting from conjunctival epithelial hyperplasia, and may be peeled off the palpebral conjunctiva. True membrane is fibrin cellular debris, which indicates a more severe inflammatory response and can cause significant bleeding when peeled.

Enlarged preauricular lymph nodes can indicate acute or severe infection. These glands often form a swollen and tender area just in front of the ear.

Conditions of the conjunctiva

Conjunctivitis

Infective conjunctivitis is extremely common and accounts for many of the cases of 'red eye' presenting to both primary and secondary care. Although a first response to red eye is often topical antibiotics, bacterial conjunctivitis is uncommon in adults. An accurate history and examination will reveal that the vast majority of conjunctivitis is viral in origin (Azari & Barney 2013) and that explanation and supportive measures are much more effective than antibiotics, which will not resolve the problem. In fact, antibiotics are likely to leave patients with this condition feeling let down, because the clinician has promised and failed to cure them.

However, bacterial conjunctivitis is common in children. Conjunctivitis can be acute, hyperacute, recurrent or chronic, depending on for how long the condition persists. It is easily transmitted, especially when there is close physical contact.

Bacterial conjunctivitis

This is inflammation of the conjunctiva, with diffuse injection of the superficial episcleral vessels, bulbar conjunctiva and occasionally papillae of the palpebral conjunctiva of the upper and lower lid. The eye is very sticky throughout the day and yellow or green pus is evident. The condition is common in children, and normally starts off in one eye before transmitting itself to the other eye. Unilateral conjunctivitis is uncommon. Even if it starts off unilaterally, it usually spreads to the other eye, so advice must be given about treatment of the fellow eye. The severity of conjunctivitis depends on the causative organism.

Pathophysiology

To protect itself, the eye has a number of defence mechanisms. For instance, the tear film contains immunoglobulin (IgA), the blink reflex moves pathogens away from the eye into the canaliculi, and the immune system tolerates general and non-pathogenic bacteria that normally colonise the eye but excludes external organisms that try to enter the eye. In the event of any of these defence mechanisms breaking down, pathogenic bacterial infection is possible. In addition, pre-existing eye conditions (such as blepharitis, dry eyes, poor contact lens hygiene, chronic infection of the lacrimal sac and the prolonged use of ophthalmic medications) can cause conjunctival inflammation.

Causative organisms

The main causative organisms are: Streptococcus pneumoniae, Staphylococcus aureus, Haemophilus influenzae, Pseudomonas aeruginosa and gonococci.

Signs and symptoms

The individual is likely to present with a red, irritable eye, describing the sensation as 'gritty' rather than painful. The lid margin and lashes are usually crusty and the eyes wet and very sticky. Eyelids are stuck together, particularly on waking up, as a result of discharge during the night. Discharge is likely to be purulent and profuse, and the lashes may be coated. The patient may be mildly photophobic and the lids may be oedematous. The conjunctiva is diffusely injected but there will be no conjunctival staining with fluorescein.

Management

Requesting cultures and sensitivity tests may be useful for accurate diagnosis but these steps are not necessary in order to give effective treatment and are expensive and uncomfortable. However, swabs *should* be taken in the case of neonates (up to 28 days), or adults with very profuse discharge where gonococcal infection might be suspected.

The eye examination must include checking:

- Upper and lower lids for any signs of oedema and discharge
- Upper and lower lashes for signs of blepharitis
- Everting the upper and lower lids and examination of the tarsal plate for any signs of follicles, which could indicate a viral rather than a bacterial infection
- Everting the tarsal plate, which can also sometimes reveal a non-adherent pseudomembrane found in severe conjunctivitis
- The tarsal and bulbar conjunctiva for a pattern of hyperaemia
- Corneal integrity: marginal corneal infiltrate can be found in staphylococcal and haemophilus infection.

Treatment

The National Institute for Health and Care Excellence's (NICE 2015) clinical knowledge summary of bacterial conjunctivitis echoes the American Academy of Ophthalmology's (2011) preferred practice pattern and suggests that the first-line treatment is advice and self-care, as bacterial conjunctivitis is entirely self-limiting and does not cause serious sequelae. Sheikh, Hurwitz *et al.*'s (2012) systematic review suggests that there is a modestly improved rate of clinical remission with antibiotic treatment (compared to placebo) in bacterial conjunctivitis and this may also help to reduce the spread of disease. NICE recommends chloramphenicol drops as the first-line treatment, with fusidic acid as the alternative.

Children with acute bacterial conjunctivitis are normally prescribed fusidic acid (Fucithalmic) because this necessitates only a twice-daily drop regimen.

In cases of severe bacterial conjunctivitis, a pseudomembrane can sometimes be seen loosely adherent to the palpebral conjunctiva. Pseudomembranes consist of coagulated exudate that adheres loosely to the inflamed conjunctiva and is a response to severe inflammation or infection. They are typically not integrated with the conjunctival epithelium (unlike the true membrane, which is fibrin cellular debris, becoming interdigitated with the vascularity of the conjunctival epithelium). It is important that the pseudomembrane be removed from the conjunctival epithelium by peeling it with forceps. A little bleeding may be encountered.

Never pad the eye in any acute eye infection. If mild photophobia is present, encourage the use of dark glasses instead.

Care

Health education information, particularly on how to control the spread of infection, should be given. Regular handwashing should take place, especially before and after drop instillation; and, if discharge is profuse, it may be wise to change pillowcases daily. Face cloths and towels should not be shared, and make-up should be discarded. Attention to hygiene should be reiterated where there are children. The use of disposable tissues to wipe the eye should be encouraged.

The clinician must ensure that the patient understands how to use the medication before leaving the department: chloramphenicol drops should be kept in a cool place, preferably in a fridge. Drops and ointment should never be shared and should be discarded at the end of the treatment period.

Artificial tears may be suggested to lubricate the eye and give further comfort.

Information on how to keep the lids clean and free from discharge may be needed (cooled, boiled water and cotton wool or tissues), especially by parents of small children, who may also need extra help and advice on instilling the prescribed medication effectively.

If a patient wears contact lenses, the use of these should be discontinued until the infection has cleared up. Disposable lenses should be discarded. Where possible, any oral information given should be reinforced with written information.

It is not necessary to review bacterial conjunctivitis, as it is self-limiting. However, before discharging patients, they must be told to come back if there is a change in visual acuity, or if they experience moderate or severe eye pain or photophobia.

Gonococcal conjunctivitis

Gonococcal conjunctivitis (Figure 16.1) is a sexually transmitted infection (STI), sometimes known as hyperacute conjunctivitis. Again, the normal mode of transmission is through sexual contact, genital/ocular or hand/ocular transmission, but casual interaction with infected individuals has also been reported as a cause. The organism responsible is Neisseria gonorrhoea. Systemically, gonococcal infections are associated with infection of the rectum, urethra and cervix.

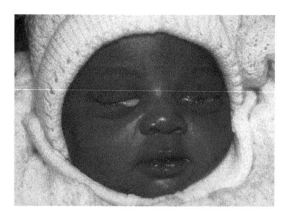

Figure 16.1 Gonococcal conjunctivitis in a baby

Symptoms

● Sudden onset – becoming severe in less than 12 hours.

Signs

● Severe purulent discharge

● Acute red eye

● Conjunctival papillae and chemosis: papillae are a common non-specific response of the conjunctival tissue to inflammation and consist of tiny elevations of various types of inflammatory cells (lymphocytes, plasma cells, eosinophils) which are tightly packed together, with a vascular core

● Corneal epithelial haze and defect

● Possible peripheral ulcers

● Severe cases of perforation.

Management

Eye swabs and conjunctival scrapings should be performed for Gram staining. With Gram stain, epithelial parasitism by Gram-negative diplococci is seen (Matejcek & Goldman 2013), which confirms the diagnosis.

Treatment

Treatment is usually systemic, as systemic infection will be present. This should be undertaken at a genitourinary medicine or sexual health clinic, and contact tracing will be needed. The 2012 European guideline suggests a 3-day regime (because of the relative avascularity of the cornea) of ceftriaxone 500mg intramuscularly as a single dose daily or, if the strain of bacteria is not resistant, azithromycin 2g as a single oral dose with doxycycline 100mg bd for 1 week and ciprofloxacin 250mg daily for 3 days (Bignell & Unemo 2012).

Care

Extreme sensitivity is required when dealing with the sexual connotations of this infection in the ophthalmic department. Partners may accompany the patient but the patient may not, as yet, wish this diagnosis to be shared. Compliance with all forms of treatment is needed in order to prevent transmission of the infection. Full and frank discussion about the connotations of the infection may need to take place to ensure concordance and compliance with treatment.

Ophthalmia neonatorum

Ophthalmia neonatorum (or conjunctivitis of the newborn) is the term used by the World Health Organization (WHO) for any conjunctivitis with discharge occurring during the first 28 days of life. The chief culprit used to be Neisseria gonococcus but, although it is still seen occasionally and appears to be increasing, Chlamydia trachomatis is by far the most common cause. Both organisms can infect the baby's eyes during delivery through the birth canal. The incubation period of Neisseria sp. is 2–3 days. If left untreated, gonococcal neonatal conjunctivitis can cause corneal ulceration, leading to endophthalmitis and blindness. The transmission rate for gonorrhoea from an infected mother to her newborn is 30–50% (Rhee and Pyfer 1999).

Chlamydial neonatal conjunctivitis is less destructive, although it can last months if left untreated and may be followed by pneumonia (British Association for Sexual Health and HIV 2015). The incubation period is 5–12 days. Other causes of infections may include staphylococci, pneumococci, Haemophilus spp. and herpes simplex virus.

The risk factors associated with ophthalmia neonatorum are premature rupture of the membranes, resulting in ascending infection from the cervix and vagina, documented or suspected STI, postpartum contact and local eye injury during delivery.

Signs and symptoms

- Lid oedema
- Purulent discharge (much more purulent and profuse in gonococcal conjunctivitis), sometimes blood-stained; often just 'sticky' in chlamydia
- Chemosis.

Management

Gonococcal neonatal conjunctivitis should be treated with ceftriaxone 25–50mg/kg Iv or IM as a single dose (Bignell & Unemo 2012).

Ophthalmia neonatorum caused by chlamydial infection is diagnosed through laboratory investigation and when a positive eye swab is made. This condition can be associated with otitis media and respiratory and gastrointestinal tract infections including pneumonia. Neonates are treated with oral erythromycin ethyl succinate suspension 12.5mg/kg four times daily for 14 days. Topical treatment is inadequate and unnecessary (British Association for Sexual Health and HIV 2015).

Nursing care

The condition must be clearly and carefully explained to both parents (if available). Both parents should be told the baby's diagnosis, how the baby came to acquire the infection and the recommended treatment. As the infection is transmitted by the mother during delivery, it is vital that both parents are screened and examined for genital infection. Tact and sensitivity are required when the parents are told to attend the sexual health clinic and informed about the problems that could arise if they or the baby do not receive treatment.

If the baby's eyes are sticky, the carers should be shown how to clean the eyes using clean cotton wool and warm water.

The importance of any follow-up care in the hospital or community must be stressed.

Viral conjunctivitis

Adenoviruses are small infectious agents (DNA viruses) and 57 different types have been identified. These viruses often cause upper respiratory tract infection, conjunctivitis (Figure 16.2) and other infections such as colds or flu.

Adenoviruses are responsible for 3–5% of acute respiratory infections in children and 2% of respiratory illnesses in adults. The virus is extremely contagious and the usual modes of transmission are through contaminated fingers and vectors such as medical instruments (e.g. applanation tonometers).

Inhalation of airborne viruses may also lead to systemic illness with eye involvement. Viral conjunctivitis is by far the most common conjunctivitis in adults. Although it usually begins in one eye, it is likely to spread to the fellow eye within days, despite the best intentions of the patient.

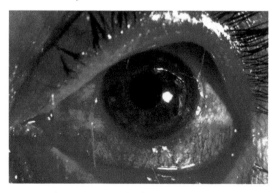

Figure 16.2 Viral conjunctivitis.

Symptoms

- Foreign body sensation
- Feeling of dryness
- Mild photophobia in some cases
- The lids are likely to be stuck together in the morning as a result of dried secretions
- Vision may be affected as a result of corneal involvement
- Corneal involvement may cause pain
- Sore throat may be present
- Other upper respiratory tract symptoms, such as a recent history of a cold.

Signs (Yanoff & Duker 2008)

- Diffuse hyperaemia
- Lid oedema may be present
- Profuse watering
- Conjunctiva may be chemosed
- May have subconjunctival haemorrhage or petechial haemorrhages on lid conjunctiva
- Tender preauricular node – unilateral or bilateral
- Follicles (multiple tiny translucent swellings) on lid conjunctiva and often at the limbus; follicles are seen on the slit-lamp as rounded, avascular white or grey structures containing lymphocytes surrounded by small vessels arising at the border and encircling it (Snell & Lemp 1998); they are inflamed lymphoid tissue
- Lesions may be seen on the corneal epithelium, which may be punctate or nummular; they may spread to stroma, producing punctate scarring (subepithelial opacities), which may compromise vision initially and last for some months before resolving spontaneously
- The tear film is likely to be poor, with a break-up time that may be instantaneous.

Management

There is no effective drug therapy for adenoviral conjunctivitis. Eye swabs are not therefore necessary unless diagnosis is uncertain, and they are expensive and can be painful (Yanoff & Duker 2008).

It is essential that patients are given a full explanation of their condition because the primary function of the management of this condition is patient awareness, and reducing discomfort through education and decreasing symptomatology. Adenoviral conjunctivitis often has symptoms out of all proportion to its importance and can be an intensely distressing condition. Advice and information should include the following points:

● The roughness of the conjunctiva (follicles – see Figure 16.3) is what makes the eyes feel so gritty and irritable.

● The patient with viral conjunctivitis often complains of dryness, along with a watery eye. The tears, although profuse, are inadequate in quality and dry up very quickly; the eye responds to the irritation and dryness by producing more tears.

● Topical antibiotics are ineffective with adenovirus conjunctivitis and secondary bacterial infection is uncommon.

● Artificial tears will help to control the feeling of dryness and irritation and these may be used frequently (e.g. half-hourly or more often).

● A bland ointment, such as simple eye ointment, may also be helpful.

● The treatment contains no drugs and can therefore be used as required to ensure comfort.

● Cold compresses on the lids may ease the irritation of this very distressing condition.

● The patient should be aware that viral conjunctivitis may persist for 3–6 weeks and the symptoms of dryness may last much longer, necessitating the use of artificial tears, sometimes for months or even years.

Adenovirus is contagious until the symptoms have peaked. It could be argued that patients should be advised to avoid work until the symptoms have peaked. However, this would not normally be advised for any other viral infection, such as a cold, so advice should be based on symptoms and the person's role. Certainly, contact in the workplace with food and children should be discouraged.

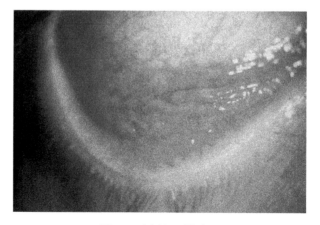

Figure 16.3 Follicles.

Infection control

Adenovirus is highly infectious and infection control is of paramount importance, both for patients – they should use their own towels and face cloths and be encouraged to wash their hands after touching their eyes or instilling drops – and for the ophthalmic department. Handwashing is the first line of defence in the control of any infection and is vital to stop the spread of viral conjunctivitis. Many major epidemics of viral conjunctivitis associated with ophthalmic units have been linked with poor handwashing techniques and inadequate disinfection of equipment. Adenovirus can survive in the desiccated state on various surfaces.

Examination equipment should be cleaned between each patient (including, for example, switches and pens which act as vectors but are often not considered). Sodium hypochlorite solution (500 parts per million) is effective against many organisms and infection control departments should be involved to ensure effective procedures. Handwashing should be supplemented by alcohol gels or wipes to ensure compliance by healthcare workers.

Epidemic keratoconjunctivitis

The onset of epidemic keratoconjunctivitis (EKC) is caused by adenovirus types 8, 19 and 37, with an acute onset, occurring first in one eye and then both; as a rule, the first eye is more severely affected. The patient complains of general discomfort and, on slit-lamp examination, follicles, petechial haemorrhages, chemosis (may be gross), and oedema of the caruncle and pseudomembrane may be seen. This type of adenoviral infection is particularly severe.

Corneal involvement is usually seen (as described earlier). The management of EKC is as already described. The use of steroids to treat infiltrate is usually thought to be unhelpful.

Pharyngoconjunctival fever

This is another adenoviral infection presenting with conjunctival findings similar to simple adenoviral infection and caused by adenovirus 3, 7 and occasionally adenovirus 4. It is characterised by a temperature of 38.3–40°C, sore throat, conjunctival injection, giant follicular conjunctivitis that begins unilaterally with the fellow eye being involved in 2–5 days. Outbreaks may be epidemic and have been linked to contamination from swimming pools. The illness is generally self-limiting, although fairly debilitating, and supportive therapy is all that is needed.

Chlamydial/adult inclusion conjunctivitis

Chlamydial conjunctivitis should be considered if conjunctivitis is unilateral with subacute onset and delayed resolution and large follicles are seen subtarsally.

Chlamydial (inclusion) conjunctivitis is caused by C. trachomatis serotypes D–K and is usually sexually transmitted (Kanski & Bowling 2011). Women seem to be more susceptible than men to systemic infection, although men are more likely to notice symptoms than women. Eye lesions may present about 1 week after sexual contact. There may be systemic signs and symptoms of vaginitis, cervicitis or urethritis. Diagnosis of inclusion conjunctivitis may be difficult, even with laboratory investigation. Infants whose mothers have untreated chlamydial infections have a 30–40% chance of developing neonatal chlamydial conjunctivitis (ophthalmia neonatorum).

Pathophysiology

Chlamydia trachomatis is an intracellular parasite and has its own DNA and RNA; it is therefore more closely related to bacteria than to viruses. It is known that subgroup A causes chlamydial infections, serotypes A, B, Ba and C cause trachoma, and serotypes D–K produce adult inclusion conjunctivitis. The incubation period is usually 2–7 days. The usual mode of transmission is through sexual exposure, hand contact from a site of genital infection to the eye, sharing infected eye make-up or towels, or the mother infecting the neonate during delivery.

Symptoms

- Subacute red eye, which was never acute and is not settling
- Foreign body sensation
- Drooping of upper lid
- Photophobia.

Signs

- Watery discharge
- Lid swelling
- Palpable preauricular node may be present
- Superficial punctate keratitis
- Micropannus
- Large follicles in upper and lower fornices
- Possibility of formation of pseudomembrane and haemorrhage.

Management

Bearing in mind its implications, suspicion of chlamydial infection should not trigger discussions about STIs. Mentioning the subject before an accurate diagnosis can be made may introduce suspicion and tension into the patient's relationships. Although informed consent should be given for the swab, as for any investigation, it might be thought sufficient to explain that this is for one of the infective agents that is treatable and not mention its possible nature of transmission. Chlamydia is very widely known about though, particularly by young people, and the discussion may be very straightforward. The treatment for chlamydial infection is simple and effective, once it has been diagnosed by a positive eye swab. Results are usually available in 3 days, although more rapid results may be possible in urgent cases. Topical treatment is not necessary as systemic treatment will manage the whole infection. Systemic treatment is with doxycycline (100mg bd for 1–2 weeks) or azithromycin (1g single dose) or erythromycin (500mg qds for 1 week if tetracycline is contra-indicated). There is ongoing debate as to which antibiotic is most effective (alone or in combination) but the single-dose treatment ensures, when given under supervision, that the infection has been treated (British Association for Sexual Health and HIV 2015).

Sensitivity and tact must be shown to the patients and their partners when a diagnosis of chlamydial infection is made. Patients and their partners must be made fully aware of the circumstances surrounding the disease, as an STI, and the importance of treating partners who may be asymptomatic because they will be at risk. Appointments must be made for the patients and their partners at a genitourinary medicine/sexual health clinic.

It is important that patients finish any course of treatment and attend all their appointments to avoid systemic complications. Untreated chlamydial infection can result in pelvic inflammatory disease, leading to infertility or long-term pelvic pain. If a woman has chlamydial infection when she is pregnant, she is at a higher risk of having an ectopic pregnancy or a premature birth. In addition to giving her newborn baby an eye infection, lung infection is also a possibility. For men, although the complications are rare, inflammation of the testicles causing infertility is a possibility. For both men and women, Reiter's syndrome and appendicitis are additional possible complications.

Herpes simplex virus conjunctivitis

Herpes simplex virus (HSV) is usually seen before or at the same time as the appearance of vesicular lesions on the eyelids. It occurs during primary infection (HSV-1 and also possibly HSV-2) or during recurrent episodes of ocular herpes (Bowling 2015). The disease usually runs for 3–4 weeks, beginning unilaterally, with the fellow eye involved within a week. Slit-lamp examination may reveal pseudomembrane and conjunctival ulceration, and there is usually tenderness of the preauricular lymph nodes. The cornea is frequently involved because of its association with herpes simplex keratitis – superficial punctate staining and formation of dendrites are common. Occasionally, uveitis may be present.

Early treatment is required and antiviral agents such as aciclovir 3% ointment or, very occasionally, older treatments such as idoxuridine 0.1% or trifluorothymidine

(F3T), are prescribed. Recurrence is common, with 50% of patients having a second episode within 2 years. Some patients with recurrent HSV keratitis are kept on long-term prophylactic oral acyclovir, although there are some worries that this may lead to HSV, which is resistant to this drug (van Velzen *et al.* 2013). Ganciclovir gel is emerging as an alternative treatment.

Molluscum contagiosum

This is a viral infection of the skin, mainly affecting children. If a molluscum lesion is located on the eyelid margin, a secondary follicular conjunctivitis may develop as an immune reaction to the pox virus particles being shed into the eye. The usual management is excision of the lid lesion and the follicular reaction will then resolve.

Axenfield conjunctivitis

This is usually mild and asymptomatic with upper large palpebral follicles. It usually runs a chronic course and treatment is unnecessary.

Measles, mumps and rubella conjunctivitis

These three conditions may be accompanied by a mild bilateral follicular conjunctivitis, which appears similar to simple adenoviral infection; therapy is usually supportive.

Toxic and irritating follicular conjunctivitis

This can be caused by long-term use of certain ocular medications, heavy make-up, environmental irritants, sensitivity to soap, etc., as a result of hypersensitivity reaction. Slit-lamp examination may reveal a mixture of papillae and follicles. The condition is usually unilateral, depending on the cause. Management consists of replacement ocular medications, encouraging better hygiene and (where possible) isolating and removing irritants. Artificial lubricants may be helpful.

Children with conjunctivitis

Although it is very common for nurseries and schools to demand either that children are withdrawn until they are better, or until they are taking antibiotics, the guidance from the Health Protection Agency and the British Infection Association (2012) specifically states that children should not be removed from school or nursery for this reason (as they would not be if they had a 'cold'). It is worth mentioning this to parents who may want antibiotics for their child when it is clinically unjustified, so that they can resume school or nursery.

Trachoma

Trachoma (also known as granular conjunctivitis or Egyptian ophthalmia) is a contagious, chronic inflammation of the mucous membranes of the eye caused by an organism called Chlamydia trachomatis, a parasite closely related to bacteria. The spread of trachoma is through discharge from an infected child's eyes passing on to hands or clothing, hand-to-eye contact or by flies that land on the faces of infected children. The infection is highly contagious in its early stages.

Trachoma occurs worldwide but most often in poor rural communities. It is widespread in the Middle East, parts of the Indian subcontinent, South Asia and China. Pockets of blinding trachoma are also found in Australia (among native Australians), the Pacific Islands and Latin America. It is one of the world's leading causes of preventable blindness, and problems occur in areas where there is overcrowding and poor sanitation.

Infection usually occurs in childhood and the early symptoms of trachoma include the development of follicles on the conjunctiva of the upper eyelids. The patient also experiences oedematous eyelids, discharge, pain and photophobia. Repeated attacks will cause scarring of the inner eyelids, leading to entropion. The continuous rubbing of the inturning lashes (trichiasis) on the cornea, as the result of the entropion, will eventually lead to severe cornea scarring, resulting in severe loss of vision and blindness. In addition, blindness is also caused through repeated secondary bacterial keratitis.

Diagnosis is based on the patient's history and slit-lamp examination of the eye. Small samples of cells can be taken from the conjunctiva and stained (Giemsa staining) to confirm diagnosis.

Trachoma is treated using the SAFE strategy developed by the World Health Organization:

- **S** Surgery
- **A** Antibiotics
- **F** Facial cleanliness
- **E** Environmental improvement.

The antibiotic of choice is a single dose of oral azithromycin which can be observed being taken. Where azithromycin is not available (it is donated in many areas of endemic trachoma) tetracycline can be used, but the home level of compliance will be unknown. Facial cleanliness in children reduces the risk and the severity of active trachoma.

Environmental improvement (including the availability of clean water) and household sanitation, particularly the disposal of human waste (which is a breeding ground for the flies which spread the disease), are important.

Trichiasis treatment and lid surgery is necessary to prevent damage to the cornea, resulting in blindness. Bilamellar tarsal rotation involves a full thickness incision of the scarred lids and external rotation of the distal margin. In many parts of the world, this surgery is undertaken by trained eye health workers and nurses.

Allergic conjunctivitis

Allergic conjunctivitis affects 6 out of 10 allergy patients and is often associated with hayfever. Allergic conjunctivitis occurs when the eye comes into contact with a substance to which the sufferers are sensitive. There are many types of allergens or substance to which the eyes can become sensitive, such as:

- **Pollen**: Flowers, trees and grasses and weeds all release pollen into the air and this is carried by the wind. When the pollen count is high, especially in spring and summer, the patient may experience allergies.

- **Pets**: Hairs from pets, particularly cats, can cause allergies. The tiny dandruff-like scales that household animals shed can become trapped in furniture and carpets.

Other common allergens include cosmetics, house mites and pollution.

Pathophysiology

Allergy may occur to normally harmless antigens (known as allergens) or to infectious agents. The allergic response is known as type 1 hypersensitivity and exists in two phases: the sensitisation phase and the effector phase.

A harmless antigen causes the production of an antibody (IgE) on first exposure. This then comes into contact with mast cells and basophils, which have receptors for IgE antibody (sensitisation). The patient will experience no symptoms after initial binding; however, introduction of the allergen stimulates the production of more IgE and increases the possibility of cross-linking with existing antibodies on the mast cell surface, causing the mast cell to degranulate. Degranulation releases a large number of inflammatory mediators such as histamine, prostaglandins and bradykinin. Histamine causes the itchy symptoms experienced by patients and induces vasodilatation and mucus secretion by goblet cells.

Prostaglandins directly stimulate nerve endings to produce sensations of itching and pain and also increase vascular permeability and vasodilatation.

Acute allergic conjunctivitis

Allergic conjunctivitis presents acutely in two distinct ways. The first is by an acute and frightening atopic reaction that involves massive chemosis or swelling of the conjunctiva, which the patient often describes as 'jelly' on the eye (Figure 16.4). The cornea appears to have sunk backwards, as the conjunctiva protrudes beyond it. This is an alarming but self-limiting condition that often occurs in children. The chemosis usually resolves spontaneously within a couple of hours, and often more quickly, so there is little need for intervention with drugs or drops and, as the eye is sensitised to allergens at this stage, reaction to drops or preservative may be potentiated. Reassurance is required; and supportive treatments, such as cold compresses, may be soothing.

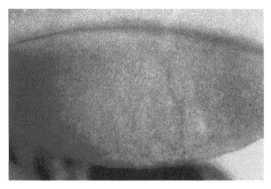

Figure 16.4 Papillae.

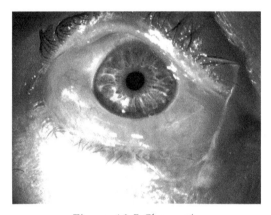

Figure 16.5 Chemosis.

The second presentation of acute allergic conjunctivitis is more common and less dramatic.

Signs and symptoms

- Itching that may be severe
- Hyperaemia
- Eyelid chemosis and erythema
- Watery discharge
- Foreign body sensation
- Burning of the eye
- Papillae
- History of seasonal or other allergies
- Lack of palpable preauricular lymph nodes
- Other systemic conditions such as rhinitis and asthma.

Treatment

The primary aim of management is alleviating the symptoms and supporting the patient. The most effective, but perhaps least practical, approach is to prevent exposure to any known allergen. As this is not always possible, mast cell stabilisers, such as lodoxamide and sodium cromoglicate, are applied four times daily. These drops prevent the onset of allergic reaction by blocking the adherence of the IgE-allergen compound to the mast cell. Side effects of these drops may include transient burning and stinging.

Once degranulation of the mast cell membrane has occurred (and histamine has been released), it will take 7–10 days for the membrane to restabilise. Mast cell-stabilising drops will therefore have no apparent effect for 7–10 days. Once an allergic reaction has occurred, antihistamine drops will be useful (ketotifen, levocabastine, emedastine) and may be used in combination with a mast cell stabiliser. One drug that combines both properties is olopatadine (Azari & Barney 2013).

Care

Individuals presenting with allergic conjunctivitis are usually aware of what to avoid in order to minimise their symptoms. Patients, especially those with a history of seasonal allergic conjunctivitis, should be told to avoid (where possible) exposure to any substances that precipitate symptoms. Prophylactic treatment with a mast cell stabiliser should be recommended, and this should be used for the duration of the patient's hayfever season to prevent symptoms.

Cold compresses, artificial tears or gel can be used together to relieve symptoms. In addition, topical decongestants (which cause vasoconstriction and thereby retard the release of the chemical mediators into the tissues from the bloodstream) can be used. The use of antihistamine systemically can also be beneficial.

Vernal conjunctivitis

This is a more serious seasonal disorder affecting children and young adults, which is more prevalent in warmer climates. The onset is typically between the ages of 3 and 25 years, and males are more affected than females.

Symptoms

- Itching
- Blepharospasm
- Photophobia
- Copious mucoid discharge
- Blurred vision.

Signs

- Giant cobblestone papillae (palpebral form of vernal conjunctivitis)
- Areas of superficial punctate keratitis
- Diffuse papillary hypertrophy on the palpebral conjunctiva, especially on superior tarsal plate
- Hyperaemia
- Chemosis
- Severe cases have superiorly located corneal shield ulcers
- Horner–Trantas dots (gelatinous, white clumps of degenerated eosinophils at the superior limbus, known as limbal form of vernal conjunctivitis).

Treatment and care

Treatment and care are as for allergic conjunctivitis. If a shield ulcer is present, topical steroids should be given four to six times a day, with a prophylactic antibiotic and cycloplegic agent in addition to mast cell stabiliser and cold compresses. Refer to Abelson *et al.* (2012) for more information on what sets vernal keratoconjunctivitis apart from other allergic conditions, and how to create targeted treatments for it.

Giant papillary conjunctivitis

This is often associated with wearing soft or gas-permeable contact lenses, and is seen as a local allergic reaction. Sometimes this condition can occur in patients with ocular prostheses and sutures. The tear levels of IgE, IgG and IgM are elevated, as in vernal conjunctivitis, in which the mast cells are activated (Pavan-Langston 2007).

Signs and symptoms

- Decreased contact lens tolerance
- Superficial punctate staining, especially superiorly
- Photophobia
- Giant cobblestone papillae
- Mucus discharge
- Hyperaemia
- Fine papillae in lower tarsal plate.

Management and nursing care.

Patients are advised to stop wearing their contact lenses for a couple of weeks until all the inflammation and superficial punctate staining are gone. It is also advisable for patients to see an optician for their contact lens check in relation to the fit, the continued suitability of their current contact lenses, and contact lens hygiene (including preservative-free solutions). If symptoms persist, it may be necessary to change to a different type of contact lens or discontinue their use permanently.

Superior limbic keratoconjunctivitis

This condition primarily affects the upper tarsus and superior bulbar conjunctiva, especially at the limbus, and is usually bilateral. It affects females more than males.

Pathophysiology

The aetiology and pathogenesis are unclear and numerous causative agents have been implicated, including infectious agents such as bacteria, viruses and fungi. An autoimmune aetiology has also been considered, based on the course of the disease – with periods of exacerbation and remission. There has also been an association with thyroid disease and other autoimmune disease. One widely regarded theory is that the loose conjunctival tissue rubs against the limbus during blinking, causing a mechanical irritation. Predisposing factors, such as prominent globe (in cases of thyroid disease) or tight lids, have been implicated as causes of the condition. A newer theory suggests that these patients have a degree of tear deficiency to the superior keratoconjunctiva, resulting in significantly reduced levels of vital tear-based nutrients reaching the affected region, as well as friction from the upper lid.

Signs and symptoms

- Burning, foreign body sensation
- Red eye
- Mild photophobia
- Nondescript pain
- Papillae on the superior palpebral conjunctiva
- Sectoral injection on the superior bulbar conjunctiva
- Fine punctate staining on superior cornea, limbus
- Superior corneal micropannus and filament.

Management

This is a chronic and recurrent disorder and there is no 100% effective treatment. The treatment of choice is usually 0.5–1.0% silver nitrate solution, applied topically to the superior bulbar and tarsal conjunctiva to cauterise the irregular tissue, thereby promoting growth of new healthy epithelium. Other treatments, such as pressure patching as well as bandage hydrogel lenses to alleviate mechanical irritation, are sometimes employed. Surgical intervention (such as surgical recession or resection of the superior bulbar conjunctiva) is another option. Vitamin A eye drops have also been somewhat effective in treating this condition. All patients presenting with superior limbic keratoconjunctivitis should have a systemic work-up.

Miscellaneous disorders of the conjunctiva

Phlyctenulosis

There are two forms of phlyctenulosis: conjunctival and corneal. There is always the appearance of a focal, staining nodule of limbal tissue on the conjunctiva, usually as a response to staphylococcal exotoxins and blepharitis. Treating the blepharitis with eyelid hygiene instructions usually causes the disappearance of phlyctenulosis. If the phlyctenulosis is severe, antibiotic drops alone are effective, although they may be combined with steroid drops.

Subconjunctival haemorrhage

Rupture of the superficial conjunctival vessels (not caused by trauma) can occur spontaneously and is usually unilateral. Sometimes the cause can be attributed to vomiting, severe eye rubbing, coughing, heavy lifting or sneezing. The possibility of blood dyscrasias cannot be ruled out in cases of recurrent or bilateral subconjunctival haemorrhage. The onset is usually sudden and it is very alarming for the patient to see an extremely red eye. The eye is examined on the slit-lamp and sometimes, in severe subconjunctival haemorrhage, a dark red mass of the bulbar conjunctiva can be seen, which spills over the lower lid margin. Depending on the extent of the subconjunctival haemorrhage, this condition normally settles within 2 weeks.

It is important to reassure patients and inform them that the haemorrhage will subside and that they will often notice a yellowish discoloration as the haemorrhage fades. If a patient is on anticoagulant, it is important that an international normalised ratio (INR) is performed or advice is sought from the anticoagulant lab. Similarly, if patients are on aspirin, they are advised to see their GP. Artificial lubricant may be prescribed to soothe any minor discomfort. It is sometimes suggested that the patient's blood pressure should be taken to detect any underlying hypertensive state or monitor cases of known hypertension but there seems to be little evidence for this.

Pinguecula

These are yellowish, slightly raised, lipid-like nodules, commonly found in the nasal and temporal limbal bulbar conjunctiva. The base of the pinguecula abuts on to the limbus but never crosses the corneoscleral frontier. Pinguecula can become vascularised and inflamed and is a common presentation in the eye emergency department; it may be associated with corneal punctate epitheliopathy and corneal dellen (corneal thinning, secondary to dryness).

Pinguecula is commonly found in patients who are middle-aged, with a history of chronic exposure to sun or living in a hot, dry, dusty atmosphere. There is no predilection for sex or race and both eyes are usually affected.

Pathophysiology

As mentioned previously, this condition typically affects the older population and is a conjunctival degenerative process that is initiated by continuous exposure to ultraviolet (UV) light or other irritants. This exposure alters the elastic and collagen tissue of the conjunctival stroma, leading to elastic tissue degeneration and deposition of abnormal elastic fibres in the conjunctival substantia propria.

Management

In general, treatment is given only if the patient complains of acute irritation and if the pinguecula is inflamed. In cases of mild pingueculitis, or when a dellen is present, suitable lubricating drops or ointment are prescribed. Patients are educated in the use of eye protection or sun wear to minimise eye exposure.

Where symptoms are severe, weak topical steroids (such as prednisolone 0.12%) may be given; or a non-steroidal medication, such as Acular (ketorolac trometamol) or Voltarol (diclofenac sodium), may be prescribed.

Pterygium

This is another degenerative condition of the conjunctival tissue. Slit-lamp examination reveals a raised, triangular, whitish wedge of fibrovascular tissue encroaching onto the nasal cornea. In some instances, the vascularised cornea may become red and inflamed and is a common presentation in the eye department. Surgery is usually indicated if it encroaches on the pupillary area.

Pathophysiology

There are potentially contributory factors to the formation of pterygium. These may include exposure to UV-A and UV-B, allergens and irritants (such as wind, dirt, dust and air pollution). These may particularly affect people who spend a great deal of time outdoors. Heredity may also be a factor.

Degeneration of the conjunctival stroma results in replacement by thickened, tortuous elastic tissue. Activated fibroblasts in the leading edge of the pterygium invade and fragment Bowman's layer as well as a variable amount of superficial corneal stroma. If left to grow, it will encroach on the visual axis.

Management

This initially involves educating the patient about taking precautions, such as avoiding dusty and smoky environments and the use of sun wear to protect the eyes in mild cases of pterygium. Ocular lubrication is also helpful. If the pterygium is inflamed, treatment is usually a mild topical steroid, applied four times daily to the affected eye. Surgery usually consists of the removal of pterygium with perhaps a small portion of superficial clear cornea beyond the area of encroachment. Antimetabolites are often used during surgery to attempt to prevent regrowth which is common. Pterygium surgery is one of the most common ophthalmic surgical procedures in hot dry countries such as Australia. It is common practice to remove the pterygium as soon as practically possible to reduce the level of corneal involvement.

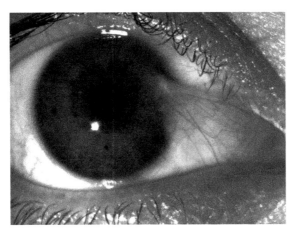

Figure 16.6 Pterygium.

Conjunctival tumours

Tumours in the conjunctiva can be either benign or malignant. Benign tumours include:

- Dermoid
- Pigmented naevus
- Granuloma
- Papilloma.

Malignant tumours include:

- Malignant papilloma
- Epithelioma
- Sarcoma (may originate from pigmented naevus)
- Rodent ulcer (as direct extension from lids).

Other miscellaneous 'lumps' and 'bumps' include:

- Concretions
- Retention cysts.

Ophthalmic care

Dermoid

A dermoid is a congenital benign tumour arising from the mesoderm and ectoderm, which may involve the cornea and sclera; it is mainly composed of collagen and is commonly located in the inferotemporal limbal area. The lesions are white (limbal dermoid) or yellow (dermolipoma), solid and have hairs protruding from them. A dermoid tumour normally remains quiescent, although it can enlarge around puberty. Surgical intervention is indicated if the vision is threatened or if a cosmetic deformity is particularly significant.

Pigmented naevus

This is usually congenital and may develop in the early years. The lesion is normally smooth and flat with well-circumscribed edges, and is most commonly seen nasally within the bulbar conjunctiva. Cysts may be seen within the lesion and are a key diagnosis of its benign nature. However, a malignant melanoma may develop from a naevus and enlargement may be an early sign of malignancy (Shields & Shields 2004). Management mainly consists of taking baseline colour photographs to document growth; and these patients may be reviewed every 6 months or 12 months. If the lesion is enlarging, or patients exhibit signs of malignancy such as ulceration, change in pigmentation, haemorrhage and development of feeder vessels, they will require a biopsy.

Granuloma

This can occur at any age and is found predominantly on the tarsal conjunctiva. Granuloma inflammation usually occurs around a site of irritation, such as a foreign body, or around a discharging chalazion and can be associated with systemic disease such as sarcoidosis and tuberculosis (Bowling 2015). Management involves incisional or excisional biopsy.

Papilloma

A papilloma can be either flat (sessile) or on a stalk (pedunculated) with an irregular surface. Papillomas are common in patients over the age of 40 years and can usually be seen in the fornix or caruncle. Two different forms can be distinguished:

- **Viral**: Recurrences are common, with multiple lesions.
- **Non-viral**: Single lesions are more common and may be pigmented; they are often thought to be pre-cancerous. Basal cell carcinoma of the conjunctiva is rare but can appear similar to a papilloma.

Malignant melanoma

Malignant melanoma of the conjunctiva is rare and presents itself as a raised, pigmented or non-pigmented lesion that appears in patients in their early 50s and is rarely seen in people younger than 20. It may resemble benign melanosis or naevus and may develop on its own (without any histological or clinical evidence of a pre-existing lesion in about 10% of cases) or in areas of previous pigmentation (about 20% of cases) (Roque 2015). Both sexes are equally affected and it predominantly affects fair-skinned people. There may be multiple lesions.

It is crucial to elicit a good history of growth characteristics of each lesion, as patients may be aware of subtle changes that may be helpful in identifying these lesions. It is also important to carry out a good physical slit-lamp examination. The clinical presentation can be variable. Conjunctival melanomas can extend onto the peripheral limbus with some growing circumferentially around the limbus (Roque 2001).

The overall tumour-related mortality rate for conjunctival melanoma is 25–26%. The treatment for conjunctival melanoma is surgical excision, after positive biopsy, which does not seem to enhance its lethality and may help avoid more drastic surgery. Exenteration of the orbit is sometimes necessary for a large melanoma that has invaded the orbit. However, this procedure does not improve the prognosis. The poor survival rate post-exenteration may suggest that metastasis has already occurred at the time of treatment, and confirmation of the extent of the disease at diagnosis is the most important factor to determine the outcome (Roque 2001). Brachytherapy and local chemotherapy (such as mitomycin C) are also used on local tumours after excision with good effect (Damato & Coupland 2009)

Concretions

These are small white to yellowish deposits, usually 1–3 mm in size, found in the lower or upper or both palpebral conjunctivae. Concretions can be seen singly or multiply, and are formed by the calcification of cell debris and conjunctival secretions within subconjunctival spaces. The patient is usually asymptomatic, unless the hard matter erodes through the overlying epithelium and causes irritation. Staining with fluorescein indicates protruding concretions; they will stain, while those remaining unexposed are unstained. Concretions that cause irritation can be removed with a sterile green needle after a drop of local anaesthetic, such as benoxinate or amethocaine. Prophylactic antibiotic ointment (such as chloramphenicol) may be given as a single dose to provide comfort and infection prophylaxis. The patient needs to know that they often recur.

Retention cysts

These are clear, fluid-filled cysts seen anywhere in the conjunctiva; they may be filled with lymphatic fluid or secretions from the glands of Krause or Wolfring (Figure 16.7). Patients are often asymptomatic; a large cyst causing irritation can be drained by piercing the conjunctiva with a sterile green needle after a drop of local anaesthetic.

These cysts have the tendency to refill so it is important for patients to perform ocular massage with topical lubricant after drainage. It is also a wise precaution to prescribe a topical antibiotic to minimise any infection.

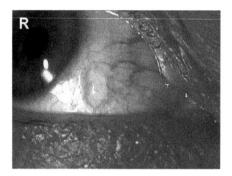

Figure 16.7 Conjunctival cyst.

Systemic conditions affecting the conjunctiva

Ocular rosacea

This condition is seen in patients with acne rosacea and occurs in people who are light skinned. On physical examination, patients will exhibit signs of erythema, pustules, and papules of the forehead, cheek and nose. Patients' main symptoms are bilateral chronic ocular irritation, foreign body sensation, hyperaemia of the eyelids and recurrent episodes of chalazion. The inferior cornea is involved, with superficial or deep vascularisation, and may extend into the stroma. The treatment consists of tetracycline 250mg, four times a day, with the dose being tapered off once relief of symptoms is obtained.

Ocular cicatricial pemphigoid

This is thought to be a type of hypersensitivity reaction with a slowly progressive cicatrising conjunctivitis. The course of the disease is characterised by periods of remission and exacerbation and it usually occurs in patients over the age of 55. On examination, there are signs of superficial punctate keratitis, inferior symblepharon, secondary bacterial conjunctivitis, entropion and trichiasis. Systemically, there are signs of scarring of the mucous membrane of the nose, mouth, pharynx, oesophagus and anus. Management consists of slit-lamp examination, work-up, conjunctival swabs, and mouth and nose examination. Treatment consists of systemic and local steroids and copious artificial lubricant. Surgical correction entropion and electrolysis of trichiasis may be considered.

Erythema multiforme major (Stevens–Johnson syndrome)

This is essentially a disease of the mucous membranes and skin resulting from acute hypersensitivity reaction. It may also be precipitated by drugs (such as tetracyclines, phenytoin or penicillin) or infectious agents (such as various bacteria, viruses, fungi and herpes). There is an acute onset of fever, red eye, rash and general malaise, and it is common in children and young adults. Signs include 'target' skin lesions (red-centred vesicles surrounded by a pale ring and then a red ring), bullous skin lesion on the hands and feet, and severe mucosal lesions on eyes and mouth (Bowling 2015). Again, corneal vascularisation, scarring of the conjunctiva, dry eyes, symblepharon, eyelid deformities, corneal ulcers, corneal perforation and endophthalmitis may develop.

Taking a good history is essential in order to determine the precipitating factor. Slit-lamp examination should include lid examination and examination of the fornices. Conjunctiva and corneal scrapings are taken if infection is suspected. Blood tests, such as electrolytes and a full blood count, are essential. Treatment consists of topical and systemic steroids, topical antibiotic and artificial lubricant. Nursing care includes support for patients and relatives and frequent oral toilet and general care of the patient's skin.

Reiter's syndrome

This is a triad of disease manifestations consisting of non-specific arthritis, conjunctivitis and urethritis. It is more common in men than women. There has been some success with treatment using oral tetracycline plus steroid for any systemic indications.

Systemic lupus erythematosus

This is a multisystem disorder that is thought to have an autoimmune aetiology, usually occurring in the third or fourth decade of life. Women are more susceptible than men. Signs and symptoms include a butterfly rash on the face, non-specific conjunctival findings such as hyperaemia, and fine papillae, keratitis and non-granulomatous inflammation. Treatment consists of aspirin, chloroquine and steroids. Uveitis is normally treated with topical steroids and cycloplegics.

Polyarteritis nodosa

This is arteritis of small and medium vessels caused by severe hypersensitivity, and occurs more frequently in men than women. There are many systemic findings such as nephritis, hypertension and pulmonary involvement. Ocular signs consist of episcleritis, scleritis and involvement of the retinal circulation (Snell & Lemp 1998).

References

Abelson, M.B., Leonardi, A. & Smith, L. (2002) The mechanisms, diagnosis and treatment of allergy. *Review of Ophthalmology.* **9**, 74–84.

Abelson, M.B., McLaughlin, J. (2012) VKC and the Allergy Rogues Gallery. *Review of Ophthalmology.* **12**, 36. http://www.reviewofophthalmology.com/content/d/therapeutic_topics/i/1777/c/32282/ (accessed 29 August 2016).

American Academy of Ophthalmology (2011) *Preferred practice pattern: conjunctivitis.* American Academy of Ophthalmology. http://www.aao.org (accessed 29 August 2016).

Azari, A.A. & Barney, N.P. (2013) Conjunctivitis: a systematic review of diagnosis and treatment. *Journal of the American Medical Association.* **310**(16), 1721–29.

Bignell, C. & Unemo, M. (2012) European guideline on the diagnosis and treatment of gonorrhoea in adults. *International Journal of STD & AIDS.* **24**, 85–92

Bowling, B. (2015) *Kanski's Clinical Ophthalmology, a systematic approach.* 8th edn. London: Elsevier.

British Association for Sexual Health and HIV (2015) *UK national guideline for the management of infection with Chlamydia Trachomatis.* http://www.bashh.org/documents/2015_UK_guideline_for_the_management_of__Chlamydia_trachomatis_final_12....pdf (accessed 29 August 2016).

Damato, B. & Coupland, S.E. (2009) An audit of conjunctival melanoma treatment in Liverpool. *Eye.* **23**(4), 801–9.

Health Protection Agency and British Infection Association (2012) *Management of infection guidance for primary care for consultation and local adaptation.* Health Protection Agency.

Kanski, J. & Bowling, B. (eds) (2011) *Clinical Ophthalmology.* 7th Edn. London: Elsevier

Knop, N. & Knop, E. (2000) Conjunctiva-associated lymphoid tissue in the human eye. *Investigative Ophthalmology & Visual Science.* **41**(6), 1270–79.

Matejcek, A. & Goldman, R. (2013) Treatment and prevention of Ophthalmia Neonatorum. *Canadian Family Physician.* **59**(11), 1187–90.

National Institute for Health and Care Excellence (2015) *Conjunctivitis – infective.* http://cks.nice.org.uk/conjunctivitis-infective#!scenario (accessed 29 August 2016).

O'Rahilly, R., Muller, F., Carpenter, S. & Swenson, R. 2008) *The Eye in Basic Human Anatomy.* http://www.dartmouth.edu/~humananatomy/part_8/chapter_46.html (accessed 30 September 2016).

Pavan-Langston, D. (2007) *Manual of Ocular Diagnosis and Therapy.* 6th edn. Boston, MA: Lippincott Williams and Wilkins.

Rhee, D.J. & Pyfer, M.F. (eds) (1999) *The Wills Eye Manual.* 3rd edn. Philadelphia, PA: Lippincott, Williams & Wilkins.

Roque, M.R. (2001) Conjunctival melanoma. http://emedicine.medscape.com/article/1191840 (accessed 29 August 2016).

Sheikh, A., Hurwitz, B., van Schayck, C., McLean, S. & Nurmatov, U. (2012) *Antibiotics versus placebo for acute bacterial conjunctivitis (Cochrane Review).* The Cochrane Library. Issue 9. John Wiley & Sons.

Shields, C.L. & Shields, J.A. (2004) Tumors of the conjunctiva and cornea. *Survey of Ophthalmology.* **49**(1), 3–24.

Snell, R.S. & Lemp, M.A. (1998) *Clinical Anatomy of the Eye.* 2nd edn. USA: Blackwell Science.

van Velzen, M., van de Vijver, D.A.M.C., van Loenen, F.B., Osterhaus, A.D.M.E., Remeijer, L. & Vejans, G.M.G.M. (2013) Acyclovir Prophylaxis Predisposes to Antiviral-Resistant Recurrent Herpetic Keratitis. *The Journal of Infectious Diseases.* **208**, 1359–65

Yanoff, M. & Duker, J.S. (2014) *Ophthalmology.* 4th edn. USA: Elsevier Saunders.

Figures 16.1 and 16.2 reprinted by permission of the International Centre for Eye Health (ICEH.)

CHAPTER SEVENTEEN

The cornea

Bradley Kirkwood

Introduction

It is essential for the cornea to maintain its clarity, as it is the 'window' that allows light rays to enter the eye. Despite its highly exposed position, the cornea (along with the tear film) acts as a robust defence system between the eye and the external environment. Optical properties and refraction rely on the maintenance of corneal shape and clarity. Even the smallest corneal change in the visual axis may result in visual distortion and disability for the patient.

Medical and surgical treatments of the cornea therefore aim to restore corneal transparency and improve functional vision. This chapter focuses on the anatomy and physiology of the cornea; some of the more common corneal diseases, disorders and dystrophies; diagnostic equipment for the cornea; and some of the surgical procedures currently used in corneal transplantation and keratoconus. The final section discusses the various keratorefractive procedures and keratoprosthetics that are currently employed.

Anatomy and physiology of the cornea

Optical properties and macroscopic anatomy

The normal cornea is made up of transparent and avascular tissue. The anterior corneal surface is covered by the tear film, and the posterior surface is directly bathed by the aqueous humour. The transitional zone between cornea and sclera is the richly vascularised limbus. The normal shape of the anterior corneal surface is convex and aspheric.

Externally, the cornea may appear round in shape but it is actually oval. Horizontally, the normal cornea measures 11–12mm, compared to 9–11mm vertically. This is due to the sclera extending over the corneal margin in the superior and inferior aspects. The central corneal thickness is approximately 0.52mm, and increases gradually toward the periphery, where it is about 0.7mm thick. The radius of curvature is between 7.5

and 8.0mm at the central 3mm optical zone of the cornea, where the surface is at its steepest and is almost spherical, to a variably less steep cornea in the periphery, giving the cornea a prolate shape. The refractive power of the cornea is 40–44 dioptres.

Microscopic anatomy and physiology

The tear film comprises three layers: lipid, aqueous and mucin. The cornea consists of three different cellular layers and two interfaces: epithelium, Bowman's layer, stroma, Descemet's membrane and endothelium. Components of the tear film and cornea, and within the layers of the cornea itself, interact with each other to maintain the integrity and function of the tissue. The individual layers are described below.

Tear film

The tear film is about 0.7mm thick and covers the surface of the cornea. The tear fluid consists of three layers. The most superficial is the lipid layer, which is produced by the meibomian glands and the glands of Zeis and Moll in the eyelids. The middle layer is the aqueous layer, produced by accessory lacrimal tissue and the lacrimal gland. The inferior layer is the mucin layer, which is derived from the secretion of goblet cells within the conjunctiva. More than 98% of the total volume of the tear is water. The tear film contains many biologically important factors, including electrolytes, glucose, immunoglobulins, lysozyme, albumin, and oxygen. Therefore, the tear film not only acts as a lubricant for the cornea, but also provides a source of nutrition, assists in the maintenance and repair of the corneal epithelium, and plays a vital part in providing an optical smooth surface for clear vision.

Corneal layers

The corneal epithelium is 50–60 μm thick and composed of two to three layers of superficial cells, two to three layers of 'wing' cells, and one layer of columnar basal cells. Only the basal cells have the ability to proliferate. The daughter cells gradually emerge to the anterior surface of the cornea, differentiating into wing cells and subsequently into superficial cells. This process can take up to 14 days, before the superficial cells are desquamated into the tear film. The outer surface layer of the superficial cells is composed of microplicae and microvilli, making their surface irregular. The tear film plays an important part in making the surface optically smooth by plugging the gaps.

Basal cells of corneal epithelium adhere to the basement membrane. The basement membrane is composed of two layers called lamina lucida and lamina densa, and adds strength to the membrane. Hemidesmosomes are located on the underside of the basal cells and are linked to anchoring fibrils. Anchoring fibrils penetrate the basement membrane and reach the stroma, where they form anchoring plaques. The health of this adhesion complex is critical in connecting the epithelium to Bowman's layer and anterior stroma.

Bowman's layer is 12µm thick and consists mainly of randomly arranged collagen fibres. Bowman's layer is considered the anterior portion of the corneal stroma and plays an important role in maintaining the epithelial structure. Bowman's layer does not regenerate after injury.

The stroma encompasses over 90% of the cornea and is crucial in maintaining its shape, strength and transparency. The stroma primarily consists of collagen fibres, keratocytes and proteoglycans. Corneal transparency relies on the regular arrangement of collagen fibres. Any disarray in the uniformity of the fixed interfibre distance, as in the case of stromal oedema or scarring, will result in a loss of corneal transparency.

There is some controversy about the presence of a distinct layer in the deep stroma, just anterior to Descemet's membrane (now known as Dua's layer or pre-Descemet stromal layer). This may be just regional stromal variation, rather than a distinct layer, and further clarification will undoubtedly come with time and further research.

Descemet's membrane is largely composed of collagen and is 7µm thick. It is firmly joined to the posterior surface of the stroma and does not regenerate following trauma.

The corneal endothelium comprises a single layer of cells that are hexagonal, uniform in shape and closely interdigitated. The most important physiological function of the endothelium is to regulate the water content of the stroma through active ion transport systems. Endothelial cells are unable to replicate, and therefore rely on neighbouring cells to enlarge and spread to cover a defective area. When the endothelial cell count decreases considerably, the endothelial transport capability becomes overwhelmed and corneal oedema results.

Innervation

The cornea is one of the most innervated structures in the body. Sensory innervation of the cornea occurs primarily through the ophthalmic branch of the trigeminal nerve (cranial nerve V). Nerve fibres penetrate the cornea in the peripheral stroma. As the fibres travel toward the central cornea, the axons become finer. Fibres also branch anteriorly to create a terminal subepithelial plexus. The nerve fibres lose their myelination soon after entering the cornea. Clinically, the loss of superficial epithelium exposes the nerve endings, which results in severe ocular pain.

Limbal stem cells

The centripetal movement of corneal epithelial cells during healing phases has been well demonstrated (described below). Limbal epithelial stem cells are located in 'limbal crypts' within the limbal palisades and are variably distributed around the limbus. Recent research suggests that there are also reservoirs of corneal stem cells located within the central and peripheral cornea as well (Yoon *et al.* 2014). These stem cells are responsible for normal homeostasis and repair of the corneal surface. Ocular injury and disease can result in a deficiency of these stem cells, and this is termed limbal stem cell deficiency. As a result, conjunctival epithelium migrates across the limbus, causing the cornea to become opaque, vascularised and inflamed. There is currently no definitive marker for limbal epithelial stem cells and this presents a challenge for identifying and sorting stem cells from a limbal biopsy (O'Callaghan & Daniels 2011).

Corneal abrasion healing phases

The processes involved in the healing of corneal epithelial wounds can be divided into three separate phases that are, in reality, part of a continuous process. These stages in epithelial healing can be described as:

- The latent phase, during which the movement of existing basal epithelial cells at the corneal wound margin occurs

- Cell migration and adhesion, when the epithelial cells spread across the wound area before mitosis commences, and extracellular matrix proteins (such as fibronectin and laminin) appear on the wound site surface to assist with epithelial adhesion

- Cell proliferation, which occurs until normal epithelial thickness is restored. An important prerequisite for stability of regenerated corneal epithelium is tight adhesion to the underlying stroma.

There are many factors that affect the healing process, including the size and depth of the wound, the quality of the tear film and the causative agent.

Slit-lamp examination

By using a slit-lamp biomicroscope, pathological processes in the cornea can be directly observed. Furthermore, the cornea is conveniently placed for observation with a slit lamp. Different lighting techniques can assist in the visualisation of corneal pathology and these techniques are discussed elsewhere in the book.

Corneal diagnostic instruments

Corneal diagnostic instruments enable the ophthalmic practitioner to carry out specialised methods of examination to yield valuable information for the diagnosis and treatment of corneal disease. The techniques discussed here will include keratometry, corneal topography, specular microscopy, confocal microscopy, pachymetry, pentacam and anterior segment optical coherence tomography.

Keratometry

This measures the radius of corneal curvature within a 4mm central optical zone. Such devices provide illuminated object mires that are reflected from the surface of the cornea, acting as a convex mirror. The radius of curvature of the anterior corneal surface is determined from four reflected points that are evaluated as two pairs. The keratometer determines the power and location of the steepest meridian and the power of the meridian 90° away; it is therefore useful in diagnosing and monitoring corneal astigmatism. It is also useful in diagnosis of steep or flat corneas. The disadvantage of the keratometry reading is that it only measures the central cornea.

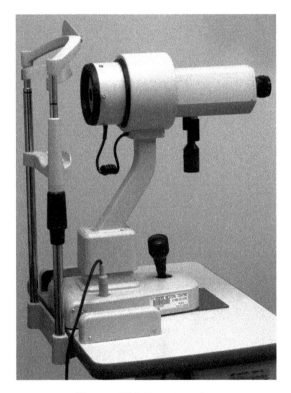

Figure 17.1 Keratometer.

Videokeratoscopy

Otherwise known as corneal topography, this provides overall mapping of the corneal shape through quantification and displays the map on a video screen. The videokeratoscope displays a colour-coded map for easy interpretation. The red or 'hot' colours depict abnormal corneal steepening. This is useful for diagnosis of corneal disorders and monitoring of both regular and irregular corneal astigmatism. Corneal topography is also used in preoperative and postoperative assessment for keratorefractive surgery.

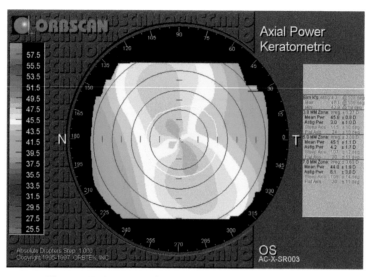

Figure 17.2 Corneal topography of astigmatism.

Specular microscopy

This produces highly magnified photography of the corneal endothelium. The specular microscope allows visual observation, examination and analysis of the number, size, shape and density of the endothelial cells. Corneal disorders, such as Fuchs' dystrophy, can be monitored with specular microscopy.

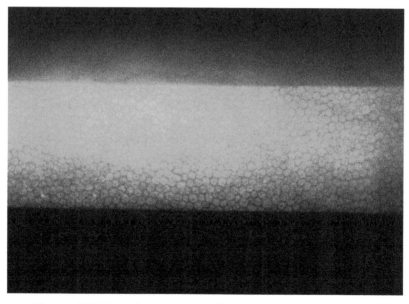

Figure 17.3 Specular micrograph of a normal endothelium.

Confocal microscopy

This is a non-invasive investigation that provides a high level of magnification and resolution. This offers the opportunity to study the different layers of the cornea at a cellular level, allowing any corneal pathology to be observed, measured and analysed over time.

Pachymetry

This is the process of measuring corneal thickness. Optical, ultrasonic and laser methods are available. A pachometer is the name given to the instrument. Pachymetry is used in preoperative assessment for keratorefractive surgery and tonometry, and can also be used when monitoring the function of the corneal endothelium.

Pentacam (Oculus, Germany)

This is an imaging instrument that utilises a 360° rotating Scheimpflug, non-contact camera to rapidly take multiple images of the cornea and anterior segment. The information captured is used to generate three-dimensional tomography and calculate measurements of the eye. Data for corneal topography (anterior and posterior surfaces), corneal wave front, corneal pachymetry, anterior chamber and lens analysis are displayed.

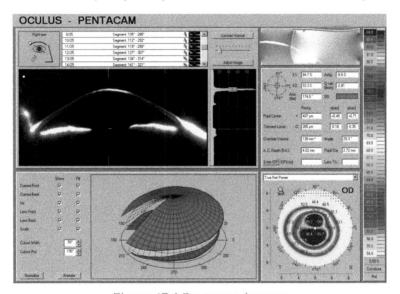

Figure 17.4 Pentacam images.

Anterior segment optical coherence tomography

This process creates high-resolution images of anterior segment structures in order to document and follow changes in the cornea, angle and anterior chamber. It uses low-coherence interferometry to produce cross-sectional tomographs. Images of the cornea are taken when fitting complex contact lenses, and when dealing with patients with keratoconus, corneal opacities and corneal dystrophies. Optical coherence tomography (OCT) images can also be useful in patients with blebs, intrastromal corneal rings, penetrating and lamellar corneal keratoplasties, iris pathology, anterior segment intraocular lenses and keratorefractive surgery.

Tear film disorders

When considering tear film disorders (see also Chapter 16), the ocular surface microenvironment of the eyelids, conjunctiva, cornea and the tear film need to be evaluated. Any alteration in this environment has the potential to cause a tear film disturbance. This section will focus on the tear film, the cornea and dry eye.

Dry eye

Dry eye is a condition that results in dryness of the ocular surface, broadly categorised as aqueous tear deficient and evaporative dry eye (Table 17.1). According to the Research Subcommittee of the International Dry Eye Workshop (2007), Sjögren's syndrome is an autoimmune condition that affects lacrimal and salivary glands. It is an example of aqueous tear deficiency. Other examples of aqueous tear deficiency (non-Sjögren's syndrome category) include lacrimal gland dysfunction and age-related dry eye. Evaporative dry eye can be intrinsic (as in meibomian gland dysfunction and reduced blink rate) or extrinsic (resulting from vitamin A deficiency, contact lens wear and ocular surface conditions).

Table 17.1 Classification of dry eye

Dry eye			
Aqueous deficient		Evaporative	
Sjögren's syndrome	Non-Sjögren's syndrome	Intrinsic	Extrinsic
• Primary	• Lacrimal gland disease / dysfunction • Reflex block • Systemic drugs	• Lipid deficient • Lid related • Reduced blink rate • Drug related	• Eye drop preservatives • Vitamin A deficiency • Contact lens related • Ocular surface change

Patients with dry eyes can present with an assortment of symptoms. The most common symptoms include foreign body sensation, burning, itching, light sensitivity and transient blurry vision. Dry eye disease is a chronic condition. The symptoms are exacerbated by environmental factors, such as humidity and air movement, which lead to increased tear evaporation. Also, the demands of certain visual tasks (such as driving, reading or using a computer/hand-held device for extended periods) reduce the blink reflex and aggravate dry eye symptoms. Ironically, patients can complain of excess tearing if the eye becomes so irritated that reflex tearing mechanisms are activated.

When diagnosing dry eye, the clinician relies upon the patient history, in conjunction with a decreased tear film break-up time and reduced Schirmer test (see Chapter 16) along with a careful slit-lamp examination of the ocular surface and eyelids. Fluorescein dye stains punctate epithelial erosions, particularly of the inferior cornea. The corneal epithelium may desquamate as filamentous threads (filamentary keratitis) (Figure 17.5). Rose bengal and lissamine green are diagnostic dyes that stain dead or devitalised epithelial cells, mucus and corneal filaments, all of which are associated with dry eyes.

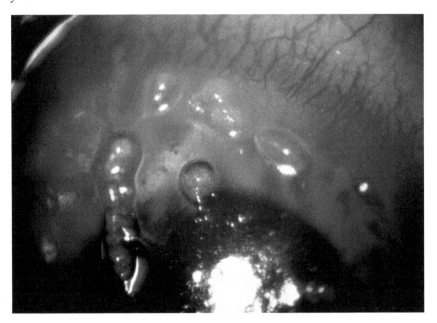

Figure 17.5 Filamentary keratitis.

Medical treatment for dry eye includes ocular surface lubrication in the form of drops, gels and ointments. These need to be used frequently in order to be therapeutic. Counselling on lifestyle changes to relieve dry eye symptoms is vital to improve quality of life. Treatment of the contributing eyelid or ocular surface inflammation is favourable. Eyelid hygiene, warm compresses, and possibly topical antibiotics are essential for chronic blepharitis and meibomian gland dysfunction. Higher dietary intake and oral supplementation of essential fatty acids, particularly omega-3, may be beneficial in the treatment of dry eye. Surgical treatment is in the form of temporary or permanent punctal occlusion to assist with tear preservation.

Nurses should remember that dry eye is a chronic condition that can often be controlled but not cured. Management of these patients is therefore commonly psychological. Nurses need to spend time counselling them, with careful explanation of the problem to assist with lifestyle changes to reduce the patient's complaints, frustrations and fears.

Corneal disorders

Microbial keratitis

Microbial keratitis is a sight-threatening ocular condition and can present in bacterial, fungal and protozoa forms. Bacterial and fungal keratitis are discussed in this section. Acanthamoeba keratitis, a protozoa form of corneal infection, is discussed in the contact lens section of this chapter (see p. 420). Microbial keratitis commonly occurs in compromised corneas – for instance, following trauma, contact lens wear and in cases of dry eyes. Clinical signs of corneal ulceration and stromal inflammation (infiltrate) are considered to be due to corneal infection until proven otherwise by negative microbial investigations.

Bacterial keratitis

Bacterial keratitis (Figure 17.6) can be caused by a wide variety of bacteria; however, the most common organisms include Staphylococcus species, Streptococcus species, Pseudomonas aeruginosa, Serratia species, Moraxella species, Enterobacteriaceae and Haemophilus influenzae (Keay *et al.* 2006, Daniell 2003, Coster 2002).

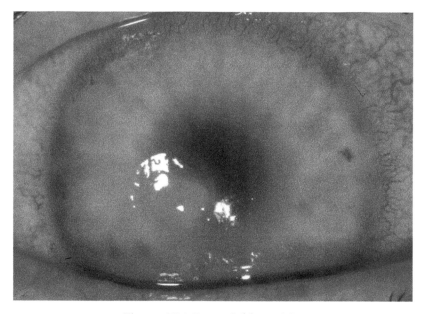

Figure 17.6 Bacterial keratitis.

When there is sufficient evidence following clinical examination to raise suspicions of a possible infectious aetiology, laboratory studies are required to identify the specific causative organism. Based on the features of clinical examination, results of laboratory investigation and knowledge of potential corneal pathogens, a therapeutic plan is initiated.

The choice of antibiotic for a patient with a corneal ulceration is based on the preference of the ophthalmologist. A combination of a fortified topical aminoglycoside (e.g. gentamicin 1%) and a first generation cephalosporin (e.g. cefazolin 5%) or monotherapy with a fluoroquinolone (e.g. ofloxacin) are possible options. The fluoroquinolones are more convenient to use but are not so effective against streptococci. Initially, topical antibiotics should be given frequently for the first 2–3 days and the clinical response should be evaluated daily for the first week, and then according to the clinical picture.

Fungal keratitis

Fungal keratitis is less common than bacterial keratitis but should be considered a differential diagnosis of any corneal infection. Fungal keratitis tends to be more common in hotter and tropical regions. Fungi from both filamentous and yeast organisms have been implicated in corneal infections. For the onset of filamentous fungal keratitis, commonly Fusarium solani and Aspergillus species, trauma most often occurs outdoors and involves plant matter (Bowling 2015). Yeast organism (Candida albicans) tends to occur in patients with chronic corneal disorders and immunosuppression (Bowling 2015). Clinically, ulcers have a feathery border, with the infiltrate extending beyond the epithelial defect. However, because it is clinically difficult to establish a diagnosis of fungal keratitis, the use of microbial investigation is extremely important.

Fungal ulcers are less responsive to medical therapy than bacterial ulcers, as topical antifungal preparations are relatively non-specific and drug penetration is limited. Natamycin and Miconazole drops are the drugs of choice. Topical corticosteroids are contraindicated in fungal keratitis. Debridement of the corneal epithelium can assist with the penetration of topical medication. Corneal perforations are common with fungal keratitis; when progression of the keratitis is noted, penetrating keratoplasty should therefore be performed.

Herpes simplex keratitis

Herpes simplex keratitis is a common condition affecting the cornea. Following primary infection, the virus travels up the sensory nerve to the trigeminal ganglion, where it resides in a latent state and can become active at any time. Reactivation triggers the virus particles to travel down the trigeminal nerves and shed onto the mucosal surface and then enter epithelial cells, creating recurrent infection.

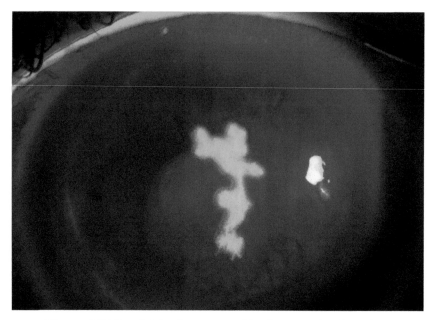

Figure 17.7 Dendritic ulcer caused by herpes simplex virus

The most common presentation of herpes simplex keratitis is the dendritic ulcer (Figure 17.7). The features of a dendritic ulcer include a branching, linear lesion with terminal bulbs and swollen epithelial borders that contain live virus. Although the diagnosis of primary and recurrent ocular herpes simplex virus infection relies on a thorough ophthalmic examination, viral polymerase chain reaction (PCR) or culture can help make a definitive diagnosis.

An enlarged dendritic ulcer that is no longer linear is referred to as a geographic ulcer (Figure 17.8). This lesion can be thought of as a widened dendritic ulcer. Like a dendritic ulcer, it is a true ulcer in that it is an epithelial lesion that extends through the basement membrane. Also, like a dendritic ulcer, it has swollen epithelial borders that contain live virus. If the corneal stroma is invaded by the virus, disciform or necrotic keratitis may occur.

Herpetic keratitis is treated with antiviral agents that impair viral replication. Acyclovir is effective in treating epithelial conditions. Other topical preparations available are ganciclovir, trifluridine and vidarabine. Oral antiviral medication, such as acyclovir, has also been shown to be effective for those patients with keratitis who have shown sensitivity to topical treatment. Gentle epithelial debridement may be performed to remove infectious virus before commencing antivirals.

The treatment of corneal stromal disease due to herpetic keratitis is aimed at reducing the stromal inflammation. This is done effectively with topical corticosteroids but is often used in conjunction with an antiviral, as topical steroids enhance viral replication in the epithelium.

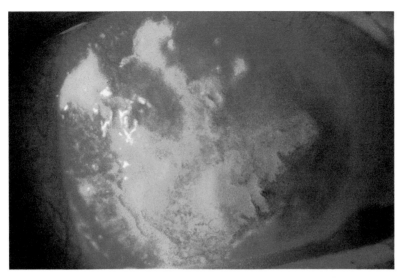

Figure 17.8 Geographic ulcer caused by herpes simplex virus

Peripheral corneal disease

Dellen

Dellen (Figure 17.9) may occur as an age-related change or secondary to other ocular abnormalities. Clinically, dellen are saucerlike depressions in the corneal surface. Although they may be idiopathic, they are more commonly found next to elevated areas of conjunctiva or conjunctival chemosis. Treatment with ocular lubricants or pressure patching will accelerate the healing process.

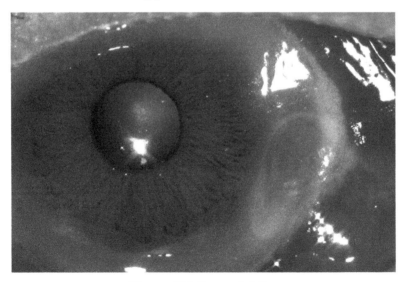

Figure 17.9 Corneal dellen

407

Marginal keratitis and phlyctenular keratitis

Marginal keratitis is most commonly caused by the Staphylococcus species, usually as a result of chronic blepharitis or blepharoconjunctivitis and is secondary to the host's antibody response to the staphylococcal antigen (Mozayeni & Lam 1998). Staphylococcal marginal keratitis begins with localised peripheral stromal infiltrates, which tend to occur along the oblique meridians (i.e. the 2, 4, 8 and 10 o'clock positions). The infiltrates are typically separated from the limbus by a thin strip of clear cornea, measuring 1–2mm in width. They may be single or multiple and tend to spread, paralleling the contour of the limbus. Topical corticosteroids, in combination with an antibiotic, are the mainstay in treating marginal keratitis. Warm compresses, eyelid hygiene, and a topical antibiotic applied to the eyelid margin are all helpful in controlling eyelid inflammation.

Phlyctenular keratitis is commonly reported as a disease of children and young adults. It is known as an inflammatory disorder leading to corneal nodules, most commonly at the limbus (Figure 17.10). It is believed to be a form of T-cell mediated (i.e. type IV) hypersensitivity caused by an antigen located in the microbe (Robin *et al.* 1998). Eyelid hygiene, with a topical antibiotic-corticosteroid ointment, is the recommended management regime. The association between phlyctenular disease and tuberculous and chlamydial infection has also been described.

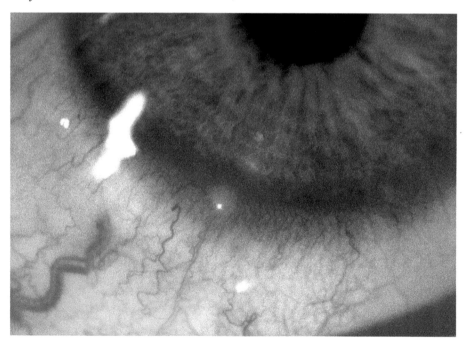

Figure 17.10 Phlycten

Corneal degenerations

Arcus senilis

Corneal arcus senilis is a degenerative change involving lipid deposition in the peripheral cornea. The lipid deposition starts clinically as a grey to yellow arc, first in the inferior cornea and then the superior cornea. As the deposition progresses, the arcs meet forming a complete ring. Corneal arcus has no visual significance, and thus no treatment is necessary. However, patients under the age of 40 with corneal arcus have an increased risk of coronary artery disease and should be evaluated for hyperlipidemia.

Lipid keratopathy

Lipid keratopathy is a collection of yellow or cream-coloured lipids containing cholesterol, neutral fats and glycoproteins deposited in the superficial cornea, usually in areas of vascularised corneal scars.

Band keratopathy

Band keratopathy is a corneal disorder characterised by the deposition of calcium salts both in Bowman's layer and the subepithelial. Clinically, it usually begins at the corneal periphery in the 3 and 9 o'clock positions; then a complete band, from limbus to limbus, may form in later stages. As the calcific deposition progresses, it becomes white and chalky and can break through the epithelial, causing ocular irritation. Treatment includes chelation with application of ethylenediaminetetraacetic acid (EDTA) and excimer laser phototherapeutic keratectomy to clear the visual axis and improve the patient's vision.

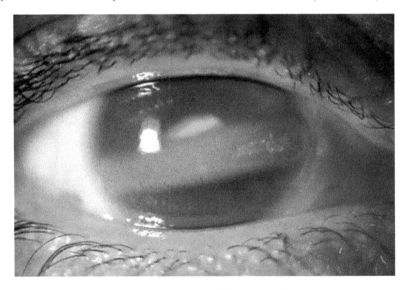

Figure 17.11 Band keratopathy

Corneal dystrophies

Corneal dystrophies can be present in any layer of the cornea. In general, corneal dystrophies are categorised into epithelial, Bowman's layer, stromal and endothelial. Diagnosis can be made with examination, clinical appearance and familial tendencies.

Anterior basement membrane dystrophy, also known as map-dot-fingerprint dystrophy, is the most common epithelial corneal dystrophy. It is bilateral, autosomal dominant dystrophy. On examination with the slit-lamp, grey patches, microcysts and/or fine lines are seen in the central epithelial layer. It is an abnormality of epithelial basement membrane, anchoring itself to Bowman's layer. As a result, patients are prone to spontaneous recurrent corneal erosions.

The treatment is the same as for recurrent corneal erosion, whether traumatic or dystrophic. It firstly consists of simple lubricating ointment at bedtime for at least 2 months. Failing this, a bandage contact lens may be used to help protect the corneal epithelium from the lids while healing; anterior stromal puncture may be instigated as a way of tacking down the abnormal area, mechanical debridement of the loosened epithelium and excimer laser phototherapeutic keratectomy may also be used to aid in the management of these patients.

Reis-Buckler's corneal dystrophy

This is an autosomal dominant hereditary disorder of Bowman's layer. The disorder presents during early childhood and affects both eyes equally. Clinical findings include opacification of the central corneal surface, which can have a honeycomb or geographic configuration. In the later stages of the disorder, scarring can occur, which reduces the vision significantly and these patients have a predisposition to recurrent corneal erosions. Treatment options include excimer laser phototherapeutic keratectomy or corneal transplantation to restore vision.

Granular dystrophy

This is a bilateral corneal disorder characterised by the deposition of small, discrete, sharply demarcated, greyish-white opacities in the anterior central stroma (Figure 17.12). It is transmitted as an autosomal dominant trait that appears in the first or second decade of life. Visual impairment is rare before the fifth decade and usually occurs secondary to the opacification of the intervening stroma. Most patients with granular dystrophy do not require treatment. If vision is markedly reduced, surgical intervention can be considered. Surgical management varies, based on the depth and extent of the stromal lesions. The surgical approach has traditionally been penetrating keratoplasty, although anterior lamellar keratoplasty techniques can be be considered as alternative surgical options.

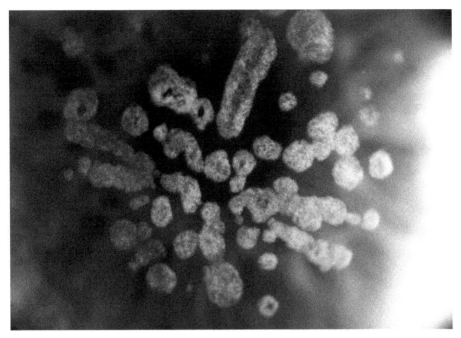

Figure 17.12 Granular dystrophy

Macular corneal dystrophy

This is characterised by bilateral corneal opacities resulting from intracellular and extracellular deposits within the corneal stroma. It is inherited as an autosomal recessive trait. Vision is usually severely affected by the time the patient reaches their twenties or thirties. In the early stages of the disease, slit-lamp examination demonstrates a ground-glass-like haze in the central and superficial stroma. With progression of the dystrophy, small, multiple, grey-white opacities, with irregular borders, are seen. These opacities are more superficial and prominent in the central cornea, and deeper and more discrete in the periphery. Penetrating keratoplasty or anterior lamellar keratoplasty techniques are the surgical modalities of choice.

Lattice dystrophy

This is a bilateral condition that commonly appears in the first decade of life. It is inherited as an autosomal dominant trait. Early features of lattice dystrophy include discrete ovoid or round subepithelial opacities, anterior stromal white dots, and small refractile filamentary lines. With time, patients may also develop a diffuse central anterior stromal haze which reduces their visual acuity. With further progression, the lesions can appear as thicker, radially oriented branching lines, giving a lattice appearance (Figure 17.13). Penetrating keratoplasty has a high rate of success in these patients, or anterior lamellar keratoplasty techniques may be employed.

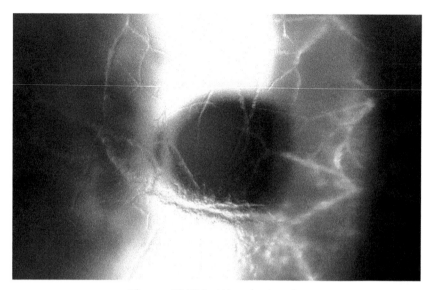

Figure 17.13 Lattice dystrophy

Fuchs' endothelial dystrophy

This has an autosomal dominant inheritance pattern with a late onset and slow progression, rarely becoming symptomatic before the age of 50. It is a bilateral process but may be markedly asymmetrical. The initial manifestation of Fuchs' dystrophy is central corneal guttata. The guttata appear as dark spots on the posterior corneal surface by direct illumination. Pigment dusting is also commonly present on the endothelium.

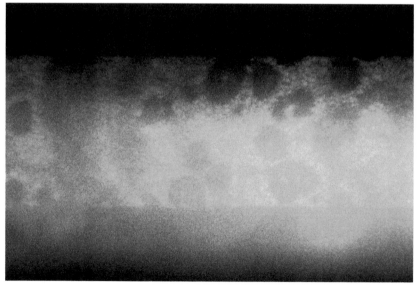

Figure 17.14 Specular micrograph of Fuchs' endothelial dystrophy

Specular microscopy may be helpful in diagnosing this condition (Figure 17.14). Patients in an early stage of the disease are not symptomatic. Progressive stromal oedema results in a ground-glass opacification, with marked thickening of the central cornea. Early medical management may include topical hypertonic saline drops, which may assist with reducing corneal oedema. Surgical management is evolving, with posterior lamellar keratoplasty being more frequently utilised to treat this condition when the corneal stroma and epithelium are healthy. If stromal scarring or epithelial changes exist, penetrating keratoplasty is employed.

Corneal ectasia

The non-inflammatory ectatic diseases of the cornea discussed in this section are keratoconus, pellucid marginal degeneration and keratoglobus. Keratoconus is the most common corneal ectasia. Corneal thinning is a hallmark of these ectatic diseases.

Keratoconus

Keratoconus is a clinical term used to describe a condition in which the cornea assumes a conical shape because of thinning of the stroma and subsequent protrusion with irregular astigmatism. Keratoconus usually occurs bilaterally, but can be asymmetrical. The onset occurs at about the age of puberty and typically progresses in a variable fashion over a period of 10 to 20 years. There is a familial predisposition to keratoconus development but cases of keratoconus are sporadic. The exact role of heredity in the development of keratoconus has not been clearly established to date, and genetic studies are currently being conducted. Keratoconus is associated with systemic conditions such as Down's syndrome and atopy.

Clinically, patients have a progression of myopia with associated irregular astigmatism. Measurement of corneal topography is valuable when diagnosing and monitoring this condition (Figure 17.15). Munson's sign is visible bulging of the lower lid when the patient looks down and is indicative of keratoconus in the later stages (Figure 17.16). Slit-lamp signs include a deposition of iron in Bowman's layer around the base of the cone, called a Fleischer ring. Also at the level of Bowman's layer, a series of fine, vertical, parallel 'stress' lines at the apex of the cone may be noted, called Vogt's striae. In very advanced cases of keratoconus, a condition called corneal hydrops may occur. This is the result of a tear in Descemet's membrane, which allows fluid into the stroma, creating an opaque cornea.

Early management of keratoconus involves spectacles for the correction of myopia and astigmatism. Rigid gas-permeable or mini-scleral contact lenses are used when spectacles become ineffective. Surgical treatment options for keratoconus involves two

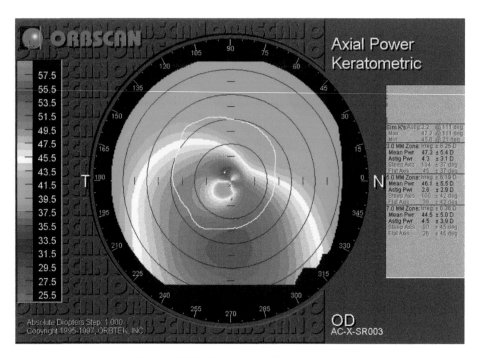

Figure 17.15 Orb scan of keratoconus

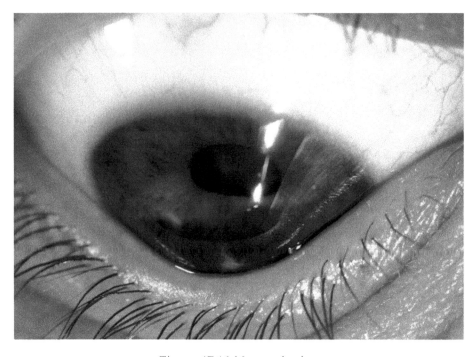

Figure 17.16 Munson's sign

important goals: slowing or halting progression, and improving vision. For progressive changes, corneal collagen cross-linking (CXL) has been shown to be beneficial in slowing advancement (Wittig-Silva *et al.* 2014). The procedure uses ultraviolet (UV) light and riboflavin to strengthen the stromal collagen. Riboflavin releases free radicals in the stroma when excited by UV exposure. This causes a cross-linking formation between the amino acids on the collagen chains, producing an increase in the spacing between collagen fibrils and a 'strengthening' effect. If the patient's central corneal thickness is less than 400µm, CXL should be avoided because of the known risks of endothelial damage (Dahl *et al.* 2012).

Intrastromal corneal ring segments (ICRS) have been shown to be effective in treating keratoconus (Poulsen & Kang 2015). Initially developed to treat myopia, these polymethylmethacrylate plastic corneal inserts are available in various arc lengths, thicknesses and designs. INTACS and Kerarings are examples of these devices. They are designed to induce a geometrical change in the central corneal curvature, thereby reducing the refractive error and optical aberrations and improving vision. The devices themselves are inserted into corneal stromal tunnels that can be made with a manual technique or by using a femtosecond laser. A significant advantage of ICRS is the procedure's reversibility.

Corneal transplantation, in the form of either penetrating keratoplasty or deep anterior lamella keratoplasty, is reserved for advanced disease when visual acuity has reached unacceptable levels.

Pellucid marginal degeneration

Pellucid marginal degeneration is a bilateral, inferior, peripheral corneal disorder characterised by a band of thinning extending from the 4 to the 8 o'clock position. The area of thinning is usually found 1–2mm central to the inferior limbus. Patients with this condition usually come for treatment between the second and fifth decades of life with complaints of blurred vision resulting from irregular astigmatism. The abnormal corneal contour induces a gross shift in the axis of astigmatism. Management is similar to keratoconus, with contact lenses or corneal surgery.

Keratoglobus

Keratoglobus is a rare, congenital, bilateral disorder characterised by the entire cornea protruding from generalised thinning, most marked in the periphery. The cornea tends to be of normal or slightly increased diameter. Management of keratoglobus follows the same principles as management of keratoconus. However, due to the extreme shape and thinning of the cornea, keratoglobus presents extreme challenges for both the contact lens practitioner and the surgeon.

Miscellaneous keratopathies

Recurrent corneal erosion

Recurrent corneal erosion is invariably caused when a sudden, sharp, abrading injury, such as a fingernail, vegetable matter or paper cut, causes a corneal abrasion. The injury heals clinically, leaving no evidence of damage. However, secondary breakdown can occur at any time following the injury, when the basal cell of the epithelium loses its adhesion to the basement membrane, which detaches and becomes loose and unstable. Anterior corneal dystrophies, diabetic patients and tear film abnormalities are some other causes of recurrent corneal erosions. It can also occur after excimer laser photorefractive keratectomy.

Classically, recurrent corneal erosion occurs at the time of awakening. During the night the pressure of the eyelid on the dry epithelium produces adhesion to the epithelium which is stronger than the adhesion of the epithelium to the basement membrane. Upon awakening, opening of the eyelid therefore separates away the epithelium. Each episode causes a variable amount of ocular pain, tearing and photophobia.

Treatment of corneal erosion aims to promote epithelial regeneration and maintain an intact ocular surface for long enough to allow reformation of the normal basement membrane complexes responsible for tight adhesion. Application of a lubricating ointment at night for at least 2 months may provide a moisture barrier between the corneal epithelium and eyelids. This may help to reduce the friction on the cornea. Debridement of abnormal epithelium may be required when it is loose. Bandage contact lens therapy is designed to relieve pain and to protect loosely adherent epithelium from the abrasive action of the eyelids so that epithelial healing can occur. Surgical treatment includes anterior stromal puncture, superficial keratectomy and excimer laser phototherapeutic keratectomy.

Bullous keratopathy

Bullous keratopathy occurs when the cornea decompensates as a result of failing endothelial cells. This can be the result of trauma, corneal endothelial dystrophy or following cataract surgery and artificial lens implantation (known as pseudophakic bullous keratopathy). As the endothelial cells reduce, the cornea swells and affects the patient's vision. This corneal swelling is also painful.

Commonly, patients with bullous keratopathy experience vision symptoms that are worse in the morning but improve as the day progresses. This occurs because the excess fluid evaporates into the air along with the tears.

The main goals in the management of bullous keratopathy are to reduce swelling, provide comfort and restore useful vision. Saline eye drops can assist with reducing some corneal swelling. A contact lens may be used temporarily for comfort, but it will not improve vision. The mainstay treatment is corneal transplantation, with posterior lamellar keratoplasty being more frequently utilised to treat this condition when the corneal stroma and epithelium are healthy. If stromal scarring or epithelial changes exist, penetrating keratoplasty is used.

Wilson's disease

Wilson's disease is an autosomal recessive disorder characterised by the generalised accumulation of copper in the blood and urine. The Kayser-Fleischer ring is a valuable diagnostic sign. The ring is golden-brown to blue-green, situated in Descemet's membrane, with characteristic progression first superiorly and inferiorly, then extending the full circumference in the peripheral cornea. This can be best appreciated by standard slit-lamp biomicroscopy.

Vortex keratopathy

Certain systemic medication can cause corneal epithelial changes. Deposits are bilateral, golden or grey in colour and appear in a whorl-like pattern. These changes, known as vortex keratopathy, seldom affect the patient's vision and enter the corneal epithelium via the perilimbal vasculature. Amiodarone and chloroquine are examples of systemic medication causing vortex keratopathy. Clinicians should also be mindful of vortex keratopathy associated with Fabry's disease, a hereditary disease involving abnormal storage of lipids that can cause kidney and cardiac problems.

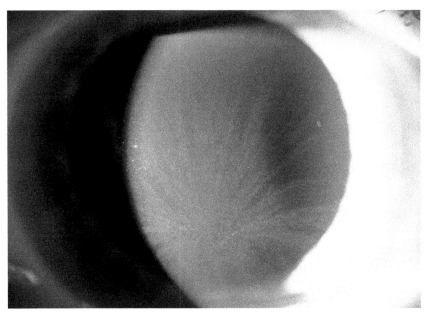

Figure 17.17 Vortex keratopathy.

Exposure keratopathy

Exposure keratopathy often follows a seventh nerve palsy or is associated with dysthyroid ophthalmopathy, leading to exposure of the inferior third of the cornea and localised drying. Small to moderate epithelial defects develop and increase the risk of corneal infection. Nocturnal lagophthalmos may also occur when the patient sleeps with their eyelids open, resulting in corneal exposure.

Management of exposure keratopathy includes artificial tears and lubricating ointments, occlusive patches and shields, and lid taping as temporary solutions. Partial or complete tarsorrhaphies should be considered if prolonged insult to the ocular surface is evident or anticipated.

Neurotrophic keratopathy

Neurotrophic keratopathy occurs in the absence of corneal sensitivity. The most common causes for corneal anaesthesia are post-herpes simplex or zoster corneal infections and damage to the trigeminal nerve through surgery or tumour. The trophic corneal defects can vary in severity, ranging from punctate epithelial staining to larger recalcitrant epithelial defects characterised by heaped, rolled edges of grey epithelial cells. These epithelial defects increase the risk of corneal infection and potential stromal melting. Although not fully understood, it appears that corneal sensation is essential for maintenance of healthy epithelial cells.

Management of neurotrophic keratopathy is directed towards preserving corneal integrity with artificial tears, lubricating ointments, occlusive patches and lid taping as temporary solutions. Partial or complete lid tarsorrhaphy is considered if prolonged insult to the ocular surface is evident.

Corneal disorders associated with contact lenses

Various types of contact lenses are available, including rigid gas permeable (RGP), scleral lenses and conventional soft contact lenses (extended wear and disposable). Patients who wear contact lenses are routinely placing foreign bodies on their corneas and ocular surface, which alters their normal anatomy and physiology. In most circumstances, any complication from contact lenses will resolve with discontinued use. Two of the more common corneal complications from contact lenses are either toxic or hypoxic changes. Contact lens-associated microbial keratitis is a potentially sight-threatening condition and is an ocular emergency that requires urgent management. Pseudomonas aeruginosa is the most commonly recovered causative organism in contact lens-related disease (Stapleton & Carnt 2012).

Toxic

Chemicals used in disinfection systems and, to a lesser degree, preservatives used in cleaning solutions can produce subepithelial opacifications similar to those seen in adenoviral keratoconjunctivitis. Inadvertent instillation of cleaning and disinfection solutions can damage the epithelium, producing diffuse epithelial staining. Typically, lenses are placed in the eye with cleaning or distinfecting solution still on the lens. This causes immediate pain, redness, tearing and photophobia. Diffuse punctate staining defects, conjunctival injection and irritative symptoms usually resolve within 1 or 2 days of lens removal. Subepithelial opacities are treated with topical corticosteroids.

Hypoxic

Contact lens wear decreases the amount of oxygen reaching the cornea. The resulting hypoxia can have the acute effect of epithelial cell death or may cause chronic changes to the superficial cornea. If acute hypoxia compromises epithelial metabolism, the epithelium becomes oedematous and eventually desquamates. In the early stages, oedema causes blurred vision; this is followed by pain, redness and photophobia. Subepithelial opacities are also seen in chronic corneal hypoxia that comprises clumps of polymorphonuclear leukocytes and mononuclear cells. Soft lenses are particularly prone to causing superficial, peripheral corneal neovascularisation called pannus (Figure 17.18).

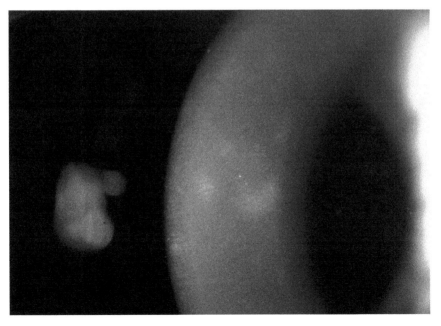

Figure 17.18 Contact lens-induced hypoxia

Corneal infection

Corneal infection is potentially the most devastating complication of contact lens wear. When clinical suspicion of corneal infection is high, the lesion should be scraped promptly for stains and cultures, and treatment should be initiated without delay. The mainstay of treatment is frequent dosage with topical broad-spectrum fortified antibiotics, modified by the results of the smears and culture results.

Two potentially sight-threatening pathogens should be considered until proven otherwise by microbial culture. The first is Pseudomonas aeruginosa (Figure 17.19), an aggressive gram-negative pathogen that has the potential to progress from a corneal ulcer to an abscess and corneal perforation within 48 hours if not treated properly. Intensive topical therapy with aminoglycoside (usually gentamicin), fortified with a cephalosporin, or monotherapy with a fluoroquinolone (usually ciprofloxacin), are generally the treatments of choice.

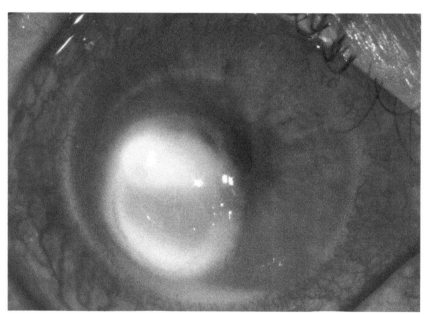

Figure 17.19 Bacterial keratitis caused by Pseudomonas aeruginosa

The second pathogen is Acanthamoeba keratitis (Figure 17.20), a ubiquitous, protozoa found in water, soil and air samples. The organism exists in two forms, a motile trophozoite and a double-walled cyst form, making eradication of this organism difficult. Acanthamoeba cysts are resistant to amoebacidal eye drops such as propamidine (Brolene) and can lie dormant for months and possibly years. Propamidine is often combined with chlorhexidine or polyhexamethylene biguanide in order to treat the cysts. Hourly treatment is needed initially and is then reduced in response to treatment. Clinical response may take 2 weeks and the total duration of therapy is a minimum of 3 weeks and perhaps up to 12 months. The clinician should have a high degree of suspicion of Acanthamoeba in any contact lens wearer with a keratitis and should culture appropriately. The pain associated with Acanthamoeba keratitis often appears out of proportion to the findings.

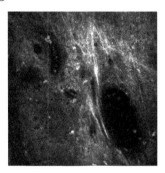

Figure 17.20 Acanthamoeba within the corneal stroma

Healthcare professionals need to remember that counselling and fully educating patients who wear contact lenses is imperative. This includes providing advice on personal hygiene, correct cleaning/disinfecting techniques, and wearing the specific lenses according to the product recommendations. Triaging skills may be utilised to give a high priority ophthalmology appointment for patients with contact lens complications.

Corneal surgery

Corneal transplantation has been carried out for many years, with the first corneal transplant being performed in 1906 by Dr Eduard Zirm. Since then, instrumentation and eye banking techniques have improved dramatically, along with the success of corneal transplantation. The main reasons why corneal transplantation is performed are, in order of prevalence: optical (to improve vision); therapeutic (to relieve pain); structural (to manage corneal thinning or perforation); and cosmetic (to restore a normal appearance) (Bowling 2015). Keratoconus is the most common reason for corneal transplantation, followed by bullous keratopathy, failed previous graft and Fuchs' dystrophy (Williams *et al.* 2012, Coster 2002).

Penetrating keratoplasty

Penetrating keratoplasty (PK) is the most common form of corneal transplantation. This refers to the surgical replacement of a full-thickness 'button' of the host cornea with a donor cornea, which is then sutured in place. Outcomes are typically excellent early after PK but are less satisfactory in the longer term. Prospective, long-term penetrating corneal graft survival is 87% at 1 year, though the survival rate drops to 46% at 15 years postoperatively (Kirkwood & Kirkwood 2010). Endothelial cell counts after PK continue to reduce for many years following the surgery with 70% loss reported after 5 years (Kirkwood & Kirkwood 2010). The likelihood of a successful penetrating keratoplasty reduces if there is corneal vascularisation, glaucoma, active anterior uveitis and previous graft failures.

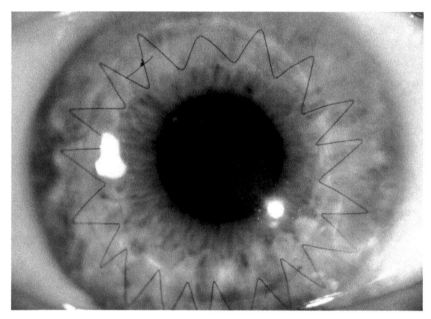

Figure 17.21 Penetrating keratoplasty

Postoperative care includes educating the patient to recognise any signs or symptoms of graft complications and the importance of seeking specialist medical assistance promptly. Long-term topical corticosteroids are maintained to help reduce any immune response.

Complications include a wound leak that may require resuturing, and loose or broken sutures requiring removal as they may precipitate a rejection episode (Figure 17.22); glaucoma and recurrence of original disease may also occur. Corneal graft rejection can occur at any stage following PK. It presents as an increase in ocular inflammation with increasing corneal oedema. Treatment of graft rejection comprises increasing dosage of topical corticosteroids and then, as the process reverses, the frequency can be reduced. Primary graft failure can also occur when the endothelium of the graft is not functioning. The graft is replaced if it does not clear within the first 2 weeks following surgery.

Postoperative graft astigmatism is the most frequent complication following PK. Regular astigmatism of less than 5 dioptres can be corrected with glasses or contact lenses. Higher degrees of astigmatism cause severe image degradation and can be reduced with intraocular lenses, keratorefractive surgery or incisional surgery.

More recently, femtosecond pulsed laser has been introduced for the preparation of donor and host tissue in PK. The femtosecond laser technology allows individual sizes and geometrically complex shapes for PK in a safe and precise fashion to maximise the surface area of the wound incision. Several preliminary studies have reported on the outcomes of femtosecond laser penetrating keratoplasty using top hat, conventional and zig zag wound configurations (Kirkwood & Kirkwood 2010). To date, this technique of PK has shown advantages including a more stable graft-host junction (resulting in reduced astigmatism) and faster wound healing (giving earlier visual recovery). However, long term results, particularly in relation to the endothelium, are not yet known.

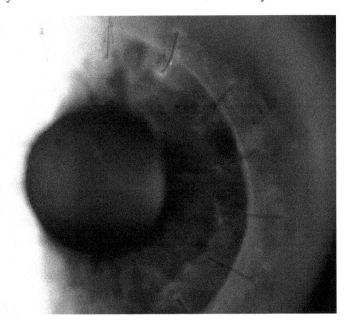

Figure 17.22 Loose corneal suture

Anterior lamellar keratoplasty

Over the last decade, there has been a noted increase in the use of lamellar keratoplasty in numerous countries. Surgical techniques such as anterior lamellar keratoplasty and deep anterior lamellar keratoplasty have emerged as alternatives to conventional pentetrating keratoplasty. Two general indications for lamellar keratoplasty are optical and structural. (Anterior lamellar keratoplasty and deep anterior lamellar keratoplasty have some distinct advantages over penetrating keratoplasty.) Firstly, lamellar keratoplasty is an extraocular procedure and therefore avoids the potential complication of endophthalmitis. Secondly, as the endothelium is not transplanted, graft rejection is significantly decreased.

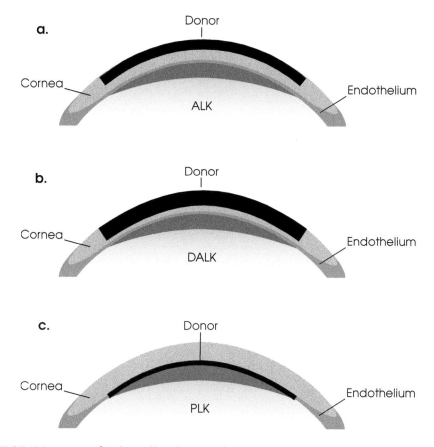

Figure 17.23 Diagram of 3 lamellar keratoplasty techniques in a cross sectional view. (a) ALK, Anterior lamellar keratoplasty: the recipient anterior corneal stroma is excised and a donor lamellar disc (black area) is transplanted and sutured in place. (b) DALK, Deep anterior lamellar keratoplasty: the recipient anterior corneal stroma is excised down to Descemet's membrane and a donor lamellar disc (black area) is transplanted and sutured in place. (c) PLK, posterior lamellar keratoplasty: the recipient Descemet's membrane is excised and a posterior lamellar disc (black area) consisting of posterior stroma, Descemet's membrane and endothelium is transplanted and positioned with an air bubble.

The surgical technique is technically more difficult to perform. It involves a partial-thickness 'button' of the host cornea with a donor cornea, which is then sutured in place. ALK can be sub-classified into two procedures, based on the depth of stromal dissection: ALK with dissection depth less than one-third or 160μm; and deep anterior lamellar keratoplasty with a dissection depth greater than one-third or 160μm. In both instances, Descemet's membrane and the endothelium remain intact. Figures 17.23a and 17.23b show how the different lamellar transplant techniques vary and which part of the cornea is replaced.

The most common indications for ALK are optical degradation followed by structural anomalies. This procedure is often performed for anterior stromal scars from various aetiologies, corneal ectatic conditions such as keratoconus, and stromal dystrophies that spare Descemet's membrane and the corneal endothelium.

Deep anterior lamellar keratoplasty (DALK) is known as a surgical procedure for removing the whole of the corneal stroma, leaving only the Descemet's membrane and endothelium. A number of different techniques are being used for DALK to facilitate separation of Descemet's membrane from the corneal stroma. Ultimately, the visual result of DALK depends on the ability to maintain clear interfaces between the tissues. With the DALK technique, there is an inherent risk of intraoperative Descemet's membrane rupture and perforation requiring conversion to PK. Other complications noted with DALK include interface lamellar haze, epithelial ingrowth and postoperative double anterior chamber formation, due to breaks in Descemet's membrane. Epithelial, subepithelial and stromal rejection can occur occasionally, but respond well to topical corticosteroid therapy.

Postoperative care includes protecting the eye from trauma and infection. Topical corticosteroids are tapered and ceased sooner than following penetrating keratoplasty.

Posterior lamellar keratoplasty

This form of PK is used in patients with endothelial dysfunction such as Fuchs' endothelial dystrophy and bullous keratopathy. With this form of corneal transplantation, a donor posterior corneal button or 'lenticule', including donor posterior corneal stroma, Descemet's membrane and corneal endothelium, is used for selective replacement of diseased corneal endothelium. The procedure is closed eye surgery, performed through scleral, limbal or corneal incision, where the donor lenticule (~150μm thick) is inserted carefully through the pocket incision and then held in place with an air bubble rather than fixation sutures (see Figure 17.23c).

The technique of removing the diseased Descemet's membrane and endothelium by 'stripping' is known as 'descemetorhexis'. The donor tissue used to be manually prepared but this procedure was subsequently replaced by automated microkeratome-assisted donor tissue dissection. This adaptation introduced the term Descemet stripping automated endothelial keratoplasty (DSAEK).

The procedure was further developed by selectively transplanting only Descemet's membrane and the endothelium – hence the name Descemet membrane endothelial keratoplasty (DMEK). Femtosecond laser has been employed to prepare the endothelial graft technique in a modification to the DSAEK procedure. Contraindications for PLK include any anterior corneal scarring or opacity affecting vision. In these cases, PK, ALK or DALK are indicated.

The benefits of DSEK, DSAEK and DMEK, over PK, include a better quality of vision, a more comfortable postoperative period and quicker visual rehabilitation. Little or no induced astigmatism and spherical error (slight hyperopic shift due to the concave shape of the graft decreasing the power of the cornea) have been reported postoperatively. Average reported visual acuity at 3–6 months has been 20/40 or 6/12 (Price & Price 2007). This postoperative visual acuity compares favourably with PK. However, few cases reach visual acuity of 6/7.5 (20/25) or better. One possible explanation for this is the stroma-to-stroma interface causing subclinical stromal interface disturbances. Stable visual recovery is much quicker than PK with high gains initially, and a lack of graft and suture-induced astigmatism. Reported complications following PLK include partial or complete graft dislocation, endothelial rejection, primary graft failure and postoperative glaucoma.

Despite not all ophthalmologists performing corneal transplantation, healthcare professionals should be familiar with the different techniques and postoperative complications because patients do not always return to their corneal surgeons when problems arise and many of these problems require immediate intervention to save the graft. Nurses and healthcare workers may also be called upon to provide preoperative and postoperative counselling and education for patients.

Keratorefractive surgery

As the cornea is responsible for two-thirds of the refraction of light rays in the eye, a number of surgical procedures have been introduced to reduce or eliminate refractive errors by altering the shape of the cornea. Keratorefractive procedures aim to flatten or shorten a myopic eye, steepen or lengthen a hypermetropic eye, and flatten or neutralise the steep meridian of astigmatism. Different procedures are able to correct varying amounts of myopia, hypermetropia and astigmatism. In general, the further the amount of correction a patient requires away from the ideal range, the less likelihood of a highly accurate final refractive outcome.

Incisional, photoablative and photothermal surgical procedures will be briefly described below; also included is a short discussion on wavefront technology and its role in photoablative surgery. A comprehensive discussion of the procedures, the exact theory and biomechanics behind incisional and laser–tissue interactions is beyond the scope of this chapter.

Incisional

Radial keratotomy (RK) is a refractive procedure to reduce a small amount of myopia. Creating radial incisions of approximately 90% thickness in the peripheral cornea with a specially designed diamond blade flattens the central cornea and reduces myopia. The advantages of RK, compared to other refractive procedures, include inexpensive instrumentation and a relatively quick recovery of vision with minimal discomfort. Disadvantages include permanent corneal weakening, fluctuating vision, glare and progressive hypermetropic shift. This procedure has largely been replaced by other methods to correct myopia.

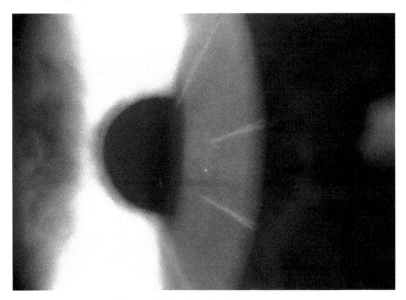

Figure 17.24 Radial keratotomy.

Astigmatic keratotomy (AK) is a surgical procedure to correct astigmatism. Corneal incisions of 85% depth are placed in the steep meridian of the astigmatism with the aim of flattening this meridian. Straight transverse or arcuate incisions can be used and are usually placed in the 7–8mm diameter optical zone. This procedure has the same advantages as RK and is utilised during cataract surgery to reduce astigmatism and for post-cataract and corneal graft astigmatism.

Intrastromal corneal ring (ICR) is a procedure in which a polymethyl methacrylate (PMMA) ring or ring segments are implanted into the peripheral corneal stroma to correct myopia. The ring or ring segments, available in different ring thickness relative to the amount of myopia correction, flatten the anterior corneal curvature with no removal of tissue from the central optical zone. The surgical technique involves making a small radial incision at

427

the 6mm diameter optical zone, and a stromal dissector creates a channel for the rings to be inserted. A 11-0 nylon suture is required to close the incision, which is removed when the wound is healed. A significant advantage of the ICR is that it is a reversible procedure.

Photoablative

The use of the excimer laser to remove corneal tissue with microscopic precision has been a major advance in the field of keratorefractive surgery.

Photorefractive keratectomy

Photorefractive keratectomy (PRK) is a procedure in which the epithelium is mechanically removed by the surgeon before the laser is applied to reshape the cornea. This procedure has achieved good refractive outcomes in low to moderate myopic correction, and is technically easy to perform. However, it has lost its appeal, due to unpleasant and unavoidable side effects, including severe pain, light sensitivity and tearing for the first few days, whilst the epithelium heals. Visually significant corneal haze as a result of the healing phase can occur in some patients, causing reduced visual acuity. Recurrent corneal erosion is also common following PRK. Refractive stability can take up to 6 months and regression can occur, particularly in higher myopic and hypermetropic patients.

Laser in-situ keratomileusis

Laser in-situ keratomileusis (LASIK) has become more popular than PRK because it offers rapid visual recovery and reduced postoperative pain. This procedure combines creating a lamellar flap of approximately 180μm thick and 10mm diameter with a specially designed microkeratome, lifting the flap, applying the laser and then replacing the flap. Complications include microkeratome malfunction and flap abnormalities such as thin or incomplete flaps and buttonholes. Femtosecond laser is being utilised to create the lamellar flap to allow more precision and safety. Epithelial ingrowth can occur when epithelial cells are lodged between the undersurface of the flap and the stromal bed. These cells often regress with time or, if they involve the visual axis, can be mechanically removed by lifting the flap and debriding the cells.

Diffuse lamellar keratitis (DLK) is a nonspecific inflammatory response, causing diffuse interface haze and reduced vision. This condition responds well to topical corticosteroids. Dry eyes occur due to reduced corneal sensation in the area of flap. This recovers slowly over a 6- to 12-month period and regular use of artificial tears is required during this time.

Keratectasia following LASIK has occurred when there is less than 250μm of stroma remaining, and the cornea becomes structurally unsound and bulges forward. Gas-permeable contact lenses, corneal cross-linking or corneal transplantation may be required as treatment if this occurs.

Laser sub-epithelial keratomileusis

Laser sub-epithelial keratomileusis (LASEK) is a procedure that provides an alternative method of manually creating and removing the epithelial flap. This eliminates the microkeratome-related complications in LASIK. The epithelium is carefully trephined, devitalised with diluted alcohol and then gently peeled back. Following the application of laser, the epithelial flap is repositioned and a bandage contact lens is applied until the epithelium is healed. The visual recovery is not as rapid as following LASIK and there is more patient discomfort, but not as severe as postoperative PRK. Corneal haze can also occur to a lesser degree than in PRK.

Phototherapeutic keratectomy

Treatment of certain corneal disorders with excimer laser has also been advocated in a procedure called phototherapeutic keratectomy (PTK). Corneal disorders such as recurrent corneal erosion, band keratopathy and anterior corneal dystrophies can be treated by photoablating the corneal surface. This improves visual function by reducing or eliminating corneal opacities and smoothing the anterior corneal surface. It also delays the need for corneal transplantation. The surgical technique is the same as PRK.

Photothermal

Thermal keratoplasty (TK) uses heat to shrink corneal collagen, thus producing corneal steepening and the correction of mild hypermetropia. A non-contact holmium: YAG laser is currently used for this procedure and eight laser treatment spots are applied to the cornea at a 6mm optical zone and then an additional eight spots are applied at the 7mm optical zone. The major advantage is the ability to correct hypermetropia without operating over the central optical zone. However, regression remains a significant disadvantage. Conductive keratoplasty (CK), a similar procedure, uses radiofrequency waves instead of laser to induce collagen shrinkage and correction of hypermetropia.

Wavefront technology

Wavefront technology reveals higher-order aberrations or a distortion of a light ray in a patient's optical system not detected with corneal topography. It is being utilised in conjunction with LASIK for a procedure called 'customised ablation'. With the production of advanced eye tracking devices, it seems theoretically possible that a small spot scanning laser, used in combination with wavefront analysis, can potentially treat spherical corneal aberrations at the time of surgery and achieve the best possible visual outcome for the patient.

Wavefront-guided treatments in eyes having large amounts of higher-order aberrations would benefit visually postoperatively, with changes in corneal asphericity and spherical aberration being targeted. Further work is required to study the interactions between aberrations and visual performance. Factors limiting optimal vision outcomes may include corneal wound healing, corneal biomechanical response, the process of capturing aberrometry and modelling the ideal outcome (Myrowitz & Chuck 2009).

Ophthalmic nurses are being exposed to patients who have had keratorefractive procedures or are being asked about the procedures and whether they are suitable candidates for a procedure. Nurses and healthcare workers may also be called upon to provide preoperative and postoperative counselling and education to patients.

Keratoprosthesis

Artificial corneal replacement or keratoprosthesis is a surgical option for patients with corneal blindness, who may not be candidates for other forms of corneal transplantation. In general, a keratoprosthesis is offered to patients with bilaterally poor vision to the degree of hand movements or light perception. One eye is usually treated and the second eye is kept in reserve.

Current designs include the Boston keratoprosthesis (type I & II devices), osteo-odonto-keratoprosthesis (OOKP), and the AlphaCor artificial cornea (Ple-Plakon and Shtein 2014). The Boston keratoprosthesis type I device is the most commonly implanted. The type I Boston keratoprosthesis consists of two polymethyl methacrylate (PMMA) plates, joined by a clear optical system surrounding a donor corneal allograft. This design is used in patients with relatively normal lid function and has a moist ocular surface. A soft contact lens is placed over the cornea on completion. The type II Boston keratoprosthesis is similar to type I but has a 2mm long anterior extension of the lens that is implanted through a surgically closed eyelid. This device is reserved for those with end-stage dry eye.

OOKP is the most technically challenging of the keratoprosthetic procedures. It involves the placement of a PMMA optical cylinder in an excised single rooted healthy tooth with a patch of buccal mucous membrane graft. OOKP implantation requires a number of stages with several surgeries. OOKP is indicated in situations with severe ocular surface disease leading to keratinisation of the surface.

The AlphaCor artificial cornea includes a nonporous transparent optic of poly-2-hydroxyethyl methacrylate (pHEMA) and a peripheral porous sponge skirt that allows for biointegration into the host cornea by stromal fibroblast ingrowth. The implantation requires a two-stage procedure. AlphaCor is indicated for failed grafts in patients without dry eyes. The most frequent complication is stromal melting, which is strongly associated with a history of herpes.

References

Bowling, B. (2015) *Kanski's Clinical Ophthalmology, a systematic approach.* 8th edn. London: Elsevier.

Coster, D. (2002) *Fundamentals of Clinical Ophthalmology. Cornea.* London: BMJ Pub Group.

Dahl, B.J., Spotts, E. & Truong, J.Q. (2012) Corneal collagen cross-linking: an introduction and literature review. *Optometry.* **83**(1), 33–42.

Daniell, M. (2003) Overview: Initial antimicrobial therapy for microbial keratitis. *British Journal of Ophthalmology.* **87**(9), 1172–74.

Keay, L., Edwards, K., Naduvilath, T., Taylor, H.R., Snibson, G.R., Forde, K. & Stapleton, F. (2006) Microbial keratitis: predisposing factors and morbidity. *Ophthalmology.* **113**(1), 109–16.

Kirkwood, B.J. & Kirkwood, R.A. (2010) Penetrating and lamellar corneal transplantation: techniques and indications. *Insight: The Journal of the American Society of Ophthalmic Registered Nurses.* **35**(3), 6–12

Mozayeni, R. & Lam, S. (1998) 'Chapter 109: Phlyctenular Keratoconjunctivitis and Marginal Staphylococcal Keratitis' in J. Krachmer, M. Mannis, E. Holland & D. Palay. *Cornea Text and Color Atlas CD-ROM.* USA: Mosby CD online.

Myrowitz, E.H. & Chuck, R.S.(2009) A comparison of wavefront-optimized and wavefront-guided ablations. *Current Opinion in Ophthalmology.* **20**(4), 247–50.

O'Callaghan, A.R. & Daniels, J.T. (2011) Concise review: limbal epithelial stem cell therapy: controversies and challenges. *Stem Cells.* **29**(12),1923–32.

Ple-Plakon, P.A. & Shtein, R.M. (2014) Trends in corneal transplantation: indications and techniques. *Current Opinion in Ophthalmology.* **25**(4), 300–305.

Poulsen, D.M. & Kang, J.J. (2015) Recent advances in the treatment of corneal ectasia with intrastromal corneal ring segments. *Current Opinion in Ophthalmology.* **26**(4), 273–77.

Price, M.O. & Price, F.W. (2007) Descemet's stripping endothelial keratoplasty. *Current Opinion in Ophthalmology.* **18**(4), 290–94.

Research Subcommittee of the International Dry Eye WorkShop (2007) Research in dry eye: Report of the Research Subcommittee of the International Dry Eye WorkShop. *The Ocular Surface.* **5**(2), 179–93.

Robin, J., Dugel, R. & Robin, S. (1998) 'Chapter 23: Immunologic disorders of the Cornea and Conjunctiva' in H. Kaufman, B. Barron & M. McDonald. *The Cornea.* 2nd edn. Boston: Butterworth-Heinemann.

Stapleton, F. & Carnt, N. (2012) Contact lens-related microbial keratitis: how have epidemiology and genetics helped us with pathogenesis and prophylaxis. *Eye.* **26**(2), 185–93.

Williams, K.A., Lowe, M.T., Keane, M.C., Jones, V.J., Loh, R.S. & Coster, D.J. (2012) *The Australian Corneal Graft Registry: 2012 Report.* Adelaide: Snap Printing.

Wittig-Silva, C., Chan, E., Islam, F.M., Wu, T., Whiting, M. & Snibson, G.R. (2014) A randomized, controlled trial of corneal collagen cross-linking in progressive keratoconus: three-year results. *Ophthalmology.* **121**(4), 812–21.

Yoon, J.J., Ismail, S. & Sherwin, T. (2014) Limbal stem cells: Central concepts of corneal epithelial homeostasis. *World Journal of Stem Cells.* **6**(4), 391–403.

All photographs in this chapter except 17.4 and 17.20 are reprinted by permission of Angela Chappell, Ophthalmic Imaging Department, Flinders Medical Centre, Adelaide, South Australia.

CHAPTER EIGHTEEN

The sclera

Agnes Lee

Anatomy and physiology of the sclera

The sclera is a white tough fibrous tissue that covers five-sixths of the eyeball and provides structural integrity for the globe. It is the eye's protective coat and it is thickest posteriorly (1mm) and thinner (0.6mm) near the junction with the cornea and where the rectus muscles are inserted (0.3mm). The outer surface of the sclera is normally smooth, except at the muscle insertions.

The colour of the sclera varies from white with a bluish tinge in children (because the sclera is normally thinner and the pigment cells of the choroid show through) to white with a yellowish tinge in elderly people as a result of deposition of fat. The sclera is for the most part avascular (much like the cornea). However, unlike the cornea, the sclera is opaque, preventing light from entering the eye other than through the cornea.

Above the sclera is the episclera, which is of similar composition to the sclera but contains blood vessels. It is the episclera that in part provides some of the nutritional requirements of the sclera. The functions of the sclera are:

- To provide a rigid insertion for the extraocular muscles
- To protect the inner structures of the eye
- To maintain the shape of the eyeball and maintain the exact position of the different parts of the optic system (Snell & Lemp 1998)
- To prevent the entry of light.

The sclera is subdivided into three layers:

- Episclera
- Scleral stroma
- Lamina fusca
- Episclera.

This external layer is made out of loose connective tissue that is connected to the fascial sheath of the eyeball (Tenon's capsule) by fine strands of tissues. The episclera has a rich blood supply from the anterior ciliary arteries. The anterior ciliary arteries normally lie quite deep in the conjunctiva and are conspicuous only in the presence of inflammation.

Scleral stroma

This layer consists of dense fibrous tissue that is intermingled with fine elastic fibres. The fibres run in concentric rings around the limbus and around the opening of the optic nerve, whereas elsewhere the fibres run in interlacing loops. The irregular arrangement of collagen fibrils, forming a mat-like structure, is responsible for the opaqueness of the sclera. This contrasts with the cornea, where the fibrils run parallel with the surface, resulting in transparency. The sclera is elastic and responds to deforming forces by lengthening (elastic response) and then stretching (viscid response) (Snell & Lemp 1998).

Lamina fusca

This is the inner aspect of the sclera, located adjacent to the choroid and separated from it by the perichoroidal space; it contains star-shaped pigment cells and thinner collagen fibres. The collagen fibres provide a weak attachment between the sclera and choroid. The lamina fusca also contains many grooves caused by the passage of blood vessels and nerves.

The limbus

This is the name given to an area about 1mm wide at the periphery of the cornea. It marks the junction between the corneal epithelium and the conjunctiva (conjunctival limbus) on one surface and the cornea and sclera on the other (corneal junction).

Just posterior to the limbus is a circular canal (canal of Schlemm), lying within and therefore forming a groove in the sclera. Posterior to the canal is a ridge of tissue, the scleral spur, which forms the attachment for the ciliary muscle.

Tenon's capsule (fascia bulbi)

This is made out of fibrous membrane, consisting of compact collagen fibres, and forms the fascial sheath of the globe. It envelops the globe and separates it from the orbital fat, forming a socket. Its inner surface is smooth and separated from the outer surface of the sclera by an episcleral space. Attaching it to the sclera are bands of connective tissue. The tendons of the extraocular muscles pierce Tenon's capsule, which forms a tubular sleeve over each tendon. Tenon's capsule is attached to the sclera 1.5mm posterior to the corneoscleral junction. Posteriorly, it fuses with the meninges around the optic nerve. It is pierced by the ciliary nerves and vessels, and the vortex veins. The globe and its fascial sheath move together on orbital fat.

Scleral apertures

The optic nerve exits the globe medial to the posterior pole. This perforation of the sclera is called the posterior scleral foramen (Snell & Lemp 1998) and the sclera is fused here with the dura and arachnoid coverings of the optic nerve. Where the sclera is pierced by the optic nerve, it has a sieve-like appearance (lamina cribrosa) and is a weakened area. (If it bulges outwards as a result of raised intraocular pressure, it produces a cupped disc.)

The apertures are as follows:

- Four vortex veins – one in each quadrant – pierce the sclera posterior to the equator of the eye.
- Smaller perforations result from the anterior ciliary arteries and veins as well as aqueous veins from Schlemm's canal.
- The long and short ciliary nerves also perforate the sclera.
- Anteriorly, there is a large aperture in the sclera where the cornea is located.

Scleral blood supply

The sclera is a relatively avascular structure. The posterior part of the sclera is supplied by the long and short posterior ciliary arteries. The episclera has a rich blood supply arising from the episcleral plexus.

Nerve supply

The nerve supply is via the short ciliary nerves (which supply the posterior portion of the sclera) and the ciliary nerve (which pierces the sclera around the optic nerve). The anterior portion of the sclera is supplied by the two long ciliary nerves.

Abnormal physiology seen in inflammatory disorders of the sclera

Ciliary flush

The episcleral plexus, which is formed by branches of the anterior ciliary arteries, exists beneath the conjunctiva. In cases of inflammation involving the cornea, iris or ciliary body, marked vasodilatation may occur, especially in the limbal area surrounding the cornea (Snell & Lemp 1998).

Localised or sectoral hyperaemia

Scleral vessels are significantly dilated, as are the overlying vessels of the episcleral and bulbar conjunctiva, as seen in cases of episcleritis and scleritis.

Dull aching pain

In cases of scleritis, dull aching pain is a result of profuse nerve innervation. In addition, the pain is made worse on extraocular movement as a result of muscle insertion in the sclera.

Diseases of the sclera

Episcleritis

Episcleritis (Figure 18.1) is a self-limiting inflammatory condition of the episcleral connective tissue, which lies between the conjunctiva and sclera. Episcleritis presents as a relatively asymptomatic acute onset of a sectoral red eye. On examination, there is sectoral injection of the episcleral and overlying conjunctival vessels. The eye's red appearance is often mistaken for conjunctivitis but there is no discharge, foreign body section or the presence of any follicles. It typically looks worse than it is.

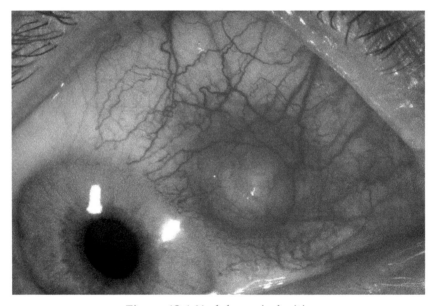

Figure 18.1 Nodular episcleritis

(Angela Chappell, Ophthalmic Imaging Department, Flinders Medical Centre, Adelaide, South Australia)

Pathophysiology

The pathophysiology is not clearly understood but this benign inflammatory condition is commonly seen in young adults. It is usually a mild, self-limiting, recurrent disease. The inflammatory response is localised to the superficial episcleral vascular network (Hampton 2001). Women are more affected than men and in most cases the disorder is idiopathic, although one-third of patients have an underlying systemic condition such as rheumatoid arthritis, gout, systemic lupus erythematosus (SLE), inflammatory bowel disease, sarcoidosis, herpes zoster virus (HZV) or herpes.

Two different clinical types of episcleritis may be found:

- Simple, where the congestion is diffuse
- Nodular, where there is localised hyperaemia and swelling which is mobile over the surface of the globe.

Simple episcleritis can recur at 1- to 3-monthly intervals and usually lasts 7–10 days; most cases resolve after 2–3 weeks, although prolonged episodes may be more common in patients with associated systemic conditions (Hampton 2001). Some patients may have an attack of episcleritis during spring or autumn. Stress and hormonal changes have also been implicated.

Patients with nodular episcleritis have prolonged attacks of inflammation that are painful. The cornea is unaffected, although long-standing or recurrent episcleritis may lead to dellen formation. The anterior chamber is deep and quiet.

Signs and symptoms

- Localised sectoral injection of episcleral vessels with perhaps some overlying conjunctival injection
- Mild to moderate discomfort or tenderness
- Nodules in nodular episcleritis
- In cases where the diagnosis is difficult, blanching the conjunctiva and episclera vessels with phenylephrine 2.5% will allow better evaluation of the underlying sclera
- History of systemic disease, as listed above
- Vision is not usually affected.

Management

All patients should have a thorough history taken. Most cases are self-limiting, with little or no permanent damage to the eye even without treatment. Therefore, many of these patients will not require any treatment. The use of artificial tears can be beneficial in cases of discomfort. Non-steroidal drugs such as diclofenac (Voltarol) can be prescribed for persistent discomfort. If patients present with more than three episodes of episcleritis, a referral to a medical physician is recommended. Steroid drops are still the treatment of choice for some clinicians.

Scleritis

This is more serious than episcleritis. Patients presenting with scleritis complain of severe ocular pain that can involve the adjacent head and facial regions (Figure 18.2).

The scleral vessels are involved with vessel dilatation, including the overlying vessels of the episcleral and bulbar conjunctiva. The inflammation has a slightly bluish hue as a result of deeper vessel involvement.

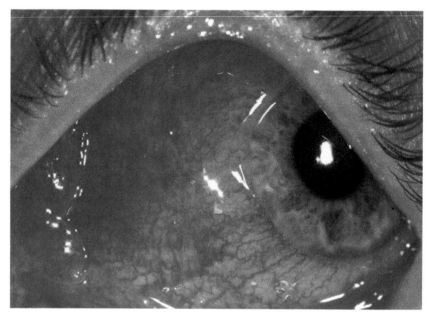

Figure 18.2 Scleritis
(reproduced by permission of Angela Chappell, Ophthalmic Imaging Department,
Flinders Medical Centre, Adelaide, South Australia).

Pathophysiology

Over 50% of scleritis cases have an underlying systemic cause. The common related disorders are: ankylosing spondylitis, rheumatoid arthritis, systemic lupus erythematosus (SLE), Wegener's granulomatosis, polyarteritis, gout, syphilis and herpes zoster virus (HZV). Scleritis may follow ocular surgery, typically presenting within 6 months postoperatively, with necrosis adjacent to the site of surgery. The cause is unknown. Scleritis may also be caused by infective spread from a corneal ulcer or from trauma (Bowling 2015).

If left untreated, scleritis has the potential to spread to the anterior and posterior segment of the eye, causing proptosis, cataract, secondary glaucoma, cystoid macular oedema, choroidal effusion, exudative retinal detachment and optic atrophy. It is therefore imperative to distinguish this disorder from episcleritis and to start treatment as early as possible after diagnosis.

Signs and symptoms

- Gradual onset of redness and pain
- Vision may be decreased

- Photophobia
- Scleral nodules
- Peripheral keratitis
- Secondary uveitis.

In cases of necrotising scleritis, the sclera takes on a bluish hue where the sclera has thinned, revealing the underlying choroids; in necrotising scleritis, an ischaemic area is visible; where there is no evidence of inflammation the condition is known as scleromalacia perforans.

It is important always to consider the underlying cause to be systemic unless proved otherwise. Patients should always be referred for a comprehensive medical examination and investigations such as full blood count (FBC), erythrocyte sedimentation rate (ESR), antinuclear antibody (ANA), HLA-B27, rheumatoid factor, angiotensin-converting enzyme (ACE), Lyme titre and chest radiograph must be performed.

Generally, topical steroids alone are insufficient to treat scleritis. Systemic treatment such as an oral non-steroidal anti-inflammatory drug (e.g. ibuprofen 600mg four times a day or indometacin 25mg) has a proven effect. However, if the inflammation is severe or necrotising, a systemic steroid such as oral prednisolone may be prescribed. In rare cases, the patient may require immunosuppressive agents and should be managed by a rheumatologist. The treatment of scleritis can be complex so the disease process must be clearly documented at each stage.

Anterior necrotising scleritis with inflammation

This is the most severe form of scleritis and is bilateral, although not necessarily simultaneous in 60% of cases. The mortality rate is 25% within 5 years of the onset of scleritis as a result of systemic vascular disease (Bowling 2015). Perforation may occur and inflammation may spread to the uveal tract. This is an intensely painful and distressing condition and patients will need a lot of support, in terms of both their eye condition and the systemic problems associated with severe vascular disease. Treatment includes oral or intravenous prednisolone, along with immunosuppressive agents such as cyclophosphamide or ciclosporin.

References

Bowling, B. (2015) *Kanski's Clinical Ophthalmology, a systematic approach*. 8th edn. London: Elsevier.

Hampton, R. (2001) Episcleritis. *Journal of Emergency Medicine*. **2**(7).

Snell, R.S. & Lemp, M.A. (1998) *Clinical Anatomy of the Eye*. 2nd edn. USA: Blackwell Science.

CHAPTER NINETEEN

The lens

Stephen Craig

Anatomy of the lens

The lens is an asymmetric oblate spheroid, located within the anterior segment of the eye. The steeper curve faces the iris and is known as the 'anterior pole'. The corresponding 'posterior pole' faces into the vitreous; 90° to this, the meridian is known as the equator. The lens possesses no nerves, blood vessels or connective tissue. It is located posterior to the iris but anterior to the vitreous face. At birth, the lens is approximately 6.5mm in diameter, increasing to 10mm in adulthood, and also increasing slightly in thickness.

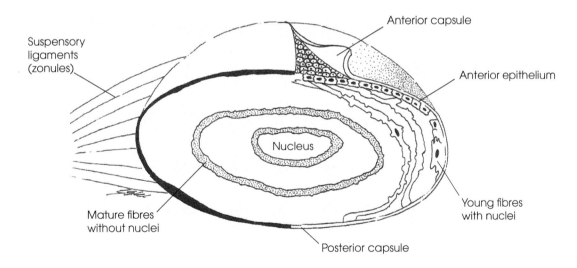

Figure 19.1 Section through the lens.

The lens contributes to approximately one-third, or approximately 20 dioptres (D) of power of the eye, the cornea provides the remaining two-thirds, or approximately 43D. The eye's total dioptric power is 58.7D and not 63D, due to approximately 4D being 'lost' because of the distance between the cornea and anterior surface of the lens. The individual property of the lens is that it can change shape in order to focus on distant and near objects.

The lens is made up of three parts: firstly, an elastic capsule, made up of collagen fibrils; secondly, the lens epithelium, which is confined to the anterior surface of the lens; and, lastly, the lens fibres.

Structure and physiology of the lens

The elastic capsule, colloquially known as 'the bag ' or 'capsule', is made up of collagen fibrils (lamellae), which are 20μm thick at the equator, thinning towards the posterior pole to 3μm. Anteriorly, the fibrils are in direct contact with the lens epithelium, while posteriorly the lens epithelium contacts the superficial lens fibres. These envelop the whole lens from this capsule in the equatorial plain. The zonular fibres, also known as suspensory ligaments, which connect the capsule to the ciliary body, are connected at this point (Tobwala *et al.* 2015).

The superficial lens fibres make up the main mass of the lens. Over time, some lens fibres lose their nuclei and start to produce crystallins. Alpha, beta and gamma crystallins, all water-soluble proteins, are found in the lens and are thought to increase its refractive index and transparency (Yanoff & Duker 2009).

In adults, the lens is approximately 10mm in diameter and 5mm from anterior to posterior surface. The lens continues to grow throughout life and these cells concentrate over time to the central portion of the lens, increasing its density. This in turn makes the lens less pliable. Snell and Lemp (1998) suggest that the lens of a 65-year-old is at least a third larger than in a 25-year-old.

The lens capsule

The capsule is a semipermeable elastic basement membrane, which surrounds the cortex and the nucleus of the lens. It also facilitates changes in the shape of the lens during the process of accommodation. It is composed of a number of lamellae (fibrils) stacked on top of each other. The capsule varies in thickness from 4μm (at the posterior pole) to 23μm close to the equator on both anterior and posterior surfaces. The capsule is highly resistant to chemical and toxic influences; however, it allows water and electrolytes from the aqueous fluid to pass through it, facilitating nourishment of the lens material.

The lens substance (cortex and nucleus)

The lens substance is composed of a single layer of cuboidal epithelial cells, which lie immediately beneath the anterior capsule. They are soft, densely packed, lens fibre cells.

The purpose of cuboid epithelial cells is to secrete to and absorb from the aqueous. A recent study notes that oxidative damage to the cuboidal epithelial cells on the anterior surface of the lens can precede and contribute to human lens cataract formation (Babizhayev & Yegorov 2015). Within the substance of the lens there is very little extracellular space.

The cells within the lens are nourished by the diffusion of proteins, minerals and enzymes, contained within aqueous fluid, which passes through the lens capsule. The cortex of the lens accounts for about 16% of the lens substance and is histologically indistinct from the nucleus of the lens, which accounts for the remaining 84% of the lens substance. The thickness of the cortex gradually increases throughout life, whereas the thickness of the lens nucleus decreases with age (Chinmayu 2011).

Functions of the lens (refraction and accommodation)

Refraction may be defined as the change in direction of light when it passes from one transparent medium into another of a different optical density: the denser the medium, the more slowly the light is able to pass through it (see Chapter 2). The change in the direction of the light as it moves from one medium to another of a different refractive index is calculated using Snell's Law, named after the Dutch physicist, Willebrord Van Roijen Snell (1850–1626).

The 'refractive index' (n) compares the speed of light through a particular material, with the speed of light through a vacuum, where 1 is the speed of light in a vacuum. If the refractive index of a material were 1.5, this would mean that light travels through a vacuum 1.5 times as fast as it does through the material. A high refractive index therefore means a denser medium to the passage of light.

Different clear media have differing refractive indices, meaning that they bend light rays at differing rates. An example of this process may be seen if a pencil is half submerged in a glass of water. Looking at this model from the side, the pencil will appear to bend in the middle where it meets the surface of the water. This is because air has a refractive index of 1.000293, while water is 1.3330, at room temperature and pressure (Zajac & Hecht 2013).

The transparent media of the eye therefore have differing refractive indices and curvatures, which means that they will bend light by different amounts. The cornea (n = 1.373–1.40), aqueous (1.336), lens (1.386–1.406), and vitreous (1.338), (Lakes & Park 1992), refract light rays travelling through to the retina.

The lens is the main refractive structure inside the eye possessing ± 20D of refractive power.

If the refractive power of the emmetropic (normal) eye was fixed and unable to change, only objects at infinity, considered to be more than 6m away, would be clearly seen. To focus the light rays from objects nearer than infinity on to the retina, the lens must be able to increase its refractive power by changing its shape. This process is known as accommodation and is enabled by contraction of the ciliary muscle, which in turn releases the tension on the suspensory ligaments, thus allowing the lens to become more spherical in shape. The stimulus to accommodation is a blurred retinal image. Within accommodation, in addition to the lens becoming more spherical in shape, the pupils constrict slightly when looking at near objects; and, in order to maintain binocular single vision, the eyes converge. When looking at distant objects, the eyes come back to the midline, the pupils enlarge slightly and the lens becomes more elliptical in shape. This whole process of focused vision depends on each component and process happening; but in relation to this chapter, it is primarily reliant on:

- The clarity of the lens
- The elasticity of the lens capsule and zonules
- The selective permeability of the lens capsule
- The ability of the lens to change its shape during accommodation.

Developmental abnormalities of the lens
Congenital aphakia

Congenital aphakia is a rare anomaly that can be subdivided into two forms: primary and secondary. Primary is thought to derive from a mutation in gene FOXE3, which results in the failed induction of ectoderm during foetal development. Secondary aphakia is thought to be due to an infective cause, such as rubella, which results in the formed lens, at whatever stage of development, being reabsorbed or extruded prior to birth (Valleix *et al.* 2006).

Spherophakia or microphakia

Spherophakia or microphakia are terms that describe smaller than normal lenses, which are more spherical. This is due to defects in the zonules which allow for lower tension on the capsule. Common causes include congenital rubella infection and Marfan's Syndrome (Lee & Higginbotham 1999).

Lenticonus and lentiglobus

This is a developmental abnormality of the lens, characterised by a localised cone-shaped protrusion of the axial portions of the anterior and posterior lens surfaces. It is usually associated with a high degree of axial lens-induced myopia. Anterior lenticonus is associated with Alport's Syndrome (deafness and nephritis), while posterior manifestations are usually idiopathic, unilateral and may be associated with persistent hyperplastic primary vitreous (Lee & Higginbotham 1999).

Degenerative changes in the lens (cataract formation)

Cataracts are responsible for half the world's blindness (WHO 2012) and 3% of visual impairment worldwide (WHO 2010). The United Kingdom shows a continuing trend in increasing cataract incidence. Minassian *et al.* (2000), state that the incidence in the UK adult population was 225,000 new cases of visually impairing cataract.

A total of 345,038 procedures were performed by the NHS in 2012–13, with 20,800 being performed in the private sector. The last projected total for the procedure, from the Health and Social Care Information Centre (2014), was 372,022 for 2013–14.

This amounts to a 10,000 per year increase since the 2000 data from Minassian *et al.* Worldwide a figure of 18 million 'cataract blind' is supported by Lansingh (2010), which equates to half of all global blindness. Treatment is usually extraction of the lens and intraocular lens (IOL) implantation.

Cataract formation is not due to a single factor. The Royal College of Ophthalmologists' 'Guidelines for Cataract' (2010) state that the causes of cataract are multifactorial. Apart from age, aetiological epidemiological studies have identified a number of risk factors for cataract, including: gender, diabetes mellitus, UV exposure, prolonged steroid use, nutritional status, socio-economic status, and lifestyle choices such as smoking and excessive use of alcohol (Dolin 1998, Congdon & Taylor 2003). Information from genetic studies estimate that the heritability of age-related cataract could be between 48–59% (Hammond *et al.* 2001).

As part of the normal aging process, the lens not only loses its flexibility and therefore some of its accommodative power (resulting in presbyopia) but also loses transparency as the lens tissue gets thicker. The thicker, denser lens has a higher refractive index and dioptric power. This combination leads to 'index myopia', where the refraction of the whole eye changes and, often, a new spectacle prescription is required to achieve good vision. With the increase in lens density, the lens changes from transparent to yellow, then to dark yellow or amber, and finally to a brown colour.

This process may take several years or decades. The visual effects are insidious and the majority of individuals may not notice their visual decline (Craig 2015). 'Senile' cataracts progress slowly, and – by their nature – are more commonly seen in elderly people or in the latter years of life.

Cataracts may also be classified as:

- Congenital
- Traumatic (due to blunt or penetrating injuries)
- Secondary, as a result of pre-existing ocular conditions, e.g. glaucoma, choroiditis and uveitis
- Secondary as a result of pre-existing systemic diseases, e.g. diabetes and metabolic disorders such as galactosaemia
- Toxic as a result of UV radiation or the side effects of certain medications, the most common being the prolonged use of oral steroids.

Cataracts that develop rapidly, particularly uniocular mature cataracts, should be considered with a high level of clinical suspicion as they may indicate the presence of ocular malignancy or underlying retinal detachment. In general, however, the following are some of the most common symptoms that individuals complain about in relation to the development of cataract:

- An overall gradual reduction in vision
- Glare while driving at night or in bright light/sunlight, and difficulty seeing objects outdoors in bright sunlight, known as reduced contrast sensitivity (mainly associated with posterior subcapsular lens opacities)
- Difficulties in reading small print
- Difficulty in seeing distant objects or, for example, people's faces on the other side of the street or bus numbers
- Colour shift: there is poor appreciation of colours; as the cataract develops, the lens becomes more absorbent at the blue end of the spectrum (mainly associated with nuclear sclerotic cataract)
- Monocular diplopia (particularly associated with cortical spoke opacities)
- Visual field loss, depending on the position and density of the lens opacity
- Probably most commonly not being able to find a pair of spectacles that enables the patient to see as well as they would like to.

In assessing the effects of cataracts, it is important not only to look at the level of visual impairment caused, but also, more importantly, to look at the impact the visual impairment has on the patient's quality of life.

Examination in relation to cataract assessment

The presence of cataract is one of the most common reasons that patients are referred to an eye department by their General Practitioner (GP) or optometrist. Alternatively, the individual notices a change in their ability to do 'close work', such as reading, because the index myopia has become so great that accommodation is inadequate to the task.

Most optometry referrals provide a detailed account of the ocular examination and pathology. Some optometry referrals may also relate their findings to the impact that any visual impairment has on the patient's lifestyle. Knudston *et al.* (2005) noted that decreased visual function, despite the cause, is associated with diminished quality of life and general functional living activities. Questionnaires exist, such as American Centers for Disease Control and Prevention', 'Health-Related Quality of Life' (HRQoL 2000) and the National Eye Institute Visual Function Questionnaire (NEI-VFQ-25), produced by Mangione *et al.* (1998), which was validated in 2000, which looks at the impact of deteriorating vision on the individual. Some countries use these scales, or other tools incorporating quality of life as well as, or instead of, visual acuity to prioritise waiting lists for surgery.

Once referred and within the healthcare services cataract pathway, patients may be screened by a medically or nursing-led outpatient clinic. Recent developments, cataract redesign projects and the introduction of one-stop services have led to nursing roles featuring much more in the overall assessment and management of cataracts.

Before examining the lens and other related ocular structures, it is essential to find out about any pre-existing underlying or long-standing ocular pathology, which may influence decisionmaking in the management of the cataract.

Although optometry referrals for assessment of cataract usually identify any pre-existing ocular pathology, such as amblyopia, strabismus, retinal disorders, age-related macular degeneration (ARMD), and any abnormalities of the optic nerve, these findings will need to be confirmed. Intraocular pressures (IOP) are always recorded and, in some instances, visual fields.

Referrals from GPs can be less detailed and tend towards the individual's report of deteriorating vision rather than a detailed ocular examination. With this in mind, it is important that whichever professionals meet the patient, they are knowledgeable and skilful in ocular examination.

In addition to this information, it is essential that the immediate preoperative assessment of an individual's suitability for cataract surgery excludes the presence of other ocular conditions that could compromise surgical intervention or outcome.

Examination of the lens and cataract

Grossly, the lens may be subdivided into three areas: the capsule (anterior and posterior); the cortex; and the nucleus (Figure 19.2). By using a slit-lamp, it is possible to examine in detail each of these structures and to observe the amount and position of any lens opacification. Noting the position of the lens, it is critical to examine the lens in a systematic fashion, starting anteriorly with the lens capsule and working backwards, through the cortex and nucleus, to the posterior capsular surface.

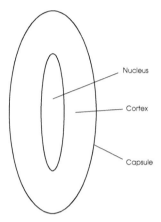

Nucleus

Cortex

Capsule

Figure 19.2 Simplified diagram of a section through the lens.

When examining the anterior lens capsule, note should be taken of any pigmented adhesions known as 'synechiae'. Remnants of small fragments of iris tissue on the anterior capsular surface indicate previous or pre-existing inflammatory disease such as uveitis.

The more serious pseudoexfoliation syndrome is a common, age-related, systemic disorder of worldwide significance, with an estimated prevalence ranging from 10% to 20% of the general population over 60 years of age (Ritch & Schlotzer-Schrehardt 2001). It can be recognised by white/grey flake-like deposits adhering to the anterior capsular surface. In pseudoexfoliation disease, fibrillar material is produced by cells in the anterior segment. Minute clumps of the fibrillar material are released into the extracellular space, some of which end up deposited on structures inside the eye. The trabecular meshwork becomes compromised, resulting in raised intraocular pressure. Iris pigment can also be released, which compounds the issue. Because of the exfoliation proliferating in the anterior segment, cataract surgery carries a greater risk of postoperative complications particularly inflammation (Ahmed 2012).

Slit-lamp examination gives the most detailed view of the lens, but direct ophthalmoscopy is also useful in determining whether the opacification is affecting the visual axis. By directing the ophthalmoscope light through the pupil to obtain a red reflex, opacities can be seen as shadows and their position can be determined in relation to the visual axis, enabling a judgement to be made as to their impact on visual acuity.

Forms of cataract

As well as classifications of cataract, there are many different types. Various example names include: blue dot, Christmas tree, lamellar (found in children), snowflake, cuneiform and stellate. Cataracts may develop in many forms. The three most common types are:

- Cortical
- Nuclear sclerotic
- Posterior subcapsular.

Table 19.1 Common variants of cataract (NICE 2010)

Cataract type	Main symptoms
Nuclear sclerotic cataract	Near vision can improve to begin with, and patients can do without reading glasses for a while. Distance vision worsens.
Cortical	Light is scattered quickly throughout the lens, causing blurring of vision. Associated with glare, loss of contrast and depth perception.
Posterior subcapsular	More common in the younger age range. Haloes and glare common during dusk, dawn or night time, particularly when driving.
Post-capsular	Visual acuity is worse when the pupil is constricted, such as in daytime and when reading.
Axial	Opacity on the visual axis in the lens.

Cortical cataract

Cortical cataracts are opacities that are confined to the lens cortex. They are commonly a shade of white in colour and may be present in either the anterior or the posterior lens cortex. Eventually the whole cortex will become opaque and is described as 'mature'. Ultimately this opacity will totally obstruct the passage of light through to the retina.

The lens cortex begins to generate small vesicles which contain abnormal amounts of crosslinked proteins, cholesterol and phospholipids. They are bordered by membranes that are rich in square arrays and have gap junctions which are 'degenerate'. Few intramembranous particles are present. It has been shown that the opaque shades represent cohorts of locally affected fibres, segregated from unaffected neighbouring fibres by 'non-leaky' membranes. This segregation is an effective mechanism, delaying the outgrowth of these opacities to cuneiform cataracts entering the pupillary space and thus becoming blinding cortical cataracts (Vrensen 2009).

This type of cataract results in wedges or spokes of opacification, usually in the inferior quadrants initially, which eventually merge. Predominant symptoms are blurring of vision, glare (particularly at dawn and dusk) and loss of contrast and depth perception (NICE 2010).

Hypermature or morganian cataracts

As the cortical cataract matures, the lens fibres degenerate. Increasing amounts of cortex degenerate over time and the globules begin to coalesce, creating large accumulations of liquefied lens protein. When the majority of the cortex is affected, the lens nucleus is left floating in the liquid cortex, forming a morganian cataract (Albert 2008). Eyes with mature or hypermature cataracts may develop a form of secondary elevated intraocular pressure, referred to as phacolytic glaucoma. An increased concentration of protein molecules under the lens capsule forces water from the aqueous into the lens capsule via osmosis. This results in a swollen, tense lens capsule. Lens proteins may leak from microscopic rents in the capsule, which can trigger a nongranulomatous inflammatory response.

Nuclear sclerotic cataract (senile cataract)

Nuclear cataracts (Figure 19.3) develop very slowly over a period of years and the patient is often unaware that they have visual difficulties until the cataract is quite advanced. Older people often simply assume that reduced vision is a natural part of the aging process. Visual disturbance is very gradual and is, more often than not, associated with reduced distance visual acuity and diminished colour perception so reading ability is less changed. The lens nucleus changes from transparent to pale yellow, through to a darker amber or brown discoloration. With time, it becomes sclerotic because of condensation of the lens nucleus and deposition of brown pigment within the lens.

Known as a 'brunescent cataract', this type of cataract causes problems in near-sightedness and in distance vision, while reading is less affected (Bollinger & Langston 2008). This discoloration is confined to the lens nucleus and can be seen on slit-lamp examination by directing the light beam obliquely through the lens.

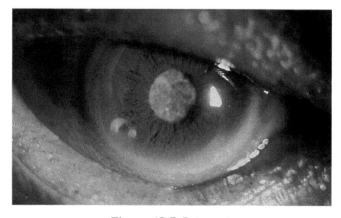

Figure 19.3 Cataract.
(Photo reprinted by permission of the International Centre for Eye Health – ICEH.)

Posterior subcapsular (polar) cataract

A posterior subcapsular cataract, in some texts described as a posterior polar cataract, is a circular, opaque mass that is composed of malformed and distorted lens fibres located in the central posterior part of the lens. The area is significant because of its proximity to, and possible adherence to, the posterior capsule. Moreover, the capsule itself may be weakened. This presents a technical challenge for the ophthalmologist during surgery. Posterior subcapsular cataracts are common in the younger patient age group. Visual symptoms include haloes and glare, particularly at dawn, dusk or night time, especially while driving (NICE 2010).

Cataract management

As the cataract develops, many patients are managed by community optometrists who manage any early index myopia with changes in their spectacle prescription.

When the patient is referred for surgery is a matter for discussion with the patient, and the optometrist or GP. Different patients will be referred at different stages of cataract development, as the timing of referral depends on the impact the cataract has on the particular individual's quality of life. A common misconception held by most patients is that, if they have cataracts, they must be removed. However, the Royal College of Ophthalmologists (2010) recommends that surgery is not performed if:

- Tolerable refractive correction provides vision that meets the patient's needs.
- Surgery is not expected to improve visual function, and no other indication for lens removal exists.
- The patient cannot safely undergo surgery due to coexisting medical or ocular conditions. Appropriate postoperative care cannot be arranged.
- The patient or surrogate decision-maker cannot give informed consent for non-emergency surgery.
- Indications for second-eye surgery are the same as for the first eye (with consideration given to needs for binocular function).

If the patient desires cataract surgery, they are referred in the UK to the Hospital Eye Service (HES), often via the Choose and Book (CaB) system, by their GP or directly by the optometrist, either to a clinic type or a clinical team.

An initial ocular report will also be completed on the General Ophthalmic Certificate # 18, more commonly abbreviated to GOS18. Within the UK, Local Optical Committee Support Units (LOCSUs) offer guidance on referral pathways, particularly in community settings.

Preoperative assessment

A comprehensive preoperative assessment is required and this may take place on the same day as the ophthalmic consultation, thus saving the patient further visits to the hospital. This approach is recommended in the Royal College of Ophthalmology (2010) *Cataract Surgery Guidelines*, although different eye units will have different practices.

At whatever point the patient is assessed, either in a 'one-stop shop' clinic or on different dates, they have to undergo appropriate preoperative assessment. This assessment is essentially in two parts. Firstly, an accurate medical/surgical history has to be taken, including details of any medications allergies and sensitivities, in order to minimise any intraoperative or postoperative risk

Secondly, a full personal and family ophthalmic history should be taken, usually consisting of:

● A medical evaluation, including details of current medication and history of allergies; this examination should make particular note of comorbidities such as diabetes and macular degeneration which may impact on the outcome of the surgery

● Measurement of visual acuity, preferably with an up-to-date refraction

● Full slit-lamp examination

● Pupil examination

● Dilated examination of the cataract and fundus. Where the fundus is not visible, the option of a 'B' scan should be considered to minimise unforeseen poor visual rehabilitation if the retina or macula is not healthy. It is important to discuss the visual possibilities with the patient, which will be reduced if other pathology is present.

● Measurement of intraocular pressure (IOP)

● Biometry

● The identification of social problems, which may require support so that services may be arranged and the surgery is not delayed.

In addition to this information, it is essential (so that it can be dealt with before surgery) that the immediate preoperative assessment of a patient's suitability for cataract surgery excludes the presence of:

● Conjunctivitis or any other bacterial or viral load

● Infective corneal ulceration

● Scleritis or episcleritis

● Blepharitis

● Infected lid lesions such as chalazion

- Entropion or ectropion
- Trichiasis
- Epiphora due to unknown cause.

Interestingly, a Cochrane review by Keay *et al.* (2012) found that routine preoperative medical testing did not reduce the risk of intraoperative or postoperative adverse medical events. There was no difference in the cancellation of surgery between patients who had preoperative medical testing and those who had no testing or limited preoperative testing. This robust evidence could be used to change practice in cataract services in future.

Core to the purpose of the preoperative consultation is the patient's safety, the minimising of pre-, intra- and postoperative risks and the maximising of the postoperative result in terms of visual rehabilitation and patient satisfaction. Integral to this is the patient's understanding of the goals of the surgery, so that they can confidently and genuinely consent to the procedure.

Biometry (IOL calculation)

Sir Harold Ridley (1906–2001), who performed the first cataract procedure in 1949, did not have the benefit of biometry, with the patient's resultant postoperative refraction being -24.0/+6.0 x 30° (Astbury & Ramamurthy 2006). It is therefore obvious that it is important to implant the correct intraocular lens in order to achieve a good result postoperatively.

The three factors that make up the refractive power of the eye are:

- The power of the cornea
- The power of the lens
- The length of the eye.

In order to calculate what lens must replace the physiological lens, the power of the cornea and the length of the eye must be accurately calculated. This involves making a series of measurements of the eye, including assessment of the corneal curvature and any axis of that curvature (keratometry) and the axial length of the globe. These processes, and the calculation from them of the IOL power required to be implanted in the eye, are collectively known as biometry. Calculating the power of the IOL required for cataract surgery is one of the most critical components of the preoperative assessment process.

There are different types of biometry machines. The common types are applanation; (acoustic) immersion, which make contact with the corneal surface; and non-contact laser interferometry machines such as the IOLMaster® and Lenstar®. Although the biometry equipment used by different ophthalmic units to calculate IOL power may differ in technical terms, the principles of measurement are essentially the same.

Refractive outcome

Deciding, with the patient, the refractive outcome required after surgery is the first step in selecting the correct IOL to implant during surgery. Emmetropia is not necessarily the outcome that would be wanted by the patient, or the surgeon. A common example of this would be to leave a high myope slightly short-sighted following surgery, as they may not tolerate emmetropia following surgery if they have been myopic since birth.

Discussions about lifestyle may also influence the decision. If the patient spends a great deal of time undertaking close work, particularly if they are not very mobile, the desired postoperative refraction may be to enable good near vision without spectacles.

The discussion about the desired results of surgery should occur *before* the patient agrees to surgery and the decision should be recorded in the patient's notes, so that the calculation of lens power is done to achieve the desired result, rather than just achieving emmetropia.

Measuring the power of the cornea: keratometry

Keratometry is the measurement of the anterior curvature of the cornea in horizontal and vertical axes. To differentiate between these three axes, the Ks are designated 'K1' and 'K2'. Readings can be given in dioptres (D) or radius of curvature of the cornea in mm. These values are convertible, one to the other, and conversion charts are easily available. These are usually noted as 'K' readings.

Most ophthalmic units still possess a manual keratometer. In complex corneal pathology patients, a manual keratometer is more suitable than an automated one, as it allows the operator to line the keratometer up to miss corneal pathology.

Automated keratometers have become popular over the last 20 years and many models are available. Corneal topography can also be used to measure K readings, as can non-contact biometry such as IOLMaster®.

To minimise postoperative refractive errors, many studies on comparative outcomes have been undertaken on the accuracy of differing machines. A study by Elbaz *et al.* (2007) suggested that some methods were reliable and repeatable between manual and automated systems. Mehravaran *et al.* (2014) suggested that keratometry in normal subjects is mostly repeatable with IOLMaster® and Topcon® automated refractometers when compared to manual keratometer, EyeSys®, and Pentacam®. Similarly, these two systems demonstrated the best agreement with a manual keratometer and they could safely be interchanged in a clinical setting.

Process

- Calibrate and check your keratometer
- Ensure you are measuring the central cornea

- Don't touch the cornea beforehand (this should be done before tonometry)

- Relax your own accommodation

- Hard contact lenses 'out' for at least 4 weeks and soft for 1 week (Royal College of Ophthalmology 2010); check, or get someone else to check, if the results are high (less than 40D) or high (more than 48D)

- Use average of 'K' readings

- Beware of scarred or abnormal corneas; if in doubt, use an average, e.g. 43.5D

- Print off results and attach to the patient's notes (Figure 19.4).

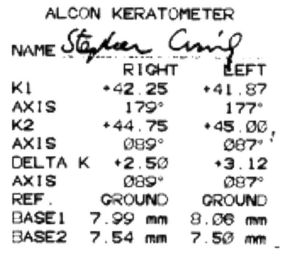

Figure 19.4 Print of 'K' reading

Factors affecting keratometry

- Technique
- Position of patient/operator
- Fixation: ocular movements/nystagmus/squint
- Cornea: ulcer/dry eyes/pterygium
- Lids: ptosis/ectropion/entropion
- Previous surgery: keratotomy/graft
- Contact lenses
- Not measuring central cornea
- High IOP
- Focus on machine not calibrated.

An error of 0.25D in K readings = IOL calculation error of approx 0.3D

Measuring the axial length of the eye

Contemporary biometry systems are usually non-contact and automatically combine all measurements necessary for the choice of IOL. Older machines use ultrasound contact or immersion technique, commonly called the 'manual technique', to measure the axial length of the eye. The two most common methods of measuring the axial length, which represent contact and non-contact forms, are 'A scan' ultrasonography and IOLMaster®.

'A scan' ultrasonography

This measures the time taken for sound to travel through the eye and converts it into a value, using a velocity formula. Sound travels faster through solids than liquids, and therefore changes velocity as it passes through the eye. As part of the sound reflects back from each structure in the eye (anterior cornea, anterior and posterior lens and internal limiting membrane of the retina), the image shows a spike. The distance between the anterior surface of the cornea and retinal spikes gives the axial length of the eye. This is usually done by placing a probe in contact with the cornea. Immersion techniques involve a water bath between the probe and the cornea.

Most A and B scans use an ultrasound frequency of 10MHz. The known sound velocity through the cornea and the lens is 1641 metres/second (m/s), with the velocity through the aqueous and vitreous being 1532 m/s. The average sound velocity through the phakic eye is 1550 m/s. The sound velocity through the aphakic eye is 1532 m/s, and the velocity through the pseudophakic eye is 1532 m/s plus the correction factor for the intraocular lens (IOL) material (Byrne 1995). This means that the 'A scan' practitioner should be mindful of the natural state of the eye and adjust the frequency accordingly, as failure to do so will render the axial length inaccurate and the IOL choice will therefore be 'incorrect '.

Technique

- Ensure the machine is calibrated
- Identify patient and notes
- Check notes for past ophthalmic history and visual acuity
- Focimetry on distance glasses
- Check no contact lenses/sign of infection/trauma
- Check for allergies
- Explain what you are going to do
- Ensure patient's co-operation
- Position patient, ensuring safety and comfort.

Keratometry:

- Record Ks x 3 (use average reading)
- Input the patient's details into machine.

Axial length measurement:

- Instil G. benoxinate
- Measure axial lengths and repeat if necessary.

IOL calculation:

- Choose the lens type and the desired refraction and the machine will calculate the lens strength to be implanted (Figure 19.5).

Print readings and secure in the patient notes or record. Any equipment numbers or disposable equipment reference numbers should also be recorded, according to local policy. Any problems obtaining the readings should also be recorded – for example, if the patient rubbed their eyes between readings.

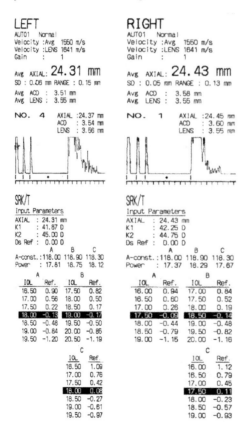

Figure 19.5 'Good' A scans with K readings and calculations for different lenses

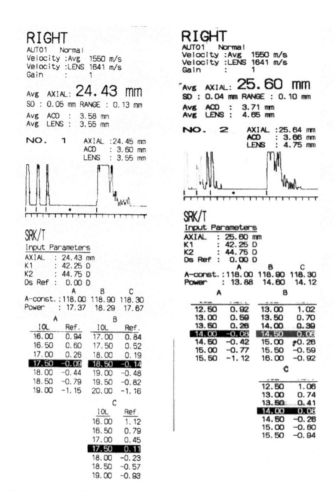

RIGHT
AUT01   Normal
Velocity :Avg   1550 m/s
Velocity :LENS 1641 m/s
Gain   :   1

Avg AXIAL: **24.43 mm**
SD : 0.05 mm RANGE : 0.13 mm

Avg ACD : 3.58 mm
Avg LENS : 3.55 mm

NO. 1   AXIAL :24.45 mm
            ACD   : 3.60 mm
            LENS : 3.55 mm

RIGHT
AUT01   Normal
Velocity :Avg   1550 m/s
Velocity :LENS 1641 m/s
Gain   :   1

Avg AXIAL: **25.60 mm**
SD : 0.04 mm RANGE : 0.10 mm

Avg ACD : 3.71 mm
Avg LENS : 4.65 mm

NO. 2   AXIAL :25.64 mm
            ACD   : 3.66 mm
            LENS : 4.75 mm

SRK/T
Input Parameters
AXIAL : 24.43 mm
K1   : 42.25 D
K2   : 44.75 D
Ds Ref : 0.00 D
             A   B   C
A-const. :118.00 118.90 118.30
Power   : 17.37   18.29   17.67

| A | | B | |
IOL	Ref.	IOL	Ref.
16.00	0.94	17.00	0.84
16.50	0.60	17.50	0.52
17.00	0.26	18.00	0.19
17.50	**-0.09**	**18.50**	**-0.14**
18.00	-0.44	19.00	-0.48
18.50	-0.79	19.50	-0.82
19.00	-1.15	20.00	-1.16

C
IOL	Ref.
16.00	1.12
16.50	0.79
17.00	0.45
17.50	**0.11**
18.00	-0.23
18.50	-0.57
19.00	-0.93

SRK/T
Input Parameters
AXIAL : 25.60 mm
K1   : 42.25 D
K2   : 44.75 D
Ds Ref : 0.00 D
             A   B   C
A-const. :118.00 118.90 118.30
Power   : 13.88   14.80   14.12

A		B	
12.50	0.92	13.00	1.02
13.00	0.59	13.50	0.70
13.50	0.26	14.00	0.39
14.00	**-0.08**	**14.50**	**0.06**
14.50	-0.42	15.00	-0.26
15.00	-0.77	15.50	-0.59
15.50	-1.12	16.00	-0.92

C
12.50	1.06
13.00	0.74
13.50	0.41
14.00	**0.08**
14.50	-0.26
15.00	-0.60
15.50	-0.94

Figure 19.6a Good scan

Figure 19.6b Poor scan, right eye of the same patient. Note the difference in axial length and then the difference in the IOL calculation.

Issues:

- Alignment is vital. If the scan is taken off the visual axis, the length of the eye will be measured incorrectly.

- The echoes from the cornea, lens and retina should be present and lined up and of a good height with peaks (and not plateaus) at the top of the responses (Figure 19.5).

- The gain should be at the lowest level at which a good reading can be obtained.

- Pushing in the cornea will distort it and give a falsely short reading.

- Often, a small amount of liquid is placed on the probe to act as a cushion between it and the cornea. Be very careful that this fluid does not add to the axial length of the eye (fluid bridge) (see Figures 19.6a normal, and 19.6b with fluid bridge).

- Average the 5–10 most consistent results. Choose the results yourself from the ones giving the lowest standard deviation (<0.06mm). Don't let the machine do it for you, as a single 'bad' scan will change the average significantly.
- If there is a difference of more than 0.3mm between the two eyes, repeat the procedure.
- If the eye seems very long (more than 25mm) or very short (less than 22mm), check the result again.

Light will behave differently in the eye depending on what materials it is passing through. The speed of light through the eye will therefore need to be changed (by altering the settings on the 'A scan') so that the light passes through the eye without attenuation or scatter and a good scan is achieved as shown in the following list:

Phakic eye	1555 m/s
Aphakic eye	1534 m/s
PMMA pseudophakic eye	1555 m/s
Acrylic pseudophakic eye	1549 m/s
Silicone pseudophakic eye	1487 m/s
Phakic eye with silicone in vitreous	1144 m/s
Aphakic eye with silicone in vitreous	1044 m/s

Non-contact biometry; IOLMaster® and Lenstar®

The technique employed by this equipment is based on laser interferometry with partial coherent light, often termed partial coherence interferometry (PCI). It measures the eye with an infra-red beam and measures from the anterior cornea to the retinal pigmented epithelium. It also measures the visible iris diameter (white to white) and measures the anterior chamber from the corneal epithelium to the anterior surface of the lens. It measures all intraocular distances parallel to the visual axis. The resolution of axial length measurements is 0.01mm.

The Lenstar employs similar methods but uses low coherence optical reflectometry and measures anterior chamber depth from the cornel endothelium to the anterior surface of the lens and can measure the thickness of both cornea and retina. Measurements take longer than with the IOLMaster, but both are very fast. The machines are comparable in their measurement accuracy

Factors affecting measurements for both instruments:

- Technique
- Position of the patient or operator

- Fixation – ocular movement/nystagmus or squint
- Dense cataract
- Pseudophakia/aphakia
- Pterygium distorting the cornea.

Technique for IOLMaster:

- At the beginning of each session, the test eye should be used to calibrate the instrument.
- Overview screen 'O' on measuring view, allows patient alignment – fixation light is yellow.
- Align the patient's eyes. Adjust to the patient distance until 6 light spots are focused on screen.
- Focus corneal reflections and align crosshairs with pupil.

Measuring the axial length:

- Press joystick button once – this takes you to axial length (AL) mode. The patient may wear their own glasses if more than +/- 4D to see fixation light for axial length calculation only.

Keratometry:

- Press 'K' on keyboard, or keratometry symbol on screen.
- Focus peripheral spots and align central spot in crosshair circle.
- Peripheral spots should have a halo around them.
- Ask the patient to blink and open eyes wide.
- Press joystick button once.
- Take second reading and compare – it should not differ by more than 0.5D.
- Highlight best K reading so it will be taken to IOL calculation by the machine.
- Artificial tears may help if patient's eyes are dry and you don't get good focus.

AC Depth/White to White is only required for specific formulae for IOL calculation such as Holladay 2.

IOL calculation:

- Once all measurements have been evaluated for both eyes, go to the IOL calculations screen ('I' or the IOL icon).
- Check that the correct formula has been selected.
- The operator can choose a surgeon from the surgeon box.
- If the desired refraction is other than 'plano', enter power in target refraction box.

- Click on the IOL button and a number will come up in each of the IOL columns.
- Print and secure in the patient's notes, recording any difficulties with the technique.

All machines are slightly different so users should refer to the manual for the machine that they are using

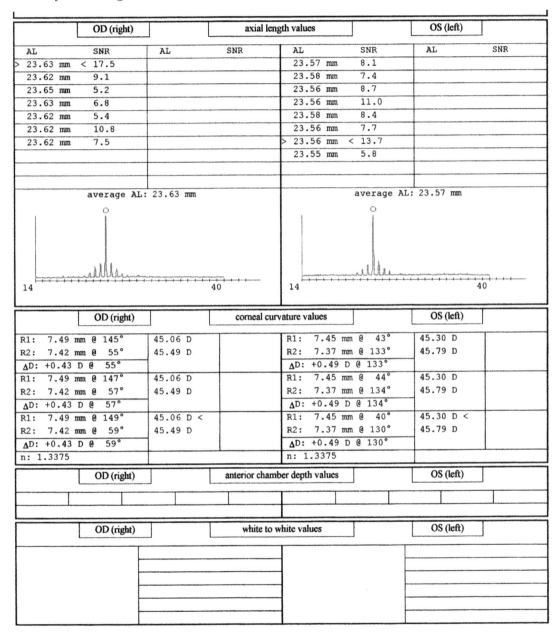

Figure 19.7 IOLMaster®, good scan showing K readings.

Which biometry technique?

The advantages of non-contact over contact biometry techniques include:

- Non-touch technique – more suitable for children/nervous/less compliant patients
- Faster to operate – bigger turnover of patients
- Faster to train staff to use
- Non-contact so no potential for corneal infection transmission or corneal damage
- Can penetrate silicone oil
- Keratometry readings are done by the machine so there is no danger of transcription errors between keratometer and axial length measurement.

All cataract services must also have ultrasound biometry available, as non-contact biometry does not work so well in some cases. Between 8 and 17% of eyes cannot be measured by optical methods (Rajan *et al.* 2002). Biometry skills in this more difficult technique must be maintained to ensure that this significant group of patients are not disadvantaged.

'A scan' ultrasonography is necessary to:

- Measure *dense* cataracts.
- In cases where the patient cannot sit up at a machine, or is non-compliant. Ultrasound biometry can be undertaken with the patient in any position, and under anaesthetic.

In all cases, for best practice:

- Use good (averaged) single scans, which are better than 'Auto' scans, as these may include poor-quality 'averages'.
- Always print out the scan, ensuring its clarity of information.
- Record/annotate if the scan was difficult to obtain.
- Re-measure if >0.3mm difference between the eyes.
- Re-measure if AL <22mm or >25mm.
- Re-measure if Ks <40D or >47D.
- Re-measure if 1D difference in IOL power or Ks that don't match preoperative refraction.
- Keep 'hard copy' of scans in patient's notes.

A difference of 1mm in AL length = to 3D in IOL power.

Formulae and 'A constants'

The formulae for calculating the power of a particular IOL for implantation into a particular eye includes the measured information as well as the 'A constant' for each particular lens. Each IOL also possesses an 'A constant' value, which relates to the position of the IOL as it sits within the eye. This value is supplied by the IOL manufacturer. The 'A constant' value is also pre-programmed into the biometry machine for use in calculation. As A constants were initially formatted for use with applanation biometry, different A constants should be used specifically for optical biometry machines.

An 'A constant', although called a constant, is actually highly variable, depending upon multiple factors – both IOL dependent (such as type, material and position of the lens) and surgeon dependent (including the technique and placement of incision).

Personalisation of 'A constants'

The Royal College of Opthalmologists' (2010) *Guidelines for Cataract Surgery* state that each surgeon should personalise their 'A constant'. This is on the basis of continuous audit of the comparison of the predicted and actual spherical equivalent of the postoperative subjective refraction. No standards for postoperative refraction are mentioned.

Gale *et al.* (2009) state that, using a Royal College of Ophthalmology formula, optimising 'A constants' and partial coherence interferometry, a benchmark standard of 85% of patients achieving a final spherical equivalent within ID of the predicted figure and 55% of patients within 0.5D should be adopted as a standard postoperative refraction outcome.

Formulae

Commonly known examples of formulae are: Holladay I, Holladay II, SRK I, SRK II, SRK/T, Hoffer Q and Haigis. These can usually be adapted (or, indeed, additional formulae installed), depending on the surgeon's preferences. Formulae for calculating the IOL have been refined over time and some are now obsolete although they may still be included on some machines. The formula used is usually identified by the individual surgeon.

The Royal College of Ophthalmologists (2010) considers a range of lengths of eye:

- **Short**: less than 22.00mm
- **Average length**: 22.00 to 24.50mm
- **Medium long**: 24.50 to 26.00mm
- **Very long**: more than 26.00mm.

The guidelines go on to state that different formulae are needed for optimum results in each of these categories.

The most recent meta-analysis of results for different formulae suggests that these formulae, in these eyes, give the best results:

- **Less than 22.00mm**: Haigis or Hoffer Q
- **22.00 to 26.00mm**: Haigis, Hoffer Q, Holladay 2 or SRK/T
- **More than 26.00mm**: Haigis, Holladay 2 or SRK/T.

Different formulae will give different lens powers, even if using the same 'A constants'. It is important to use the correct formula for the individual eye and this is usually specified by the unit's protocol, depending on the axial length of the eye.

Exam Date: **01/04/2010**		Formula: **HofferQ**

Preoperative Data:		**OD**
AL: **23.63 mm**	Refraction:	
R1: **7.49 mm @ 149°**	Visual Acuity: **20/20**	
R2: **7.42 mm @ 59°**	Eye Status: **phakic**	right
opt. ACD:	Target. Ref.: **plano**	

118		118.4		115.4		118.4	
pACD Const: 4.96		pACD Const: 5.21		pACD Const: 3.34		pACD Const: 5.21	
IOL (D)	REF (D)	IOL (D)	REF (D)	IOL (D)	REF (D)	IOL (D)	REF (D)
19.0	−1.2	19.0	−0.9	16.5	−1.2	19.0	−0.9
18.5	−0.8	18.5	−0.5	16.0	−0.8	18.5	−0.5
18.0	−0.5	18.0	−0.2	15.5	−0.4	18.0	−0.2
17.5	**−0.1**	**17.5**	**0.2**	**15.0**	**0.0**	**17.5**	**0.2**
17.0	0.2	17.0	0.5	14.5	0.3	17.0	0.5
16.5	0.6	16.5	0.8	14.0	0.7	16.5	0.8
16.0	0.9	16.0	1.2	13.5	1.1	16.0	1.2
Emme. IOL: 17.33		Emme. IOL: 17.75		Emme. IOL: 14.95		Emme. IOL: 17.75	

Preoperative Data:		**OS**
AL: **23.57 mm**	Refraction:	
R1: **7.45 mm @ 40°**	Visual Acuity: **20/20**	
R2: **7.37 mm @ 130°**	Eye Status: **phakic**	left
opt. ACD:	Target. Ref.: **plano**	

118		118.4		115.4		118.4	
pACD Const: 4.96		pACD Const: 5.21		pACD Const: 3.34		pACD Const: 5.21	
IOL (D)	REF (D)	IOL (D)	REF (D)	IOL (D)	REF (D)	IOL (D)	REF (D)
18.5	−0.9	19.0	−1.0	16.5	−1.4	19.0	−1.0
18.0	−0.6	18.5	−0.6	16.0	−1.0	18.5	−0.6
17.5	−0.2	18.0	−0.3	15.5	−0.6	18.0	−0.3
17.0	**0.1**	**17.5**	**0.1**	**15.0**	**−0.2**	**17.5**	**0.1**
16.5	0.5	17.0	0.4	14.5	0.2	17.0	0.4
16.0	0.8	16.5	0.7	14.0	0.6	16.5	0.7
15.5	1.1	16.0	1.0	13.5	1.0	16.0	1.0
Emme. IOL: 17.17		Emme. IOL: 17.58		Emme. IOL: 14.79		Emme. IOL: 17.58	

Figure 19.8 (above and opposite) SRK/T and Hoffer Q calculations on the same eye, showing the difference in recommended lens due to the use of different formulae.

Preoperative Data:		OD
AL: **23.63 mm**	Refraction:	
R1: **7.49 mm @ 149°**	Visual Acuity: **20/20**	
R2: **7.42 mm @ 59°**	Eye Status: **phakic**	right
opt. ACD:	Target. Ref.: **plano**	

118		118.4		115.4		118.4	
A Const:	118	A Const:	118.4	A Const:	115.4	A Const:	118.4
IOL (D)	REF (D)	IOL (D)	REF (D)	IOL (D)	REF (D)	IOL (D)	REF (D)
19.5	−1.12	20.0	−1.15	17.0	−1.24	20.0	−1.15
19.0	−0.77	19.5	−0.81	16.5	−0.85	19.5	−0.81
18.5	−0.43	19.0	−0.47	16.0	−0.45	19.0	−0.47
18.0	**−0.09**	**18.5**	**−0.13**	**15.5**	**−0.07**	**18.5**	**−0.13**
17.5	0.25	18.0	0.20	15.0	0.32	18.0	0.20
17.0	0.59	17.5	0.53	14.5	0.70	17.5	0.53
16.5	0.92	17.0	0.85	14.0	1.07	17.0	0.85
Emme. IOL: 17.87		Emme. IOL: 18.30		Emme. IOL: 15.42		Emme. IOL: 18.30	

Preoperative Data:		OS
AL: **23.57 mm**	Refraction:	
R1: **7.45 mm @ 40°**	Visual Acuity: **20/20**	
R2: **7.37 mm @ 130°**	Eye Status: **phakic**	left
opt. ACD:	Target. Ref.: **plano**	

118		118.4		115.4		118.4	
A Const:	118	A Const:	118.4	A Const:	115.4	A Const:	118.4
IOL (D)	REF (D)	IOL (D)	REF (D)	IOL (D)	REF (D)	IOL (D)	REF (D)
19.5	−1.19	19.5	−0.87	17.0	−1.32	19.5	−0.87
19.0	−0.84	19.0	−0.54	16.5	−0.93	19.0	−0.54
18.5	−0.50	18.5	−0.20	16.0	−0.54	18.5	−0.20
18.0	**−0.16**	**18.0**	**0.13**	**15.5**	**−0.15**	**18.0**	**0.13**
17.5	0.18	17.5	0.46	15.0	0.23	17.5	0.46
17.0	0.51	17.0	0.78	14.5	0.61	17.0	0.78
16.5	0.84	16.5	1.10	14.0	0.99	16.5	1.10
Emme. IOL: 17.76		Emme. IOL: 18.19		Emme. IOL: 15.31		Emme. IOL: 18.19	

The importance of skill, judgement and accuracy

The addition of all of these component investigations should provide the surgeon with the necessary detail to choose the best IOL to potentiate the accurate postoperative refraction in the patient. A printout from any machine should be correctly annotated and presented in the patient's notes for this purpose and for future reference.

As with all technical diagnostic systems, the manufacturer's instructions should be adhered to, and practitioners should be fully conversant with the system's capabilities, as well as its limitations, to ensure that the systematic and accurate assessment of the eye is used. Keratometry must be carried out, and axial length must be accurately measured and used with the surgeon's preferred 'A constant' to arrive at the 'best' IOL choice.

During the biometry and calculation process, a strict protocol must be maintained to minimise errors and reduce the need for high-powered spectacle lenses or, at worst, IOL exchange. Accuracy in biometry can be maintained through:

- Adequate training
- Understanding of basic optics
- Practising regularly and annual updates
- Establishing protocols
- Checking results a second time, if in doubt
- Maintaining equipment.
- Acknowledging the limitations of one's own practice.

The non-contact machines, in particular, appear to be 'idiot proof' – all that is needed is to push a button. However, whichever method is used, professional judgement and a high level of critical skill (knowing why, how, what and when), is crucial to achieving consistently good results.

Implanting the wrong lens (which is often a result of incorrect biometry) is the largest cause of medical negligence claims in ophthalmology. Mistakes are easy to make but much more difficult to rectify.

Auditing results

The only way of knowing what you are doing is correct is to audit the results. All cataract services should have audit programmes to ensure that benchmark standards are achieved. Personal biometrist audits should be carried out, as well as audits at surgeon and unit level. Continued learning from unexpected outcomes, good-quality training and education of those who undertake biometry, and good communication between them and surgical teams, are all needed to ensure good outcomes for patients.

Cataract surgery
The history of cataract surgery

'Couching', a technique that involved pushing the cataract down into the vitreous and away from the visual axis, used to be the method of choice in removing the block to light getting into the eye. Much more complex ophthalmic surgery is also described in texts on ancient Indian and Arabian medicine. Couching is still used by traditional healers to improve vision in parts of the world today.

Pierre Brisseau (1631–1717) identified the lens as the site of cataract and this was corroborated by Antoine Maitre-Jan (1650–1725) in 1707. Before this, ancient texts proposed differing reasons why vision fails due to cataract. The first successful removal of a cataractous lens, via a corneal incision, was undertaken in 1750 by Jacques Daviel (1693?–1762) who performed what was essentially an extracapsular extraction, removing the anterior capsule first and then expressing the lens matter. Soon after this, Samuel Sharp of London developed a strategy to extract the full unbroken lens via an incision by placing pressure next to the incision with his thumb.

Since the lens was removed whole in this technique and it was undesirable for lens matter to be left behind, it was considered important that the lens was hard or 'ripe–', a belief that persists in some patients to the present day. Once removed, with no IOL being available, the patient remained aphakic. No sutures were available until Henry Willard Williams (1821–1895) used corneal sutures for the first time in 1865 (Albert & Edwards 1996). Williams also routinely used anaesthesia for cataract operations. Carl Koller (1857–1944), described the effects of cocaine on the eye in 1884. Postoperative aphakia was the norm until Harold Ridley's innovation in 1947.

Three main advances in cataract surgery are worth identifying:

- Intracapsular lens extraction
- Extracapsular lens extraction
- Phacoemulsification.

Intracapsular lens extraction (ICCE)

This is an almost redundant procedure in contemporary times. In this procedure, popularised by Hermann Knapp (1832–1911), the whole of the lens, including the lens capsule, was removed through a large corneal or limbal incision. The zonules were dissolved using chemical agents, and in later times Zonulysin®. A cryotherapy machine was then prepared in order to freeze a cryoprobe tip. When excess moisture was removed from all surfaces, contact was made between the lens and cryoprobe, causing adhesion, so that the lens could be removed.

This technique was clumsy compared with current methods and carried with it a high risk of retinal detachment, resulting from the shifting and displacement of the vitreous gel into the space left by removing the lens. Damage to the structure that would support the lens caused difficulty in IOL insertion (when used). A large rate of refractive error occurred because of no IOL insertion or, latterly, poorly 'measured' or poorly placed IOLs. (This was before the use of biometry techniques.)

The large 180° incision, usually from the 3 to 9 o'clock position, left problematic correction surgery, leaving patients to use aphakic glasses of +10D power or more.

Patients needed to have both eyes operated on within a short timescale in order to be fitted with their corrective spectacles, and many experienced problems with unsatisfactory postoperative refraction.

Early developments in the use of intraocular lenses helped ease this problem, and patients could either be fitted with iris clip or anterior chamber lens implants, and spectacle prescriptions of more acceptable powers could be used. The corneal section was usually sutured with five interrupted sutures, leading to the possibility of iris prolapse through a slipped or broken suture and longstanding astigmatism until the section was stabilised. Tight sutures might cause astigmatic problems. Suture sites had the potential to become infected.

Extracapsular lens extraction (ECCE)

Considered safer than ICCE, this technique was the 'gold standard ' until the late 1990s, when it was superseded by phacoemulsification. It remains the default procedure when phacoemulsification is considered inappropriate or if a phacoemulsification procedure requires converting to ECCE. Extracapsular lens extraction requires a large corneal or limbal incision, with the potential problems discussed above. However, with foldable lenses currently being used, the incision is smaller, though it remains large by contemporary standards.

The main advantage over ICCE was that the lens cortex was removed, expressed from the globe in its entirety, through an aperture manufactured in the anterior lens capsule using a 'can opener' technique and leavening a serrated edge on the anterior capsule. This lens matter was delivered using a squint hook, or a similar instrument and a 'Vectis', a small looped instrument to cradle the lens from the globe. The use of a viscoelastic medium to bathe the internal structures, offering some protection to them, improved intraoperative complication rates greatly. After expression of the lens nucleus, remaining soft lens matter (cortex) can be removed by irrigation and aspiration techniques. Variations in the technique for creating the capsular opening in order to facilitate removal of the lens contents are common.

For some time, different lens positions were used, such as posterior chamber, anterior chamber or pupil suspension. As ECCE established itself as the norm, posterior lenses became standard, located within the remaining lens capsule. This allowed for greater stability of lens position and, with the emphasis on IOL calculation, postoperative visual outcome was improved. Refraction was easier for the optometrist to establish. Other positions used for the IOL were a matter of clinical need.

The ECCE is still the procedure of choice in many areas of the developing world because the instrumentation associated with it is much less complex and expensive than for phacoemulsification surgery (which requires 'disposables', the single-use technical equipment needed for modern phacoemulsification surgery). However, the eye does not recover as quickly as a result of the larger incision; and removal of the sutures can change the contour of the eye and induce astigmatism, which will need to be corrected to achieve the best visual potential for the patient.

Phacoemulsification.

This is currently the standard form of cataract surgery in developed countries. Pioneered by Charles Kelman (1930–2004) in 1967, phacoemulsification involves using ultrasonic vibrations, at 40,000Hz, to sculpt and break up the lens cortex and nucleus, before irrigation and aspiration of the remaining lens fragments. Kelman took inspiration from his dentist's ultrasonic teeth cleaning system (Pandey *et al.* 2004).

Phacoemulsification is undertaken through a small incision (about 2–3mm long). A single continuous circular tear is made in the anterior capsule, capsulorhexis, and then, using hydrodissection, under a protective layer of a viscoelastic substance, the nucleus and cortex are separated. Some surgeons 'chop' the cataract, some 'divide' and some 'flip.' This will depend on the particular surgeon and clinical need. Aspiration of the nucleus is performed, and this is followed by irrigation and aspiration to remove the remaining soft lens matter (cortex). The technique only requires a small incision, due to the development of flexible IOL materials that can be preloaded into a small 'injector', re-inserted through the small incision and 'injected' into the capsule, where they unfurl into position. Prior to this development, the small incision needed for phacoemulsification had to be enlarged to implant the lens, although techniques involving 'stepped' incisions through the sclera into the anterior chamber allowed sutureless surgery.

The much smaller, contemporary incision minimises wound leaks, due to the stepped incision and interior intraocular pressure forcing the wound shut; this also minimises iris prolapse problems. Sculpting of the lens nucleus before removal makes it a much more refined technique, with reduced incidence of capsular rupture. Surgically induced astigmatism is less common, and the wound to the eye generally heals much more quickly, making it easier for patients to return to normal day-to-day activities within a relatively short time period.

(Manual) small incision cataract surgery (MSICS)

This procedure can be considered a hybrid of ECCE and phacoemulsification. A larger corneal incision than phacoemulsification is required, or often, a scleral tunnel incision which can be sutureless. A rigid IOL is generally used as they are less expensive, but foldable lenses can be used when available. The procedure is sutureless and is quick to perform. With cheaper disposables than phacoemulsification, it gives similar postoperative visual results to phacoemulsification, at a fraction of the cost. It is therefore ideal in developing countries and or in high-volume performing clinics.

A study by Haripriya *et al.* (2012) stated that, for experienced surgeons using both phacoemulsification and MSICS, intraoperative complication rates were comparably low. However, for trainee surgeons, the complication rate was significantly higher with phacoemulsification, suggesting that MSICS may be a safer initial procedure to learn for inexperienced cataract surgeons in the developing (and perhaps also the developed) world.

The development of intraocular lenses (IOLs)

The first lens for implantation within the eye was introduced by Ridley in 1949 and manufactured by Rayner's of Brighton and Hove, in conjunction with their chief optical scientist, John Pike (Apple & Sims 1996). The first substance used in the manufacture was polymethylmethacrylate (PMMA), usually known by its trade name Plexiglas®. Apple and Sims (1996) note that the quality of the PMMA was thought to be causing issues with infection and approached the PMMA manufacturers, particularly the chemist, John Holt at Imperial Chemical Industries (ICI), to ask if it would be possible to improve the purity. This was achieved by removing free monomers. The trade name of this modified version is Plexiglas CQ® ('CQ' meaning 'clinical quality'). It is worth noting the altruism of Ridley, Pike and Holt, who sought no financial reward and did not patent or copyright the original IOL.

Various generations of IOLs have existed and continue to evolve, but in the main, four main substances are used in their manufacture; polymethylmethacrylate (PMMA), silicone, hydrophobic acrylate, hydrophilic acrylate and collamer. IOLs can be divided into three major types:

- Monofocal
- Multifocal
- Toric.

Monofocal IOLs

Monofocal IOLs are designed for either near or distance vision. This type of IOL will require the patient to wear some prescription eyewear after the procedure, due to the limitation of the IOL's ability. It is common for IOLs to be chosen to provide better distance vision than near vision. After surgery and following refraction, glasses are used to achieve sharp near vision.

Multifocal (or accommodative) IOLs

Multifocal IOLs allow correction for both near and distance vision; and both near and far objects can be in focus at the same time. The brain learns to select the visual information it needs to form an image of either near or distant objects, so multifocal IOLs may require some adjustment. A patient may adjust to multifocal IOLs if they are placed in both eyes. Multifocal lenses are not included in normal NHS contract agreements, which may consider them to be a 'premium lens', which may not be an option for the majority of patients within a public health service such as the NHS. In addition, depending on the clinical findings, this lens may not be suitable for some patients.

Toric IOLs

Toric IOLs are a type of monofocal IOL that helps correct astigmatism. It may also be considered a premium lens, so it might cost more than a monofocal IOL and again may not be available in the NHS.

Different permutations of lens design appear at regular intervals on the commercial market – so much so that IOL manufacturing has become a global, multimillion-pound enterprise. By 2020, the market in IOLs is expected to be, in the United States alone, worth $4.7b, by 2020 (Research and Markets 2015).

Anaesthesia

Generations of different anaesthetics have been used for cataract surgery. There has been an overall shift from predominantly general anaesthetic (GA), local (or regional) anaesthetic (LA) to topical anaesthetic, with general anaesthesia now only being used in the main for patients who are unable to lie still or cooperate with the needs of the surgery. While general anaesthesia was introduced in the nineteenth century, topical anaesthetic was an early development, with the introduction of cocaine anaesthesia by Kolle in 1884. In the same year, Knapp introduced retrobulbar anaesthesia.

Peribulbar and retrobulbar techniques are associated with a risk of complications such as globe perforation, optic nerve damage, retrobulbar haemorrhage and muscle injury, as well as life-threatening complications of stimulation of the oculocardiac reflex arc, intravenous or intra-arterial injection or brain stem anaesthesia.

Introduction of the sub-tenon's anaesthesia technique reduced the risk of complications of peribulbar/retrobulbar anaesthesia. These techniques were all designed to block the area enough to stop the eye moving (akinesia). Evolving surgical techniques have reduced the need for akinesia, and the anaesthetic of choice is now often topical with intracameral or sub-tenon's anaesthesia.

An anaesthetist should be present if retrobulbar, peribulbar and sharp-needle sub-tenon's techniques are used. An anaesthetist is not essential when topical, subconjunctival or blunt-cannula sub-tenon's techniques without sedation are used (Royal College of Ophthalmologists 2010).

It could be argued that the risks of retrobulbar anaesthesia in particular (with the skill degradation which results from its rare use) make it a technique that should no longer be used.

Sedation rates for cataract extraction in the UK are very low, and explanation and hand-holding can alleviate much of the anxiety associated with the procedure.

Complications of cataract surgery

Table 19.2 Possible complications and errors in cataract surgery (Royal College of Ophthalmologists 2010)

Area	Preoperative	Intraoperative	Postoperative
Incision	Wrong site	Perforation Descemet's Detachment Thermal burns	Wound leak Would dehiscence
Cornea	Missed endothelial pathology		Astigmatism Oedema/bullous keratopathy
Anterior segment		Haemorrhage	Pressure rise (5.3%) Long-term raised pressure (2.3%) Endophthalmitis (0.072–0.3%)
Capsule		Radial tears in anterior capsule Rhexis too small Rupture with hydrodissection Rupture during Phako	Capsule block syndrome Late tear with IOL posterior Posterior capsule opacification
Zonules	Missed phacodonesis	Subluxation	IOL/Bag decentration
	Missed lens subluxation	Dislocation	Sunset syndrome
Nucleus		Trapped nucleus (non-rotating) Subluxation Dropped nucleus (0.3%–1.1%)	
Iris		Prolapse Phaco damage	Pupil capture Epithelial ingrowth
IOL	Wrong power calculation	Insertion damage Incorrect positioning	Inflammation
Retina/ Vitreous		Incarceration in the section Retinal tear Choroidal haemorrhage (0.04%–0.20%). Only 45% of affected eyes will achieve 6/60 or better, on recovery.	Cystoid macular oedema (1–12%) Retinal detachment (0. 1–0.8%)

Complications in surgery are categorised in three time slots: preoperative (issues occurring up to the procedure); intraoperative (issues occurring during the procedure); and postoperative (issues occurring after the procedure, either immediately or up to discharge). The Royal College of Ophthalmologists' *Cataract Surgery Guidelines* (2010) clearly set out these complications in each period, with the last percentages included where available (Table 19.2).

Some of the above complications are described in greater detail below.

Raised intraocular pressure

Raised IOP is often due to the blockage of the aqueous outflow channels with the viscoelastic substance used. The pressure may also rise as a reaction to the surgery or as a result of inflammation. The patient is likely to experience pain and blurring of vision, which occurs some hours after surgery. Oral Diamox is used in some cases, both preoperatively and postoperatively.

Posterior capsule rupture

Rupture of the posterior capsule during surgery may result in the nucleus dropping back into the vitreous, necessitating vitrectomy either during surgery or later. Posterior capsule rupture may also result in the need to insert a different type of IOL.

Shallow anterior chamber

A shallow anterior chamber may be caused by inhibition of aqueous production, a wound leak resulting from surgery or postoperative trauma, or raised pressure. If the chamber becomes very shallow, the corneal endothelium may be damaged by touching the iris and this may result in permanent corneal oedema.

Uveitis

Uveitis occurs as an inflammatory response to surgery. It is a rare consequence of surgery and so patients will be treated postoperatively, with eye drops containing a steroid, to reduce and control this inflammation. Increased pain and redness of the eye may occur if the inflammation increases, and modification of the drop therapy may be required. Infection is always a possible complication of surgery and, for this reason, prophylactic antibiotic drops will also be prescribed after cataract extraction.

Retinal detachment

Retinal detachment may occur after cataract surgery in a very small number of cases.

Cystoid macular oedema

Oedema of the retina at the macula (cystoid macular oedema) is also recognised as a complication of cataract extraction and is likely to cause some disturbance of central vision. It often disappears over time with treatment with oral steroids.

Posterior capsular opacification (PCO)

PCO is the most frequent long-term complication of surgery, and is reported in 10–50% of all cases (Apple *et al.* 2001). The posterior portion of the remaining lens capsule becomes opacified and the patient reports a reduction in vision. Posterior capsular opacities are easily dealt with in a painless and fast outpatient procedure, using a laser to burn a hole in the capsule with a ND-Yag laser (Neodymium-Doped Yttrium Aluminium Garnet) (Figure 19.10).

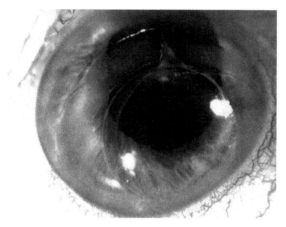

Figure 19.9 Dislocated IOL

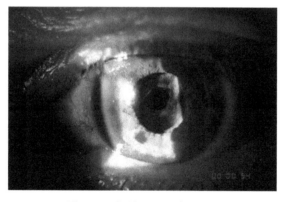

Figure 19.10 Capsulotomy

Approaches to care of the cataract patient

Cataract is a common cause of visual impairment affecting about 30% of the population over the age of 65 years. In parallel with the improvements in the anaesthetic and surgical techniques used in cataract extraction, trends towards day-case care have developed.

Changes in attitudes, roles and the working relationships between ophthalmic healthcare professionals have greatly influenced the development of day-case care. Probably one of the most influential factors is the expanded role of ophthalmic nurses in the preoperative assessment and postoperative management of cataract patients.

It is the expanded nursing role, from the initial screening of GP or optometrist referral, through to increased nursing input into patient care in preoperative assessment clinics, that has created flexibility in the coordinating of theatre lists, transport arrangements and admission routines, which have influenced the rapid development of day-case care.

The preoperative (surgical) assessment clinic facilitates better opportunities to provide more detailed information in relation to the perioperative management of cataract for patients. Increased patient involvement and subsequent cooperation in care planning leads to the negotiation of much more flexible approaches to perioperative care.

In the postoperative management of cataract patients, the increased use of local anaesthesia, whether by facial blocks or sub-tenon's or subconjunctival injections, or the more recent use of topical anaesthetic drops, removes the need to keep patients in hospital overnight.

Small-incision phacoemulsification and the subsequent shortening of the recovery time needed after cataract surgery have also assisted in shortening the length of hospital stay for patients.

Surgical (wound) healing rates are much faster and the delicate nature of the surgical techniques used usually results in much less disruption to the anterior chamber and fewer postoperative complications.

All the above factors have helped in the development of one-stop cataract services, which have also influenced the development of nurse-led postoperative ocular examination (also known as first dressing) in both hospital and community settings.

References

Ahmed, I.K. (2012) The Art of Managing PXF Glaucoma. *Review of Ophthalmology.* (4),104.

Albert, D.M. & Edwards, D.D. (1996) *The History of Ophthalmology.* Oxford: Blackwell Science.

Albert, D., Miller, J., Azar, D. & Blodi, B. (2008) *Mechanism of cataract formation: Albert & Jakobiec's Principles and Practice of Ophthalmology.* Philadelphia: Saunders Elsevier Inc.

Apple, D.J. & Sims J. (January 1996) Harold Ridley and the Invention of the Intraocular Lens. *Survey of Ophthalmology.* **40** (4), 279.

Apple, D.J., Peng, Q., Visessook, N., Werner, L., Pandey, S.K., Escobar-Gomez, M., Ram, J. & Auffarth, G.U. (2001) Eradication of posterior capsule opacification: documentation of a marked decrease in Nd:YAG laser posterior capsulotomy rates noted in an analysis of 5416 pseudophakic human eyes obtained postmortem. *Ophthalmology.* **108**, 505–18.

Astbury, N. & Ramamurthy, B.L. (2006) How to Avoid Mistakes in Biometry. *Community Eye Health.*19(60), 70–71.

Babizhayev, M.A. & Yegorov, Y.E. (2015) *Telomere Attrition in Human Lens Epithelial Cells Associated with Oxidative Stress Provide a New Therapeutic Target for the Treatment, Dissolving and Prevention of Cataract with N-Acetylcarnosine Lubricant Eye Drops. Kinetic, Pharmacological and Activity-Dependent Separation of Therapeutic Targeting: Transcorneal Penetration and Delivery of L-Carnosine in the Aqueous Humor and Hormone-Like Hypothalamic Antiaging Effects of the Instilled Ophthalmic Drug Through a Safe Eye Medication Technique. Recent Patents on Drug Delivery and Formulation.* June 2015.

Bollinger, K.E. & Langston, R.H. (2008) What Can Patients Expect From Cataract Surgery? *Cleveland Clinic Journal of Medicine.* **75**(3), 193–96.

Byrne, S.F. (1995) *A-Scan Axial Eye Length Measurements. A Handbook for IOL Calculations.* Mars Hill: Grove Park Publishers.

Centers for Disease Control and Prevention (2000) *Measuring Healthy Days.* Atlanta: CDC.

Chinmayu, S. (2011) *Comprehensive Notes in Ophthalmology.* New Delhi: Jaypee Brothers Medical Publishers.

Congdon, N., Taylor H. (2003) 'Chapter 8: Age Related Cataract' in G.J. Johnson, D.C. Minassian, S. West & R. Weale (eds.) *The Epidemiology of Eye Disease.* London: Arnold Publishers.

Craig, S. (2015) Nurses' Role in Early Detection of Cataracts. *Nursing Times.* **111**(17), 12–14.

Dolin P. (1998) 'Chapter 5: Epidemiology of Cataract' in J.G. Johnson, D.C. Minassian & R. Robert Weale. *The Epidemiology of Eye Disease.* London: Chapman & Hall Medical.

Elbaz, U., Barkana, Y., Gerber, Y., Avni, I. & Zadok, D. (2007) Comparison of different techniques of anterior chamber depth and keratometric measurements. *American Journal of Ophthalmology.* **143**, 48–53.

Gale, R.P., Saldana, M., Johnston, R.L., Zuberbuhler, B. & McKibbin, M. (2009) Benchmark Standards for Refractive Outcomes after NHS Cataract Surgery. *Eye.* **23**, 149–52.

Hammond, C.J., Duncan. D.D., Snieder. H., de Lange, M., West, S.K., Spector, T.D. & Gilbert, C.E. (2001) The Heritability of Age-Related Cortical Cataract: The Twin Eye Study. *Investigative Ophthalmology and Visual Science.* **42**, 601–605.

Haripriya, A., Chang, D.F., Reena, M. & Shekhar, M. (2012) Complication Rates of Phacoemulsification and Manual Small-Incision Cataract Surgery at Aravind Eye Hospital. *Journal of Cataract & Refractive Surgery.* **38**(8), 1360–69.

Health and Social Care Information Centre (2014) *Hospital Episode Statistics: Main Procedures and Interventions: 2011–14.* London: HSCIC.

Keay, L., Lindsley, K., Tielsch, J., Katz, J. & Schein, O. (2012). *Routine Preoperative Medical Testing for Cataract Surgery (Review).* London: Cochrane Eyes and Vision Group.

Knudston, M.D., Klien, B.E.K., Kline, R., Cruickshanks, K.J. & Lee, K.E. (2005) Age Related Eye Disease, Quality of Life and Functional Activity. *Archives of Ophthalmology.* **123**, 807–14.

Lakes, R.S. & Park, J. (1992) *Biomaterials: An Introduction* (2nd ed.). Springer Science & Business Media.

Lansingh, V. (2010) *Cataract and Public Health*. International Council of Ophthalmology.

Lee, D.A. & Higginbotham, E.J. (1999) *Clinical Guide to Comprehensive Ophthalmology*. New York: Thieme Medical Publishers.

Mangione, C.M., Berry, S., Spritzer, K., Janz, N.K., Klein, R., Owsley, C. & Lee P.P. (1998) Identifying the content area for the 51-item National Eye Institute Visual Function Questionnaire: results from focus groups with visually impaired persons. *Archives of Ophthalmology*. **116**, 227–33.

Mehravaran, S., Asgari, S., Bigdeli, S., Shahnazi, A. & Hashemi, H. (2014) Keratometry with five different techniques: a study of device repeatability and inter-device agreement. *International Ophthalmology*. **34**, 869–75.

Minassian, D.C., Reidy, A., Desai, P., Farrow, S., Vafidis, G. & Minassian, A. (2000). The Deficit in Cataract Surgery in England and Wales and the Escalating Problem of Visual Impairment: Epidemiological Modelling of the Population Dynamics of Cataract. *British Journal of Ophthalmology*. **84**, 4–8.

National Institute for Health and Care Excellence (2010). *Clinical Knowledge Summaries – Cataracts*. London: NICE.

Pandey, S.K., Milverton, E.J. & Maloof, A.J. (2004). A Tribute to Charles David Kelman MD: Ophthalmologist, Inventor and Pioneer of Phacoemulsification Surgery. *Clinical & Experimental Ophthalmology*. **32**(5), 529–33.

Rajan, M.S., Keilhorn, I. & Bell, J.A. (2002) Partial coherence laser interferometry vs conventional ultrasound biometry in intraocular lens power calculations. *Eye*. **16**, 552–56.

Research and Markets (2015) Global Intraocular Lens Industry Report.

Ritch, R. & Schlotzer-Schrehardt, U. (2001). Exfoliation Syndrome. *Survey of Ophthalmology*. **45**, 265–315.

Royal College of Ophthalmologists (2010). *Cataract Surgery Guidelines*. London: RCO.

Snell, R.S. & Lemp, M.A. (1998) *Clinical Anatomy of the Eye*. 2nd edn. USA: Blackwell Science.

Tobwala, S., Humerya, K. & Ercol, N. (2015) 'Antioxidant defense networks in the lens and benefits of glutathione prodrugs in cataracts' in M. Babizhayev, D. Wang-Chen Li, A. Kasus-Jacobi, L. Zoric & J.L. Alio (eds) *Studies on the Cornea and Lens*. New York: Human Press.

Valleix, S., Niel, F., Nedelec, B., Algros, M.P., Schwartz, C., Delbosc, B., Delpech, M. & Kantelip, B. (2006) Homozygous nonsense mutation in the FOXE3 gene as a cause of congenital primary aphakia in humans. *American Journal of Human Genetics*. **79**(2), 358–64.

Vresen, G.F. (2009) Early Cortical Lens Opacities: A Short Overview. *Acta Ophthalmologica*. **87**(6), 602–10.

World Health Organization (2010) *Global Data on Visual Impairment*. Geneva: WHO.

World Health Organization (2012) *Visual Impairment and Blindness Factsheet, Number 282*. Geneva: WHO.

Yanoff, M. & Duker, J.S. (2014) *Ophthalmology*. 4th edn. USA: Elsevier Saunders.

Zajac, A. & Hecht, E. (2003). *Optics*. 4th edn. Harlow: Pearson Higher Education.

CHAPTER TWENTY

The uveal tract

Carol Slight and Susanne Raynel

with material from Bronwyn Ward and Gayle Catt

Anatomy and physiology

The uveal tract makes up the middle layer of the globe and is protected by the cornea and sclera. Although it is a continuous layer, it has three distinct parts: the choroid, ciliary body and iris, which differ in location and structure. The term 'uvea' is derived from the Italian uva, a grape, because the uveal tract is the vascular layer of the globe and so, when it is examined, it looks like the inside of a dusky grape skin. The choroid has cells containing melanin pigment, which also contribute to the 'grape-like' colour.

The iris

The iris is the most anterior structure of the uveal tract arising from the ciliary body; it is situated behind the cornea and in front of the lens. It is a coloured diaphragm separating the anterior and posterior chambers of the globe and has a central hole, the pupil, through which aqueous passes between the two chambers and light rays enter the globe. Although the iris appears rigid, it is in fact 'floppy' and is supported, to remain in place, by the lens. Without this support, it trembles (iridodonesis). The iris is made up of a vascular stroma located anteriorly and pigmented epithelium located posteriorly. The stroma is divided into an anterior border (loose collagen tissues with densely packed pigmented or non-pigmented cells) and a deeper stroma. The anterior border forms the pupillary zone, which is about 1.5mm wide. The remaining, wider area of iris is the ciliary zone with iris crypts formed by irregular atrophy. The border of the anterior area is known as the collarette, which is a circular ridge and the site of the minor vascular circle of the iris.

The sphincter and dilator muscles of the iris are found within the stroma. The sphincter muscle is about 1mm wide and surrounds the pupil, facilitating constriction of the pupil; it is innervated by the parasympathetic fibres of the third cranial nerve. The dilator muscle consists of multiple radial fibres in the periphery, facilitating pupil dilatation and innervated by sympathetic fibres. The sphincter muscle is stronger than the dilator muscles and, if the normal functioning of the muscles is interrupted, the sphincter muscle will overpower the dilator muscle. This is demonstrated in patients presenting with iritis when the pupil is small.

The stroma of the iris also has melanin-containing pigment cells and the density of these cells determines the colour of the iris. At birth, pigment is absent from the iris but by the age of 1 year the pigment is laid down and this is why Caucasian babies all appear to have blue eyes at birth; this may change by the time they are aged 1 year but iris colour will not change after this. In brown eyes, the surface of the iris is smooth and heavily pigmented; in blue eyes it is irregular with multiple crypts.

The iris receives its blood supply from the long posterior ciliary artery and the anterior ciliary artery. These join to form the major circle of the iris, which lies in the pars plicata and sends branches posteriorly into the ciliary body, as well as forward into the iris; this then forms the minor circle of the iris. The venous return of the iris is via the vortex veins.

The ciliary body

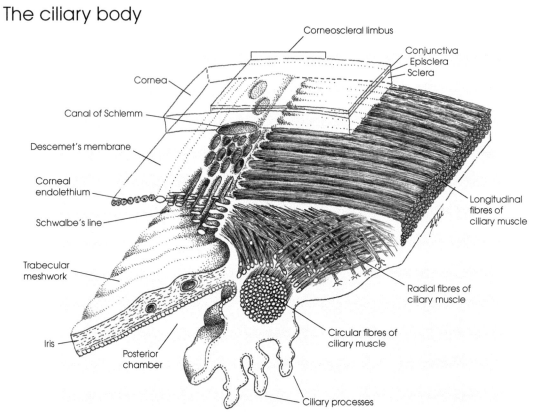

Figure 20.1 Cross-section through the iris and ciliary body.

The ciliary body (Figure 20.1) is between 4 and 6mm wide, roughly triangular in shape, and situated between the anterior choroid and the root of the iris. It is adherent to the sclera just behind the limbus, continuous with the iris and extends from the scleral spur to the ora serrata. Blood is supplied to the ciliary body by the anterior ciliary arteries and long posterior ciliary arteries, and drainage is via the anterior ciliary veins, long posterior ciliary veins and vortex vein. The nerve supply comes from the oculomotor nerve via the short ciliary nerve.

The ciliary body can be divided into three distinct sections: the pars plicata, pars plana and ciliary muscles. The pars plicata is the anterior part of the ciliary body and lies between the pars plana and iris. It appears corrugated and is about 2mm long. It is from the pars plicata that the ciliary processes arise. There are about 70 ciliary processes and these are composed of vascular tissue (mainly capillaries and veins), covered by epithelium. The ciliary processes can be divided into two layers: the outer layer is an extension of the pigment epithelium of the retina; and the inner layer is unpigmented and continuous with the neural retina. The ciliary processes are responsible for the formation and secretion of aqueous: first into the posterior chamber; and then via the pupil to the anterior chamber. The lens is also held in situ by fine suspensory ligaments that arise in the ciliary processes and valleys, known as zonular fibres (zonules of Zinn).

The pars plana is the posterior part of the ciliary body; it is about 4.5mm long and lies next to the ora serrata. Whereas the pars plicata appears corrugated, the pars plana is generally flat and it is via the pars plana that vitreoretinal surgery is undertaken. There is also some attachment of zonular fibres from the lens to the pars plana.

The ciliary muscles form the bulk of the ciliary body, and lie adjacent to the sclera; they are made up of a combination of longitudinal, circular and radial fibres, which are controlled by the oculomotor nerve. It is the ciliary muscles, specifically the circular fibres, that are responsible for accommodation. The circular fibres contract and relax the ciliary processes, thus allowing the lens to become more convex and enabling light rays to be focused on the retina when looking at objects nearer than 'infinity'. The longitudinal fibres are responsible for influencing the microscopic channels of the trabecular meshwork, facilitating the outflow of aqueous and thereby assisting with the regulation of intraocular pressure.

The choroid

The choroid is a vascular layer situated between the retina and sclera; it is about 0.22mm thick posteriorly, thinning to 0.1mm at the periphery; it is firmly attached to the margins of the optic nerve posteriorly and anteriorly joins the ciliary body. Blood is supplied to the choroid by the short posterior ciliary artery and drainage is via the choroidal and vortex veins; the nerve supply comes from the oculomotor nerve via the posterior ciliary artery. The choroid extends from the optic nerve towards the ora serrata and is continuous with the ciliary body and iris.

The choroid can be divided into three distinct layers: the basal lamina, blood vessels and lamina fusca. The basal lamina, more commonly called Bruch's membrane, is very thin (2–3µm); it is the inner layer of the choroid and is situated between the retinal pigment epithelium and the choriocapillaris. It consists of two layers, the outer made up of collagen and the inner being the basement membrane of the pigment epithelium.

The middle layer of the choroid is a meshwork of blood vessels where the arteries and veins are external, whereas a dense network layer of capillaries, the choriocapillaris, is internal. This meshwork of blood vessels is sandwiched between the basal lamina and lamina fusca. The lamina fusca is the outer layer of the choroid and, as the name suggests, is a supporting structure between the blood vessel layer and the sclera.

The primary function of the choroid is to nourish the outer layer of the retina but it also has a role in reducing internal reflection of stray light rays via pigment cells (melanin) and helps disperse heat that may collect in the retina.

Uveitis

Uveitis refers to inflammation of the uveal tract. Initial presentation for uveitis is usually between the ages of 20 and 50 years of age, with children making up about 5% of cases. In the United States, uveitis accounts for around 10% of permanent blindness; and in developing countries the equivalent figure is around 24%.

Classification of uveitis

This is based on the Standardisation of Uveitis nomenclature. Uveitis may be classified in many ways but a simple classification is on the basis of disease course, laterality, granulomatous or non-granulomatous and anatomical location in the eye (Huang & Gaudio 2010, Trusko *et al.* 2013).

Careful classification can help in identifying potential underlying causes of uveitis, as shown below.

Disease course

- Acute: Disease course of less than 3 months with sudden onset and limited duration
- Chronic: Persistent uveitis with relapse in less than 3 months, whether on or off treatment
- Recurrent: Repeated episode separated by inactivity of more than 3 months, whether on or off treatment.

Unilateral or bilateral

Granulomatous or non-granulomatous: Defines size and type of keratic precipitates on endothelium.

Main anatomical location

- Anterior uveitis: This involves the iris and/or ciliary body. The anterior chamber cells are more plentiful than the vitreous cells.
- Intermediate uveitis: Chronic inflammation of the pars plana, the extreme periphery of the retina and choroid. Vitreous cells are greater than anterior chamber cells.
- Posterior uveitis: The choroid is the principal site of inflammation.
- Pan uveitis: This involves diffuse inflammation with involvement of anterior and posterior ocular structures. The cells in the anterior chamber are similar to those in the vitreous.

Aetiology

Exogenous uveitis is caused by either external injury or invasion of micro-organisms or other agents external to the patient.

Endogenous uveitis is caused by inciting factors that originate within the patient and subsequently cause inflammation within the eye. Bowling (2015) suggests five main types of endogenous uveitis:

- Associated with systemic disease
- Infections with micro-organisms such as bacteria (tuberculosis [TB] or Lyme disease), viruses (herpes zoster, herpes simplex or HIV) or fungi (Histoplasma spp., Candida spp.)
- Infestations, such as with Pneumocystis carinii or Toxoplasma canis
- Idiopathic specific uveitis entities, which are a group of disorders associated with systemic disease but with specific features of their own (Fuchs' heterochromic cyclitis)
- Idiopathic uveitis (which makes up around 25% of cases).

Other endogenous causes include a response to soft lens matter in hypermature cataract, scleritis and sympathetic ophthalmia. Some diseases that primarily affect other structures (such as toxoplasmosis, which primarily affects the retina) may cause an overspill of inflammation into the choroid and vitreous (American Academy of Ophthalmology 2015).

Anterior uveitis

Anterior uveitis is the inflammation of the iris and/or ciliary body (anterior uvea). This is the most common form of uveitis and is often unilateral and acute in onset. It may also be referred to as iritis (inflammation of the iris) or iridocyclitis, if the iris and ciliary body are involved.

Causes of uveitis

There is a wide range of causes of uveitis, as described above, but description may also be based on the type of inflammation. Most types of anterior uveitis are sterile inflammatory reactions.

Granulomatous uveitis is more likely to be part of a systemic disease process or an ocular syndrome but this is not always the case, as diagnosis does not definitively indicate an underlying systemic process.

Clinically, the keratic precipitates (KPs) associated with this are described as large, wet clusters of white cells on the endothelium (mutton-fat) or iris nodules.

Non-granulomatous uveitis is associated with the human leukocyte antigen (HLA) B27 in over 55% of cases (Dahl 2015). The KPs are small, dry, discrete white cells on endothelium. Some conditions can present in either way, which sometimes makes this classification unreliable.

Table 20.1 Types of uveitis

Non-granulomatous	Granulomatous
Acute	Sarcoidosis
Idiopathic	Syphilis
Ankylosing spondylitis	Tuberculosis
Reiter's syndrome	Systemic lupus erythematosus
Inflammatory bowel disease	Brucellosis
Psoriatic arthritis	Leprosy
Glaucomatocyclitic crisis	Vogt–Koyanagi–Harada syndrome
Herpes simplex or zoster, or varicella zoster	
Lyme disease	
Behçet's disease	
Trauma toxoplasmosis	
Chronic	
Juvenile rheumatoid arthritis	
Chronic iridocyclitis	
Fuchs' heterochromic iridocyclitis	

Symptoms of uveitis

Symptoms depend on the type of inflammation (acute or chronic).

Pain: This may range from mild to severe pain, localised or referred to the periorbital region and aggravated by light. This type of pain is mainly caused by ciliary spasm and may be referred, so that it feels as though it radiates over a large area served by the trigeminal nerve.

Photophobia: This may range from mild to severe, with associated blepharospasm, resulting from the irritation of the trigeminal nerve.

Lacrimation: This is caused by irritation of the trigeminal nerve by the lacrimal gland.

Decreased vision: The decrease in vision may be moderate or marked according to the level of clouding of the media, compromised tear film, macular involvement or change in lens position.

Uveitis may be found on routine clinical examination in chronic presentations such as Fuchs' heterochromic iridocyclitis.

Signs of uveitis

Conjunctival hyperaemia is present, without any discharge and focal perilimbal or circumcorneal injection may be referred to as 'ciliary flush'. Conjunctival vessels are often tortuous rather than smooth (Figure 20.2).

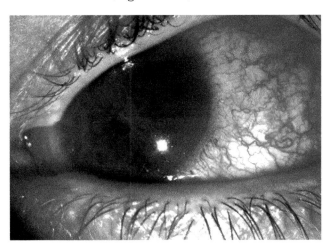

Figure 20.2 Diffuse tortuous conjunctival vessels with deeper inflammation seen perilimbally.

Distortion of the pupil may be present: This is due to reactive miosis of the pupil as a result of dominance of sphincter muscle, iris spasm and/or synechiae.

Cells and flare in the anterior chamber: Both need to be graded. More severe inflammation may lead to fibrin in the anterior chamber (Figure 20.3).

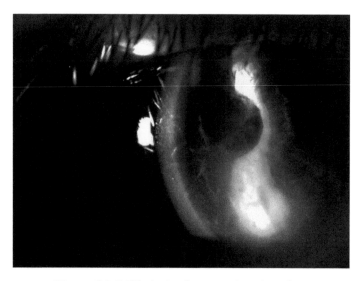

Figure 20.3 Fibrin in the anterior chamber.

Keratic precipitates may be present: These are cellular deposits on the corneal endothelium. Their distribution and characteristics can indicate the type of uveitis present.

Hypopyon: This consists of layering of inflammatory cells in the inferior angle due to a large number of cells in the anterior chamber (Figure 20.4). There are also abnormalities in the iris colour, which may appear 'muddy'. Nodules may be present and are categorised as Koeppe or Busacca. Koeppe nodules appear as white fluffy precipitates on the inner surface of the pupillary margin, while Busacca nodules are larger and appear on the surface of the iris.

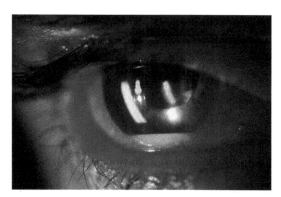

Figure 20.4 Hypopyon.

Heterochromia: The iris may be a different colour to the unaffected eye, with loss of iris stromal detail, and this is characteristic of Fuchs' heterochromic iridocyclitis. The iris may appear a slightly different colour on examination, due to the examiner looking at the iris through a hazy anterior chamber.

Posterior synechiae (PSs): These are adhesions between the anterior surface of the lens and the iris. PSs occur when part or all of the pupillary zone of the iris adheres to the anterior surface of the lens because there is an inflamed, swollen and slightly 'sticky' iris in close proximity to the lens. This obstructs the flow of aqueous through the pupil, resulting in the build-up of pressure in the posterior chamber. As a result, the iris bulges forward and this is known as iris bombé.

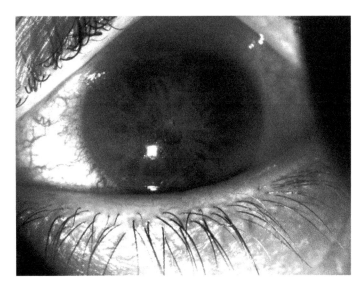

Figure 20.5 Distortion of the pupil due to adhesions between the iris and the lens (posterior synechiae).

Peripheral anterior synechiae (PAS): This may follow where the peripheral anterior surface of the iris bombé adheres to the peripheral posterior surface of the cornea.

Increased or decreased intraocular pressure: Inflammation of the ciliary process will reduce the production of aqueous, resulting in a low intraocular pressure. Increased intraocular pressure will result if secondary glaucoma has occurred.

Other signs of uveitis include:

- Anterior vitreous cells
- Cystoid macular oedema
- Neovascularisation of choroid or optic nerve.

The inflammatory response
An inflammatory response to infectious, traumatic, neoplastic or autoimmune processes produces the signs of uveitis as a result of the chemical mediators of the acute stages of inflammation such as serotonin and complement. Other chemicals

involved in inflammation include leukotrienes, kinins and prostaglandins. The lymphocyte is the predominant inflammatory cell in uveitis; and other cells, including mast cells, also contribute to the inflammatory response. These chemical mediators result in dilatation of blood vessels and ciliary flush, increased vascular permeability (resulting in aqueous flare), and the release of inflammatory cells into the eye (leading to aqueous or vitreous cells).

Grading of flare

Anterior chamber flare, resulting from extra protein in the aqueous, is usually present and can be graded, using the SUN Working Group Grading Scheme for Anterior Chamber Flare (Jabs *et al.* 2005), as follows:

- 0 = None
- 1+ = Faint
- 2+ = Moderate (iris and lens detail clear)
- 3+ = Marked (iris and lens detail hazy)
- 4+ = Intense (fibrin or plastic aqueous).

Grading of cells

This should be undertaken using a narrow (1mm) beam of light, about 3mm high and at maximum intensity and high magnification, and is best observed with the beam of light at a 45–46° angle. Cells are counted and graded as follows:

0 < 1
0.5 = 1–5 cells
1+ = 6–15 cells
2+ = 16–25 cells
3+ = 26–50 cells
4+ = More than 50 cells
(Jabs *et al.* 2005)

Hypopyon is suggestive of diseases associated with HLA-B27; with Behçet disease; or, less commonly, with an infection-associated iritis.

Diagnosing uveitis

As in other conditions, the diagnosis is based on history and examination. A comprehensive history must include an ophthalmic history with current or previous medication usage as well as a detailed systemic health history to determine possible aetiology. There should be a targeted systemic physical examination of the skin and joints.

Because uveitis can result from a large number of systemic causes and because a large proportion of it is idiopathic, comprehensive testing of all patients with uveitis is not recommended. It is expensive to carry out huge numbers of non-targeted investigations so testing should be based on the patient history and presenting symptoms.

Not all patients presenting with uveitis should undergo any testing; often, the first episode of uveitis will be the only episode. Generally, then, the first episode of non-granulomatous uveitis with an unremarkable medical history should not be tested. However, uveitis that is significant, recurrent, responding poorly to therapy or bilateral should be investigated thoroughly (Dahl 2015).

Once a range of possible causes for the uveitis has been identified, a range of patient specific tests (Table 20.2) may be organised – this is common to all forms of uveitis.

Table 20.2 Possible tests in intermediate uveitis, depending on history and examination (from Janigian 2014)

Table reprinted with permission from Medscape Drugs & Diseases

Type of inflammation	Associated factors	Suspected disease	Laboratory tests
Acute/sudden onset, severe with or without fibrin membrane or hypopyon	Arthritis, back pain, GI/genitourinary symptoms	Seronegative spondyloarthropathies	HLA-B27, sacroiliac films
	Aphthous ulcers	Behçet disease	HLA-B5, HLA-B5I
	Postsurgical, post-traumatic	Infectious endophthalmitis	Vitreous tap, vitrectomy
	Medication induced	Rifabutin	None
	None	Idiopathic	Possibly HLA-B27
Moderate severity of pain and redness	Shortness of breath, African descent, subcutaneous nodules	Sarcoidosis	Serum ACE, lysozyme, chest radiograph or chest CT scan, gallium scan, biopsy
	Posttraumatic	Traumatic iritis	
	Increased IOP, sectorial iris atrophy, corneal dendrite	Herpetic iritis	
	Poor response to steroid, manifestations of 2° or 3° syphilis, HIV	Syphilis	Rapid plasma reagent (RPR) or VDRL, FTA-ABS
	Post cataract extraction, white plaque on posterior capsule	Endophthalmitis, intraocular lens (IOL)- related iritis	Vitrectomy and/or culture, consider anaerobic and fungal cultures
	Medication induced	Etidronate (Didronel), metipranolol (OptiPranolol), latanoprost (Xalatan)	
	History of HIV, alcohol abuse, exposure to infected individuals, residence in endemic regions	Tuberculosis	Purified protein derivative (PPD), QuantiFERON®-TB Gold, chest radiograph, referral to infectious disease specialist

Chronic, minimal signs of redness or pain	Child, especially with arthritis	Juvenile idiopathic arthritis (JIA) related iridocyclitis	Antinuclear antibody (ANA), erythrocyte sedimentation rate (ESR)
	Heterochromia, diffuse stellate keratic precipitate, unilateral	Fuchs uveitis syndrome	None
	Postsurgical	Low-grade endophthalmitis, IOL	Vitrectomy, capsulectomy with culture
	None	Idiopathic	Lyme titers (possibly)
	Child, especially with arthritis	JIA-related iridocyclitis	Antinuclear antibody (ANA), erythrocyte sedimentation rate (ESR)
	Heterochromia, diffuse stellate keratic precipitate, unilateral	Fuchs' uveitis syndrome	None
	Postsurgical	Low-grade endophthalmitis, IOL	Vitrectomy, capsulectomy with culture
	None	Idiopathic	Lyme titers (possibly)

Intermediate uveitis

Chronic inflammation of the pars plana peripheral retina and vitreous is known as intermediate uveitis and is non-granulomatous with unknown aetiology and insidious onset. It typically affects people aged between 5 and 40 years and there are two peaks in this age range: from 5 to 15 and then from 20 to 40. Some patients may have self-limiting, short, low-grade episodes. Others may have a lingering chronic bout with sub-acute exacerbation and incomplete remissions. It accounts for up to 15% of all cases of uveitis (American Academy of Ophthalmology 2015).

Table 20.3 Specific tests in intermediate uveitis (from Janigian 2014)

Table reprinted with permission from Medscape Drugs & Diseases

Clinical entity	Diagnostic tests
Idiopathic (pars planitis)	None
Sarcoidosis	ACE, chest radiography, gallium scan, biopsy (possibly)
Multiple sclerosis	MRI and neurologic consultation if history of neurologic symptoms or optic neuritis, HLA-DR2
Lyme disease	Lyme serology (immunoglobulin [Ig]G/IgM Western immunoblot testing) if from endemic area and/or presence of systemic signs
Syphilis	VDRL, FTA-ABS
Inflammatory bowel disease	GI consultation
Whipple disease	GI consultation
Lymphoma	Vitreous cytology with immunophenotyping, lumbar puncture for cytology, neuroimaging

Cause of intermediate uveitis

The cause is mostly unknown, although it is certainly a feature of sarcoidosis and 10–15% of patients go on to develop multiple sclerosis (MS).

Symptoms of intermediate uveitis

Intermediate uveitis may be painless and the patient may present with an increase in floaters. Macular oedema results in loss of central vision and this may also be a presenting symptom.

Signs of intermediate uveitis

- Minimal anterior chamber cells or flare
- Cells in the anterior vitreous indicate vitritis, which varies in severity, from individual cells only and including 'snowballs' (which are gelatinous exudates and cells) to, occasionally, a completely opaque vitreous
- 'Snow-banking', which involves fibrovascular exudates along the inferior pars plana
- Optic disc swelling
- Cystoid macular oedema
- Posterior vitreous detachment.

Complications of intermediate uveitis

- Cystoid macular oedema is the most common cause of visual loss
- Secondary cataract develops in eyes with severe and prolonged inflammation
- Tractional detachment may occur
- Vascularisation of exudate behind the posterior lens capsule may cause ciliary detachment, with consequent reduced aqueous secretion, hypotony and, eventually, phthisis bulbi.

Posterior uveitis

This applies to the posterior structures of the eye and may include retinitis, choroiditis, vasculitis and vitritis. These conditions may occur in combination or separately. Patients with posterior uveitis complain of decreased vision, floaters, metamorphopsia and scotoma, or a combination of these.

Examination shows areas of retinitis or choroiditis as well as cells in the vitreous. There may be posterior vitreous detachment and precipitates on the posterior hyaloid face, which are similar to KPs. Retinitis gives the retina a white, cloudy appearance with obscured vessels, and the areas of inflammation tend to have indistinct edges. Vasculitis is seen as fluffy white haziness surrounding blood vessels, and veins are more often affected than arteries.

Causes of posterior uveitis

Posterior uveitis can be caused by infection or endogenous inflammation or it can be neoplastic.

Infection and infestations

- Viral: Herpes zoster, herpes simplex, cytomegalovirus (CMV), HIV
- Bacterial: TB, syphilis, Lyme disease, brucellosis, Whipple disease
- Fungi: Candida spp., Aspergillus spp., histoplasmosis
- Parasites: Toxocariasis, toxoplasmosis, onchocerciasis.

Systemic disease

- Sarcoidosis
- Behçet's disease
- Vogt–Koyanagi–Harada disease
- Toxoplasmosis
- Multiple sclerosis
- Systemic lupus erythematosus (SLE)
- Inflammatory bowel disease
- Wegener's granulomatosis
- Large cell lymphoma.

Complications include cystoid macular oedema, macular scarring, epiretinal membrane formation, retinal detachment (which may be tractional, rhegmatogenous or exudative), scotomata from chorioretinal scarring or vascular occlusions.

Panuveitis

This may also be referred to as diffuse uveitis, because there is diffuse inflammation of all anterior and posterior structures of the eye. In most cases, the aetiology is unknown but it is often associated with sarcoidosis, TB and syphilis, and less commonly with sympathetic ophthalmia, Vogt–Koyanagi–Harada syndrome and Behçet's disease.

Treatment of uveitis

Treatment aims to:

- Alleviate acute symptoms and suppress inflammation
- Preserve vision and prevent complications
- Treat the cause of inflammatory process if known.

Mydriatics and cycloplegics

These are used in anterior uveitis, or in intermediate or posterior uveitis when there is overspill of inflammation into the anterior segment.

Mydriatics and cycloplegics dilate the pupil and are used to break down or prevent posterior synechiae. This may include subconjunctival or topical instillation of a combination of drops, such as cyclopentolate 1%, phenylephrine hydrochloride 2.5 or 10%, atropine 1% and homatropine 2%. There may be an initial period of intensive instillation if synechiae are present in order to break down the adhesion between the lens and iris.

These drops also have an analgesic effect via the paralytic effect of cycloplegic eye drops, which will reduce the iris sphincter spasm. A side effect will be limitation of accommodation affecting close and fairly near work (as with computers).

Practitioner experience shows that application of heat to the eye during intensive dilatation may aid its effectiveness. Heat may be applied in various ways – for example, by asking the patient to lean over a bowl or jug of boiling water; a novel method involves filling a surgical glove with hot water, firmly tying a knot in the wrist and asking the patient to apply it, perhaps wrapped in a cover, to the closed eye. Many patients find the application of heat extremely soothing.

If the pupil fails to respond to topical therapy, a subconjunctival drug may be given, often combined with a steroid.

Corticosteroids

The mainstay of management in most cases of uveitis is steroids, which may be delivered as topical, periocular, subconjunctival (useful for severe acute uveitis or cystoid macular oedema), intravitreal and/or systemic treatment. Their primary action is to suppress the inflammatory response within the eye and they are used only where infection has been ruled out as a possible cause.

Topical treatment can be intensive, initially (every 30 minutes to 1 hourly) with a tapering of drops over a prescribed period. Sudden stopping of steroid drops may result in rebound inflammation.

Patients need to be aware of the importance of compliance, possible side effects and the need to complete prescribed treatment. This may impact on patients' lifestyles if they are working; and, if they are unable to self-medicate, frequent assistance may be needed. An ointment may be used at night or if the patient has trouble instilling frequent drops.

Topical steroids are effective for anterior uveitis although they may have useful effects on vitritis or macular oedema if the patient is aphakic. Drugs used include prednisolone acetate, prednisolone sodium phosphate and dexamethasone phosphate.

Periocular or subconjunctival treatment is an option in severe cases of anterior uveitis that are uncontrolled by drops, intermediate uveitis or in cases where limiting systemic steroids are preferable. Drugs used include methylprednisolone acetate, hydrocortisone sodium succinate, dexamethasone and triamcinolone acetonide. Periocular routes include sub-Tenon's or trans-septal routes into the orbital floor.

Intravitreal steroids may be given by injection or implantation of a sustained release device. This has been shown to be useful in chronic uveitis and cystoid macular oedema (Antcliff *et al.* 2001).

Systemic steroids can be used in patients with chronic, vision-threatening uveitis and in severe uveitis that is not responding to other treatments or when systemic causes must be treated concurrently. They are therefore usually used only for posterior and some intermediate forms of uveitis.

Practitioners and patients need to be aware of the possible complications of steroid use, particularly in the long term. Corneal integrity may be compromised, susceptibility to opportunistic infections increased, or cataracts (usually posterior subcapsular) or glaucoma may develop.

Systemic side effects of oral steroid use are varied. Patients will complain of mood alterations with high doses, which resolve as the dose is reduced. There can be a classic cushingoid appearance but this is dose dependent. Long-term steroid use can cause bone depletion, with increasing osteoporosis, and the clinician might consider the use of bisphosphonate in long-term corticosteroid treatment. Hypertension, hypercholesterolemia and atherosclerosis are also serious side effects of systemic corticosteroid use.

Appetite increases and can cause weight gain (Huang & Gaudio 2010). Proton pump inhibitors are used to reduce the risk of stomach irritation with the use of high-dose steroids.

Non-steroidal anti-inflammatory drugs (NSAIDs)

These may be indicated if underlying conditions are present, such as arthritis, or juvenile, psoriatic or ankylosing spondylitis.

Immunosuppressants

Although steroids suppress the immune system, the use of immunosuppressants benefits patients with severe sight-threatening uveitis or those who are resistant to or intolerant of steroids. The most commonly used steroid-sparing immunosuppressives include antimetabolites, T-cell inhibitors and alkylating agents. These types of medication are being used more frequently in both severe and moderate uveitis, due to the complications of long-term steroid use. Drugs include methotrexate, azathioprine (antimetabolites), cyclophosphamide, chlorambucil (alkylating agents) and cyclosporine (T-cell inhibitor). Newer medications that have become available include Mycophenolate Mofetil and Infliximab.

Medications are often initially used in combination with oral corticosteroids until therapeutic levels are achieved; then steroids are tapered. Treatment choices depend on the individual patient and disease being treated. Biologics, which are monoclonal antibodies, are now being investigated for the treatment of uveitis.

Patients must be monitored closely by practitioners who are experienced in the use of these agents. Regular blood tests (including blood count, and renal and hepatic tests) should be taken. Serious complications include renal and hepatic toxicity and bone marrow suppression, and there is a heightened risk of infection. Some of these drugs are associated with sterility and they are all potentially teratogenic, so pregnancy should be avoided.

Antibiotic or antiviral therapy
Topical and/or systemic delivery may be indicated if uveitis is caused by a pathogen. This can include oral antiviral treatment. Tuberculosis treatment can be indicated for some TB-induced uveitis with complications. Treatment is indicated with penicillin for neurosyphilis, which includes ocular syphilis.

Anti-glaucoma therapy
This may be necessary to lower the intraocular pressure if secondary glaucoma has occurred. In the acute stage, intensive topical treatment and/or systemic acetazolamide is used.

Surgery
Vitrectomy may be useful in vitritis or cystoid macular oedema; and other types of surgery may be needed to deal with the complications of uveitis, such as tractional detachment and cataract.

Education
Education about the condition is crucial in aiding compliance with drop regimens. The patient may need to be taught how to instil eye drops and should understand any possible side effects of treatment. Understanding of the condition will also help to reinforce the importance of attending associated clinics – for instance, for radiographs or blood tests.

As a result of its dense vascular make-up, the uveal tract mirrors all systemic vascular diseases and uveitis can be an initial presentation of many systemic diseases.

Results from diagnostic tests performed in the ophthalmic unit may confirm or discover associated immunological disorders; and it therefore commonly falls to the ophthalmic health professional to tell the patient of their diagnosis. Ophthalmic nurses may find that they are educating patients on their ophthalmic condition and treatment, and associated systemic diseases.

Complications of uveitis
Secondary glaucoma
This is the most common complication of anterior uveitis. It may be the result of anterior, posterior or peripheral anterior synechiae or a response to steroids. Presence of a hypopyon may cause debris to block the angle and drainage canals, leading to increase in pressure.

Visual impairment
This can take various forms, depending on the cause: inflammation, use of mydriatics, floaters, cataract and glaucoma with visual field loss. If visual impairment is present as a result of cystoid macular oedema, referral to a low-vision assessment clinic may be needed.

Cataract
Formation of a cataract may be secondary to inflammation and steroid use or impairment of metabolism. Corneal band keratopathy may also occur.

Syndromes/conditions and uveitis
Fuchs' heterochromic cyclitis (Fuchs' uveitis syndrome)
This is an uncommon cause of chronic uveitis, affecting fewer than 5% of all patients diagnosed with uveitis. It generally affects those aged over 30 years and is usually unilateral. The common signs and symptoms of uveitis (of redness, pain and photophobia) are minimal. However, the patient does complain of blurred vision, often from a cataract – because cataracts eventually occur in most patients. Often the colour of the iris is affected as a result of stromal atrophy, leading to a lighter-coloured iris.

On examination, changes are seen in the architecture of the iris and there is a large pupil as a result of iris changes. Anterior synechiae are sometimes present but posterior synechiae are never seen. Slit-lamp examination reveals KPs, usually present over the entire corneal endothelium. Flare may be present, and there are never more than 2+ cells present. Rubeosis is a common finding.

The two complications of Fuchs' syndrome are cataract and secondary glaucoma as a result of the rubeosis. Cataract surgery is usually successful, and the glaucoma is treated with topical medications.

Glaucomatocyclitic crisis (Posner–Schlossman syndrome)

This type of chronic uveitis is characterised by recurrent episodes of secondary open-angle glaucoma; it generally affects young adults, and episodes are unilateral. However, 50% of patients will have bilateral episodes at different times. The 'classic' signs and symptoms of uveitis are minimal and the patient usually complains of rainbow-like haloes around lights. These haloes are the result of corneal oedema; however, pain is not a common presenting symptom despite intraocular pressure (IOP) being elevated as high as 40–60mmHg.

On examination, corneal oedema is present but (as with open-angle glaucoma) the anterior chamber depth is normal. No flare is present; there may be a few cells in the aqueous and KPs are present, but posterior synechiae do not develop.

Treatment during an active episode is designed to reduce the IOP. Over time, some patients may develop a chronic rise in IOP, which can lead to optic disc cupping and visual field loss, as with any glaucoma.

Vogt–Koyanagi–Harada (VKH) syndrome

This syndrome predominantly affects those in populations prone to pigmented skin; it is reasonably common among the Japanese population. It is a multisystem disorder associated with alopecia, poliosis, vitiligo, neurological irritation (headaches, etc.) and auditory disturbances. This syndrome is often divided into different types, depending on what the patients present with. If they have mainly skin involvement and anterior uveitis, it is described as Vogt–Koyanagi syndrome; and if there is neurological and retinal involvement, it is described as Harada's disease.

On ocular examination, there may be anterior involvement (usually iridocyclitis), or posterior involvement with the presence of posterior synechiae, secondary glaucoma and retina involvement such as retinal detachments or disc oedema.

Sympathetic uveitis
(sympathetic ophthalmitis, sympathetic ophthalmia)

This is a very rare presentation of uveitis in the second eye (sympathising eye) which occurs after a penetrating injury to the other eye (exciting eye), generally as a result of trauma but occasionally after intraocular surgery. In most cases there may have been exposure of some uveal tissue. The patient presents with a mild anterior uveitis in the sympathising eye 2–3 weeks to several years after the initial injury, although 65% of cases present within 3 months and 90% within 1 year.

The patient presents with photophobia and blurred vision in the sympathising eye. On examination, the 'classic' signs of uveitis are not present in the sympathising eye, but there are cells present in the retrolental space, and the exciting eye shows evidence of the original injury and may be injected. However, both eyes eventually develop a severe, chronic inflammation, eventually resulting in a panuveitis; in addition, posterior synechiae form if not treated early with mydriatics.

Most patients with sympathetic uveitis eventually develop cataract, glaucoma and phthisis bulbi, but in some instances the disease is self-limiting with no long-term effects. Treatment options for patients with sympathetic uveitis are few and often drastic: enucleation of the injured eye within 2 weeks, which seems to have an impact on the incidence, steroid therapy and immunosuppressive therapy.

Systemic disorders and uveitis
HLA-B27

All animals with white blood cells express cell surface glycoproteins (major histocompatibility complex [MHC]) and those in humans are known as human leukocyte antigens (HLAs). HLA-B27 is expressed on the short arm of chromosome 6. Although it is present in only 1–8% of the general population, about 50% of patients with acute anterior uveitis express the HLA-B27 molecule and many of these patients also have other immune disorders such as Reiter's syndrome, inflammatory bowel disease or ankylosing spondylitis (Chang, McCluskey & Wakefield 2006). The mechanism of these immune reactions is still unknown, but it is thought (from animal models) that bacterial gut infection may predispose to arthritis and Reiter's syndrome.

The combination of systemic and ocular disease can be devastating for patients who not only have to manage a disease process but may also have to align themselves to diminishing sight. Here is a brief look at some of the more common systemic diseases; this area is covered more fully in texts dealing with particular systemic diseases.

Ankylosing spondylitis

As previously mentioned, there is a strong association between HLA-B27 and this disease. Uveitis almost always occurs at some stage. Ankylosing spondylitis affects men more than women, involves the sacroiliac joints and axial skeleton and ranges in severity from asymptomatic to crippling. Radiographs of the sacroiliac joints show sclerosis and narrowing of joint spaces. HLA-B27 is found in up to 90% of patient with ankylosing spondylitis. Pain, redness and photophobia are the initial complaints and synechiae formation is common. It may be accompanied by iridocyclitis. The iritis is usually recurrent and may lead to permanent damage if not adequately treated.

Reiter's syndrome

This is characterised by a triad of symptoms: non-specific urethritis, polyarteritis and conjunctival inflammation, often with uveitis. It is most common in young adult males.

It may be triggered by an episode of diarrhoea caused by a pathogen such as Chlamydia spp., Shigella spp. or Salmonella spp., which acts to trigger inflammation. In most patients, arthritis begins within about 30 days of infection. HLA-B27 is found in up to 95% of these patients.

Crohn's disease and ulcerative colitis

These are both associated with acute uveitis and HLA-B27. Ulcerative colitis affects the colon, whereas Crohn's disease can affect the whole bowel. Around 12% of patients with ulcerative colitis develop an associated uveitis and this decreases to about 2.4% of patients with Crohn's disease.

Behçet's disease

Behçet's disease is a generalised occlusive vasculitis of unknown cause and typically affects young men from the eastern Mediterranean region and Japan (Bowling 2015). Its effects include recurrent aphthous ulceration, skin rashes, genital ulceration and uveitis, vitritis or retinitis. Ocular signs with this disease occur in about three-quarters of cases. The uveitis is characterised by the sudden onset of a hypopyon; visual loss is frequent and posterior involvement occurs despite treatment. Combination therapy is often used (steroid plus immunosuppressive) and this can help to reduce visual loss (Huang & Gaudio 2010).

Juvenile idiopathic uveitis (juvenile rheumatoid arthritis and Still's disease)

Uveitis presents in about 50% of patients with juvenile rheumatoid arthritis disease. Low-grade bilateral iridocyclitis may precede or follow joint involvement. Females are more commonly affected and in most cases the onset is insidious. The uveitis may precede the arthritis by 3–10 years; the average age at which the uveitis is detected is 5 years. Corticosteroids and mydriatics are of value in acute episodes but their long-range effect is possibly only to delay the inevitable, which may be severe visual impairment. In 50% of cases, the uveitis is moderate to severe and persists for more than 4 months; and in 25% of cases the uveitis is very severe and lasts several years, resulting in cataract, secondary glaucoma and band keratopathy (Huang & Gaudio 2010).

Treating children with uveitis presents some unique problems. There may be a risk of amblyopia in young children; there are different dose requirements for children that may be unique to a particular child; and there are drug-associated risks (such as growth retardation) with systemic steroids. Gaining cooperation for examination and treatment may also be difficult. Loss of vision in a child will have a greater impact over their lifespan, in terms of earning potential and financial burden, and adequate education may also be a problem (Holland & Stiehm 2003).

Sarcoidosis

This is a chronic granulomatous disease of unknown cause, characterised by multiple cutaneous and subcutaneous nodules. Almost all organs of the human body can be affected but respiratory is suspected in 90% of patients characterised by hilar lymphadenopathy. Neurosarcoidosis, cutaneous and liver are also common sites to develop sarcoid lesions.

The most common ocular presentation is bilateral granulomatous anterior uveitis, which can be characterised by inflammatory nodules on the pupillary border (Koeppe nodules) or on the iris surface (Busacca nodules). Posterior involvement includes clumps of inflammatory cells in the vitreous (snowballs), the development of chorioretinal granulomas, cystoid macula oedema and sheathing of retinal veins with periphlebitis. (Slight, Marsden & Raynel 2013).

This type of uveitis may lead to severe visual impairment due to cataract formation and secondary glaucoma. Corticosteroid therapy given early in the disease may be effective, but recurrences are common and the long-term visual prognosis is poor.

Tuberculosis

Tuberculosis causes a granulomatous type of uveitis and is rare in patients with active pulmonary TB. If the anterior segment is involved, iris nodules and mutton-fat KPs will be visible on slit-lamp examination. It is the nodules and the localised nature of tuberculous uveitis that help to make a clinical differentiation from sympathetic ophthalmia.

Disseminated choroiditis is the most posterior sign in TB uveitis. TB should be suspected in patients who travel to countries where TB is endemic. Treatment can be prolonged and can include systemic TB treatment. The course of the disease can be prolonged. Blurred vision may remain as a result of scarring of the retina.

Infections and uveitis

Infections associated with uveitis include toxoplasmosis and toxocariasis (see Chapter 22) and onchocerciasis (see Chapter 13).

Ocular melanoma

Melanoma is a malignancy that develops from cells that produce melanin, the dark-coloured pigment found in skin, hair and the lining of internal organs. The highest incidence of melanoma occurs in the skin and less frequently in other organs of the body such as the eye. The strong link between skin malignant melanoma and exposure to ultraviolet light from the sun is well documented, but the exact cause of ocular melanoma is unknown. The incidence of ocular melanoma is about 28 per million head of population.

Ocular melanoma may involve any part of the eye but the uveal tract is the most common site for a primary intraocular malignant tumour. The tumour can affect any of the three parts that make up the uveal tract: the iris, the ciliary body or the choroid.

These tumours can also be secondary to primary sites in patients with a history of cancer elsewhere in the body. In particular, in women the breast and lung, and in men the genitourinary and gastrointestinal tracts with the liver are the most common primary sites for all secondary ocular melanomas.

The discovery of an ocular melanoma is often an incidental finding from an ophthalmic examination. The patient often has no ocular symptoms (unless there is macular involvement) and they may complain of blurred vision. Sometimes the patient presents with a retinal detachment and will describe the symptoms associated with a retinal detachment.

Iris melanoma

Melanoma of the iris accounts for about 5% of all ocular melanomas. Most are slow-growing tumours and the prognosis is good. The presence of a tumour may discolour the iris or distort the shape of the pupil and so may be noticed by the patient and the family, although they are unlikely to know what the diagnosis is. Often the patient is referred with a differential diagnosis of naevus or melanoma. These tumours are generally observed until growth is noted and then removed by iridectomy.

Ciliary body melanoma

Melanoma of the ciliary body accounts for about 10% of all ocular melanomas. Unlike melanoma of the iris, ciliary body melanoma cannot be visualised without the pupil being dilated and it is therefore difficult to diagnose. Patients may present with a variety of signs and symptoms that, on ocular examination, may include: secondary astigmatism caused by anterior displacement of the lens from pressure by the tumour; dark mass present on the sclera; dilated episcleral blood vessels; or the anterior chamber invaded by the iris root resulting from erosion, or even retinal detachment, and the patient may present with an anterior uveitis but this is uncommon.

The treatment of choice for ciliary body tumours is enucleation for large melanomas but iridocyclectomy (local resection of the ciliary body) may be undertaken if the tumour does not involve more than one-third of the iridocorneal angle. In selected cases radiotherapy may be the treatment of choice.

Choroidal melanoma

Choroidal melanoma is by far the most frequently diagnosed malignancy of the uveal tract, accounting for about 85% of cases and is the most common primary ocular tumour in adults. The tumour predominantly affects those aged between 50 and 60 years, with only 4% of cases diagnosed in those aged under 30 years.

Patients often have no symptoms until the tumour is quite large and is an incidental finding on ocular examination of the posterior segment. Alternatively, the patient may present with decreased vision, visual field loss, photopsia or a retinal detachment. The tumour is usually seen as an elevated, oval mass of the choroid, which may be pigmented or non-pigmented.

The diagnosis of choroidal melanoma is made only after numerous examinations and investigative tests, including:

- Ocular examination by slit-lamp with a 60 + -D lens, indirect ophthalmoscopy (as long as the ocular media are clear) and transillumination (differentiates between pigmented tumour and dense retinal haemorrhage)
- Fluorescein angiography, which may assist in diagnosis but does not differentiate between melanoma and other choroidal tumours (haemangiomas)
- Ultrasonography with a 'B scan', which is the most helpful tool in detecting ocular tumours
- Computed tomography, which has no advantage over a 'B scan' in aiding the diagnosis but does detect any extension of the tumour extraocularly
- Magnetic resonance imaging
- Other tests such as colour-coded Doppler imaging and intraocular biopsy.

The treatment of choroidal melanoma remains controversial and each patient should be assessed individually to determine the best line of treatment for them. The patient's current visual acuity in the affected eye, the size, extent and location of the mass, the state of the unaffected eye and the patient's general health should all be taken into consideration when deciding on a course of treatment or intervention. The aim of any treatment is to retain what vision the patient has, destroy the cancer and prevent recurrence.

There are various treatment options available to patients presenting with choroidal malignant melanoma: enucleation, radioactive plaques, external radiotherapy, photo-coagulation, transpupillary thermotherapy, interferon and surgical resection (Damato 2012).

Treatment of Ocular Melanoma

Enucleation

This is undertaken if the tumour is extensive, particularly if the patient has lost all sight in the affected eye. During the procedure, the surgical team must take care to avoid any chance of leakage of malignant cells. A prosthesis should be fitted 4–6 weeks after enucleation and the patient must be followed up at regular intervals for possible recurrence of the tumour in the orbit.

Radioactive plaques

These are generally used for treating small- to medium-sized choroidal melanomas and they deliver radiotherapy directly to the tumour. Two types of plaques are commonly used – iodine-125 or ruthenium – and the ophthalmologist's preference determines which type of plaque is chosen. Insertion of the plaque requires a surgical procedure, with hospital admission (usually lasting between 1 and 7 days).

At the time of surgery, the plaque is positioned at the site of the tumour, left in place for a predetermined length of time and then removed during a later surgical procedure. The length of time that a radioactive plaque is left in situ is determined by the strength of radiation remaining in the plaque, which defines the required treatment time calculated by an oncology physicist.

Iodine plaques require staff, patients and their families to take more protective precautions than are required for ruthenium plaques. The following general precautions apply irrespective of what type of 'radiation' is used:

- The plaques must be stored in the correct lead-lined container
- All uses of plaques must be logged
- Staff providing care for the patient must be provided with radiation monitoring meters and signage warning of radioactive material in use, and have a Geiger counter available.

Refer to local hospital policies for specific procedures.

External radiotherapy

This treatment is undertaken using conventional radiotherapy machines and aims to cause as little damage as possible to surrounding healthy tissue. Before the radiotherapy, a minor surgical procedure is undertaken to attach 'tags' to specific parts of the eye, which act as 'markers' to isolate the area to be treated. The treatment is given over several days, in small doses.

Photocoagulation

A laser can be used to seal the blood supply of a tumour but this treatment modality is only suitable for very small melanomas. The patient will require several treatments.

Transpupillary thermotherapy

This is a relatively new laser treatment option for ocular melanomas; it can be used to treat small tumours and may be used in combination with radiotherapy, but is not readily available in all countries. The transpupillary thermotherapy laser heats the tumour cells, which are more susceptible to heat than normal cells, and destroys them. The patient requires several treatments.

Interferon

Although it is uncertain what interferon may offer in the treatment of ocular melanoma, it is being looked at as a possible future treatment option.

Surgical resection

This is an eye-salvaging procedure for selected uveal tumours. There are two possible resection techniques, and the choice depends on the site of the tumour. For tumours anteriorly involving the ciliary body and/or iris, a transcleral or 'exoresection' via a partial lamellar sclero-uvectomy is undertaken. This technique is reserved for small tumours covering less than one-third of the globe's circumference; whereas posterior tumours without ciliary body involvement are undertaken transretinally or by 'endoresection'.

Possible complications from treatment of ocular melanomas include the following, particularly for treatments involving radioactive material:

- Telangiectasis, a permanent dilatation of superficial capillaries and vessels
- Keratinisation, a process by which the epithelial cells of the cornea are exposed to the external environment, lose moisture and are replaced by horny tissue
- Corneal vascularisation, which occurs when corneal tissue becomes vascular and develops proliferating capillaries
- Radiation retinopathy, which involves changes in retinal vessels resulting from exposure to radiation
- Radiation cataract, resulting from exposure to radiation.

Nursing care of patients with ocular melanoma

The role of the nurse in treating patients with ocular melanoma is varied, ranging from providing routine outpatient clinic care to specialist nursing roles within the service to providing care to patients throughout the continuum (clinic, ward and sometimes operating rooms). Perhaps the nurse's most important role is providing support for the patient and their family and ensuring that they understand, and are familiar with, all care procedures and processes.

As with any cancer diagnosis, patients and their families experience fears that must be dealt with. The nurse is ideally situated to recognise patient concerns, provide support, act as advocate at every decision point for treatment options, and refer the patient to appropriate specialist services within oncology if required.

References

American Academy of Ophthalmology (2015) *Intraocular Inflammation and Uveitis*. San Francisco, CA: AAO.

Antcliff, R.J., Spalton, D.J., Stanford, M.R., Graham, E.M., Ffytche, T.J. & Marshall, J. (2001) Intravitreal triamcinolone for uveitic cystoid macular edema: an optical coherence tomography study. *Ophthalmology*. **108**, 765–72.

Bowling, B. (2015) *Kanski's Clinical Ophthalmology, a systematic approach*. 8th edn. London: Elsevier.

Chang, J.H., McCluskey, P.J. & Wakefield, D. (2006) Toll-like receptors in ocular immunity and the immunopathogenesis of inflammatory eye disease. *British Journal of Ophthalmology*. **90**(1),103–108

Dahl, A.A. (2015) *Uveitis, Anterior, Nongranulomatous Workup*. http://emedicine.medscape.com/article/1209595-workup (accessed 13 September 2016).

Damato, B. (2012) Progress in the management of patients with uveal melanoma. The 2012 Ashton Lecture. *Eye*. **26**, 1157–72; doi:10.1038/eye.2012.126; published online 29 June 2012.

Holland, G.N. & Stiehm, E.R. (2003) Special considerations in the evaluation and management of uveitis in children. *American Journal of Ophthalmology*. **135**, 867–78.

Huang, J.J. & Gaudio, P.A. (2010) *Ocular inflammatory disease and uveitis manual*. Philadelphia: Lippincott Williams and Wilkins.

Jabs, D.A., Nussenblatt, R.B. & Rosenbaum, J.T. (2005) Standardization of uveitis nomenclature for reporting clinical data. Results of the First International Workshop. *American Journal of Ophthalmology*. **140**(3), 509–16.

Janigian, R.H. Jr. (2014) *Uveitis Evaluation and Treatment*. http://emedicine.medscape.com/article/1209123-overview#a3 (accessed 13 September 2016).

Medscape Drugs & Diseases *Other Entities Reported to Cause or Confused With Intermediate Uveitis* (http://emedicine. medscape.com/), 2016, available at: http://emedicine.medscape.com/article/1209123-overview.

Medscape Drugs & Diseases *Various Clinical Scenarios Encountered by Practitioner of Uveitis* (http://emedicine. medscape.com/), 2016, available at: http://emedicine.medscape.com/article/1209123-overview.

Slight, C., Marsden, J. & Raynel, S. (2013) Sarcoidosis: the disease and its ocular manifestations. *International Journal of Ophthalmic Practice*. 4(1), 20–23.

Trusko, B., Thorne, J., Jabs, D., Belfort, R., Dick, A., Gangputra, S., Nussenblatt, R., Okada, A. & Rosenbaum, J. (2013) Standardization of Uveitis Nomenclature (SUN) Project Development of a clinical evidence base utilizing informatics tools and techniques. *Methods of Information in Medicine*. **52**(3), 259–65.

CHAPTER TWENTY-ONE

The angle and aqueous

Agnes Lee

The drainage system of the eye

To understand glaucoma, it is important first to consider the drainage system of the eye and aqueous dynamics. Abnormalities of the drainage system and the imbalance between the production and drainage of aqueous can lead to glaucoma.

The drainage system includes the anterior and posterior chamber, trabecular meshwork and canal of Schlemm (Figure 21.1).

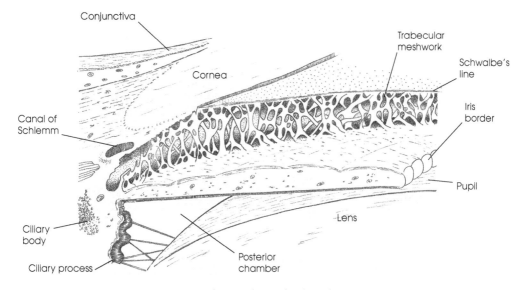

Figure 21.1 The angle and related structures.

The anterior chamber

This is a space that is bounded anteriorly by the inner surface of the cornea and posteriorly by the anterior face of the ciliary body, the iris and the lens. The area where the inner cornea meets the iris is known as the angle and is the location for the trabecular meshwork (Snell & Lemp 1998). The depth of the anterior chamber is 2.6–4.4mm and this decreases by 0.06mm per year of life. The anterior chamber deepens, in general, by 0.06mm for each dioptre of myopia and its average volume is 220µl. It is filled with aqueous humour secreted by the ciliary processes. The blood supply to the anterior segment is shown in Figure 21.2.

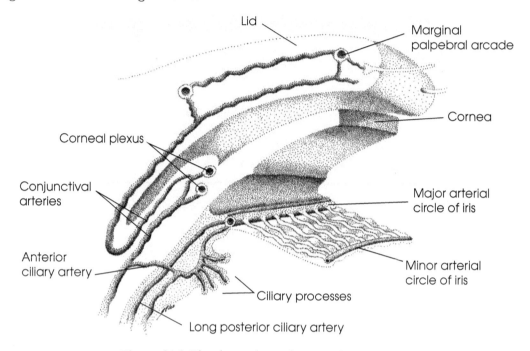

Figure 21.2 Blood supply to the anterior segment.

The posterior chamber

This is bounded anteriorly by the iris peripherally and the ciliary processes and posteriorly by the lens and the suspensory ligaments (Snell & Lemp 1998). Aqueous first enters the posterior chamber and then flows through the pupil into the anterior chamber.

Trabecular meshwork

This is a sponge-like porous network of connective tissue beams arranged as sheets and consisting of three portions: uveal meshwork, corneoscleral and juxtacanalicular. The uveal meshwork portion lies closest to aqueous humour and this portion extends from the ciliary body in the angle recess to Schwalbe's line. The uveal meshwork covers the anterior face of the ciliary body, the scleral spur and the trabecular meshwork. The corneoscleral portion extends from the scleral spur to Schwalbe's line. The endothelial portion (also known as the juxtacanalicular meshwork) is the deepest layer within the trabecular meshwork and is the last layer that the aqueous crosses before entering Schlemm's canal.

This canal offers the most resistance to aqueous outflow and consists of endothelial cells, the primary function of which is to digest foreign materials, after which the cells migrate away from the trabecular beams into Schlemm's canal. With age and repeated insult, the endothelial cells decrease and so does the flow of aqueous through the trabecular meshwork. Endothelial cells lining the trabecular meshwork have larger and less prominent cells borders than corneal endothelial cells.

Canal of Schlemm

This is a vein-like tube, containing septa, located at the base of the scleral sulcus. If the intraocular pressure (IOP) is high, the canal can collapse, so resistance to outflow subsequently increases. The canal's primary function is to collect aqueous from the trabecular meshwork and it also drains aqueous into the venous circulation.

Longitudinal muscles, situated in the ciliary body, open the canal by pulling on the scleral spur (which is made out of a ring of collagen fibres running parallel to the limbus).

Aqueous humour

Production

Aqueous humour (or 'aqueous') is a clear fluid produced by the non-pigmented portion of the ciliary processes through active secretion, ultrafiltration and diffusion. It is derived from plasma but, unlike plasma contains no protein. It contains predominantly water with electrolytes, glucose, amino acids and a high concentration of ascorbic acid and dissolved gases, and provides nourishment for the posterior cornea and lens as well as maintenance of the shape of the eyeball. The rate of aqueous flow is 2–6µl/min and turnover in the eye is less than 2 hours.

Drainage

There are two routes of drainage – via the trabecular and uveoscleral routes. The trabecular route accounts for 90% of aqueous drainage. Aqueous flows from the anterior chamber into the trabecular meshwork and Schlemm's canal and is drained by the episcleral veins. This is a pressure-sensitive route, in that increasing the pressure will increase outflow. Trabecular outflow can be increased by drugs such as miotics, sympathomimetics, laser trabeculoplasty and trabeculectomy.

The uveoscleral route accounts for the remaining 10% of aqueous outflow. Aqueous passes across the ciliary body into the suprachoroidal space (the space between the sclera and choroid) and is drained away by the venous circulation in the ciliary body choroid and sclera. Uveoscleral outflow can be decreased by miotics, and increased by atropine sympathomimetics and prostaglandin analogues.

A very small amount of aqueous is also drained away via the corneal endothelium, iris vessels and anterior vitreous surface (Bowling 2015).

Pathological resistance to outflow can be the result of an increase in the thickness of trabecular sheets, caused by an accumulation of collagen and basement membrane material, as well as a decrease in the number of trabecular cells.

Understanding intraocular pressure (aqueous dynamics)

Three factors determine the level of IOP:

- The rate of aqueous secretion by the ciliary processes
- The resistance encountered by the drainage of aqueous through the trabecular meshwork
- The level of episcleral venous pressure, which is normally relatively stable, except when resulting from alterations in body positions and in certain diseases of the head, neck and orbit. This in turn will obstruct the venous return to the heart, or shunt blood from the arterial to the venous system.

According to Alward (2000), a wide range of normal IOPs exists. Pooled data from large epidemiological studies indicate that the mean IOP is about 16mmHg, with a standard deviation of 3mmHg (American Academy of Ophthalmology 2015a).

Intraocular pressure can be influenced by the time of day (it is higher in the morning and lower in the afternoon and evening – the diurnal curve). It is also affected by:

- Heartbeat
- Respiration
- Blood pressure
- Age
- Sleep
- Exercise
- Race
- Thickness of the cornea (a thicker cornea will give a higher IOP reading and vice versa)
- Refractive error
- Topical and systemic drugs
- Fluid intake
- Caffeine
- Alcohol
- Cannabis.

For these reasons, a single IOP reading is not a sufficient basis on which to make a diagnosis of glaucoma.

Glaucoma

The term 'glaucosis' is derived from ancient Greek, meaning cloudy or blue-green hue, and over the years the concept of glaucoma has been extensively refined.

Glaucoma is now understood to refer to a large group of disorders characterised by widely diverse clinical and pathological denominators. It is a silent progressive disease and is one of the leading preventable causes of blindness if arrested before it significantly affects the vision. The common denominators of all glaucomas are optic neuropathy, visual field loss and irreversible blindness. One of the risk factors associated with most types of glaucoma is a raised IOP.

Classification of glaucoma

The classification of glaucoma depends on the following factors:

- The appearance of the drainage angle (open or closed)
- The presence of any other factors that may contribute to the rise in IOP
- Primary glaucoma has no other ocular disorders associated with a rise in IOP
- Secondary glaucoma is associated with another condition such as inflammation, neovascular disease, etc, and accounts for one-third of all glaucoma cases.

Primary open-angle glaucoma (POAG)

Epidemiology

Primary open-angle glaucoma (POAG) is the most common form of glaucoma in the UK. Glaucoma is also the second leading cause of blindness worldwide. An estimated 13.5 million people may have glaucoma and 5.2 million of those may be blind. It is the leading cause of blindness in African–American individuals in the USA, and it is responsible for 12% of blind registration in the UK and the USA.

Risk factors for POAG

There are a number of risks factors associated with POAG.

Raised IOP

A number of population-based studies have demonstrated that the prevalence of POAG increases with the level of IOP. According to Alward (2000), when the IOP is >21mmHg, the risk of developing POAG increases 16-fold when compared with eyes in which the IOP is <16mmHg. It is clear though that there is huge individual variation in the susceptibility of the optic nerve to damage from raised IOP; and the American Academy of Ophthalmology (2015) suggest that using a figure of >21mmHG is an arbitrarily chosen level for screening or diagnosis, which is a poor predictor of glaucoma.

It should be remembered that an increase in IOP is a risk factor associated with the development of the disease, and is not the disease in itself.

Ethnicity

Ethnicity affects both the chance of an individual developing glaucoma and the prognosis of their disease. The Barbados Eye Study (Leske *et al.* 1994) highlighted the public health importance of POAG in the African–Caribbean region. The prevalence of POAG by self-reported race was 7.0% in black, 3.3% in mixed-race and 0.8% (1 in 33) in white or other participants. In black and mixed-race participants, the prevalence reached 12% at the age of 60 and older and was higher in men (8.3%) than in women, with an age-adjusted male:female ratio of 1.4. Among participants aged 50 or older, 1 in 11 had POAG and prevalence increased to 1 in 6 at 70 or older.

Age

Glaucoma affects 1 in 200 of the general population over the age of 40, and the incidence increases with age. Population-based studies show that the prevalence of POAG ranges from 0.4% to 8.8% in those aged over 40. POAG is uncommon before the age of 40 (Rivera *et al.* 2008).

Genetic factors

There is little doubt that familial factors play an important role in POAG. First-degree relatives of POAG patients run a 4–16% risk of developing glaucoma, compared with 1–2% for the general population (Alward 2000). The Barbados Family Study (Leske *et al.* 2001) found a high prevalence of open-angle glaucoma in Barbados and identified a family history of glaucoma as a major risk factor. Everyone with a positive family history should therefore undergo an annual IOP check.

In addition to family history, certain genes have been implicated in POAG. Tamm (2002) reported the discovery of gene GLCIA or MYOC, which produces a protein called myocilin. Mutations in the MYOC gene that encodes for myocilin are causative for some forms of juvenile and adult-onset POAG. Myocilin has been detected in several ocular tissues such as the trabecular meshwork, ciliary body and retina. A genetic marker, endothelial leukocyte adhesion molecule 1 (ELAM-1), has also been identified, which could predict the chances of developing glaucoma. The ELAM-1 molecule is found to be the earliest marker for arteriosclerosis.

Myopia

Some studies have demonstrated a correlation between myopia and POAG. However, it must be acknowledged that some selection bias could have occurred because myopic patients are more likely to attend for their regular optometry examinations than their emmetropic counterparts.

Diabetes mellitus

Several older studies have demonstrated a higher prevalence of elevated mean IOP and POAG among patients with diabetes, compared with non-diabetic patients, although the epidemiological evidence for an association between the two conditions remains inconclusive (Wong *et al.* 2011). However, Nakamura *et al.* (2005) found that diabetes not only affects vascular tissues but also compromises neuronal and glial functions and metabolism in the retina, which ultimately gives rise to apoptotic death of retinal neurons including retinal ganglion cells (RGCs). The impaired metabolism of neurons and glia by diabetes may render RGCs susceptible to additional stresses related to OAG such as elevated intraocular pressure. Gordon *et al.* (2002) noted that the presence of diabetes seemed to protect patients against developing glaucoma. However, this finding is controversial because it is thought that patients with diabetes are prone to small vessel involvement; the optic disc of a patient with diabetes is therefore more susceptible to pressure-related damage.

Other risk factors

A history of migraine or cold hands and feet (a condition associated with vasospasm), Raynaud's phenomenon, is one of the risk factors and may play a role in the development of POAG. Other risk factors include systemic hypertension, systemic hypotension with nocturnal pressure drops and smoking, which have been associated with an increased risk in some studies.

Pathophysiology of POAG

There are multiple theories about the possible role of IOP as one of the factors that initiates glaucomatous damage in a patient's optic nerve. The exact cause of glaucomatous optic nerve damage is unknown and is probably the result of a combination of factors. It is thought that the increase in IOP increases vascular resistance, thereby causing decreased vascular perfusion of the optic nerve and ischaemia. The increased pressure can also cause impaired axoplasmic flow in the ganglion cell axons, resulting in aponeurosis and cell dysfunction. As the ganglion cells die, the neuroretinal rim of the optic nerve thins and the optic cup enlarges. This is known as glaucomatous cupping. The increased pressure can also cause mechanical dysfunction by compressing the lamina cribrosa, a sieve-like structure through which the axons pass.

The cause of elevated IOP is generally accepted to be a decreased facility of aqueous outflow through the trabecular meshwork. The increased resistance to the outflow can be associated with:

- Age and increased loss of trabecular endothelial cells

- Obstruction of the trabecular meshwork
- Loss of normal phagocytic activity
- Loss of giant vacuoles in the inner wall endothelium and a reduction in the trabecular pore density and size in the inner wall endothelium of Schlemm's canal.

Patients with POAG are normally asymptomatic at presentation; the suspicious features are usually detected by an optometrist and include a rise in IOP measured on several occasions, optic disc changes and visual field defects.

Optic disc changes in glaucoma include asymmetry of the neuroretinal rim or cupping and asymmetry of the cup:disc ratio between the two eyes. Other features may include localised thinning or notching of the rim, optic disc haemorrhage and vasculature abnormalities.

Table 21.1 A brief overview of guidelines from glaucoma clinical trials

Ocular hypertension study: Risk factors for development of POAG (Gordon et al. 2002)
1. Older age
2. Higher IOP
3. Greater pattern standard deviation
4. Thinner central corneal thickness
5. Larger vertical cup-disc ratio
Collaborative normal tension glaucoma study: Risk factors for progression (Anderson 2003)
1. Female gender
2. Recurrent disc haemorrhages
3. History of migraines
Early manifest glaucoma treatment trial: Risk factors for progression (Leske et al. 2004)
1. Higher IOP
2. Exfoliation
3. Older age
4. Bilateral disease
5. Worse mean deviation on VF
6. Recurrent disc haemorrhages

A systematic assessment of a patient with POAG

All new patients presenting to the outpatient department as glaucoma suspects should be methodically assessed. Building a good rapport with patients should be the starting point of any assessment because this is crucial in obtaining a complete history with valid information. It is essential to be a good listener as well as an approachable healthcare professional. According to NICE guidelines (2009) on glaucoma care, all new patients with POAG should have:

- A comprehensive medical, surgical and ophthalmic history (including family history)
- Social assessment, including any disability that might hinder concordance/compliance in treatment
- Slit-lamp examination: anterior segment, IOP measurement, gonioscopy and fundal examination, including optic disc and retinal nerve fibre examination
- Measurement of anterior chamber by van Herick's or Smith's method
- Pupillary examination for relative afferent pupillary defect
- Pachymetry
- Optic disc assessment
- Visual field examination
- Optic disc photographs.

In addition, NICE guidelines (2009) advocate that the following documentation must be available at each clinical episode to all healthcare professionals involved in a person's care:

- Records of all previous tests and images relevant to COAG and OHT assessment
- Records of past medical history, which could affect drug choice
- Current systemic and topical medications glaucoma medication record
- Records of drug allergies and intolerances
- Records of previous investigations
- Results of slit-lamp examination.

This is the same as for any other patient; glaucoma-specific findings might include the following:

- Lids: Port wine stain (which may accompany Sturge–Weber syndrome) or naevi
- Cornea: Krukenberg's spindle (a line of deposited pigment on the endothelium, indicative of pigment dispersion syndrome), flecks of extra tissue which may indicate pseudoexfoliation syndrome
- Anterior chamber depth is important and the angle should be assessed
- Iris: Transillumination defects may suggest pigment dispersion syndrome, posterior synechiae, new vessels on the iris (rubeosis), deposition of pseudoexfoliative material, heterochromia, iris atrophy, evidence of trauma
- Pupils: Differing responses may indicate damage to the optic disc
- Lens: Deposition of pigment, pseudoexfoliative material, red blood cells; anterior capsule opacities may indicate a previous attack of angle-closure glaucoma (glaukomflecken).

Pupillary assessment

It is important to evaluate the pupillary reaction between the two eyes because a relative afferent pupillary defect may indicate that there is an inequality in the severity of glaucomatous optic nerve damage between the two eyes of a patient. Careful evaluation and documentation serve as a baseline for future evaluations.

Measuring the IOP

Accurate measurement of the IOP is extremely important in the management of glaucoma patients. In the Collaborative Normal Tension Glaucoma Study (1998), eyes that had a reduction in IOP of 30% had a lower rate of visual field progression than those eyes that did not have their IOP lowered. Grant and Burke, as far back as 1982, made a retrospective study of the long-term relationship between IOP, stage of glaucomatous damage and progressive visual field loss, and commented that the worse the eye is on first presentation, the lower the pressure needs to be to prevent further loss or blindness.

The measurement of IOP is based on the Imbert–Fick principle, which states that, in an ideal, dry, thin-walled sphere, the pressure inside the sphere (P) is equal to the force necessary to flatten the surface (F), divided by the area (A) of flattening, calculated thus: $P = F/A$.

In the eye, a force is applied to the cornea to flatten a specific area of it and the Imbert–Fick principle is used to calibrate instruments to calculate the pressure inside the globe.

The area of flattening by a prism in Goldmann applanation tonometry (the gold standard) is 3.06mm of cornea. The cornea is flattened and the IOP determined by measuring the applanating force and the area flattened. The force necessary to flatten the cornea is adjusted on a drum wheel on the instrument and measured in gram force pressure. The gram force is converted to millimetres of mercury (the international standard unit for pressure measurement) by multiplying the force by 10.

Other methods of intraocular measurements include:

- 'Air puff' tonometry, which is widely used by community optometrists. This non-contact tonometer uses a pulsed jet of air to deform the corneal apex. This method carries less risk of cross-infection and is useful in mass screening. However, it is less accurate than Goldmann tonometry and the sudden burst of air can cause the patient to jump and inadvertently give a higher IOP reading.
- 'Tonopen', which is a light portable instrument that applanates a small area of cornea. It is useful for immobile or poorly compliant patients. The Tonopen

has inbuilt software that automatically self-calibrates after each use and selects the acceptable measurements. It takes the average of three 'good' readings and rejects the inappropriate readings. It is slightly less accurate than the Goldmann tonometer.

- Schiøtz tonometer, which is rarely used in developed countries. A preset weight is placed on the tonometer, which is then placed on the anaesthetised cornea. The amount the plunger sinks is measured off the scale and the reading is converted to millimetres of mercury from a conversion table. This can only be used for a recumbent patient.

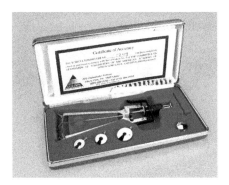

Figure 21.3 Schiøtz tonometer.

Figure 21.4 Goldmann tonometer.

Figure 21.5 Tonopen.

- The Perkins' tonometer, which is a hand-held tonometer that is based on the same principle as the Goldmann tonometer. It is useful for bed-bound, anaesthetised patients or patients who are impossible to examine on the slit-lamp. This instrument may be difficult to master initially.

- Rebound tonometry, which determines IOP by bouncing a small probe against the cornea and processing its interaction with the eye. Probes are disposable, with a rounded end to minimise the risk of corneal damage. These devices (e.g. icareTM) are very easy to use and their results are comparable with those of Goldmann tonometry. Devices exist which can be used by the individual to record pressure frequently in order to examine variations in pressure over the course of 24 hours, or a number of days, with results feeding back to the clinic so that target IOPs can be based on the whole range of pressures, rather than just those obtained in clinic.

- Digital tonometry, a crude method of measuring how 'hard' the affected eye is in comparison to the normal 'softer' eye by gently palpating the eyeball using the first finger of each hand.

Tonometer readings can be affected by:

- Tight collars
- Breath holding
- Thick or thin corneas
- Astigmatism > 3D
- Pressure against the globe from the operator's finger when holding the patient's upper lid
- Valsalva's manoeuvre
- Squeezing of the eyelids
- Corneal refractive surgery
- Inaccurately calibrated tonometer
- Excessive fluorescein results in wide mires, giving an artificially high IOP reading, or insufficient fluorescein with an extremely thin mire, giving an artificially low IOP reading.

Step-by-step guide to measuring IOP using the Goldmann tonometer

The Goldmann tonometer is used together with the slit-lamp. The tonometer consists of two main parts: (1) a small Perspex cylinder containing a prism (or a disposable equivalent) that is applied to the eye by (2) a lever attached to a coiled spring, the tension of which is controlled by a calibrated drum at the side of the instrument. Extreme care should be taken when handling the tonometer to avoid damage to the spring-loaded device. It is good practice to calibrate the tonometer before each clinic or at the very least weekly to ensure accurate IOP measurement. Any defective tonometer (> 2mmHg on calibration) must be sent away for repair.

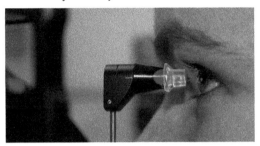

Figure 21.6 Goldmann tonometry.

Method

A clear, concise explanation is given to the patient to ensure cooperation. Putting the patient at ease also makes measurement much easier.

Contact lenses should be removed and Minims of lidocaine (lignocaine)/fluorescein or proxymetacaine/fluorescein drops should be instilled into each eye.

The tonometer prism is sterilised in lens cleaning solution according to local policy. The use of disposable prisms or prism covers is good practice to minimise the spread of infections.

The prism should be placed in the clip at the end of the tonometer arm. While attaching the prism to the tonometer arm, the lever should be supported with a finger to minimise damage to the spring lever. The prism is placed with the 0 aligned with the white mark on the clip. In patients with astigmatism of 3D or more, readings should be taken with the bi-prism horizontally and vertically and the two readings averaged. To take the vertical reading, the prism is aligned to the red mark (about 43°) on the tonometer arm.

The tonometer calibration arm is turned to 1 so that the arm is exerting a slight forward pressure.

The complete tonometer is placed on the mounting plate on the viewing arm of the slit-lamp and the slit-lamp magnification is set to 10×, with a blue filter in place.

The illuminating arm of the slit-lamp is placed at an angle of 60° to the slit-lamp.

The patient should be instructed to look straight ahead and the slit-lamp advanced until a bright blue hue is seen just before touching the apex of the cornea.

Up to this point it is best observed from the side. If the patient is unable to keep their eyes from blinking, the lids can be held open, provided that the supporting fingers do not exert any pressure on the eye.

While looking down the viewing piece of the slit-lamp microscope, the tonometer prism is brought gently into contact with the cornea. As there are two prisms within the tonometer head, on contact with the cornea, two half-circles are seen through the tonometer, adjacent to each other. The two half-circles must be symmetrically placed on the apex of the cornea. It is important that the slit-lamp be pulled slightly away from the cornea should any fine adjustment be needed. This is to minimise any corneal epithelial damage.

The calibrated wheel is turned until the half-circles just overlap.

The IOP is read when the inside edges of the half-circles are just touching.

The IOP in the individual varies over the course of a day (diurnal variation) and patients may need a series of readings, taken over the course of a day (phasing or day phasing) to determine the range of pressures particular to their eyes. Figure 21.3 shows the correct placement of mires when undertaking Goldmann applanation tonometry.

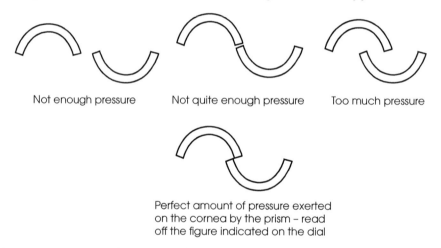

Not enough pressure   Not quite enough pressure   Too much pressure

Perfect amount of pressure exerted
on the cornea by the prism – read
off the figure indicated on the dial

Figure 21.7 Correct placement of mires when undertaking applanation tonometry.

Pachymetry

The accurate measurement of IOP is a cornerstone of the diagnosis and management of glaucoma. The influence of corneal thickness on IOP measurements using Goldmann applanation tonometry measurement is well recognised. Research has shown that a thick cornea can cause an elevated IOP reading, whereas a thin cornea can give a false reading. Central corneal thickness should be taken into account when assessing the risk of ocular hypertension patients developing glaucomatous damage. Underestimation of

IOP, as a result of lower corneal thickness, might lead to under-recognition of glaucoma. It has been suggested that a thin cornea could possibly also have a thin lamina cribrosa or perhaps a more susceptible optic nerve.

Studies have also shown that patients who have had photorefractive keratectomy and laser in situ keratomileusis have shown significantly lower IOP measurements. Other pathological corneal variations causing an alteration in the IOP included: corneal oedema, corneal scars, keratoconus, flat anterior chamber, penetrating keratoplasty, bandage contact lenses, and patients with pituitary adenoma and resultant acromegaly. Corneal thickness should be routinely measured in all patients suspected of having POAG. Pachymetry should be done before gonioscopy.

Measuring the width of the angle
Van Herick method
Van Herick's system is a method of estimating the angle width by making use of the slit-lamp. This system was devised by van Herick and is an alternative to gonioscopy if clinical circumstances rule out gonioscopy – for example, when people with physical or learning disabilities are unable to participate in the examination (NICE 2009).

To estimate the angle width, an optic section (narrow slit beam) is placed near the corneal limbus with the light source at 60°. The examiner then compares the depth of the anterior chamber with the thickness of the cornea. If the anterior chamber is thicker than the cornea, the angle is incapable of closure and is thus graded a 4 (wide open angle). The angle is graded a 3 if the anterior chamber depth is between a half and a quarter of the corneal thickness. In this case, the angle remains incapable of closure. However, if the thickness of visible aqueous is a quarter (grade 2) or less (grade 1) of the corneal thickness, the angle is probably in danger of closure. A slit (grade 0) indicates that the angle is extremely narrow and that closure is imminent.

Gonioscopy
All patients with suspected glaucoma should undergo gonioscopy examination (Figure 21.8). When performing gonioscopy or tonometry, it is important to adopt a strict infection control measure to avoid the risk of transmitting infective agents. Gonioscopy is performed to assess and identify the following:

- The drainage angle
- Estimation of the width of the chamber angle – open/closed angle
- Abnormal angle structures
- The effect of anterior chamber-deepening procedure.

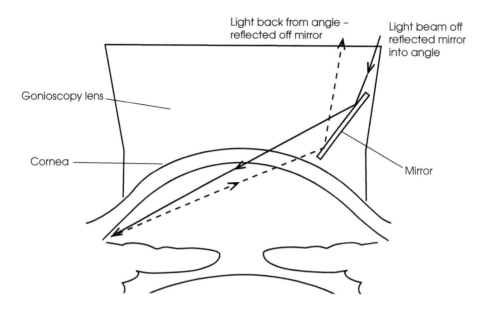

Figure 21.8 Single-mirror gonioscopy lens.

The angle of the anterior chamber cannot be visualised directly so a complex lens is placed onto the cornea, enabling the operator to direct light into the angle and thus see its structures, as a result of the placement of reflecting surfaces in the lens.

This lens is generally called a goniolens and there are a number of different types. The most common ones used are the triple mirror or single mirror Goldmann goniolens or the Zeiss goniolens. The Goldmann lenses require a 'coupling fluid', usually a carbomer gel, which is placed on the lens before it is placed on the cornea. This forms the interface between the cornea and the lens.

Although not painful, this may be an uncomfortable procedure and topical anaesthetic is instilled into the patient's eye to remove corneal sensation. Adequate explanation of the procedure will help ensure patient cooperation.

In an ideal world, gonioscopy should be carried out at yearly intervals because it cannot be assumed that the angle configuration will remain constant. As a patient gets older, cataracts can develop and cause a pupillary block, and the angle becomes more shallow or even closes in some instances.

The following are the angle structures that can be visualised from a gonioscopy examination:

- Posterior surface of the cornea
- Schwalbe's line (the point where the cornea and trabecular meshwork meet); a build-up of pigmentation on Schwalbe's line is known as Sampaolesi's line.

- The trabeculum (which stretches from Schwalbe's line to the scleral spur) is divided into two parts – the anterior non-pigmented part and the posterior pigmented part; trabecular pigmentation may be visible
- The scleral spur is the most anterior part of the sclera and can be seen as a shiny band on gonioscopy
- The ciliary body lies posterior to the scleral spur and appears as a dull brown/slate-grey band.
- Schlemm's canal can occasionally be seen as a darker line deep to the trabeculum
- Iris processes are thin extensions of the iris that insert into the scleral spur
- Radial blood vessels are often seen in healthy eyes.

Angle width grading

The angle is graded according to the structures seen and grading allows an estimation of the likelihood of angle-closure (Bowling 2015):

- Grade 4: Ciliary body easily seen and this angle cannot close.
- Grade 3: Scleral spur is visible and this angle cannot close.
- Grade 2: Trabecular meshwork seen and this angle may close but it is unlikely.
- Grade 1: Schwalbe's line and top of trabecular meshwork are visible and this represents a high angle-closure risk.
- Slit angle: An angle that is in danger of imminent closure.
- Grade 0: A closed angle.

Abnormal angle findings

- Abnormal angle blood vessels which may be rubeotic glaucoma
- Increased pigmentation of the angle which may indicate pigment dispersion, pseudoexfoliation
- Peripheral anterior synechiae, adhesions of the iris to the angle that prevent aqueous drainage
- Angle recession as a result of blunt trauma.

Optic disc assessment

Primary angle-closure glaucoma causes damage and loss of ganglion cell axons, leading to changes in the optic nerve head and nerve fibre layer. Significant nerve fibre damage and ganglion cell loss can precede any visual field defect and so the detection of any early pathological signs in the nerve fibre layer and optic nerve head will enable the ophthalmologist to come to an early diagnosis. Documenting the appearance of the optic disc at the time of the first clinical assessment and subsequent follow-up is as important as taking coloured optic disc photographs (Figure 21.9).

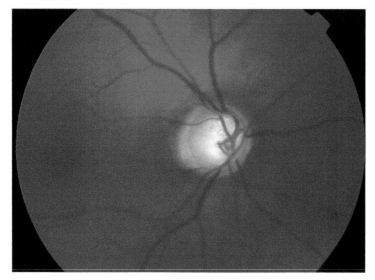

Figure 21.9 Cupped optic disc
(reprinted with permission of Richard Hancock).

Examination and assessment of the optic nerve head should take into account:

- Size
- Symmetry
- Shape/contour
- Colour
- Cup:disc ratio – progressive enlargement or deepening of the cup, asymmetry and vertical elongation all give rise to suspicions of glaucomatous changes
- Thickness of rim-localised nerve rim thinning, known as notching, is significant and this corresponds to visual field changes and nerve fibre layer loss
- Vasculature
- Depth
- Peripapillary atrophy (PPA), caused by poor perfusion from the short posterior ciliary arteries, producing visible PPA of the choroid and retinal pigment epithelial layer
- Any haemorrhages, found most commonly temporally and in patients with normal tension glaucoma
- Nerve fibre layer, in which defects may be visible.

When assessing the optic disc, one of the biggest drawbacks is the huge variation in the appearance of both the normal and the abnormal disc (Alward 2000). The other problem is that early changes in the optic disc are often very subtle. They may be within the range of normal diversity and can therefore be easily missed, even with careful and accurate documentation of the disc. There is currently no quick, simple, inexpensive, specific and sensitive method of optic nerve head analysis by which glaucoma can be easily and reliably diagnosed and all subtle progression noted.

Assessment of the optic disc routinely involves the direct ophthalmoscope or, more commonly, slit-lamp biomicroscopy, combined with an indirect lens such as a 90-D, 78-D or 66-D lens. Drawing the optic disc, measuring the vertical height of the disc and estimating the cup:disc ratio will all have to be incorporated in the patient's record. Regular disc photographs can be useful, giving an objective view of the disc.

When the optic disc is being assessed for signs of glaucomatous changes, it must be compared with a presumed previous appearance or prior documented evidence. Four basic patterns of glaucomatous damage are:

- Concentric enlargement of the cup
- Notching (focal extension of the cup)
- Development of an acquired pit
- Development of pallor of the neuroretinal rim.

In addition to these, the examiner must look for other changes in the optic disc such as 'nasal excavation', which is a form of concentric enlargement of the disc.

During this excavation process, 'overpass' or 'flyover' vessels may occur. In this scenario, the appearance of a flyover vessel is caused by unsupported neural tissue and the vessels appear suspended over the cup. Normal blood vessels usually follow the contour of the cup as it crosses the disc.

Peripapillary atrophy has also been noted in eyes with maximal excavation of the optic disc. Optic nerve head haemorrhages occurring at the disc margin can predate future excavation, especially in patients with suspected normal tension glaucoma.

It is also important to examine the nerve fibre layers (NFLs) at the same time because the NFL defects may precede visual field defects by as much as 5 years.

Visual field assessment

The visual field is the extent of the area that the eye can see – 'an island of vision surrounded by a sea of darkness' (Bowling 2015). The visual field extends around 50° superiorly, 70° inferiorly, 60° nasally and 90° temporally. Vision is sharpest at the fovea and reduces gradually towards the periphery of the visual field. There is a single area within the visual field where there is no vision. This is known as the blind spot and represents the optic nerve head. As the size and brightness (luminance) of a point are decreased, the visual field within which it can be seen gets smaller in a series of concentric rings called isopters.

Effects of glaucoma on the visual field

One of the features of glaucoma is a reduction in the visual field. There are a number of contributory factors but essentially this is the result of damage to optic nerve fibres caused by a combination of pressure-induced vascular disease of the optic nerve head and direct pressure on the axons passing through the lamina cribrosa, disrupting the axoplasmic flow.

Several IOP-independent variables have been found to be associated with glaucomatous field loss, such as disc haemorrhage, altered and disadvantageous blood flow, and haemodynamic characteristics. Nerve fibre bundles passing on to the optic nerve head on the temporal side of the disc, above or below the horizontal, are selectively damaged, resulting in paracentral defects in the nasal visual field (scotomata), which eventually merge to form an arc-shaped area of vision loss (arcuate scotoma). As glaucoma progresses, the cup in the optic nerve head becomes larger, with a correspondingly enlarged field defect eventually resulting in a small island of central vision and an island of vision on the temporal side that also disappears.

Perimetry

Perimetry can be extremely useful in diagnosing patients with glaucoma as well as measuring its progression. Perimetry is a standardised way of evaluating the visual field, which attempts to remove all possible variables of patient response and reaction. However, no test can control for all human variables, and individual patient characteristics should always be taken into account when interpreting perimetry results.

Dynamic perimetry involves a moving stimulus of known size and brightness that moves from a non-seeing into a seeing area until it is perceived by the patient. The stimulus is brought into the visual field along a straight meridian, often corresponding to clock hours, and the point at which it is perceived by the patient is plotted on a chart. Different sizes and intensities of stimulus can be used for different plots so that the concentric field isopters can be identified.

There are several ways of undertaking kinetic perimetry, including confrontation, where the patient sits opposite the clinician with one eye occluded, fixes the other eye on the eye of the clinician (who can then see any lack of fixation) and tells the clinician when the stimulus comes into view. Other strategies include the tangent screen and the Goldmann perimeter.

Static perimetry forms a three-dimensional assessment of both the visual field and the different light sensitivities of different areas of the retina. Static perimetry involves showing the patient static stimuli of varying luminance in the same position. Suprathreshold perimetry (such as Henson's) is often used for screening and presents targets over the normal threshold to the patient. Targets that are noticed indicate areas of grossly normal function; missed targets indicate areas of lowered sensitivity. Threshold perimetry can then be undertaken to quantify the missed areas.

Accurate perimetry takes commitment on behalf of the patient, who needs to fix on a target and remain alert throughout the process, which may be quite difficult. For this reason, the patient's abilities should always be taken into account, along with the printout from any machine.

Factors that can affect all visual field testing include patient fatigue or lack of concentration, the spectacle frame, miosis (from pilocarpine drops) and opacities of the ocular media such as cataract.

Goldmann kinetic perimetry

The flexible and interactive nature of this form of perimetry makes this test more suitable for those patients who are unable to cope with automated techniques. Referral criteria include patients with gross visual field loss (such as those with extensive retinitis pigmentosa or very extensive glaucoma defects) or visually impaired individuals who require assessment of functional fields. The use of full-threshold fields is probably advisable in the optic neuropathies, provided the central acuity is sufficient, i.e. 6/60 or better. However, Goldmann perimetry is recommended for chiasmal or post-chiasmal field defects or in selected cases of anterior pathway lesions with poorer acuity.

Henson's suprathreshold perimetry

Perimetrists will use the extended Henson's 136-point examination, which is an excellent threshold testing for the detection of defects. As this test is much quicker and easier for patients to comply with (in addition to having a more patient–perimetrist-centred interaction), it may also be a more suitable strategy for those patients in whom concentration may otherwise be a problem. For more serious concentration difficulties, Goldmann perimetry is still recommended. The criteria for referring patients for Henson's suprathreshold perimetry include all new patients in whom visual fields are indicated and follow-up patients who do not manifest a defect or patients at 'low risk' of developing field loss. Suprathreshold perimetry will also be useful for patients in whom static perimetry is desirable, but who have difficulty complying with the lengthy full-threshold testing.

Humphrey: threshold strategies

Humphrey's perimeter consists of a white bowl with low background illumination. Target size and luminance of targets on this background can be altered. Only the luminance is altered while the test is in progress. The stimuli are accompanied by sound.

The patient must fix on a target for a considerable period of time while stimuli are shown to them. Humphrey's perimeter gives a reliability index for the patient log with the printout, which includes fixation losses and false negatives and positives.

A target is presented to where the physiological blind spot should be if the patient were fixating. If they respond, a fixation loss is recorded. A false positive is recorded when a sound is presented without an accompanying visual stimulus and the patient responds; a highly false-positive score indicates an unreliable field. False negatives are indicated when the machine presents a brighter stimulus at an area where a positive has already been indicated and no response is given. This may indicate inattention on behalf of the patient.

Other tests include: confocal laser scanning ophthalmoscope, pulsatile ocular blood flow and ultrasound Doppler velocimetry.

Lasers: other diagnostic uses in glaucoma

Retinal nerve fibre layer analysis (RNFLA) can be seen as complementary to IOP measurements, visual field analysis and optic disc photographs. RNFLA can be used as a diagnostic tool to quantify damage to the optic disc and NFL.

Three main devices currently available for retinal nerve fibre analysis are optical coherence tomography (OCT), scanning laser ophthalmoscopy such as the Heidelberg retinal tomograph and nerve fibre analysers such as the GDX.

The retinal thickness analyser works by projecting a narrow slit (20μm) of green light on the fundus and the image is acquired on digital fundus camera. The image thus represents an optical cross-section of the retina and the computer algorithm provided will register the thickness maps of the posterior pole and surrounding peripapillary areas.

The RNFLA gives a measurement of macular NFL thickness and the optic nerve (and cup) contour.

The OCT is primarily a retinal tool and uses the interference patterns of reflected laser light to build up pictures of retinal layers. It is very effective at outlining the retinal nerve fibre layer with precision which is important in glaucoma as this layer thins as ganglion cells are lost. Software allows a 3-dimensional picture of the optic nerve head to be produced and very small changes from previous scans can be evaluated. Ganglion cell analysis is possible and a 3D 'picture' of the nerve fibre layer can be produced. Reproducibility of scans has been demonstrated so that this technique is useful for detecting early changes and progression of retinal damage and is widely used for this purpose.

Confocal scanning laser ophthalmoscopy uses scanning laser and moving pinhole aperture to acquire multiple image planes and creates a three-dimensional image to determine the optic disc and retinal topography. The edge of the disc is marked by the operator. Subjective marking also determines the cup (area below the retinal surface, red), neuroretinal rim (at the surface, green) and area of slope (blue). The procedure gives information about NFL thickness and quantitative information about the cup is also generated. Retinal topography (contour analysis) indirectly measures the RNFL thickness and requires a reference plane for all measurements.

Making the diagnosis of POAG

When considering the diagnosis of a patient with POAG, the following features may be in evidence:

- Elevated IOP on more than one occasion
- Glaucomatous optic nerve changes
- Typical visual field defects
- May affect only one eye initially.

Some ophthalmologists would wait for evidence of progressive change in disc or field appearance before making the diagnosis. Other options to consider are:

- Glaucoma suspected – only one suspicious feature
- Ocular hypertension – raised IOP but no disc or field changes
- Normal tension glaucoma – normal IOP but optic disc and visual field changes
- Secondary open-angle glaucoma
- Angle-closure glaucoma that may be asymptomatic if it is chronic.

Usually if there are optic disc changes and typical visual field defects are present, treatment for glaucoma is commenced. However, if there is insufficient information to diagnose POAG, repeat assessment for signs of progression will be undertaken. In glaucoma suspects or ocular hypertensive patients, assessments are repeated and the patient is monitored for signs of progression. Measuring IOP throughout a day spent in the ophthalmic unit (phasing) can also provide useful information about the patient's range of IOP.

Informing patients that they have glaucoma

It is never easy to inform patients that they have a condition that requires lifelong management, which involves medication that may cause them to have side effects as well as lifelong visits to the hospital for monitoring of their condition.

These patients also have to come to terms with their diagnosis and prognosis and to live with the uncertainty of long-term visual loss. If the patient is the main breadwinner and faces the possibility of having to take a lower-paid job as a result of further visual field loss at some later stage of the disease, their quality of life may be affected. In addition to the financial and social costs, there may be psychological costs. The patient may have the burden of not only coping with a physically disabling environment but also with the additional self-identity issues involved in learning to be visually impaired in a sighted world, especially if the patient has presented late in the disease (Green *et al.* 2002).

Before informing patients of their diagnosis, it is important to understand from the patient's perspective the impact that this diagnosis will have. Some patients can feel inhibited and intimidated by healthcare professionals. The quality of the patient–healthcare professional relationship is an important factor in patient compliance.

The quality of this interaction can be improved by showing tact, sensitivity and empathy for the patient in light of the diagnosis. Spending time talking to patients may not always be possible in a busy clinic so a contact telephone number of someone to whom they can talk can be very useful.

Patients may also have a poor understanding of what is being said to them initially. Always keep any explanation short and simple and, if necessary, repeat the information that you have given, using simple words and short sentences.

Allow time and opportunity for patients to ask any questions. Important information regarding compliance with prescribed medication and regular assessment should be given early in the discussion because research has shown that people tend to remember first those items that are mentioned at the beginning of a conversation or interaction (Robinson 2000).

The discussion should include the treatment options that are available and any side effects of prescribed medication. When patients leave the clinic, they should do so with as much information as possible about their condition. It is also important to check on subsequent visits that the relevant information has been understood and remembered by patients. This is particularly applicable to elderly patients who can be forgetful. Where possible, any verbal information given should therefore be backed up with appropriate written information in a language that is appropriate for the patient.

NICE guidelines (2009) on the management of COAG and OHT recommend that all patients must be given the opportunity to discuss their diagnosis, prognosis and treatment, and be provided with relevant information in an accessible format at initial and subsequent visits. This may include:

- Their specific condition (OHT, suspected COAG and COAG), its life-long implications and their prognosis for retention of sight
- The fact that COAG in the early stages and OHT and suspected COAG are symptomless
- That most people treated for COAG will not go blind
- That loss of sight cannot be recovered
- That glaucoma can run in families and that family members should be encouraged to be tested for the disease
- The importance of the patient's role in their own treatment – for example, the ongoing regular application of eye drops to preserve sight
- The different treatment options, including mode of action, frequency and severity of side effects, and risks and benefits of treatment, so that people can be active in the decision-making process
- How to apply eye drops, including technique (punctal occlusion and devices) and hygiene (storage)
- The need for regular monitoring as specified by the healthcare professional
- Methods of investigation during assessment
- How long each appointment is likely to take and whether the person will need any help to attend (or example, driving soon after pupil dilatation would be inadvisable)
- Information on support groups
- Information on compliance aids (such as dispensers) available from their GP or community pharmacist
- Letter of Vision Impairment (LVI), Referral of Vision Impairment (RVI) and Certificate of Vision Impairment (CVI) registration
- Driver and Vehicle Licensing Agency (DVLA) regulations.

Managing POAG

The goal of glaucoma management is to preserve a patient's vision by reducing IOP to a level safe for the optic nerve by increasing outflow facility while preserving the patient's quality of life. Glaucoma therapy can involve:

- Medical therapy
- Laser therapy
- Surgical therapy.

A decision on the best type of treatment option for the individual patient must not be solely based on likely clinical outcome but also on the overall well-being of the patient because glaucoma is a chronic lifelong disease. Ophthalmologists and other healthcare workers managing this group of patients must therefore base their assessment on a range of considerations, such as physical and social functioning and quality-of-life parameters (Robinson 2000).

It is also worth remembering that any treatment regimen selected for patients must take into consideration not only the financial costs but also the psychological costs. Patients have to live not only with the chronic disease but also with the uncertainty of visual loss and blindness. These patients also face a lifetime of clinic appointments and regular assessments, in addition to the numerous potential side effects associated with treatment. Patients' quality of life will be altered, including lifestyle changes, relationships and loss of independence at a later stage.

The impact of sight loss for an individual clearly depends on a combination of environmental, social and psychological factors, including physical environment, family circumstances, work roles and adaptive responses to symptoms, rather than medically defined measures of disability (Green *et al.* 2002).

Target pressure

In recent years, ophthalmologists have come to realise that simply reducing the IOP to the upper normal range is not sufficient; treatment that is merely aimed at achieving pressures in the upper normal range has resulted in substantial under-treatment (Palmberg 2001).

Due to the insidious nature of POAG, visual field loss often goes unrecognised as a result of the tendency to compare only the more recent visual field results with the last few obtained and, over 5–10 years, a proportion, perhaps as many as 34% of people, will go blind (King *et al.* 2000).

Target pressure has been defined by Hitchings (2001) as an IOP level below which further optic nerve damage does not occur. However, in clinical practice, there is a limit on the extent of achievable IOP reduction as a result of the inherent danger of increased ocular morbidity caused by low pressure.

Identifying a target IOP can often be fraught with difficulties and ophthalmologists often have to make their decision based on the mean IOP from a diurnal curve, the peak pressure from day phasing (repeated IOP measurements over the course of a day) or an isolated pressure reading.

Different theories exist – for example, that IOP-induced damage may be related to peak rather than mean pressure or that it is reasonable to rely on mean IOP and identify it from a diurnal curve and then use that as a baseline from which to calculate the target IOP. When using readings from the diurnal range, it should be remembered that the diurnal IOP range does not cover the nocturnal sleep period (about one-third of our daily life). It is thought that the nocturnal fall in blood pressure, combined with higher IOP (caused by an elevation of episcleral venous pressure at night), may compromise optic nerve circulation at night.

It may be that relying solely on elevated IOP is therefore not a good measure for identifying the potential for conversion to glaucoma. Other risk factors (such as family history, race and age) have to be taken into account. Other considerations in the decision-making process include the risks, as well as the benefits, of reaching target IOP, including the age of the patient (long life expectancy requires lower target IOP) and quality of life. It is also important to identify current treatments that would lower the IOP effectively and have the fewest side effects.

Setting a target IOP

Currently, lowering the IOP is the only proven way of preventing further glaucomatous nerve damage. In the Collaborative Normal Tension Glaucoma Study (1998), eyes that showed a reduction of the IOP by 30% had a lower rate of visual field progression than those eyes that did not have their IOP lowered.

Target IOP may be defined as the mean IOP obtained that prevents further damage by glaucoma in the individual under consideration. As we have seen, individuals can vary so there is no absolutely safe standard target pressure. However, it has been suggested that the following points must be considered when setting a target pressure for patients:

- The target must be based on the general assessment of each individual patient's disease. No absolute level or percentage change from baseline will be correct for every patient.
- It must be an accurate estimate and the cost of reaching the target IOP should be weighed against the likely benefit.

It needs to be determined in advance and re-evaluated at regular intervals, especially in light of any unacceptable disease progression.

Other factors to be considered when setting target IOP included the following:

- The IOP level before treatment – the higher the IOP at which damage occurred, the higher the target pressure.
- The greater the pre-existing damage, the lower the target IOP should be.
- The rate of progression.
- The age of the patient, their general condition and expected lifespan.
- The presence of any other risk factors already mentioned.

However, there are also a few limitations to setting target pressures and these are summarised below:

- The frequency at which the IOP is measured – the eye is subjected to IOP all the time, yet we have an idea of a patient's IOP only at a given time when the patient attends the clinic. This limits our ability to gauge the level of IOP at which the damage has already occurred.
- The diurnal fluctuation of IOP.
- Patients must get worse in terms of optic nerve damage before the ophthalmologist knows that they did not set the target pressure low enough.

Medical therapy for glaucoma

Medical therapy, in the form of eye drops, is still the mainstay of primary therapy for POAG. The European Glaucoma Society (2014) guidelines suggest that, in order to improve compliance, the number, drug concentration and frequency should be kept to a minimum so that inconvenience caused by the medication can also be kept to a minimum. The NICE guidelines (2009) recommend that treatment with a prostaglandin analogue should be offered to newly diagnosed patients with early or moderate COAG, and at risk of significant visual loss in their lifetime.

There are five classes of topical medications (for further details see Chapter 3):

- Prostaglandin analogues
- β-adrenergic antagonists and adrenergic agonists
- Carbonic anhydrase inhibitors
- Parasympathomimetics: direct and indirect
- Hyperosmotics.

There are a number of combined preparations on the market. The greatest advantage of a combined preparation is increased patient compliance and a reduction in side effects.

General principles of prescribing

When prescribing treatment for glaucoma patients, it is important that all healthcare personnel take into consideration not only the clinical parameters of the disease but also the effect of the disease and treatment on the patient's overall well-being. The main goal should be to preserve vision for a lifetime with as little inconvenience to the patient as possible (Robinson 2000).

- A target IOP should always be set before starting treatment.
- If topical medication is ineffective, always consider switching before adding another medication. Only consider additional medication if there is a reasonable response

but the target has not been achieved. For most patients, the 'maximum medical therapy' should be two bottles of drops.

- Discuss side effects with patient and review any side effects.
- Check on the patient's compliance.
- Avoid long-term carbonic anhydrase inhibitors if possible.

Managing compliance/concordance issues in glaucoma patients

The term 'non-compliance' is seen by healthcare personnel as:

- Failure to take medication
- Taking too much medication
- Taking a drug for the wrong reason
- Improper timing of administration
- Not filling the prescription
- Defaulting on the follow-up care.

Various factors that have been associated with non-compliance are:

- Dissatisfaction with treatment
- Dissatisfaction with the consultation
- Health beliefs and attitudes
- Lack of understanding of the disease treatment
- Little subjective reward for a disease with marginal symptoms
- Lack of comprehension/memory
- Unexpected side effects
- Complex regimen
- Visual/physical disability
- Lifelong treatment.

The issue of compliance can suggest an underlying authoritarian, dictatorial tone on the part of the healthcare personnel and a yielding acquiescent patient who just does as they are told by 'those who know better'. In fact, concordance involves a partnership and negotiation between the healthcare professional and patient. It takes into account the wishes of patients and respects their beliefs. As a result of concordance, the health professionals and patients, to some extent, determine how and when medicines are to be taken. This takes into account factors that may reduce 'non-compliance' and involves negotiation and agreement with the patient.

Glaucoma is usually an asymptomatic chronic disease requiring lifelong management, with very little subjective reward in terms of visual improvement as perceived by the patient. In view of this, healthcare professionals must continuously strive to convince patients that not taking the prescribed therapy can lead to blindness. The use of fear can be an effective way to alter patients' attitudes and behaviour, as long as the suggested consequences of non-compliance are realistic. Continuity of care by the same healthcare professional can also optimise compliance, although it is acknowledged that this might not always be possible.

To summarise, the various strategies used to promote concordance among glaucoma patients include:

- Providing patient education about the condition, the treatment, and how to use it
- Minimising the treatment regimen
- Minimising inconvenience to the patient
- Providing patient self-help groups, such as the International Glaucoma Association
- Ensuring good lines of communication between patients and healthcare providers
- Strengthening the quality of interaction between patients and healthcare providers.

More glaucoma clinics led by other trained healthcare professionals for stable glaucoma patients may allow more contact time between patient and healthcare professional and encourage partnership in care (see also Chapters 3 and 6).

Monitoring patients with glaucoma

According to NICE (2009), the monitoring of patients with COAG or OHT should take into account their risk of conversion.

At each monitoring visit, the following investigations must be performed:

- Goldmann applanation tonometer
- Repeated CCT measurement as necessary – for example, following laser refractive surgery or at onset or progression of corneal pathology
- Repeated gonioscopy where a previous examination has been inconclusive or where there is a suspicion of a change in clinical status of the anterior chamber angle-closure
- Offer standard automated perimetry (central thresholding test) to all patients who have established COAG and those suspected of having visual field defects who are being investigated for possible COAG. People with diagnosed OHT and those suspected of having COAG whose visual fields have previously been documented by standard automated perimetry as being normal may be monitored using

supra-threshold perimetry (see Tables 21.2 and 21.3 for recommended monitoring intervals)

- Where a defect has previously been detected, use the same visual field measurement strategy for each visual field test.
- Offer stereoscopic slit-lamp biomicroscopic examination of the optic nerve head to all people with COAG, who are suspected of having COAG or who have OHT at monitoring assessments (see Tables 21.2 and 21.3 for recommended monitoring intervals).
- When a change in optic nerve head status is detected by stereoscopic slit-lamp biomicroscopic examination, obtain a new optic nerve head image for the person's records to provide a fresh benchmark for future assessments.
- When an adequate view of the optic nerve head and surrounding area is unavailable at a monitoring visit, people undergoing stereoscopic slit-lamp biomicroscopy should have their pupils dilated before the assessment.
- Monitor at regular intervals people with OHT or suspected COAG recommended to receive medication, according to their risk of conversion to COAG (see Table 21.2).

Table 21.2 Monitoring intervals for people with OHT or suspected COAG who are recommended to receive medications

Clinical assessment		Monitoring intervals (months)		
IOP at target (a)	Risk of conversion (b)	Outcome (c)	IOP alone (d)	IOP, optic nerve head and visual field
Yes	Low	No change in treatment plan	Not applicable	12 to 24
Yes	High	No change to treatment plan	Not applicable	6 to 12
No	Low	Review target IOP or change treatment plan	1 to 4	6 to 12
No	High	Review target IOP or change treatment plan	1 to 4	4 to 6

- **a)** Person is treated and IOP is at or below target. If IOP cannot be adequately controlled medically, refer to consultant ophthalmologist.
- **b)** To be clinically judged in terms of age, IOP, CCT, appearance and size of optic nerve head.
- **c)** For change in treatment plan, refer to treatment recommendations.
- **d)** For people started on treatment for the first time, check IOP 1 to 4 months after start of medication.

Table 21.3 (below) shows the NICE (2009) recommended monitoring intervals for people with COAG according to their risk of progression to sight loss.

Table 21.3 Monitoring intervals for people with COAG

Clinical assessment		Monitoring intervals (months)		
IOP at target (a)	Risk of conversion (b)	Outcome (c)	IOP alone (d)	IOP, optic nerve head and visual field
Yes	No (e)	No change in treatment plan	Not applicable	6 to 12
Yes	Yes	Review target IOP and change treatment plan	1 to 4	2 to 6
Yes	Uncertain	No change in treatment plan	Not applicable	2 to 6
No	No	Review target IOP or change treatment plan	1 to 4	6 to 12
No	Yes/uncertain	Change treatment plan	1 to 2	2 to 6

a) IOP or below target
b) Progression = increased optic nerve damage and/or visual field change confirmed by repeated test where clinically appropriate
c) For change of treatment plan refer to treatment recommendations
d) For people started on treatment for the first time, check IOP 1 to 4 months after start of treatment
e) No = not detected or not assessed if IOP check only following treatment change

Surgical treatment for glaucoma

Although the mainstay of glaucoma management is medical, other options have to be considered if medical treatment is insufficient to halt the progression of the disease. Less developed countries may consider laser or surgical intervention as their first choice if patients live in a rural area and are unable to get to a clinic setting, or if the cost or availability of medical treatment present problems. Some surgical procedures have been recommended as first-line treatments, with effectiveness similar to first-line medical therapy (Latina et al. 2002, Katz et al. 2012).

The obvious advantage of surgery is that it eliminates compliance issues, it negates the consequences of the side effects of the medical therapy and it may, over a period of time, be more cost-effective.

NICE (2009) recommends surgery with pharmacological augmentation (mitomycin

C [MMC] or 5-fluorouracil [5-FU]) for people with COAG who are at risk of progressing to sight loss despite treatment.

As with all surgery, patients must be given information on the risks and benefits associated with surgery. At the time of publication of the NICE guidelines in 2009, MMC and 5-FU did not have UK marketing authorisation for this indication. Informed consent should therefore be obtained and documented. As both drugs are cytotoxic, they must be handled with caution and in accordance with guidance issued by the Health and Safety Executive.

Surgery is indicated:

- When target IOP cannot be reached despite maximal medical treatment
- If there is further progression of the disease, such as further optic nerve damage
- If the patient is unable to tolerate or comply with medication.

Laser trabeculoplasty

Argon laser trabeculoplasty (ALT)

The argon laser produces a therapeutic burn to a pre-selected area of the eye, causing minimal damage to the surrounding tissue, and it emits a blue–green light. The delivery of the argon laser can be done through a slit-lamp via a contact lens, using an indirect laser or endolaser. More recent developments include the development of solid-state diode lasers, which have the same effects as the argon laser procedure.

(ALT) involves the application of laser energy to the trabecular meshwork. The rate of outflow of aqueous humour is improved and the IOP is lowered.

The precise mechanism of ALT is unknown and two main theories have been proposed. It is thought that argon photocoagulation damages the trabecular meshwork, causing collagen shrinkage and scarring of the trabecular meshwork. This tightens the meshwork in the area of each burn, and opens up the adjacent, untreated intertrabecular spaces. This is known as the mechanical theory. The second theory is that the laser induces coagulative necrosis, causing migration of macrophages, which phagocytose and clear the trabecular meshwork of debris.

Laser trabeculoplasty is contraindicated in a situation where the trabeculum is not visible as a result of narrowing of the angle, in situations where the cornea is cloudy, and in advanced glaucoma where there is a known poor compliance with medical therapy and when there is insufficient time to assess the response to ALT before proceeding to a surgical laser trabeculectomy. It is also contraindicated in paediatric glaucoma and most secondary glaucomas, except pigmentary and pseudoexfoliation glaucomas. The laser beam is usually applied to the pigmented portion of the trabecular meshwork.

Usually, 180° of the trabecular meshwork is treated in the first instance. The effects of the ALT may not be obvious for several weeks. The IOP is usually reduced by about 25%, and 80% of patients show an initial beneficial effect. In up to 50% of these patients, the effect is lost in the first 5 years.

The most common complication of ALT is a sudden transient rise in IOP after treatment. The cause of this is not certain, but increased laser energy has been implicated because greater energy may result in an increased inflammatory response in the anterior chamber. To lessen this risk, topical apraclonidine and oral acetazolamide (Diamox) are prescribed before the laser treatment and immediately afterwards to prevent a spike in IOP.

After laser trabeculoplasty, patients should have their IOP checked within the first 6 hours and again the next day. Topical steroids may be prescribed four times a day for up to 1 week and patients should continue with all their glaucoma medications until they are seen in the clinic. The optimal effect for ALT is usually seen within 4–6 weeks. The glaucoma medications are withdrawn gradually, although complete topical medication withdrawal may not always be possible. The aim of ALT is a safe IOP and not a complete cessation of medication.

Other side effects of ALT include transient iritis and peripheral anterior synechiae, especially if the burns are placed too posteriorly. In addition, there is field loss associated with IOP spikes as well as loss of effect and a late rise in IOP.

Selective laser trabeculoplasty (SLT)

SLT requires a specially designed laser with a frequency that doubles the Nd:YAG (neodymium:yttrium–aluminium–garnet) laser, which is 532nm. This laser delivers less energy because the specific wavelength is only absorbed by the pigmented cells in the trabecular meshwork, without causing collateral thermal damage to adjacent non-pigmented trabecular meshwork. It causes a biological response in the trabecular meshwork by provoking a release of cytokines, which triggers macrophage recruitment and other changes.

SLT has certain advantages over ALT:

- The laser beam bypasses surrounding tissue, leaving it undamaged. This is why, unlike ALT, SLT can be repeated several times.
- SLT delivers less than 1% of the energy of ALT, further emphasising the lack of thermal damage.
- The IOP-reducing effects of SLT and ALT seem to be comparable and there are fewer side effects with SLT.
- SLT can be an additional IOP-lowering treatment in patients who have had previous failed ALT.

There is an increasing body of research suggesting that SLT could be used as a first-line treatment and is comparable with the IOP-lowering effects of prostaglandin analogues (Katz *et al.* 2012)

In summary, laser trabeculoplasty has been subjected to much investigation and is generally recognised as playing a part in primary glaucoma treatment, especially in patients known to be non-compliant. ALT, and its newer counterpart SLT, are relatively easy to perform with a low complication rate.

Care and management of patients undergoing laser treatment as outpatients

For patients who have never had any laser treatment, this can be an extremely daunting prospect. Laser trabeculoplasty is usually performed on an outpatient basis.

Patient explanation of the treatment must include a full explanation of the procedure and what to expect during and after it, including:

- The fact that a contact lens will be placed on the front of the eye after topical anaesthetic and that flashing lights and clicks will accompany the treatment. Normally the procedure will take 10–15 minutes and it is imperative that the patient remains still during the treatment.

- Appropriate communication methods must be used between the patient and the ophthalmologist so that the patient can attract the ophthalmologist's attention during treatment.

- After treatment, the patient should be warned that their vision will be dazzled for about half an hour and the eye may be slightly red and uncomfortable for 2 days.

- The patient should be advised about appropriate pain management afterwards and who to contact (and when) in case of complications such as an acute rise in IOP.

- Patients must continue with all anti-glaucoma therapy after ALT, although reduction may subsequently be possible.

Trabeculectomy

The most common surgical procedure for glaucoma is trabeculectomy. In trabeculectomy, a channel is created into the anterior chamber from underneath a partial thickness scleral flap to allow for aqueous outflow from the eye. The aqueous flows into the subconjunctival space, usually leading to an elevation of the conjunctiva, referred to as a filtering bleb. After this, it is suggested by Allingham *et al.* (2005) that aqueous is filtered through the conjunctiva into the tear film, absorbed by vascular or perivascular conjunctival tissue, as well as flowing through lymphatic vessels near the margins of the surgical area, and draining through aqueous veins.

Trabeculectomy has been proved to lower IOP more consistently than anti-glaucoma eye drops or laser trabeculoplasty. However, it can be associated with complications. The trabeculectomy may fail either because of scarring around the scleral flap or closure of the internal ostium. Another complication associated with trabeculectomy is cataract, which may progress rapidly.

To increase the success rate of the procedure, topical anti-metabolites (such as 5-fluorouracil or mitomycin) can be used intraoperatively or immediately postoperatively to increase the success rate of the trabeculectomy procedure.

Other surgical procedures for glaucoma include the following (AAO 2015a, 2015b):

- Aqueous shunts, which consist of a tube that diverts aqueous to an end plate located under the conjunctiva and tenon's capsule. There is a resistance to flow across a fibrous capsule that develops around the end plate and this ensures that a pressure is kept within the eye. Some shunts have valves; others are valveless. Common types include the Molteno implant (non-valved) and the Ahmed glaucoma valve (valved).

- Combined procedure (glaucoma/cataract surgery with IOL) – cataract surgery alone can result in a lower IOP but a combined procedure is generally not as effective as glaucoma surgery alone, so if only mild cataract is present, glaucoma surgery alone may be the best option, with the cataract being removed later (Jampel *et al.* 2002).

Non-penetrating glaucoma surgery avoids a continuous passage from the anterior chamber to the subconjunctival space. This type of surgery can take the following forms:

- Deep sclerectomy – excision of sclerocorneal tissue under a partial thickness scleral flap, leaving a thin lamina of trabecular meshwork and Descemet's membrane to provide resistance to aqueous outflow, often with an antifibrotic agent

- Viscocanalostomy, which includes a deep sclerotomy with expansion of Schlemm's canal using a viscoelastic to also allow the passage of aqueous through the lamina mentioned above and into the canal of Schlemm

- Canaloplasty – involves viscodilation of the whole of Schlemm's canal with a microcatheter, in combination with deep sclerectomy.

Micro-invasive glaucoma surgery procedures are commonly combined with phacoemulsification and done from within the eye (ab interno). They include procedures such as ab interno trabeculectomy, which removes a strip of trabecular meshwork and Schlemm's canal using electrocautery. Other procedures include the trabecular microbypass stent. These are much newer surgeries with little long-term data as yet.

Cyclodestruction procedures reduce the rate of aqueous production by reducing ciliary body function. This can be done by cryotherapy (cyclocryotherapy) and by laser (cyclophotocoagulation). These procedures have traditionally been used for glaucoma, where other therapies have not worked, and have been associated with a subsequent decrease in visual acuity.

Other glaucomas
Normal tension glaucoma

Patients diagnosed with normal tension glaucoma (NTG) have optic nerve head cupping and visual field loss but with normal document IOP readings. According to Alward (2000), patients who develop glaucomatous changes at normal or low pressures appear to have a more vascular type of damage, compared with patients with POAG. NTG patients tend to have notching of the neuroretinal rim, and optic disc haemorrhages are also more common. The management of these patients can be challenging because it is more difficult to lower what is already a 'normal' IOP. NTG is treated in the same way as POAG.

Ocular hypertension

Unlike NTG patients, ocular hypertension (OH) patients have IOPs over 21mmHg but with normal optic nerve head and normal visual field. Some ophthalmologists will advocate treatment only if the IOP has reached a level at which the risk of damage outweighs the costs and side effects of treatment (Alward 2000). If no other risk factors from developing glaucoma are present, the patient should be monitored regularly.

Congenital glaucoma

Congenital glaucoma is present at or near birth and is relatively rare. It can also appear at any time during the first 3 years of life (Figure 20.10). It occurs in only 1 out of 10,000 babies, and is significant by virtue of the young age of the patients. It occurs as a result of malformation of the angle development or secondary to another eye condition. It is referred to as infantile when it is present within the first 3 years of life and juvenile when it occurs after 3 years of age. According to Alward (2000), 60% of cases are diagnosed by the age of 6 months and 80% by 1 year old. The disease affects boys more often (65%) than girls and 70% of cases are bilateral.

As there is very little production of aqueous in the first few months of life, most cases are not manifest at birth. A baby's ocular tissues are quite elastic and stretch easily. As the pressure becomes elevated, the eye becomes enlarged and distended (a condition known as buphthalmos). Sometimes the elevated pressure can cause cracks to appear in Descemet's membrane, known as Haab's striae. In addition, the corneal diameter is also enlarged. The normal newborn corneal diameter is 10.0–10.5mm and any corneal diameter greater than 12mm is suggestive of glaucoma. Corneal oedema is another classic sign of glaucoma and the infant cornea can become oedematous at levels of IOP that would be considered only mildly elevated in the adult eye.

Congenital glaucoma can also be associated with many systemic conditions such as neurofibromatosis, congenital rubella and Sturge–Weber syndrome, and related eye problems such as Axenfield, Rieger's and Peter's anomalies, aniridia, nanophthalmos and microcornea.

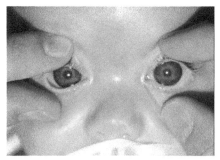

Figure 21.10 Buphthalmos.

Presentation

Presentation is often related to the corneal oedema – parents become concerned that the child's eye appears 'milky' and telephone the unit for advice. Parents often report that the child has very large, blue eyes normally. The child should be seen urgently because, obviously, early intervention is likely to lead to a better outcome. Any parent worried about a child's eyes or vision should be taken extremely seriously – parents see subtle changes that healthcare professionals often do not notice, and conditions such as buphthalmos may be overlooked by non-specialist healthcare professionals.

Treatment

The normal treatment for congenital glaucoma is a surgical procedure called goniotomy where a goniolens is used to visualise the angle and the anterior portion of the trabecular meshwork is incised (just below Schwalbe's line). Trabeculectomy can also be performed instead of goniotomy. Both give similar IOP control.

Secondary glaucomas

Secondary glaucomas, as the name implies, are secondary to another ophthalmological disease, such as inflammation or neovascular disease, and they account for one-third of all glaucoma cases (Table 21.4). Patients with secondary glaucomas are typically younger than those with POAG and it is important to rule out secondary glaucoma in patients with POAG and NTG. The angle in patients with secondary glaucoma may be closed or open.

Table 21.4 Secondary glaucoma: features of the angle

Secondary glaucomas	Angle
Pigmentary	Open
Pseudoexfoliation	Open
Steroid induced	Open
Neovascular	Closed
Lens induced	Open or closed
Inflammatory	Open or closed
Early or late traumatic	Open or closed

Pigment dispersion syndrome

Pigment dispersion syndrome (PDS) is an aggressive form of glaucoma that typically affects myopic men in their mid-twenties. It is usually bilateral but may be asymmetrical. During blinking, aqueous is driven from the posterior to the anterior chamber. The aqueous from the anterior chamber causes an increase in iridozonular contact, liberating pigment from the posterior surface of the iris and depositing it in the anterior and posterior chambers. The pigment epithelium may be abnormally prone to shedding, and exercise may precipitate acute episodes.

One of the key findings is deposition of pigment on the corneal endothelium in a spindle shape (Krukenberg's spindle), along with iris atrophy and transillumination.

IOP rise is a result of obstruction of intertrabecular spaces and up to 50% of people with PDS will go on to develop ocular hypertension or pigmentary glaucoma (Kanski 2003). This is often quite an 'aggressive' disease and management and treatment are as for POAG.

Pseudoexfoliation glaucoma

Pseudoexfoliation (PEX) syndrome involves the deposition of a grey-white, fibrogranular material on all structures in the anterior segment as well as the anterior vitreous face and conjunctiva. Systemic changes may also be found with deposition elsewhere in the body. The material is produced by aging abnormal epithelial cells and may have a genetic component. The trabecular meshwork is blocked by deposits, resulting in secondary glaucoma. The risk of glaucoma in people with PEX increases with time and a yearly ocular examination should be part of the management of the condition. Medical treatment is as for POAG but surgery is often needed.

Steroid-induced glaucoma

Steroids are thought to change the trabecular meshwork ability to process aqueous; and both topical and oral steroids can cause a rise in IOP. About two-thirds of people are thought to be steroid responders, and response depends on frequency of application and dose. Patients with myopia and POAG are at increased risk. Treatment is by stopping steroids if possible or by using drop therapy or surgery to lower the IOP. Patients with uveitis who are steroid responders will need therapy to control their IOP, along with their treatment for uveitis.

Neovascular glaucoma

This is relatively common and potentially devastating. Retinal hypoxia leads to neovascularisation of the iris and the new vessels will proliferate on to the iris, known as iris rubeosis (open angle), with contraction of the fibrovascular membrane (closed angle). It may follow central retinal vein occlusion (36%), diabetic retinopathy (32%) and other carotid disease (13%), central retinal artery occlusion, chronic uveitis and intraocular tumours. Prompt panretinal photocoagulation (PRP) is required if the media are clear, or cryotherapy if the view is poor. Atropine and steroids will reduce flare and improve the vascular component. Surgery may be needed to control IOP and eventually, if the eye becomes blind and painful, enucleation may be discussed with the patient.

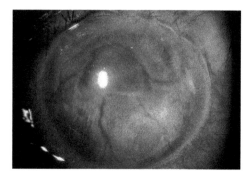

Figure 21.11 Neovascularisation causing glaucoma.

Lens-induced glaucoma

Phakolytic glaucoma is caused by lens protein leaking through the intact lens capsule into the aqueous and then obstructing the trabecular meshwork. It is more common in less developed countries where people with cataract may often present late or be unable to access treatment. Treatment involves control of IOP and surgery to remove the cataract and lens material.

Phakomorphic glaucoma is acute, secondary angle-closure caused by a large, swollen, cataractous lens. The lens moves anteriorly as a result of slackened suspensory ligaments and the size of the lens precipitates pupillary block. Treatment is by control of the IOP, laser iridotomy when IOP is controlled and cataract surgery when the eye has settled.

Inflammatory glaucoma: uveitic glaucoma

Glaucoma may occur secondary to intraocular inflammation and may be transient or persistent and damaging. Secondary glaucoma is the most common cause of blindness in children and young people with chronic anterior uveitis (Kanski 2003). Uveitis can result in posterior synechiae. If 360° of posterior synechiae occur, aqueous outflow into the anterior chamber is obstructed, the angle will close as the iris moves forward and the IOP will rise rapidly. Treatment is with topical therapy and laser iridotomy.

Posner–Schlossman syndrome (glaucomatocyclitic crisis)

Unilateral, acute, secondary open-angle glaucoma occurs in association with mild anterior uveitis. The rise in the IOP is presumed to be a result of trabeculitis. It is most common in young people and more common in men. Patients who have repeat episodes are often a good source of information about their condition. Treatment combines uveitis therapy with topical therapy to suppress the production of aqueous.

Traumatic glaucoma

Glaucoma can result from blunt trauma, immediately or months to years later, and in late presentations it is the result of angle recession. Patients with blunt trauma should be encouraged to have follow-up assessments, perhaps in the form of regular eye tests with an optometrist to ensure that any IOP rise is identified promptly.

Primary angle-closure glaucoma

Primary angle-closure glaucoma (PACG) is a condition in which the iris is apposed to the trabecular meshwork at the angle of the anterior chamber of the eye. Angle-closure may occur by two mechanisms: pupillary block or plateau iris, which is rare and not considered here.

There are three interrelated factors that predispose to pupillary block:

- Lens size: the lens continues to grow in all dimensions throughout life. Growth in diameter allows the suspensory ligaments to slacken and the lens may then move forward, nearer to the iris; along with this, it also becomes 'fatter' and this, again, leaves its anterior surface nearer to the front of the eye. Both these factors lead to a shallower anterior chamber.
- A smaller corneal diameter ensures a smaller anterior chamber.
- A short eye, one with a smaller than average axial length, ensures that there is a smaller corneal diameter and more crowded structure within the eye.

Primary pupillary block glaucoma is most prevalent in elderly individuals with hypermetropic eyes. Races with an anatomically narrower angle, such as Asians and Inuit people, have a higher incidence of angle-closure than Caucasians. Among the latter, the incidence of angle-closure glaucoma is three times higher in women. Women have a slightly smaller mean axial length than men, but the calculated ocular volume of the average female eye is 10% less than that of men (Quigley *et al.* 2003). In other races, men and women are equally affected and PACG is uncommon in people with an African heritage.

Several studies have found a bimodal peak, with the first peak at age 53–58 years and the second at 63–70 years.

Aqueous is normally produced by ciliary, non-pigmented, epithelial cells in the posterior chamber and flows through the pupil to the anterior segment, where it drains out of the eye through the trabecular meshwork and Schlemm's canal. If contact occurs between the lens and iris, aqueous accumulates behind the pupil, increasing posterior chamber pressure and forcing the peripheral iris to shift forward and block the anterior chamber angle. The anterior surface of the iris may be apposed to the posterior surface of the cornea, as with total posterior synechiae, or to the trabecular meshwork as in relative pupillary block.

Newer theories seem to suggest that expansion of choroidal volume, leading to increased vitreous cavity pressure and poor vitreous fluid conductivity, may also be responsible for the occlusion. Each of these features can appear as an isolated dominant cause in a single condition (nanophthalmos and malignant glaucoma, respectively) or they may be contributory features in acute primary angle-closure. The full pathogenesis of PACG is not yet fully understood.

Recent literature on PACG has highlighted the importance of this disease as a worldwide cause of blindness. According to Foster *et al.* (2002), in a population-based survey people with PACG are three times more likely to be blind than those with POAG; they concluded that PACG may be the leading cause of glaucoma blindness in the world today. There is therefore a need to develop screening tests that will identify both people with occludable angles and those likely to develop frank angle-closure and angle-closure glaucoma.

Signs and symptoms of PACG

- Haloes around lights as a result of corneal oedema
- Rapidly progressive visual loss caused by corneal oedema
- Severe pain, in and around the eye, and headache as a result of the acute rise in IOP
- Nausea, vomiting and abdominal pain caused by vagal stimulation
- Lacrimation
- In general settings, acute glaucoma (Figure 21.12) may be missed or the patient's systemic symptoms of nausea, abdominal pain, vomiting or headache may lead to clinicians overlooking eye signs and symptoms.

On examination, the following are found:

- A 'red eye'
- Corneal oedema caused by the acutely raised IOP overcoming the pumping action of the corneal endothelium and forcing fluid into the corneal tissue
- Shallow or flat anterior chamber with peripheral contact between iris and cornea
- The iris may be bowing forwards (iris bombé)
- Flare and cells in the aqueous (once oedema has settled) as a result of breakdown of the blood–aqueous barrier
- An oval (vertically) fixed, unreactive and semi-dilated pupil
- Dilated iris vessels
- Raised IOP (50–100mmHg).

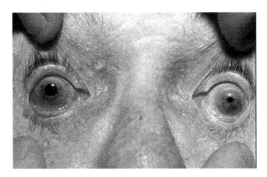

Figure 21.12 Acute glaucoma.

Gonioscopy and optic disc evaluation

Once the pressure is controlled and corneal oedema has resolved, gonioscopy should be undertaken to assess the angle in both eyes. It is also important to evaluate and assess the optic disc for any glaucomatous damage.

Even a short elevation of acute IOP can result in a posterior displacement of the lamina cribrosa. The most likely explanation for the IOP-dependent changes of the topography of the optic disc is a mechanical displacement of the optic nerve head tissues. An elevation of IOP could compress, rearrange and/or displace the tissues of the optic nerve head, resulting in a larger cupping.

Immediate medical and nursing management

Acute angle-closure glaucoma is a common ophthalmic emergency that requires early recognition, followed by appropriate treatment to minimise visual loss. There is considerable variation in the details of treatment, but it is generally accepted that treatments should be aimed at reducing any acutely raised IOP (thereby limiting any ischaemic sequelae and reducing pain, as well as clearing corneal oedema) (AAO 2015b) and removing any element of pupil block (to minimise further iris–trabecular meshwork apposition) through use of IOP-lowering medications, followed by laser peripheral iridotomy or (in some cases) filtration surgery to relieve pupillary block.

Immediate medical treatment

- Intravenous acetazolamide (Diamox) 500mg, followed by an oral dose of 500mg, provided that the patient is not vomiting.
- Alpha-adrenergic agonists – Apraclonidine is an α2-agonist that acts primarily by decreasing aqueous production. Its effects are additive to topically administered beta blockers. It has been reported to be effective in treating acute angle-closure glaucoma.
- Beta-adrenergic antagonists are also used to decrease aqueous production and, as above, can be used in combination with alpha adrenergic agonists.
- Pilocarpine 2% drops – the use of pilocarpine to induce pupillary constriction, which leads to the opening of the narrow angle and thus facilitates aqueous outflow, can also cause shallowing of the anterior chamber by increasing axial lens thickness, and induce anterior lens movement, particularly if a 4% concentration is used. Cholinergic agonists must be used only after the IOP has decreased sufficiently to allow perfusion of the iris (< 40mmHg). The few cases of cholinergic toxicity reported from pilocarpine are typically the result of over-administration of this drug during attacks of acute angle-closure glaucoma. *There is no place in the treatment of acute glaucoma for intensive miotic therapy* (Kanski 2003).
- If there is secondary pupil block from vitreous, oil, the lens or an IOL, mydriatics (rather than miotics) may be more effective in breaking the pupil block.
- Analgesics and antiemetics as required.
- Lying down for a period of time will not only be more comfortable for the patient, but will also aid pressure reduction.
- Intravenous fluid should be administered if the patient is dehydrated.
- Oral 50% glycerol 1g/kg may be administered if the IOP does not fall quickly and intravenous 20% mannitol 1–2g/kg may be used subsequently, or if the patient is unable to tolerate glycerol.
- Topical hyperosmotic agents may be used to reduce corneal oedema so that laser therapy can take place.

It is vital to offer the patient reassurance and explanation in order to alleviate anxiety and fears.

Subsequent nursing management

Patients with an acute attack of angle-closure are usually admitted (although not in all cases) for further monitoring. These patients are often elderly and may be in a great deal of pain in addition to feeling nauseous. They may have been feeling unwell for a few days before seeking treatment. They may be dehydrated, which further adds to their confusional state. On admission to the ward, a full nursing assessment must be carried out. The assessment and care should include issues such as:

- Maintaining a safe environment, taking into account the mental, visual and mobility state of the patient
- Controlling pain and nausea
- Communication issues – hearing, language barriers, speech
- Ensuring patient understanding of condition and treatment
- Nutrition, including the care of any intravenous fluids (input and output chart)
- Care of intravenous infusion
- Observations as necessary – pulse, blood pressure, temperature
- Investigations as necessary, such as bloods for urea and electrolytes, especially if the patient has had nausea and vomiting for some time
- Skin integrity assessment using a Waterlow score
- Care of any other relevant medical problems, such as diabetes, cardiovascular and respiratory issues
- Identification of relevant previous ophthalmic problems
- Medications
- Allergies
- Social assessment and communication with relatives, carers and others who need to know about the patient's admission.

Subsequent medical treatment

When the IOP has been brought under control, a laser (peripheral) iridotomy (LPI) is carried out on both the affected and unaffected eye because the fellow eyes of acute angle-closure patients are at very high risk of developing PACG. Acute angle-closure in the fellow eye occurs most frequently during the period between the initial onset of symptoms in the acute eye and the end of the first month of outpatient follow-up. Contralateral eyes of patients with acute ACG are at significant risk of an acute attack and iridotomy virtually eliminates this risk (AAO 2015b).

Laser iridotomy creates an opening in the iris, through which aqueous humour trapped in the posterior chamber can reach the anterior chamber and trabecular meshwork. As aqueous flows into the anterior chamber through the iris defect, pressure behind the iris falls, allowing the iris to recede towards its normal position. The procedure opens the anterior chamber angle and relieves the blockage of the trabecular meshwork. A number of laser burns are delivered to the mid-peripheral iris until a hole is seen and aqueous flows through.

Possible adverse side effects include development of posterior synechiae and, in theory, endothelial changes in the cornea. Many eyes treated with peripheral iridotomy will eventually require medication to control chronic pressure elevation and some will need filtering surgery.

The use of argon laser peripheral iridoplasty (ALPI), where a ring of contraction burns is placed on the peripheral iris to contract the iris stroma near the angle, has been reported to be an efficient and effective option in opening up the angle. This mechanically pulls open the angle, thus lowering the IOP and thereby allowing the eye to become quiet before definite treatment is performed (Smythe & Ngo 2012). ALPI is most useful when LPI cannot be performed because of corneal oedema or a very shallow anterior chamber. The usual practice is to perform ALPI 3–6 hours after maximal medications fail to control IOP.

References

Allingham, R.R., Damji, K.F., Freedman, S., Moroi, S.E., Shafranov, G. & Shields, M.B. 'Filtering surgery' in J. Pine & J. Murphy (eds) (2005) *Shields' Textbook of Glaucoma*. 5th edn. Philadelphia, Pennsylvania: Lippincott Williams and Wilkins.

Alward, W. (2000) *Glaucoma: The requisites in ophthalmology*. New York: Mosby.

American Academy of Ophthalmology (AAO) (2015a) *Preferred Practice Patterns: Primary Open Angle Glaucoma*. San Francisco, CA: AAO

American Academy of Ophthalmology (AAO) (2015b) *Preferred Practice Patterns: Primary angle closure glaucoma*. San Francisco, CA: AAO

Anderson D.R. (2003) Collaborative normal tension glaucoma study. *Current Opinions in Ophthalmology*. **14**(2), 86–90.

Bowling, B. (2015) *Kanski's Clinical Ophthalmology, a systematic approach*. 8th edn. London: Elsevier.

Collaborative Normal Tension Glaucoma Study Group (1998) Comparison between glaucomatous progression between untreated patients with normal tension glaucoma and patients with therapeutically reduced intraocular pressures. *American Journal of Ophthalmology*. **126**, 498–505.

European Glaucoma Society (2014) *Terminology and Guidelines for Glaucoma* 4th edition. EUGS Savona http://www.eugs.org/eng/EGS_guidelines4.asp (accessed 15 September 2016).

Foster, P.J., Buhrmann, R., Quigley, H.A. & Johnson, G.J. (2002) The definition and classification of glaucoma in prevalence surveys. *British Journal of Ophthalmology*. **86**, 238–42.

Gordon, M.O., Beiser, J. & Arandt, J.D. (2002) The Ocular Hypertension Treatment Study: baseline factors that predict the onset of primary open angle glaucoma. *Archives of Ophthalmology*. **120**, 714–20.

Grant W.M., Burke J.F. (1982) Why Do Some People Go Blind From Glaucoma? *Ophthalmology*. **89**(9), 991–98.

Green, J., Siddall, H. & Murdoch, I. (2002) Learning to live with glaucoma: a qualitative study of the diagnosis and the impact of sight loss. *Social Science & Medicine*. **55**, 257–67.

Hitchings, R. (2001) Target pressure. *Journal of Glaucoma*. **10**(5, suppl 1), 68–70.

Jampel, H,D., Friedman, D.S., Lubomski, L.H., Kempen, J.H., Quigley, H., Congdon, N., Levkovitch-Verbin, H., Robinson, K.A. & Mass, E.B. (2002) Effect of technique on intraocular pressure after combined cataract and glaucoma surgery. An evidence-based review. *Ophthalmology*. **109**(12), 2215–24.

Kanski, J.J. (2003) *Clinical Ophthalmology*. 5th edn. London: Butterworth Heinemann.

Katz, L.J., Steinmann, W.C., Kabir, A., Molineaux, J., Wizov, S.S. & Marcellino, G. (2012) Selective Laser Trabeculoplasty Versus Medical Therapy as Initial Treatment of Glaucoma: A Prospective, Randomized Trial. *Journal of Glaucoma*. **21**(7), 460–68.

King, A.J., Reddy, A. & Thompson, J.R. (2000) The rates of blindness and of partial sight registration in glaucoma patients. *Eye*. **14**, 613–19.

Latina, M.A. & Tumbocon, J.A.J. (2002) Selective laser trabeculoplasty: a new treatment option for open angle glaucoma. *Current Opinion in Ophthalmology*. **13**(2), 94–96.

Leske, M.C., Connell, A.M.S., Schachat, A.P. & Hyman, L. (1994) The Barbados Eye Study: prevalence of open angle glaucoma. *Archives of Ophthalmology*. **112**, 821–29.

Leske, M.C., Nemesure, B. & He, Q. (2001) Patterns of open angle glaucoma in the Barbados Family Study. *Ophthalmology*. **108**, 1015–22.

Leske, M.C., Heijl, A., Hyman, L., Bengtsson, B. & Komaroff, E. (2004) *Factors for progressions and glaucoma treatment: the Early Manifest glaucoma trial*. **15**(2), 102–6.

Nakamura, M.I., Kanamori, A. & Negi, A. (2005) Diabetes mellitus as a risk factor for glaucomatous optic neuropathy. *Ophthalmologica*. **219**(11), 1–10.

National Institute for Health and Care Excellence (NICE) (2009) *Glaucoma: Diagnosis and management of chronic open angle glaucoma and ocular hypertension.*
http://www.nice.org.uk/guidance/cg85/chapter/1-Guidance (accessed 15 September 2016).

Palmberg, P. (2001) Risk factors for glaucoma progression. Where does intraocular pressure fit in? *Archives of Ophthalmology.* **119**, 897–98.

Quigley, H.A., Friedman, D.S. & Congdon, N.G. (2003) Possible mechanisms of primary angle closure and malignant glaucoma. *Journal of Glaucoma.* **12**, 167–80.

Rivera, J.L., Bell, N.P. & Feldman, R.M. (2008) Risk factors for primary open angle glaucoma progression: what we know and what we need to know. *Current Opinion in Ophthalmology.* **19**(2), 102–6.

Robinson, R. (21 December 2000) How to inform patients about glaucoma. *Glaucoma World.* 17–18.

Smythe, B.A. & Ngo, Y. (2012) An Overview of Laser Iridoplasty. *Glaucoma Today.*
http://glaucomatoday.com/2012/04/an-overview-of-laser-iridoplasty/ (accessed 15 September 2016).

Snell, R.S. & Lemp, M.A. (1998) *Clinical Anatomy of the Eye.* 2nd edn. USA: Blackwell Science.

Tamm, E. (2002) Myocillin and glaucoma: facts and ideas. *Progress in Retinal and Eye Research.* **21**(4), 395–428.

Wong, V.H.Y., Bui, B.V. & Vingrys, A.J. (2011) Clinical and experimental links between diabetes and glaucoma. *Clinical and Experimental Optometry.* **94**(1), 4–23

CHAPTER TWENTY-TWO

The retina and vitreous

Susanne Raynel and Olga Brochner

The posterior segment is the area of the eye behind the posterior capsule of the lens. It is difficult to visualise without dilation and equipment, including ophthalmoscopes, slit-lamp and lenses. But it is worth it, as the posterior segment is the 'home' of the retina (also referred to as the fundus), the most complex ocular tissue. The retina lines the inner two-thirds of the wall of the globe, extending from the ora serrata to the optic nerve head.

Anteriorly is the vitreous gel (humour), and the choroid and sclera are posterior to the retina. The anterior ocular structures (cornea and lens) are designed to refract and focus light on to the retina and must be transparent to allow an unobstructed passage of light, as the process of sight commences in the retina. The retina's neurosensory components receive the light photons and transmit the resulting electric impulse of visual information to the occipital cortex in the brain. (Batterbury & Bowling 1999). Any condition that affects the retina and associated structures may therefore have a negative impact on an individual's vision and/or visual outcomes.

The retina

It is only relatively recently that technology has enabled us actually to 'see' and 'explore' the posterior segment in enough detail to understand the pathology of (especially) retinal conditions. But to begin to understand the posterior segment and retina, it is necessary to have an understanding of normal anatomy and physiology.

Retinal anatomy and physiology

The optic cup develops from the optic vesicle in the first 6–7 weeks of gestation. This consists of two layers of neuroectoderm separated by a space. The outer layers form the retinal pigment epithelium (RPE), whereas the inner layers form the neurosensory retina, with a potential space between them. This space is an important factor in the development of retinal detachments.

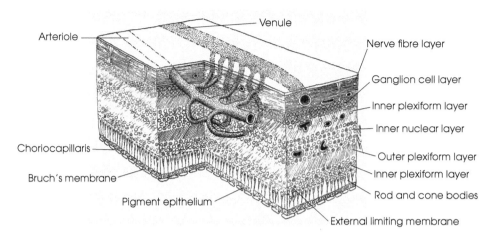

Figure 22.1 Anatomical diagram of the layers of the retina.

The retina is a semi-transparent, multi-layered sheet of neural tissue with the RPE at the 'bottom' and nine neural layers on top. It is important to know how the layers interact because a healthy retina is essential to vision and any disruption in the retinal layers will interfere with how they interact and support each other.

There are two functional layers in the retina: the RPE and the neural retina (Table 22.1).

Table 22.1 Functions of the layers of the retina

Function layer	Function/Purpose
Retinal pigment epithelium (RPE)	RPE is a single layer of cells that provides the metabolic support for the neurosensory retina, recycles vitamin A (essential for the photoreceptor cells: rods and cones) and reduces photoreceptor damage by absorbing scattered light.
Neural retina consisting of several identified layers: photoreceptors, external limiting membrane, outer nuclear, outer plexiform, inner nuclear, inner plexiform, ganglion cell, nerve fibre layers and internal limiting membrane	The retina is transparent, as light must pass through all the neural layers to reach the photoreceptor cells. Light (photons) interact with the photoreceptors, causing a chemical and then a neural response (nerve impulse) that is transferred to the brain. The neural layers include the photoreceptor cells (rods and cones), bipolar cells and ganglion cells. This is only 100–200um thick. These neural cells are connected though the different layers, e.g. the bipolar cells transmit signals from the photoreceptor cells through to the ganglion cells. The impulses pass from the outer plexiform layer, through the inner nuclear and inner plexiform layer to the ganglion cell layer itself. Cones function best with light. There are 6–7 million cones, which are mainly situated in the macula, with the central fovea comprising only cones. Cones allow the most accurate visual acuity (VA). For example, when someone is reading, watching TV or looking at a person, the eyes will move so that the object that they are watching is fixed on the fovea. This is because cones have a direct one-to-one connection with the

The labels on the figure read:
Arteriole, Venule, Nerve fibre layer, Ganglion cell layer, Inner plexiform layer, Inner nuclear layer, Choriocapillaris, Outer plexiform layer, Inner plexiform layer, Bruch's membrane, Rod and cone bodies, Pigment epithelium, External limiting membrane

cont.	ganglion cells (large neurons responsible for conducting impulses from the retina to the brain). The cones' connective 'wiring' to the rest of the neural cells therefore allows for their accuracy. Cones are also responsible for our colour vision. They contain pigments that are sensitive to blue, green and red wavelengths (Figure 22.2).
	Rods are mainly situated in the periphery of the retina. They are more numerous than cones, there are 120 million rods, and they function in dim light (scotopic). Rods contain the photoreceptor protein molecule rhodopsin, which is very light sensitive. But it takes the rods about 20 minutes to become properly dark adapted, because rhodopsin is 'bleached' by bright light. Hence that dazzled feeling when one moves from darkness into a brightly lit room, or why it takes some time to be able to 'see' in a darkened area.

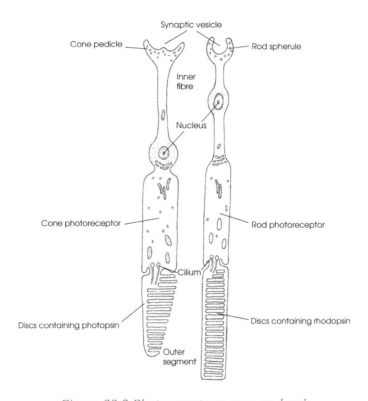

Figure 22.2 Photoreceptors: cone and rod.

Retinal blood supply

The central retinal artery enters the eye at the optic nerve and branches into four large vessels in each of four quadrants (four arcades) and then to smaller vessels. These in turn connect to the venous vessels, and four quadrant veins, which then drain into the central retinal vein, which leaves the eye through the optic nerve. The retinal blood vessels have tight junctions, forming a blood–retinal barrier similar to the blood–brain barrier. The inner retina (inner nuclear, inner plexiform and ganglion layers and the inner limiting membrane) receive their blood supply from retinal arteries and capillaries, whereas the choroid supplies the outer areas of the retina and the macular region (from the photoreceptors to the outer plexiform layer), as nutrients cross the Bruch's membrane separating the choroid and retina.

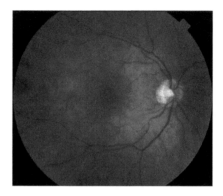

Figure 22.3 Normal retina including the macula area of a right eye
(reprinted by permission of Ophthalmic Imaging Department, Manchester Royal Eye Hospital).

The vitreous

The vitreous occupies the posterior segment cavity and is the largest structure within the globe, occupying about 80%. Embryologically, the vitreous develops in two stages: primary and secondary. The primary vitreous is forming at the same time as the retina, 6–7 weeks, between the neural ectoderm and the lens vesicle. The hyaloid vascular system (hyaloid canal) runs through the primary vitreous, nourishing the developing lens. In months 6–7, the hyaloid system begins to atrophy; and the primary vitreous is replaced by the transparent secondary vitreous. If the primary vitreous is not replaced, the patient is diagnosed with persistent hyperplastic primary vitreous.

The secondary vitreous (humour/gel) is a clear, avascular, gelatinous body made up of 99% water and 1% collagen and hyaluronic acid molecules, which are necessary to bind this large volume of water. Vitreous has an outer surface, the hyaloid membrane, which is firmly attached to the posterior capsule of the lens, the posterior surface of the zonules, the retina and the optic disc, especially when one is young. It is a normal part of aging for the vitreous to shrink, collapse in on itself and separate posteriorly from the retina, and this is known as a posterior vitreous detachment (PVD). The aging process of the vitreous is known as syneresis. And spaces left in the vitreous cavity after a PVD are filled by aqueous. However, if the vitreous attachment to, for example, the retinal structures results in traction to the retina, holes or tears may form, which can result in retinal detachment.

Vitreous base

This straddles the ora serrata. It is about 3.2mm wide and consists of a firm attachment of vitreous to the retina and pars plana.

Retinal landmarks

Pars plana

This is a posterior segment landmark at the posterior region of the ciliary body, situated behind the lens and above the retina.

Ora serrata

This the junction between the retina and pars plana (posterior to the ciliary processes), where the retina ends. The ora comprises a series of crescent-shaped indentations, making it look like a scallop shell.

Macula and fovea

The macula is situated in the central part of the retina, 3mm temporal to the optic disc. The macula differs structurally and functionally from the rest of the retina and has a high concentration of cones, whereas the peripheral retina has a high concentration of rods. The fovea is the centre of the macula, with the foveola in the centre of the fovea. The fovea receives all nutrients from the choroid, and is free from retinal capillaries (foveal avascular zone). This area enables fine, detailed vision.

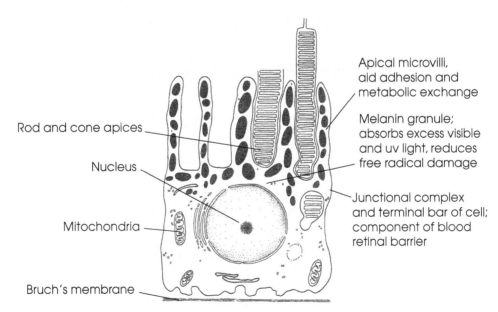

Figure 22.4 Diagram showing the main structures of the retinal pigment epithelium.

Optic disc

The optic disc is a relatively pale, almost circular area at the posterior pole, where retinal nerve fibres leave and retinal blood vessels enter and leave the interior of the eye. The optic disc is 1.5mm in diameter and the disc is often used as a unit of measurement within the retina: 'disc diameter'. This is the portion of the optic nerve that is clearly visible for examination.

The choroid

The choroid is the posterior aspect of the uveal tract, sitting under the retina, with aspects of the retinal tissue integrating with it. It has a vascular structure and has the highest rate of blood in the body. Diseases of the choroid will negatively affect the retina.

Assessment of retinal disorders

The retina reacts in a limited way to pathology and can exhibit only a limited range of physical signs. Similar fundus appearances may be produced by a number of different 'disease' processes. Also due to the position of the retina in the globe, it is difficult to view and there are limited but specific modulates in which assessments of conditions or disease are undertaken. However, it is possible to see the retina, disc and retinal vessels. Clinicians can therefore take the opportunity to see actual neural tissue and to observe changes caused by ocular or systemic diseases. Patient history is always important, as even subtle symptoms (including the increased presence of vitreous floaters or distortion) can be offer clues to the underlying condition.

Generic symptoms of retinal disorders

Any ocular examination must begin with the patient history, including their current problem and their ocular and medical history. Patients presenting with a variety of retinal conditions may provide a similar description of symptoms. Retinal disorders, unless associated with trauma, are painless. In particular, the patient should be asked about any metamorphopsia (distortion in vision), photopsia (flashing lights), sudden increase in floaters, a curtain-like appearance in visual field and/or a sudden loss of vision. Such symptoms are associated with specific retinal disorders.

Floaters

Vitreous floaters may present in one or more 'shapes' and patients usually describe them as cobwebs, threads, spots or blobs in the visual field. They are more commonly seen against a uniform background, such as looking up at the sky. Floaters can be the sign of something innocuous or more sinister.

They are usually the result of the clumping of collagen and hyaluronic acid molecules in the vitreous as one ages, i.e. vitreous degeneration/syneresis resulting in harmless but sometimes annoying floaters.

Floaters can also be caused by vitreous haemorrhages. Such haemorrhages can be secondary to a rupture of retinal vessels caused by trauma, retinal traction or the bleeding of abnormal vessels as occurs in proliferative diabetic retinopathy (PDR). Any disruption to visual acuity (VA) depends on the cause of the floater or size of the haemorrhage. A large retinal bleed into the vitreous may even cause a reduced red reflex (Chawla 1999). Usually no treatment is required for floaters. Small haemorrhages are left to clear on their own, unless the pathology (as in PDR) signifies the need for vitreoretinal surgery to preserve sight.

There is no associated ocular pain with vitreous floaters, unless they are the result of trauma; however, the underlying cause should be identified, particularly if the patient notices a sudden increase in number or if they are associated with 'flashing lights'.

Flashes

Flashing lights (photopsia) can have many possible causes, including migraines. However, regarding a retinal condition, the description of flashing lights is most often due to the photoreceptors responding to retinal traction (see retinal detachment section).

Signs include:

- the presence and pattern of sub-, intra- or vitreous haemorrhage
- other vasculature abnormalities
- retinal scars, naevi or other lesions
- fibrous or other membranes.

The above signs will be discussed in relation to specific retinal conditions later in this chapter.

Examination

Visual acuity (VA) and anterior segment assessment also need to be undertaken, and findings documented, before the posterior segment is examined. For retinal conditions, VA is often normal unless there is macula involvement or a large vitreous opacity resulting, for example from a haemorrhage or an inflammatory process in the posterior segment. It is also important to determine if a decrease in VA has been gradual or sudden.

Anterior segment examination should include:

- Presence of red reflex
- Relative afferent pupillary defect (RAPD)

Posterior segment examination.

- Pupil dilation is required for an accurate retinal examination.

- The use of either an indirect ophthalmoscope using a 20D lens with indentation of the sclera to view the peripheral retina or a slit-lamp with, for example, a 90D lens is required. The view through a direct ophthalmoscope is smaller and somewhat limited, nor does it provide a stereoscopic view.

- Other specific posterior segment investigations are discussed below.

Diagnostic tools and investigations in retinal disorders

Optical coherence tomography

Optical coherence tomography (OCT) is a scanning laser, similar to a 'B scan' but using infrared light waves rather than sound waves. It is has become a vital tool in the assessment, monitoring and diagnosis of, in particular, conditions affecting the macula (such as age-related macular degeneration and other maculopathies). Optical coherence tomography provides a non-invasive topographical map of the retina/macula as a cross-sectional, almost three-dimensional image. It allows an accurate assessment of macula thickness and is also useful as an educational tool for the patient and their carers. OCT is also used when assessing the optic nerve head/disc, especially by the glaucoma team (Hassenstein & Meyer 2009).

Retinal photography

The main function of retinal photographs is to document retinal findings and for serial assessment of retinal disorders such as naevi/lesions, presence of new vessels or even retinal tears. Retinal photography is also an acknowledged part of diabetic retinopathy (DR) screening programmes (see p. 578). Wide field imaging systems have been developed to enhance the view of the peripheral retina with an almost 200° field of view. Innovative new ways to image the fundus, such as use of mobile phone technology are being developed to aid telemedicine. Current retinal/fundus cameras, complete with digital technology, also offer patients a chance to view their retinal images, providing a fantastic educational opportunity.

Fundus fluorescein angiography (FFA)

Fluorescein is used extensively in ophthalmic practice to aid in the diagnosis of maculopathy and retinal circulation abnormalities caused by a number of conditions, as it enables imaging of ocular circulation. Fluorescein, a mineral-based dye, is injected intravenously and quickly reaches the retinal circulation. The progress and action of the dye as it passes through the retinal circulation can assist in diagnosing and monitoring many conditions. For example, fluorescein dye will not leak from healthy retinal vessels but where they have been damaged or if new vessels have developed (neovascularisation) the fluorescein will leak and show up as hyperfluorescent areas, as in diabetic retinopathy or age-related macular degeneration (AMD).

FFA is not without risk, and should be treated as any medication (with allergy status discussed before administration). Dosages vary, but a common prescription is 2.5ml of 20% fluorescein, given intravenously in the antecubital fossa while the patient is positioned at a posterior segment camera. Patients should be told that their skin may appear yellow and their urine will be bright yellow/green until all the fluorescein has been excreted. They should be encouraged to drink copious amounts of fluid to aid in excretion (Hassenstein & Meyer 2009).

Indocyanine green (ICG)

This type of angiography highlights the choroidal circulation and is used as an adjunct when diagnosing macular disorders such as AMD. It is administered in a similar way to fluorescein, and images are taken as the dye passes through the choroidal and then retinal circulation. However, indocyanine green angiography (ICG) is used in patients with choroidal pathology because it enables diagnosis of the choroid vasculature, as ICG binds with proteins in the blood and so will not leak – for example, in patients not responding to a treatment or suspected of choroidal polypoidal vasculopathy (CPV). In such cases, ICG and FFA will often be undertaken simultaneously to allow review of the retina and choroidal vascular network. ICG is not indicated for those who have an iodine or shellfish allergy, as they may have an allergic reaction to indocyanine green (Hassenstein & Meyer, 2009).

Autofluorescence imaging

Fundus autofluorescence (FAF) works by using the fluorescence in the neural retina, so no dye is required. However, the light source in a laser with a 488nm wavelength is extremely bright and some patients find it very uncomfortable. The resulting image is in black and white, and areas that are dark may mean a decrease in photoreceptors. FAF is used particularly for assessment of lipofuscin in the RPE. In excess, lipofuscin will interfere with normal cell function and result in cell death (Hassenstein & Meyer 2009).

Amsler grid

This is a grid of black lines on a white background, or white lines on a black background, that is used to assess macular function. If macular pathology is present, the lines are distorted, or there may be areas where they appear absent. Patients with AMD are often given Amsler grids to use for regular self-monitoring, and given guidance on what to do (attend the eye unit) if changes are noted. To use an Amsler grid, one eye must be occluded and the patient should look at the central spot on the grid and describe or draw any areas that are distorted (Mattice & Wolfe 1986).

Two-dimensional ultrasound ('B scan')

If no view of the retina is possible, a 'B scan' may be undertaken to aid diagnosis. This is the ophthalmic equivalent of the ultrasound scan that is used in other specialties. Sound waves are projected through the closed eyelid, providing a two-dimensional image of the interior of the globe. The images appear as white or black. White corresponds to known structures but also signifies abnormalities, such as a retinal haemorrhage. Black is the vitreous cavity and anterior segment.

Electroretinography

This is commonly referred to as electrophysiology testing, and is used for the diagnosis of hereditary dystrophies. Electroretinography (ERG) is to the eye what an electrocardiogram (ECG) is to the heart. When the retina is stimulated by a light source, the resultant action potential is recorded between two electrodes; rod and/or cone responses are then analysed to determine the visual potential.

Other diagnostic tools in retinal disorders

Other types of investigation include:

● Electro-oculography (EOG), which measures the activity of the RPE and photo-receptors.

● Heidelberg retinal tomography, a laser scanning system that ultimately provides a three-dimensional image. It can be used for disc and nerve fibre layer evaluation in glaucoma, and to assess conditions such as macular oedema. Its use has largely been surpassed by the OCT.

● Retinal thickness analyser, a laser scan used to calculate retinal thickness.

● Watzke-Allen test, in which a narrow slit beam of light is projected onto the macula to detect macular pathology. It is considered to be a crude method for detection of abnormality and, with the current diagnostic aids available, has become obsolete.

Age-related macular degeneration (AMD/ARMD)

This is the leading cause of irreversible loss of central vision in people aged over 65 in the western world, and its incidence will continue to increase with an aging population. AMD affects the macula, an individual's central vision, but peripheral vision is maintained, which allows the retention of 'navigational' vision. However, the loss of central vision severely affects a person's vision as they are then unable to, for example, recognise faces, read, write, watch television or drive. This can result in a loss of independence and have a negative impact on quality of life. There is a recognised link between AMD and depression (Caster & Rovner 2008).

The exact cause of AMD is unknown and there is currently no 'cure'. However, a range of management options has helped maintain the vision of many patients. AMD affects the outer layers of the retina and portions of the choroid. The areas involved include the photoreceptors, the RPE, Bruch's membrane and the choroidal circulation. AMD is divided into two main types: atrophic non-neovascular (dry) and neovascular (wet).

Atrophic (non-neovascular) AMD

Atrophic AMD is the more common form, affecting roughly 10% of people aged over 60. There is no associated vascularisation – hence the term 'dry' AMD. Atrophic AMD progresses slowly and usually has little impact on vision until significant atrophy develops. This form of AMD causes thinning and loss of the RPE layer, progressive damage to the photoreceptors, and corresponding destruction in central vision if the fovea is involved.

Drusen are the characteristic sign of atrophic AMD; these are yellowish deposits occurring under the RPE and above Bruch's membrane. However, there are different types and sizes of drusen. They can be a common retinal lesion but, when large, confluent and occurring in the macula, drusen are recognised as an early sign of atrophic AMD.

On examination the retina will appear patchy from the RPE atrophy, with areas of depigmentation in the macula, seen as 'geographic atrophy'. Geographic atrophy describes the thinned retina appearance of the non-functioning retina affected by AMD. End-stage AMD is therefore characterised by large areas of geographic atrophy in an affected patient's macula (Bourla & Young 2006).

Exudative (neovascular) AMD

Severe and rapidly progressing vision loss is characteristic of the neovascular ('wet') form of AMD, which affects roughly 2% of people over 60. It is also referred to as exudative, or choroidal neovascularisation (CNV), as it is characterised by a network of choroidal vessels.

These abnormal vessels proliferate into the subretinal space, leaking blood and fluid into the subretinal and/or retinal layers – hence the term 'wet AMD'. Breaks in Bruch's membrane provide sites through which CNV may grow and proliferate.

The RPE can detach from the outer aspect of Bruch's membrane, which can damage the RPE and photoreceptors, leading to rapid, widespread and significant loss of vision. This process is accompanied by a build-up of fibrous tissue.

CNV is divided into subtypes, depending on the stage of the exudative leak identified with FFA; these include 'classic' (early leak) or 'occult' (late leak). CNV can also be defined by position as 'extra' or 'subfoveal'. Other variants include pigment epithelial detachment (PEDs). These are clearly seen on OCT as elevated RPE and retina neural layers in a circular form. Much larger than drusen, PEDs can be associated with subretinal fluid (SRF).

Polypoidal choroidopathy (PCV) was originally thought to occur mainly in Asian people but is now seen in many racial groups. ICG is required to correctly identify the abnormal choroidal polyps. ICG is also useful for diagnosis of retinal angiomatous proliferation (RAP).

A RAP lesion is suspected when, on examination, there are small intraretinal haemorrhages and OCT shows intraretinal oedema. The RAP variant can be an aggressive form of 'wet' AMD (Hassenstein & Meyer 2009).

Pathological myopia can also cause a CNV, but this most commonly occurs in individuals under the age of 50 (Tan, Chew & Lim 2014).

The cause of exudative AMD, and why some patients with 'dry' AMD develop the new vascularisation, is unknown. It is thought that RPE that is damaged, due to atrophy, may produce vascular endothelial growth factors (VEGFs), which stimulate the growth of abnormal new vessels (angiogenesis) and increase vascular permeability (Jager *et al.* 2008). Chronic inflammation may also be a factor.

The natural history of exudative AMD shows fibrocyte build-up between and within the RPE and photoreceptors. Disc-like fibrovascular structures (called disciform scars) are formed, which replace the RPE, photoreceptors and inner choroid in the fovea, resulting in central vision loss.

Almost half of patients with bilateral neovascular AMD are likely to be legally blind within 5 years of diagnosis (without treatment) because 42% of patients with neovascular AMD will develop it in the other eye within 5 years (Macular Photocoagulation Study Group 1997).

Risk factors for AMD

AMD is related to increasing age, but other risk factors have also been identified, including cigarette smoking (Arnold & Sarks 2000). Cessation of smoking is highly recommended for those with AMD. Smoking is a possible modifiable risk factor for AMD. Other factors that may be associated with AMD include Caucasian ethnicity, hypertension and possibly obesity (Jager, Mieler & Miller 2008).

Although the actual aetiology of AMD has not yet been determined, it is suspected to be multifactorial (including genetic and environmental factors). It is thought that this combination may involve free radicals, disrupting the normal metabolic activity of the RPE.

Findings from the Age-Related Eye Disease Study and AREDS2 trial recommended high levels of antioxidants, lutein, zeaxanthin and zinc to reduce the risk of advanced AMD. However, it is recognised that such supplements are not without risk and not indicated for those with early or mild AMD (AREDS Research Group 2001, 2013).

AMD symptoms

There is no pain associated with AMD and, if unilateral, the patient may be unaware of any reduction in vision until there is already significant foveal damage.

Some patients present with normal visual acuity but report distortion (metamorphopsia) of central vision. Patients generally notice this distortion only when they close one eye and see distortion of normally straight lines such as door frames or lines on the road. Metamorphopsia is indicative of foveal pathology but other symptoms are not as specific. Many patients report a 'black spot' or central blur or feel their vision is not quite clear, especially when reading. There is also a decrease in contrast sensitivity. However, many patients feel that distorted vision is 'normal' (indeed an expected result of 'old age') and may not present until they have already lost central vision in one eye.

As severe loss of vision is often a consequence of the CNV variant, strategies for early detection of this condition are extremely important. Recognising sudden changes in visual acuity as early as possible could limit vision loss. Patients with recognised AMD should monitor their own sight by noting their ability to carry out daily activities or by use of an Amsler grid, one eye at a time, to recognise when their sight is deteriorating. Any changes must be reported promptly for accurate diagnosis and possible treatment. Many support groups aim to publicise the need to have regular eye/retina checks and to report as early as possible any new or sudden vision disturbances to an ophthalmic unit or ophthalmologist.

AMD signs

Fundus examination confirms the presence of drusen, pigmentary changes and atrophy, depending on the stage of AMD. In the case of neovascular AMD, subretinal haemorrhage is the distinguishing feature.

Diagnostic tests for AMD

Since 2005, OCT macular scans have become the standard for detection, diagnosis and monitoring of AMD.

Historically, FFAs were used to obtain accurate visualisation of the retina and choroidal vascular network to identify not only atrophic or neovascular AMD, but also the variant, size and location of the CNV. Areas of CNV and leakage appear as hyperfluorescence, and if part or all of the lesion is under the centre of the foveal avascular zone, the lesion is defined as subfoveal. Lesions within 200μm of the foveal centre, but not beneath it, are defined as juxtafoveal; and extrafoveal lesions are those where lesions are at least 200μm from the foveal centre (Figure 22.5).

ICG is a useful diagnostic adjunct to investigate the choroidal circulation, especially when PCV or RAP lesions are suspected. The findings of these tests assist in determining treatment options. OCT allows the early detection of subretinal fluid, often before it is clinically evident, and is therefore vital for AMD assessment.

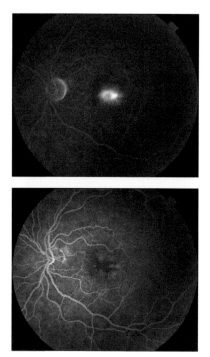

Figure 22.5 (a) Early and (b) late phase fluorescein angiography of wet macular degeneration

(Reprinted with permission of Ophthalmic Imaging Department, Manchester Royal Eye Hospital.)

Treatment options

There are no treatment options at present for atrophic AMD. Low vision support services are effective in assisting patients to learn to make use of their peripheral vision, and low vision aids in combination with good lighting enable patients to make the best use of their remaining vision. It is also important to recognise any depression and mobility issues patients may be experiencing and address these needs.

When CNV has developed in both eyes, it is also vital to maximise existing vision. If some central vision remains, low-vision aids and lightning can improve visual function significantly. Referral to support agencies and low-visual aid assessors is paramount to assist the patient. Where registration as visually impaired is available and brings with it access to services, this should be highlighted and facilitated for patients. However, disturbances, such as metamorphopsia, make visual rehabilitation more challenging. In view of the association between depression and severe AMD, offering emotional support is also important, as is reassuring the patient that AMD does not affect their total peripheral vision.

Lifestyle modifications and dietary supplements

Education regarding smoking cessation is indicated, in combination with advice regarding reducing weight, reducing fat consumption and maintaining a healthy blood pressure, which is important for those with atrophic and exudative AMD. Diet advice is also recommended, consisting of an increase in green leafy vegetables and carotenoid consumption. However, such interventions do not necessarily halt progression of the disease. Daily high-dose supplements, including vitamins A, C and E, zinc oxide, lutein and zeaxanthin, may be prescribed if indicated. Early AREDS formulas contained β-carotene. But it was recognised that smokers and ex-smokers should not take the β-carotene component because of the increased risk of lung cancer.

Ultraviolet light avoidance

Protection against ultraviolet (UV) light has also been recommended, but a recent review (Yam & Kwok 2014) concluded that there is still insufficient evidence to determine any relationship between UV exposure and AMD.

Anti-angiogenic VEGF drugs

Until approximately 2005, there were very limited options for treatment of exudative AMD. Now, unless the patient has end-stage exudative AMD with fibrosis, anti-VEGF agents have revolutionised the management of exudative AMD.

CNV, together with many other conditions, is attributed to vascular endothelial growth factors (VEGF). These stimulate angiogenesis and vessel permeability. A number of anti-angiogenic therapies were developed as therapies for tumour treatments and have since been successfully used in ophthalmology to treat AMD. Bevacizumab/Avastin was first developed for the treatment of colorectal cancer.

Rosenfeld (2005), an ophthalmologist, noted the anti-VEGF effect of Bevacizumab and, with an astounding degree of lateral thinking, thought of angiogenesis with AMD. This led to the off-label use of Avastin for patients with exudative AMD. Some patients even had an improvement in VA. Given the natural history of AMD, this had never happened before. Regular monitoring and Avastin injections suddenly meant exudative AMD did not progress to the fibrotic stage: truly a revolutionary outcome. For individuals with AMD the realisation that anti-VEGF agents could be helpful was life-changing.

While not a cure, VEGF inhibitors aim to stop any further loss of vision and, if detected and treated early, an individual can maintain central vision, something no other treatment has previously offered for AMD (Avery *et al.* 2006). A specific ocular anti-VEGF, Ranibizumab/Lucentis, was developed and a number of clinical trials demonstrated the safety and efficacy of Ranibizumab, including the MARINA and ANCHOR trials (Rosenfeld *et al.* 2006).

Anti-VEGF agents are injected into the intravitreal cavity, into the vitreous at the pars plana. Both Ranibizumab and Bevacizumab are monoclonal antibodies. However, the cost of Ranibizumab, compared with Bevacizumab, combined with the apparent lack of difference in visual outcomes of the two agents, led to a National Eye Institute head-to-head trial: The CATTT study: Comparisons of Age-Related Macular Degeneration Treatments Trial (Martin *et al.* 2011). The results compared the safety and efficacy of the two agents but found little difference in outcome.

The anti-VEGF agent Aflibercept (Eylea) has also been approved for use for exudative AMD. It is a cytokine or VEGF trap, with two arms. In this way it 'traps' VEGF receptors 1 and 2 (Heier *et al.* 2012).

Initial Ranibizumab trials indicated that regular monthly injections were associated with the best vision outcomes. However, this places a large burden not only on patients, but on ophthalmic clinics. Current practice suggests an induction series of a monthly anti-VEGF injection for 3 consecutive months, followed by a treat and extend protocol if successful. This means an injection at each visit, but increasing the time between each visit if the exudative AMD has not been active – i.e. there is no new haemorrhage or subretinal fluid (Toalster, Russell & Ng 2013). Some practices may use PRN (as required) or continue with monthly injections.

Naturally any intravitreal injection (IVI) procedure has associated ocular risks, including infection and retinal detachment. There have also been reports of systemic risks, including stroke, but the majority of anti-VEGF injections are well tolerated with few serious complications (Toalster, Russell & Ng 2013. (See 'IVI' section below)

The agent Pegaptanib sodium (Macugen) was developed to inhibit a VEGF isoform, VEGF-A. However, it does not reverse any loss of vision or stop progression of CNV (Avery *et al.* 2006). Agents to address the impact of chronic inflammation on retinal cells and the development of AMD are also under consideration.

Intravitreal injections

As this is an intraocular procedure, the preparation is as for surgery. It should be done in an approved theatre or clean room setting, in line with guidelines set by the ophthalmology standards applicable in the particular setting.

These consist of an injection of a substance into the vitreous cavity, i.e. an anti-VEGF agent. Ophthalmic units will have different protocols regarding pre- injection analgesia – for example, only topical drops or a combination with a local injection of subconjunctival anaesthetic prior to the injection. Common side effects are: discomfort, subconjunctival haemorrhage, vitreous floaters and corneal abrasion. Rare events include: endophthalmitis, retinal detachment, cataract, glaucoma and inflammatory responses.

Comprehensive information about setting up an intravitreal injection service, including training and dealing with critical incidents is available in Waqar *et al.* 2014.

Other treatments for exudative AMD

Intravitreal steroid

Steroid agents (such as triamcinolone) have also been used in the past, as there is thought to be an inflammatory factor in the development of AMD. Steroid agents are also injected into the intravitreal cavity.

Argon laser

For a minority of patients affected by exudative AMD in the past, thermal laser photocoagulation was applied to 'seal' off, or cauterise, the leaking vessels. But this had limited use and was only effective if the CNV was located outside the fovea. This is because the laser burns and would therefore damage the fovea and all other normal tissues, along with the CNV. Well-demarcated extrafoveal and juxtafoveal lesions have been successfully treated with photocoagulation for several years, and maintenance of vision has been achieved for an extended interval, but CNV does recur frequently, and certainly photocoagulation does not reverse any loss of vision (Gliem *et al.* 2013).

Photodynamic therapy

Non-thermal laser treatment, known as photodynamic therapy (PDT), was developed as a treatment option for exudative AMD. This combines a photosensitising drug (Verteporfin) with non-thermal laser therapy in an attempt to close the leaking vessels. The procedure is time critical and the patient must be well prepared for it. Verteporfin is metabolised mainly in the liver and cleared primarily via the bile and faeces, with less than 1% cleared via the kidneys and urine. Verteporfin is taken up slowly by the skin, and can be activated in the peripheral vasculature by light. Precautions must therefore be taken against skin photosensitivity after a Verteporfin infusion, and patients should avoid direct sunlight and bright lights for 48 hours after treatment and wear a brimmed hat, sunglasses and be fully covered with clothes when out of doors after treatment.

The use of a bracelet to inform the patient and other healthcare professionals about the needs of the patient after Verteporfin therapy is recommended. Some patients report severe back pain following infusion of the drug and the mechanisms for this are not fully understood.

Multiple treatments are required and studies have indicated that PDT is useful only for some patients. To restrict the loss of vision, patients must be referred early. PDT does not restore vision and in some countries, such as New Zealand, it is available only through the private sector, so the expense of the multiple treatments required puts it out of reach of many elderly, retired individuals. It may still be used in combination with other agents and for some variants of exudative AMD (Gliem *et al.* 2013).

Surgery

Vitreoretinal surgical intervention with macular translocation, or rotation, has been investigated to offer such patients some chance of regaining central vision. This surgery involves a three-port pars plana vitrectomy, after which there is a planned retinectomy and then a retinal detachment is created, allowing the retina to be 'spun' around. The result is that the macula/fovea is translocated to a site away from the underlying CNV. Laser photocoagulation is used to seal the retinectomy. Further surgery is then required to correct the resultant strabismus, and there is a high risk of postoperative complications, including PVD, retinal detachment and macular folds. Again, this does not reverse any macular damage and, due to all the associated risks, should not be undertaken lightly if at all (Singerman *et al.* 2005).

AMD consequences

The end-result of either atrophic or exudative AMD can be a central scotoma (blind spot) and associated loss of vision but the progression of AMD varies in different patients. Some patients with AMD may experience a phenomenon known as Charles Bonnet syndrome, where the person with visual impairment/central scotoma may have hallucinations that are well defined, organised, clear images (Menkhaus *et al.* 2003). The precise mechanism is unknown but is believed to originate from the visual association areas of the cerebral cortex. Charles Bonnet syndrome has been described as 'phantom vision' and likened to the phantom limb phenomenon. It is important to discuss this with patients, as they may be experiencing such disturbances and questioning their sanity.

AMD has far-reaching implications not only for the affected patient's quality of life, but also for the cost of social care and healthcare. In an attempt to offer some support to affected patients, it has often been stressed that they will not become totally blind because 'only central vision is lost', although they will be classified as legally blind. This view is, however, likely to be of little comfort to anyone (which must include nearly everyone) who is reliant on their central vision for a normal life.

For those with atrophic AMD, there are no treatment options. Exudative AMD management now involves regular review (initially 4–6 weekly) and intravitreal injections as indicated. Although anti-VEGF agents have revolutionised outcomes and resulted in a more positive prognosis for many patients with exudative AMD, the uptake of use has also meant an increased demand and cost for ophthalmology departments. The search for a curative therapy continues.

Central serous retinopathy (CSR)

Also known as central serous chorioretinopathy, this is a serous detachment of the neural retinal layers. Unlike exudative AMD, there is no break in Bruch's membrane, but OCT confirms the presence of subretinal fluid. The cause is unknown, but it is common in young to middle-aged men and is often stress related. Most patients have a sudden onset of decreased vision and metamorphopsia. FFA will confirm the diagnosis with the CSR characteristic 'smokestack' hyperfluorescence. Around 80% of cases will spontaneously resolve, but some patients develop a chronic form. In persistent cases, if juxta-foveal, argon laser may be indicated. PDT has also been used. Anti-VEGF agents are not indicated, as there is no VEGF drive for this retinopathy (Ehrlich *et al.* 2012).

Diabetic retinopathy

Diabetes mellitus (DM) is a metabolic disorder characterised by defects in insulin secretion resulting in chronic hyperglycaemia and disturbances of carbohydrate, fat and protein metabolism. DM is classified as type 1 (no insulin produced) or type 2 (decreased or diminished insulin production or insulin resistance) diabetes and is reaching epidemic proportions in many countries. Long-term DM can cause a number of macro- and microvasculature complications. Type 1 and 2 diabetes can affect a variety of ocular structures, but one of the most universal complications is diabetic retinopathy (DR).

Studies have shown that a person with diabetes is 10–20 times more likely to go blind than a non-diabetic person. It is also the leading cause of vision loss in people of working age in the western world. Diabetic retinopathy is part of the spectrum of microvasculature complications that are similar to changes found in other regions of the body (nephropathy and neuropathy) as a result of diabetes. It is a microangiopathy where the retinal vasculature is pathologically altered, and the result is DR.

The likelihood of having a degree of DR increases with the duration of diabetes, with almost all type 1 and 60% of those with type 2 diabetes developing some form of retinopathy after 20 years. The development and progression of DR is also influenced by several factors, the most important of which is chronic hyperglycaemia, but also includes poorly controlled hypertension and pregnancy. If left untreated, the retinopathy will progress, causing loss of vision (Batterbury & Bowling 1999). To date, there is no cure for DM or DR.

The dense network of capillary vessels in the retina is vulnerable to microvascular disease. The exact mechanisms causing the development of DR are not yet completely understood; yet chronic levels of hyperglycaemia affect retinal blood vessels, resulting in features of microvascular occlusion and leakage, thickening of the capillary basement membrane and endothelial damage that are believed to contribute to retinal microvascular occlusion, which may begin the cascade of DR changes that can result in blindness. The development of DR is progressive and the clinical manifestations of different stages are related to the changes occurring in the retinal vasculature and different stages may exist together. The classification of stages and clinical features observed as retinopathy develops are outlined in Table 22.2 (below).

Vision loss due to DR can occur from two pathways:

- Ischaemic, affecting predominantly the peripheral retina
- Leakage/increased vessel permeability, affecting the macula (maculopathy).

The ischaemic pathway has identifiable signs that are used to categorise it into stages reflecting the progress of DR, from nil to minimal, to moderate, to severe. Diabetic maculopathy does not have such defined stages and can progress relatively quickly. Unfortunately for the patient, there are no symptoms until the vision is affected, which means that treatment options are often limited and it is not always possible to restore any vision.

Stages and signs of diabetic retinopathy

Table 22.2 Classification and visible clinical features of diabetic retinopathy (adapted from Hamilton *et al.* 1996).

Classification	Clinical features	Visual symptoms
Non-proliferative diabetic retinopathy (NPDR) mild to moderate	Microaneurysms & small intraretinal haemorrhages (dots) Larger intraretinal haemorrhages – 'blots' 'Hard' exudates Retinal oedema	→asymptomatic
Pre-proliferative diabetic retinopathy Moderate to severe NPDR	Changes to venous vessels – 'beading' or 'looping' Intraretinal microvascular abnormalities IRMA	→asymptomatic
Proliferative diabetic retinopathy (PDR)	Neovascularisation: new vessels at optic disc (NVE), or elsewhere in retina (NVE) or on iris Fibrous traction bands Vitreous haemorrhage	→asymptomatic →sudden ↓ in vision
Diabetic maculopathy	Macular exudates and oedema Clinically significant macular oedema (CSMO) with foveal thickening	→↓in visual acuity →↓central vision

Non-proliferative diabetic retinopathy (NPDR)

This is when there are no signs of DR. This stage can last many years. But a patient should still have regular retinal reviews to ensure early detection of any signs.

Mild non-proliferative DR is an early stage, when changes are characterised by microaneurysms or small 'dot' intraretinal haemorrhages. Microaneurysms are 'outpunchings' from the walls of the capillaries (Figure 22.6). These are the earliest signs and this stage is also known as 'background retinopathy' and/or mild non-proliferative DR (NPDR), as there is no growth of new vessels (neovascularisation). Changes can be reversed with good glycaemic and hypertensive control, and there is no reduction in vision.

Moderate non-proliferative DR

This occurs when the retinopathy progresses and microaneurysms from the basement membranes of the capillaries thicken, resulting in impaired cell integrity. Pericytes are responsible for structural integrity in the retinal capillary walls and chronic hyperglycaemia may lead to pericyte and capillary wall damage. Advanced glycation end-products (AGEs) have also been indicated in the development of basement membrane abnormalities. The affected retinal capillary basement membranes thicken and may become entirely blocked, thus cutting off the blood supply to the cells served by that capillary network. The vessels also become more permeable, resulting in vascular leakage of blood, protein and lipid.

Moderate NPDR is characterised by larger 'blot' haemorrhages, as the distended capillary vessels burst, and the presence of exudates results from the diminished permeability of the capillary walls. Exudates are yellow in appearance, composed of lipoproteins and deposit in the outer plexiform area/layer of the retina. Exudates can be seen even if there is no current capillary leakage or oedema and take some time to resolve. They were previously referred to as 'hard' exudates to differentiate them from drusen, especially when occurring in the macula.

Flame-shaped haemorrhages occur in the nerve fibre layer, and they are a sign of hypertensive retinopathy. 'Cotton wool spots' (CWS) indicate retinal ischaemia. Although they were part of the DR grading classification in early DR studies (i.e. ETDRS: Early Treatment Diabetic Retinopathy Study) they are now considered to be more a sign of hypertensive retinopathy. CWS lie in the retinal nerve fibre layer and appear as white and fluffy. They do not interfere with vision and are transient.

Severe or pre-proliferative NPDR

The microvasculature changes and resulting capillary non-perfusion lead to the progression of DR and the development of retinal ischaemia. This stage is characterised by intraretinal microvascular abnormalities (IRMA) and beaded or looped blood vessels. These are all signs of worsening retinal ischaemia and the increased probability of the development of proliferative vessels, neovascularisation (PDR).

Proliferative diabetic retinopathy (PDR)

Proliferative diabetic retinopathy (Figure 22.7) is defined as 'the presence of new vessels on the surface of the retina or optic disc' (Ferris et al. 1999, p. 669). This is associated with advanced retinal vessel disease and, if left untreated, will always impede vision. Ischaemia is the major influencing factor in the progression to PDR. In an attempt to correct this and improve the retinal circulation, vaso-endothelial angiogenic factors (VEGFs) are released, stimulating the proliferation (growth) of new blood vessels (neovascularisation). They can grow from the remaining retinal vessels at the edge of the non-perfused retinal areas (new vessels elsewhere/NVE) or at the optic disc (new vessels at disc/NVD).

These vessels do not resolve the ischaemia. Instead, they can 'grow upwards' off the retina's surface and into the vitreous, using it as scaffolding. The vitreous shrinks forward and the vessels are pulled forward and bleed, resulting in a haemorrhage known as a vitreous or intragel haemorrhage. This haemorrhage may obscure a patient's vision and be their first presenting symptom, despite having pathological DR changes for some time.

The new vessels are fragile and tend to bleed, which also results in haemorrhages between the posterior hyaloid membrane and the retinal surface: preretinal/subhyloid. Or they can even bleed into the vitreous cavity (vitreous haemorrhage). They have an accompanying fibrotic glial tissue or scar-like component, which can also grow up into the vitreous, using it as scaffolding. This tissue is white and non-transparent so it interferes with visual acuity as well as behaving like any scar tissue and contracting. As this occurs, the tissue pulls on retinal vessels, leading to breaks and/or haemorrhages. It also pulls on the retina, causing distortion and retinal breaks, leading to retinal detachment and severe visual loss.

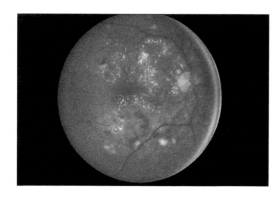

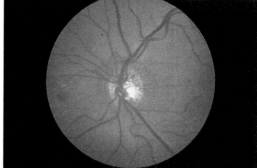

Figure 22.6 Non-proliferative diabetic retinopathy.

Figure 22.7 Proliferative diabetic retinopathy.

In PDR sudden loss of vision is secondary to bleeding from the new vessels, often with a large vitreous haemorrhage. In the contraction stage, vision loss occurs secondary to traction complications of the neovascular fibrotic membrane effect on the retinal surface, causing neurosensory retinal separation from RPE. The detachment may be localised, causing loss of vision if it involves the macula, or it may be a larger traction. This occurs due to tractional forces on the retina and may cause a retinal tear/s and a secondary rhegmatogenous retinal detachment and resulting loss of vision from the PDR.

Diabetic maculopathy

DR can damage the capillaries and result in increased blood vessel permeability. When this occurs at the macula, exudates, oedema or both can be seen. Vascular permeability is associated with macular thickening and the development of maculopathy. Long-term thickening or clinically significant macular oedema (CSMO) will cause permanent loss of central vision as a result of the separation of neurosensory retina from the RPE. CSMO is the principal mechanism of visual loss in NPDR, but it can occur at any time during the progression of retinopathy. OCT has become a valuable tool in assessing the level of maculopathy and foveal thickening.

Diagnosing DR

Diabetic retinopathy does not cause any visual symptoms until late in the ischaemic pathway when, for example, a vitreous haemorrhage occurs; by then, the retinopathy can be quite advanced. With diabetic maculopathy, vision may initially be blurred. But, if unilateral, this may not be noticed. There is no associated pain or a red eye with DR. The diagnosis of DR is made by either visual examination or retinal photography. This is why all those patients with diagnosed diabetes require regular and accurate checks to assess the state of the retina in relation to diabetes. Early diagnosis and treatment are always more effective and give better results in the long term. Failing this, the aim is to diagnose and treat before permanent vision loss occurs.

DR prevention

The rate of development of diabetes-related complications, such as DR, is affected by diabetic/glycaemic control. Management of diabetes is the only viable option to reduce the occurrence of blinding DR. This involves education about factors that affect diabetes, including glucose and blood pressure control, diet, physical activity and pharmacological agents. Patient education should begin early in the patient's disease process, and diabetic liaison nurses, GP nurses and diabetic clinics have an important role in assisting patients by empowering them to gain the knowledge and skills required to help prevent complications. Management therefore also involves regular review of a patient's glycaemic status. The advent of measurement of HbA1c (glycosylated haemoglobin) has enabled a better review of glycaemic status and trends.

Patients with diabetes need to understand the importance of regular eye examinations for the management of DR, due the lack of symptoms early in the disease process. A health intervention plan for a patient with diabetes must include education about the importance of regular ophthalmic assessments because the rate and development of retinopathy progression in an individual cannot be accurately predicted. Again, patients with DR may remain asymptomatic, unaware of their condition and the potential for loss of vision, and the retinopathy can be well advanced before visual symptoms occur and the patient presents for assessment and treatment.

DR screening

Diabetic retinopathy screening consists of retinal imaging, ophthalmoscope examination (fundoscopy) or a combination of both. Once screened, patients with retinopathy changes can receive appropriate follow-up or treatment modalities as indicated (Hamilton *et al.* 1996). There are three main ways in which the retina is imaged to aid in the diagnosis monitoring of DR and to decide on treatment options: retinal photography, fluorescein angiography and optical coherence tomography.

Retinal photography

This involves photographing the retina to accurately document signs of retinopathy and has therefore become an integral part of DR screening programmes. With new wide-field imaging systems, there is also a possible role for retinal photography monitoring of those with more advanced DR who have exited photoscreening programmes.

Retinal photoscreening is a process whereby patients with diabetes are screened on a regular basis, using retinal photography, for signs of DR. For those with nil, minimal or mild DR, photoscreening can provide a safe and viable option to dilated retinal ophthalmoscopy. Photographs of the retina are taken and reviewed for signs of retinopathy and graded on these findings. Outcome and follow-up depends on the grade of DR. In some countries, DR photoscreening is undertaken annually; in others the expectation is every 2 years if no DR is present. The frequency of subsequent retinal photoscreening episodes depends on the presence of the retinal disease, or other factors (such as poor glycaemic control), or severe hypertensive retinopathy. Primary screening can be undertaken by nurses and other trained personnel, with support and auditing screening by consultant ophthalmologists for photographs of patients identified as abnormal or significant pathology (Shah & Brown 2000).

In the original landmark Early Treatment Diabetic Retinopathy Study Research Group protocol (1985), imaging involved obtaining seven-field fundus images. While this resulted in a large coverage of the retina for observation of DR signs, it takes some time to complete for each patient. Most DR screening programmes today involve less imaging – i.e. a macula and nasal views and sometimes also superior and inferior images. Wide-field imaging systems offer a nearly 200° image, as opposed to the 45° image provided by a standard fundus camera.

At present, however, standard fundus imaging is most often used in photoscreening programmes. Digital cameras are now used for retinal photoscreening because the images can be transmitted electronically, which has several advantages over celluloid images. The image can be viewed by ophthalmologists as necessary in the clinical setting. Also, for tertiary screening, the screener can be offsite and the images can be used for teaching purposes with healthcare personnel (Ryder 1995). However, perhaps most importantly, the images can be used as a teaching tool for the patient and the family to assist them in understanding the degree of retinopathy and the possible outcome or treatment required. The photographs are a hard record of the presence or absence of DR and offer a safer alternative to a retinal drawing, which could be misinterpreted.

Digital cameras also allow flexibility in the provision of screening services, with outreach facilities closer to the patients, making attendance easier than asking them to come to a large hospital.

Patient preparation depends on whether the camera is non-mydriatic or mydriatic. Non-mydriatic cameras do not require the patient to have the pupil dilated, whereas pupil dilatation is required for a mydriatic camera.

Fluorescein angiography (FFA)

FFA is undertaken for diagnosis of ischaemia in the retina, maculopathy and to aid in decisions about photocoagulation.

Optical coherence tomography (OCT)

OCT is used in diagnosis of diabetic maculopathy, even at subclinical levels. It can accurately show the presence of intraretinal macula oedema and foveal thickening and has become an important tool for monitoring of diabetic maculopathy.

DR treatment options

Photocoagulation

Two ground-breaking trials, the Diabetic Retinopathy Study (DRS Group 1978) and the Early Treatment of Diabetic Retinopathy Study (ETDRS Research Group 1985), demonstrated that the risk of severe visual loss from PDR can be reduced by the use of retinal photocoagulation (laser). Before this, there was no established form of treatment for PDR, and patients with PDR would inevitably lose their sight. Maculopathy is more difficult to treat with laser. There are a number of lasers that are currently suitable for use in treating DR; yet, despite the proven effectiveness of photocoagulation treatment, it does not improve or restore any lost vision. Photocoagulation can only delay the progression of retinopathy and reduce loss of vision if it is instigated (for example, in PDR) when there are signs of ischaemia.

The rationale for PDR photocoagulation is to destroy abnormal new vessels by treating retinal areas where the capillaries are not perfused; consequently, the stimulation for neovascularisation is reduced. Panretinal photocoagulation (PRP) laser for PDR treatment involves applying thermal energy to the peripheral retina in order to ablate the ischaemic retina, causing a reduction in its oxygen need and therefore decreasing the stimulation of vasogenic factors, leading to regression of neovascularisation (Figure 21.8). Although the peripheral retina is 'burnt' by the laser, central vision should be maintained as the macula is preserved. Destruction of the ischaemic areas in the peripheral areas has been shown to lead to shrinkage of new vessels at the optic disc.

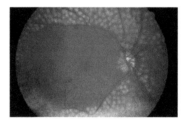

Figure 22.8 Panretinal photocoagulation for retinopathy
(reprinted by permission of the National Eye Institute, National Institutes of Health, USA).

Focal or grid macular photocoagulation consists of precise focal points of laser burns to blood vessels leaking into the macular area. Laser treatment destroys or occludes leaking vessels near the macula, thereby reducing the leakage of fluid accumulation and lipid deposits. If retinal neural cells are already destroyed, treatment cannot heal them or improve the visual acuity, but macular laser instead aims to maintain vision at the current level. Before the advent of anti-VEGF agents, this was the only treatment option for diabetic maculopathy.

Patient preparation for laser:

- Dilate pupil
- Provide information about the procedure – bright flashes are occasionally uncomfortable; laser burns for PRP may be uncomfortable and they will often require more than one PRP treatment
- Regional anaesthesia may be used if the patient finds the procedure very painful, and this will need to be planned into each treatment session
- Obtain informed consent.

Side effects may include headache, choroidal detachment and macular oedema.

Intravitreal treatments

Vaso-endothelial growth factors drive angiogenesis and increase vascular permeability. The anti-VEGF agents (currently Bevacizumab, Ranibizumab and Aflibercept) have therefore become part of the DR treatment modalities. Patients with PDR may have an anti-VEGF intravitreal injection prior to vitreoretinal surgery or PRP treatment. However, their main use is for diabetic maculopathy, either with leaking capillaries too close to the fovea for laser, or prior to laser treatment to reduce oedema. Anti-VEGF agents have had a positive impact in the management of diabetic maculopathy.

Intravitreal steroid (triamcinolone) has also been effective for maculopathy. However, the associated risks of cataract development and steroid-induced glaucoma mean that it is not seen as a first-line treatment. These treatments are not a cure, but aim to reduce vision loss. However, the most effective method of preventing loss of vision is to prevent NPDR from progressing.

Vitreoretinal surgery

In the early 1960s, the concept of a controlled removal of vitreous was realised when Kasner performed a planned 'open sky vitrectomy'. Machemer went on to develop the pars plana vitrectomy, which has made visual rehabilitation possible for many patients with previously untreatable retinal conditions. Vitrectomy for traction detachments and other such complications of PDR resulted in the preservation of vision for many patients.

Indications for a vitrectomy in diabetic eye disease include:

- Severe non-clearing vitreous haemorrhage
- Traction retinal detachment, especially when involving the macula
- Combined traction and rhegmatogenous retinal detachment
- Severe progressive fibrovascular proliferation.

Surgical steps are similar to vitreoretinal (VR) surgery for other reasons. However, if there is localised retinal traction from PDR fibrous tissue, VR surgery will include a membranectomy to dissect off and remove the proliferating tissue and relieve the traction. PRP can also be undertaken via indirect laser or with an endolaser probe at the time of VR surgery. If there is a combined tractional-rhegmatogenous detachment, the surgical procedure will also involve the identification of retinal breaks, removal of subretinal fluid, photocoagulation to seal the breaks, insertion of an internal tamponade, possible external explant, and postoperative posturing for the patient.

In cases of severe persistent retinal traction, a retinectomy (planned incision of the scleral surface of the retina) may need to be performed in order to salvage the macula and central vision.

Postoperative complications can include:

- Infection
- Cataract formation
- Recurrent vitreous haemorrhage
- Rhegmatogenous retinal detachment
- Fibrin clot formation
- Neovascular glaucoma
- Flat anterior chamber
- Transient rise in IOP and possible pain.

Pharmacological control of diabetic retinopathy

Research into the possibility of pharmacological control includes the pharmacological control of angiogenesis to reduce proliferative diabetic neovascularisation and a drug to dissolve the vitreous, thereby reducing vitreoretinal traction. However, at present these are not viable options (Ferris *et al.* 1999).

The prevalence of diabetes is predicted to increase, reflecting changing demographic factors (including increased population size and changes in population age structure) and epidemiological factors (such as obesity and physical inactivity). The rising incidence of diabetes will inevitably mean that diabetes-related complications, such as DR, will have an increasing impact on society, healthcare and economics.

Hypertensive retinopathy

Hypertensive retinopathy occurs secondary to an elevated systemic blood pressure, resulting in changes in the vasculature of the retina and choroid. The elevated systemic blood pressure can cause either primary hypertension or secondary hypertension as a result of renal disease or toxaemia of pregnancy. Sustained hypertension causes disruption of the blood–retina barrier, with a resulting increase in vascular permeability.

Specific ocular manifestations associated with systemic hypertension are: retinal vein occlusion, retinal artery occlusion, exudative retinal detachment and ischaemic optic neuropathy.

The incidence of hypertensive retinopathy depends on the control of the patient's systemic hypertension. The initial response is narrowing of the retinal arterioles; however, if there is a lot of involution sclerosis in older patients, the same degree of narrowing does not occur, despite the presence of hypertensive retinopathy.

Patient symptoms and signs

Symptoms depend on the severity of the retinopathy present.

- Minimal retinopathy is generally asymptomatic.
- The patient will complain of blurred or distorted vision with moderate to severe hypertensive retinopathy. These symptoms are caused by haemorrhages and exudates affecting the macula, and consequently affecting central vision.
- If moderate to severe hypertensive retinopathy is present, the patient may also complain of headaches.

Signs include:

- The retinal image is characterised by vasoconstriction, 'flame' haemorrhages, CWS, exudates and leakage of vessels.
- A narrowing of the veins at arterial–venous crossing points is known as 'AV nipping' and is a significant sign of hypertensive retinopathy
- Hypertensive retinopathy has four distinct grades (Table 22.3).

Treatment

Control of hypertension is the key to controlling hypertensive retinopathy.

Table 22.3 The grading and visible clinical features of hypertensive retinopathy

Grading of hypertensive retinopathy	Clinical features	Visual symptoms
Grade 1: Mild	Arteriolar narrowing Broadening of arteriolar light reflex	→asymptomatic
Grade 2: Moderate	Arteriovenous crossing changes Cottonwool spots	→asymptomatic
Grade 3: Severe	Flame-shaped haemorrhages, mainly in nerve fibre layer Microaneurysms Hard exudates 'Copper wiring' of arterioles Marked arteriolar constriction Secondary telangiectasias Serous detachment	→generally asymptomatic →symptomatic if retinal involvement
Grade 4: Malignant	Signs as for grade 3 Disc swelling/ischaemic papillopathy Macular star from hard exudates around fovea	→symptomatic only if macular involvement

Retinal vein occlusion

Central retinal vein occlusion (CRVO) and branch retinal vein occlusion (BRVOs) are second only to diabetic retinopathy as a cause of vision loss due to a retinal vascular disorder. Factors that predispose to retinal vein occlusions can be systemic or ocular

Table 22.4 Causes of retinal vein occlusion (adapted from Recchia & Brown 2000)

Cause	Contributing factors
Systemic	Age
	Hypertension
	Blood abnormalities (dyscrasias), e.g. sickle-cell disease
Ocular	Raised intraocular pressure
	Hypermetropia
	Congenital anomalies
	Periphlebitis, e.g. Behçet's disease

Branch retinal vein occlusion (BRVO)

Occlusion of a vein draining any section of the retina results in stagnation of blood flow and hypoxia of the corresponding retinal area, and increased vessel permeability. The occlusion can occur in the periphery or the macula. The latter may result in macular oedema with a noticeable decrease in the patient's visual acuity.

In the acute stage, features seen include tortuous veins, flame-shaped haemorrhages and retinal oedema, which may resolve in 6–12 months, but which may be replaced by vascular sheathing, chronic macular oedema and RPE degeneration at the macula. The larger the area affected by the BRVO, the poorer the visual recovery prognosis. With a main vessel BRVO (for instance, involving one of the four retinal arcade vessels), vitreous haemorrhage may be present; although this will usually clear over a number of months. Complications of BRVO include secondary neovascularisation, due to ischaemia, and chronic macular oedema, due to the increased permeability of the vessels.

Management

It is important to make the patient aware that, in 5% of cases, both eyes can be affected by a BRVO, and control of systemic hypertension is paramount. The following are alternatives for the management of secondary complications:

● If an FFA shows macular oedema, as opposed to macular ischaemia, laser photocoagulation may be useful.

● Anti-VEGF agents can be used for maculopathy or as an adjunct to laser.

- Laser photocoagulation is indicated for neovascularisation.
- Persistent or recurring vitreous haemorrhage requires a vitrectomy.

Previously, vitrectomy and sheathotomy were undertaken by opening the sheath surrounding the retinal vessels, as this was thought to provide a release of the arteriovenous (AV) pressure and enable the occlusion to resolve. However, this procedure did not prove successful.

Prognosis

Visual prognosis is reasonably good unless the macula is involved. In about 50% of patients, collateral vessels develop and take over the role of the occluded vein. However, if the perifoveal capillary network is too badly affected, the visual prognosis is poor. Laser as for PDR is used if there is ischaemia, to halt the development of neovascularisation.

Central retinal vein occlusion

CRVO can be divided into three specific groups; and the treatment and prognosis vary according to which group the vein occlusion falls into (Table 22.5).

Table 22.5 Central retinal vein occlusion (CRVO)

Groups	Clinical features	Symptoms	Prognosis	Treatment
Non-ischaemic	Tortuous and dilated branches of CRV Retinal haemorrhages Disc oedema Macular oedema	Loss of VA Slight Marcus–Gunn pupil	50% regain near normal VA Loss of VA is the result of chronic cystoid macular oedema	Inconclusive if laser beneficial for macular oedema Anti-VEGF agents useful to help manage macular oedema if the capillary bed is not too damaged
Ischaemic	Tortuous and engorged veins Retinal haemorrhages Cottonwool spots Disc oedema Macula Haemorrhages and cystoid changes	Loss of VA (6/60) Marcus–Gunn pupil	Poor Potential development of neovascular glaucoma and vitreous haemorrhage	Laser photocoagulation to prevent neovascularisation
Young individuals (rare)	Optic disc vasculitis and oedema Retinal haemorrhages	Mild decrease in VA, worse in the morning	Good as little retinal ischaemia	Observe

Treatment is as for BRVOs. Previously, surgical intervention (vitrectomy and optic neurotomy) was undertaken. After the vitreous was removed, the surgeon would 'stab' an outer area of the optic disc to widen the lamina cribrosa, allowing more room for the central retinal vein and decreasing the pressure on the vein, thereby decreasing the amount of the occlusion. However, this did not prove to be a successful procedure.

Retinal artery occlusion

This can be central retinal artery occlusion (CRAO) or branch retinal artery occlusion (BRAO); they are commonly associated with an embolic blockage from the heart or carotid artery disease such as cholesterol plaques. They may also be caused by systemic conditions that result in arteritis and secondary occlusion of the artery, e.g. giant cell arteritis. A severe rise in IOP may also cause an RAO but this is rare and tends to be a complication associated with pressure on the globe or secondary to a gas tamponade.

Central retinal artery occlusion

This is an ophthalmic emergency and is most often the result of an atheroma or embolus. The patient presents with sudden, complete, painless loss of vision.

Externally, the eye will look quiet. The fundal image is of a pale, swollen retina with an absence of red reflex. As the fovea does not have the thick nerve fibre layers present in the rest of the retina, the reflex from choroidal vessels is still evident so the fovea stands out as a 'cherry-red spot'; this spot will disappear after a few weeks. Although retinal veins appear normal, the arteries are narrowed.

Treatment needs to be prompt and is aimed at increasing retinal perfusion. Medically, intravenous acetazolamide can help lower the IOP, as can intermittent ocular massage, with the added aims of increasing blood flow and dislodging the arterial blockage. Re-breathing (into a paper bag) as a strategy to increase CO_2 levels and cause vessel dilatation, which may allow the embolus to move to a branch artery, may also be used. Other options are: an anterior chamber paracentesis to reduce IOP (again, to take pressure off the central retinal artery and allow the embolus to travel to a branch artery); or a gas exchange if the raised IOP is caused by a gas tamponade. However, the visual prognosis for patients with CRAO is usually poor.

Branch retinal artery occlusion

These occlusions are commonly the result of emboli and patients present with a painless sudden defect noticed in their visual field. On examination, a pale ischaemic area of the retina is seen. Over time, the inner retinal layers atrophy and the patient is left with a permanent visual field defect.

In both CRAO and BRAO, retinal emboli suggest carotid artery disease and the patient should be investigated for cardiovascular disease to prevent a CVA stroke.

Retinal detachment

Retinal detachment refers to the separation of the neural retina from the RPE. Retinal detachments are generally divided into two main types: rhegmatogenous and non-rhegmatogenous. Rhegmatogenous is derived from the Greek *rhegma*, meaning 'break' or 'tear'.

This detachment recreates the potential space between the two layers of the original embryonic cup that was briefly discussed earlier in this chapter (see p. 555).

Rhegmatogenous retinal detachments

This type of detachment is caused by a full-thickness break (hole or tear) in the continuity of the retina, allowing fluid to collect between the neural retina and RPE as a result of the tension between the vitreous and the retina. The break cannot close without intervention. This is the most common type of detachment, with an incidence of 1 in 10,000 in Western populations, 10% being bilateral. The retinal break most often described is a horseshoe-shaped tear.

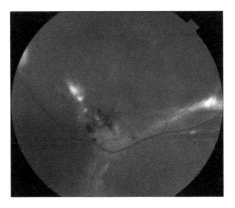

Figure 22.9 Retinal detachment

(reprinted with permission of Ophthalmic Imaging Department, Manchester Royal Eye Hospital.)

This break can occur spontaneously as a consequence of PVD, or as a result of trauma to the globe, allowing fluid through the break. This fluid then accumulates, precipitating separation of the neural retina and RPE. The cause of spontaneous retinal detachments is often not found, and not all patients presenting with PVD will progress to retinal detachment because, if the vitreous detaches evenly, there is no traction on the retina to produce a hole. These breaks most frequently occur in the periphery of the retina, making viewing difficult.

People with myopia make up only 10% of the population but have 42% of all retinal detachments as a result of increased incidence of lattice degeneration in this group of patients and a high frequency of PVD at a younger age (Taylor *et al.* 1995).

Another common cause of retinal breaks is degeneration of the retina. Lattice degeneration is present in about 7% of the population, and about 40% of eyes with a retinal detachment have lattice degeneration.

There are several other ophthalmic conditions that may also contribute to the development of rhegmatogenous detachments: cataract extraction (resulting from movement of the vitreous; rare in phacoemulsification), peripheral cystic retinal tufts and senile retinoschisis. Blunt trauma may result in detachment because the retina may become detached at the ora serrata (retinal dialysis), or in retinal holes which may occur at the time of injury or months later (Newell 1996). Penetrating trauma may damage the retina directly or result in tears and lead to detachment at a later date.

Timing of surgery is important. If the macula is not affected, or has only recently become involved, detachment surgery is likely to be undertaken as a matter of urgency in order to preserve macular function. If the macular area has been detached for some time, there is less chance of recovering macular function and surgery may be delayed (Ross & Kozy 1998).

Non-rhegmatogenous retinal detachments

There are two types of non-rhegmatogenous retinal detachments: traction and exudative.

Traction detachments

These occur when there is a proliferation of vitreoretinal membranes creating a localised traction on the retina, pulling the neural retina away from the RPE. This type of detachment is associated with proliferative diabetic retinopathy (PDR), proliferative vitreoretinopathy (PVR) and retinopathy of prematurity (ROP). Traction membranes grow on the surface of the retina and can even grow into the vitreous cavity, using the vitreous as a type of scaffolding. Membranes, as in PVR, can create traction, which cause new retinal breaks or result in the recurrence of retinal detachments. PVR is often the cause of failed detachment procedures.

To restore vision, the traction needs to be removed; and to gain access to the membranes, the vitreous must be removed. Vitreoretinal surgery is currently the only treatment option.

Exudative detachments

Exudative detachments occur when there is damage to the RPE due to choroidal or retinal disorders. The conditions associated with this type of detachment are: AMD, tumours of the choroid, choroidal haemorrhage, inflammation and retinopathies. These have a poor prognosis and there are few treatment options. Although anti-VEGF agents are proving successful in maintaining VA in those patient with exudative AMD, and are often used with other conditions, success is limited and, as yet, does not constitute a cure.

Signs and symptoms of retinal detachment

Patients presenting with retinal detachments provide a similar description of their symptoms, irrespective of the type of detachment. Symptoms that patients complain about are photopsia (flashing lights), floaters, distorted vision or straight lines appearing wavy (metamorphopsia), loss of some of the visual field (peripheral or central), with no associated pain.

As vitreous separates from the retina and moves within the eye, floaters may be seen by the individual. They appear as spots, curly lines or rings, and may be dark or clear. They move with the eye and may be especially troublesome when looking at a pale surface or the sky. Vitreous 'tugging' on the retina stimulates it and this is interpreted by the brain as a flashing light. The appearance of photopsia may, therefore, be an indication of traction on the retina, a PVD or even precursor to a retinal tear and detachment.

If a retinal blood vessel is damaged, blood may emerge into the vitreous (vitreous haemorrhage). A small amount of blood may be seen as a shower of spots, and larger amounts of blood can cause darker patches in the field of vision.

A retinal detachment may appear as a patch of vision that is missing, or as something moving around in the periphery of vision. Another common visual symptom described by patients is that they can see a spider's web, or even that they have been trying to brush away stray hairs that appear to be over their vision.

Examination for retinal detachment

Anterior segment:

- There may be an absence of the red reflex.
- Relative afferent pupillary defect may be noted with extensive retinal detachment.
- There may be an intraocular pressure (IOP) difference between the affected and normal eye of up to 5mmHg.
- A mild anterior uveitis may be present.
- If major, the pupil may appear white (leukocoria) as a result of the detached retinal tissue floating behind the lens.

Posterior segment:

- The detached retina has the appearance of a tissue waving in the breeze, whereas retina that remains intact and attached appears red from the choroidal circulation.

- Tobacco dust, pigment from the RPE, may be seen in the vitreous.
- Haemorrhage may be present if there is trauma or the detachment has occurred directly over a vessel.

If no view of the retina is possible, a three-dimensional ultrasound scan ('B scan') may be undertaken to aid diagnosis.

Treatment of retinal detachment

The choice of treatment depends on the type and severity of detachment, and treatments are either surgical or non-surgical. Before the 1920s there was no recognised successful treatment option available for any type of retinal detachment; people eventually lost their sight. The goal of any intervention is the preservation of vision, and to restore pre-detachment vision when possible. The aim of treatment is therefore to close the retinal break and realign the neural retinal epithelium and the RPE.

Retinopexy

This is the least complex method of repairing (i.e. closing) a retinal break. It is the least invasive option and is used only when the break is small.

Pre-procedure

Explain the procedure to the patient, including the feeling of an uncomfortable pressure when indenting and the need for positioning/posturing post-procedure, and probable visual disturbance from the introduced gas.

The pupil of the affected eye is dilated, the patient is positioned supine, local anaesthetic eye drops are instilled, and sometimes local infiltrate is required. A gas bubble of an expandable agent is inserted intravenously at the pars plana, and the paracentesis (see below) is undertaken.

Post-procedure

The patient requires positioning or posturing; this allows the gas bubble to provide an internal tamponade to the break. Positioning is vital to the successful outcome of this procedure. Regular IOP checks are required and the patient must be warned about visual disturbance from the injection of gas (Shelswell 2002). Changes in atmospheric pressure can alter the size and therefore the effect of the gas bubble. Air travel must be avoided, as must driving at high altitude, as the lower pressure can allow the bubble to expand, leading to a raised IOP and retinal ischaemia. Diving may cause the bubble and therefore, potentially, the eye to collapse. The patient must inform their surgeon and anaesthetist if any other non-ophthalmic operative procedures are to be undertaken while gas is in the eye. SF6 absorbs in around 3 weeks and C3F8 in around 3 months (see Chapter 11).

The procedure

An expandable gas is injected into the posterior segment through a 30-gauge needle at the pars plana (pneumatic retinopexy). Two commonly used gases are perfluoropropane (C3F8) and sulphur hexafluoride (SF6). The bubble of gas acts as a tamponade to prevent more fluid entering the retinal break and thus allows the RPE and choroid to reabsorb the subretinal fluid.

A paracentesis is frequently required to reduce IOP because the gas goes into a cavity that has a finite capacity. The injected gas is absorbed over a few weeks.

Indirect laser (photocoagulation) or cryotherapy is applied around the retinal break to create a chorioretinal scar and permanently seal the break. The use of cryotherapy is not influenced by the presence of excessive subretinal fluid and may be used if a laser is not available, but the patient usually experiences more pain as a result of postoperative conjunctival oedema.

If laser is the preferred treatment option, this may be a staged procedure because excessive subretinal fluid prevents sufficient uptake of laser. However, after positioning following insertion of a gas bubble, subretinal fluid is reduced as a result of the pump action of the RPE. Laser can then be effectively applied to create scarring and seal the retinal break.

Scleral explant surgery

Scleral explant surgery is often referred to as a conventional retinal detachment repair and used when there is a peripheral retinal break or breaks. This procedure not only closes the retinal break, but also reduces the vitreous tension on the retinal surface caused by the indentation created by an external tamponade. The external tamponade may be a scleral buckle, tyre, band or 'plomb'. It is essential that there is a good view of the break/s if this option is to be successful. The explants are generally made out of silicone because of the material's properties. Before the advent of vitreoretinal surgery, this was the treatment of choice for most retinal detachments.

Pre-procedure

Preparation as for retinopexy.

Post-procedure

Positioning is required only if air or gas has been inserted in the posterior segment. See above and Chapter 11. Adequate analgesia is required.

The procedure

The break is closed with cryo- or indirect laser therapy. The application of an external tamponade (explant) aims to bring the RPE, choroid and sclera into contact with the retinal break. Although the vitreous may still be causing a traction-like force on the retina, this inward force will be decreased as the wall of the eye is indented by the explant. There are many different shapes and sizes of scleral explants, and use depends on the size of the break and often the surgeon's preference.

Subretinal fluid may be drained to aid the contact of the retinal break to the underlying RPE.

Air or expandable gas may also be inserted into the posterior segment, acting as an internal tamponade.

Vitreoretinal surgery

This is more commonly known as a three-port pars plana vitrectomy or just 'vitrectomy'. The vitrectomy has revolutionised the treatment of complicated retinal detachment repairs. A vitrectomy may also be performed in combination with a scleral buckling procedure, especially in complicated retinal detachment repairs such as giant retinal tears (where the retinal edge has rolled in on itself).

Pre-procedure

Prepare as for retinopexy.

Post-procedure

Positioning or posturing will always be required.

The procedure

A vitrectomy involves making three incisions (sclerotomies) at the pars plana; this is the safest method of gaining access to the posterior segment. As the word suggests, 'vitrectomy' is the removal of the vitreous. However, as vitreous is a gel, it cannot simply be sucked out of the eye; instead, a special device that cuts as well as sucks the vitreous is required to remove vitreous safely. As a result of the shape of the eye and the presence of the lens, it is physically impossible to remove all the vitreous, but careful attention ensures that the posterior hyaloid and as much vitreous as necessary are removed, thereby releasing the traction on the retina and enabling it to be reapposed to the RPE. Originally the instrumentation was 20 gauge, now they can be as small as 23g or even 25g.

Subretinal fluid can be drained via the retinal break or another retinotomy (retinal hole made by the operator/surgeon).

Heavy liquid (perfluorocarbon liquid) is injected into the vitreous cavity to reappose the neural epithelium to the RPE to assist in the repair of the retinal detachment, but this substance is toxic to the retina and so is used only as a temporary tamponade. The retinal break/s is then closed with the formation of a chorioretinal scar by laser, which may be either endo (internal) or indirect, or even cryotherapy.

The vitreous does not regenerate, so something is needed to replace it. During the operation an ocular compatible solution (such as balanced salt solution/BSS) is used to maintain IOP, but postoperatively BSS would not create the required internal tamponade to ensure a successful detachment repair. For this reason, an expandable gas or silicone oil is inserted into the vitreous cavity, thus providing an intraocular tamponade. The substance used depends on the retinal break/s and the patient's ability to position postoperatively.

If an expandable gas is used, it will naturally be a much larger volume than that used for a pneumatic retinopexy or during a scleral buckle retinal detachment procedure, where the vitreous has not been removed. To reduce the risk of central retinal artery occlusion, the gases are mixed with non-expandable air to create an appropriate mix. Expandable gases are absorbed after a few weeks (as described earlier) and aqueous fills the remaining space. A large break may require a longer-acting tamponade, in which case silicone oil may be a better option than a gas replacement for the removed vitreous.

If silicone oil is used, a further surgical procedure is required to remove the oil.

Retinal tamponades

Unlike other organs in the body, it is impossible to apply direct pressure to the eye without potential damage to the ocular structure and so tamponades are used. These tamponades can be external (scleral explants) or internal. The internal tamponades consist of air, expandable gases (such as SF6 or C3F8), silicone oil or heavy liquid (perfluorocarbon liquids), and it is essential that the implications of these substances are understood when providing care for patients, particularly for discharge information. Complications of tamponade use include increased IOP and cataract formation. If an internal tamponade is likely to be required during a surgical procedure, there is potential for cataract development. Preassessment for retinal surgery should therefore involve a preoperative 'A scan', as for any cataract surgery.

Patients are required to posture postoperatively to ensure that the tamponade is effective, irrespective of which substance (oil or gas) is used. Positioning also depends on where the tamponade needs to be applied. Macular hole repair requires face-down posturing, whereas a superior temporal hole may require the patient to posture 'cheek to pillow'.

Air

This is seldom used as a tamponade because it is absorbed too readily from the vitreous cavity.

Gases

As discussed, there are a number of expandable gases available for use. However, with all gases, atmospheric pressure and nitrogen and oxygen pressure affect the rate of expansion, and activities such as diving or flying could adversely affect the gas, causing further expansion, resulting in occlusion of the central retinal artery. For this reason, the patient must be educated, particularly if they intend to fly immediately after surgery, because alternative arrangements may need to be made – either to their planned travel or to the treatment. Nitrous oxide is a commonly used general anaesthetic agent, but when there is an expandable gas in the vitreous cavity, the use of nitrous oxide will adversely affect the rate of the gas's expansion, as described above.

An application of some sort of identification of the patient having had insertion of a gas (i.e. a 'gas bracelet') is recommended. This reminds the patient of the potential complications of the gas and also highlights to other medical staff the presence of the gas in the eye. An example of an appropriate wording for the bracelet would be: 'No nitrous oxide, expandable gas in eye.' This bracelet would be removed by the ophthalmologist when there is no further viable presence of gas in the vitreous cavity.

Silicone oil

Unlike gas, silicone oil cannot be absorbed; it requires a surgical procedure for removal. Silicone oil is a transparent substance that is lighter than water. It is indicated for use in giant retinal tears, diabetic retinopathy, post-traumatic retinal detachments, if the patient has to travel by air postoperatively or if the patient may not be compliant with positioning.

The removal of the oil is undertaken 3–6 months postoperatively but the timeframe depends on the stability of the retina and the oil may be left in situ in some cases. A cataract extraction and insertion of an intraocular lens (IOL) is often performed when removing the silicone oil, if required.

Heavy liquids

These have a low viscosity that makes them easily injected and aspirated during vitreoretinal surgery. They are a useful tool for repairing retinal detachments such as unfolding the edge of a giant retinal tear, but they are never left in situ long term because of ocular toxicity.

Other potential vitreous substitutes are under development.

Other reasons for vitreoretinal surgery

Epiretinal membrane

VR procedures can also be undertaken to remove an epiretinal membrane (ERM). Such membranes are not those of PDR. Instead they are localised, akin to a thickening of the inner limiting membrane at the retinal–vitreous interface. If there is significant vitreomacular traction, distortion and vision reduction, VR surgery and membrane peel may be indicated. ERMs can be seen on examination or with an OCT scan, but many are asymptomatic. Surgery is not indicated if there is a long history of an ERM or if there are already macular structural changes, i.e. a lamellar hole, related to the ERM.

Removal of foreign body

Following penetrating trauma with retained matter in the vitreous, or cataract surgery if lens matter has been lost into the posterior segment, VR surgery is indicated. If the foreign body is glass or wood, intravitreal forceps will be used, or a magnet for metallic objects, to extract the foreign material after the vitreous is removed. If a retinal hole or tear has occurred, this will be sealed and repaired as per VR detachment surgery.

Regarding retained lens matter, after the vitreous is removed, heavy liquids can be used to help 'float' lens matter off the retina, which can then be removed by use of a fragmatome (ultrasound) for large pieces of lens matter or by the vitrector cutter.

Vitreous biopsy

A vitrectomy allows collection of vitreous matter in the case of endophthalmitis.

Macular hole repair

A macular hole can occur secondary to vitreoretinal traction or other unknown factors. If it is a new lesion, with a new decrease in VA, surgical repair is indicated. This involves a vitrectomy, peel of the internal limiting membrane (assisted by a dye to stain the membrane), insertion of a gas tamponade and post-procedure positioning by the patient.

Other retinal conditions

Retinoschisis

In retinoschisis, the neural retina splits and separates, generally in the outer plexiform layer. There are three major types of retinoschisis: congenital, acquired/degenerative or secondary to other retinal trauma or disease. It affects a small proportion of the population and is more common in hypermetropic individuals. For most people, it is asymptomatic with no visual impairment.

Congenital retinoschisis is uncommon and always bilateral and causes a vitreoretinal degeneration; the patient has impaired visual acuity as a result of maculopathy. Congenital retinoschisis is found almost exclusively in males.

No treatment is necessary for most patients with retinoschisis, except when there are complications such as retinal detachment.

Retinopathy of prematurity

Retinopathy of prematurity (ROP) was first described in 1942 as retrolental fibroplasia (RLF). It was initially thought that the tissue developed postnatally and the white retrolental mass might be a congenital cataract. However, the cause was unknown and different aetiologies were proposed, including infection transmitted by either the mother or another source, vitamin E deficiency and/or anoxia.

History of ROP

In 1948, Owens and Owens ophthalmoscopically observed normal fundi in pre-term infants undergoing a transformation over several weeks, but it was not until the early 1950s that hyperoxia was implicated in the incidence of RLF. Although the judicious use of inspired oxygen for pre-term infants reduced the amount of RLF, there was an increase in the incidence of death and brain damage. However, with the technological developments of the 1960s, low-birthweight pre-term infants (who would have previously died) survived, but required the use of oxygen to do so and the incidence of RLF continued to increase in the 1960s and 1970s, despite sophisticated oxygen-measuring techniques. In the 1980s, ROP replaced RLF as the accepted terminology to describe this condition.

Incidence of ROP

Low birthweight infants are increasingly susceptible to ROP and, despite meticulous monitoring of oxygen therapy, this continues to be the case today. It is now thought that prematurity and associated low birthweight (<1000g) are the primary contributors to ROP, as opposed to over-zealous use of oxygen, as suggested in the past.

Causes of ROP

Although it is not fully understood how or why ROP develops, the retinal vasculature is not completely developed in a very pre-term infant. The nasal ora is reached by the inner retina vasculature at about 8 months' gestation, and the temporal ora is not reached until 9 months' gestation, and once vascularisation is complete, oxygen use does not affect the retina. Currently it is thought that the pre-term baby is at higher risk as a result of ischaemic areas of the retina. Since 1984, the International Classification of Retinopathy of Prematurity (ICROP) has been used. This classification defined the location of disease and the extent of developing vasculature. The location is divided into three zones and the abnormal vascularisation is divided up into five progressive stages.

The most common outcome for most babies who develop ROP is regression; this occurs spontaneously and does not require intervention. However, a small minority progress to advanced ROP requiring intervention.

Treatment for ROP

All pre-term low birthweight babies must be monitored, particularly those at or below 26 weeks' gestation, because they have an increased risk of developing ROP.

It is necessary to dilate pupils to examine these babies with an indirect ophthalmoscope, and indenting of the retina as retinal pathology in ROP begins at the periphery.

Advanced ROP requires cryotherapy or laser treatment to ablate the ischaemic areas, resulting in regression of the abnormal vasculature. Rarely, babies with ROP develop retinal detachments and these require surgical intervention.

New wide-field imaging cameras can be used for detection, surveillance and monitoring in at-risk babies

Nursing care for ROP

It is essential that the parents are supported and provided with education and given time to absorb information and encouraged to ask questions, irrespective of the extent of the disease. Managing the pre-term neonate through this procedure can be challenging, and partnership between the ophthalmology team, the neonatal team and the parents is vital at all stages.

Retinoblastoma

Retinoblastoma is a rare ocular malignant tumour of the retina. It is the most common childhood intraocular malignancy and can be life threatening if undiagnosed and untreated, although with the current treatment modalities available the survival rate is over 90%. An accurate diagnosis and prompt initiation of treatment interventions that are ongoing for several years are necessary to save the child's life and, where possible, to maintain vision. The development of retinoblastoma can occur in the embryo in utero and up to 7 years of age, with 18 months as the average age of diagnosis. Retinoblastoma affects about 1 in 20,000 live births and is generally diagnosed within 3 years of birth, although it can be diagnosed at any age.

Retinoblastoma is a complex ocular 'disease' process that can be unilateral, bilateral or even trilateral (involving the pineal gland); it can also be familial or sporadic in origin. Familial retinoblastoma occurs from an autosomal dominant gene mutation to chromosome 13 and accounts for only about 6% of cases (Bowling 2015). Children with familial retinoblastoma tend to have an early onset of the disease, are generally bilateral and are at risk of developing other tumours late in life. Sporadic retinoblastoma cases can be either unilateral or bilateral and the cause is unknown. However, if the child with a sporadic presentation has bilateral retinoblastoma, they are considered to have a gene mutation (the same as familial cases) and are therefore carriers of the disease.

Presentation and diagnosis of retinoblastoma

Occasionally retinoblastoma is 'picked' up as an incidental finding on a regular ultrasound scan during pregnancy. The child commonly presents with leukocoria and/or strabismus, with about 60% of cases presenting with leukocoria. Parents may notice 'something strange' about their child's eye, and report a cat's eye appearance, a twinkling easily seen in photographs, or even an absence of the normal red reflex from photographs.

All such signs require prompt investigation and referral to an ophthalmologist. Although not all of these children will have retinoblastoma, any strabismus or leukocoric eye requires investigation.

A suspicion of retinoblastoma requires an ophthalmic examination of all ocular media, in particular the retina, and this is generally done under general anaesthesia. At the same time the child may undergo ultrasonography, computed tomography (CT) or magnetic resonance imaging (MRI) and bone marrow biopsy, depending on the facility in which the ophthalmic examination takes place.

Bilateral indirect ophthalmoscopy, with both pupils fully dilated, is the most important ophthalmic examination undertaken. The examination must include scleral indentation to ensure that tumours located anteriorly in the retina are seen and documented.

Documentation of the tumour may be recorded in a variety of ways, including hand-drawn sites of the tumour or retinal photographs (conventional celluloid or digital 'reteam'). The tumour appears nodular and from there it can seed out to form a multitude of small retinoblastoma intraocular tumours; there may be a retinal detachment present. It is essential to determine the location of the tumour in relation to the optic nerve because malignant cells can track back to the brain via the optic nerve.

Adjunctive investigations are generally undertaken in collaboration with a paediatric oncology service and include radiological investigations, such as CT and MRI, which highlight involvement of other organs, e.g. the optic nerve and pineal gland. Bone marrow biopsies are also taken at this time to exclude any metastasis.

Treatment of retinoblastoma

As retinoblastoma typically occurs in pre-school children, the treatment involves not only the patient, but also the family and significant others. A large part of the care involves education and support, not only concerning the initial diagnosis, but also during the ongoing monitoring necessary for the child.

There are a variety of options, depending on the size and location of the tumour. An examination under anaesthetic is performed in order to assess the tumour; this may also involve obtaining retinal photographs (commonly digital) of the tumour. The major contributors to the current survival rate in children with retinoblastoma are the treatment modalities available. The treatment modality may differ from one child to the next because these are often tailored to the individual patient.

Before the development of other therapies, enucleation was the treatment of choice. Today this may still be required if the tumour does not respond to other treatment modalities or if it is encroaching on the optic nerve. Postoperatively, the socket will be assessed and the child will need to be fitted for a prosthesis.

Photocoagulation and/or cryotherapy to the cancer destroys the tumour and prevents it seeding. These treatments are used for treating small tumours and also in combination with chemotherapy agents. Photocoagulation (laser) applies burns to the tissue surrounding the tumour, destroying its blood supply without direct treatment. During cryotherapy, the cryoprobe is placed on the sclera, as in a retinal detachment repair. As with all cryo-treatments, the eye may appear oedematous after the procedure.

Chemotherapy has been the major advance and, over the last few decades, has had the most impact on saving sight and the long-term survival rate for children with retinoblastoma. Chemotherapy works by preventing cell division and replication; it interferes with the DNA and is used to treat retinoblastoma that has become metastatic. In cases of bilateral disease and advanced unilateral disease, it can be used to decrease the size of the tumour, in combination with focal treatment to the lesions with laser therapy or cryotherapy to destroy the tumour. There are a number of side effects associated with chemotherapy, and the child's family will also require support and education about these.

External beam radiotherapy is also used in some cases. However, side effects include cataract formation and disruption to the structure of the bony orbit, resulting in deformity, so it is a rarely used treatment option. Radiotherapy is also used in some cases, but is rarely a treatment of choice today.

New treatments, such as thermotherapy, can be used alone for very small tumours. For larger tumours, thermotherapy can be used along with chemotherapy (called thermos-chemotherapy) or with radiation therapy (called thermos-radiotherapy). It is thought that heat helps these other treatments to work more effectively (American Cancer Society 2015).

Advances in gene technology have enabled some centres to offer retinoblastoma identification markers, so parents are aware of the potential risk to their offspring.

All children born to parents with retinoblastoma or who have siblings diagnosed with retinoblastoma are routinely examined and followed up to ensure early detection of the development of a tumour. This is a type of screening where the children are followed regularly, initially with retinal examinations under anaesthetic. As the child grows older, retinal examinations can occur in an outpatient setting and generally cease when the child is about 5 years old.

It is common for families to be offered genetic counselling and screening, particularly if their child with retinoblastoma is the first, to determine whether there is a genetic cause of the tumour. Although counselling can be undertaken in any ophthalmic unit, the screening will generally have to be done at a major centre and it will take time to get the results, during which time the family will require support.

Patient and family care and support

A diagnosis of retinoblastoma is devastating for the parents of the child and it is essential that education and support are provided, particularly as ocular examinations and treatments will be frequently required, often for several years.

Perhaps the most important role for the nurse is providing support for the patient and the family, and ensuring that they understand all the procedures and processes in their care. Nurses in units that provide care for retinoblastoma patients come to know the children and their parents very well. The parents meet each other frequently and offer support to each other that healthcare personnel cannot; the children also often form friendships.

Many ophthalmic units have nurses who have a pivotal role in coordinating the care of children with retinoblastoma: they organise follow-up visits, liaise with oncology departments, liaise with cancer societies, liaise with ophthalmologists, etc. Some units also have the services of a play therapist, who helps the children understand what is happening to them and makes their frequent visits for ocular examinations 'fun', rather than something to be 'dreaded', which in turn helps the parents. Most ophthalmic care for children with retinoblastoma is undertaken on a daycare basis, There is therefore little specific nursing care for these children, other than what has already been outlined, and the routine preparation undergone by any patient having a retinal examination through dilated pupils.

To manage retinoblastoma successfully, early detection is vital. It would make a big difference if a test as simple as checking for a red reflex could be incorporated into the newborn health assessment checks as an early assessment for retinoblastoma.

Retinitis pigmentosa (RP)

This a hereditary degenerative ocular disease causing a photoreceptor dystrophy with resultant progressive loss of RPE and photoreceptor function. There is also an atypical retinitis pigmentosa, which may be associated with a variety of systemic disorders (including Usher's syndrome), characterised by profound deafness and blindness.

RP is a bilateral condition, affecting more males than females. Although both rods and cones are affected, the damage to the rods is predominant so patients present because they are having problems with dark adaptation, often described as night blindness (nyctalopia). Patients frequently present in their teenage years with nyctalopia and by the age of 30 over 75% are symptomatic, with progressive loss of peripheral vision (and often tunnel vision) occurring by the time the patient is in their fifties.

In patients with retinitis pigmentosa there are few signs in the early stages, but – with progression of the disease – coarser pigmentary changes occur, and these are seen as clumping of retinal pigment on ocular examination. There is no known treatment for this condition and patients are generally referred to supportive organisations. Genetic counselling may be offered to patients who carry the gene.

Sickle-cell disease

Sickle-cell disease is the most common haemoglobinopathy affecting humans; it is caused by the presence of abnormal haemoglobins in the red blood cells. In conditions such as hypoxia and acidosis, the abnormal haemoglobin cells become sickle shaped and more rigid than normal. These sickle cells obstruct small blood vessels, resulting in tissue ischaemia locally. Once ischaemia is present, a cycle begins where more sickling occurs. It is predominantly found in people of African or Afro-Caribbean background, affecting about 8% of that population in the US. There are varying degrees of sickle-cell disease and the severity depends on the amount of normal versus abnormal haemoglobins present.

A proliferative retinopathy can develop secondary to a sickle-cell disease, and this has five distinct stages:

- Arteriolar occlusion
- Ischaemia
- Neovascularisation
- Vitreous traction
- Retinal detachment.

Treatment, as for other retinopathies, is laser photocoagulation to stop neovascularisation.

Asteroid hyalosis

These vitreous opacities are a form of vitreous gel degeneration where calcium 'soaps' aggregate in the vitreous. They are usually unilateral and asymptomatic and rarely impair the individual's vision. On examination, asteroid hyalosis appears like stars in the vitreous; and; if dense; can impede a full examination of the retina. 'B scan' shows bright 'spots' in the vitreous body.

Macular dystrophies

Family history, electrophysiological tests and the retinal appearance are all important for the diagnosis of these inherited macular dystrophies. There are no current treatment options, so ongoing support is vital, along with prompt referral to low-vision agencies.

Cone dystrophy

This is a progressive deterioration of the cones and most cases are sporadic rather than inherited; however, the disease is linked to an autosomal dominant gene and has a poor visual prognosis. As discussed previously, the cone photoreceptors are responsible for colour vision and central vision, so a cone dystrophy results in a decreased visual acuity, a decrease in colour sensitivity and photophobia. On examination, the retina may appear normal until late in the disease progression when RPE changes and an atrophic macula may be seen. A 'bull's-eye' pattern of depigmentation, with a surrounding zone of hyperfluorescence and a central spot of non-fluorescence, is indicative of a cone–rod dystrophy on FFA.

Electrophysiological tests assist in the diagnosis, as ERG shows a decreased cone function with some loss of rod function. There is currently no treatment for cone–rod dystrophy.

Best's dystrophy

Best's dystrophy is also known as vitelliform dystrophy and is linked to an autosomal dominant trait, with the onset of the disease process affecting those aged between 4 and 20 years. Presenting symptoms vary from none to decreased visual acuity and, for some, strabismus. On ophthalmoscopy examination, the retinal appearance varies from a mild pigmentary disturbance in the fovea to a yellow material resembling 'egg yolk'. Degeneration of the macula may lead to subretinal neovascularisation, extensive macular scarring and subretinal haemorrhage.

Stargardt's disease

Stargardt's disease is caused by an autosomal recessive gene and is bilateral. Children will often present with a loss of central vision but, at whatever age the patient presents, this disease generally results in an untreatable loss of central vision. Early symptoms include a decrease in vision, followed by a decrease in night vision as a result of poor dark adaptation. The retina usually has the appearance of creamy-white flecks that change with time. Initially, the macula appears normal but then develops changes that ultimately result in the macula appearing like 'beaten bronze'. The visual prognosis is poor.

Retinopathies

Diabetic retinopathy and hypertensive retinopathy are the most common presentations, but the other retinopathies that patients may present with include the following.

Valsalva's retinopathy

This can follow a rise in intrathoracic or intra-abdominal pressure against a closed glottis/Valsalva's manoeuvre. The result is a rupture in superficial retinal veins, causing small inter-retinal haemorrhages without any leakage. These are asymptomatic and there is no loss of vision or permanent retinal damage.

Solar retinopathy

This is caused by intense exposure to visible light in the blue and near UV wavelengths (250–441mm). This can be a result of observing the sun or a solar eclipse without using the correct safety filters. There are also case reports of people using hallucinatory drugs and staring at the sun, or unconsciously exposing their eyes to the sun, with a resultant macular burn. A larger pupil size will naturally result in more damage. Initially the retina may appear normal, but the retinal burn will result in RPE depigmentation and may even cause a macular cyst or hole. In mild cases, the photoreceptors and RPE will regenerate in time.

Inflammation in the posterior segment

There are a number of conditions that can cause severe posterior segment inflammations. Some are systemic, such as the human immunodeficiency virus (HIV), which allows opportunistic retinal infections resulting in retinal necrosis and loss of vision. Other infections (such as herpes infections, toxoplasmosis and tuberculosis) can cause posterior uveitis, chorioretinal inflammation and lesions, and vitritis. As with management of any infection, a range of interventions (from topical and systemic medication regimens to surgical procedures) may be indicated.

Toxoplasmosis

This is caused by the Toxoplasma gondii, a protozoon with the domestic cat as the primary host although other felines also carry the disease. Oocysts are excreted in cat faeces, and infection occurs directly or indirectly through ingestion of undercooked meat or even transplacentally. Toxoplasmosis is a common cause of posterior segment inflammation worldwide, and presentations may be congenital or acquired.

The clinical features in congenital toxoplasmosis are bilateral macular lesions; whereas in acquired toxoplasmosis the more typical ocular features are focal retinitis adjacent to the chorioretinal scar/lesion but in some cases without the presence of a scar/lesion.

The acquired infection tends to result in a subclinical illness and detection is often an incidental finding of chorioretinal scars/lesions, with the majority of those infected remaining asymptomatic. However, these lesions may be reactivated and cause symptoms, the main symptom being blurred vision. Other symptoms may vary from nil to floaters and, in severe cases, pain and photophobia.

On ocular examination, a vitritis (an inflammatory process in the vitreous) can be seen, which may be mild or dense enough to obscure the retina from view. The inflammatory process can be associated with a progressive and recurring necrotising retinitis, resulting in vision-threatening complications such as choroidal neovascularisation, retinal detachment and glaucoma.

OCT and FFA are used in the assessment and treatment of ocular toxoplasmosis. Testing for the presence of toxoplasma antibodies is not routine, because many people may be positive without the presence of active disease. Therefore, diagnosis is usually based on clinical observations.

Treatment is not normally required, because most cases of reactivation resolve spontaneously. However, if the patient's vision is threatened or affected, antimicrobial treatment is necessary. Steroids may be indicated to help reduce the inflammation. Treatment regimens vary but generally treatment is required for a minimum of 6 weeks with a combination of medications. If left untreated, toxoplasmosis may lead to vision loss.

Toxocariasis

This is caused by roundworms passed from dogs and cats to humans. Ocular manifestations of toxocariasis may appear without systemic involvement and usually affect children from 7 years of age, because they tend to have a close association with family pets and may also eat dirt that harbours the toxocara ova.

This disease tends to be unilateral and the child may present with a red eye, complain of blurred vision or have leukocoria. On examination, the patient may have a vitritis and choroidal granuloma or possibly chronic endophthalmitis.

Vitreous inflammation

Known as 'vitritis', this is a sign of inflammatory cells in the vitreous. Vitritis can be a result of posterior uveitis or lesions in the retina or choroid, such as toxoplasmosis, or tumours such as lymphoma. The inflammation can be localised and small, causing only a few cells to appear as floaters. However, if there is a larger amount of infiltrate, the resulting opaque vitreous will cause a decrease in visual acuity. In such cases, a vitrectomy may be indicated to clear the media. Vitritis of unknown origin may be an indication for a vitrectomy or a vitreous biopsy to identify the underlying pathology.

Human immunodeficiency virus (HIV)

HIV is associated with a range of ocular diseases and in the retina it can present within a spectrum, from minimal ocular symptoms and signs to those infections secondary to the patient's immunodeficiency, with consequences including loss of vision.

HIV microvasculopathy is a non-sight-threatening, non-infective condition with cottonwool spots and is the most common ocular sign seen in patients with HIV. The cottonwool spots are transient and, although retinal microaneurysms may also be seen, no treatment is indicated. These signs are also seen with other retinal conditions, including hypertension, highlighting the need to obtain an accurate, detailed health and social history from the patient.

Cytomegalovirus

This is an opportunistic infection associated with the common herpes virus but was rarely seen in ophthalmology departments until the advent of AIDS. Retinal cytomegalovirus (CMV) causes a severe retinal infection known as CMV retinitis, causing in turn an inflammation that results in a necrotic, thinned retina that has a high risk of developing retinal breaks and an associated retinal detachment. CMV retinitis can occur in any immunocompromised patient, but it is most commonly seen to affect a large percentage of patients with advanced AIDS.

Initial presentation may be when the patient complains of painless blurred vision, but on examination the retinal picture provides the diagnosis. CMV retinitis causes a 'pizza' appearance of the retina as a result of flame-shaped haemorrhages along the retinal vessels and large areas of yellow–white exudates. There have been cases when a patient presents with CMV retinitis and a diagnosis of AIDS is made at the same time, which can be devastating for the patient and the family.

The CMV infection is treated with antiviral medications, including Ganciclovir and Foscarnet. Any retinal detachments occurring secondary to CMV are difficult to repair because of retinal necrosis. For this reason, CMV retinitis is commonly sight threatening.

Care of retinal patients

Although the retina can be affected by many different diseases and conditions that affect its function and ultimately impact on the patient's vision, there are many similarities when providing care for this group of patients. Rather than providing advice for specific diseases and conditions, it is more appropriate to provide general guidelines because the care of retinal patients differs from one country to the next and according to the individual doctor's preference. The retina is a new frontier for advances in ophthalmic care and preservation of vision (both surgically and non-surgically) so the way care is provided is changing all the time. However, there are some specific requirements that apply to care for retinal patientsrequiring surgical intervention.

As with any other ophthalmic disorder, one of the most important factors is providing adequate, comprehensive and timely information, in a form that can be understood by the patient.

Nurses are generally the first healthcare professionals that the patients and their family members will see, whether they present to a hospital service, private clinic or GP's surgery. However, patients may interact with many ophthalmic professionals over the duration of their disease. It is therefore essential to establish a rapport with the patients and family from the outset, because this will assist both the individual clinician and the whole clinical team in dealing with the patient and family in the future. For most patients who have a retinal problem, interaction with healthcare professionals is likely to continue for the rest of their lives, so it is essential to establish a good relationship in order to ensure the best outcome for the patient.

Many retinal patients will not regain their vision once it is lost and will often require referral to and input from specialised services such as low-vision clinics and charities associated with low vision or specific diseases, and this should occur in a timely fashion. All clinicians must be aware of the resources available to such patients, who often 'slip through the net' because everyone thinks this aspect of care is someone else's role.

Posturing after surgery

Patients are often required to position or posture postoperatively and this is the greatest challenge not only for the patient but also for nursing staff. The patient is required to lie in specified positions, such as head down, and the sensory deprivation and physical deprivation experienced by the patient in this situation are often not fully appreciated. If the patient has initial care in hospital, make sure that you tell the patient who you are when you enter the room, explain what you are going to do, position anything they need within easy reach and answer call bells promptly.

Positioning and posturing are important for a successful visual outcome from surgical intervention when internal tamponades are used (see section on 'Retinal detachment', p. 590). Patients often find it difficult to maintain a particular posture for any length of time and again, depending on the doctor, the patient may be permitted to stop posturing for periods of time during the day.

There are several aids that can assist patients to maintain the required position but these may vary from one country to another. Positioning aids with an area that allows the patient to position correctly, but also to continue to read or work, such as massage-type chairs or beds with a head support with an opening, are sometimes used.

Analgesia after surgery

Analgesia is generally required and, if prescribed analgesia does not relieve pain postoperatively, the IOP should be checked. Some patients may have their IOP monitored at regular intervals after surgery, again depending on the particular hospital and doctor. A raised IOP requires urgent intervention to preserve vision. Some surgeons give the patient a sub-Tenon's block at the end of the surgical procedure, which provides excellent postoperative analgesia without the use of opiates, and reduces the incidence of postoperative nausea and vomiting. Pain after ophthalmic surgery should not be underestimated and must be assessed and managed effectively.

References

Age-Related Eye Disease Study Research Group (2001) A randomised, placebo controlled, clinical trial of high-dose supplementation with vitamins C and E, beta-carotene, and zinc for age-related macular degeneration and vision loss. *Archives of Ophthalmology.* **119**, 1417–36.

Age-Related Eye Disease Study 2 Research Group (2013 Lutein + zeaxanthin and omega-3 fatty acids for age-related macular degeneration: the Age-Related Eye Disease Study 2 (AREDS2) randomized clinical trial. *Journal of the American Medical Association.* **309**(19), 2005–15.

American Cancer Society (2015) http://www.cancer.org/cancer/retinoblastoma/detailedguide/retinoblastoma-treating-thermotherapy (accessed 18 September 2016).

Arnold, J.J. & Sarks, S.H. (2000) Age related macular degeneration. *British Medical Journal.* **321**, 741–44.

Avery, R.I., Pieramici, D.J., Rabena, M.D., Castellarin, A.A. & Nasir Giust, M.J. (2006) Intravitreal Bevacizumab (Avastin) for Neovascular Age-Related Macular Degeneration. *Ophthalmology* **113**,3. 363–72.

Batterbury, M. & Bowling, B. (1999). *Ophthalmology: An illustrated colour text.* London: Churchill Livingstone.

Bowling, B. (2015) *Kanski's Clinical Ophthalmology, a systematic approach.* 8th edn. London: Elsevier.

Bourla, D.H. & Young, T.A. (2006) Age-Related Macular Degeneration: A Practical Approach to a Challenging Disease. *Journal of American Geriatrics* **54**(7), 1130-1135.

Casten, R. & Rovner, B. (2008) Depression in Age-Related Macular Degeneration. *Journal of Visual Impairment and Blindness.* **102** (10), 591–99

Chawla, H.B. (1999) *Ophthalmology – A symptom-based approach.* 3rd edn. London: Reed Educational and Professional Publishing Ltd.

Diabetic Retinopathy Study Research Group (1978) Photocoagulation treatment of proliferative diabetic retinopathy: the second report of Diabetic Retinopathy Study findings. *Ophthalmology.* **85**, 82–106.

Early Treatment Diabetic Retinopathy Study Research Group (1985) Photocoagulation for diabetic macular edema. Early Treatment Diabetic Retinopathy Study report number 1. *Archives of Ophthalmology.* **103**, 1796–806.

Ehrlich R., Mawar, N.P., Mody, C.H., Brand, C.S. & Squirrell, D. (2011) Visual function following photodynamic therapy for central serous chorioretinopathy: a comparison of automated macular microperimetry versus best-corrected visual acuity. *Clinical and Experimental Ophthalmology.* **40**(1), 32–39

Ferris, F.L., Davis, M.D. & Aiello, L.M. (1999) Drug therapy: treatment of diabetic retinopathy. *New England Journal of Medicine.* **341**, 667–78.

Gliem, M., Finger, R.P., Fimmers, R., Brinkmann, C.K., Holz, F.G. & Charbel Issa, P. (2013) Treatment of choroidal neovascularization due to angioid streaks: A comprehensive review. *Retina.* **33**(7), 1300–314.

Hamilton, A.M.P., Ulbig, M.W. & Polkinghorne, P. (1996) *Management of Diabetic Retinopathy.* London: BMJ Publishing Group.

Hassenstein, A. & Meyer, C.A, (2009) Clinical use and research applications of Heidelberg retinal angiography and spectral-domain optical coherence tomography – a review. *Clinical & Experimental Ophthalmology.* **37**, 130–43.

Heir, J.S., Brown, D.M., Chong, V. *et al.* (2012) Intravitreal Aflibercept (VEGF Trap-Eye) in Wet Age-related Macular Degeneration. *Ophthalmology.* **119**(12), 2532–48.

Jager, R.D., Mieler, W.F. & Miller, J.W. (2008) Age-Related Macular Degeneration. *New England Journal of Medicine.* **358**, 2606–17.

Kanski, J.J. (2003) *Clinical Ophthalmology.* 5th edn. London: Butterworth-Heinemann.

Macular Photocoagulation Study Group (1997) Risk factors for choroidal neovascularisation in the second eye of patients with juxtafoveal or subfoveal neovascularisation secondary to age related macular degeneration. *Archives of Ophthalmology.* **115**, 741–47.

Martin, D. F., Maguire, M.G., Fine, S.L., Ying, G., Jaffe, G.J., Grunwald, J.E., Toth, C., Redford, M. & Ferris, F.L. (2012) Ranibizumab and Bevacizumab for Treatment of Neovascular Age-Related Macular Degeneration: 2-Year Results *Ophthalmology.* **119**(7), 1388–98.

Martin, D. F., Maguire, M.G., Fine, S.L., Ying, G., Jaffe, G.J., Grunwald, J.E., Toth, C., Redford, M. & Ferris, F.L. (2012) Comparison of Age-related Macular Degeneration Treatments Trials (CATT) Research Group. *Ophthalmology.* **119** (12), 2537–48

Mattice, E.& Wolfe, C.P. (1986). Using the Amsler grid. *Journal of Ophthalmic Nursing Technology.* **5**(1) 34.

Menkhaus, S., Wallesch, C.W. & Behrens-Baumann, W. (2003) Charles-Bonnet syndrome. *Ophthalmology.* **100**, 738–39.

Newell, F.W. (1996) *Ophthalmology: Principles and concepts.* St Louis, MO: Mosby.

Owens, W.C. & Owens, E.U. (1948) Retrolental fibroplasia in premature infants. *Transactions of the American Academy of Ophthalmologists and Otolaryngologists.* **53**, 18–41.

Recchia, F. & Brown, G.C. (2000) Systemic disorders associated with retinal vascular occlusion. *Current Opinion in Ophthalmology.* **11**, 462–67.

Rosenfeld, P.J., Moshfeghi, A.A. & Puliafito, C.A. (2005) Optical coherence tomography findings after intravitreal injection of bevacizumab (AvastinR) for neovascular age-related macular degeneration. *Ophthalmic Surgery, Lasers & Imaging.* **36**, 331–35.

Ross, W.H. & Kozy, D.W. (1998) Visual recovery in macula-off rhegmatogenous retinal detachments. *Ophthalmology.* **105**, 2149–50.

Ryder, B. (1995). Screening for diabetic retinopathy. *British Medical Journal.* **311**, 207–8.

Shah, G.K. & Brown, G.C. (2000) 'Photography, angiography, and ultrasonography in diabetic retinopathy' in H.W. Flynn & W.E. Smiddy (eds) *Diabetes and Ocular Disease: Past, present and future therapies.* San Francisco, CA: Foundation of the American Academy of Ophthalmology.

Shelswell, N. (2002) Perioperative patient education for retinal surgery. *Association of periOperative Registered Nurses (AORN) Journal.* **75**, 801–7.

Singerman, L.J., Brucker, A.J., Jampol, L.M., Lim, J.I., Rosenfeld, P., Schachat, A.P. & Spaide, R.F. (2005) Neovascular Age-Related Macular Degeneration: Roundtable. *Retina.* **25**(7), 1–22.

Tan, C.S., Chew, M.C. & Lim, T.H. (2014) Comparison of foveal-sparing with foveal-involving photodynamic therapy for myopic choroidal neovascularisation. *Eye.* **28**, 17–22.

Taylor, R.H., Shah, P. & Murray, P.I. (1995) *Key Topics in Ophthalmology.* Oxford: BIOS Scientific.

Toalster, N., Mattew, R. & Ng, P. (2013) A 12 Month Prospective Trial of Injection and Extended Regimen for Ranibizumad Treatment of Age-Related Macular Degeneration. *Retina.* **33**(7), 1351–58.

Waqar, S., Park, J.C. & Cole, M.D. (2014) *Intravitreal Injections: a handbook for ophthalmic nurse practitioners and trainee ophthalmologists.* London: World Scientific.

Yam, J.C.S. & Kwok, A.K.H. (2014) Ultraviolet light and ocular diseases. *International Ophthalmology.* **34**(2), 383–400.

CHAPTER TWENTY-THREE

The orbit and extraocular muscles

Rosie Auld
with material by Allyson Ryder

This chapter describes the anatomy of the orbit and discusses some orbital problems, including thyroid eye disease, orbital infection, orbital inflammatory disease and orbital tumours. It then looks at the extraocular muscles, eye movements and strabismus (squint) and its management. This is followed by an overview of a basic orthoptic assessment.

Anatomy of the orbit

The bony orbits are pyramid-shaped cavities composed of four walls (roof, floor, medial and lateral), converging on the apex posteriorly (Figure 23.1). The medial walls are parallel and the lateral walls make an angle of about 90° with each other. The widest part of the orbit is about 15mm behind the orbital margin, or rim. The orbital rim generally protects the globe from injury.

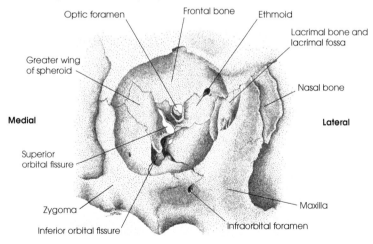

Figure 23.1 The bones of the orbit.

The average height of an adult orbit is 35mm and the average width 40 mm. In an adult the average volume of the orbit is 30ml (Bron *et al.* 1998).

Seven bones form the four walls of the orbit: frontal, maxilla, zygoma, sphenoid, ethmoid, lacrimal and palatine (Snell & Lemp 1998). There are several openings within and adjacent to the orbits, through which nerves and blood vessels supply the globe, extraocular muscles and nearby structures.

Table 23.1 Orbital structures

Structure	Travels through...
Motor nerves to ocular muscles and ophthalmic nerve and vein	Superior orbital fissure and inferior orbital fissure
Optic nerve	Optic foramen
Supraorbital nerves and vessels	Supraorbital notch
Infraorbital nerve and artery	Infraorbital foramen

Roof

The very thin orbital plate of the frontal bone primarily forms the roof. The lesser wing of the sphenoid lies posteriorly at the apex, perforated by the optic canal.

Relationships

Above, the roof is indented by the convolutions of the frontal lobe and the frontal sinus lies anteriorly.

Anteromedially, 4mm behind the orbital rim, lies a small depression called the fovea, for the pulley (trochlear) of the superior oblique. The supraorbital notch lies on the supraorbital margin, approximately one-third of the way along from the medial wall.

Anterolaterally in the frontal bone lies the fossa for the lacrimal gland; this is bounded below by the suture between the frontal and zygomatic bones.

Immediately below the roof lie the frontal nerve, supraorbital artery and levator palpebrae superioris, with the superior oblique between the roof and the medial wall.

Medial wall

From front to back, the medial wall is made up of the frontal process of the maxilla, the lacrimal bone, the very thin lamina papyracea of the ethmoid, which forms the major part of the wall, and then a small part of the body of the sphenoid.

Relationships

Anteriorly the lacrimal sac lies in the lacrimal fossa, which leads down into the lacrimal canal.

Medially lie the ethmoidal air cells and posteriorly the sphenoidal air cells.

The medial rectus runs along the medial wall, and the superior oblique runs along the angle between the medial wall and the roof. The nasociliary nerve and the anterior part of the ophthalmic artery lie between the two muscles.

Floor

The floor is mainly formed by the orbital plate of the maxilla. The orbital surface of the zygoma forms the anterolateral part, with the apex formed by the orbital process of the palate.

Relationships

Below the floor lies the maxillary antrum and above lies the inferior rectus. Posteriorly the inferior rectus is in contact with the floor, whereas anteriorly it is separated from the floor by the inferior oblique and orbital fat. The inferior oblique rises from an area lateral to the opening of the nasolacrimal canal. It then crosses the floor outwards and backwards.

Posteriorly the inferior orbital fissure separates the floor from the lateral wall and the infraorbital sulcus runs forwards from the middle of this fissure. Anteriorly the sulcus becomes a canal, emerging in the infraorbital foramen, about 4mm from the orbital rim.

Lateral wall

This is formed by the orbital surface of the zygoma anteriorly and the orbital surface of the greater wing of the sphenoid posteriorly. The superior and inferior orbital fissures separate the sphenoidal part of the wall from the roof and floor, respectively.

Relationships

The lateral rectus originates from a small bony spur on the lower margin of the superior orbital fissure, at the junction of the narrow and wide parts. The muscle then runs forward in contact with the lateral wall. The lacrimal nerve and artery run above the muscle.

The zygomatic nerve runs within the zygomatic groove, from the anterior end of the inferior orbital fissure to the zygomatic foramen.

Superior orbital fissure

The superior orbital fissure is the largest opening between the middle cranial fossa and the orbit. It is a gap about 22mm long, lying between the lesser wing of the sphenoid in the roof of the orbit and the greater wing of the sphenoid in the lateral wall. It is closed anteriorly by the frontal bone. Medially it lies below the optic foramen, separated from it by the posterior root of the lesser wing of the sphenoid; from here it runs upwards and laterally.

The superior orbital fissure consists of two parts – a wider medial portion and a narrow lateral portion; these are separated by the spine of the lateral rectus muscle. There is an oval tendinous ring, the annulus of Zinn, which divides the wide portion into two and also encloses the optic foramen. This ring is the common origin of the four rectus extraocular muscles.

Passing through the fissure above the annulus are, from above down, the lacrimal, frontal and fourth (trochlear) nerves, with the superior ophthalmic vein below and lateral. Passing within the annulus, from above downwards, are the superior division of the third (oculomotor) nerve, the nasociliary and sympathetic root of the ciliary ganglion, the inferior division of the third nerve and then the sixth (abducens) nerve. Occasionally the inferior ophthalmic vein passes through the fissure below the annulus.

Inferior orbital fissure

The inferior orbital fissure lies between the greater wing of the sphenoid on the lateral wall and the maxilla on the floor of the orbit. It starts below and lateral to the optic foramen, close to the medial end of the superior orbital fissure, and then runs forwards and laterally to about 20mm from the inferior orbital margin.

It forms a communication between the orbit and the pterygopalatine fossa and transmits the infraorbital nerve, the zygomatic nerve, branches from the pterygopalatine ganglion to the orbital periosteum and a communication between the inferior ophthalmic vein and the pterygoid plexus.

Optic canal

Within the optic canal, and adherent to its roof, runs the optic nerve, with its covering of dura, arachnoid and pia mater. The ophthalmic artery runs alongside, first below and then lateral to the nerve.

The canal runs forwards, laterally and slightly downwards from the optic groove of the sphenoid bone in the middle cranial fossa, between the two roots of the lesser wing of the sphenoid, and opens into the apex of the orbit at the optic foramen.

Orbital disorders

As a result of the rigid bony structure of the orbit, with only an anterior opening for expansion, anything that causes an increase in the orbital contents will displace the globe. Pressure behind the globe will push it forward (proptosis), whereas pressure to one side will push it to the opposite side. Displacement of the globe will result in diplopia (double vision). Pressure, which affects the blood supply to the optic nerve and retina, will result in reduced vision and constricted visual field.

Thyroid eye disease (TED)

Thyroid eye disease (TED) is also referred to as Graves' orbitopathy. TED is part of Graves' disease, a systemic autoimmune disorder.

The thyroid gland is the largest endocrine gland in the body, situated just below the cricoid cartilage in the neck. It has numerous small follicles, which secrete thyroxine (T4) and triiodothyronine (T3). Secretion of thyroid hormones is initiated by the hypothalamus, which secretes thyrotrophin-releasing hormone (TRH). This stimulates the pituitary gland to release thyroid-stimulating hormone (TSH), which binds to receptors on the thyroid gland. This new protein, thyroid-stimulating hormone receptor protein (TSH-R), activates a complex system that regulates the functions of the thyroid gland and results in secretion of the two thyroid hormones (Newell 1996).

Graves' disease (thyrotoxicosis) is a systemic disease secondary to excessive secretion of thyroid hormones (hyperthyroidism), with a female to male ratio of 5:1 – 10:1. Hyperthyroidism is a direct result of an abnormal circulating antibody (TSH receptor Ab), which targets the TSH receptor and mimics the effect of normal TSH, resulting in overstimulation of the thyroid gland, its enlargement (goitre) and the excess release of thyroid hormones (Ansons & Davis 2014).

Thyroid eye disease commonly occurs in patients with a history of thyroid dysfunction, specifically Graves' disease. Eye problems may precede, coincide with or follow the hyperthyroidism. Around 25% of patients present to an ophthalmologist with eye signs and symptoms before the discovery of hyperthyroidism. About 4% of patients with TED, Graves' orbitopathy are hypothyroid, with thyroid hormone levels depressed but the TSH level increased, and 6% are euthyroid.

Thyroid eye disease is believed to be an organ-specific autoimmune disorder in which an antibody is responsible for hypertrophy of the extraocular muscles (caused by round cell infiltration), lymphocyte infiltration of the interstitial tissue and proliferation of orbital fat, connective tissue and lacrimal glands.

Environmental factors play a part in the development and severity of autoimmune disease; and severe TED has been linked with smoking, which is known to affect the immune system. Patients with TED are four times more likely to be smokers or former smokers (Vestergaard 2002). Smoking affects the immune system, either by altering the function of the T cell, thus changing the balance of the immune chain, or because the products of the cigarette smoke have a direct immunological effect.

Signs and symptoms of TED

Signs of TED:

- Upper eyelid retraction caused by sympathetic overaction of Müller's muscle

- Contraction of the levator (affects 90–98% of patients at some stage)
- Lid lag (von Graefe's sign)
- Staring, frightened appearance (Kocher's sign)
- Periorbital and lid swelling
- Chemosis: oedema of the conjunctiva
- Conjunctival hyperaemia
- Superior limbic keratoconjunctivitis
- Proptosis – axial
- Mechanical restriction of ocular movements
- Increased intraocular pressure
- Compressive optic neuropathy
- Corneal exposure.

These signs may be unilateral or bilateral, but if unilateral it is likely that the other eye will be affected at a later stage.

Symptoms of TED (most common during the active phase):

- Pain/discomfort from soft tissue involvement
- Photophobia
- Lacrimation
- Grittiness/discomfort from corneal exposure
- Diplopia
- Progressive impairment of central vision
- Defective red–green colour vision.

Classification of ocular changes (Wiersinga & Kahaly 2010)

Clarifying the presence or absence of both symptoms and signs is best achieved in conjunction with the protocol of the European Group on Graves' orbitopathy (EUGOGO) atlas (http://www.eugogo.eu).

Using the Clinical Activity score, one point is given for each of the following features:

- Painful oppressive feeling on or behind the globe
- Pain on attempted up, side or downgaze
- Redness of the eyelids
- Redness of the conjunctiva
- Chemosis

- Inflammatory eyelid swelling
- Inflammation of the plica
- Increase of 2mm or more in proptosis in the last 1–3 months
- Decrease in visual acuity in the last 1–3 months
- Decrease in eye movements of 8 degrees or more in the last 1–3 months

Alternative classification using the acronym NO SPECS:

- Class 0 – no signs or symptoms
- Class 1 – only signs, no symptoms (signs limited to upper lid retraction with or without lid lag)
- Class 2 – soft tissue involvement
- Class 3 – proptosis
- Class 4 – extraocular muscle involvement
- Class 5 – corneal involvement
- Class 6 – sight loss – optic nerve involvement.

Natural history of TED

Thyroid eye disease has two identifiable phases: the active inflammatory (wet) phase, in which the eyes are red and painful; and the later inactive (dry) phase.

The active inflammatory (wet) phase

The inflammatory process that affects the extraocular muscles and eyelids gives rise to most of the characteristic features of TED. This is caused by activation of the muscle fibroblasts, which differentiate into orbital fat and secrete increased glycosaminoglycans which attract water.

Ultrasound and CT scans show extraocular muscle enlargement early in the disease process. Proliferation of orbital fat and connective tissue increases the orbital volume and causes proptosis, which can lead to corneal exposure.

Intraorbital pressure can rise and the blood supply to the optic nerve may be compromised. This risk of optic neuropathy has been found to be directly linked to the size of the extraocular muscles. Upper lid retraction and lid lag in this phase are thought to be the result of sympathetic over-stimulation, secondary to high levels of thyroid hormone, resulting in overaction of Müller's muscle.

The inactive (dry) phase

The inflammatory phase is followed by fibrosis of the extraocular muscles and secondary muscle contracture. The muscle swelling subsides, the proptosis gradually reduces and the risk of optic neuropathy also reduces. Ocular movement restriction becomes more symmetrical and there is a gradual development of a large, vertical, fusional amplitude, which means that diplopia may be less troublesome.

Eyelid retraction normally persists and may be caused by contraction of the levator, and fibrosis between it and the overlying orbital tissues, or by secondary increased innervation to the superior rectus, in order to try to elevate the eye after the fibrosis of the inferior rectus.

Management of thyroid dysfunction

Hyperthyroidism:

The aim is to achieve a euthyroid state by:

- Immunosuppression – intravenous steroids are more effective than oral
- Radioactive iodine to irradiate the thyroid gland
- Thyroidectomy.

Hypothyroidism:

- Replacement of thyroid hormone usually with thyroxine.

Management of TED

Soft tissue involvement

This includes periorbital and lid swelling, chemosis, conjunctival hyperaemia, especially over the insertion sites of the horizontal recti, keratoconjunctivitis sicca and superior limbic keratoconjunctivitis. Classification of the soft tissue signs is best undertaken by using a photographic comparative atlas (Wiersinga & Kahaly 2010).

Management is often unsuccessful but the following may benefit the patient to some extent:

- Topical therapy: Using lubricants (such as artificial tears) during the day and ointment at night, may help if there is ocular irritation resulting from corneal exposure, conjunctival inflammation and keratoconjunctivitis sicca. Patients with superior limbic keratoconjunctivitis may need 1% topical adrenaline (epinephrine) and 5% acetylcysteine.
- Head elevation: increasing pillows during sleep may help to reduce periorbital oedema.
- Taping lids: during sleep may aid patients with exposure keratopathy.
- Diuretics: at night may reduce periorbital oedema in the morning.
- Patients should be advised to stop smoking
- Eyelid retraction.

Around 50 % of patients with Graves' disease have lid retraction, which may be mild, moderate or marked. Patients with mild lid retraction do not normally need treatment and it may improve spontaneously or after treatment of associated hyperthyroidism.

Surgical treatment is indicated in cases of marked, but stable, lid retraction with exposure keratopathy and poor cosmesis. The following are the main surgical procedures:

- Botulinum toxin injected into the levator muscle
- Inferior rectus Botulinum toxin or recession – if the fibrotic inferior rectus is thought to be causing the lid retraction
- Disinsertion of an overactive Müller's muscle
- Lengthening a contracted levator with donor sclera
- Lateral tarsorrhaphy – sewing the upper and lower lids together at the lateral canthus. This is rarely used because it is unsightly and does not benefit corneal exposure.

Proptosis

Thyroid eye disease is the most common cause of proptosis in adults. It may be unilateral or bilateral and is permanent in about 70 % of patients. It is uninfluenced by any hyperthyroidism treatment and, if severe, will prevent adequate lid closure, leading to exposure keratopathy, corneal ulceration and endophthalmitis.

Management of proptosis can involve systemic steroids, radiotherapy and/or surgical decompression.

Systemic steroids

These are used during the early stages of the disease where there is rapidly progressing and painful proptosis. Oral prednisolone 80–100mg/day is prescribed, with relief of symptoms expected within 48 hours. Ciclosporin can be used in addition and this permits a reduction in the dosage of prednisolone. Steroids should be discontinued after 3 months.

Radiotherapy

This can be considered in patients who are unresponsive to steroids or where steroid therapy is contraindicated. The aim is to reduce the size of the extraocular muscles and relieve intraocular pressure.

Surgical decompression

This can be considered when medical treatment has failed or is contraindicated. The aim is to create space for the orbital contents and reduce proptosis by removing one or more of the orbital walls. The most common procedure is to remove part of the floor and the posterior portion of the medial wall, allowing the orbital contents to prolapse into the maxillary and ethmoidal sinuses. This achieves 3–6mm retroplacement of the globe. Significant ocular movement restriction is common following orbital decompression. Decompression should therefore be considered if radiotherapy fails to achieve improvement, and decompression should be carried out before any extraocular muscle surgery.

Optic nerve involvement

About 5% of patients have optic neuropathy, caused by direct compression of the optic nerve or its blood supply (Char *et al.* 1997). Patients present with decreasing visual acuity, defective red–green colour vision and central or paracentral field defects. Optic atrophy will develop if treatment is delayed.

The threat to vision is classed as a medical emergency and management is the same as for severe proptosis:

- Systemic steroids
- Orbital radiotherapy
- Surgical decompression.

Extraocular muscle involvement

Between 30% and 50% of patients develop ophthalmoplegia and diplopia can be a persistent problem through the active (wet) phase and the inactive (dry) phase. Diplopia may be vertical, horizontal or a combination of both.

The extraocular muscles become enlarged during the inflammatory stage, followed by a mechanical restriction of movement in the field of gaze opposite to the affected muscle. This is caused by an inability to relax the muscle due to oedema in the infiltrative stage and fibrosis in the inactive (dry) stage. A single muscle in one eye may be affected or a number of muscles in both eyes. As the disease process develops, the degree of restriction changes.

In order of frequency the affected muscles are:

- Inferior rectus: restricting elevation (most common)
- Medial rectus: restricting abduction (lateral gaze)
- Superior rectus: restricting depression
- Lateral rectus: restricting adduction (medial gaze).

Management may be conservative or surgical.

Conservative management of TED

This aims to monitor the process of the disease, by recording and measuring changes in the condition.

Conservative management also aims to overcome symptoms and maintain binocular single vision (BSV) by:

- Prism therapy: Using prisms to join the diplopia and restore BSV. This treatment is not always viable due to the variability of the eye movement restrictions in different positions of gaze that cannot be corrected by a prism of one strength.

- Botulinum toxin (BT): Injection into the affected muscle/s in the inflammatory stage to reduce the mechanical restriction. This can be successful in helping to regain BSV.

- Occlusion of one eye: This can be used as a last resort to eliminate diplopia when other conservative methods have failed.

Surgical management of TED

Extraocular muscle surgery should be carried out only when the TED is inactive and the ocular muscle restrictions have been stable for between 3 and 6 months; the patient should ideally be euthyroid for at least 6 months. The aim of surgical management is to achieve a field of BSV (binocular single vision) in the primary position and the reading position (i.e. down-gaze) and to improve cosmetic appearance. The patient should be aware that binocularity in all positions of gaze is difficult to achieve, and further surgery may be necessary.

Surgery is tailored to the affected individual muscle, but the most commonly performed surgery is an inferior rectus recession and/or medial rectus recession, using adjustable sutures. A Forced Duction Test and Forced Generation Tests should be carried out to confirm the presence and degree of mechanical restriction before commencing surgery. Adjustable sutures are commonly used in TED extraocular muscle surgery in view of the unpredictable effect of surgery on fibrotic muscles.

Orbital infections

Preseptal cellulitis

This is an inflammation and infection of the eyelid and skin around the eye, anterior to the orbital septum. It must be differentiated from orbital cellulitis, which is an ophthalmic emergency requiring immediate intravenous antibiotics. Rapid progression to orbital cellulitis can occur in some patients.

Preseptal cellulitis can be a result of trauma to the skin, infected insect bites or sinus infection. Local infection (such as infected chalazion or dacryocystitis) may spread to become preseptal cellulitis, or a more remote infraction such as a middle-ear infection may be transmitted via the blood supply to the lids.

Presentation will be as a unilateral, tender and red periorbital area with some lid oedema. Treatment is with a course of oral antibiotics such as flucloxacillin or amoxicillin.

Orbital cellulitis

Orbital cellulitis is a bacterial infection of the soft tissue behind the orbital septum and is caused by the same organisms that cause acute sinusitis, i.e. pneumococci, streptococci or staphylococci (Figure 23.2). These enter the orbit from the infected frontal, maxillary, ethmoidal or sphenoidal sinuses via the vascular channels or by direct extension. This infection may also be post-traumatic or postoperative, following retinal, lacrimal or orbital surgery. It may also result from an extension of preseptal cellulitis through the orbital septum or spread locally from, for example, dacryocystitis.

If not treated successfully, infection can spread to the cavernous sinus or meninges, resulting in cavernous sinus thrombosis, meningitis or abscess of the brain. It is therefore potentially life threatening and, although it can occur at any age, it is more common in children (Bowling 2015). Orbital abscess can occur in post-traumatic or postoperative cases.

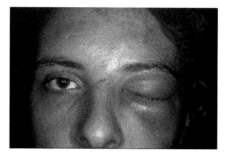

Figure 23.2 Orbital cellulitis.

Signs and symptoms

Orbital cellulitis is almost always unilateral, with a sudden onset. Mild cases involve swelling and redness of the eyelids, chemosis, proptosis, discharge and dull pain. In more severe cases, the pain is more intense and there is pain on eye movements, which will be restricted. In advanced cases, there may be signs of optic nerve dysfunction, with optic neuritis after severe inflammatory reactions. Other symptoms can range from mild fever and malaise to high fever and marked debility.

Differential diagnosis

- Tendonitis
- Orbital periostitis
- Cavernous sinus thrombosis
- Rhabdomyosarcoma in children.

Treatment

Immediate treatment is very important. The patient will be admitted to hospital and assessed frequently as orbital cellulitis presents a risk to vision and can even be life threatening. However, almost all cases respond well to large doses of systemic intravenous antibiotics. Visual prognosis is good in the absence of complications, although emergency canthotomy may need to be performed if an orbital compartment syndrome is diagnosed, and surgical drainage of sinuses and subperiosteal or orbital abscesses may be required. In cases of fungal infection, surgical debridement of the orbit may be indicated and, in extreme disease, exenteration of the orbit and the sinuses (Harrington 2016).

Investigations include white cell count, blood culture and magnetic resonance imaging (MRI) of the orbit and brain. Optic nerve function should be monitored every 4 hours while the orbital cellulitis is in its acute phase. If improvement is noted within 48 hours, antibiotics may be changed from intravenous to oral. Pupil reactions, visual acuity, colour vision and brightness appreciation should form part of this monitoring and patients must have sufficient information and awareness of their condition to recognise the importance of these investigations at a time when they may well be feeling very ill.

Monitoring may be more of a problem in children with orbital cellulitis because it is likely that they will be nursed in a specialist paediatric area. It is essential that children are referred to an ophthalmologist for investigation and specialist management. A multispecialty approach is required for the successful treatment of patients with orbital cellulitis and this may include ophthalmology, ENT, radiology, infectious diseases and neurosurgery. Immediate diagnosis and effective treatment are essential.

Cavernous sinus thrombosis

Cavernous sinus thrombosis is normally caused by a bacterial infection spreading along the venous channels draining the orbit, central face, throat and nasal cavities. The thrombosis restricts the venous drainage flow from the brain, resulting in pressure in the cavernous sinus. If left untreated, the infection will spread, causing sepsis.

Signs and symptoms

The condition is normally bilateral, with proptosis, orbital oedema, swelling of the eyelids, diminished or absent pupillary reflexes, papilloedema and reduced vision. There may be involvement of the cranial nerves that traverse the cavernous sinus, i.e. nerves III and IV, and the ophthalmic division of nerves V and VI, thus diplopia is likely. There will be severe headache, fever, nausea and vomiting.

Differential diagnosis

It is important to differentiate between this and orbital cellulitis, which is unilateral, with normal pupillary reflexes, no papilloedema and less severe pain.

Treatment

High doses of systemic antibiotics will normally ensure good visual recovery.

Orbital inflammatory disease

Idiopathic orbital inflammatory disease (pseudotumour)

Orbital pseudotumour is a benign, nongranulomatous orbital inflammatory condition characterised by extraocular, orbital and adnexal inflammation with no known cause.

Signs and symptoms

Patients typically present with rapid onset unilateral painful proptosis, oedema and conjunctival injection. There may also be ptosis, chemosis and motility dysfunction and optic neuropathy. The exact cause is unknown, but infectious and immune-mediated mechanisms have been proposed. There may be optic nerve dysfunction if the inflammation involves the posterior part of the orbit.

Differential diagnosis

- Orbital cellulitis
- Thyroid eye disease
- Orbital tumours
- Ruptured dermoid cyst.

Treatment

- Observation in mild cases, because there may be a remission.
- Systemic steroids (usually prednisone) are successful in over 50% of moderate to severe cases.
- Radiotherapy is carried out if there is no improvement after 2 weeks of steroid therapy.
- Cytotoxic drugs (usually cyclophosphamide) are used if there is no improvement after treatment with steroids or radiotherapy.

Orbital tumours

Costin *et al.* (2013) classify orbital tumours into:

- **Cystic**
- **Vascular**
- **Myogneic**
- Lipomatous
- Melanocytic

- **Lacrimal gland and sac**
- Lymphoproliferative
- **Neural**
- Fibrous
- Hystiocytic
- Bone
- **Metastatic**
- Secondary.

The more common orbital tumours are considered here, as shown in bold.

Cystic

Dermoid cysts are the most common cystic lesions and are congenital, arising from epithelial cells trapped underneath surface epithelium during embryogenesis. They are benign and often appear at the orbital rim close to the zygomaticofrontal suture.

Vascular tumours

Capillary haemangioma is the most common type of childhood orbital and periorbital tumour. It may present as a small isolated lesion or a large disfiguring mass, causing impairment of vision due to stimulus deprivation amblyopia, caused by inadequate visual stimulation during the critical period of visual development.

Signs

The tumour presents at birth and may be superficial, subcutaneous or deep. If superficial, there will be the classic strawberry naevi on the eyelids.

If subcutaneous, the skin on the eyelids will appear dark blue or purple and there may be displacement of the globe.

A deep tumour will cause unilateral proptosis with no skin discoloration.

About 25% of cases have coexisting capillary haemangiomas on other parts of the body and large tumours may be associated with high-output cardiac failure.

Treatment

Around 40% of patients spontaneously resolve by the age of 4 and this increases to 70% by the age of 7. Early treatment is indicated if there is a threat to visual acuity, poor cosmesis, necrosis or infection, or high-output cardiac failure. The methods of choice are steroid injections (effective in the early stages of subcutaneous tumours) or systemic steroids, which are used if there is a large orbital component.

Cavernous haemangioma

This is the most common type of benign orbital tumour in adults, normally presenting in the fourth to fifth decades. It consists of large dilated veins with an endothelial lining and normally occurs in the fat space behind the globe.

Signs

There is slow progressive unilateral axial proptosis, which may be associated with disc oedema and chorioretinal folds.

Treatment

Surgical excision is required in most cases as the tumour enlarges. It is usually well encapsulated and relatively easy to remove.

Lymphangiomas

These are rare benign vascular malformations, normally presenting in early childhood.

Signs

If anterior, there will be soft bluish masses in the upper nasal quadrant, with conjunctival cysts. If posterior, there may be slow progressive proptosis; or, if the tumour initially lies dormant, there may be a sudden onset of painful proptosis, following a spontaneous haemorrhage.

Treatment

These are difficult to treat, due to the fact that they are not encapsulated. There is a tendency to haemorrhage easily and they may infiltrate normal orbital tissue. They may be treated by drainage or by controlled vaporisation using a carbon dioxide laser.

Myogenic

Rhabdomyosarcomas represent the most common type of myogenic orbital tumour and the most common malignant orbital neoplasm in childhood. This is mainly a disease of younger children, with 90% of cases occurring before the age of 16, and many within the first decade.

Signs

There is rapid progressive proptosis with displacement of the globe. It can involve any part of the orbit but the most common location is retrobulbar followed by superior. Around 33% of cases have ptosis, with a palpable mass. Swelling and injection of skin develop later. A CT scan will show a poorly defined, irregular orbital mass, which may extend into adjacent bones or sinuses. There may be metastatic spread to the lungs, bone or, rarely, the lymphatic system.

The treatment approach relies on accurate staging of the tumour. Treatment involves a combination of surgery, irradiation and chemotherapy, depending on the stage and location of the tumour.

Orbital RMS should be considered in the differential diagnosis of any child with unilateral proptosis.

Lacrimal tumours

Pleomorphic lacrimal gland adenoma

This is a benign mixed-cell type of tumour and is the most common epithelial tumour affecting the lacrimal gland (about 50% of cases). It normally presents in the fifth decade as a slowly progressive, firm, painless swelling in the superotemporal orbit. There may be proptosis and downward and medial displacement of the globe with diplopia, especially in the field of action of the superior rectus. Treatment is by surgical excision.

Lacrimal gland carcinoma

This is a very rare tumour, presenting in the fourth to sixth decades, with a high morbidity and mortality. There will be a fast-growing, often painful, lacrimal gland mass, causing downward and medial displacement of the globe, with associated diplopia. Around 25% of cases have swelling of the optic disc and 25% have hypoaesthesia in the region supplied by the trigeminal nerve.

Prognosis for life is poor. Radical surgery involving orbital exenteration or mid-facial resection is normally unsuccessful because the tumour is past surgical excision. Radiotherapy may reduce pain and prolong life.

Neural tumours

Optic nerve glioma (juvenile pilocystic astrocytoma)

This is a primary tumour of the glial cells of the optic nerve, which presents in the first decade, normally before the age of 5. Bowling (2015) reports that 25–50% of cases have associated neurofibromatosis, whereas Levine and Larson (1993) indicate a figure of 60% of cases.

There is slow, painless, progressive loss of vision and axial proptosis. Due to the contours of the orbital walls, the globe is eventually displaced outwards and downwards. The optic nerve is initially swollen and then becomes pale. A CT scan will show a smooth fusiform enlargement of the optic nerve.

Treatment is by observation only if vision is good and the tumour is confined to the orbit.

Surgical excision, with preservation of the globe, is carried out if the tumour is growing towards the optic foramen, vision is reducing and cosmesis is poor.

Radiotherapy, combined with chemotherapy, is indicated in cases where the tumour has extended into the cranium.

Neurofibroma

Diffuse or plexiform neurofibroma is the most common peripheral nerve tumour of the orbit. It presents in early childhood and occurs in patients with neurofibromatosis 1.

There is diffuse orbital involvement, with overgrowth and hypertrophy of periorbital tissues and a mechanical ptosis following eyelid involvement. Kanski (2011) reports that on palpation the tissues 'feel like a bag of worms'.

Treatment is difficult because of the close involvement of the extraocular muscles and lacrimal gland.

Metastatic tumours

Extraocular metastases are uncommon, being identified in less than 1% of cases, though identified post mortem in more.

In around 40% of patients who are symptomatic from orbital metastases (except for breast cancer metastases), orbital symptoms occur before any symptoms from the primary tumour and may therefore be the first indication of advanced disease (Char *et al.* 1997).

Signs and symptoms depend on the exact position of the tumour although orbital metastases more usually present with diplopia than proptosis. There will be displacement of the globe, diplopia and inflammation, similar to orbital pseudotumour. If the orbital apex is affected, there will be involvement of the cranial nerves (II, III, IV, V, VI) and mild proptosis.

Treatment is aimed at relieving pain and preserving vision. Radiotherapy, chemotherapy and hormonal therapy in breast metastases are the options of choice, although surgery may be an option where there is isolated involvement without an identifiable primary.

The discovery of orbital metastases usually indicates advanced and widespread metastatic disease and the prognosis is very poor.

Eye removal – enucleation

This is the surgical removal of the globe and a portion of the optic nerve from the orbit. The indications for enucleation are: primary intraocular malignant tumours, irreparable trauma, where there is a possibility of sympathetic ophthalmia and blind painful eyes. The patient is likely to need a great deal of psychological support both preoperatively and postoperatively. One of the greatest concerns for the patient is often that the incorrect eye might be removed. Marking of the forehead preoperatively, part of the requirements of safe surgery, helps to reassure the patient that this will not happen and this can be confirmed by the usual preoperative checks at the theatre door and, later, in the theatre.

Procedure

A 360° limbal periotomy is performed, preserving as much of the conjunctiva as possible. The conjunctiva is then undermined back to the four rectus muscles, which are isolated, tagged and severed from their insertions. The two obliques are identified, severed and allowed to retract. Fascial bands, nerves and vessels are cut to allow exposure of the optic nerve, which is identified and transected 5mm from the globe. This can then be removed.

Procedures to remove the eye should always address the subsequent appearance of the orbit. Whenever possible, volume replacements should be placed in the socket at the time of surgery to ensure that the postoperative socjet is as 'normal' as possible. Implants in the socket can be used later, to support a prosthesis, or to integrate a prosthesis, which can achieve prosthesis movement, using the remaining muscle, and achieve a good cosmetic appearance.

Hydroxyapetite was one of the first materials used as an integratable orbital implant. Because it is porous, fibrovascular tissues will grow into it, anchoring the extraocular muscles and providing good movement. Hydroxyapetite is rough and therefore wrapped before being placed in the orbit. Wrappings include donor sclera or autologous tissue grafts such as temporalis facia or fascia lata, or synthetic meshes. The muscles are sutured to the wrapping material. Subsequent developments in implant material include porous polyethylene, which is smoother and does not need wrapping. The muscles can be sutured directly to the implant. The implant, wrapped or unwrapped, is placed into the muscle cone. The sutures used to tag the rectus muscles are attached to the anterior lip of windows cut in the wrapping material where used, so that the muscle is in direct contact with the implant. This will aid in vascularisation of the implant. Tenon's capsule and then the conjunctiva are sutured closed.

The patient is likely to return to the ward with a pressure dressing in situ and nurses must be aware of possible complications of surgery (haemorrhage particularly) and should check the dressing very frequently. Pressure on the dressing may be maximised by nursing the patient on their operated side.

A shaped conformer or shell is placed in the socket at surgery in order to maintain the shape of the socket. The patient must know how to remove, clean and reinsert the shell, before discharge to avoid discomfort and infection, and become adept at manipulating the shell and later the prosthesis. This is obviously a very upsetting time for both the patient and their relatives or carers and they may find the whole process extremely distasteful. Enough time must be allowed so that the patient can be supported adequately through this period.

Socket implants may be integrated or non-integrated. Integrated implants are more commonly used now because of the potential for a much better cosmetic effect. A biointegrated implant reduces the incidence of migration and extrusion. The position of the implant and the fibrovascular ingrowth allow it to be drilled, and a peg is introduced for direct coupling of a prosthesis. The peg fits into the back of the prosthesis and, in this way, movement of the artificial eye is equal to that of the other eye. The peg also supports the weight of the prosthesis, taking the pressure off the lower lid (Leatherbarrow 2003).

A prosthesis can be fitted in 4–6 weeks and, later, when the implant has vascularised, the implant can be drilled and a peg placed.

Evisceration

This is the removal of the contents of the globe while leaving the sclera and the optic nerve intact. The advantages over enucleation are that there is less disruption of orbital anatomy, reduced socket deformity, with potentially better mobility of a prosthesis and better cosmesis as well as less pain after surgery due to the reduction of tissue disruption. The disadvantages are that it does not remove any unsuspected intraocular tumour (although the incident of this is very rare), and does not stop the theoretical development of sympathetic ophthalmia, although, again, the incidence of this is so low as to be thought negligible (Phan *et al.* 2012). Evisceration is the procedure of choice when endophthalmitis is present, to reduce the spread of infection via the cut dura and has gained popularity over recent years because of the advantages mentioned above.

Exenteration

Exenteration is the removal of the entire contents of the orbit and is usually performed to remove life-threatening malignancy. Exenteration may be total, subtotal or extended. Subtotal exenteration spares the eyelids and is performed when the disease is behind the globe. Extended exenteration removes surrounding bone. There is a considerable loss of tissue during exenteration and, often, a skin graft is needed, which may be taken at the time of surgery. A split skin graft lining the cavity will heal faster than a cavity that is left to granulate. The patient must be aware of the need for skin grafting and that there will be a second painful site postoperatively. The donor site must be prepared preoperatively and must be an area where there is minimal growth of hair, such as the inner thigh or arm. When the exenteration site has healed, osseo-integrative techniques can help to achieve a good cosmetic effect for the patient.

Extraocular muscles

There are six extraocular muscles, which allow the eye to move into different positions: four recti (medial, lateral, superior and inferior); and two obliques (superior and inferior).

Table 23.2 Summary of the nerve supply and actions of the extraocular muscles

Muscle	Nerve supply	Primary action	Secondary action	Tertiary action
Lateral rectus (LR)	VI	Abduction		
Medial rectus (MR)	Inferior division III	Adduction		
Superior rectus (SR)	Superior division III	Elevation in Abduction	Adduction	Intorsion
Inferior rectus (IR)	Inferior division III	Depression in Abduction	Adduction	Extorsion
Superior oblique (SO)	IV	Intorsion, greatest in Abduction	Depression greatest in Adduction	Abduction
Inferior oblique (IO)	Inferior division III	Extorsion greatest in Abduction	Elevation greatest in Adduction	Abduction

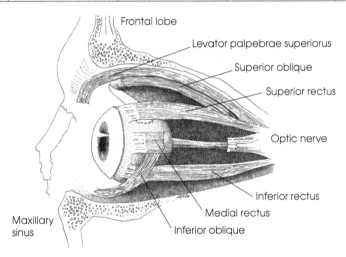

Figure 23.3 Extraocular muscles.

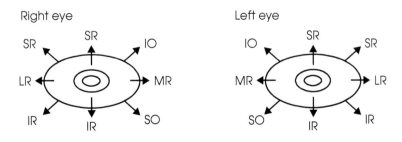

Figure 23.4 Actions of the extraocular muscles.

Lateral rectus

Action
Abducts, i.e. pulls the eye laterally.

Origin
The lateral rectus originates from the lateral part of the tendinous annulus of Zinn, where it bridges the superior orbital fissure. Lateral to this tendinous ring is a small spine rising from the surface of the greater wing of the sphenoid, to which the lateral rectus is also attached.

Insertion
The lateral rectus passes forward along the lateral wall, pierces Tenon's capsule and is inserted into the sclera 6.9mm from the limbus by a tendon 8.8mm long. The line of insertion is almost vertical.

Relationships
- Above lie the lacrimal nerve and artery and then the superior rectus
- Below is the orbital floor
- Laterally is the lateral wall and anteriorly lies the lacrimal gland
- Medially lie nerve VI, the ophthalmic artery, the ciliary ganglion and then further forward the tendon of the inferior oblique.

Nerve supply
- Nerve VI (abducens).

Blood supply
- Lacrimal artery
- Lateral muscular branch of the ophthalmic artery.

Medial rectus

Action
Adducts, i.e. pulls the eye medially.

Origin
The medial rectus originates from the medial part of the annulus of Zinn and is attached to the dural sheath of the optic nerve. It is the largest of the extraocular muscles.

Insertion
It passes forwards along the medial wall, pierces Tenon's capsule and is inserted into the sclera 5.5mm from the limbus by a tendon 3.7mm long. The line of insertion is almost vertical.

Relationships
- Above lie the superior oblique, the ophthalmic artery, with its anterior and posterior ethmoidal branches, and the nasociliary nerve

- Below is the orbital floor
- Laterally is the optic nerve and orbital fat
- Medially is the orbital plate of the ethmoid bone and the ethmoidal air cells.

Nerve supply

- Inferior division nerve III (oculomotor).

Blood supply

- Medial muscular branch of the ophthalmic artery.

Superior rectus

Action

Elevates, i.e. pulls the eye up.

Adducts

Intorts, i.e. rotates the eye medially.

Origin

The superior rectus originates from the superior part of the annulus of Zinn, above the optic foramen. Like the medial rectus, it is attached to the dural sheath of the optic nerve.

Insertion

It passes forwards and laterally, making an angle of 25° with the median plane, pierces Tenon's capsule and is inserted into the sclera 7.7mm from the limbus by a tendon 5.8mm long. The line of insertion is oblique and slightly curved.

Relationships

- Above lie the levator palpebrae superioris, the frontal nerve and the orbital roof
- Below are the optic nerve, the ophthalmic artery, the nasociliary nerve and orbital fat
- Laterally lie the lacrimal artery and nerve and then the lateral rectus
- Medially lie the ophthalmic artery, the nasociliary nerve, the medial rectus and the superior oblique.

Nerve supply

- Superior division nerve III (oculomotor).

Blood supply

- Lateral muscular branch of the ophthalmic artery.

Inferior rectus

Action

Depresses, i.e. pulls the eye down.

Adducts

Extorts, i.e. rotates the eye laterally.

Origin

The inferior rectus is the shortest of the recti, originating from the inferior part of the annulus of Zinn, below the optic foramen.

Insertion

It passes forwards and laterally, making an angle of 25° with the median plane, pierces Tenon's capsule and is inserted into the sclera 6.5mm from the limbus by a tendon 5.5mm long. The line of insertion is oblique and slightly curved.

Relationships

- Above lie the inferior division of nerve III, the optic nerve and orbital fat, and then the globe

- Below is the orbital floor, the infraorbital vessels and nerve, in their canal, and the maxillary sinus; the inferior oblique crosses below, between the inferior rectus and the orbital plate of the maxilla, and here the two muscle sheaths are united

- Laterally lies the nerve to the inferior oblique.

Nerve supply

- Inferior division nerve III (oculomotor).

Blood supply

Medial muscular branch of the ophthalmic artery.

Superior oblique

Action

- Intorts

- Abducts

- Depresses.

Origin

The superior oblique is the longest and thinnest of the extraocular muscles. It originates outside the annulus of Zinn, above and medial to the optic canal. The muscle runs forward between the roof and the medial wall of the orbit, giving rise to a rounded tendon, about 10mm behind the trochlea.

Trochlea

This is a U-shaped pulley of fibrocartilage, attached to the trochlear fossa on the frontal bone, a few millimetres behind the orbital margin. It is lined by a synovial sheath, which surrounds the tendon as it runs through the pulley and then continues with it until its insertion.

Insertion

As the tendon emerges from the trochlea, it bends downwards, backwards and laterally, at an angle of about 55°. It pierces Tenon's capsule, passes beneath the superior rectus, fans out and is inserted into the sclera, posterior to the equator of the globe.

Relationships

- Above are the orbital roof and the supratrochlear nerve
- Below lie the nasociliary nerve, the ophthalmic artery and its posterior and anterior ethmoidal branches.

Nerve supply

- Nerve IV (trochlear).

Blood supply

- Superior muscular branch of the ophthalmic artery.

Inferior oblique

Action

- Extorts
- Elevates
- Abducts.

Origin

The inferior oblique is the only muscle that has its origin at the front of the orbit. It arises from a small depression in the orbital floor, just behind the orbital margin and lateral to the nasolacrimal canal.

Insertion

The inferior oblique passes backwards and laterally, parallel with the reflected tendon of the superior oblique, making an angle of 50° to the median plane. It follows the curve of the lower surface of the globe, running between the inferior rectus and the orbital floor. It is inserted into the sclera at the posterolateral part of the globe, under the lateral rectus. The line of insertion is oblique and convex above.

Relationships

- Above lie the inferior rectus and the globe
- Below are the orbital floor and then laterally the lateral rectus.

Nerve supply

- Inferior division III nerve (oculomotor).

Blood supply

- Infraorbital artery
- Medial muscular branch of the ophthalmic artery.

Remembering the actions

An easy way to remember the secondary and tertiary actions of the muscles is: **RADSIN** **R**ecti – **AD**duct – **S**uperior muscles – **IN**tort.

Therefore:

- Obliques abduct
- Inferior muscles extort.

Ocular movements

Normal ocular movements are dependent on the integrity of the ocular muscles, the infranuclear and internuclear pathways and the oculomotor nuclei. Ocular movements take place around three axes of Fick:

- X: The horizontal axis around which vertical movements are made
- Y: The sagittal or anteroposterior axis around which torsional movements are made
- Z: The vertical axis around which horizontal movements are made.

Ocular movement terminology

Ductions

These are uniocular movements around the axes of Fick from the primary position. They are:

- Adduction – moving the eye medially
- Abduction – moving the eye laterally
- Elevation
- Depression
- Intorsion
- Extortion.

Versions

These are binocular conjugate movements of the eyes, i.e. the eyes move in the same direction:

- Dextroversion: right gaze
- Laevoversion: left gaze
- Dextroelevation: up and right
- Laevoelevation: up and left
- Dextrodepression: down and right
- Laevodepression: down and left.

Vergences

These are binocular disjugate movements of the eyes, i.e. in opposite directions. They are:

- Convergence: both eyes moving in
- Divergence: both eyes moving out.
- Positions of gaze.

There are six cardinal positions of gaze:

- Dextroversion: right gaze
- Laevoversion: left gaze
- Dextroelevation: up and right
- Laevoelevation: up and left
- Dextrodepression: down and right
- Laevodepression: down and left.

Smooth pursuit ocular movements

These are assessed in nine positions of gaze – the six cardinal positions, plus:

- Primary position: straight ahead
- Elevation
- Depression.

Laws of ocular movements

Sherrington's law of reciprocal innervation

This states that when there is increased innervation to one muscle to contract, there is decreased innervation to its direct antagonist, which is therefore relaxed. In other words, when the right lateral rectus contracts, the right medial rectus relaxes. This is a uniocular law.

Hering's law of equal innervation

This states that when an impulse to contract is sent to one muscle, a simultaneous and equal impulse is sent to its contralateral synergist or yoke muscle. In other words, to look to the right, the right lateral rectus and the left medial rectus receive equal innervation to contract. This is a binocular law, aiding the maintenance of binocular single vision.

Antagonists are pairs of muscles in the same eye, which move the eye in opposite directions, e.g. right superior oblique and right inferior oblique.

Synergists are pairs of muscles in opposite eyes, which move both eyes in the same direction, e.g. right superior oblique and left inferior rectus (Table 23.3).

The term 'ipsilateral' is used to define an antagonist in the same eye, and 'contralateral' is used to define a synergist or antagonist in the opposite eye.

Table 23.3 Synergists and antagonists

Muscle	Contralateral synergist	Ipsilateral antagonist	Contralateral antagonist
RMR	LLR	RLR	LMR
LMR	RLR	LLR	RMR
RLR	LMR	RMR	LLR
LLR	RMR	LMR	RLR
RSR	LIO	RIR	LSO
LSR	RIO	LIR	RSO
RIR	LSO	RSR	LIO
LIR	RSO	LSR	RIO
RSO	LIR	RIO	LSR
LSO	RIR	LIO	RSR
RIO	LSR	RSO	LIR
LIO	RSR	LSO	RIR

See Addendum (p. 650) for abbreviations. R and L at the beginning of each abbreviation here signify right and left.

Muscle sequelae of these laws

These are the series of changes that take place in line with Hering's and Sherrington's laws of ocular movement:

- Primary underaction
- Overaction of contralateral synergist (Hering's law of equal innervation)
- Contracture of ipsilateral antagonist (Sherrington's law of reciprocal innervation)
- Secondary inhibition of contralateral antagonist (Hering's law).

The overaction of the contralateral synergist will occur at the onset of the defect but the other sequelae take time to develop.

Testing smooth pursuit ocular movements

The patient sits straight, with a straight head and without spectacles.

A light fixation target is held at a distance of 50cm.

The light is initially held in the primary position, the corneal reflections observed and a cover test performed. The light is slowly moved into each of the extreme positions of gaze in turn. The corneal reflections are observed and any asymmetry noted.

A cover test is carried out to detect any abnormal movement and to differentiate between defects found on version (both eyes) and duction testing (one eye).

- The light is moved back into the primary position.
- The patient must not move the head to look, only the eyes.
- The patient is asked to report any diplopia, pain/discomfort in any positions of gaze.
- Any abnormal movements are noted and are compared to any manifest deviation present in the primary position.
- Changes in palpebral fissures, lids and globe position should be noted, e.g. ptosis, lid retraction, lid lag, globe retraction.
- Any nystagmus or jerky eye movements should be noted.

Recording smooth pursuit ocular movements

Ocular movements can be recorded in various ways: written in descriptive form, graphic or photographically.

Hess and Lees Screen can be used to record ocular movements. These are also useful in quantifying the degree of defect (Figure 23.5).

When recording ocular movements, it is important to note:

- The type of defect, i.e. Overaction/underaction or restriction
- Which eye
- Which position(s)
- Size of defect, i.e. slight, small, moderate, marked or numerical grading.

Underaction

This is where the eye does not move fully on a vergence movement (both eyes open), but on duction (where the other fixing eye is covered) the eye moves fully. For example, on dextroelevation the right eye does not move fully up but when the left eye is covered, the right eye moves up to take up fixation. Underactions are usually associated with defects in the neurogenic supply to the extra ocular muscle(s).

This is recorded as:

small underaction of the right eye on dextroelevation.

Overaction

This is where the eye moves past the position that it should be in and moves back to take up fixation when the other eye is covered. For example, on dextroelevation when the right eye fixates the light, the left eye moves upwards. When the right eye is covered, the left eye moves down to take up fixation. Overactions arise due to neurogenic supply defects to synergist or antagonist muscles.

This is recorded as:

small overaction of the left eye on dextroelevation.

As mentioned previously, the development of muscle sequelae means that an underaction of a muscle of one eye in a particular position of gaze is accompanied by overaction of its contralateral synergist. In the above example, the underacting muscle is the right superior rectus and the overacting muscle is the left inferior oblique.

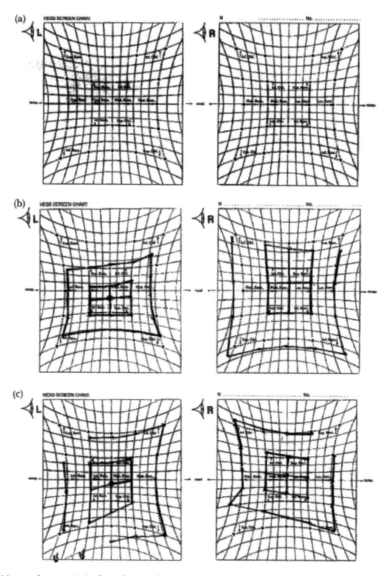

Figure 23.5 Hess charts: (a) the chart; (b) mechanical limitation of elevation in the left eye; (c) right fourth nerve palsy.

Restriction/Limitation

This is where the eye does not move fully on either version or duction. These restrictions arise due to mechanical defects of the extraocular muscle itself or lesions within the orbit that mechanically restrict the movement of the eye.

Written notation

As seen in the above example, this indicates the size (small), action (underaction), eye (right) and direction of gaze (dextroelevation).

Graphic method of notation of ocular movements

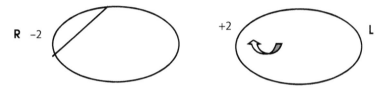

Figure 23.6 This is a graphic recording of the same ocular movements.

 indicates overaction

 indicates overaction

Slight $= \pm 1$ Small $= \pm 2$ Moderate $= \pm 3$ Marked $= \pm 4$

Hess/Lees screen

This test plots the function of the extraocular muscles and is used in cases of incomitant squint, paralytic squint and to provide a baseline in cases such as TED where defective ocular movements change during the course of the disease. It also provides a record of improving eye movements in a recovering muscle palsy.

The test is based on foveal projection, and therefore cannot be used in patients with suppression or abnormal retinal correspondence, Hering's and Sherrington's laws of innervation and dissociation of the eyes.

Method

The patient sits in front of a screen, which is a large version of the grid on the chart (see Figure 23.5). Their eyes are dissociated either by red and green goggles (Hess screen) or by a double-sided plane mirror (Lees screen). Each eye is tested in turn as the patient fixates on the different points on the grid and indicates with a pointer where they see the points projected. The position of the points is then recorded on the chart.

Interpretation

The position of the central dot in each field indicates the deviation in the primary position.

Each small square on the grid subtends 5° so the measurement of the deviation can be calculated in the different positions of gaze.

As it is based on foveal projection, patients must have normal retinal correspondence; otherwise the field plotted will not be an accurate representation of the eye position. On the chart the position of the field reflects the position of the eye; the higher field is the higher eye, as opposed to diplopia where the higher image belongs to the lower eye.

As a result of Hering's law, the smaller field belongs to the eye with limitation or underaction of movement; underactions are noted by the inward displacement of the dots towards the centre of the chart. There will be maximum displacement in the direction of action of the affected muscle. Overactions have an outward displacement of dots, with the maximum displacement occurring in the field of action of the ipsilateral antagonist or contralateral synergist, depending upon the stage of muscle sequelae.

A squashed or narrow field indicates a mechanical restriction of ocular movements (see Figure 23.5c).

Orthoptics

Orthoptists investigate, diagnose and treat disorders of binocular vision, ocular motility and visual development. The role of the orthoptist, in line with other non-medical professions within ophthalmology, is changing to encompass additional roles, such as glaucoma and low vision assessment and management. The work includes patients of all ages, especially children.

Up to the age of 7, about 8% of children have impaired vision (as a result of a need for spectacles) and 5% have a squint. Visual development can be monitored from birth and abnormalities diagnosed at an early stage; no child or baby is too young to be assessed by the orthoptist. Vision develops quickly during the first year of life and finishes developing at about 7 years of age, so early detection and treatment lead to a more successful outcome.

The orthoptist normally sees adults if they complain of diplopia. This could be sudden onset or a more long-standing problem. The orthoptist's role is to detect which muscles are causing the problem and which cranial nerves may be affected and deduce where the lesion may be. Diplopia has many causes, e.g. trauma, cerebrovascular accident (CVA), tumour, hypertension, diabetes or thyroid disorders. It may also be the first sign of multiple sclerosis (MS) or myasthenia gravis, so an inaccurate diagnosis by the orthoptist can have serious consequences for the patient (McNamara 1995).

Squint (strabismus)

Strabismus or squint (colloquially known as 'turn', 'cross eyed', 'wall eyed') is a condition where the eyes are not parallel, so only one of the visual axes is directed towards the fixation object, whereas the other deviates horizontally, vertically or a combination of both. A squint can be manifest (heterotropia) or latent (heterophoria). It may be concomitant (the same in all positions of gaze) or incomitant (paralytic), varying according to the position of gaze and the affected muscle (Ansons & Davis 2001).

Heterotropia

This is the term for a manifest deviation where one of the visual axes is not directed towards the fixation point. It may be constant (present all the time) or intermittent (present only at certain distances or under certain circumstances, e.g. when tired or unwell):

- Esotropia: Convergent squint – one eye deviates nasally, i.e. turns in
- Exotropia: Divergent squint – one eye deviates temporally, i.e. turns out
- Hypertropia: One eye deviates up
- Hypotropia: One eye deviates down.

Heterophoria

This is the term for a latent deviation where both eyes are directed towards the fixation point when both eyes are open, but deviate on dissociation, i.e. when one eye is covered.

- Esophoria: Latent convergent squint
- Exophoria: Latent divergent squint
- Hyperphoria: Latent upwards deviation
- Hypophoria: Latent downwards deviation
- Concomitant squint.

Concomitant squints are predominantly horizontal and the size of the deviation is the same whichever eye is fixing in the primary position. The onset is in childhood, usually before the age of 6 years, with infantile strabismus developing between 2 and 6 months of age.

Aetiology

Anything that disrupts the development of binocular vision during the developmental period will result in squint and there are a number of factors that may contribute to this.

Heredity: Around 60% of children with squint have a close relative with a squint and a child with a parent who has a squint is four times more likely to develop one.

Refractive error: Uncorrected refractive error can influence the development of squint; specifically moderate hypermetropia which is associated with accommodative esotropia.

Neurological defects: Pre-term, low-birthweight and brain-damaged babies, especially those with cerebral palsy, have a higher incidence of squint.

Febrile illness: Squint is often reported after chickenpox or measles but often these children have a predisposition for squint and the illness precipitated it rather than caused it.

Incomitant (paralytic) squint

In incomitant squints, the size of deviation differs depending on the position of gaze and according to which eye is fixing, with the size of deviation increasing in one or more positions of gaze depending on the underlying cause of the underaction or limitation of movement. The aetiology may be:

- Neurogenic palsy, as a result of a cranial nerve palsy of nerve III, IV or VI

- Mechanical restriction caused by elements within the orbit that either interfere with muscle contraction and relaxation or prevent free movement of the globe (Ansons & Davis 2014); causes such as orbital fracture, thyroid eye disease, etc.

- Myogenic, palsy due to a problem affecting the muscle itself, e.g. caused by myasthenia gravis, orbital myositis, rhabdomyosarcoma.

Detection of squint

The methods of detection are observation of appearance, observation of corneal reflections and the cover test.

Observation of appearance

Any obvious ocular deviation, abnormal head posture, abnormal lid position or other anomaly, which may indicate an oculomotor defect, should be noted.

Corneal reflections

The patient is asked to look at a pen light held at a distance of 33cm, and the positions of the corneal reflections in each eye are noted. If the corneal reflections are central and symmetrical the eyes are straight, but if the reflections are asymmetrical there is a manifest deviation present.

The reflection will be central in the fixing eye and displaced in the deviating eye. Temporal displacement indicates a convergent squint, medial displacement a divergent squint and vertical displacement a vertical squint.

The amount of displacement also indicates the size of squint: 1mm of displacement represents about 7° of deviation so if the corneal reflection is on the border of the pupil the deviation is about 15°.

Pseudostrabismus

The corneal reflection test is also useful for detecting a pseudostrabismus or pseudosquint.

Often children have flat noses with the presence of skin folds on the inner canthi, called epicanthic folds. This results from the fact that their facial features are not fully formed. Many babies and young children may appear to have a convergent squint as a result of their facial appearance but the corneal reflections will be central and symmetrical in either eye, showing that the eyes are straight. Epicanthus normally resolves as the facial skeleton develops.

Cover test

This is the most accurate assessment of a deviation and, as Ansons and Davis state (2014), the cornerstone of the investigation of squint. It is an objective dissociative test, which elicits the presence of a latent or manifest squint, relying on observing the behaviour of the eyes while each eye is covered and uncovered in turn.

The cover test is performed for near (33cm), distance (6m) and far distance (in the case of divergent deviations) and with and without spectacles. The test is carried out first with a pen light for near and then with an accommodative target.

There are two types of cover test:

- The cover–uncover test
- The alternate cover test.

Performing the cover–uncover test

The test consists of two parts: cover, then uncover.

Part 1 – cover:

- The patient sits comfortably facing the examiner.
- The patient fixes a pen light held in the primary position (straight ahead) at 33cm while the examiner observes the corneal reflections.
- One eye is covered and any movement of the uncovered eye to take up fixation is noted.
- If there is no movement to fix, the test is repeated, covering the other eye, and any movement of the uncovered eye is noted.
- A movement out to fix indicates esotropia and a movement in to fix indicates exotropia. A movement down to fix indicates hypertropia, whereas a movement up to fix indicates hypotropia. An inward rotation of the eye to take up fixation indicates an Extorted eye and any outward rotation of the eye to take up fixation indicates an Intorted eye.

Part 2 – uncover:

The test is repeated but now the eye behind the occluder is observed.

- The right eye is occluded for a few seconds and then the cover is removed, with the examiner noting any movement of the right eye.

- If the eye moves out as the cover is removed, the eye has been deviated inwardly, indicating an esophoria or latent convergent squint.
- If the eye moves in when the cover is removed, it has been deviated outwards, indicating an exophoria or latent divergent squint.
- Downward movement indicates a hyperphoria, whereas upward movement indicates a hypophoria.
- The test is repeated by occluding the other eye.

No movement indicates orthophoria (no manifest or latent deviation).

The cover–uncover test is repeated, using an accommodative target for near, suitable for the vision and age of the patient, then at 6m and, if required, at the far distance.

Performing the alternate cover test

This is the repeated alternate covering of each eye in turn so that binocular vision is prevented and fusional stimuli are eliminated. It reveals the total deviation: tropia + phoria. It should be performed only after the cover–uncover test, otherwise it will be impossible to differentiate between the manifest and latent components of the squint:

- The patient fixes the light or accommodative target while the examiner covers the right eye for about 2 seconds.
- The occluder is quickly transferred to cover the left eye completely, ensuring that there is no opportunity for binocular interaction between the two eyes.
- The left eye is covered for a couple of seconds and then the occluder is moved back to the right eye.
- As the occluder is moved alternately between the two eyes a few more times, the eye movements are noted. The eyes will be completely dissociated and so the maximum deviation will be elicited.
- When the cover is removed the eyes return to their pre-dissociated state and the examiner notes the speed and smoothness of recovery.

Information gained from the cover test

- Direction of deviation: eso-/exo-/hyper-/hypo-/torsional
- Type of deviation: manifest or latent
- Size: small/slight/moderate/marked
- Variations between near and distance: this aids in the classification of squint
- Comitance or incomitance: if the size of the deviation differs according to which eye is fixing

- The effect of any optical correction on the deviation
- The effect of accommodation on the deviation

In a latent squint, the rate and speed of recovery (the speed at which the eye moves to take up fixation following removal of the occluder) to binocular single vision (BSV) indicates the ability to control the deviation.

Management of squint

Concomitant squint

The aims of management of a concomitant squint are to:

- Attain and maintain the best possible visual acuity by correcting any refractive error and treating amblyopia
- Achieve BSV where there is the potential for it
- Restore a good cosmetic appearance.

The methods of achieving these aims are:

- Conservative
- Surgical
- A combination of the two.

Conservative treatment

Optical/spectacles. All children attending an orthoptic clinic will have a cycloplegic refraction, fundus and media examination carried out by the ophthalmologist or optometrist. If there is a significant refractive error, spectacles will be prescribed:

- To correct vision
- To correct the squint – certain lenses can reduce the angle of a squint and possibly restore BSV, e.g. a hypermetropic correction in an esotropia may reduce the angle of squint and may allow it to be controlled to an esophoria.

Prisms may also be used to correct a deviation to restore BSV

Occlusion (patching) or drug penalisation

These are the most effective ways to treat amblyopia (lazy eye). The aim of occlusion is to achieve the best possible visual acuity in the amblyopic or lazy eye by occluding or temporarily blurring the vision in the good eye using a cycloplegic drug (usually Atropine). If a patch is used, it should preferably be on the face (to avoid peeping) either full time (FTTO), i.e. all day, or part time (PTTO), i.e. for a specific period. The amblyopia studies have shown that in children aged 3–7 with severe amblyopia, full time patching produced a result similar to that of patching for only 6 hours each day and that in moderate amblyopia, in this age group, 2 hours of patching produced similar effects to 6. While amblyopia is most responsive to treatment in children up to age 7, it has been demonstrated that even previously treated amblyopia responds to 2–6 hours of patching in children aged 7–12. In patients aged 13–17 visual acuity improved in almost half those that had never been treated and a quarter of those who had previously been treated with patching Holmes *et al.* 2003, Repka *et al.* 2003, Scheiman *et al.* 2005 Pediatric Eye Disease Investigator Group (PEDIG) 2009).

The optimum results are achieved from occlusion therapy if:

- The treatment is commenced as soon as possible after onset of the amblyopia
- The child is in the critical period of visual development, i.e. up to the age of about 7 years
- Spectacles, if needed, are worn with the patch or atropine
- Most importantly of all, compliance is good, the patch is worn as prescribed and the child attends regularly.

Occlusion is continued until equal, or the best possible, vision has been achieved.

Orthoptic exercises

Exercises are used in a number of different ways and in different types of squint. They are most frequently used to help a patient control a latent squint, which may be causing asthenopic symptoms, i.e. headache, blurred vision or diplopia, or to teach control of an intermittent squint.

Surgical treatment

Surgery is performed to:

- Restore BSV where this is possible
- Improve a cosmetically poor appearance.

The following are the two main methods of surgical procedure used in squint surgery:

- Recession – weakening: Where the muscle is detached from its insertion and reattached further back towards its origin.
- Resection – strengthening: Where the muscle is detached from the globe, a piece is cut out, thereby shortening the muscle, and the shortened muscle is then reattached to the original muscle insertion position.

The choice and amount of surgery depend on the type and size of the squint. In the case of a left esotropia, where the left eye turns in and therefore needs to be pulled laterally into a straight ahead position, the left medial rectus will be recessed or weakened and the left lateral rectus will be resected or strengthened.

Incomitant squint

The aims of management of an incomitant squint are to:

- Diagnose which muscles are underacting and overacting
- Establish the type of limitation, i.e. neurogenic, mechanical or myogenic
- Differentiate between a long-standing and a recently acquired palsy
- Diagnose and treat the cause of the palsy
- Monitor the progress of the condition by maintaining an accurate and repeatable record of the condition
- Alleviate symptoms until there is spontaneous recovery, or squint surgery can be carried out if full recovery does not take place.

Orthoptic assessment

An orthoptic assessment uses different methods to assess and measure visual acuity, detect the presence of squint or abnormal ocular movements, to measure any deviation present and to assess binocular functions (see also Rowe 2012).

There follows an overview of a basic orthoptic assessment, giving examples of orthoptic terminology that may be seen in an orthoptic report.

History

A detailed history will always be taken, eliciting the reason for attendance, what has been noticed, what the symptoms are, when it first occurred and how often it is noticed now, if there were any precipitating factors and if there has been any previous ophthalmic treatment.

Visual acuity

This is always assessed monocularly to ascertain the level of visual acuity in each eye. The test used depends on the age and ability of the patient. LogMAR-based tests are accepted as being the most accurate.

Cover test

This is carried out (as above) to establish the type of deviation.

Smooth pursuit ocular movements

These are assessed (as above) to determine if there is an ocular motility problem and which muscles are involved. Other ocular movement systems may be assessed, sacaddic, vestibular, vergence, opto-kinetic, in order to localise the site of the lesion causing the ocular motility defect.

Binocular functions

The aim of the assessment of binocular functions is to determine if the patient has binocular vision or the potential for binocular vision, as this will affect the course of treatment undertaken. Tests used to assess binocular functions are:

- Bagolini glasses
- Worth's lights
- Prism fusion range (PFR) or prism reflex test in young children
- Stereoscopic tests, e.g. Wirt, TNO, Frisby.

Measurement

A squint can be measured using the following methods:

- By approximation using the corneal reflections (see above), recorded in degrees.
- By the prism cover test (PCT), recorded in prism dioptres (Δ), $2\Delta = 1°$. Prisms are used in conjunction with the cover test to neutralise the movement of the eyes and so determine the size of the squint.
- By the synoptophore, recorded in degrees.

Examples of orthoptic reports

Case 1: Child aged 4 years

VA	c gls R 0.4 LogMAR (6/15 Snellens)	L 0.0 LogMAR (6/6 Snellens)	Vision with spectacles using Keeler Crowded LogMAR
Cover test	c gls n & d sl/mod RCS s gls n & d mod RCS		Right convergent squint Increasing without spectacles
Smooth pursuit ocular movements	Slight limitation RE on abduction		
Convergence	with deviation to nose		
PCT	c gls	n 20ΔPBO d 18ΔPBO	Measurement with prisms
	s gls	n 40ΔPBO d 35ΔPBO	
Synoptophore	c gls	obj + 10° subj R suppression	Measurement with synoptophore
	s gls	obj + 20°	

Diagnosis: partially accommodative right esotropia with amblyopia

Treatment: PTTO LE – 2 hours a day (part-time total occlusion left eye)

To see again: 4/52 (4 weeks)

Case 2: Adult aged 60

VA	s gls R 0.0	L 0.1 LogMAR (6/7.5 Snellens)
	LogMAR (6/6 Snellens)	

CT n sl Right hypertropia c diplopia
d sl latent Right hyperphoria c fair recovery – diplopia before recovery

OM moderate underation (u/a) RE on laevodepression
moderate updrift RE of laevoversion
moderate (overaction) o/a RE on laevoelevation
slight underaction LE on laevoelevation

Diplopia: vertical for near in all pos > separation on laevodepression
Saccades: horiz + vert – normal response to 8cm
Convergence
(Conv)

PFR n no demonstrable fusion   Prism fusion range
d 8ΔPBO – 2^ PBI

PCT n 10Δ prism base down RE   Prism cover test
D 4Δ prism base down RE

Diplopia joined for near c 8Δ BD RE BSV proven using Worth's lights control test for binocular vision

Worth's lights test n vertical diplopia image from RE
lower
d BSV resp
n with 8Δ Prism base down PBD RE
BSV response
c 8Δ BD RE 55 seconds of arc

Frisby Stereotest   Stereopsis

Lees no, 1 Right superior oblique palsy

Diagnosis: recently acquired Right IVth nerve palsy

Diplopia: joined with 8Δ prism BD RE

For further investigations

Addendum
Orthoptic abbreviations

ACS	alternating convergent squint
ADS	alternating divergent squint
AHP	abnormal head posture
ARC	abnormal retinal correspondence
BD	base down
BE	both eyes
BEO	both eyes open
BI	base in
BO	base out
BSV	binocular single vision
BT or BTX	botulinum toxin
BU	base up
BV	binocular vision
BVA	binocular visual acuity
CC or CAC	Cardiff acuity cards (vision test for babies)
CI	convergence insufficiency
c/o	complains of
Conv	convergence/convergent
CPEO	chronic progressive external ophthalmoplegia
CT	cover test
D	dioptre
Dep	depression
Dist	distance
Div	divergence/divergent
DVD	dissociated vertical deviation
DVM	delayed visual maturation
EE	either eye
EF	eccentric fixation
Elev	elevation
EP	esophoria
Eso	esotropia/-phoria
Exo	exotropia/-phoria
ET	esotropia
FCPL	forced choice preferential looking (vision test for babies)
FEE	fixing either eye
FLE	fixing left eye
FRE	fixing right eye
FTTO	full-time total occlusion
H/A	headaches
HES(1)	hospital eye service prescription
HM	hand movements
INO	internuclear ophthalmoplegia
IO	inferior oblique
IR	inferior rectus
Kay Pics	Kay pictures (vision test for children)
LCS	left convergent squint
LDS	left divergent squint

LE	left eye
LogMAR	LogMAR based tests of visual acuity (most commonly used – Keeler Crowded, Bailey Lovey, Lighthouse)
LPS	levator palpebrae superioris
LR	lateral rectus
L/R	left over right (left hypertropia/-phoria or right hypotropia/-phoria)
LVA	low visual aid or left visual acuity
MR	medial rectus
N	nerve
NAD	no apparent deviation
NPA	near point of accommodation
NPC	near point of convergence
NRC	normal retinal correspondence
NPL	no perception of light
NVA	near visual acuity
o/a	overaction
OKN	optokinetic nystagmus
OM	ocular movements
PBD	prism base down
PBI	prism base in
PBO	prism base out
PBU	prism base up
PCT	prism cover test
PFR	prism fusion range
PH	pin hole
PL	perception of light
PMT	post-mydriatic test
PRT	prism reflection test
PTTO	part-time total occlusion
RAF	Royal Air Force rule measurement of convergence and accommodation
RAPD	relative afferent pupillary defect
RCS	right convergent squint
RDS	right divergent squint
Recess	recession
Resect	resection
R/L	right over left (right hypertropia/-phoria or left hypotropia/-phoria)
ROP	retinopathy of prematurity
rr	rapid recovery (as in latent deviations)
RVA	right visual acuity
SI rec	slow recovery (as in latent deviations)
Sn	Snellen's
SO	superior oblique
SP	simultaneous perception
SR	superior rectus
u/a	underaction
VA	visual acuity
VEP	visual evoked potential
VER	visual evoked response
VF	visual field
VOR	vestibulo-ocular reflex
XP	exophoria
XT	exotropia

References

Ansons, A. & Davis, H. (2014) *Diagnosis and Management of Ocular Motility Disorders.* 4th edn. Oxford: Wiley Blackwell.

Bowling, B. (2015) *Kanski's Clinical Ophthalmology, a systematic approach.* 8th edn. London: Elsevier.

Bron, A., Tripathi, R. & Tripathi, B. (1998) *Wolff's Anatomy of the Eye and Orbit.* 8th edn. Oxford: Taylor & Francis.

Char, D.H., Miller, T. & Kroll, S. (1997) Orbital metastases: diagnosis and course. *British Journal of Ophthalmology.* **81**(5), 386–90.

Cleary, M. (2000) Efficacy of occlusion for strabismic amblyopia: can an optimal duration be identified? *British Journal of Ophthalmology.* **84**, 572–78.

Costin, B.R., Perry, J.D. & Foster, J.A. (2013) Classification of Orbital Tumors. *Clinical Ophthalmic Oncology.* **04** November, 9–14

European Group on Graves Orbitopathy. http://www.eugogo.eu (accessed 28 September 2016).

Harrington, J.N. (2015) *Orbital Cellulitis.* http://emedicine.medscape.com/article/1217858-overview (accessed 19 September 2016).

Holmes, J.M., Kraker, R.T., Beck, R.W., Birch, E.E., Cotter, S.A., Everett, D.F., Hertle, R.W., Quinn, G.E., Repka, M.X., Schieman, M.M. & Wallace D.K., Pediatric Eye Disease Investigator Group (2003) A randomized trial of prescribed patching regimens for treatment of severe amblyopia in children. *Ophthalmology.* **110**(11), 2075–87.

Leatherbarrow, B. (2004) *Oculoplastic Surgery.* London: Taylor & Francis Group.

Levine, M. & Larson, D. (1993) 'Orbital tumours' in R. Tenzel (ed.) *Orbit and Oculoplastics. Textbook of ophthalmology,* Vol. 4. London: Mosby-Wolfe.

McNamara, R. (1995) 'Orthoptics' in J.P. Perry & A.B. Tullo (eds) *Care of the Ophthalmic Patient.* 2nd edn. Springer.

Newell, F.W. (1996) *Ophthalmology: Principles and concepts.* 8th edn. St Louis, MO: Mosby.

Kanski, J. & Bowling, B. (2011). *Clinical Ophthalmology: A Systematic Approach.* 7th Edn. London: Elsevier.

Pediatric Eye Disease Investigator Group (PEDIG) (2009) Treatment of severe amblyopia with weekend atropine: Results from two randomized clinical trials. *J AAAPOS.* **13**(3), 258–63

Phan, L.T., Hwang, T.N. & McCulley, T.J. (2012) Evisceration in the Modern Age. *Middle Eastern and African Journal of Ophthalmology.* **19**(1), 24–33.

Rowe, F.J. (2012) *Clinical Orthoptics.* Oxford: Wiley & Sons.

Repka, M.X., Beck, R.W., Holmes, J.M., Birch, E.E., Chandler, D.L., Cotter, S.A., Hurtle, R.W., Kraker, R.T., Moke, P.S., Quinn, G.E. & Scheiman, M.M. (2003) A randomized trial of patching regimens for treatment of moderate amblyopia in children. *Archives of Ophthalmology.* **121**(5), 603–11.

Scheiman, M.M., Hertle, R.W., Beck, R.W., Edwards, A.R., Cotter, S.A., Crouch, E.R., Cruz, O.A., Davitt, B.V., Holmes, J.M., Lyon, D.W., Repka, M.X., Sala, N.A., Silber, D.I., Suh, D.W., Tamkins, S.M. Pediatric Eye Disease Investigator Group (2005) Randomized trial of treatment of amblyopia in children aged 7 to 17 years. *Archives of Ophthalmology.* **123** (4), 437–47.

Snell, R.S. & Lemp, M.A. (1998) *Clinical Anatomy of the Eye.* 2nd edn. USA: Blackwell Science.

Vestergaard, P. (2002) Smoking and thyroid disorders – a meta-analysis. *European Journal of Endocrinology.* **146**(2), 153–61.

Wiersinga, W.M. & Kahaly, G.J. (2010) *Graves' Orbitopathy – A multi disciplinary approach. Questions and Answers.* 2nd edn. Amsterdam: Karger.

CHAPTER TWENTY-FOUR

The visual and pupillary pathways and neuro-ophthalmology

Yvonne Needham

The complexity of the visual system though the brain's hemispheres often leads to confusion, but knowledge of the primary pathways and their progress will assist the ophthalmic practitioner in supporting patients with visual, pupillary and neurological problems. The anatomy and physiology of the visual pathway must be understood in order to put it into perspective for patients, to explain and help them deal with the issues that they face with a variety of conditions.

This chapter provides an overview and a basis for further study. It initially identifies the relevant anatomy and physiology of the visual pathway, from the optic nerve to the visual cortex, and goes on to discuss how damage to the pathway affects the patient's vision and in some cases movement and balance. In some conditions, medical or surgical interventions may be advised, and in all cases patients and their relatives will need advice and support in managing their condition and maintaining a healthy lifestyle. Visual disturbances can often lead to isolation and loss of confidence. For ophthalmic health care practitioners, there are several websites that support the content of this chapter and are a good resource. These are included in the references.

Components of the visual pathway

The primary visual pathway in humans consists of the retina (see Chapter 22), optic nerve, optic chiasma, optic tracts, lateral geniculate bodies, optic radiations and the visual cortex (Figure 24.1). The visual pathways travel horizontally though the brain, using parallel systems in each hemisphere, from the retina to the cortex. The whole pathway is regarded as part of the 'central nervous system', growing forward from the brain into the orbital cavities.

Optic nerve

The second cranial nerve is known as the optic nerve. Each optic nerve is about 51mm in length, commencing at the optic nerve head in the globe and ending as the two optic nerves joined at the chiasma situated in the third ventricle. It is surrounded by cerebrospinal fluid contained within the meninges. The optic nerve contains oligodendrocytes, astrocytes and microglia, rather than the Schwann cells, fibroblasts and macrophages of peripheral nerves. It has the same structure as the brain's white matter and therefore has no powers of regeneration. It is not myelinated in the same way as peripheral nerves (by oligodendrocytes rather than Schwann cells) and is covered by the meninges (pia, arachnoid and dura mater). It is the only cranial nerve that is visible and can be seen though the eye at the optic disc.

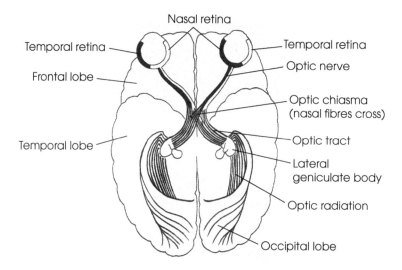

Figure 24.1 Visual pathways.

Visual development commences with the optic stalk identified at day 27 of foetal gestation; by week 8 the ganglion cells of the optic nerve and the optic nerve sheath can be identified clearly. The optic nerve can be split into four distinct sections: intraocular, orbital, intracanalicular and intracranial (Forrester *et al.* 2016).

The intraocular portion of the optic nerve is about 1mm in length. The optic disc is the commencement of the optic nerve, and is visible when the eye is viewed internally though the pupil. The optic disc is pale in comparison to the retina and, on examination, may appear yellowish and vertically ovoid. The optic disc is about 1.5mm in diameter; it contains 1.2 million ganglion cell axons in the nerve fibre layer, which converge to form a raised area known as the papilla. The protrusion of the optic disc through the retina creates an area with no visual receptors – hence the blind spot.

The optic nerve exits the eye though the choroid and sclera. At the exit point the nerve fibres thicken, doubling the size of the optic nerve. In some individuals the optic nerve exits the sclera at less than a 90° angle. This elevates the disc margin, giving it a tilted appearance known as tilted disc. Tilted discs are usually small and bilateral and are often associated with astigmatism (Ragge & Easty 1999). When viewing the optic disc, this is considered as a common normal variant.

The blood supply to this part of the optic nerve is by branches from four sources: central retinal vessels, scleral vessels (circle of Zinn–Haller), choroidal vessels and pial vessels. The first three are derived from the central retinal artery, with the pial vessels from the internal carotid artery.

The orbital portion of the optic nerve is about 30mm long and extends backwards medially from the sclera to the optic canal at the apex of the orbit. It is covered by the meninges and surrounded by the four rectus muscles. The dura and arachnoid blend with the sclera. The orbital portion of the optic nerve has an S-shaped bend, which enables the full range of eye movement and up to 8mm of proptosis without the optic nerve being stretched. The central retinal vessels travel though this space before entering the optic nerve 1cm behind the globe. The central retinal vessels must cross the subarachnoid space, making them vulnerable to compression when raised intercranial pressure occurs.

The intracanalicular portion of the optic nerve is about 10mm in length and passes though the optic canal, accompanied by the optic artery and the sympathetic nerves. The optic canal is formed by the two roots of the lesser wing of the sphenoid bone.

The intracranial portion of the optic nerve is 10mm in length and travels from the optic canal medially backwards and slightly upwards, coming together with the other nerve to form the optic chiasma in the fold of the third ventricle. The olfactory tract, frontal lobe and anterior cerebral arteries lie above the optic nerve with the internal carotid arteries laterally.

Optic chiasma

The optic chiasma is situated at the junction of the floor and the anterior wall of the third ventricle. It is quadrangular in shape and approximately 12 × 8mm in size, consisting of a flattened bundle of nerve fibres. The posterior angles form the optic tract. In the chiasma, the fibres from the nasal half of each retina (those that collect light from the temporal side), including the nasal half of the macula, cross over and enter the optic tract on the opposite side. The fibres from the temporal retina pass backwards along the optic tract on the same side. This partial crossing of the nerve fibres is essential for binocular vision.

Optochiasmal glioma may have its origins in the differentiation of cells during month 4 of foetal development.

The optic tracts

The optic tracts extend as cylindrical bands of fibres from the chiasma backwards towards the midbrain. Most of the fibres terminate in the lateral geniculate body and are concerned with conscious vision. Around 10% pass the lateral geniculate body and enter the pretectal nucleus; these are concerned with visual body and light reflexes. The nerve fibres conducting these reflexes synapse in the pretectal nuclei with neurons connecting to the Edinger–Westphal nuclei.

Lateral geniculate bodies

The lateral geniculate bodies are oval in shape and are highly differentiated structures lying in the thalamus. The function of these bodies is to transmit the visual information from the eye, via the lateral root of the optic tract, to the cortex. As a result of the crossing of fibres in the chiasma, each of the lateral geniculate bodies receives information from both retinas (Forrester *et al.* 2016).

Optic radiations

Optic radiations consist of nerve fibre bundles, the bodies of which lie in the lateral geniculate bodies with their axons terminating in the visual cortex of the occipital lobe. As a result of their path though the temporal lobe along the lateral aspect of the lateral ventricle, they are of major clinical significance because they are frequently disturbed during cerebrovascular disturbances or tumour growth. The optic radiations stimulate the whole of the visual cortex. Those stimulating the lower visual cortex carry information from the peripheral retina and those supplying the upper visual cortex carry information from the macular area of the retina.

The visual cortex

The visual cortex is found in the occipital lobe of the brain. Very simplistically, the cortex differentiates between impulses sent from the peripheral and those sent from the central retina. Damage to any part of the visual pathway will result in characteristic field loss.

Congenital optic nerve problems
Malformation of the optic nerve head

Failure of the posterior optic fissure to close leads to the formation of an optic nerve head coloboma with bulging of the sclera. The coloboma may be seen as a small recess on the rim of the disc. This will be associated with visual loss resulting from the leakage of fluid from the optic pit, and formation of exudates beneath the macula (Forrester *et al.* 2016).

Axial coloboma or morning glory syndrome

This presents with a symmetrically enlarged and excavated optic disc, which may be unilateral or bilateral (Forrester *et al.* 2016). This malformation of the optic nerve causes a displacement into the optic meninges of the optic nerve; the meninges contain fat and smooth muscle. This distortion of the normal optic nerve structure results in severe visual loss and the nerve impulses cannot be transmitted for interpretation in the visual cortex.

Congenital optic disc abnormalities

Optic disc colobomas prevent visual development in babies and children. It is essential that children's visual development and stimulation be maximised from an early stage. Parents will need information about this condition and the effects it will have on their child's sight. Often, parents who have children with congenital abnormalities feel responsible for the child's problems. It is important to allow the parents time to come to terms with their child's condition and it would not be unexpected for the parents to go through the stages of grieving. Parents need to know that their reaction to the news that they have been given is normal, and what to expect in terms of the rollercoaster of emotion that they will go through during the years to come. It is essential to make parents aware of services that exist to support them with their child's visual impairment and how to access that support. Referrals need to be made promptly so parents are not left for a long period without support after the initial diagnosis.

Ophthalmic nurses may rarely see these children and parents when they visit as outpatients, so it is important to let parents know that they can still access support from outpatient clinics. It is therefore valuable to make information available about the locations of local child development centres and educational development centres and their telephone numbers. Specialist child development teams will assist parents in caring for their child before they start school; and educational development teams will support the child and parents though the school years. These services (along with mobility officers and local, national and international organisations for people with visual disability) will assist the parents in enabling the child to maximise the vision that they have. Parents will need ongoing support from social workers, counsellors and health visitors because having a child with such a condition requires adjustments to be made to family life, and the potential for isolation is great in families with children with disabilities (Goffman 1990, Daniels 2001).

Optic nerve hypoplasia (ONH)

This may be accompanied by other ocular or forebrain abnormalities and visual function may be good or poor. Where optic disc hypoplasia is bilateral, there is poor vision and nystagmus. As a rule, the smaller the disc, the poorer the visual acuity. Although the cause is unknown, various studies have linked a number of maternal and pregnancy-related issues to the development of ONH. Maternal diabetes has been linked to optic disc hypoplasia (Liu *et al.* 2010), as has intake of toxic substances such as alcohol, quinine, phenytoin and lysergic acid diethylamide (LSD) (Glaser 1990). A recent study (Garcia Filion *et al.* 2010) challenged many previously suggested risk factors such as alcohol and substance use, but confirmed young maternal age and primaparity as associated risk factors, also suggesting maternal weight loss and early gestation bleeding as possible correlates.

ONH is one of the leading causes of childhood vision impairment in the US and Europe, affecting up to 12% of visually impaired children (Hatton *et al.* 2007). While other causes of visual impairment have reduced, ONH appears to have risen dramatically (Blohme *et al.* 2000). Care of the child and parents will follow similar routes to those identified above for optic nerve coloboma. However, if parents have researched the condition, older studies on causation may lead to feelings of guilt and blame, and ophthalmic clinicians must be able to share up-to-date findings and resources to help parents come to terms with their child's condition.

Nystagmus

Normally, when the head rotates about any axis, the place of distant visual images is maintained by rotating the eyes in the opposite direction on the same axis. The semicircular canals within the vestibular system sense head turning, sending signals to the nuclei for eye movement in the brain. A response is sent to the extraocular muscles, allowing the gaze to remain on one object as the head moves. Nystagmus occurs when the vestibulo-ocular reflex is damaged, or does not develop effectively, often due to lack of stimulation. Nystagmus may be optokinetic (eye related) or vestibular (inner ear related). Optokinetic nystagmus tends to develop in children where central vision is lost before the age of 2 years – movements may be horizontal (right, left), vertical (up, down) or rotary and this is known as sensory defect nystagmus.

Some children are born with nystagmus and this is known as congenital idiopathic nystagmus. Neurological nystagmus is the result of lack of development of the mechanism of smooth pursuit.

There are three types of movement, which are known as:

- Pendulum – movements of equal velocity in each direction (similar to a pendulum)
- Jerk nystagmus – slow movement in one direction and fast in the other

- Mixed nystagmus – pendulum movements that occur in the primary position and jerk movements when the eyes deviate laterally.

Due to the constant eye movement, accommodation is very difficult and objects appear blurred. Because the intensity of nystagmus movement varies with the direction of gaze, a zone where the intensity is smallest (the null zone), is often used for seeing and this results in an abnormal head posture.

Visual development in children may be restricted by nystagmus, and accurate assessment of vision will assist in planning how to use the vision they have for mobility and education. Early identification of nystagmus is needed so that strategies can be put in place to help the child to align the fovea with the object of fixation during the period when the fovea is developing. Failure to do this will restrict focal development and thus visual potential.

Nystagmus may also be acquired, with the most important differential diagnosis being ischaemia of the brainstem or cerebellum. Chronic nystagmus may result from neurodegenerative, inflammatory disorders or tumours (Strupp *et al.* 2011).

Acquired optic nerve problems

Optic neuritis

Optic neuritis in children presents with bilateral visual loss with disc swelling associated with viral illness such as measles, mumps and chickenpox (Wormald *et al.* 2004, Schatz 2015).

Optic neuritis normally presents in adults between the ages of 20 and 50, with an acute unilateral loss of vision and with pain behind the eye and on movement, and possibly brow ache. This pain may precede or accompany the visual loss. Vision loss may be exacerbated by heat or exercise (Uthoff phenomenon) and, because of the asymmetric conduction between the optic nerves, things moving in a straight line may appear to have a curved trajectory (Pulfrich phenomenon).

Decreased colour vision is often obvious because objects appear drab and 'washed out' and this may be more obvious to the patient than the loss of vision.

The optic disc may appear swollen (optic neuritis) but is more often normal in appearance because the nerve is swollen behind the globe and the condition is then known as retrobulbar optic neuritis (Wormald *et al.* 2004). Contrast sensitivity, central scotoma or other field defects and a relative afferent pupillary defect are also seen on examination.

Causes in adults

Optic or retrobulbar neuritis is the first presentation of multiple sclerosis (MS) in a large number of patients, with about 70% of women and 35% of men going on to develop other neurological problems associated with MS later (Maclean 2002). These figures do vary between different authors but the risk is very significant.

Optic neuritis may also develop secondary to inflammation of sinuses, orbit or meninges (Liu *et al.* 2010). Syphilis, sarcoidosis, tuberculosis and cytomegalovirus infection have also been implicated (Liu *et al.* 2010), although many cases are idiopathic.

Management

Management of the patient involves full blood count (FBC); erythrocyte sedimentation rate (ESR); Venereal Disease Reference Laboratory (VDRL) test, anti-nuclear antibodies; angiotensin-converting enzyme (ACE); thyroid function tests and other tests to exclude vasculitic and other causes of optic neuropathy (Ergene 2015). Magnetic resonance imaging (MRI) is highly sensitive and specific in the assessment of inflammatory changes in the optic nerve. Visual evoked potentials (VEPs) are useful and can show problems in nerve function even when the MRI is normal.

High-dose corticosteroids may be used in severe cases. Studies (Wormald *et al.* 2004, Arnold 2005) have found that this may speed up visual recovery but it does not affect long-term outcome or lessen the frequency of recurrence. Furthermore, the use of high-dose corticosteroids may have side effects such as insomnia, mild mood changes, stomach upsets, oedema and weight gain.

Visual loss is rapid and progressive, reaching its lowest level after around a week. Visual loss may be partial or total but normally begins to improve in the second or third week and may be back to normal by the fourth week. In the Optic Neuritis Study Group treatment trial, the mean visual acuity was 6/5, with only 7% having a visual acuity of 6/12 after 1 year (Beck & Cleary 1993).

With the rapid loss of vision, patients need to be assured that in 75% of cases vision is restored to normal within a few weeks, although it is likely to worsen initially. Timescales for visual recovery and colour sensitivity need to be conveyed accurately. In this way, as the patient's vision recovers, they will be reassured. In cases where visual recovery is not within the expected timescale, patients need to be kept informed of their progress and improvements from the initial loss identified.

Time should be taken to listen to patients' concerns, and support and advice should be given about the difficulties that they may be encountering. Each patient is an individual and recovery of vision will vary. Discussion of how the visual loss is affecting the patient must include home and work, and advice and assistance should be offered. Loss of binocular vision (and how this will affect the patient) will need identifying. Patients may be more prone to tripping or misjudging depth and generally appearing clumsy, thus increasing their anxiety, especially if the cause of the optic neuritis has been linked to MS.

Where another systemic disease is identified as the cause, additional support will be necessary. Information about the need to treat the underlying cause will assist the patient in dealing with their uncertainty while undergoing the tests required. When

MS is suspected, referral to a neurologist is indicated, and it could be argued that the possibility of MS should be discussed only by a neurologist, or an ophthalmologist together with a neurologist, so that the patient gains the best possible advice from someone who will be able to discuss all the disease possibilities.

A number of these patients are likely to be followed up in the ophthalmic department and, after being informed of the possibility that the cause of the visual loss may be MS, they are likely to be extremely shocked because a confirmed diagnosis will have a profound effect on their future health and life. During this time, it is helpful if the patient has assistance from friends or family members who will be able to offer support and retain information that can be discussed at a later time. There is some evidence (Matti *et al.* 2010) that educating patients in relation to their symptoms will improve their engagement with treatment.

It is common for patients not to hear important information or to focus solely on the negative when receiving bad news. Although MS may be potentially life altering, patients can experience long periods of remission and, as with all disease, progression varies in different individuals. It is important that patients are aware of support from social workers, counselling services and support groups. Family support should not be overlooked because, if the diagnosis of MS is confirmed, this may require changes. Although it is not likely that the nurse in the ophthalmic clinic will be required to provide all this information, it is useful to know what the patient will experience when it comes to the referral and possible tests needed to confirm the diagnosis. Fear of the unknown, in terms of the next stage in the process, can often cause distress and referral to the neurologist may take several weeks, during which time the patient and family may feel very isolated, so providing a contact number for the clinic or social worker may be valuable.

Optic neuropathies

Anterior ischaemic optic neuropathy

This involves the 1mm segment of the optic nerve head (optic disc) and results in visible disc swelling with sudden, painless reduction in vision. It is presumed to be caused by circulatory insufficiency or an acute infarction of the optic nerve head and may be divided into non-arteritic and arteritic ischaemic optic neuropathy. Although the pathophysiology of the two types differs, ischaemia of the optic nerve is the result of both, and the consequences for vision are similar.

Non-arteritic ischaemic optic neuropathy

This affects individuals aged 45 and over (Liu *et al.* 2010), with the average age of onset being around 60 (Wormald *et al.* 2004). Visual loss is sudden and painless and mostly irreversible but non-progressive.

Various vascular risk factors have been associated with non-arteritic ischaemic optic neuropathy (NAION), such as hypertension and diabetes mellitus. Tests will include an ESR to exclude giant cell arteritis; blood pressure and blood sugar tests to check for risk factors will need to be recorded. An RAPD is common. Up to 97% of patients have a small optic disc, with a small or absent cup, typically less than 0.3. Although the contribution of this to the condition is unclear, it is felt that a 'crowded' disc can exacerbate chronic mechanical obstruction to axoplasmic flow, resulting in secondary compression and ischaemia.

Many therapies have been attempted, but most have not been adequately studied (Atkins *et al.* 2010). No benefit has been found from surgical intervention and there are currently no class one studies showing benefit from medical or surgical treatment (Atkins *et al.* 2010). While there is no widely accepted treatment, a range of therapies have been proposed, which act on thrombosis, on the blood vessels, on the disc oedema, or are presumed to have a neuroprotective effect. These may include aspirin and other antiplatelet agents, thrombolytics, oral or intravitreal steroids, anti-VEGFs and optic nerve decompression. As aspiring and other antiplatelet therapies are well evidenced for the prevention of cerebral and myocardial infarction, Atkins *et al.* (2010) suggest that these therapies would be considered even in the absence of class evidence.

While effective therapy as well as prevention in the other eye are still not well evidenced, the NAION patient should have their risk of vascular disease assessed initially by their GP. Patients are now more aware that aspirin is prescribed to help prevent the risk of myocardial infarctions and strokes. Once vascular diseases such as these are mentioned, they may question the use of aspirin if it is not advised. Nurses must be ready to support patients with information in such cases and advise them to ensure that they get the vascular risk assessment done. If patients smoke, they may need to be advised of the possible links between smoking and their NAION. National and local helpline numbers and other information about smoking cessation assistance may also be useful.

Arteritic ischaemic optic neuropathy

The most common cause of arteritic ischaemic optic neuropathy (AION) is giant cell/ temporal arteritis. Giant cell arteritis is considered to be a severe variant of polymyalgia rheumatica, with a combination of genetic and environmental factors thought to play a role in its aetiology (Huang *et al.* 2001). Inflammation reduces blood flow in the ophthalmic artery, thus producing ischaemia of the optic nerve.

Adults over the age of 50 are affected, with the mean age of onset being 70. Loss of vision is initially in one eye and may be profound, reducing vision to perhaps 'count fingers', but may be followed rapidly by loss of vision in the other eye if treatment is not started (Wormald *et al.* 2004). In 30% of patients, visual acuity may improve over 2 years. Loss of vision may be accompanied by other signs of arteritis such headache, which is temporal over the scalp; patients may also complain of pain when brushing their hair. Jaw claudication may be present, with pain occurring on chewing and being relieved by rest. Morning muscle stiffness, anorexia, anaemia, fever and fatigue may also be present.

Tests needed to confirm giant cell arteritis are: ESR, CRP and temporal artery biopsy. The presence of jaw claudication, anaemia and European origin have been significantly correlated with biopsy results that are positive for giant cell arteritis (Liu *et al.* 2010).

Treatment involves initial intravenous hydrocortisone, followed by 60–80mg orally daily as a starting dose. This will be tapered as the ESR is reduced (Wormald *et al.* 2004). Patients may have to continue treatment for up to 2 years and will require frequent visits to outpatients during this time. Information in relation to giant cell arteritis and the risk of the other eye being affected must be discussed with patients because, in 40% of patients, the other eye was subsequently found to be affected.

Patients will need referral for treatment of anaemia and any underlying rheumatic disease, and this may involve referral to the GP and/or a rheumatologist. Steroid use and its possible side effects must be explored with patients. These side effects may include: osteoporosis, peptic ulcer, diabetes, hypertension, immunosuppression, weight gain, psychiatric disturbances, and ocular complications such as cataract and glaucoma.

Patients may need to adapt to field loss, and can learn to move their eyes or head in the direction of field loss. In older adults, there is a greater risk of falls until these skills are acquired. Both patients and family members therefore need to be aware of these risks. It is important that the team caring for the patient and family – nurse, orthoptist, low-visual aid optician and/or social worker – spend time discussing how the treatment and visual loss may impact on daily life.

Taking a team approach in this way will provide the best support for the patient and their family. Nurses can give information and advice on the use of steroids, and the orthoptist will advise on prisms to combat any diplopia and using the visual field the patient has. Some patients may not be able to tolerate prisms for walking and this should be assessed before dispensing. Patients may be able to have prisms for reading, watching television or computer work (Melore 1997).

Social workers will be able to advise on services available to assist at home, in mobility and with work if this is relevant. The low-visual aid optician will dispense and advise on the use of low-visual aids and lighting (Melore 1997). Throughout the patient's care, nurses in the outpatient department will be able to assess and discuss how the patient is coping with treatment and managing at home. These interactions are crucial because the patient could potentially become depressed and isolated. Clear documentation of the patient's appearance, mobility and concerns will ensure continuity of care.

Leber's optic neuropathy

This is a rare hereditary disorder and is transmitted by mitochondrial DNA (most of which comes from the mother), rather than by nuclear DNA. It normally affects healthy young men but there is no transmission down the male line. Women transmit the disease to sons and the carrier state to their daughters, although some carrier females are also affected. It is the most common inherited mitochondrial disorder. Visual loss is initially monocular and painless, and progresses to bilateral over weeks or months. These young people will need extensive support because their visual impairment may have a profound effect on their lives. It will be important for family members to be examined (Liu *et al.* 2010) and counselling about the hereditary aspect of this condition will be necessary.

Depending on their visual acuity, the patient will need different types of support and advice about mobility, and life and work options. The process of acceptance and rehabilitation may be lengthy and patients may be at risk of becoming depressed and isolated. Friends and family will play a large part in rehabilitation, but will need advice and support and, with the patient's permission, must be included in discussions. New research linked to understanding of mitrochondrial DNA is being carried out and could give some treatment options in the future (Quiros *et al.* 2006, Sadun & Carelli 2006).

Toxic optic neuropathies

Toxic amblyopia typically affects heavy drinkers and pipe smokers who have a diet that is deficient in B vitamins. Visual loss is gradual, progressive and bilateral. Vision will improve with treatment of hydroxycobalamin for 10 weeks. The classic field defect is bilateral central or caecocentral scotomata. Patients need advice on reduction of alcohol and/or smoking cessation, and may need social work involvement to enable them to access a treatment programme. Without reduction of the cause, the condition will recur.

Drug-induced optic neuropathy

Ethambutol can cause optic neuropathy and this is dose related (Liu *et al.* 2010). Patients who become toxic often have concurrent alcoholism or diabetes. Onset is sudden and associated with loss of red–green colour vision. Visual recovery is normally complete but may take up to 12 months. As ethambutol is part of the treatment for tuberculosis, it is vital that the treatment be continued. These requirements will need to be fully explained to the patients to ensure compliance. Patients may need help with daily life and mobility and need to have any associated underlying condition treated.

Papilloedema

This is swelling of the optic nerve head produced by raised intracranial pressure. Finding the cause and treating the pressure will relieve the papilloedema and prevent long-term visual loss. Visual loss may initially be in the form of diplopia and an enlarged blind spot. Other signs may include: loss of consciousness, headache worsened by coughing or straining, and vomiting without nausea. Papilloedema is invariably bilateral unless there is previous disease of the optic nerve.

There are three stages of papilloedema:

- Early papilloedema, where there is minimal hyperaemia of the disc and oedema.
- Acute papilloedema, which includes haemorrhages and exudates, in addition to the early symptoms. Visual acuity is normal unless there is macular oedema. The disc margins become indistinct and the central cup is obliterated.
- Vintage papilloedema, when the acute haemorrhagic and exudative components resolve. Once oedema resolves, the optic disc is pale and nerve fibre visual field defects are seen on field testing (Liu *et al.* 2010, Bowling 2015).

Initial referral to an ophthalmologist will be at an ophthalmic clinic and may come via an optician or GP. Patients will require detailed explanations of the possible causes and what tests will be required to identify the underlying cause. The main causes of papilloedema are tumours in the cranium, and urgent referral to a neurologist or neurosurgeon will be required.

Optic nerve tumours
Glioma

Gliomas present in two different forms. Benign tumours are found in children between the ages of 4 and 8 years, with unilateral proptosis and visual impairment (Liu *et al.* 2010). Investigations include radiographs, computed tomography and ultrasonography and these will identify the size and extent of the tumour. According to Bowling (2015), about 55% of patients will also have neurofibromatosis. If proptosis becomes aesthetically unacceptable and the eye is blind from optic atrophy, a local resection is the treatment of choice. Intracranial extensions to the tumour may need the assistance of a neurosurgeon, and radiation is used for tumours that are too big for surgical excision. Parents and children will require support and information about the condition and treatments. Loss of vision will require additional support for the child in terms of education.

In adults (normally men aged 40–60), the presence of the tumour may mimic optic neuritis, with rapid monocular visual loss, retrobulbar pain and disc oedema. Even with steroid treatment, complete blindness ensues within several weeks. Radiotherapy and/or chemotherapy may be of some value but death usually occurs within months.

Meningioma

These are invasive tumours that typically affect middle-aged women (Bowling 2015). The meningiomas spread along the lines of least resistance, along the subarachnoid space, and are usually encapsulated by intact dura (Liu *et al.* 2010). Visual loss is slow but progressive, with loss of acuity and central scotoma, and loss of colour vision. Treatment for intracranial tumours is surgical but prognosis is poor (Liu *et al.* 2010). By contrast, primary optic nerve sheath meningiomas, when removed by stripping the optic nerve sheath with its blood supply, are not normally fatal although they do have a profound effect on visual acuity.

Pituitary tumour

These tumours affect the chiasma as they grow so visual field loss is normally bitemporal. Headaches may initially accompany the blurring of vision and diplopia would indicate that the third, fourth or sixth nerve may be involved. As the pituitary gland is responsible for producing hormones, depending on which tumour is present, different features may present (Bowling 2015).

Care for patients with tumours varies depending on the treatment required but nurses must ensure that the patient and family are fully informed throughout all the investigations and treatments. Coming to terms with a potentially life-threatening illness requires skilled support and may need the intervention of specialist nurses in this field and referral to local hospice services. For those patients who survive, the loss of vision will require significant adjustment.

Aneurysms

The proximity of the carotid artery to the chiasma when a carotid aneurysm occurs initially causes a unilateral nasal hemianopia. As the aneurysm becomes larger, it may press against the opposite carotid artery (Bowling 2015).

Supranuclear disorders of eye movement

In these conditions, patients may be unaware of visual disturbance, such as the inability to see food on their plate, and may attribute problems that they are experiencing to simple solutions such as inappropriate spectacles (Liu *et al.* 2010). Differentiation between problems with fixation and the location of objects will determine which area of the visual pathway is affected and determine the underlying cause, such as sixth nerve palsy, Huntington's disease, Parinaud's syndrome or internuclear ophthalmoplegia

(Bowling 2015). Patients may adopt varying head postures to accommodate visual disturbances. Given that the patient may not attribute problems to visual disturbances, after diagnosis nurses may initially need to spend time listening to the patient in order to determine to what extent the visual loss is affecting their life.

Nerve palsies (see also Chapter 22)

About 25% of third, fourth or sixth nerve palsies have no known cause and 50% of these will resolve spontaneously (Bowling 2015). Nerve palsies may be the first sign of patients developing complications of systemic disease and conditions such as diabetes, hypertension and atherosclerosis are the most common causes. Other causes may include: herpes zoster, tuberculosis, basal meningitis, syphilis, otitis media and Guillain–Barré syndrome. The nerves are susceptible to trauma as a result of their pathways and this is a common cause of palsy. Aneurysms may cause third nerve palsies (Bowling 2015).

Generally, in nerve palsy, surgical intervention will be carried out only after symptoms have been present for about 6 months. This is to allow time for spontaneous resolution. During this time, depending on the visual disturbances, patients may benefit (apart from in fourth nerve palsy) from the use of prisms applied to spectacles, or even occlusion of the affected eye. Support and advice on how to manage at home and work may require referral to a specialist social worker.

Third nerve (oculomotor)

The third nerve is situated in the midbrain (Bowling 2015) and supplies the medial, inferior and superior rectus, superior oblique and lid levator muscles (Liu *et al.* 2010). Paralysis of the nerve may be complete or partial, leading to a variety of different symptoms. Complete third nerve palsy will lead to ptosis, which may mask diplopia. Paralysis and unopposed action of extraocular muscles will cause diplopia, and loss of pupillary function as a result of interruption of the parasympathetic pathway to the sphincter pupillae causes a fixed, dilated pupil that is non-reactive to direct or consensual light (Bowling 2015). Vascular disease often causes pupil-sparing third nerve palsy. A painful palsy may be associated with diabetes but should be investigated thoroughly because it may be a sign of a more sinister causation. Posterior communicating artery aneurysm is an important cause of a painful third nerve palsy with pupil involvement.

Fourth nerve palsy (trochlear)

The fourth cranial nerve lies in the midbrain at the caudal aspect of the oculomotor nuclear complex and exits the brain stem dorsally (Liu *et al.* 2010). It innervates the superior oblique muscle. Bilateral palsy is common and is characterised by hyperdeviation in gaze. There is limitation in adduction as a result of superior oblique weakness; diplopia is vertical, torsional and worse on looking down. Diplopia may be reduced by abnormal head posture. Frequent causes of fourth nerve palsies are congenital lesions that may manifest later in life. Trauma is also an important cause, as are vascular lesions.

Sixth nerve (abducens)

This nerve lies in the mid-portion of the pons, inferior to the floor of the fourth ventricle. There is frequently a facial nerve palsy, and weakness of the lateral rectus prevents abduction. If palsy is complete, there will be no abduction beyond the midline and patients may adopt face turning in order to reduce diplopia. Acoustic neuroma is an important cause of sixth nerve palsy, and hearing and corneal sensitivity should be tested because these are the first signs and symptoms of acoustic neuroma. Other causes include nasopharyngeal tumours, pituitary adenoma (Saffra *et al.* 2011), raised intracranial pressure and basal skull fractures as well as vascular causes.

Pupillary pathways

The pupil changes size as a result of the actions of two opposing muscles in the iris: the constrictor and dilator pupillae. The size of the pupil at any given time is the result of a balance of the innervations of the two (Figure 24.2).

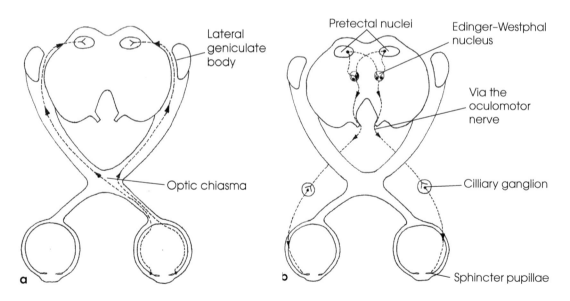

Figure 24.2 The pupillary light reflex: (a) to the pretectal nuclei – the afferent pathway; (b) from the pretectal nuclei to the Edinger–Westphal nuclei – the pretecto oculomotor pathway, and from there to the sphincter pupillae – the efferent pathway.

As photoreceptors in the retina are stimulated by light, impulses travel through the optic nerve to the lateral geniculate body as described earlier. Those fibres that bypass the lateral geniculate body synapse on nerve cells in the pretectal nucleus. The impulse travels via axons of the pretectal nerve cells to the Edinger–Westphal nuclei of the oculomotor nerve (parasympathetic nuclei) on each side (which accounts for the consensual response). This forms the afferent pathway. From here, the fibres synapse and travel through the oculomotor nerve to the ciliary ganglion within the orbit. The short ciliary nerves take the impulses to the constrictor pupillae muscle – the efferent pathway.

The pupil also constricts in response to accommodation, which consists of a triad of convergence, accommodation and miosis. The three light reflexes are therefore:

- The direct light reflex occurs when light is focused on the eye.
- At the same time, the pupil of the other eye constricts as well – the consensual reflex.
- The near reflex in accommodation.

The dilator pupillae is under sympathetic nerve control from the hypothalamus via the spinal cord and superior cervical ganglion and then in the sympathetic fibres that run alongside the carotid artery and ciliary nerves to the eye. Stimulation of these nerve pathways causes the pupil to dilate, in low intensity light and when the person is experiencing excitement or fear.

The size of the pupil is in a constant state of movement (hippus), adjusting to changes in illumination, fixation distance and psychosensory stimuli. Pupillary sizes tend to be smaller in children and older adults than young adults and smaller in brown eyes than blue (Liu *et al.* 2010).

Examining the pupils

To examine the pupil, the light should be dim and preferably directed onto the face from below so that both pupils are seen simultaneously; the size should be measured with a millimetre rule (Bowling 2015). Anisocoria, a difference in pupillary size between the two eyes, may normally be found in 41% of people examined (Liu *et al.* 2010). To determine whether this is normal, the pupillary dimensions of the individual should be reassessed, varying the amount of illumination in the room; anisocoria that varies with the degree of illumination is pathological (Bowling 2015). Reaction to light should be brisk and full, and should be tested when the patient is fixating at distance to prevent constriction caused by the near response.

Pupillary pathway defects
Afferent pupil defect

If the afferent pathway is completely compromised, no light impulse will reach the Edinger–Westphal nucleus and therefore no direct response is possible. The pupil will still show a consensual response if light is shone into the other eye because the efferent pathway is susceptible to impulses directed to it from the fellow eye. Complete afferent pupillary defects are uncommon but relative afferent pupillary defects (RAPDs) are a sensitive measure of optic nerve damage or disease.

The test for this is commonly known as the swinging flashlight test and should take place in a dimly lit room. Both pupils must be observed at once so complete darkness is unhelpful. A bright light is shone on to the unaffected eye and the pupil's direct response and the consensual response of the other eye are noted. The light is swung to the affected eye and, if a defect of the afferent pathway is present, the pupil appears to dilate to a greater or lesser degree. Both pupils are larger at this phase of the test as a result not of not dilating, as such, but of a lesser degree of constriction because of a compromised afferent pathway of the affected eye, and therefore a lesser impulse reaching the unaffected eye through its efferent pathway. (To put it simply, if only 50% of the optic nerve is working on the affected eye, then only 50% of the 'signal' can reach the Edinger–Westphal nucleus and only 50% return down each of the efferent routes.) As the flashlight is swung back to the unaffected eye, the pupil constricts further and the pupil of the affected eye does the same (100% of impulse reaching the Edinger–Westphal nucleus means 100% down each efferent pathway).

RAPDs should be recorded according to an agreed taxonomy such as 'mild', 'moderate' or 'severe'. Although RAPDs are felt to be characteristic of optic nerve disease, they can also be present in some retinal lesions, including detachment, age-related macular degeneration and retinal vein occlusion. RAPDs may also be seen in some people with amblyopia, although the mechanism is not clear and the severity of the RAPDs is not related to the degree of amblyopia.

Efferent pupil defect

If there is damage to the nerve parasympathetic pathway controlling the action of the constrictor pupillae, the pupil will respond poorly to both direct and consensual stimulation. Abnormalities of the efferent pathway may be caused by lesions anywhere from the midbrain to the pupillary sphincter muscle. The cause and site of the nerve damage will need to be determined in order to make a diagnosis.

Light-near dissociation

The light reflex is absent or sluggish and the near response is normal. Compression of the dorsal midbrain can selectively damage the dorsally located light reflex fibres while leaving the more ventrally located near reflex fibres intact. The most commonly seen bilateral light-near dissociation is an Argyll Robertson pupil, whereas a common cause of unilateral near-light dissociation is Adie pupil (or Adie's tonic pupil).

Argyll Robertson pupil

Argyll Robertson pupils are small (<2mm), irregular and react to near but not to light. They are the result of tertiary syphilis involving the central nervous system. Iris atrophy is frequent and dilatation is poor after mydriatic instillation. It is important to assess visual acuity accurately in these patients because optic atrophy, which may also cause light-near dissociation, is also a consequence of syphilis. Argyll Robertson (-like) pupils are also seen in diabetes, chronic alcoholism and some degenerative disorders as well as encephalitis.

Adie pupil/Adie's tonic pupil/Adie syndrome

Adie pupil is a common cause of anisocoria and is commonly seen in young adults (Bowling 2015). This pupillary abnormality is caused by damage to the postganglionic supply to the sphincter pupillae and the ciliary muscle. The cause is not understood but it is a benign condition and does not indicate any underlying pathology.

The affected pupil is larger and does not react to light, although it reacts slowly to near stimuli. A tonic near response is one where the pupil remains constricted after accommodative effort has ceased. Accommodation may also be tonic, giving the person blurred vision for some time after they have stopped accommodating. Deep tendon reflexes are diminished in many patients but the reasons for this are unclear (Holmes–Adie syndrome). The palsy of the sphincter pupillae is almost always segmental. Slit-lamp examination reveals bunching of the iris stroma in those areas where the sphincter pupillae is intact. The segmental response may be described as vermiform or worm-like.

A test for Adie pupil is the instillation of 0.05–0.125% pilocarpine. Many of these patients have a hypersensitivity to this strength of pilocarpine.

A change in anisocoria of more than 1mm after 45 minutes is considered to be a positive result. The test should not be carried out within 24 hours of any other test that changes the corneal permeability (because this will affect the results – perhaps giving a false positive as a result of increased uptake of the pilocarpine), such as instillation of topical anaesthetic, applanation tonometry, etc., so the patient may have to come back to the department to have this carried out.

Patients with Adie pupil may have photophobia or accommodative symptoms but they often have no symptoms and state that the anisocoria was noted by a friend or relative. Accommodative problems tend to resolve within months. About half of Adie pupils will resolve within 2 years but involvement of the second eye is common.

Horner's syndrome

Lesions at any point along the sympathetic pathway results in Horner's syndrome. Here, one pupil is smaller as a result of paralysis of the dilator muscle, along with a moderate degree of ptosis and mild lower lid elevation. Anisocoria is more apparent in dim light and there is delayed dilatation (dilation lag). Reactions to light and near are normal. The lesion may be congenital (associated with birth injury to the brachial plexus) or associated with acquired lesions of the pathway. These will result in a degree of anhidrosis (lack of sweating) in the areas of the body innervated by the pathway in which the lesion occurs – the entire side of the body, the same side of the face or just the forehead.

The first-order neuron originates in the hypothalamus and descends through the brainstem into the lateral column of the spinal cord, synapsing at the cervicothoracic junction. Causes involving first-order neurons include central nervous system lesions such as vascular occlusion, tumours and cervical disc problems.

The second-order neuron (preganglionic) leaves the spinal cord and travels over the apex of the lung to synapse at the superior cervical ganglion at the level of the carotid artery bifurcation. Second-order neuron lesions may be caused by lung tumours and thoracic surgery, carotid or aortic aneurysm, and trauma to the brachial plexus.

The third-order neuron (postganglionic) follows a course along the internal carotid artery, passing through the cavernous sinus. The fibres then travel with the long ciliary nerve through the superior orbital fissure, and end within the iris dilator muscle and the retractor muscles of the upper and lower eyelids (Müller's muscles). Third-order neuron lesions include tumours in the neck, cluster headaches and carotid artery surgery.

Location of the lesion is important so patients may have to undergo a battery of investigations that they feel are irrelevant to their eye problem.

Instillation of cocaine 4% into both eyes confirms the diagnosis. The normal pupil will dilate as a result of the cocaine blocking the reuptake of noradrenaline (norepinephrine) which terminates its action. There is therefore an accumulation of adrenaline (epinephrine) at the postganglionic sympathetic nerve endings and the pupil dilates. There is no noradrenaline released in the pupillary pathway of the eye with Horner's syndrome and therefore cocaine has no effect.

The use of cocaine has been supplanted by 0.5% apraclonidine, an alpha-2 adrenergic receptor agonist with weak alpha-1 activity. This is more readily available and penetrates the cornea well. The affected eye has denervation supersensitivity of the alpha-1 receptors on the dilator muscle. After instillation of apraclonidine, the affected pupil dilates and the lid elevates, with no effect in the unaffected eye (American Academy of Ophthalmology 2016).

Support from ophthalmic clinicians will be needed at this time so that the patient understands the relevance of the tests and investigations.

References

American Academy of Ophthalmology (2016) *Pupil Efferent Defects.* http://www.aao.org/focalpointssnippetdetail. aspx?id=db4df9ab-f6ac-4331-91dd-9dec5fc34c47 (accessed 20 September 2016).

Arnold, A.C. (2005) Evolving management of optic neuritis and multiple sclerosis. *American Journal of Ophthalmology.* **139**(6),1101–108.

Atkins, E.J., Bruce, B.B., Newman, N.J. & Biousse, V. (2010) Treatment of Nonarteritic Anterior Ischemic Optic Neuropathy. *Survey of Ophthalmology.* **55**(1), 47–63.

Beck, R.W. & Cleary, P.A. (1993) The Optic Neuritis Study Group: Optic Neuritis Treatment Trial one year follow up results. *Archives of Ophthalmology.* **111**, 773–75.

Blohme, J., Bengtsson-Stigmar, E. & Tornqvist, K. (2000) Visually impaired Swedish children. Longitudinal comparisons 1980–1999. *Acta Ophthalmologica Scandinavica.* **78**, 416–420.

Bowling, B. (2015) *Kanski's Clinical Ophthalmology, a systematic approach.* 8th edn. London: Elsevier.

Daniels, E. (2001) *Losing Your Sight.* London: Robinson.

Ergene, E. (2015) *Adult Optic Neuritis.* http://emedicine.medscape.com/article/1217083-overview 2015 (accessed 20 September 2016).

Forrester, J.V., Dick, A.D., McMenamin, P.G., Roberts, F. & Pearlman, E. (2016) *The Eye: Basic sciences in practice.* 4th edn. Edinburgh: Elsevier.

Garcia-Filion, P., Fink, C., Geffner, M.E. & Borchert, M. (2010) Optic nerve hypoplasia in North America: a re-appraisal of perinatal risk factors. *Acta Ophthalmologica.* **88**, 527–34.

Glaser, J.S. (1990) *Neuro-Ophthalmology.* 2nd edn. Philadelphia, PA: JB Lippincott.

Goffman, E. (1990) *Stigma Notes on Management of Spoilt Identity.* Harmondsworth: Penguin Books.

Hatton, D.D., Schwietz, E., Boyer, B. & Rychwalski, P. (2007) Babies Count: the national registry for children with visual impairments, birth to 3 years. *Journal of AAPOS.* **11**, 351–55.

Huang, D., Zhou, Y. & Hoffman, G.S. (2001) Pathogenesis immunogenetic factors. *Best Practice and Research in Clinical Rheumatology.* **15**, 239–58.

John A. Moran Center Neuro-Opthalmology Collection. http://novel.utah.edu/Moran/ (accessed 20 September 2016).

Liu, G.T., Volpe, N.J. & Galetta, S.L. (2010) *Neuro-Ophthalmology: Diagnosis and Management.* 2nd edn. Philadelphia: Saunders Elsevier.

Maclean, H. (2002) *The Eye in Primary Care.* Oxford: Butterworth-Heinemann.

Matti, A.I., Keane, M.C., McCarl, H., Klaer, P. & Chen, C.S. (2010) Patients' knowledge and perception on optic neuritis management before and after an information session. *British Journal of Ophthalmology.* **10**, 7.

Melore, G.G. (1997) *Treating Vision Problems in the Older Adult.* St Louis, MO: Mosby.

North American Neuro-Opthalmology Society. http://www.nanosweb.org/i4a/pages/index.cfm?pageID=3954 (accessed 20 September 2016).

Quiros, P.A., Torres, R.J., Salomao, S., Berezovsky, A., Sherman, J., Sadun, F., De Negri, A., Belfort, R. & Sadun, A.A. (2006) Colour vision defects in asymptomatic carriers of the Leber's hereditary optic neuropathy (LHON) mtDNA 11778 mutation from a large Brazilian LHON pedigree: a case-control study. *British Journal of Ophthalmology.* **90**(2), 150–53.

Ragge, N.K. & Easty, D.L. (1999) *Immediate Eye Care.* London: Wolf Publications Ltd.

Sadun, A.A. & Carelli, V. (2006) The role of mitochondria in health, ageing, and diseases affecting vision. *British Journal of Ophthalmology.* **90**(7), 809–10.

Saffra, N., Kaplow, E., Mikolaenko, I., Kim, A., Rubin, B. & Jafar, J. (2011) Isolated sixth cranial nerve palsy as the presenting symptom of a rapidly expanding ACTH positive pituitary adenoma: a case report. *British Journal of Ophthalmology.* **11**, 4.

Schatz, M. P. (2015) *Childhood Optic Neuritis.* http://emedicine.medscape.com/article/1217290-overview#a5 (accessed 20 September 2016).

Snell, R.S. & Lemp, M.A. (1998) *Clinical Anatomy of the Eye.* 2nd edn. USA: Blackwell Science.

Strupp, M., Hüfner, K., Sandmannn, R., Zwergal, A., Dieterich, M., Jahn, K. & Brandt, T. (2011) Central Oculomotor Disturbances and Nystagmus: A Window Into the Brainstem and Cerebellum. *Deutsches Ärzteblatt International.* *108*(12), 197–204.

Wormald, R., Smeeth, L. & Henshaw, K. (2004) *Evidence Based Ophthalmology.* London: BMJ Books.

CHAPTER TWENTY-FIVE

The eye and systemic disease

Dorothy E. Field

For the physician, or the expert ophthalmic nurse, the eye may provide a window to the general health of the body. Examination through a dilated pupil will deliver a view of retinal blood vessels – an indicator of the relative health of the retina – and the optic disc may reveal evidence of raised intracranial pressure. The ophthalmic nurse should be aware of these possible eye changes, which may be relevant to an ophthalmic diagnosis or form the basis for giving further, more general health advice. As systemic health may affect the eye, producing a 'new' condition, care should be taken to note a general history in terms of family eye problems, the patient's general health and any current medications being taken.

This chapter is an overview of systemic health and the eye under the following headings:

- Congenital problems
- Acquired eye conditions
- General conditions requiring health advice.

Congenital problems

The subheadings below provide brief indications of some of the problems with each syndrome. Ophthalmic nurses who may come across these, or other unlisted problems are advised to make separate detailed studies to heighten their awareness of systemic disease and its ocular consequences. Nurses in paediatric areas and others who deal with children, particularly those requiring anaesthesia, are advised to develop information folders to ensure that they provide safe, informed care for children and their families. However, children become adults, so this information is also necessary for every ophthalmic nurse. Helpful information regarding anaesthesia for children with congenital syndromes may be found in Butler *et al.* (2000).

Sight problems in people with a learning disability

Emerson and Baines (2010) note that the incidence of visual problems in people with learning difficulties is higher than in the general population. The more profoundly disabled a person appears, the more likely they are to have sensory disabilities. About 40% of learning-disabled people have a hearing problem and 6 out of 10 need spectacles, and support in learning to use them. Adults with learning disabilities are 10 times more likely to be blind or partially sighted than the general population (RNIB 2010).

Many difficulties, both of eye problems and of focusing due to refractive errors, occur within the learning disabled population, and may remain unrecognised and, even if easily managed, may go untreated. The RNIB cautions that people who have difficulties communicating their needs to others may, in frustration, develop self-injuring behaviour that can result in eye injury, e.g. detached retinas. This too, may go unrecognised.

Cerebral palsy syndrome

Systemic problems

Cerebral palsy is a physical condition affecting movement, posture and co-ordination. It is usually diagnosed at birth, or in early childhood. No two people will be affected in exactly the same way and it can range from mild to severe. Systemic problems vary from mild to acute, according to the severity of the syndrome, which is not in itself a specific disorder. These problems include: movement disorders, epilepsy, bladder and bowel control difficulties.

Eye problems

Where the eye is the cause of visual impairment, visual acuity will be reduced; and this is reasonably straightforward to measure and to ascertain whether or not the child has visual impairment. Because damage to the brain is usually the cause of visual impairment in children with cerebral palsy, it is not just visual acuity that can be reduced but there may also be difficulties associated with the processing or recognition of objects. The person has the potential for good visual acuity, but they may not be able to fully interpret what they are viewing. These visual difficulties are more complicated both to assess and to describe and are known as cerebral (or cortical) visual impairment (CVI). Even if children have good visual acuity, processing difficulties can result in severe visual impairment.

Children with cerebral palsy may have:

- Reduced visual acuity
- Visual field loss
- Difficulty using their vision to move parts of their body or to move around

- Difficulty in recognising where objects are in space
- Difficulty recognising objects
- Difficulty in differentiating an object from its background
- Problems focusing for near objects
- Short- or long-sightedness
- Problems making accurate fast eye movements
- Problems keeping fixation still on an object (Blaikie 2016).

Strabismus and hypermetropic disorders are more common in people with cerebral palsy.

Down or Down's syndrome – Trisomy 21

Systemic problems

People with Down syndrome have varying degrees of learning disability, and may have congenital cardiac anomalies, ENT problems, recurrent chest infections, gastro-oesophageal reflux disorder (GERD), hearing loss and earlier onset of Alzheimer's disease.

Eye problems

- People with this syndrome have upslanting, narrow palpebral fissures, hyper-plasia of the iris, congenital blue-dot lens opacities and a tendency to high myopia.
- They are likely to have decreased corneal thickness, which may give an artificially low intraocular pressure measurement by applanation tonometry (Evereklioglu *et al.* 2002).
- Keratoconus is much more common than in the general population and develops in late adolescence and early adulthood. It is really important that it is screened for and found early, as, because of the thinner cornea, it progresses more quickly. Corneal cross-linking is most useful earlier in the progression of keratoconus, and later identification leads to a greater likelihood of penetrating keratoplasty (Down's Syndrome Vision Research Unit 2016).
- The Down's Syndrome Association (accessed in 6/4/2015) note that people with the syndrome are particularly likely to require spectacles. Hypermetropia is fairly common, and is often associated with convergent squint. Some are myopic, and some have astigmatism.
- Focusing difficulty may persist, even when using spectacles. Children and adults with Down's often manage better with bifocals.
- Around 15% have nystagmus, tending to tilt their heads into positions in which the nystagmus movements are minimalised.
- The nasolacrimal duct is slightly narrowed, and eye infections, watery eyes and blepharitis are more common.

- Eyelash anomalies are common, especially in adults and can be a cause of severe irritation if not identified (Down's Syndrome Vision Research Unit 2016)
- Cataracts develop earlier in life.

Edwards' syndrome, Trisomy 18

This is caused by an extra copy of chromosome 18 in some or all body cells, disrupting development and often causing miscarriage or stillbirth. Of those who survive birth, around half will die within 2 weeks. As few as one child in 12 will survive the first year of life, and only a small proportion survive into their teens and twenties (NHS Choices 2015).

Systemic problems

Learning disability and developmental problems, multiple congenital heart defects, renal, digestive and physical problems.

Eye problems

- Corneal and lens opacities, unilateral ptosis and optic atrophy.
- Although many of those affected do not have associated ocular abnormalities that might affect vision, visual acuity is difficult to measure as a result of the profound developmental delay.

Galactosaemia

Systemic problems

Galactosaemia, a rare inherited genetic condition, affects galactose metabolism. If left untreated, galactosaemia may lead to failure to thrive, lethargy, vomiting, diarrhoea, enlarged liver, renal disease, anaemia, deafness and learning disability. Treatment requires a galactose-restricted diet.

Long-term follow-up of these patients by Bosch *et al.* (2002), showed that, in spite of a severely galactose-restricted diet, most still develop abnormalities such as disturbed mental and/or motor development, dyspraxia and hypergonadotrophic hypogonadism.

Eye problems

- Early diagnosis and treatment is essential to prevent the growth of severe cataracts, which develop rapidly in the first few weeks of the child's life (Karadag *et al.* 2013).
- Infants with severe galactosaemia are prone to vitreous haemorrhages and cloudy pupils, due to developing cataracts.

Bardet–Biedl syndrome

This is an autosomal recessive multisystem genetic disorder.

Systemic problems

Obesity, learning disability, additional fingers or toes, impaired sexual development

– average age at diagnosis is 9 years (Beales *et al.* 1999). This debilitating condition develops slowly, with neurological problems, speech and language deficits, behavioural traits, facial dysmorphism and dental anomalies. The findings of Beales *et al.* may facilitate earlier diagnosis of this rare syndrome, and could have implications for the care of these patients and their apparently unaffected relatives.

Eye problems

Gradual loss of vision, with night vision impairment beginning in mid-childhood, followed by peripheral blind spots and blurred central vision. Retinitis pigmentosa may develop in infancy or early teens.

Weill-Marchesani syndrome

Systemic problems

Features of this disorder include: slight maxillary underdevelopment, narrow palate, malformed and misaligned teeth. Late ossification of the ends of the long bones is a general feature of this condition. Children may also have squat, stiff fingers and be short in stature. Cardiac defects present an anaesthetic challenge.

Eye problems

- Small shallow orbits, small lenses (microspherophakia) and resultant myopia.
- Connective tissue disorder contributes to possible lens dislocation.
- Peripheral iridectomy may be indicated to prevent pupil block.
- If there is an ectopic lens, early removal is required to prevent glaucoma.
- Trabeculectomy may be required in advanced chronic angle closure.
- Tsilou and Macdonald (2013) advise avoidance of miotics and mydriatics to avoid pupillary block.

Marfan's syndrome

Systemic problems

Unusually long limbs and fingers, scoliosis, muscular under-development, circulatory problems such as aortic aneurysm, aortic root dissection, thickening and prolapse of either or both atrioventricular valves and premature mortality are associated with this disorder (Judge & Dietz 2005).

Eye problems

- Dislocated lenses
- Megalocornea, keratoconus, severe refractive problems
- Glaucoma resulting from angle anomaly
- Lattice degeneration and retinal detachment.

Oculocerebrorenal syndrome (OCLR), or Lowe's syndrome

Systemic problems

This rare genetic condition causes problems with the eyes, brain and kidneys. Boys with this may go on to develop Fanconi-type renal tubular dysfunction by the age of about a year. The renal dysfunction ranges from mild to severe.

Eye problems

- Affected males are born with bilateral cataracts.
- Around 50% of these boys will develop glaucoma.

Patau's syndrome – Trisomy 13

Systemic problems

This condition causes brain and central nervous system defects, cleft palate, heart problems, additional fingers or toes and haemangiomas. Death by the age of 6 months is common.

Eye problems

- Anophthalmia – eyes do not develop.
- Microphthalmia – eyes are very small.
- Hypotelorism – there is a reduced distance between the eyes, with, on occasion, only a single central eye being present (cyclops).
- Cataracts and retinal problems.

Refsum's syndrome

Systemic problems

This stems from mutations in two genes. It is an enzyme/metabolic disorder, which may cause peripheral polyneuropathy, ataxia, deafness, skin disorder, cardiac arrhythmias and cardiomyopathy. It is rarely detected at birth, as raised plasma levels of phytanic acid only begin to occur in late childhood/adolescence.

Symptoms arise as the child begins to consume a common diet. This raises the plasma levels of phytanic acid. Diagnosis and treatment will result in a strict diet, which avoids many common foods.

Eye problems

- Retinitis pigmentosa
- Night blindness
- Cataracts.

Rubella

If a foetus in utero is infected by the mother via the transplacental route during the first 24 weeks of pregnancy, physical malformations may occur, depending on when organogenesis is complete.

Systemic problems

This condidition causes congenital heart problems, deafness, learning difficulties, enlarged liver and many others.

Eye problems

- Retinopathy, microphthalmos and glaucoma.
- Maternal rubella is responsible for a high percentage of congenital cataracts.

Stickler's syndrome

Systemic problems

This condition is associated with deafness, cleft palate, skeletal abnormalities and mitral valve prolapse. Stickler *et al.* (2001) found wide variations of symptoms and signs among affected people, even within the same family. They highlighted delays in diagnosis, lack of understanding among family members and denial about the risk of serious eye problems.

Eye problems

- High myopia
- Presenile cataract
- Dislocation of the lens (caused by dysfunction of the lens zonule fibres)
- Early retinal detachment.

Sturge-Weber syndrome

Systemic problems

The prevalence is 1:50,000 births, and both sexes are equally affected. It is characterised by unilateral facial naevus ('port wine stain'), which may also affect the meninges and eyes. It may be associated with epilepsy, hemiparesis and learning disability (Di Rocco & Tamburrini 2006).

Eye problems

- Involvement of the eyelid and conjunctiva generally indicates eye problems, particularly glaucoma, possible diffuse choroidal haemangioma, and haemangioma of the iris and ciliary body.
- Hemianopia may result from brain involvement.

Tuberous sclerosis (Bourneville's disease)

Systemic problems

This is multisystem and develops throughout life. Haematomas are likely to occur in the brain, skin, kidneys, eyes, heart and lungs as the person proceeds from childhood to adulthood. Symptoms in children may include epilepsy, infantile spasms, learning difficulties, adenoma sebaceum – numerous pink or red–brown facial papules, mostly around the nose. Renal or cardiac tumours occur in about 50% of cases. It is usually diagnosed when the child reaches about three years (Curatolo *et al.* 2008).

Eye problems

- Slowly maturing retinal tumours in 50% of cases.

Turner syndrome

Systemic problems

This affects girls, causing growth retardation, impaired sexual development, cardiovascular defects, renal abnormalities, lymphatic system defects, hypothyroidism and orthopaedic problems. Lawrence *et al.* (2003) discovered that people with the condition show problems remembering faces and classifying 'fear' in facial images. Anxiety, shyness, and difficulty understanding social cues are reported.

Eye problems

- Ptosis, strabismus and amblyopia
- Impaired colour vision
- Pterygia, keratoconus, blue sclera.

Usher's syndrome

Systemic problems

Usher's syndrome is responsible for about 5% of all congenital severe deafness and about half of all cases of deaf blindness (Kanski 2001).

Eye problems

- Progressive pigmentary retinopathy.

Acquired eye conditions

Amaurosis fugax

Amaurosis fugax is a transient, often complete, loss of vision experienced in one or both eyes and is indicative of transient retinal ischaemia. Causes of ischaemic transient visual loss include giant cell arteritis, cerebrovascular ischaemia and retinal arteriolar emboli. Babikian *et al.* (2001) found extracranial internal carotid artery occlusion or stenosis in 22% of cases, in a study of 77 patients – making it the largest aetiological subgroup. Transient visual loss can be a symptom of a serious vision or life-threatening condition, requiring urgent investigation and treatment, or it may have a more benign origin (such as migraine).

Significantly, Babikian *et al.* (2001) found that further adverse health events followed in 18% of patients, within 1 month, and in 8% of patients at the 3-month follow-ups. This included two myocardial infarctions and two deaths.

Diabetes and the eye

Diabetic retinopathy (see also Chapter 22)

This is a microvascular complication of diabetes mellitus that is a significant cause of blindness. Intensive glycaemic control is essential in reducing the risk of onset and progression of diabetic eye disease and other microvascular complications of diabetes. Severe and moderate visual loss from diabetes is essentially preventable with early detection, treatments, and effective long-term follow-up.

Laser photocoagulation is the treatment for proliferative diabetic retinopathy and diabetic macular oedema. Ophthalmic professionals should note that, as with patients with open-angle glaucoma, eye diseases appear to have a more aggressive course in some individuals than in others, despite the patient's efforts, so it is important to avoid 'victim blaming'.

Clinicians should take their educational role in preventing and alleviating the complications of disease seriously. There are many reliable studies demonstrating that improved control of blood glucose reduces the risk of major diabetic eye disease.

Cataract formation

The exact mechanism for cataract formation in people with diabetes is still uncertain. However, people with Type 2 diabetes do not develop true diabetic cataracts but tend to develop age-related cataracts on average 10 years earlier than people who do not have diabetes. Fluctuating vision and rapid-onset myopia, caused by shifts in the glucose, electrolyte and water balance within the lens, are early symptoms of diabetes.

Macular oedema after cataract surgery in people with diabetes

Clinicians managing postoperative cataract clinics are aware that swelling of the central retina (macular oedema) is fairly common among patients with diabetes after cataract surgery. It causes reduced central visual acuity and is an important risk consideration for patients with diabetes. Staff involved with obtaining patients' written consent should ensure that people with diabetes who are considering cataract surgery understand that macular oedema may worsen during the first year after surgery, reducing visual acuity. Fortunately, the condition often resolves spontaneously. Therapy with intravitreal steroids may be indicated.

Pupil dilatation

Ophthalmic nurses are aware of difficulties in dilating the pupils of people with diabetes, particularly on clinic visits. Pupillary autonomic neuropathy is considered to be an early sign of the development of systemic autonomic neuropathy, and is related to the duration of diabetes and the development of systemic dysfunction, e.g. trouble with circulation to the feet, development of silent cardiac ischaemia, etc.

Blood pressure and the eye

Hypotension

Systemic hypotension is being increasingly scrutinised as a possible factor in low-tension glaucoma. Studies indicate that damage may be worse at night, and patients with systemic hypotension and others on treatment for hypertension (some of whom are quite hypotensive at night) have also been studied. Greenfield *et al.* (2011) have examined the effects of Brimonidine versus Timolol in preserving visual function and have concluded that Brimonidine is the drug of choice for these patients.

Hypertension

A routine blood pressure check on a person who has attended an ophthalmic emergency department with a subconjunctival haemorrhage may reveal hypertension as a possible causative factor. Further blood pressure checks by the practice nurse should be advised before the GP will be able to make a firm diagnosis of hypertension.

A prolonged rise in blood pressure will cause microvascular changes in the retinal and choroidal blood vessel walls, causing them to narrow due to spasm or oedema. If left untreated, this may eventually lead to fibrosis, blurred vision and visual field defects.

Autoimmune disorders

Behçet's syndrome

This is a multisystem disease, associated with an increased incidence of HLA-B51. It is very rare in the UK, but genetically it is more common in the Middle East, Japan and South East Asia.

Among a range of disseminated symptoms, patients may exhibit stomatitis, skin lesions, recurrent genital ulceration, and arthritis of knees and ankles. Generally, only a few symptoms occur in each individual, the most serious of which is eye inflammation. Patients may present with floaters, loss of vision and pain. Manifestations include recurrent iridocyclitis, frequently accompanied by hypopyon and occlusive vasculitis of the retinal vessels.

Rheumatoid arthritis

Rheumatoid arthritis is a cause of multisystem disorders, including a variety of eye problems listed below.

Sjörgen's syndrome

This can also occur as a primary problem, or may be linked with rheumatoid arthritis. Symptoms are scleritis, dry eyes, redness and pain. It most commonly affects women of 40–60, due to the immune system attacking body tissues, particularly the salivary and lacrimal glands, reducing secretions and causing keratitis sicca. Very rarely, Sjörgen's may also cause lymphoma of glands within the axilla, neck or groin. There are a number of means of diagnosing Sjörgen's, but a raised ESR is generally the first signpost.

Scleritis

Inflammation of the sclera may be caused by rheumatoid arthritis, causing scleral and corneal thinning. Patients complain of a deep, boring pain in the eye.

Uveitis

Inflammation, pain, redness, blurred vision and photophobia are symptoms. If left untreated, this may lead to sight loss.

Retinal vascular occlusion

Small blood vessels become blocked, causing visual loss. If an artery is blocked, visual loss is sudden, but a blocked vein causes more gradual visual loss.

Secondary glaucoma

This may be a result of inflammation of the trabecular meshwork, giving rise to raised intraocular pressure and pain.

Earlier cataracts

These are due to inflammation of the eye.

Illicit drug use and the eye

Aspergillus is a rare cause of endophthalmitis, in connection with drug misuse. Weishaar *et al.* (1998) commented that it usually begins with acute intraocular inflammation and often presents with a characteristic chorioretinal lesion located in the macula, although patients may be asymptomatic. They noted that treatment with pars plana vitrectomy and intravitreous Amphotericin B or Voriconozole may eliminate the ocular infection, but the visual outcome is poor.

Firth (2005), detailing visual problems from abuse of Class A drugs mentions that cocaine and crack cocaine dilate pupils, which may lead to angle closure glaucoma. Its vasoactive properties can lead to vessel spasm or haemorrhage in the eye or brainstem, affecting vision. Inhaling these drugs may destroy bony tissue from the nasal septum, which may extend to the walls of the orbit, causing motor problems as well as preseptal cellulitis and orbital cellulitis

Phenytoin may be added to cocaine, causing nystagmus, bilateral ophthalmoplegia, ptosis, orbital infection and cerebral vasculitis. Contaminated IV drugs may cause endophthalmitis; and corneal ulcers may develop, due to the irritation caused by smoke from the drugs being inhaled.

Leukaemia and eye problems

Leukaemia may invade the eyes of adults and children, and occasionally the eye problem presents first, pointing the clinician to the systemic problem. Patients may have symptoms that include increasing hypermetropia, caused by posterior uveal infiltration with leukaemic cells, pushing the retina forward. Similarly, the front of the eye may be infiltrated, causing thickening of the anterior uvea, resulting in a rare secondary glaucoma (Sharma *et al.* 2004).

Myeloid leukaemia may also cause white cells to block the smallest blood vessels of the eye, causing a range of problems. Additionally, people being treated for leukaemia are more prone to infections, ranging from bacterial conjunctivitis to endophthalmitis. Sterile ring ulcers may occur on the cornea, and the choroid and ciliary body may be infiltrated, changing the iris colour and causing pseudohypopyon. Leukaemias have been identified as the cause of uveitis in 5% of paediatric cases (Soylu *et al.* 1997).

Lyme disease

Lyme disease is carried by ticks in the UK, and is common in children, who frequently present at eye units with ticks in their eyelids and eyebrows. Prophylactic antibiotics are not used after tick removal. However, the tick must be very carefully removed to avoid it regurgitating its stomach contents into the host. Ophthalmic departments should have a policy for safe tick removal and should provide information leaflets for their patients.

A tick on the body will not necessarily lead to Lyme disease. A characteristic rash spreading from the original tick bite, which starts about 2–30 days after the bite, indicates the likelihood of infection, as does headache and fever, and urgent medical advice must be sought. Lyme disease can affect the heart, joints and nervous system. Clinical diagnosis is supported by blood tests.

Ophthalmic involvement in Lyme disease is most commonly seen in the second and third stages, without the original tick bite being near to the eye. Mora *et al.* (2009) advise checking with the patient if there has been any tick contact if the following occur:

- Conjunctivitis and/or influenza-like symptoms may occur in the first stage of the illness.
- Keratitis may occur in the second and third stages, even after antibiotic treatment.
- Episcleritis is rare and relates to late stages of the disease.
- Retinal infection may occur as part of the neuroborreliosis.

Sarcoidosis (see also Chapter 20)

Sarcoidosis is a common, multisystem, idiopathic, granulomatous disease that often involves the lungs. It may also cause neurological symptoms, a variety of skin problems and affect kidneys, liver, bones and heart.

Heiligenhaus *et al.* (2011) demonstrated that the eye is a common site for the early clinical manifestation of sarcoidosis. Between 25 and 50% of patients have ocular manifestations that are likely to cause significant sight-threatening problems. The frequency and course of sarcoid eye disease, and its severity, vary with age and ethnicity.

Baughman *et al.* (2010) describe ophthalmic presentations as including the vasculature of the eye, optic nerve, extraocular muscles, bony orbit, lacrimal glands and the skin surface around the eye. Uveitis is common, and orbital disease may lead to eye entrapment and diplopia.

HIV

There are many ophthalmic manifestations of HIV infection, involving both anterior and posterior segments. Anterior problems include tumours of the periocular tissues such as Kaposi's sarcoma, as well as external infection. Posterior segment problems include HIV-associated retinopathy and opportunistic infections of the retina and choroid.

Therapies for HIV have made it an infection which is lived with for many years and therefore more patients may present with opportunistic infection. It is important to recognise infections early so that appropriate treatment can be instituted. Effective antiretroviral therapy may modify the presentation of opportunistic infection, making it more difficult to diagnose, and modified presentation can also affect the response to treatment.

Kaposi's sarcoma is a highly vasocular tumour which appears as purple to red nodules on skin and mucous membranes. It can affect eyelids, conjunctiva and, rarely, the orbit but does not invade the eye. It tends not to be treated unless it is causing symptoms.

Other findings may include;

- External eye – multiple molluscum lesions of the lids, severe herpes zoster ophthalmicus, orbital cellulitis
- Anterior segment – herpes simplex keratitis, anterior uveitis
- Posterior segment microvascular changes – including cytomegalovirus retinopathy, microaneurysms, retinal haemorrhages, areas of capillary non- perfusion, cottonwool spots, HIV retinopathy, slightly swollen optic discs, anterior ischaemic optic retinopathy.

Chlamydial genital infection

Chlamydia is spread through sexual contact with vagina, anus or mouth. Infection is spread to the eye by hands contaminated with infected discharge. Babies' eyes are contaminated via the birth canal.

Patients develop follicular conjunctivitis with mucopurulent discharge that is resistant to conventional ophthalmic preparations. It is diagnosed by the presence of superior micropannus (infiltration of the cornea with blood vessels). Chlamydial swabs will confirm the ophthalmic diagnosis and the patient will be referred to the genitourinary clinic for treatment, advice, and identification of contacts (see also Chapter 16).

Ophthalmia neonatorum

Babies may present with gonococcal infection (2–3 days after delivery), chlamydial eye infections (3–14 days) or herpes simplex virus 2 (HSV-2) keratoconjunctivitis (2–3 days), having become contaminated during the birth process.

Gonococcal infections, which may lead rapidly to corneal ulceration and even perforation, need to be treated urgently. A Gram stain will demonstrate the broad type of bacteria involved, and, prior to identification of the organism, the eyes will be treated with appropriate eye drops and systemic antibiotics. Following identification, the most appropriate systemic and ophthalmic treatments are prescribed. Parents will need treatment and advice (see also Chapter 16).

Shaken baby syndrome

Unexplained retinal haemorrhages in children under 3, without external evidence of head injury, should be investigated as possible child abuse. All ophthalmic professionals should be conversant with the child protection procedures in their units.

Stevens–Johnson syndrome (toxic epidermal necrolysis)

The pathogenesis of Stevens–Johnson syndrome is unknown. It may stem from hypersensitivity to some drugs, a weakened immune system, hereditary factors and to a gene called HLA-B 1502. It has been linked to infections, possibly by mycoplasma pneumoniae and herpes simplex. It might even follow a hypersensitive reaction to food. Children are most susceptible to this syndrome.

Symptoms include painful skin blisters and mucous membrane involvement. It is sometimes preceded by flu-like symptoms and a high fever. As the condition develops, skin from the lesions may slough off. Ocular involvement includes severe conjunctivitis, iritis, lid oedema, conjunctival and corneal blisters, corneal erosions and perforation.

There is no specific treatment for this disorder. Antibiotics, corticosteroids and IV immunoglobin are used as indicated.

Temporal arteritis (giant cell arteritis)

This condition is rare before the age of 50, and the mean age of onset is 70. It is more common in females. History of recent 'new' headaches, combined with recent visual loss, jaw or tongue pain, should prompt the clinician to consider temporal artery biopsy, which may give a conclusive diagnosis. It is a symptom of a generalised inflammation of the tunica intima (inner lining) of the medium and large arteries of the body. Prompt diagnosis and treatment will prevent monocular or binocular blindness. Corticosteroid treatment relieves the condition, which is monitored with regular ESR checks. (See also Chapter 24.)

Thyroid eye disease

Thyroid eye disease (TED) is, in many patients, mild and non-progressive, but Bartalena *et al.* (2002) state that in 3–5% of cases it is severe. Non-severe TED requires only supportive measures, such as eye ointments, sunglasses and prisms, but severe TED requires aggressive treatment, either medical (high-dose glucocorticoids, orbital radiotherapy) or surgical – orbital decompression.

People with TED require emotional support, as the change in cosmetic appearance is emotionally upsetting, as evidenced by the publications of the TED patients' organisation.

It is important that patients discontinue smoking, as it is a risk factor in thyroid-associated ophthalmopathy. Stable patients may require surgery to correct lid retraction and strabismus surgery with adjustable sutures to relieve diplopia.

Uveitis and systemic disease

Uveitis is a collective name for a number of intraocular inflammatory problems. It is linked with arthritis of various types, intraocular infections, toxocariasis, bacterial, fungal and systemic infections. It is sight threatening. Berthelot *et al.* (2002) have suggested that understanding the mechanisms of latent bacteria persisting within cells may point the way to fresh treatment approaches by using antibiotic therapy to kill dormant bacteria. (See also Chapter 20.)

In a study of 2,619 patients, Barisani-Asenbauer *et al.* (2012) demonstrated the strong link between uveitis and systemic diseases. Of all the subjects studied, 49.4% tested positive for HLA-B27 antigen, demonstrating their potential to suffer from ankylosing spondylitis, Crohn's disease, reactive arthritis, sacroiliitis and uveitis. A total of 37% had uveitis associated primarily with arthritic problems and systemic non-infectious diseases, and 10% had non-systemic diseases such as Behçet's disease, and sarcoid and multiple sclerosis.

Patients presenting with non-ophthalmic problems

Patients may appear at an eye unit complaining of an eye problem. However, it is not always directly related to the eye and patients may find it difficult to understand that there are a variety of general health problems underlying what seems to be an eye problem.

Cerebro-vascular accident (CVA)

Occasionally a patient may visit the ophthalmic department and try to describe a visual problem in a rather muddled manner. Full history and a visual field test may reveal that the problem is related to a CVA and requires immediate medical referral.

Migraine

Many migraine sufferers have visual aura symptoms. These may be transient (only lasting for seconds, or they may last about an hour. The episode may or may not be followed by a headache. Migraine accounts for many visits to ophthalmic accident and emergency departments. Encouraging the public to telephone before attendance helps to reassure patients and reduce the number of attendances.

A key question that the ophthalmic nurse needs to ask the patient who is complaining about flashing lights, shimmering zig zag lines, multicoloured stars and squiggles is whether the phenomenon is affecting both eyes. If it is, and the visual aura lasts for about 30 minutes, and clears, the symptom that the patient is reporting is most likely to be caused by migraine. A GP appointment is then indicated.

Comoglu *et al.* (2003) demonstrated a possible relationship between the pathophysiology of migraine, visual field defects and glaucomatous optic neuropathy, and suggest visual field screening for normal tension glaucoma in patients who have regular migraine attacks. There is no need for the person to attend the eye department for this. Recommend regular visits to the ophthalmic optician instead.

Optic neuritis (see also Chapter 24)

A young adult may present with vague unilateral symptoms of vision being 'a bit washed out', particularly the reds. Pain might have preceded the symptoms and the optic nerve head may look normal, but is possibly slightly swollen. Normal vision gradually returns in about a year, or will be significantly improved. Isolated optic neuritis is the initial symptom of multiple sclerosis (MS) in a proportion of cases and the patient should be referred for further investigation.

An MRI scan is used for diagnosis by identifying brain lesions. If no lesions are detected, the person has a 25% likelihood of developing MS within 15 years. If one or more lesions are detected, there is a 75% risk of developing MS (Shams & Plant 2009).

Acquired ptosis (see also Chapter 15)

Droopy eyelid (ptosis), whether minimal, moderate or severe, is a symptom rather than a disease. Possible causes include: weakened eyelid muscles due to ageing, orbital tumour, diabetes, cluster headaches. Rarer causes include: Horner's syndrome, intercranial mass, ocular amyloidosis, myasthenia gravis, strokes, cat scratch disease.

Visual loss in one or both eyes

Two possible causes of this may be: pituitary tumour, causing loss of peripheral vision; or tobacco and alcohol amblyopia.

Xanthelasma

These are fatty lesions that characteristically present around the eye. In a series of 100 patients with xanthelasma (age- and sex-matched with a group of people without xanthelasma), Ozdol *et al.* (2008) found cardiac risks to be similar within the two groups. No relationship between lipoprotein levels and xanthelasma was found.

References

Babikian, V., Wijman, C., Koleini, B., Malik, S., Goyal, N. & MaDucha, I. (2001) Retinal ischemia and embolism – etiologies and outcomes based on a prospective study. *Cerebrovascular Disease*. **12**, 108–13.

Bartalena, L., Marcocci, C., Tanda, M.L. & Pinchera, A. (2002) Management of thyroid eye disease. *European Journal of Nuclear Medicine and Molecular Imaging*. **29**(2), S458–65.

Barisani-Asenbauer, T., Maca, S., Mejdoubi, L., Machold, K. & Auer, H. (2012) Uveitis – A rare disease often associated with systemic diseases and infections – A systemic review of 2619 patients. *Orphanet Journal of Rare Diseases*. **7**, 57. https://ojrd.biomedcentral.com/articles/10.1186/1750-1172-7-57 (accessed 21 September 2016).

Baughman, R., Lower, E. & Kaufman, A. (2010) *Clinical aspects of ocular sarcoidosis*. http://www.med.unc.edu./tarc/events/event-files/ocular%20sarcoid..pdf (accessed 21 September 2016).

Beales, P., Elcioglu, N., Woolf, A., Parker, D. & Flinter, F. (1999) New criteria for improved diagnosis of Bardet-Biedl syndrome: results of a population survey. *Journal of Medical Genetics*. **36**, 437–46.

Berthelot, J.M., Glemarec, J., Guillot, P., Laborie, Y. & Maugars, Y. (2002) New pathogenic hypotheses for spondyloarthropathies. *Joint Bone Spine*. **69**, 114–22.

Blaikie, A. (2015) *Cerebral Palsy and Visual Impairment in Children: Experience of Collaborative Practice in Scotland*. Scottish Sensory Centre http://www.ssc.education.ed.ac.uk/resources/vi&multi/cpvi/ch1.html (accessed 21 September 2016).

Bosch, A., Bakker, H., van Gennip, A., van Kempen, J., Wanders, R. & Wijburg, F. (2002) Clinical features of galactokinase deficiency: a review of the literature. *Journal of Inherited Metabolic Disease*. **25**, 629–34.

Butler, M., Hayes, B., Hathaway, M. & Begleiter, M. (2000) Specific Genetic Diseases at risk for sedation/anaesthetic complications. Special Article. *Anaesthesia and Analgesia*. **91**, 837–55.

Comoglu, S., Yarangumeli, A., Koz, O., Elhan, A. & Kural, G. (2003) Glaucomatous visual field defects in patients with migraine. *Journal of Neurology*. **250**, 201–206.

Curatolo, P., Bombardieri, R. & Jozwiak, S. (2008) Tuberous Sclerosis. *Lancet*. **23**(372), 657–68.

Di Rocco, C. & Tamburrini, G. (2006) Sturge Weber Syndrome. *Child's Nervous System*. **22**(8), 909–21.

Down's Syndrome Association. http://www.downs-syndrome.org.uk/ (accessed 21 September 2016).

Down's Syndrome Vision Research Unit. http://www.cardiff.ac.uk/research/downs-syndrome-vision-research-unit/downs-syndrome-and-vision/common-vision-problems (accessed 28 September 2016).

Emerson, E. & Baines, S. (2010) *Health Inequalities and people with Learning Disabilities in the UK: 2010*. Improving Health and Lives: Learning Disabilities Observatory

Evereklioglu, C., Yilmaz, K. & Bekir, N.A. (2002) Decreased central corneal thickness in children with Down syndrome. *Journal of Pediatric Ophthalmogy and Strabismus*. **39**, 274–77.

Firth, A.Y. (2005) Class A drug abuse: an ophthalmologist's problem? *Eye*. **19**, 609–10.

Greenfield, D., Ritch, R. & Gardiner, S. (2011) A randomized trial of Brimonidine versus Timolol in preserving visual function: results from low pressure glaucoma treatment study. *American Journal of Ophthalmology*. **151**(4), 671–81.

Heiligenhaus, A., Wefelmeyer, D., Wefelmeyer, E., Rosel, M. & Schrenk, M. (2011) The eye as a common site for early clinical manifestation of sarcoidosis. *Ophthalmic Research*. 46(1), 9–12

Judge, D.P. & Dietz, H.C (2005) Marfan's Syndrome. *Lancet*. **366** (9501). 1965–76.

Kanski, J. (2001) *Systemic Diseases and the Eye*. London: Mosby.

Karadag, N., Zenciroglu, A., Dilli, D., Kundak, A., Dursun, A., Hakan, N. & Okumus, N. (2013) Literature Review and outcome of classic galactosaemia diagnosed in the neonatal period. *Clinical Laboratory*. **59** (910), 1139–46.

Lawrence, K., Campbell, R., Swettenham, J., Terstegge, J., Akers, R., Coleman, M. & Skuse, D. (2003) Interpreting gaze in Turner syndrome: impaired sensitivity to intention and emotion, but preservation of social cueing. *Neuropsychologia*. **41**, 894–905.

Mora, P. & Carta, A. (2009) Ocular manifestations of Lyme borreliosis in Europe. *International Journal of Medical Sciences.* **6**(3) 124–25.

NHS Choices (2016) http://www.nhs.uk/conditions/edwards-syndrome/Pages/Introduction.aspx (accessed 21 September 2016).

Ozdol, S., Sahain, S. & Tokgozoglu, L. (2008) Xanthelasma palpebrarum and its relation to atherosclerotic risk factors and lipoprotein (a). *International Journal of Dermatology.* **47**(8), 785–89.

RNIB (2010) *Estimates of the number of adults in the UK with learning disabilities and visual impairment.* London: RNIB.

Shams, P. & Plant, G. (2009) Optic Neuritis: A Review. *International M.S. Journal.* **16**, 82–89.

Sharma, T., Grewal, T., Gupta, S. & Murray, P. (2004) Ophthalmic manifestations of acute leukaemias: the ophthalmologist's role. *Eye.* **18**, 663–72. http://www.nature.com/eye/journal/v18/n7/full/6701308a.html (accessed 21 September 2016).

Soylu, M., Ozdemir, G. & Anli, A. (1997) Paediatric Uveitis in Southern Turkey. *Ocular Immunology and Inflammation.* **5**(3), 197–202.

Stickler, G., Hughes, W. & Houchin, P. (2001) Clinical features of hereditary progressive arthroophthalmopathy (Stickler syndrome): a survey. *Genetic Medicine.* 3, 192–96.

Tsilou, E. & MacDonald, I. (2013) Weill Marchesani Syndrome. Gene Reviews (Internet). http://www.ncbi.nlm.nih.gov/books/NBK1114/ (accessed 21 September 2016).

Weishaar, P., Flynn, H., Murray, T.G., Davis, J.L., Barr, C.C., Gross, J.G., Mein, C.E., McLean, W.C.Jr. & Killian, J.H. (1998) Endogenous aspergillus endophthalmitis – clinical features and treatment outcomes. *Ophthalmology.* **105**, 57–65.

Glossary

Accommodation	The adjustment of the eye for seeing at near distances. The shape of the lens is changed through action of the ciliary muscle, focusing a clear image on the retina.
Achromatopsia	Colour blindness.
Agnosia	The inability to recognize common objects despite an intact visual apparatus, e.g. prosopagnosia – the inability to recognise faces.
Amaurosis fugax	Transient loss of vision, often caused by carotid artery disease.
Amblyopia	Reduced visual acuity (uncorrectable) in the absence of detectable anatomical defects in the eye or visual pathways.
Ammetropia	An optical defect preventing light rays from being brought to a focus on the retina.
Amsler grid	A chart with vertical and horizontal lines and a central spot, used in the assessment of macular disease.
Angiography	A diagnostic test in which the retinal vascular system is examined. Intravenous injection of fluorescein demonstrates the retinal circulation, whilst that of indocyanine green demonstrates the choroidal circulation.
Aniridia	Congenital absence of the iris.
Anisocoria	Unequal pupillary size.
Anisometropia	Difference in refractive error of the eyes.
Anophthalmos	Absence of a true eyeball.
Aphakia	Absence of the lens.
Asthenopia	Eye fatigue from muscular, environmental or psychological causes.
Astigmatism	Refractive error preventing the light rays from coming to a focus on the retina because of different curvatures of the meridians of the cornea (or lens).
Binocular vision	Ability of the eyes to focus on one object and then to fuse the two images into one.
Bitot's spots	Keratinization of the conjunctiva near the limbus, resulting in raised spots – caused by vitamin A deficiency.
Blepharitis	Inflammation of the lid margins.
Blepharoptosis	Drooping of the eyelid, usually known as ptosis.

Blepharospasm	Involuntary spasm of the eyelids.
Blind spot	Missing area of the visual field, corresponding to where light falls on the optic nerve head.
Botulinum toxin	Neurotoxin A of the bacterium Clostridium botulinum used in very small doses to produce temporary paralysis of the extraocular muscles.
Buphthalmos	Large eyeball in congenital glaucoma resulting from raised pressure.
Canthotomy	Usually a lateral canthotomy – cutting of the lateral canthal tendon in order to widen the palpebral fissure. Usually after trauma because of haematoma in the orbit.
Canthus	The angle formed at the junction of the upper and lower lids, inner (medial) and outer (lateral).
Capsulorrhexis	Removal of the anterior capsule of the lens before phakoemulsification, using a single circular tear.
Capsulotomy (posterior)	Laser treatment after extracapsular cataract extraction involving the making of a hole in the posterior capsule of a lens that has become opaque.
Cartella	Protective eye shield.
Chalazion	A granulomatous swelling of a meibomian gland. Painless on the whole, but painful if infected
Chemosis	Conjunctival oedema.
Coloboma	Congenital cleft in ocular tissue resulting from the failure of a part of the eye or adnexae to form completely.
Concave lens	Lens having the power to diverge rays of light; also known as a diverging or minus (–) lens.
Cones	Retinal receptor cells, concerned with visual acuity and colour discrimination.
Convex lens	Lens having the power to converge rays of light; also known as converging or plus (+) lens.
Cyclodestructive procedures	Surgical techniques to reduce aqueous production by destroying part of the ciliary body using cryotherapy (cyclocryotherapy), laser (cyclophotocoagulation) or diathermy.
Cycloplegic	A drug that temporarily paralyses the ciliary muscle.
Cyclitis	Inflammation of the ciliary body.
Cylindrical lens	A segment of a cylinder (the refractive power of which varies in different meridians) used to correct astigmatism.

Dacryoadenitis	Infection of the lacrimal gland.
Dacryocystitis	Infection of the lacrimal sac.
Dacryocystorhinostomy	A procedure by which a channel is made between the nasolacrimal duct and the nasal cavity to bypass an obstruction in the nasolacrimal duct or sac.
Dark adaptation	The ability to adjust to decreased illumination.
Dellen	An area of epithelial loss on the cornea caused by drying because of shadowing by conjunctiva swollen as a result of chemosis or subconjunctival haemorrhage.
Dendritic ulcer	A corneal ulcer caused by the herpes simplex virus – named thus because of the characteristic pattern of the ulcer on the cornea.
Dioptre	Unit of measurement of the refractive power of lenses.
Diplopia	Double vision – the eyes' inability to fuse two images into one – disappears when one eye is covered.
Echymosis	'Black eye'.
Ectropion	Turning out of the eyelid (eversion).
Emmetropia	An eye with no refractive error.
Endolaser	Application of laser from a probe inside the globe.
Endophthalmitis	Intraocular infection.
Enophthalmos	Abnormal retrodisplacement of the eyeball.
Entropion	A condition where the eyelid turns inwards (inversion).
Enucleation	Surgical removal of the eyeball.
Epicanthus	Congenital skin fold that overlies the inner canthus.
Epiphora	Watering eye – tearing.
Evisceration	Removal of the contents of the globe.
Exenteration	Removal of the entire contents of the orbit, including the globe and lids. Can be more or less radical.
Exophthalmos	Abnormal protrusion of the eyeball (proptosis).
Field of vision	The entire area that can be seen without moving the point of gaze.
Floaters	Moving images in the visual field as a result of vitreous opacities.
Fornix	The junction of the bulbar and palpebral conjunctivae.
Fovea	Depression in the macula adapted for most acute vision.
Fundus	The posterior portion of the eye visible through an ophthalmoscope.

Glaukomflecken	Opacities on the anterior lens capsule indicative of a previous episode of acute, angle-closure glaucoma.
Gonioscopy	An examination technique for the anterior chamber angle, using a corneal contact lens containing a mirror and a light source.
Hemianopia	Blindness in one-half of the field of vision of one or both eyes (bitemporal where both temporal fields are missing or homonymous where the defect is on the same side).
Hippus	Spontaneous rhythmic movements of the iris.
Hordeolum, external (stye)	Infection of the glands of Moll or Zeiss.
Hordeolum, internal	Meibomian gland infection – which is likely to result in a chalazion.
Hypermetropia (far-sightedness)	A refractive error in which the focus of light from a distant object is behind the retina.
Hyphaema	Blood in the anterior chamber.
Hypopyon	Pus in the anterior chamber.
Hypotony	Abnormally soft eye from any cause.
Injection	Congestion of blood vessels.
Iridodialysis	Detachment of the iris from the ciliary body, usually caused by blunt trauma.
Iridodonesis	Trembling of the iris after cataract extraction.
Ishihara colour plates	A test for colour vision based on the ability to see patterns in a series of multicoloured charts.
Isopter	A line of equal retinal sensitivity in the visual field which maybe represented in Goldmann perimetry as lines of different colours
Keratic precipitate (KP)	Accumulation of inflammatory cells on the corneal endothelium in uveitis.
Keratitis	Corneal inflammation.
Keratoconus	Cone-shaped deformity of the cornea.
Keratomalacia	Corneal softening, usually associated with vitamin A deficiency.
Keratometer	An instrument for measuring the curvature of the cornea.
Keratoplasty	Corneal graft – may be lamellar or full thickness. An area of opaque cornea is replaced in order to achieve corneal clarity.
Keratotomy	An incision in the cornea. Radial keratotomy is a procedure in which radial incisions are made in the cornea to change the curvature of the cornea and correct refractive error.

Leukocoria	White pupil.
Limbus	Junction of the cornea and sclera.
Macula lutea	The small avascular area of the retina surrounding the fovea, containing yellow xanthophyll pigment.
Megalocornea	Abnormally large cornea.
Metamorphopsia	Distortion of vision.
Microphthalmos	Abnormally small eye with abnormal function.
Miotic	A drug causing pupillary constriction.
Mydriatic	A drug causing pupillary dilatation.
Myopia (near-sightedness)	A refractive error in which the focus for light rays from a distant object is in front of the retina, so images from a distance appear blurred.
Nanophthalmos	Abnormally small eye with normal function near point – the point at which the eye is focused when accommodation is fully active.
Nystagmus	An involuntary movement of the globe that may be horizontal, vertical, torsional or mixed.
Ophthalmia neonatorum	Conjunctivitis in the newborn.
Optic disc	Ophthalmoscopically visible portion of the optic nerve.
Pannus	Infiltration of the cornea with blood vessels.
Panophthalmitis	Inflammation of the entire globe.
Papillitis	Optic nerve head inflammation.
Perimeter	An instrument for measuring the visual field.
Peripheral vision	Ability to perceive the presence or motion of objects outside the direct line of vision.
Phacoemulsification	Technique of extracapsular cataract extraction in which the nucleus of the lens is disrupted into small fragments by ultrasonic vibrations, allowing aspiration of lens matter through a small wound, leading to faster visual recovery.
Phlycten	Localised lymphocytic infiltration of the conjunctiva or corneal margin resulting in a small, raised, staining area.
Photocoagulation	Thermal damage to tissues, in ophthalmology, usually as a result of laser energy.
Photophobia	Abnormal sensitivity to light.
Photopsia	Appearance of flashes of light within the eye as a result of traction on the retina.

Phthisis bulbi	Atrophy of the globe with blindness and decreased intraocular pressure, caused by end-stage ophthalmic disease.
Pinguecula	A thickening of the conjunctiva, usually medial to the cornea, bilateral and a normal finding.
Placido's disc	A disc with concentric black and white rings used to determine the regularity of the cornea by observing the ring's reflection on the corneal surface.
Presbyopia	Physiologically blurred near vision, caused by a reduction in the ability of the eye to accommodate, because of increasing size and rigidity of the lens, with age.
Pseudophakia	Presence of an artificial intraocular lens after cataract extraction.
Pterygium	A triangular growth of tissue that extends from the conjunctiva over the cornea.
Ptosis	Drooping of the eyelid.
Puncta	External orifices of the upper and lower canaliculi.
Refraction	(1) Deviation in the course of light rays passing from one transparent medium into another of different density. (2) Determination of refractive errors of the eye.
Retinal detachment	A separation of the neurosensory retina from the pigment epithelium.
Retinitis pigmentosa	A hereditary degeneration of the retina.
Retinoscope	An instrument designed for objective refraction of the eye.
Rods	Retinal receptor cells concerned with peripheral vision and vision in decreased illumination.
Rubeosis	Aberrant blood vessels, often on the iris (rubeosis iridis).
Scleral spur	The protrusion of sclera into the anterior chamber angle.
Scotoma	A blind or partially blind area in the visual field.
Staphyloma	A thinned part of the coat of the eye resulting in protrusion of ocular contents.
Strabismus	Misalignment of the eyes – a squint.
Subconjunctival haemorrhage	Haemorrhage, generally idiopathic, underneath the conjunctiva.
Symblepharon	Adhesions between the bulbar and palpebral conjunctivae.
Sympathetic ophthalmia	Inflammation in a normal eye resulting from inflammation in the fellow eye.
Synechiae	Adhesion of the iris to the cornea (anterior synechiae) or lens (posterior synechiae).

Syneresis	A degenerative process within the vitreous involving a drawing together of particles. within the gel, separation and shrinkage of the gel.
Tarsorrhaphy	A surgical procedure by which the upper and lower lid margins are joined.
Tonometer	An instrument for measuring intraocular pressure.
Trabeculectomy	Surgical procedure for creating a channel for additional aqueous drainage in glaucoma.
Trabeculoplasty	Laser photocoagulation of the trabecular meshwork to aid aqueous outflow.
Trachoma	A serious form of infectious keratoconjunctivitis.
Trichiasis	Inversion and rubbing of the eyelashes against the globe.
Uveal tract	The iris, ciliary body and choroid.
Uveitis	Inflammation of one or all portions of the uveal tract.
Visual acuity	Measure of central vision.
Visual axis	A theoretical line connecting a fixation point with the fovea centralis.
Vitritis	Inflammation of vitreous.
Xerosis	Drying of tissues lining the anterior surface of the eye.
Zonule	The suspensory ligaments that stretch from the ciliary processes to the lens equator and hold it in place.

Index